Key to map pages

REYKJAVÍK

• Towns with a town plan

D0996923

Symbol	Country	Symbol	Country	Symbol	Country	Symbol	Country	Symbol	Country	Symbol	Country
(A)	Austria	(CS)	Czechoslovakia	(F)	France	(IRL)	Ireland	(NL)	Netherlands	(SF)	Finland
(AL)	Albania	(D)	West Germany	(GB)	Great Britain	(IS)	Iceland	(P)	Portugal	(SU)	Russia
(B)	Belgium	(DDR)	East Germany	(GR)	Greece	(L)	Luxembourg	(PL)	Poland	(TR)	Turkey
(BG)	Bulgaria	(DK)	Denmark	(H)	Hungary	(M)	Malta	(R)	Rumania	(YU)	Yugoslavia
(CH)	Switzerland	(E)	Spain	(I)	Italy	(N)	Norway	(S)	Sweden		

MICHELIN
Road Atlas of
EUROPE

This edition first published in 1989 exclusively for
Marks and Spencer plc
by arrangement with The Hamlyn Publishing Group Limited
a division of the Octopus Publishing Group
Michelin House, 81 Fulham Road, London SW3 6RB

ISBN   0 862 73549 1

Printed and bound in Spain by Cayfosa, Barcelona

St Michael

MICHELIN
Road Atlas of
EUROPE

MICHELIN
Touring Services

Michelin

MICHELIN tyres and road maps have a reputation unsurpassed throughout Europe for quality and technical excellence in their respective fields.

It is appropriate that, at a time when the twelve member states of the European Economic Community are preparing for a single European market in 1993, Michelin should provide a new Road Atlas of Europe, compiled from their authoritative cartography, designed to meet the needs of the professional driver and holidaymaker alike.

There are over a hundred pages of mapping in this Atlas, showing the road network from North Cape to Gibraltar and from the Atlantic to the Black Sea. A full range of symbols show road categories and widths, towns and cities and places of interest as well as numerous other details, in keeping with Michelin's reputation for accuracy, legibility and up-to-date information.

Seventy town plans are included to help the driver negotiate built-up areas and the 'Driving in Europe' section provides details of national motoring regulations which are useful to know when crossing national frontiers. The comprehensive index locates about 30 000 towns and features.

The map showing 'Climates in Europe' will assist travellers in deciding which is the best season to visit a particular country.

The indispensable road mapping can be used in conjunction with other Michelin publications which provide complementary information on accommodation and sightseeing. The Red Guides, in particular the 'Europe' volume which contains a selection of hotels and restaurants in major European cities, and the Green Guides to the various countries of Europe are ideal companions for this Atlas.

Michelin are always happy to receive suggestions and comments from readers of their publications; taking these into account when preparing new editions can only improve their service to the public.

Thank you in advance and have a good journey!

MICHELIN maps and guides complement one another: use them together!

Contents

Inside front cover

Key to symbols

IV	Michelin
VI	**Route Planning**
X	**Distances in Europe**
XII	**Driving in Europe**

1	**Key to symbols**
2	**Western Europe** at a scale of 1: 1 000 000
78	**Greece** at a scale of 1: 700 000
94	**Scandinavia** at a scale of 1: 1 500 000
110	**Eastern Europe** at a scale of 1: 3 000 000

116	**Index of place names**

Inside back cover

Climates in Europe

Plans of cities and principal towns

118 ● Amsterdam	**136** ● Dijon	**155** ● Lausanne	**174** ● Oslo
120 ● Antwerpen	**137** ● Dublin	**156** ● Liège	**69** ● Palermo
86 ● Athína	**137** ● Düsseldorf	**157** ● Lille	**176** ● Paris
122 ● Barcelona	**138** ● Edinburgh	**158** ● Lisboa	**180** ● Porto
123 ● Basel	**139** ● Essen	**159** ● Liverpool	**62** ● Roma
124 ● Belfast	**140** ● Firenze	**160** ● London	**184** ● Rotterdam
125 ● Berlin	**141** ● Frankfurt a. M.	**163** ● Luxembourg	**188** ● Salzburg
126 ● Bern	**143** ● Genève	**162** ● Lyon	**190** ● Sevilla
127 ● Birmingham	**143** ● Genova	**164** ● Madrid	**192** ● Stockholm
128 ● Bologna	**142** ● Gent	**165** ● Manchester	**193** ● Strasbourg
129 ● Bonn	**144** ● Glasgow	**33** ● Marseille	**194** ● Stuttgart
130 ● Bordeaux	**145** ● Göteborg	**166** ● Milano	**196** ● Torino
46 ● Bremen	**46** ● Hamburg	**167** ● Monaco	**197** ● Toulouse
130 ● Brugge	**147** ● Hannover	**168** ● München	**199** ● Valencia
131 ● Bruxelles-Brussel	**107** ● Helsinki	**170** ● Nantes	**200** ● Venezia
	149 ● Istanbul	**65** ● Napoli	**203** ● Wien
130 ● Budapest	**152** ● København	**171** ● Nice	**205** ● Zürich
146 ● Den Haag	**153** ● Köln	**172** ● Nürnberg	

Route planning

ATLANTIC OCEAN

OCÉAN ATLANTIQUE

ENGLISH CHANNEL
LA MANCHE

MER MÉDITERRANÉE

MER

Mer Ligure
Mare Ligure

Islas Baleares

Symbol	Country	Scale
(A)	Austria.	1: 1 000 000
(AL)	Albania.	1: 700 000
(AND)	Andorra.	1: 1 000 000
(B)	Belgium.	1: 1 000 000
(BG)	Bulgaria.	1: 3 000 000
(CH)	Switzerland.	1: 1 000 000
(CS)	Czechoslovakia.	1: 3 000 000
(D)	West Germany.	1: 1 000 000
(DDR)	East Germany.	1: 1 000 000
(DK)	Denmark.	1: 1 500 000
(E)	Spain.	1: 1 000 000
(F)	France.	1: 1 000 000
(FL)	Liechtenstein.	1: 1 000 000
(GB)	Great Britain.	1: 1 000 000
(GR)	Greece.	1: 700 000
(H)	Hungary.	1: 3 000 000
(I)	Italy.	1: 1 000 000
(IRL)	Ireland.	1: 1 000 000

Ⓘ Iceland . . . . 1 : 2 400 000	Ⓟ Portugal . . . . 1 : 1 000 000	Ⓢ Russia . . . . 1 : 3 000 000
Ⓛ Luxembourg . . . . 1 : 1 000 000	Ⓟ Poland . . . . 1 : 3 000 000	Ⓣ Turkey . . . . 1 : 3 000 000
Ⓜ Malta . . . . 1 : 1 000 000	Ⓡ Rumania . . . . 1 : 3 000 000	Ⓥ Vatican City . . . . 1 : 140 000
Ⓜ Monaco . . . . 1 : 1 000 000	Ⓡ San Marino . . . . 1 : 1 000 000	Ⓨ Yugoslavia . . . . 1 : 1 000 000
Ⓝ Norway . . . . 1 : 1 500 000	Ⓢ Sweden . . . . 1 : 1 500 000	
Ⓝ Netherlands . . . . 1 : 1 000 000	Ⓢ Finland . . . . 1 : 1 500 000	

Amsterdam

Athina — 2836

Barcelona — 1547 3090

Bari — 1971 2621 1792

Basel — 745 2466 1029 1226

Belfast — 1341 3874 2046 2690 1508

Beograd — 1718 1118 1972 1503 1348 2756

Bergen — 1817 4017 3178 3244 2187 3112 2899

Berlin — 669 2584 1853 1811 862 1906 1466 1463

Bilbao — 1424 3422 607 2124 1174 1755 2304 3196 1990

Birmingham — 782 3316 1487 2131 950 535 2198 2554 1348 1196

Bordeaux — 1081 3240 633 1942 831 1412 2122 2853 1647 334 853

Brest — 1098 3501 1242 2278 1096 1244 2383 2870 1664 965 686 622

Brussel/Bruxelles — 204 2792 1365 1777 551 1150 1674 1969 781 1229 591 886 903

București — 2221 1238 2611 2142 1987 3259 639 3200 1711 2943 2701 2761 2886 2177

Budapest — 1393 1510 1952 1482 1073 2431 392 2372 883 2283 1873 2041 2058 1349 828

Clermont-Ferrand — 902 2752 648 1485 477 1337 1634 2636 1311 706 779 371 752 706 2273 1614

Dublin — 1053 3586 1758 2402 1220 165 2468 2824 1618 1467 247 1124 956 862 2971 2143 1049

Dubrovnik — 2024 1265 2049 1580 1425 2892 525 3204 1771 2381 2333 2199 2480 1970 1164 787 1711 2604

Edinburgh — 1289 3823 1994 2638 1457 251 2705 3061 1855 1703 484 1360 1193 1098 3208 2380 1286 416 2840

Firenze — 1391 2115 1075 720 646 2098 997 2664 1231 1407 1539 1225 1686 1197 1636 976 883 1810 1074 2046

Frankfurt A. M. — 446 2396 1318 1553 327 1549 1278 1864 566 1502 991 1159 1176 402 1781 953 776 1261 1583 1498 973

Genève — 885 2446 770 1203 259 1492 1328 2446 1121 1102 934 681 1080 703 1967 1307 310 1204 1405 1441 611 586

Göteborg — 1005 3205 2366 2432 1375 2300 2087 812 651 2384 1742 2041 2058 1157 2388 1560 1824 2012 2392 2249 1852 1052 1634

Hamburg — 441 2780 1802 2007 811 1736 1662 1384 289 1820 1178 1477 1494 593 2026 1198 1260 1448 1967 1685 1427 488 1070 572

Hannover — 386 2637 1659 1864 668 1623 1519 1527 288 1707 1065 1364 1381 498 2022 1194 1117 1335 1824 1572 1284 345 927 715 151

Helsinki — 1204 2540 2388 2346 1397 2441 1422 1186 505 2525 1883 2182 2199 1316 1858 1030 1846 2153 1893 2390 1766 1101 1656 662 776 823

Istanbul — 2665 1171 2919 2450 2295 3703 947 3846 2413 3251 3145 3069 3330 2621 692 1339 2581 3415 1326 3362 1944 2225 2275 3034 2609 2466 2369

Kijev — 2017 2311 3114 2644 2187 3254 1336 2844 1383 3338 2696 2995 3012 2129 1073 1162 2636 2966 1861 3203 2138 1914 2339 2032 1670 1636 1146 489

København — 738 2938 2099 2165 1108 2033 1820 1079 384 2117 1475 1774 1791 890 2121 1293 1557 1745 2125 1982 1585 785 1367 267 305 448 795 2767 1765

Köln — 264 2579 1342 1714 488 1361 1461 1802 575 1440 803 1097 1114 211 1964 1136 802 1073 1766 1310 1134 189 747 990 426 292 1110 2408 1923 723

Leningrad — 1637 2973 2821 2779 1830 2874 1855 1619 938 2958 2316 2615 2632 1749 2625 1463 2279 2586 2326 2823 2199 1534 2089 1095 1209 1256 433 2041 1552 1228 1543

Lille — 283 2910 1308 1836 610 1046 1792 2055 849 1139 487 796 813 116 2295 1467 617 758 2088 994 1256 520 668 1243 679 566 1384 2739 2197 976 329 1817

Lisboa — 2322 4320 1285 3022 2072 2653 3202 4094 2888 907 2094 1232 1863 2127 3841 3181 1604 2365 3279 2601 2305 2400 2000 3282 2718 2605 3423 4149 4236 3015 2338 3856 2037

971 3504 1676 2320 1138 416 2386 2742 1536 1385 165 1042 874 780 2889 2061 967 167 2522 365 1728 1179 1122 1930 1366 1253 2071 3333 2884 1663 991 2504 676 2283 **Liverpool**

719 3252 1424 2068 886 722 2134 2490 1284 1133 196 790 622 528 2637 1809 715 434 2270 612 1476 927 870 1678 1114 1001 1819 3081 2632 1411 739 2252 424 2031 **London**

391 2637 1148 1560 334 1338 1519 1994 767 1290 779 947 964 218 1993 1165 608 1050 1758 1286 980 248 486 1182 618 484 1302 2466 2115 915 193 1735 334 2188 **Luxembourg**

917 2559 630 1292 400 1415 1441 2548 1223 962 857 549 1003 735 2080 1421 178 1127 1518 1364 690 688 141 1736 1172 1029 1758 2388 2548 1469 711 2191 678 1860 **Lyon**

1812 3760 686 2462 1562 2143 2642 3584 2378 397 1584 722 1353 1617 3281 2622 1094 1855 2719 2091 1745 1890 1440 2772 2208 2095 2913 3589 3726 2505 1828 3346 1527 658 **Madrid**

2360 4086 1012 2788 2025 2691 2968 4132 2849 945 2132 1270 1901 2165 3607 2948 1644 2403 3045 2639 2071 2314 1766 3320 2756 2643 3384 3915 4110 3053 2376 3817 2075 634 **Málaga**

1228 2621 493 1323 710 1727 1503 2859 1534 825 1168 643 1315 1046 2142 1483 454 1439 1580 1675 606 999 451 2047 1483 1340 2069 2450 2645 1780 1023 2502 989 1723 **Marseille**

1088 2128 973 878 343 1810 1010 2493 1040 1305 1251 1123 1398 894 1649 989 629 1522 1087 1758 298 670 323 1681 1117 974 1575 1957 2151 1414 831 2008 953 2203 **Milano**

2463 3169 3630 3306 2639 3700 2194 2313 1829 3784 3142 3441 3458 2575 1931 1918 3088 3412 2705 3649 2800 2360 2898 1789 2116 2082 1127 1347 858 2211 2369 694 2643 4682 **Moskva**

837 2063 1370 1224 399 1794 945 2018 585 1615 1236 1272 1421 769 1506 678 918 1506 1184 1743 644 397 599 1206 781 638 1120 1892 1744 939 580 1553 887 2513 **München**

887 3290 945 1923 847 1168 2172 2659 1453 669 609 326 296 622 2675 1847 452 880 2125 1116 1331 965 726 1847 1283 1170 1988 3119 2801 1580 903 2421 602 1567 **Nantes**

1878 2602 1562 261 1133 2585 1484 3151 1718 1894 2026 1712 2173 1684 2123 1463 1370 2297 1561 2533 490 1460 1098 2339 1914 1771 2253 2431 2620 2072 1621 2686 1743 2792 **Napoli**

1387 2434 656 1136 658 1886 1316 2808 1355 988 1327 806 1474 1205 1955 1295 613 1598 1393 1834 419 985 472 1996 1432 1289 1890 2263 2457 1729 1146 2323 1148 1886 **Nice**

666 2171 1427 1391 436 1715 1053 1867 434 1668 1157 1325 1342 622 1556 728 885 1427 1351 1664 811 226 695 1055 610 467 969 2000 1759 788 409 1402 740 2566 **Nürnberg**

1321 3521 2682 2748 1691 2616 2403 496 967 2700 2058 2357 2374 1473 2704 1876 2140 2328 2708 2565 2168 1368 1950 316 888 1031 690 3350 2348 583 1306 1123 1559 3598 **Oslo**

2599 3322 2283 691 1853 3305 2204 3872 2439 2614 2747 2432 2893 2404 2843 2184 2091 3017 2281 3254 1210 2180 1818 3060 2635 2492 2974 3151 3346 2793 2341 3407 2464 3512 **Palermo**

504 2912 1091 1735 553 965 1794 2275 1069 922 407 579 596 308 2297 1469 399 677 1937 914 1143 587 537 1463 899 786 1604 2741 2417 1196 520 2037 219 1820 **Paris**

2143 4147 1167 2843 1893 2474 3023 3915 2709 728 1915 1053 1684 1948 3662 3002 1425 2186 3100 2422 2126 2221 1821 3103 2539 2426 3244 3970 4057 2836 2159 3677 1858 314 **Porto**

950 2154 1711 1596 720 1999 1036 1839 350 1952 1441 1609 1626 906 1361 533 1169 1711 1261 1948 1016 510 979 1027 665 603 859 1983 1389 760 693 1292 1024 2850 **Praha**

1665 2389 1349 449 920 2372 1271 2938 1505 1681 1813 1499 1960 1471 1910 1250 1157 2084 1348 2320 277 1247 885 2126 1701 1558 2040 2218 2412 1859 1408 2473 1530 2579 **Roma**

2483 4683 3844 3910 2853 3778 3565 2824 2129 3862 3220 3519 3536 2635 3866 3038 3302 3490 3870 3727 3330 2530 3112 1528 2050 2193 837 4512 2557 1745 3288 1005 2721 4760 **Rovaniemi**

980 1932 1539 1172 536 1952 814 2161 728 1772 1393 1429 1578 927 1363 535 1076 1664 1052 1900 660 540 736 1349 924 781 1263 1761 1601 1082 723 1696 1045 2670 **Salzburg**

2295 4117 1043 2819 2056 2626 2999 4067 2880 880 2067 1205 1836 2100 3638 2979 1577 2338 3076 2574 2102 2345 1797 3255 2691 2578 3415 3946 4141 2988 2311 3848 2010 417 **Sevilla**

2104 818 2358 1889 1734 3142 386 3285 1852 2690 2584 2508 2769 2060 420 778 2020 2854 765 3091 1383 1664 1714 2473 2048 1905 1808 561 1493 2206 1847 2241 2178 3588 **Sofia**

1368 3568 2729 2795 1738 2663 2450 1021 1014 2747 2105 2404 2421 1520 2751 1923 2187 2375 2755 2612 2215 1415 1997 497 935 1078 165 3397 2395 630 1353 598 1606 3645 **Stockholm**

634 2438 1110 1371 145 1450 1320 2076 751 1264 892 921 1077 439 1881 1053 568 1162 1559 1399 791 216 404 1264 700 557 1286 2267 2076 997 377 1719 545 2162 **Strasbourg**

622 2302 1258 1404 267 1592 1184 2046 631 1413 1034 1070 1219 558 1745 917 716 1304 1423 1541 824 204 526 1234 670 527 1166 2131 1956 967 365 1599 676 2311 **Stuttgart**

2350 511 2604 2135 1980 3388 632 3531 2098 2936 2830 2754 3015 2306 727 1024 2266 3100 779 3337 1629 1910 1960 2719 2294 2151 2054 660 1800 2452 2093 2487 2424 3834 **Thessaloniki**

1154 2263 779 997 409 1699 1145 2596 1157 1110 1140 864 1287 905 1784 1124 492 1411 1222 1647 395 736 252 1784 1220 1077 1692 2092 2286 1517 897 2125 961 2008 **Torino**

1199 2994 388 1696 933 1611 1876 3082 1757 447 1053 245 853 1003 2515 1856 397 1323 1953 1560 979 1222 674 2270 1706 1563 2292 2823 3018 2003 1246 2725 914 1345 **Toulouse**

3041 5241 4402 4468 3411 4336 4123 1893 2687 4420 3778 4077 4094 3193 4424 3596 3860 4048 4428 4285 3888 3088 3670 2570 2608 2751 1367 5070 3087 2303 3028 1535 3279 5318 **Tromsø**

1865 4065 3226 3292 2235 3160 2947 717 1511 3244 2602 2901 2918 2017 3248 2420 2684 2872 3252 3109 2712 1912 2494 1394 1432 1575 949 3894 2892 1127 1850 1382 2103 4142 **Trondheim**

1892 3435 361 2137 1374 2391 2317 3523 2198 606 1832 771 1402 1710 2956 2297 993 2103 2394 2339 1420 1663 1115 2711 2147 2004 2733 3264 3459 2444 1687 3166 1653 924 **Valencia**

1283 1878 1229 760 605 2072 760 2512 1079 1561 1513 1379 1660 1156 1399 739 891 1784 837 2020 254 891 585 1700 1275 1132 1614 1707 1901 1433 1026 2047 1215 2459 **Venezia**

1223 2188 2390 2066 1399 2460 1070 2050 589 2544 1902 2201 2218 1335 1506 678 1844 2172 1465 2409 1560 1120 1658 1238 876 842 352 2017 794 971 1129 785 1403 3442 **Warszawa**

1150 1862 1833 1341 830 2188 744 2131 642 2141 1630 1798 1815 1106 1071 243 1370 1900 969 2137 835 710 1030 1319 957 951 924 1691 1309 1052 893 1357 1224 3039 **Wien**

1337 1499 1591 1122 967 2375 381 2518 1085 1923 1817 1741 2002 1293 1020 350 1253 2087 618 2324 616 897 947 1706 1281 1138 1287 1328 1512 1439 1080 1720 1411 2821 **Zagreb**

831 2416 1058 1176 86 1594 1298 2267 852 1260 1036 917 1182 637 1816 988 597 1306 1375 1543 596 412 287 1455 891 748 1387 2245 2054 1188 573 1820 696 2158 **Zürich**

Distances in Europe

Distances are calculated from centres and along the best roads from a motoring point of view - not necessarily the shortest

Example: **Luxembourg – Warszawa** 1321 km

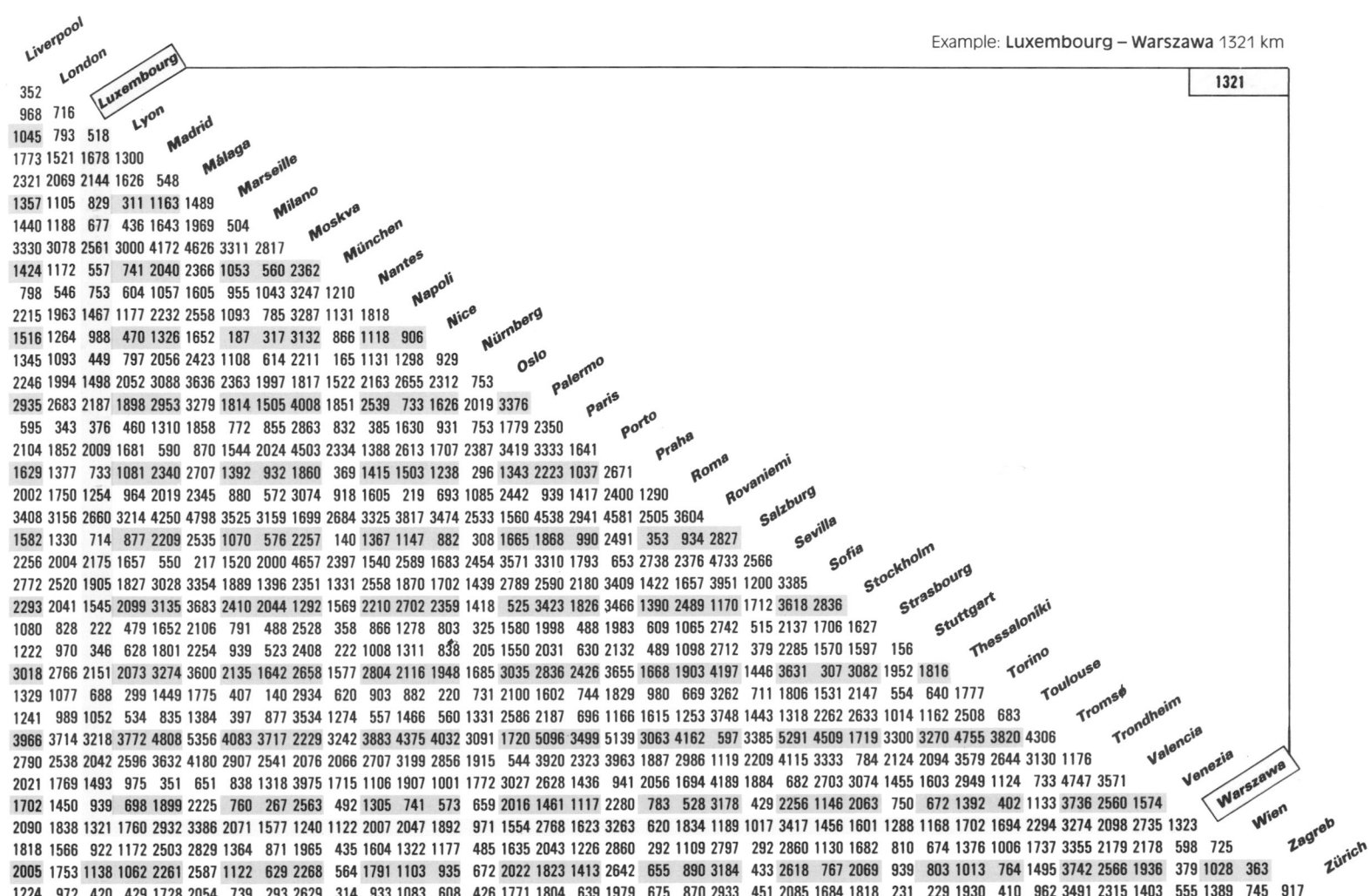

Driving in Europe

Introduction

The information panels which follow give the principal motoring regulations for all the countries included in this atlas; an explanation of the symbols is given below, together with some additional notes.

🔧 The name, address and telephone number of the national motoring organisation or organisations; the initials FIA and AIT indicate membership of the international touring associations, the Fédération Internationale de l'Automobile and the Alliance Internationale de Tourisme

🕙 Speed restrictions in kilometres per hour applying to:

   🚉 motorways
   🛣 dual carriageways
   🛤 single carriageways
   🏙 urban areas

   Where restrictions for 'trailers' or 'towing' are given, it may be assumed that these apply to both trailers and caravans

🍷 The maximum permitted level of alcohol in the bloodstream. This should not be taken as an acceptable level; it is NEVER sensible to drink and drive

🔖 Whether the wearing of seat belts is compulsory

🔲 Restrictions applying to children

△ Whether a warning triangle must be carried

✚ Whether a first aid kit must be carried

💡 Whether a spare bulb kit must be carried

⬜ Whether crash helmets are compulsory for motorcyclists

🚉 Whether tolls are payable on motorways and/or other parts of the road network

⛽ Whether petrol concessions or restrictions apply

☺ The minimum age for drivers

🗎 Documentation required; note that while insurance for driving at home usually provides the legally required minimum third party cover abroad, it will not provide cover against damage, fire, theft or personal accident; for this reason, an International Motoring Certificate (Green Card) is recommended for all countries and essential where 'Green Card required' is given

★ In this section are given any other regulations not falling into the categories above

Andorra

🔧 **Automobil Club d'Andorra**, FIA, Babet Camp 4, Andorra-la-Vella   Tel: 20-8-90

🚉	🛣	🛤	🏙
🕙	70	70	40 km/h

🍷 0.08%

🔖 Compulsory if fitted for drivers and front seat passengers

🔲 Children under 10 years of age not allowed in front seats

△ Not compulsory unless vehicle exceeds 3000 kg, but advised

✚ Recommended

💡 Compulsory

⬜ Compulsory for motorcyclists and passengers

🚉

⛽

☺ 18

🗎 Valid driving licence; Vehicle registration document or Vehicle on hire certificate; Green Card recommended; National vehicle identification plate

Austria

🔧 **Österreicher Automobil-, Motorrad- und Touring Club (ÖAMTC)**, FIA & AIT, Schubertring 1-3, 1010 Wien 1   Tel: (01) 9276510

🚉	🛣	🛤	🏙
🕙 130	100	100	50 km/h
70	60	60	50 km/h
			if towing trailer over 14.5 cwt
100	100	100	50 km/h
			if towing trailer under 14.5 cwt

🍷 0.08%

🔖 Compulsory if fitted for driver and front and rear seat passengers

🔲 Children under 12 years of age not allowed in front seats

△ Compulsory

✚ Compulsory

💡

⬜ Compulsory for motorcyclists and passengers

🚉 Tolls payable on most motorways and some roads (especially Austrian trans-Alpine routes)

⛽

☺ 18

🗎 Valid driving licence; Vehicle registration document or Vehicle on hire certificate; Green Card recommended; National vehicle identification plate

Belgium

🔧 **Royal Automobile Club de Belgique (RACB)**, FIA, 53 rue d'Arlon, 1040 Bruxelles Tel: (02) 2300810
   Touring Club Royal de Belgique (TCB), AIT, 44 rue de la Loi, 1040 Bruxelles Tel: (02) 2332211
   Vlaamse Automobilistenbond, Sint Jakobs Markt 45, 2000 Antwerpen Tel: (03) 2003434

🚉	🛣	🛤	🏙
🕙 120	90	90	60 km/h

🍷 0.08%

🔖 Compulsory if fitted for drivers and front seat passengers

🔲 Children under 12 years of age not allowed in front seats

△ Compulsory

✚ Recommended

💡

⬜ Compulsory for motorcyclists

🚉 None at present

⛽

☺ 18

🗎 Valid driving licence; Vehicle registration document or Vehicle on hire certificate; Green Card recommended; National vehicle identification plate

Bulgaria

🔧 **Union of Bulgarian Motorists (SBA)**, FIA & AIT, 6 Sveta Sofia St., Sofia C Tel: (02) 87 88 01/87 88 02

🚉	🛣	🛤	🏙
🕙 120	90	90	60 km/h

🍷 0.03%

🔖 Compulsory if fitted for drivers and front seat passengers

🔲 Children under 10 years of age not allowed in front seats

△ Compulsory

✚ Compulsory

💡

⬜ Compulsory for motorcyclists

🚉

⛽ Foreign motorists must buy fuel with coupons available in unlimited quantities at border posts and within Bulgaria

☺ 18

🗎 Valid driving licence plus authorized translation into Bulgarian or International Driving Permit; Vehicle registration document or Vehicle on hire certificate; Green Card required; National vehicle identification plate

Czechoslovakia

🔧 **Ustřední Automotoklub ČSSR**, FIA & AIT,
Na Strži 9, 14000 Praha 4   Tel: (02) 432 987

🚗	🛣	🛤	🏭
🕐 110	90	90	60 km/h

🍷 0.0%   any amount of alcohol found in the blood may result in prosecution

🔖 Compulsory if fitted for drivers and front seat passengers

🧒 Children under 12 years of age not allowed in front seats

△ Compulsory

✚ Compulsory

💡

🪖 Crash helmets and goggles compulsory for drivers of motorcycles over 50cc; crash helmets only for passengers

🚏

⛽ Tuzex petrol coupons can be purchased with foreign currency at frontier posts, Tuzex shops and banks; also from Czech Tourist Bureau Cedok (London) Ltd

⊖ 18

🪪 Valid driving licence; Vehicle registration document or Vehicle on hire certificate; Green Card recommended; National vehicle identification plate

Denmark

🔧 **Forenede Danske Motorejere (FDM)**, AIT,
FDM-Huset, Blegdamsvej 124, 2100 København Ø
Tel: (31) 38 21 12

🚗	🛣	🛤	🏭
🕐 100	80	80	50 km/h
70	70	70	50 km/h if towing

🍷 0.08%

🔖 Compulsory if fitted for drivers and front seat passengers over 15 years

🧒

△ Compulsory

✚ Recommended

💡

⊙ Compulsory for motorcyclists and passengers

🚏

⛽

⊖ 17

🪪 Valid driving licence; Vehicle registration document or Vehicle on hire certificate; Green Card recommended; National vehicle identification plate

Finland

🔧 **Autoliitto (Automobile and Touring Club of Finland) (ATCF)**, FIA & AIT, Kansakoulukatu 10, 00101 Helsinki 10   Tel: (90) 6940022

🚗	🛣	🛤	🏭
🕐 120	60-100	60-100	50 km/h
80	60-80	60-80	50 km/h towing if trailer has brakes
50	50	50	50 km/h towing if trailer unbraked

🍷 0.05%

🔖 Compulsory if fitted for drivers and front and rear seat passengers

⬤

△ Recommended

✚ Recommended

💡

⊙ Compulsory for motorcyclists and passengers

🚏

⛽

⊖ 18

🪪 Valid driving licence; International Driving Permit required for car hire or after 3 months; Vehicle registration document or Vehicle on hire certificate; Green Card recommended; National vehicle identification plate

★ Compulsory use of headlights at all times outside built-up areas

France

🔧 **Automobile Club de France**, FIA, 6-8 Place de la Concorde, 75008 Paris   Tel: (01) 42 65 08 26
Association Française des Automobiles-Clubs (AFA), FIA & AIT, 9 rue Anatole de la Forge, 75017 Paris   Tel: (01) 42 27 82 00

🚗	🛣	🛤	🏭
🕐 110-130	110	90	60 km/h
100-110	100	80	60 km/h if wet

🍷 0.08%

🔖 Compulsory if fitted for drivers and front seat passengers

🧒 Children under 10 years of age not allowed in front seats

△ Compulsory unless hazard warning lights are fitted

✚ Recommended

💡 Compulsory

⊙ Compulsory for motorcyclists and passengers

🚏 Tolls payable on most motorways although short urban sections of motorway around Paris and some other major cities are free; tolls also payable on some major bridges and in some tunnels

⛽

⊖ 18

🪪 Valid driving licence; Vehicle registration document or Vehicle on hire certificate; Green Card recommended; National vehicle identification plate

FDR (West Germany)

🔧 **Allgemeiner Deutscher Automobil-Club (ADAC)**, FIA & AIT, Am Westpark 8, 8000 München 70   Tel: (089) 76760
Automobil-Club von Deutschland (AvD), FIA, yonerstraße 16, 6000 Frankfurt am Main 71
Tel: (069) 66060

🚗	🛣	🛤	🏭
🕐 130*	130*	100	50 km/h
80	80	80	50 km/h if towing

*recommended

🍷 0.08%

🔖 Compulsory if fitted for drivers and front and rear seat passengers

🧒 Children under 12 years of age not allowed in front seats

△ Compulsory

✚ Compulsory

💡

⊙ Compulsory for motorcyclists and passengers

🚏

⛽

⊖ 18

🪪 Valid driving licence; Vehicle registration document or Vehicle on hire certificate; Green Card recommended; National vehicle identification plate

DDR (East Germany)

🔧 **Allgemeiner Deutscher Motorsport Verband der DDR**, FIA, 60 Charlottenstraße, 108 Berlin (Ost)   Tel: (02) 2071931/2071932

🚗	🛣	🛤	🏭
🕐 100	80	80	50 km/h
80	80	80	50 km/h if towing

🍷 0.0%   any amount of alcohol found in the blood may result in prosecution

🔖 Compulsory if fitted for drivers and front seat passengers

🧒 Children under 7 years of age not allowed in front seats

△ Compulsory

✚ Compulsory

💡 Compulsory

⊙ Compulsory for motorcyclists; smoking not allowed whilst driving

🚏 Tolls levied on private cars depending on distance travelled; may be paid in Marks obtained by currency exchange; information available at frontier posts

⛽ Reduced price petrol coupons available at main frontier posts; indefinite validity but cannot be returned

⊖ 18

🪪 Valid driving licence; Vehicle registration document or Vehicle on hire certificate; Green Card recommended; National vehicle identification plate

Great Britain

🔧 **Automobile Association (AA)**, FIA & AIT, Fanum House, Basingstoke, Hampshire RG21 2EA Tel: (0256) 20123
Royal Automobile Club (RAC), FIA & AIT, Lansdowne Road, Croydon CR9 2JA Tel: (01) 686 2525

	🚗	⚠	🅰	🏭
🕐	112	96	96	48 km/h
	96	96	80	48 km/h if towing

🍷 0.08%
🎗 Compulsory if fitted for drivers and front seat passengers
⬤
△
➕ Recommended
💡
🛑 Compulsory for motorcyclists and passengers
🚗
⛽
🔞 17
🪪 Valid driving licence; Vehicle registration document or Vehicle on hire certificate; Green Card recommended; National vehicle identification plate
★ Drive on the left!

Hungary

🔧 **Magyar Autóklub (MAK)**, FIA & AIT, Rómer Flóris utca 4a, Budapest 11   Tel: (01) 152 040

	🚗	⚠	🅰	🏭
🕐	120	80-100	80-100	60 km/h
	80	70	70	50 km/h if towing

🍷 0.0%   if the alcohol test changes colour, the driver is taken to a hospital for a blood test and his driving licence confiscated
🎗 Compulsory if fitted for drivers and front seat passengers
⬤ Children under 6 years of age not allowed in front seats
△ Compulsory
➕ Recommended
💡 Compulsory
🛑 Compulsory for motorcyclists and passengers
🚗
⛽ IBUSZ vouchers available (no price reduction); diesel for foreign vehicles must be bought with coupons paid for in foreign currency from exchange offices and travel agencies; unused coupons not refundable
🔞 18
🪪 Valid driving licence; Vehicle registration document or Vehicle on hire certificate; Green Card strongly recommended; National vehicle identification plate

Ireland

🔧 **Automobile Association (AA)**, FIA & AIT, 23 Suffolk Street, Dublin 2   Tel: (01) 779481
Royal Automobile Club (RAC), FIA & AIT, 34 Dawson Street, Dublin 2   Tel: (01) 775141

	🚗	⚠	🅰	🏭
🕐		88	64-88	48 km/h
		56	56	48 km/h if towing

🍷 0.10%
🎗 Compulsory if fitted for drivers and front seat passengers
⬤
△ Recommended
➕ Recommended
💡
🛑 Compulsory for motorcyclists and passengers
🚗 Toll payable on one bridge over River Liffey
⛽ Contact Irish Tourist Board for current information
🔞 17
🪪 Valid driving licence; Vehicle registration document or Vehicle on hire certificate; Green Card recommended; National vehicle identification plate
★ Drive on the left!

Greece

🔧 **The Automobile and Touring Club of Greece (ELPA)**, FIA & AIT, 2-4 Messogion, 115 27 Athína   Tel: (01) 779 1615
Hellenic Touring Club, AIT, 12 Politechniou, 104 33 Athína   Tel: (01) 524 0854

	🚗	⚠	🅰	🏭
🕐	100	80	80	50 km/h

🍷 0.05%
🎗 Compulsory if fitted for drivers and front seat passengers
⬤ Children under 10 years of age not allowed in front seats
△ Compulsory
➕ Compulsory
💡
🛑 Compulsory for motorcyclists and passengers
🚗 Tolls payable on most 'national' roads
⛽
🔞 17
🪪 Valid driving licence; Vehicle registration document or Vehicle on hire certificate; Green Card required; National vehicle identification plate
★ Fire extinguisher compulsory

Iceland

🔧 **Felag Islenskra Bifreidaeigenda (FIB)**, FIA & AIT, Borgatun 33, 105 Reykjavik Tel: (01) 29999

	🚗	⚠	🅰	🏭
🕐		70	70	50 km/h

🍷 0.05%
🎗 Compulsory for drivers and front seat passengers; rear seat belts recommended
⬤
△ Recommended
➕ Recommended
💡 Recommended
🛑 Compulsory for motorcyclists and passengers
🚗
⛽
🔞 17
🪪 Driver's passport; Valid driving licence; Vehicle registration document or Vehicle on hire certificate; Green Card required; Temporary importation permit; National vehicle identification plate
★ Vehicle mud flaps are compulsory; headlights must be used at all times

Italy

🔧 **Automobile Club d'Italia (ACI)**, FIA & AIT, Via Marsala 8, 00185 Roma   Tel: (06) 49981
Touring Club Italiano (TCI), AIT, Corso Italia 10, 20122 Milano   Tel: (02) 85261

	🚗	⚠	🅰	🏭
🕐	110*-130	110*-130	90	50 km/h
	110*-130	110*-130	90	50 km/h if towing

as at May 1989
* Saturdays, Sundays, public holidays and holiday periods

🍷 Severe penalties for drinking and driving
🎗 Compulsory if fitted
⬤
△ Compulsory
➕ Recommended
💡
🛑 Compulsory for motorcyclists
🚗 Tolls payable on most motorways
⛽ Coupons at a discount available at RAC, AA, and Port Offices and frontier Automobile Clubs to personal callers; must be paid for in foreign currency
🔞 18; visitors under 21 years of age may not drive a private car capable of exceeding 180 km/h
🪪 Valid driving licence; Vehicle registration document or Vehicle on hire certificate; Green Card recommended; Temporary importation document; National vehicle identification plate

Luxembourg

🔧 **Automobile Club du Grand Duché de Luxembourg (ACL)**, FIA & AIT, 13 rue de Longwy, 8080 Bertrange Tel: (012) 311031

🏛	⚠	🅰	🏘
🕐 120	90	90	60 km/h

🍷 0.08%

🔖 Compulsory if fitted for drivers and front seat passengers

👤 Children under 10 years of age not allowed in front seats

△ Compulsory

➕ Recommended

💡

🔲 Recommended

🏛

⛽

🔄 18

📋 Valid driving licence; Vehicle registration document or Vehicle on hire certificate; Green Card recommended; National vehicle identification plate

Norway

🔧 **Kongelig Norsk Automobilklub (KNA)**, FIA, Parkveien 68, Oslo 2   Tel: (02) 562690
Norges Automobil-Forbund (NAF), AIT, Storgata 2, Oslo 1   Tel: (02) 429400

🏛	⚠	🅰	🏘
🕐 80-90	80-90	80-90	50 km/h
80	80	80	50 km/h if towing trailer with braking system
60	60	60	50 km/h if towing trailer without braking system

🍷 0.05%

🔖 Compulsory if fitted for drivers and front and rear seat passengers

👤 Children under 12 years of age not allowed in front seats

△ Compulsory

➕ Recommended

💡

🔲 Compulsory for motorcyclists and passengers

🏛 Tolls payable on most new major roads

⛽

🔄 17 for temporarily imported vehicle; 18 to hire or borrow local vehicle

📋 Valid driving licence; Vehicle registration document or Vehicle on hire certificate; Green Card recommended; National vehicle identification plate

★ Dipped headlights compulsory at all times

Portugal

🔧 **Automóvel Club de Portugal (ACP)**, FIA & AIT, Rua Rosa Araújo 24-26, 1200 Lisboa Tel: (01) 563931

🏛	⚠	🅰	🏘
🕐 120	90	90	60 km/h
100	70	70	50 km/h if towing

🍷 0.05%

🔖 Compulsory if fitted for drivers and front seat passengers outside built-up areas

👤

△ Compulsory

➕ Recommended

💡

🔲 Compulsory for motorcyclists

🏛 Tolls payable in certain directions on some motorways and bridges

⛽

🔄 17

📋 Valid driving licence; Vehicle registration document or Vehicle on hire certificate; Green Card required; National vehicle identification plate

Netherlands

🔧 **Koninklijke Nederlandsche Automobiel Club (KNAC)**, FIA, Westvlietweg 118, Leidschendam   Tel: (070) 99 74 51
Koninklijke Nederlandsche Toeristenbond (ANWB), AIT, Wassenaarseweg 220, Den Haag Tel: (070) 26 44 26

🏛	⚠	🅰	🏘
🕐 100-120	80	80	50 km/h
80	80	80	50 km/h if towing

🍷 0.05%

🔖 Compulsory if fitted for drivers and front seat passengers

👤 Children under 12 years of age not allowed in front seats unless using child's safety seat and under 4 years of age

△ Compulsory

➕ Recommended

💡

🔲 Compulsory for motorcyclists and passengers

🏛 Tolls payable on: Zeeland Brug, Kiltunnel (from Dordrecht – Hoekse Waard), Waal Brug, Prins Willem Alexander Brug

⛽

🔄 18

📋 Valid driving licence; Vehicle registration document or Vehicle on hire certificate; Green Card recommended; National vehicle identification plate

Poland

🔧 **Polski Zwiazek Motorowy (PZM)**, FIA & AIT, Kazimierzowska 66, 02-518 Warszawa Tel: (022) 499361/499212
Auto Assistance, Krucza 6-14, 00-537 Warszawa   Tel: (022) 293541/210467

🏛	⚠	🅰	🏘
🕐 110	90	90	60 km/h
70	70	70	60 km/h if towing

🍷 0.02%

🔖 Compulsory if fitted for drivers and front seat passengers

👤 Children under 10 years of age not allowed in front seats

△ Compulsory

➕ Recommended

💡

🔲 Compulsory for motorcyclists and passengers

🏛

⛽ Coupons available at frontier offices or branches of Polish Tourist Office (ORBIS) in Poland; also from Fregata Travel Ltd, 100 Dean Street, London; unused coupons refundable

🔄 18

📋 Valid driving licence; International Driving Permit after 3 months; Vehicle registration document or Vehicle on hire certificate; Green Card required; National vehicle identification plate

Romania

🔧 In the event of breakdown or accident contact the National Tourist Office Carpaţi-Bucureşti, Bd Magheru 7, Bucureşti   Tel: (00) 145160

🏛	⚠	🅰	🏘
🕐 70-90*	60-90*	60-90*	60 km/h

*according to cylinder capacity

🍷 0.0%   any alcohol found in the bloodstream may result in immediate imprisonment

🔖 Recommended if fitted

👤 Children under 12 years of age not allowed in front seats

△ Compulsory

➕ Recommended

💡

🔲 Compulsory for motorcyclists and passengers

🏛

⛽ Coupons compulsory; obtainable with convertible currency only at frontier posts, tourist offices and some hotels; for use at PECO filling stations

🔄 17

📋 Valid driving licence; Vehicle registration document or Vehicle on hire certificate; Green Card required; National vehicle identification plate

Spain

🔧 **Real Automóvil Club de España (RACE)**, FIA & AIT, José Abascal 10, 28003 Madrid
Tel: (91) 447 3200

	🚗	🛣	🛤	🏙
〰	120	90-100	90-100	60 km/h
	80	70	70	60 km/h if towing

these limits are increased by 20 km/h for overtaking

🍷 0.08%
🔌 Compulsory if fitted for drivers and front seat passengers outside built-up areas
🧒 Children in front seats not recommended
△ Two are compulsory for vehicles with 9 or more seats; recommended for other vehicles
➕ Recommended
💡 Compulsory
⛑ Compulsory for motorcycles but not for mopeds
🚗 Tolls payable on most motorways and Cadí tunnel
⛽
🔞 18
📖 International Driving Permit required if 'pink' EEC licence not held; Vehicle registration document or Vehicle on hire certificate; Green Card required; Bail Bond strongly recommended; National vehicle identification plate

Switzerland

🔧 **Automobile Club de Suisse (ACS)**, FIA, Wasserwerkgasse 39, 3000 Bern 13
Tel: (031) 22 47 22
Touring Club Suisse (TCS), AIT, 9 rue Pierre-Fatio, 1211 Genève 3   Tel: (022) 37 12 12

	🚗	🛣	🛤	🏙
〰	120	80	80	50 km/h
	80	80	80	50 km/h if towing – up to 20 cwt trailer
	60	60	60	50 km/h if towing – over 20 cwt trailer

🍷 0.08%
🔌 Compulsory if fitted for drivers and front seat passengers
🧒 Children under 12 years of age not allowed in front seats
△ Compulsory
➕ Compulsory
💡
⛑ Compulsory for motorcyclists and passengers
🚗 Vignette compulsory: obtainable from frontier posts, post offices, garages, motoring organisations or Swiss National Tourist Office (London); separate vignette required for trailer or caravan
⛽
🔞 18
📖 Valid driving licence; Vehicle registration document or Vehicle on hire certificate; Green Card recommended; National vehicle identification plate

USSR

🔧 In the event of breakdown or accident contact officer of State Automobile Inspection (Militia) or nearest office of Intourist (obliged to give tourists assistance)

	🚗	🛣	🛤	🏙
〰	90	90	90	60 km/h

🍷 0.0%
🔌 Compulsory if fitted for drivers and front seat passengers
🧒 Children under 12 years of age not allowed in front seats
△ Compulsory
➕ Compulsory
💡 Recommended
⛑ Not applicable; motorcycles may not be hired
🚗 Road tax payable on entry to USSR though some foreign cars exempt
⛽ Petrol coupons compulsory; obtainable at border posts
🔞 18
📖 Valid driving licence meeting requirements of International Convention on Road Traffic; Vehicle registration document or Vehicle on hire certificate; Car insurance obtainable on entry to USSR at Ingosstrakh offices; Itinerary card, service coupons and motor routes map issued by Intourist; Customs obligation to take the car out of the country on departure; National vehicle identification plate
★ Fire extinguisher must be carried

Sweden

🔧 **Motormännens Riksförbund (M)**, AIT, Sturegatan 32, Stockholm   Tel: (08) 7 82 38 00

	🚗	🛣	🛤	🏙
〰	110	70-110	70-110	50 km/h
	70	70	70	50 km/h if towing with braking device
	40	40	40	40 km/h if towing with no braking device

🍷 0.05%
🔌 Compulsory if fitted for drivers and front and rear seat passengers
🧒
△ Recommended
➕ Recommended
💡
⛑ Compulsory for motorcyclists and passengers
🚗
⛽
🔞 18
📖 Valid driving licence, Vehicle registration document or Vehicle on hire certificate; Green Card recommended; National vehicle identification plate
★ Dipped headlights compulsory at all times

Turkey

🔧 **Turkiye Turing ve Otomobil Kurumu (TTOK)**, FIA & AIT, Halaskargazi Cad. 364, 80222 Sisli, Istanbul   Tel: (01) 1314631/6

	🚗	🛣	🛤	🏙
〰	130	90	90	50 km/h
	110	70	70	40 km/h if towing

🍷 0.0%
🔌 Compulsory if fitted for drivers and front and rear seat passengers
🧒 Children in front seats not recommended
△ Two must be carried – one to place in front of the vehicle, one behind
➕ Recommended
💡
⛑ Compulsory for motorcyclists
🚗
⛽
🔞 Normally 18, but drivers holding a valid foreign driving licence who are not yet 18 are allowed to drive foreign registered vehicles
📖 Valid driving licence; International Driving Permit advised and compulsory if driving Turkish vehicle; Vehicle registration document or Vehicle on hire certificate; Green Card compulsory – must cover European & Asian regions; National vehicle identification plate

Yugoslavia

🔧 **Auto-Moto Savez Jugoslavija (AMSJ)**, FIA & AIT, Ruzveltova 18, 11001 Beograd
Tel: (011) 401699

	🚗	🛣	🛤	🏙
〰	120	80-100	80-100	60 km/h
	80	80	80	60 km/h if towing

🍷 0.05%
🔌 Compulsory if fitted for drivers and front and rear seat passengers
🧒 Children under 12 years of age not allowed in front seats
△ Compulsory – two are necessary if towing trailer or caravan
➕ Compulsory
💡 Compulsory
⛑ Compulsory for motorcyclists and passengers
🚗 Tolls payable on several major roads, Tito Bridge and Ucka tunnel
⛽ Concessionary petrol coupons available at frontier posts for purchase with convertible currency; unused coupons refundable
🔞 18
📖 Valid driving licence; Vehicle registration document or Vehicle on hire certificate; Green Card required, National vehicle identification plate

Signos convencionales

Para más información ver el interior de la cubierta anterior

Importancia de los itinerarios

Autopista con calzadas separadas
con calzada única
Autovía con calzadas separadas
Número de acceso
Accesos: completo – medio acceso
parcial – sin precisión
Carretera de comunicación internacional o nacional asfaltada.
calzadas separadas
4 carriles – 3 carriles
2 carriles anchos – 2 carriles
Carretera de comunicación interregional asfaltada:
calzadas separadas
2 carriles o más – 2 carriles estrechos
Sin asfaltar: transitable, con macadán

Otra carretera asfaltada – sin asfaltar
Pista o camino forestal, sendero
Carretera en construcción
10-1989   Fecha prevista de entrada en servicio

Distancias en kilómetros (totales o parciales)

12   en autopista:
tramo de peaje
12   tramo libre
12   en carretera

Transporte

Línea férrea – Tren-coche
Barcaza – Barcaza (DK, N, S, SF)
Enlace marítimo: permanente – de temporada
Aeropuerto

Zeichenerklärung

Vollständige Zeichenerklärung siehe Umschlaginnenseite

Verkehrsbedeutung der Straßen

Autobahn mit getrennten Fahrbahnen
mit nur einer Fahrbahn
Schnellstraße mit getrennten Fahrbahnen
Nummer der Anschlußstelle
Anschlußstellen: Autobahnein- und/oder
-ausfahrt – ohne Angabe
Internationale bzw. nationale Hauptverkehrsstraße mit Belag:
getrennte Fahrbahnen
4 Fahrspuren – 3 Fahrspuren
2 breite Fahrspuren – 2 Fahrspuren
Überregionale Verbindungsstraße mit Belag:
getrennte Fahrbahnen
2 u. mehr Fahrspuren – 2 schmale Fahrspuren
Ohne Belag: befahrbar, mit Makadam

Sonstige Straßen: mit Belag, ohne Belag
Wirtschaftsweg – Weg, Pfad
Straße im Bau
10-1989   Voraussichtliches Datum der Verkehrsfreigabe

Entfernungsangaben in Kilometern (Gesamt- und Teilentfernungen)

12   auf der Autobahn:
gebührenpflichtiger Abschnitt
12   gebührenfreier Abschnitt
12   auf anderen Straßen

Transport

Bahnlinie – Autoreisezug
Fähre – Fähre (DK, N, S, SF)
Schiffsverbindung: ganzjährig – während der Saison
Flughafen

Légende

Voir la légende complète à l'intérieur de la couverture

Importance des itinéraires

Autoroute à chaussées séparées
à une seule chaussée
Double chaussée de type autoroutier
Numéro d'échangeur
Échangeurs: complet – demi-échangeur
partiel – sans precision
Route de liaison internationale ou nationale revêtue:
chaussées séparées
4 voies – 3 voies
2 voies larges – 2 voies
Route de liaison interrégionale revêtue:
chaussées séparées
2 voies et plus – 2 voies étroites
Non revêtue: carrossable, en macadam

Autre route revêtue – non revêtue
Chemin d'exploitation, sentier
Route en construction
10-1989   Date de mise en service prévue

Distances en kilomètres (totalisées et partielles)

12   sur autoroute:
section à péage
12   section libre
12   sur route

Transport

Voie ferrée – Train-auto
Bac – Bac (DK, N, S, SF)
Liaison maritime: permanente – saisonnière
Aéroport

Segni convenzionali

Vedere la legenda completa all'interno della copertina

Importanza degli itinerari

Autostrada a carreggiate separate
a carreggiata unica
Doppia carreggiata di tipo autostradale
Numero dello svincolo
Svincoli: completo – semi-svincolo
parziale – non precisato
Strada di comunicazione internazionale o nazionale rivestita:
a carreggiate separate
a 4 corsie – a 3 corsie
a 2 corsie larghe – a 2 corsie
Strada di comunicazione interregionale rivestita:
a carreggiate separate
a 2 corsie e più – a 2 corsie strette
Non rivestita: carrozzabile, in macadam

Altre strade con rivestimento – senza rivestimento
Strada per carri, sentiero
Strada in costruzione
10-1989   Apertura prevista

Distanze in chilometri (totali e parziali)

12   su autostrada:
tratto a pedaggio
12   tratto esente da pedaggio
12   su strada

Trasporti

Ferrovia – trasporto automobili per ferrovia
Su chiatta – su chiatta (DK, N, S, SF)
Collegamento via-traghetto: tutto l'anno – stagionale
Aeroporto

Verklaring der tekens

Zie voor de volledige verklaring der tekens de binnenzijde van het omslag

Belang van het wegennet

Autosnelweg met gescheiden rijbanen
met één rijbaan
Dubbele rijbaan van het type autosnelweg
Nummer knooppunt/aansluiting
Knooppunten/aansluitingen: volledig – half
gedeeltelijk – niet nader aangegeven
Internationale of nationale verharde verbindingsweg:
gescheiden rijbanen
4 rijstroken – 3 rijstroken
2 brede rijstroken – 2 rijstroken
Regionale verharde verbindingsweg:
gescheiden rijbanen
2 of meer rijstroken – 2 smalle rijstroken
Onverhard: berijdbaar, macadamweg

Andere weg: verhard – onverhard
Bedrijfsweg, pad
Weg in aanleg
10-1989   Vermoedelijke datum ingebruikneming

Afstanden in kilometers (totaal en gedeeltelijk)

12   op de autosnelweg:
gedeelte met tol
12   tolvrij gedeelte
12   op de weg

Vervoer

Spoorweg – Autotrein
Veerpont – Veerpont (DK, N, S, SF)
Scheepvaartverbinding : permanent – alleen in het seizoen
Luchthaven

Key to symbols

A full key to symbols appears inside the front cover

Road classification

Motorway: dual carriageway
single carriageway
Dual carriageway with motorway characteristics
Interchange number
Interchange: complete – half
limited – unspecified
International and national surfaced road network:
dual carriageway
four lanes – three lanes
two wide lanes – two lanes
Interregional surfaced road network:
dual carriageway
two lanes or more – two narrow lanes
Unsurfaced: suitable for vehicles, macadam

Other surfaced road – unsurfaced
Service road or cart track, footpath
Road under construction
10-1989   Scheduled opening date

Distances in kilometres (total and intermediate)

12   on motorway:
toll section
12   free section
12   on other roads

Transportation

Railway – Motorail
Ferry – Ferry (DK, N, S, SF)
Car ferry: all the year – seasonal
Airport

1

2

3

4

Cape Wrath

Butt of Lewis
Port of Ness
A 857
16
LEWIS
Barvas
A 858
12
Carloway
A 857
292
34
Stornoway
Garynahine
A 858
A 859
574
36
Broad Bay
Portnaguran
Tiumpan Head
12
A 866
Eye Peninsula

Durness   Whiten He
Kinlochbervie   A 838
20
908 △ Foinaven   Tongue
△ 927
Scourie   A 894   Ben Hope
Laxford Bridge
A 838
Eddrachillis
Bay
Kylestrome   Altnaharra
A 837
19   A 894
34
39   40   Ben
Inchnadamph   △ 961
△ 998   A 838
Ben More Assynt
Lochinver
849
A 837
Ledmore
Coigach   18
743   A 835
27 A 899
A 837
31

WESTERN

Flannan I.

HEBRIDES

A 859
Hushinish
B 887
Clisham
799 △
Tarbert
Toe Head
24
Harris
A 859
Leverburgh
Rodel
Renish Point
572
Kebock Head

ISLES

Rubha Cóigeach

Ullapool   Bonar Bridge

North Uist
Tigharry
25   A 865
A 865   9
A 867
13 △ 347
Balivanich
Benbecula
A 865
Creagorry
Sound of Monach
South Uist
22
21
A 865   620
Daliburgh
Lochboisdale

Sound of Harris

Laide   Gruinard
Bay
Rubha Réidh   15
Dundonnell   29   12
△ 1062
Gairloch   A 832   A 832   1084
△ Beinn Dearg
Sgurr Mór △   1110
△ 980   57
Ben Wyvis
Wester   Ross   1046
Liathach   15
Torridon   △ 1054   Kinlochewe   19
A 832   Garve   Dingwall
A 896   9   Achnasheen
Shieldaig   19   A 890   Contin
Glen Carron   1083
896 △   A 896   24   △   A 831
Lochcarron   Muir of Ord
15
Stromeferry   Cannich   A 831   Drumnadrochit
A 890   Carn Eige
Dornie   △ 1183
Eilean Donan Castle   HIGHLA
G

Waternish
Point
Loch
Snizort
Uig
A 855
Staffin
34
A 856
The Storr
719
22
16
A 850
Dunvegan
Portree
Bracadale
Idrigill Point
A 863
9
Sligachan
SKYE
The Cuillins
993

Dunvegan
Head

SEA OF
THE HEBRIDES

Rona
Rona
Inner Sound
Raasay
444
Sound of Raasay

Barra
A 888
383
Castlebay   Bayhirivagh

Mingulay

Barra Head

Sconser
Scalpay
Kyle of
Lochalsh   A 850   5
Broadford   Kyleakin   Glenelg
14   8   Kylerhea
Isleornsay   Glenelg
A 851   17
Elgol   A 851
Ardvasar   Sound of Sleat

Shiel Bridge   Invermoriston   Foyers
A' Chrálaig   32   50   B 862   White Bridge
△ 1120   80   16   69
43
13   7   Fort Augustus
Sgurr na Ciche   Invergarry
1040   15   25   Newton
Loch Quoich   40   Laggan

Coll

Arinagour

Tiree

Scarinish

Canna

Rhum

Eigg

Muck

Mallaig
19
Arisaig   76
46
Glenfinnan
A 830
A 861   882
27
33   A 861
Loch Shiel
888
Kilchoan   528   Salen   Strontian   A 861   13
B 8007   Sound of Sunart   Corran
Tobermory   B 801
Dervaig   19   A 884   Kentallen
A 848   10   Portnacroish
Lochaline

Spean Bridge   A 86
1130   30
10   Dalwhinnie
Caledonian Canal   Fort William   1148
9 △ 1344   Ben Alder △
Ben Nevis
Inchree   Schie
Onich   5   SC   OM
Ballachulish   Blackwater Resr.
Bidean   Glen Coe   33
nam Bian   A 82   GRAM
1141 △   Kinloch Rannoc
Loch Rannoc

D E F

Westray
Pierowall
The North
Sound
North Ronaldsay
Kettletoft
Sanday
Rousay
Westray Firth
Eday
Brough Head
Mainland 38 A 967 A 966
Stronsay Firth
Stronsay
Shapinsay
Stromness
Stenness 15 A 965
Kirkwall
Scalloway
20 A 964
A 960 10
Skaill
A 961
ORKNEY
ISLANDS
Rora Head
479
Lyness
Hoy
Scapa Flow
St Margaret's Hope
South Ronaldsay
Burwick
Aberdeen
Pentland Firth

Herma Ness
Haroldswick
11 A 968
Unst
Gutcher B Belmont
18 Fetlar
Isbister
450 △ Mid Yell
Hillswick A 970 Toft B Ulsta Yell
17 A 968
St Magnus Bay
Muckle Roe A 970 10
Papa Stour Laxo
Sandness Voe B Whalsay
Walls 31 A 870
A 871 18 Mainland
Whiteness
B Bressay
Scalloway Lerwick
293 △
Tørshavn
(Færøerne)
Seydisfjördur
Bergen
Aberdeen
Foula 418 △
SHETLAND
ISLANDS
Kirkwall
27 A 970
Sumburgh
Sumburgh Head

Strathy Point
Scrabster Dunnet Head
Bettyhill Melvich 27 A 836 Thurso 20 Duncansby Head
A 836 16 A 836 Dunnet John o' Groats
Roadside A 836 Castletown
B 876 A 9
Reiss
290 △ 21 Noss Head
A 882 Wick
A 885 24
17 A 9
Latheron
706 △ 20
Morven
A 897
237 A 9
147 Helmsdale
21 Brora
Golspie

Fair I. 217 △

18 A Dornoch
949 Dornoch Firth
Tarbat Ness
ergordon
Tain
Moray Firth

112
180

Cromarty
Lossiemouth
A 941 4
Nairn 10 Forres 13 Elgin A 96 Buckie Cullen
A 939 39 A 96 A 98
16 Fochabers 23 Banff Macduff
63 13 17 A 95 B 9031 Kinnairds Head
A 940 A 941 Rothes 12 Keith 21 Fraserburgh
22 Craigellachie A 95 A 96 B 9025 A 947 26 A 98
A 98 Deveron B 9025 18 Rattray Head
Dava Dufftown A 920 Turriff 13 A 952
24 A 939 11 22 Mintlaw
549 △ 840 △ Huntly New Deer B 9029 9 Peterhead
Grantown-on-Spey 15 A 97 A 947 18 B 1970 A 950 Buchan Ness
A 938 A 95 68 A 920 44 A 948 14
Carrbridge 28 109 23 Oldmeldrum 71 A 952
15 Dulnain 25 Rhynie Ellon Cruden Bay
Bridge Tomintoul Mossat A 97 Inverurie A 920 A 875 Stromness
Aviemore A 939 A 944 Don A 947 Newburgh Lerwick
Glen More 39 Alford Kintore 18
Forest Park Craigievar 17 A 944 A 96
Cairn Gorm 1245 △ Colnabaichin A 939 Castle A 980 34 ABERDEEN
Cairngorm Mountains 871 △ 27 A 97 A 93
Ben Macdui Aboyne A 93 Crathes 17 A 92
1309 △ Ballater 25 Castle Dee 18
Braemar 17 A 93 Balmoral Castle Banchory A 957
Dee 14
M O U N T A I N S N. Esk Stonehaven
1155 △
Devil's Elbow 1068 △ 89
Beinn a' Ghlò 665 Glas Maol 55 A 92
1120 △ 52 Inverbervie
Laurencekirk 22
L A N D Marikirk
T A Y S I D E S. Esk Brechin A 935
B 8019 Kirriemuir
Pitlochry Montrose

1

2

3

4

5

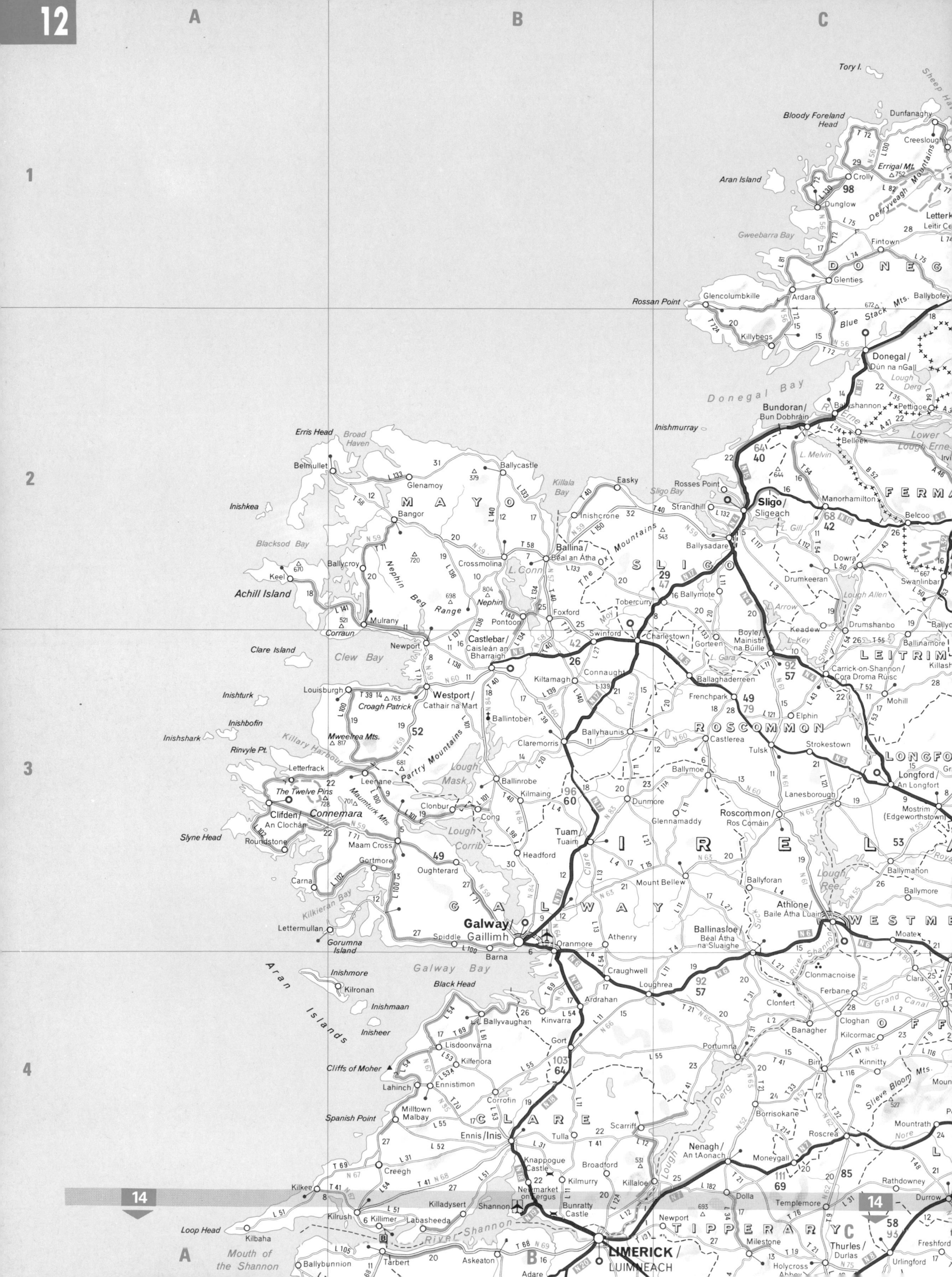

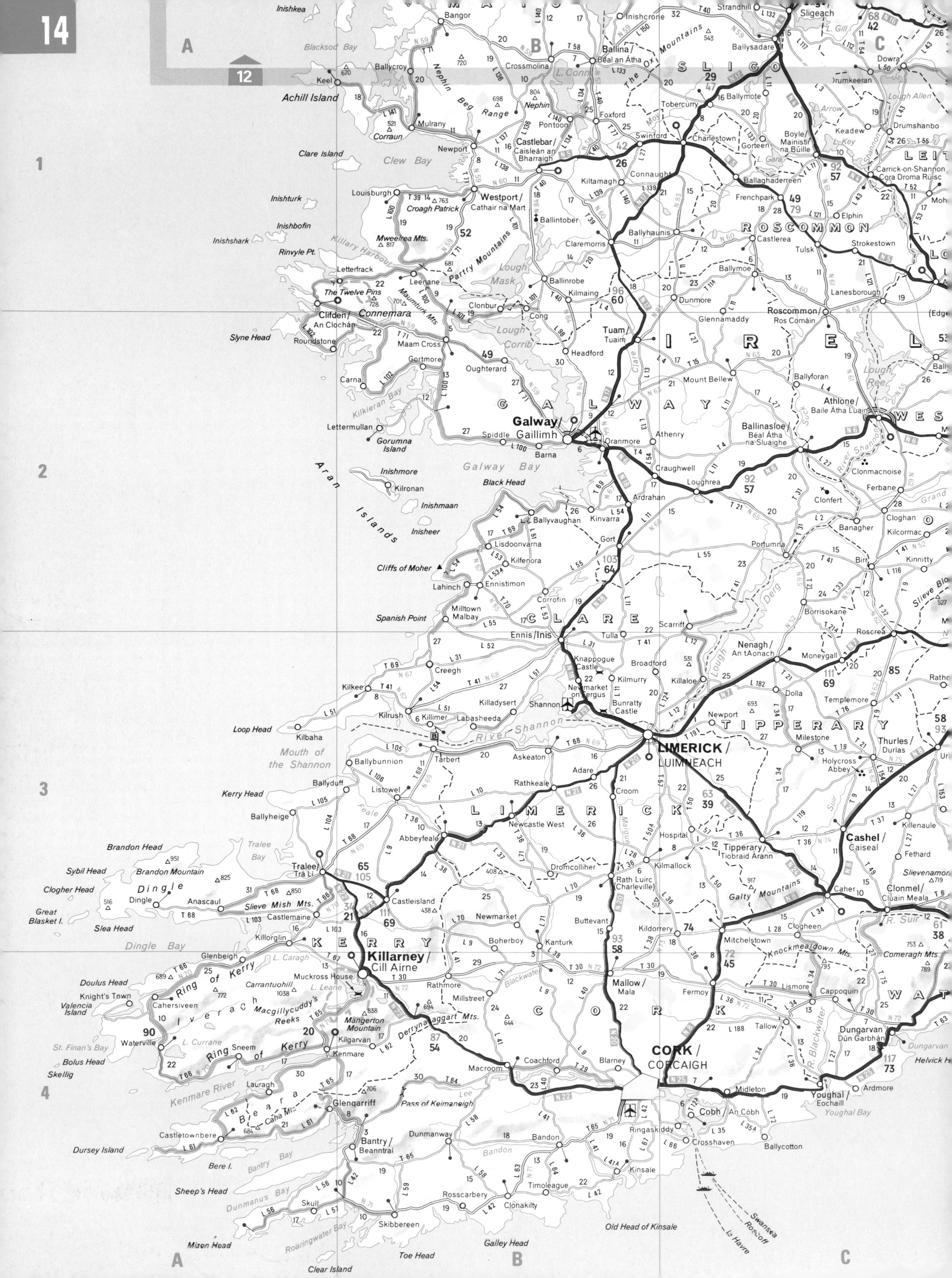

A　　B　　C

12

1

Inishkea
Bangor
Inishcrone 32
Strandhill　L 132　Sligeach / Sligo
L. Gill
68 42 N 16
Blacksod Bay
Ballycroy
Crossmolina
Ballina / Béal an Átha
L 133　L. Conn
SLIGO
Dowra
L 50
Drumkeeran
Lough Allen
LEI
Keel
Achill Island
Mulrany
Nephin
Foxford
Swinford
Tobercurry
Charlestown
Ballymote
Boyle / Mainistir na Búille
Keadew
Drumshanbo
Corraun
Newport
Castlebar / Caisleán an Bharraigh
Kiltamagh
Connaught
Ballaghaderreen
Carrick-on-Shannon / Cora Droma Rúisc
Clare Island
Clew Bay
Louisburgh
Westport / Cathair na Mart
Ballintober
Claremorris
Ballyhaunis
Castlerea
Tulsk
Strokestown
Inishturk
Croagh Patrick
Mweelrea Mts.
ROSCOMMON
Inishbofin
Inishshark
Rinvyle Pt.
Partry Mountains
Lough Mask
Ballinrobe
Kilmaing
Dunmore
Roscommon / Ros Comáin
Lanesborough
Letterfrack
Leenane
Clonbur
Cong
Tuam / Tuaim
Glennamaddy
Ballyforan
Lough Ree
The Twelve Pins
Maumturk Mts.
Maam
Headford
Mount Bellew
Athlone / Baile Átha Luain
Clifden / An Clochán
Connemara
Maam Cross
Oughterard
GALWAY
Athenry
Ballinasloe / Béal Átha na Sluaighe
WES
Slyne Head
Roundstone
Gortmore
Craughwell
Clonmacnoise
Carna
Galway / Gaillimh
Spiddle
Barna
Loughrea
Ferbane
Lettermullan
Gorumna Island
Galway Bay
Oranmore
Ardrahan
Clonfert
Cloghan
Kilcormac
Aran Islands
Inishmore
Kilronan
Black Head
Ballyvaughan
Kinvarra
Gort
Portumna
Banagher
Inishmaan
Inisheer
Lisdoonvarna
Kilfenora
Birr
Kinnitty
Cliffs of Moher
Lahinch
Ennistimon
Corofin
Borrisokane
Slieve Blo
Spanish Point
Milltown Malbay
CLARE
Scarriff
Roscrea
Ennis / Inis
Tulla
Nenagh / An tAonach
Moneygall
Creegh
Knappogue Castle
Broadford
Killaloe
Templemore
Kilkee
Kilmurry
Newmarket on Fergus
Bunratty Castle
Newport
Dolla
Kilrush
Killimer
Killadysert
Shannon
Milestone
Thurles / Durlas
Loop Head
Kilbaha
River Shannon
LIMERICK / LUIMNEACH
Holycross Abbey
Mouth of the Shannon
Ballybunnion
Tarbert
Askeaton
Adare
TIPPERARY
Kerry Head
Ballyduff
Listowel
Rathkeale
Croom
Cashel / Caiseal
Ballyheige
LIMERICK
Newcastle West
Hospital
Tipperary / Tiobraid Árann
Fethard
Brandon Head
Abbeyfeale
Dromcolliher
Kilmallock
Slievenamo
Sybil Head
Brandon Mountain
Tralee / Trá Lí
Castleisland
Newmarket
Rath Luirc (Charleville)
Galty Mountains
Caher
Clonmel / Cluain Meala
Clogher Head
Dingle
Anascaul
Slieve Mish Mts.
Buttevant
Kildorrery
Mitchelstown
Cloghen
Great Blasket I.
Slea Head
Killorglin
Castlemaine
KERRY
Boherboy
Kanturk
Knockmealdown Mts.
Lismore
Cappoquin
Dingle Bay
Glenbeigh
Killarney / Cill Airne
Rathmore
Mallow / Mala
Fermoy
Tallow
Doulus Head
Knight's Town
Cahersiveen
Muckross House
Ring of Kerry
Iveragh
Macgillycuddy's Reeks
Carrantuohill
Millstreet
CORK
Lismore
Valencia Island
Mangerton Mountain
Derrynasaggart Mts.
Blarney
Midleton
Youghal / Eochaill
Ardmore
St. Finan's Bay
Waterville
Kilgarvan
Coachford
Macroom
Cobh / An Cobh
Bolus Head
Ring of Kerry
Sneem
Kenmare
Blackwater
CORK / CORCAIGH
Ringaskiddy
Ballycotton
Skellig
Lauragh
Glengarriff
Pass of Keimaneigh
Crosshaven
Dursey Island
Beara
Caha Mts.
Castletownbere
Bantry / Beanntraí
Dunmanway
Bandon
Kinsale
Sheep's Head
Bantry Bay
Skull
Rosscarbery
Timoleague
Clonakilty
Mizen Head
Dunmanus Bay
Skibbereen
Old Head of Kinsale
Roaringwater Bay
Galley Head
Clear Island
Toe Head

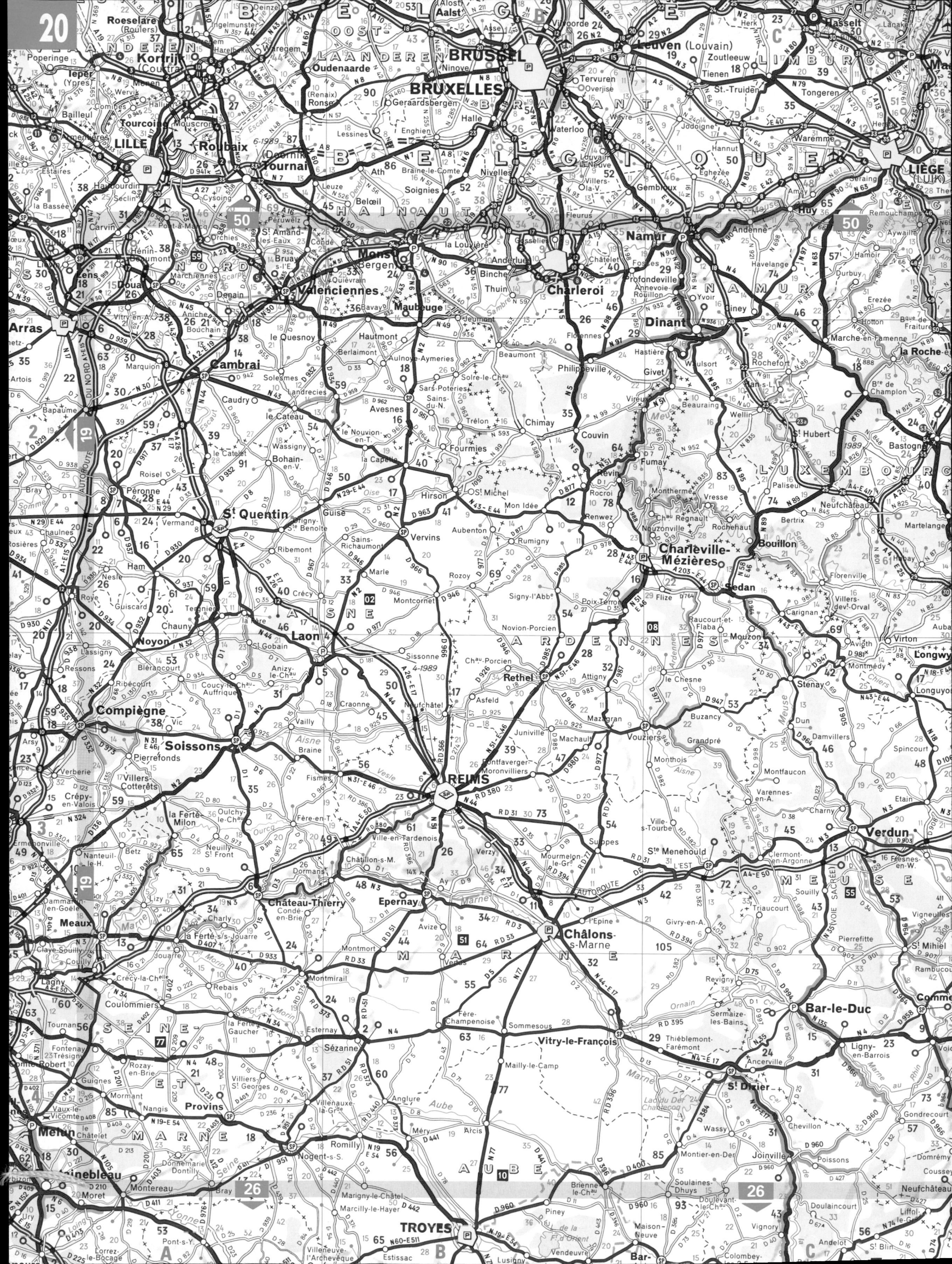

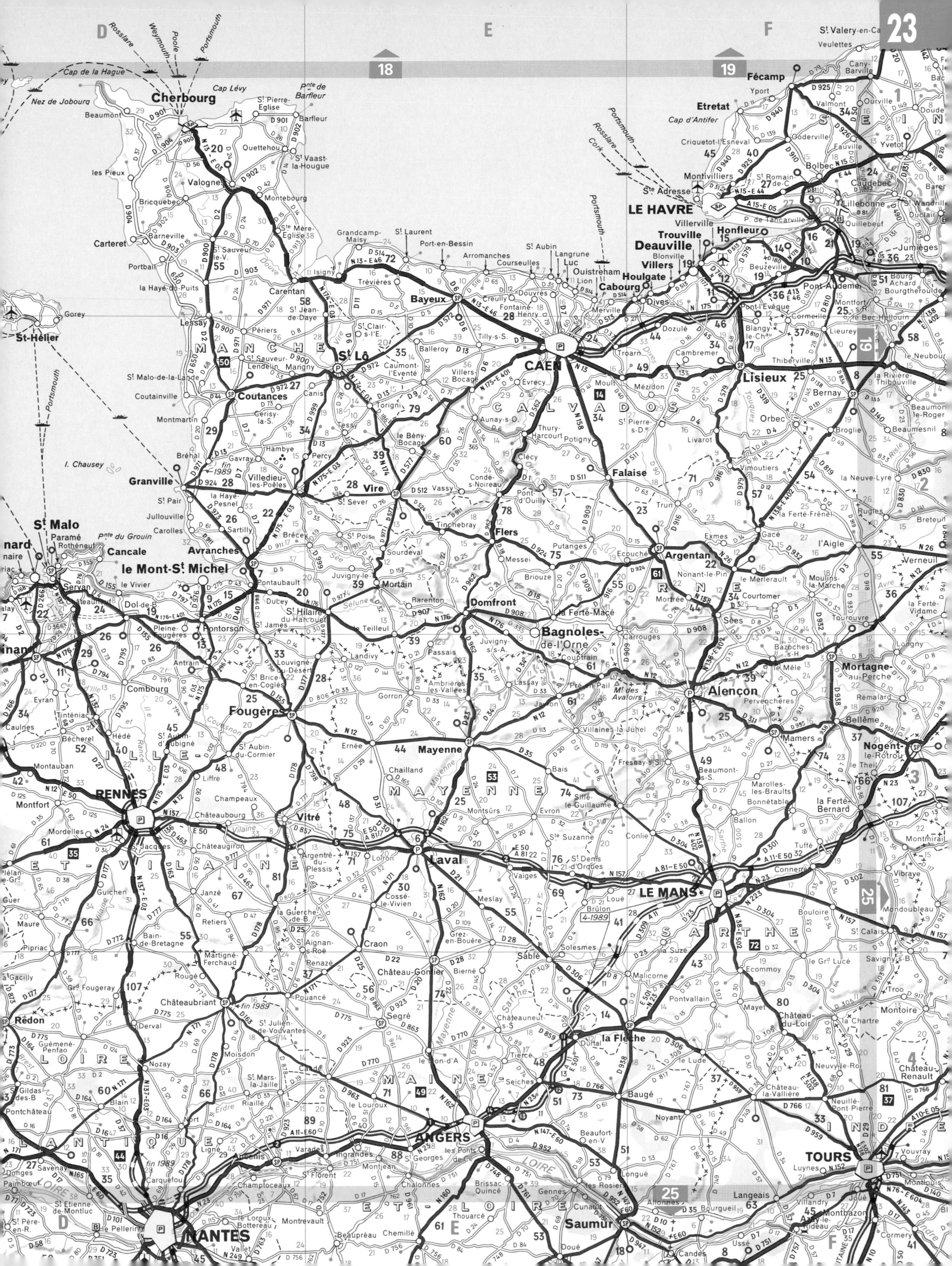

D | **E** | **F**

18 | 19

Cherbourg
Cap de la Hague
Nez de Jobourg
Cap Lévy
Pte de Barfleur
Beaumont
St Pierre-Eglise
Barfleur
Quettehou
St Vaast-la-Hougue
Valognes
les Pieux
Montebourg
Bricquebec
Carteret
Barneville
Ste Mère-Eglise
Portbail
la Haye-du-Puits
Grandcamp-Maisy
St Laurent
Port-en-Bessin
Arromanches
Courseulles
St Aubin
Langrune
Luc
Ouistreham
Lion
Fécamp
Yport
Etretat
Cap d'Antifer
Criquetot-l'Esneval
Montivilliers
Ste Adresse
LE HAVRE
Villerville
Honfleur
Trouville
Deauville
Blonville
Villers
Houlgate
Cabourg
Dives
Merville
St Valery-en-Ca
Veulettes
Goderville
Bolbec
Lillebonne
Quillebeuf
Pont-Audemer
Bourgtheroulde
Cormeille
Lieurey
Bernay
Beaumont-le-Roger

Isigny
Carentan
St Jean-de-Daye
Lessay
Périers
St Clair-s-l'E.
St Lô
Bayeux
Trévières
Creully
Balleroy
Tilly-s-S.
Caumont-l'Eventé
Villers-Bocage
CAEN
Troarn
Cambremer
Lisieux
Orbec
Broglie
Beaumesnil
la Neuve-Lyre

Coutances
Marigny
Canis
Torigni
Tessy
le Bény-Bocage
Aunay-s-O.
Thury-Harcourt
Potigny
Evrecy
St Pierre-s-D.
Livarot
Vimoutiers

St Malo-de-la-Lande
Cerisy-la-S.
Montmartin
Gavray
Hambye
Percy
Granville
Bréhal
Villedieu-les-Poêles
Vire
Vassy
Condé-s-Noireau
Falaise
Trun
Gacé
l'Aigle
Verneuil

St Pair
la Haye-Pesnel
St Sever
Tinchebray
Flers
Putanges
Briouze
Ecouché
Argentan
Nonant-le-Pin
le Merleraut
Moulins-la-Marche

Jullouville
Carolles
Sartilly
Brécey
St Pois
Sourdeval
Messei
Exmes
Mortrée
Sées
Courtomer

St Malo
Paramé
Rothéneuf
Cancale
Avranches
le Mont-St Michel
Pontaubault
Juvigny-le-T.
Mortain
Domfront
la Ferté-Macé
Bagnoles-de-l'Orne
Carrouges
le Mêle
Mortagne-au-Perche

le Vivier
Servan
Dol-de-B.
Pontorson
Ducey
St Hilaire-du-Harcouët
St James
Barenton
Passais
Juvigny-s/s-A.
Couptrain
Pré-en-Pail
Alençon
Pervenchères
Bellême
Mamers

Pleine-Fougères
Antrain
Louvigné-du-Désert
St Brice-en-Coglès
Landivy
Ambrières-les-Vallées
Lassay
Mt des Avaloirs
Villaines-la-Juhel
la Ferté-Bernard

Combourg
Fougères
Ernée
Gorron
Bais
Fresnay-s-S.
Beaumont-les-S.
Nogent-le-Rotrou

Bécherel
Liffré
St Aubin-du-Cormier
Mayenne
Montsûrs
Sillé-le-Guillaume
Marolles-les-Brauls
Bonnétable

RENNES
Montfort
Châteaubourg
Vitré
Evron
Conlie
Ballon
Tuffé
Connerré

Mordelles
Argentré-du-Plessis
Loiron
Ste Suzanne
LE MANS
Bouloire

Guichen
Janzé
Meslay
Vaiges
St Denis-d'Orques
Brûlon
Parigné-l'E.

Maure
Retiers
Cossé-le-Vivien
Laval
La Suze
Ecommoy
Vibraye

Pipriac
Bain-de-Bretagne
la Guerche-de-B.
Craon
Grez-en-Bouère
Sablé
Solesmes
Malicorne
Mayet
Château-du-Loir
Montoire

Redon
Martigné-Ferchaud
Renazé
Château-Gontier
Bierné
Pontvallain
la Chartre

la Gacilly
Grd Fougeray
Rougé
Pouancé
Segré
Châteauneuf-s-S.
la Flèche
Baugé
le Lude
Château-la-Vallière
Château-Renault

Châteaubriant
Derval
St Julien-de-Vouvantes
Moisdon
Candé
Tiercé
Seiches
Noyant
Beaufort-en-V.
TOURS

Blain
Nort
le Louroux-Bottereau
ANGERS
les Ponts-de-Cé
Brissac-Quincé
Langeais

NANTES
Ancenis
St Georges
Champtoceaux
Saumur
Doué

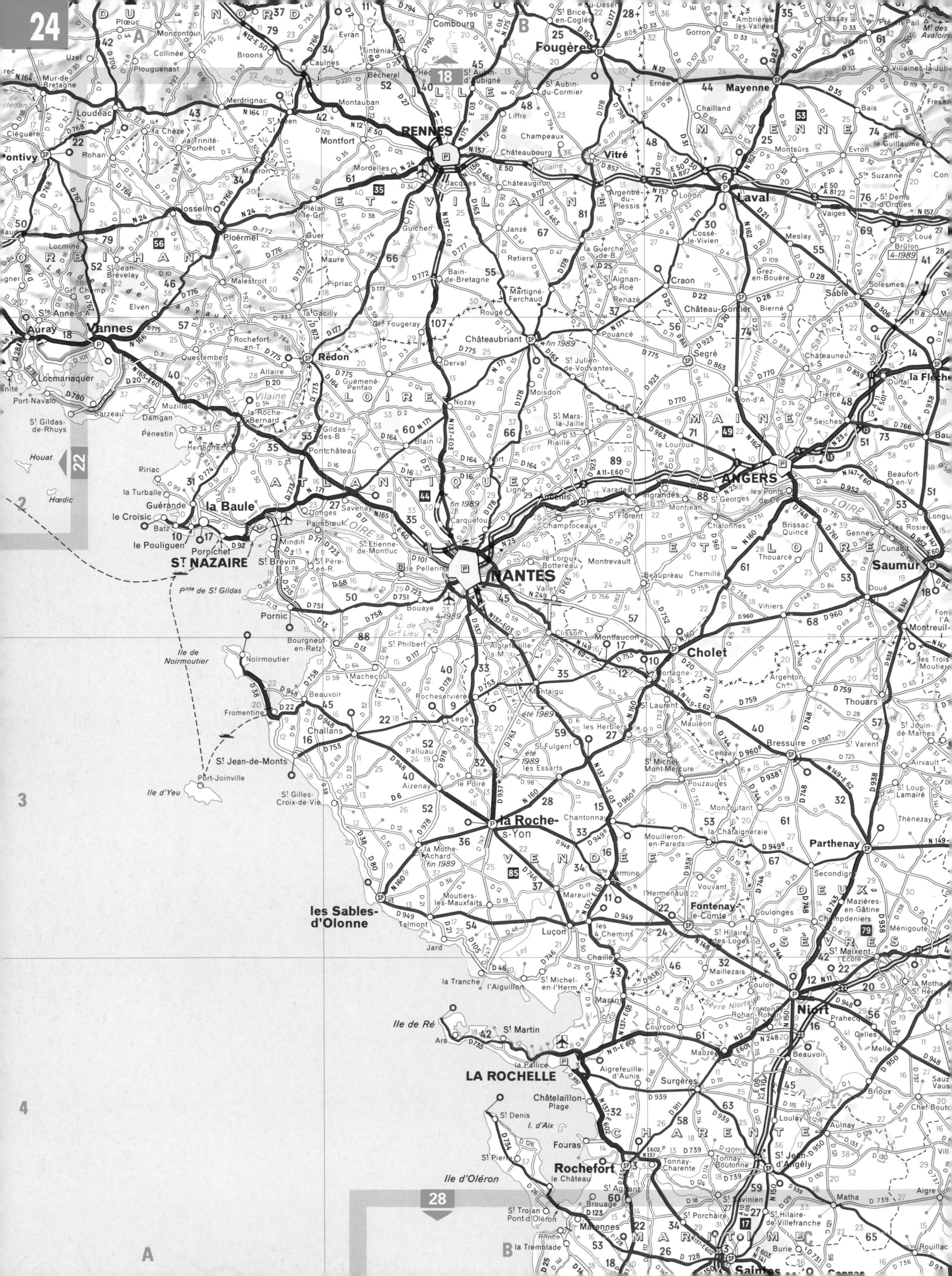

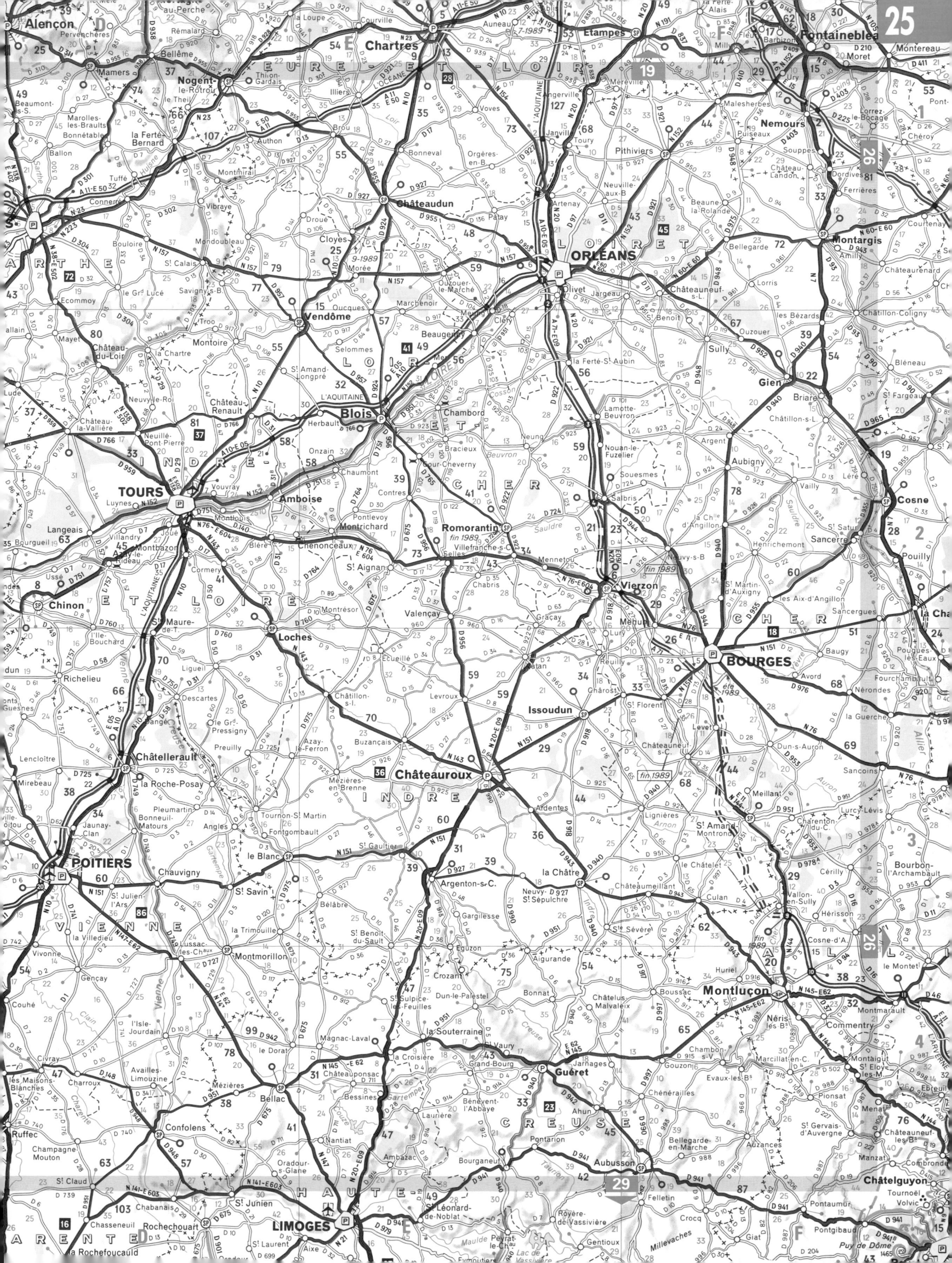

TROYES
Sens
Montargis
Joigny
Auxerre
YONNE
Chaumont
HAUTE-MARNE
Langres
Bar-s-Aube
Bar-s-Seine
Châtillon-s-S.
Tonnerre
Chablis
Avallon
Vézelay
Clamecy
Cosne
Sancerre
Montbard
Semur-en-Auxois
CÔTE-D'OR
DIJON
Saulieu
Beaune
Nuits-St Georges
NIÈVRE
la Charité
Nevers
Château-Chinon
Autun
le Creusot
Chalon-s-S.
Montceau-les-Mines
SAÔNE-ET-LOIRE
Tournus
Mâcon
Moulins
Decize
Digoin
Paray-le-Monial
Charolles
Cluny
Louhans
Bourg-en-Bresse
AIN
VICHY
Roanne
RHÔNE
Villefranche-s-Saône
LYON
Riom
CLERMONT-FERRAND
Thiers
Montluçon
Gannat
Commentry
Châtelguyon
Royat
Feurs
LOIRE
ALLIER
Saint-Pourçain
Lapalisse
Cusset
Montmarault

A   B   C

16
103 Chabanais
Chasseneuil Rochechouart

St Trojan
Pont-d'Oléron
Brouage
St Porchaire
St Hilaire-
de-Villefranche
St Savinien
65
la Rochefoucauld

Marennes 22 34 26 17 D 728
Ronce
la Tremblade 53 18
Saujon
Saintes 26 Cognac
Jarnac Hiersac Ruelle Angoulême
Châteauneuf Segonzac la Couronne
Montbron
Bussière-
Badil St Mathieu

Pnte de la Coubre

Royan 38
St Georges-
de-Didonne
le Verdon Cozes
Meschers Gémozac Pons Archiac
St Genis-
de-Saintonge Barbezieux Blanzac Villebois-
Lavalette Mareuil 85 Nontron St Pardoux-
la-Rivière
Soulac Mortagne 50 Jonzac Baignes-
Ste-Radegonde Montmoreau Verteillac Bouteilles 78 Thiviers
St Palais 37 23 91 Brossac 95 Montlieu Chalais Ribérac Brantôme Champagnac-
de-Belair

Montalivet St Vivien-
de-Médoc 88 Mirambeau St Ciers Montendre Aubeterre Montagrier St Astier **Périgueux**
Lesparre
Médoc Montguyon la Roche-Chalais 24
Hourtin Pauillac Blaye St Savin 90 Mussidan Vergt
St Laurent-
Médoc Lamarque Bourg Guitres Coutras Isle Montpon-
Ménestérol le Bugue
Carcans-Plage 64 Castelnau-
de-Médoc Ambès St André-
de-Cubzac Villefranche-
de-Lonchat Bergerac
Maubuisson Carcans Ste Hélène 59 Blanquefort Libourne St Emilion Castillon-
la-Bataille Vélines Ste-Foy-
la-Grande Monbazillac Beaumont Issigeac
Lacanau-Océan Lacanau St Médard-
en-Jalles Bassens Carbon
Blanc 31 87 Branne Dordogne Pujols 58 Duras 60 Castillonnès
Mérignac **BORDEAUX** Créon Targon Sauveterre-
de-Guyenne Eymet Villeréal
Arès 66 Andernos Audenge la Brède Cadillac Pellegrue Miramont-
de-Guyenne Lauzun Cancon Monflanquin
Arcachon Gujan-
Mestras Facture 47 Podensac Ste Croix-du-Mont la Réole Seyches Tombebœuf
Cap Ferret 45 St Macaire Monségur **Marmande** Castelmoron Villeneuve-
s-Lot
Pyla
Pilat-Plage la Teste 65 49 33 Langon GARONNE 37 Tonneins 53 47
Cazaux 55 Auros le Mas
d'Agenais été
1989
Biscarrosse-Plage Sanguinet Belin-
Béliet Villandraut Bazas Grignols 58 28 33 29 Agen
Biscarrosse Parentis-en-Born Eyre St Symphorien 46 Casteljaloux Damazan Aiguillon Port-Ste Marie
Pissos Sore Captieux Houeillès 65 30 Lavardac 31 Puymirol Valence
Mimizan-Plage Labouheyre Sabres Labrit Nérac 35 Astaffort Auvil
Mimizan 94 Morcenx 40 74 Roquefort St Justin Barbotan Gabarret Mézin Condom 71 Lavit Beaumont-
de-Lomagne
Lit-et-Mixe Onesse-et-
Laharie 83 69 Cazaubon Montréal Lectoure St Clar
St Girons-Plage 18 Castets Mont-de-Marsan Villeneuve-de-M. Eauze 67 Valence Fleurance
Vieux-Boucau Léon Tartas 65 Grenade 29 Nogaro 82 Vic-Fézensac Jegun Mauvezin
Soustons fin 1989 89 St Sever Adour Riscle Plaisance Aignan **Auch** Gimont
Hossegor Dax Mugron 54 Aire-s-l'Adour Nogaro Vic-en-Bigorre Montesquiou l'Isle-de-Noé Mirande Saramon
Capbreton St Vincent-de-Tyrosse Hagetmau Eugénie-
les-Bains Garlin Castelnau-
Rivière-Basse Marciac Masseube Seissan
BIARRITZ Tarnos Amou Geaune Riscle Lembeye Maubourguet Mielan Lombez
St-Jean-de-Luz St Martin-
de-Seignanx Peyrehorade Arzacq-
Arraziguet 37 48 Rabastens-
de-Bigorre Trie
Bayonne Bidache Orthez Salies-
de-Béarn Thèze Vic-en-Bigorre Pouyastruc Castelnau-
Magnoac
Hendaye Bidart Labastide-
Clairence Lacq Mourenx Morlaàs **Tarbes** Galan Lannemezan
Suéthary Ustaritz Hasparren Salvetat-
de-B. Navarrenx Monein Lescar **PAU** Nay Tournay
Ascain Cambo-
les-Bains St Palais Mauléon-
Licharre Oloron-
Ste Marie Ossun Lestelle Aureilhan
Vera de
Bidasoa Espelette Ainhoa St Jean-Pied-de-Port Tardets-Sorholus Aramits Lurbe-
St Christau Canyon Boussens

A   B   C

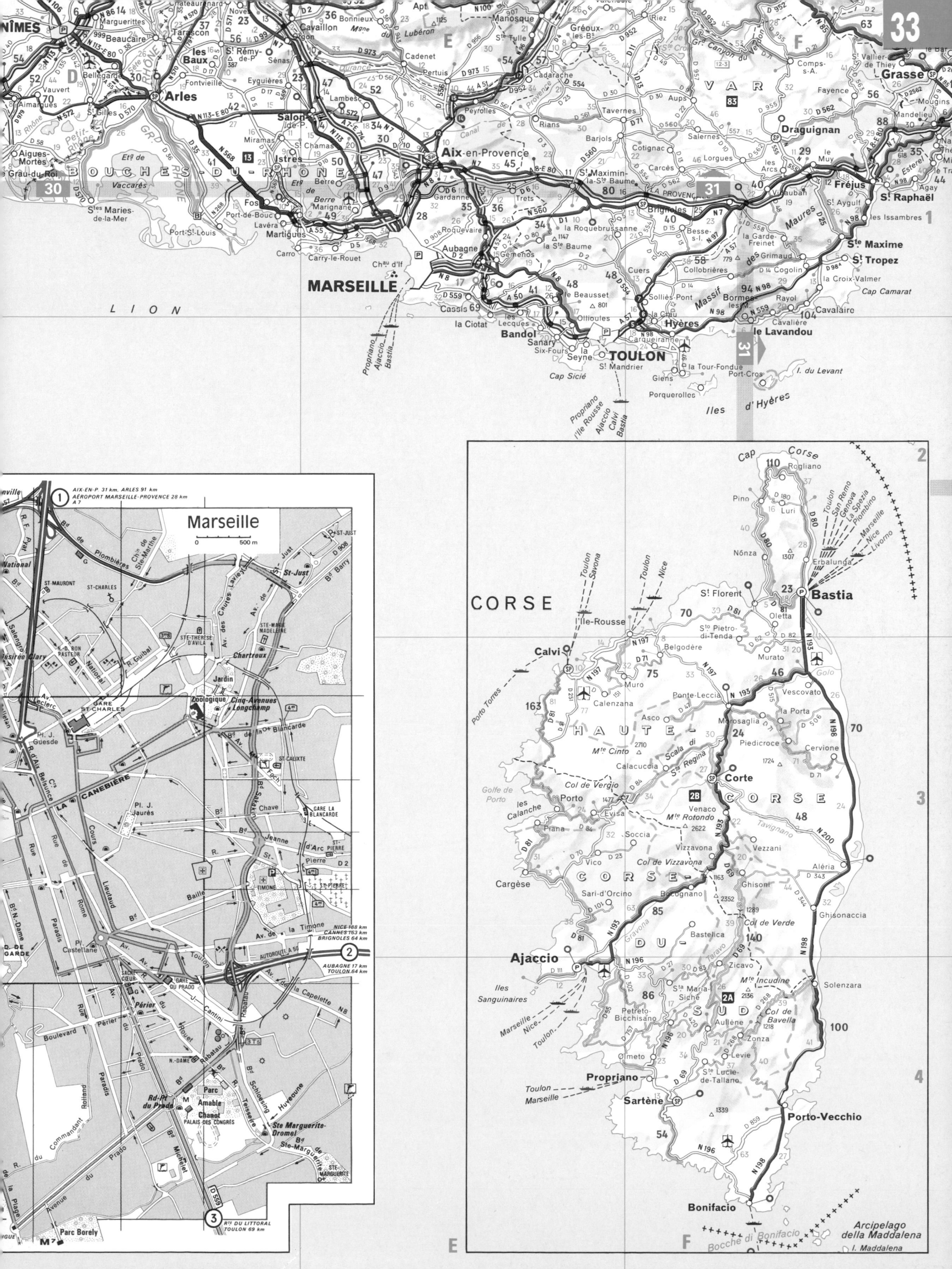

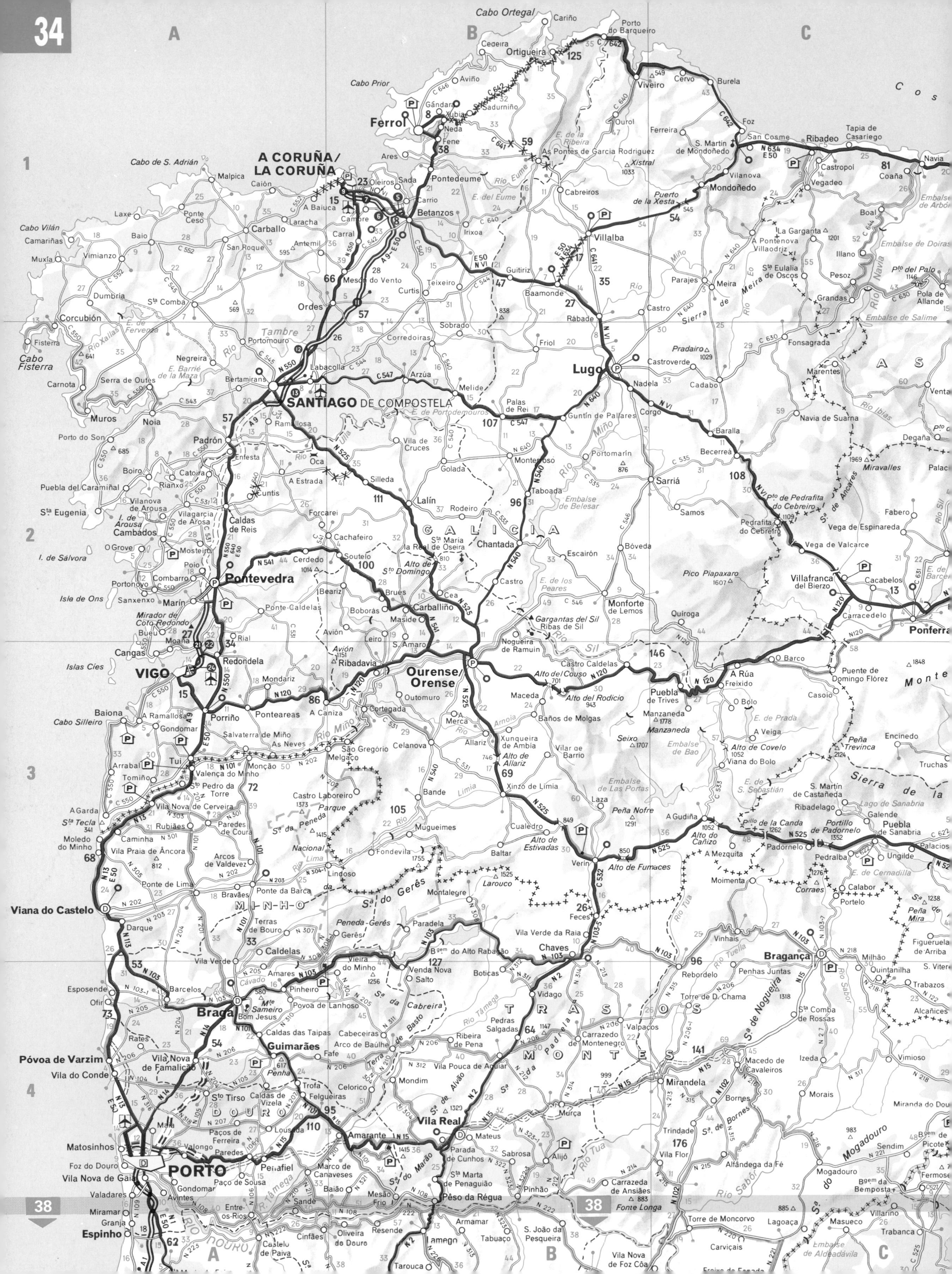

A   B   C

Cabo Ortegal
Cariño
Porto do Barqueiro
Cedeira
Ortigueira   125
Avaño   C 642   Cervo   Burela
Ferrol   Viveiro   Foz
Gándara   8   Xubia   Ourol   Ferreira   S. Cosme   Ribadeo   Tapia de Casariego
Neda   59   As Pontes de Garcia Rodriguez   S. Martin de Mondoñedo   San Cosme   81   Navia
Fene   38   Xistral   Vilanova   Castropol   Coaña
Ares   Mondoñedo   Vegadeo   Boal
A CORUÑA/LA CORUÑA   Pontedeume   Villalba   A Pontenova   Illano
Oleiros   Sada   54   Villaodriz
Malpica   Caión   Carrio   Cabreiros   Sta Eulalia de Oscos   Pesoz
Laxe   A Baiuca   Betanzos   Irixoa   17   35   Parajes   Meira   Grandas   Pola de Allande
Camariñas   23   Cambre   Carral   Guitiriz   Baamonde   Castro   Fonsagrada
Muxía   Carballo   Antemil   27   Rábade   Embalse de Salime
Vimianzo   San Roque   66   Meson do Vento   47   Friol   **Lugo**   Castroverde
Baio   Ordes   Teixeiro   Pradairo   Marentes
Dumbría   57   Curtis   Sobrado   Corgo
Corcubión   Sta Comba   Corredoiras   Nadela   Cadabo   Navia de Suarna
Fisterra   Portomouro   Labacolla   Friol   Guntín de Pallares   Baralla   Degaña
Cabo Fisterra   Negreira   Arzúa   Melide   107   Becerreá
Carnota   Serra de Outes   Bertamirans   **SANTIAGO DE COMPOSTELA**   Palas de Rei   108   Pedrafita do Cebreiro
Muros   Noia   Ramallosa   Monterroso   Samos   Miravalles
Porto do Son   Padrón   Taboada   Sarriá   Fabero
Boiro   Enfesta   Oca   111   Lalín   96   Pedrafita do Cebreiro   Vega de Espinareda
Puebla del Caramiñal   Catoira   Silleda   Rodeiro   Samos   Villafranca del Bierzo   Cacabelos
Sta Eugenia   Rianxo   A Estrada   Forcarei   **GALICIA**   Escairón   13   Carracedelo
I. de Arousa   Vilanova de Arousa   Caldas de Reis   Cuntis   Cachafeiro   Sta Maria la Real de Oseira   Chantada   Bóveda   Monforte de Lemos   **Ponferrada**
Cambados   Cerdedo   100   Souteto   Alto de Sto Domingo   Castro   Quiroga
O Grove   Mosteiro   Bearíz   Brués   Cea   146   A Rúa   Puente de Domingo Flórez
I. de Sálvora   Poio   Combarro   **Pontevedra**   Ponte-Caldelas   Carballiño   Nogueira de Ramuin   Castro Caldelas   Freixido   O Barco   Casoio   O Bolo
Portonovo   Sanxenxo   Avión   Maside   Alto del Couso   Puebla de Trives   A Veiga
Bueu   Moaña   27   Rial   Avión   Leiro   S. Amaro   Manzaneda   Encinedo
Cangas   Redondela   34   Ribadavia   **Ourense/Orense**   Maceda   Alto del Rodicio   Peña Trevinca
VIGO   15   Porriño   Ponteareas   86   Outomuro   Merca   Baños de Molgas   Manzaneda   Viana do Bolo   S. Martin de Castañeda
Baiona   A Ramallosa   Gondomar   A Caniza   Cortegada   Allariz   Xunqueira de Ambia   Ribadelago   Puebla de Sanabria
Cabo Silleiro   Tui   Salvaterra de Miño   As Neves   São Gregório   Celanova   Vilar de Barrio   A Gudiña   Portillo de Padornelo
Arrabal   Tomiño   Valença do Minho   Monção   72   Castro Laboreiro   Bande   69   Xinzo de Limia   Laza   Peña Nofre   Padornelo   Puebla de Sanabria
A Garda   Sta Tecla   Rubiães   Paredes de Coura   Parque Peneda   105   Muguemes   Cualedro   A Mezquita   Moimenta   Palacios
Moledo do Minho   Caminha   Arcos de Valdevez   Nacional   Fondevila   Lindoso   Baltar   Verín   Alto de Fumaces   Corraes   Peña Mira
68   Vila Praia de Âncora   Ponte de Lima   Bravães   **MINHO**   Ponte da Barca   Montalegre   Vila Verde da Raia   26   Feces   Vinhais   Portelo
Viana do Castelo   Darque   Vila Verde   Caldelas   Paradela   Chaves   96   **Bragança**   Figueruela de Arriba
53   Esposende   Barcelos   Amares   127   Venda Nova   Boticas   Vidago   Rebordelo   Penhas Juntas   Alcañices
Ofir   73   **Braga**   Póvoa de Lanhoso   Cabeceiras   Ribeira de Pena   64   Carrazedo de Montenegro   Valpaços   141   Macedo de Cavaleiros   Izeda
Póvoa de Varzim   Rates   54   **Guimarães**   Arco de Baúlhe   Mondim   Vila Pouca de Aguiar   Mirandela   Trabazos
Vila do Conde   Vila Nova de Famalicão   Fafe   Celorico   Murça   176   Mogadouro
Matosinhos   Sto Tirso   Caldas de Vizela   Trofa   Felgueiras   95   **Vila Real**   Mateus   Alfândega da Fé
Foz do Douro   110   Amarante   Sta Marta de Penaguião   Alijó   Vila Flor   Torre de Moncorvo
PORTO   Penafiel   Marco de Canaveses   **Péso da Régua**   Pinhão   Carrazeda de Ansiães   Mogadouro
Vila Nova de Gaia   Paços de Ferreira   Baião   Mesão Frio   S. João da Pesqueira
Valadares   Gondomar   Entre-os-Rios   Sande   Resende   Armamar   Tabuaço   Vila Nova de Foz Côa
Miramar   Granja   Avintes   Cinfães   Oliveira do Douro   222   Fonte Longa   Torre de Moncorvo
Espinho   62   Castelo de Paiva   Tarouca

A B C

Espinho
Miramar
Granja
Entre-os-Rios
RIO DOURO
Cinfães
Oliveira do Douro
Resende
Armamar
S. João da Pesqueira
Lamego
Tabuaço
Castelo de Paiva
S. Maria da Feira
Arouca
Montemuro
Tarouca
Penedono
S. João de Tarouca
Moimenta da Beira
Furadouro
S. João da Madeira
Vale de Cambra
Castro Daire
108
Sernancelhe
Vila Nova de Paiva
Ovar
Oliveira de Azeméis
Chãs de Arada
Vila Nova das ...
Torreira
Sever do Vouga
S. Pedro do Sul
Aguiar da Beira
Trancoso
Estarreja
Murtosa
Angeja
Oliveira de Frades
Vouzela
RIO Vouga
Penalva do Castelo
Sátão
Aveiro
Ílhavo
Albergaria-a-Velha
N 2
Viseu
N 16 E 51 46
Fornos de Algodres
Celorico da Beira
29
Vagos
Águeda
Caramulo
Campo de Besteiros
Mangualde
Nelas
Praia de Mira
Mira
Mamarrosa
Anadia
Tondela
Canas de Senhorim
ESTRELA
Vale de Estrela
Gua...
Cantanhede
Tocha
Arazede
Realhada
Luso
Buçaco
Sta Comba Dão
Mortágua
Carregal do Sal
Oliveira do Hospital
S. Romão
Seia
Manteigas
Valhelhas
Praia de Tocha
Cabo Mondego
Buarcos
Montemor-o-Velho
Penacova
Tábua
138
Loriga
Penhas da Saúde
Belmonte
Figueira da Foz
COIMBRA
25
Vila Nova de Poiares
Arganil
SERRA
Unhais da Serra
Teixoso
Caria
Condeixa-a-Nova
14
Miranda do Corvo
S. Pedro de Açor
Covilhã
Soure
Lousã
Góis
Fundão
Louriçal
Degracias
Penela
Castanheira de Pêra
Pampilhosa da Serra
Silvares
Vale de Prazeres
Alpedrinha
Pedrógão
54
56
Pombal
Sicó
Pontão
Pedrógão Grande
Orvalho
S. Vicente da Beira
Praia da Vieira
Vieira
Monte Redondo
Ansião
Figueiró dos Vinhos
Cambas
Foz Giraldo
Idanha a Nova
Monte Real
Bgem do Cabril
Oleiros
Salgueiro do Campo
Alcains
Escalos de Cima
S. Pedro de Moel
Marinha Grande
Barqueiro
Alvaiázere
Sarzedas
Martinganca
Leiria
Cernache de Bonjardim
Sertã
Castelo Branco
Ladoeiro
Nazaré
Batalha
Cruz da Légua
Vila Nova de Ourém
Ferreira do Zêzere
Proença-a-Nova
Vila Velha de Ródão
Rosmaninhal
Alcobaça
57
Cova da Iria
Porto de Mós
63
Vila de Rei
Bgem de Cedillo
Malpica
S. Martinho do Porto
Fátima
Mira de Aire
Cedillo
Cabo Carvoeiro
Alfeizerão
50
Tomar
Sardoal
Mação
Montalvão
Herrera de Alcántara
Foz do Arelho
Serra de Aire
Torres Novas
Castelo de Bode
58
Santiago de Alcántara
Ilha Berlenga
Baleal
Alcanena
Constância
Nisa
Peniche
Caldas da Rainha
Óbidos
18
Alcanede
Entroncamento
Almourol
Abrantes
Arez
Castelo de Vide
Atouguia da Baleia
Rio Maior
46
Golegã
Vila Nova da Barquinha
Tramagal
Rossio
Gavião
Tolosa
Marvão
Valencia de Alcántara
Lourinhã
Bombarral
33
Cadaval
Alcanhões
Chamusca
Bemposta
Alpalhão
24
Galegos
Praia de Sta Cruz
Cercal
44
Santarém
Alpiarça
Chouto
Mo da Pedra
Flor da Rosa
Crato
Portalegre
S. Vicente de Alcántara
Torres Vedras
Atalaia
47
Cartaxo
Aveiras de Cima
Almeirim
Muge
Ponte de Sor
Galveias
Alter do Chão
La Codosera
Ericeira
102
Alenquer
Azambuja
São José da Lamarosa
Bgem de Montargil
Avis
Cabeço de Vide
Arronches
Pto de los Conejeros
Mafra
Sapataria
Sobral de Mte Agraço
Arruda dos Vinhos
Vila Franca de Xira
Benavente
Montargil
Bgem do Maranhão
Fronteira
Monforte
Bgem do Caia
Malveira
35
Alverca do Ribatejo
Samora Correia
Coruche
Mora
Casa Branca
Sousel
59
Sta Eulália
Campo Maior
Cabo da Roca
Colares
Sintra
23
Loures
Bucelas
35
Sto Estêvão
85
Couço
Pavia
Vimieiro
Vila Fernando
Elvas
Malveira
Lousa
Amadora
Sacavém
Alhos
Brotas
Évoramonte
Estremoz
Vila Boim
Cascais
Estoril
25
Oeiras
LISBOA
Alcochete
Montijo
Tajpadas
Canha
Lavre
Arraiolos
68
Vila Viçosa
Juromenha
Trafaria
Almada
Barreiro
Moita
Pinhal Novo
Cruzamento de Pegões
Vendas Novas
37
Montemor-o-Novo
46
Borba
47
Alandroal
Costa da Caparica
Seixal
Maratega
Azaruja
Vila Fresca de Azeitão
39
Palmela
21
Sesimbra
Setúbal
Arrábida
Cabo Espichel
Península de Tróia
30
S. Miguel de Machede
Redondo
Terena
60
Alcácer do Sal
Comporta
Évora
Santiago do Escoural
S. Cristóvão
Bgem de Pego do Altar
Monsaraz
Casa Branca
Montoito
Aguiar
Cheles
Alconchel

A B C

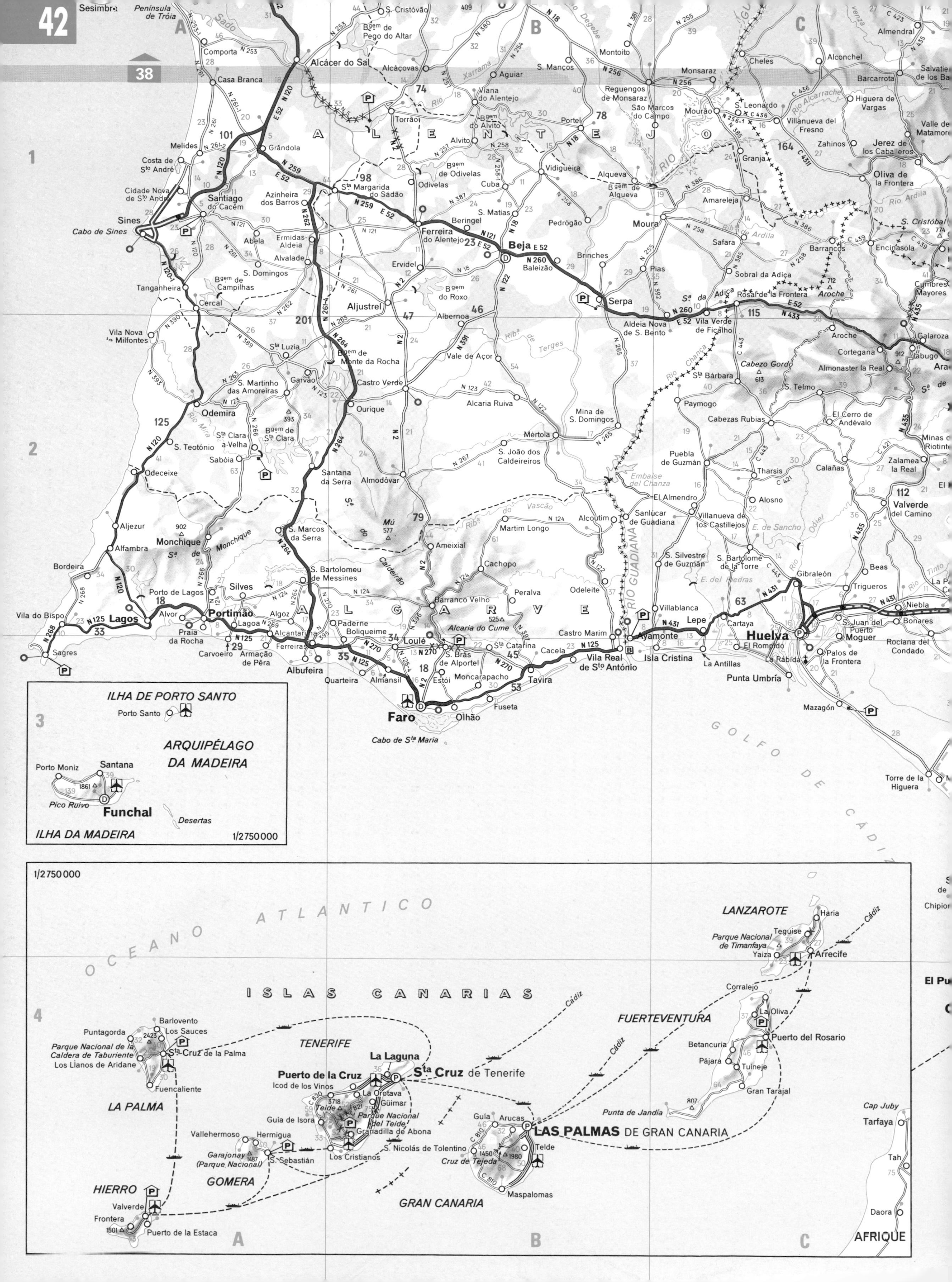

Page header / grid references
A B C
1 2 3 4

Portugal / Alentejo / Algarve region

Sesimbra
Península de Tróia
S. Cristóvão
409
N 18
N 253
Sado
44
Comporta N 253
28
Casa Branca N 261
Alcácer do Sal
Alcáçovas
S. Manços
Montoito
Monsaraz
Cheles
Barcarrota
Salvaterra de los Ba
Bgem de Pego do Altar
N 253
Aguiar
N 256
N 256
S. Leonardo
Higuera de Vargas
Grândola
N 259
Torrão
Viana do Alentejo
Portel
Reguengos de Monsaraz
Mourão
Villanueva del Fresno
Jerez de los Caballeros
101
E 52
Bgem do Alvito
N 2
78
N 18
Rio Ardila
164
Oliva de la Frontera
Melides
N 120
Sta Margarida do Sadão
98
Odivelas
Alvito
Bgem de Odivelas
Vidigueira
Alqueva
Bgem de Alqueva
N 386
Granja
Amareleja
Zahinos
Santiago do Cacém
Azinheira dos Barros
N 259
N 258
S. Matias
Cuba
Pedrógão
Moura
Rio Ardila
S. Cristóbal
73
Sines
N 121
N 262
Ermidas-Aldeia
Abela
Ferreira do Alentejo
Beringel
23
Beja E 52
Brinches
Safara
N 258
Barrancos
Cabo de Sines
Alvalade
N 121
N 121
Baleizão
Pias
Sobral da Adiça
Encinasola
S. Domingos
Ervidel
N 2
Albernoa
46
Serpa
N 260
Aldeia Nova de S. Bento
Vila Verde de Ficalho
Rosal de la Frontera E 52
Aroche
115 N 433
Galaroza
Tanganheira
Cercal
201
Aljustrel
47
Vale de Açor
Sa da Adiça
712
Cumbres Mayores
Cabezo Gordo
613
Cortegana
912
Jabugo
Ara
Vila Nova de Milfontes
Sta Luzia
Bgem de Monte da Rocha
Ribª de Terges
Rio Chança
Sta Bárbara
Almonaster la Real
Aroche
S. Martinho das Amoreiras
Garvão
Castro Verde
N 123
Paymogo
S. Telmo
Odemira
125
Sta Clara-a-Velha
Bgem de Sta Clara
Ourique
N 2
Mina de S. Domingos
Cabezas Rubias
El Cerro de Andévalo
Zalamea la Real
Riotinto
S. Teotónio
Sabóia
Santana da Serra
Alcaria Ruiva
N 122
Mértola
Rio Chança
Puebla de Guzmán
Calañas
112
Valverde del Camino
Odeceixe
Almodôvar
S. João dos Caldeireiros
Embalse del Chanza
Tharsis
Aljezur
902
Monchique
Sª
Mú 577
79
do Vascão
N 124
Alcoutim
El Almendro
Sanlúcar de Guadiana
Villanueva de los Castillejos
Alosno
Alfambra
Monchique
S. Marcos da Serra
Ameixial
Martim Longo
Rio Guadiana
E. de Sancho
Bordeira
N 266
S. Bartolomeu de Messines
Cachopo
N 122
S. Silvestre de Guzmán
S. Bartolomé de la Torre
Beas
Porto de Lagos
Silves
N 124
Peralva
Odeleite
E. del Piedras
Gibraleón
N 435
Triqueros
Vila do Bispo
N 125
Lagos
18
Alvor
Portimão
Lagoa
Algoz
Paderne
Boliqueime
Barranco Velho
525
Alcaria do Cume
Castro Marim
Villablanca
Lepe
63 N 431
Huelva
Sagres
33
29
Praia da Rocha
N 125
Alcantarilha
Ferreiras
Loulé
34
N 270
S. Brás de Alportel
N 270
Ayamonte
Isla Cristina
La Antillas
El Rompido
Rociana del Condado
Carvoeiro
Armação de Pêra
35
N 125
18
N 2
Estói
Moncarapacho
45
Cacela
N 125
Vila Real de Sto António
Punta Umbría
Albufeira
Quarteira
Almansil
Faro
Olhão
Fuseta
53
Tavira
Mazagón

ILHA DE PORTO SANTO
Porto Santo

ARQUIPÉLAGO DA MADEIRA
Porto Moniz
Santana
1861
139
Pico Ruivo
Funchal
Desertas
ILHA DA MADEIRA
1/2 750 000
Cabo de Sta Maria
GOLFO DE CÁDIZ
Torre de la Higuera

ISLAS CANARIAS
1/2 750 000
OCEANO ATLÁNTICO

LANZAROTE
Haria
Cádiz
Parque Nacional de Timanfaya
Teguise
Yaiza
Arrecife

FUERTEVENTURA
Corralejo
La Oliva
Puerto del Rosario
Betancuria
Pájara
Tuineje
Gran Tarajal
Punta de Jandía
Cap Juby
Tarfaya

La Palma
Barlovento
Los Sauces
Puntagorda
2423
Parque Nacional de la Caldera de Taburiente
Sta Cruz de la Palma
Los Llanos de Aridane
Fuencaliente
LA PALMA

TENERIFE
La Laguna
Puerto de la Cruz
Icod de los Vinos
La Orotava
Güimar
Sta Cruz de Tenerife
3718
Teide
Parque Nacional del Teide
Guía de Isora
Granadilla de Abona
Abona
Los Cristianos
S. Nicolás de Tolentino

Vallehermoso
Hermigua
Garajonay (Parque Nacional)
1487
S. Sebastián
GOMERA

HIERRO
Valverde
Frontera
1501
Puerto de la Estaca

Guía
Arucas
LAS PALMAS DE GRAN CANARIA
Telde
Cruz de Tejeda
1980
Maspalomas
GRAN CANARIA

El Pu
Chipio

AFRIQUE

1

2

3

4

Hamburg

KIEL
KIEL, FLENSBURG
LANGENHORN
LÜBECK
Pinneberger Str.
432
433
LANGENHORN
Langenhorner Chaussee
Brombeerweg
WELLINGSBÜTTEL
Alte Landstr.
HUSUM ITZEHOE
7
HAMBURG EIDELSTEDT
SCHNELSEN
HAMBURG SCHNELSEN
447
Friedrich-Ebert-Str.
NIENDORF
FUHLSBÜTTEL
OHLSDORF
Berner Chaussee
Fuhlsbütteler Str.
BRAMFELD
Chaussee
A 23
E 45-A 7
HAMBURG NORDWEST
ALSTERDORF
ADAC
Kieler Str.
Holsteiner Chaussee
Alsterkrug-chaussee
Alster
BARMBEK
LÜBECK
Pinneberger Chaussee
EIDELSTEDT
TIERPARK HAGENBECK
STELLINGEN
EPPENDORF
WINTERHUDE STADTPARK
U Bahn
Friedrich-Ebert-Damm
LURUP
STADION
VOLKSPARK
MOSCHEE
8
AuBenalster
S Bahn
WANDSBEK
Ahrensburger Str.
431
BAHRENFELD
7
6
Wandsbeker Chee.
A 24
GUDOW LÜBECK
WEDEL
HAMBURG BAHRENFELD
Stresemannstr.
ALTONA
1
Sievekingsallee
Horner Landstr.
FLOTTBEK
OTTENSEN
5
2
3
BLANKENESE
OTHMARSCHEN
ELBE (Niederelbe)
Norderelbe
HAMM
HORNER RAMPE
5
LAUENBURG
BILLBROOK
HÄFEN
4
ELBBRÜCKE
HAMBURG WALTERSHOF
FINKENWERDER
AUTOBAHN
HAMBURG SÜD-OST
LÜBECK GUDOW
KÖHLBRANDBRÜCKE
WILHELMSBURG
Georg-Wilhelm-Str.
Wilhelmsburger Reichsstr.
HAMBURG SÜD
E 22-A 1
A 25
ALTENWERDER
HAMBURG MOORBURG
KIRCHDORF
MOORFLEET
LAUENBURG
SPADENLAND
STADE CUXHAVEN
73
Stader Str.
Buxtehuder Str.
HAMBURG STILLHORN
HAMBURG-HEIMFELD
NEULAND
HARBURG
HARBURGER BERGE
E 45-A 7
Bremer Str.
HAMBURG HARBURG
75
4
E 22-A 1
ADAC
BREMEN HANNOVER
ROTENBURG SOLTAU
LÜNEBURG
HANNOVER BREMEN

0   3 km

Bremen

BREMERHAVEN
INDUSTRIEHÄFEN
2 km
BREMERHAVEN
E 234-A 27
WORPSWEDE, BORGFELD
GRÖPELINGEN
Gröpelinger Heerstr.
FREIHÄFEN
HORN-LEHE
HAFEN
Werftstr.
Wetterungs-weg
Unterer Burger
HORN-LEHE
WESER
Nordstr.
Bremer Burger
FINDORFF
SCHWACHHAUSEN
RADIO BREMEN
NEUE-
WOLTMERSHAUSEN
Woltmershauser Str.
5
PARK
Parkallee
VAHR
Senator-Apelt-Str.
4
1
Kurfürstenallee
WESERSTADION
HUCHTING
3
2
Osterdeich
75
NEUSTADT
Kornstr.
Neuenlander Str.
HUCKELRIEDE
HABENHAUSEN
Habenhauser Landstr.
HEMELINGEN
OLDENBURG WILHELMSHAVEN GRONINGEN
Oldenburger Str.
AUTOBAHN (E 37-A 1): BRINKUM MINDEN, OSNABRÜCK
ARSTEN
AUTOBAHN (E 37-A 1): HEMELINGEN

NOORDZEE

N O O R D

D U I N

NORD

Waddeneilanden
Oosterend
Hollum
West-Terschelling
Terschelling
Oost-Vlieland
Vlieland
Leeuwarden
A 31
Harlingen
34
Francker
FRIES
De Koog
Texel
Bolsward
A 7-E 22
N 31
Den Burg
N 359
Den Helder
Den Oever
Afsluitdijk
Workum
N 9
54
N 99
Sloten
Staveren
44
NOORD-
IJsselmeer
Schagen
Medemblik
NEDER
78
Enkhuizen
Bergen
Bergen aan Zee
HOLLAND
Hoorn
Urk
Egmond aan Zee
Alkmaar
N 302
Markermeer
Lelystad-Haven
Lelystad
A 9
90
102
Heerhugowaard
Hoorn
Purmerend
Edam
Volendam
Beverwijk
Wormerveer

50

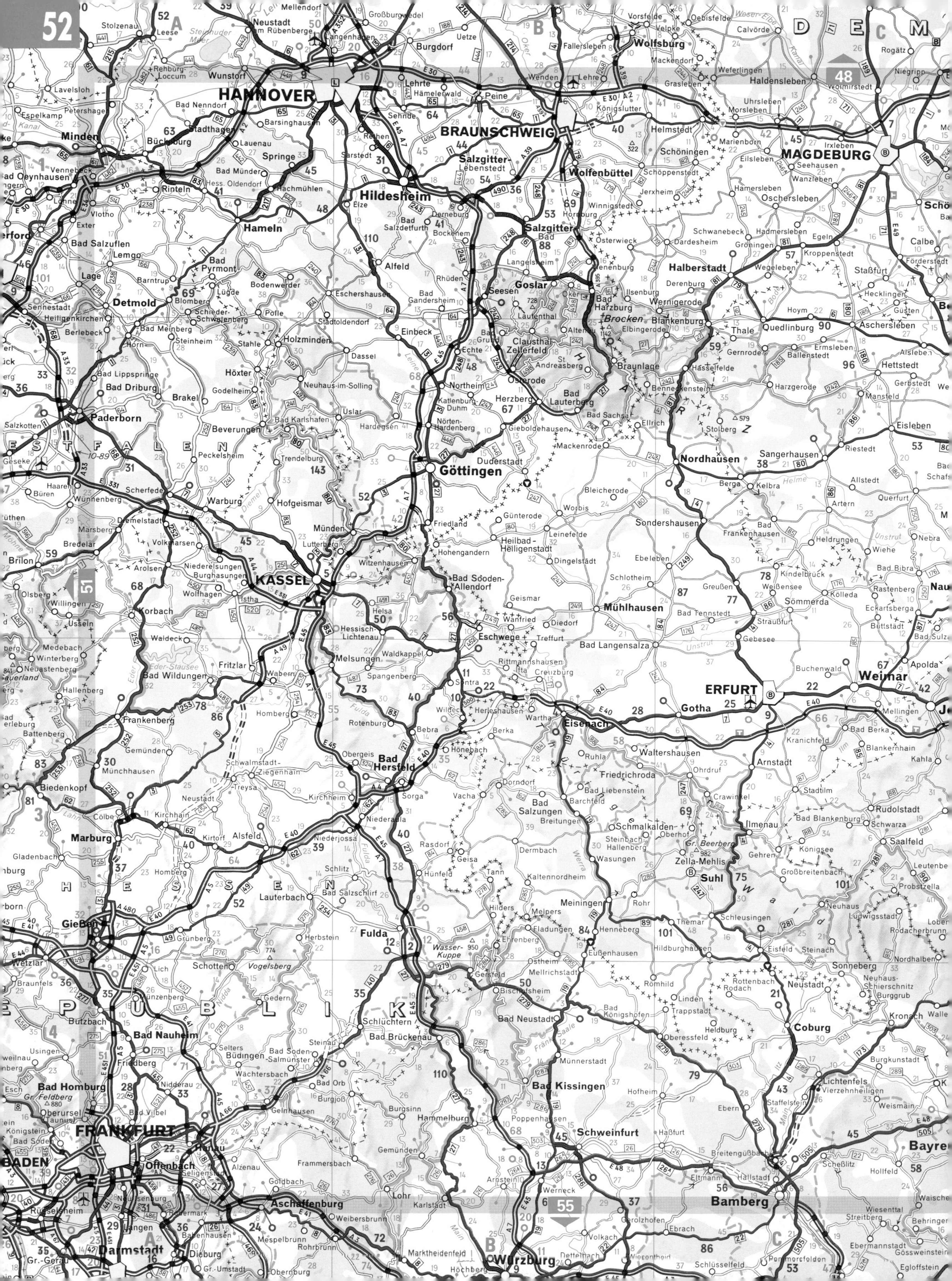

HANNOVER
BRAUNSCHWEIG
MAGDEBURG
Wolfsburg
Haldensleben
Hildesheim
Hameln
Salzgitter
Wolfenbüttel
Goslar
Halberstadt
Quedlinburg
Aschersleben
Detmold
Paderborn
Göttingen
Nordhausen
Mühlhausen
Sangerhausen
KASSEL
Eschwege
Eisenach
Gotha
ERFURT
Weimar
Bad Hersfeld
Marburg
Fulda
Meiningen
Suhl
Hildburghausen
Coburg
Gießen
Bad Nauheim
FRANKFURT
Offenbach
Aschaffenburg
Bad Kissingen
Schweinfurt
Bamberg
WÜRZBURG

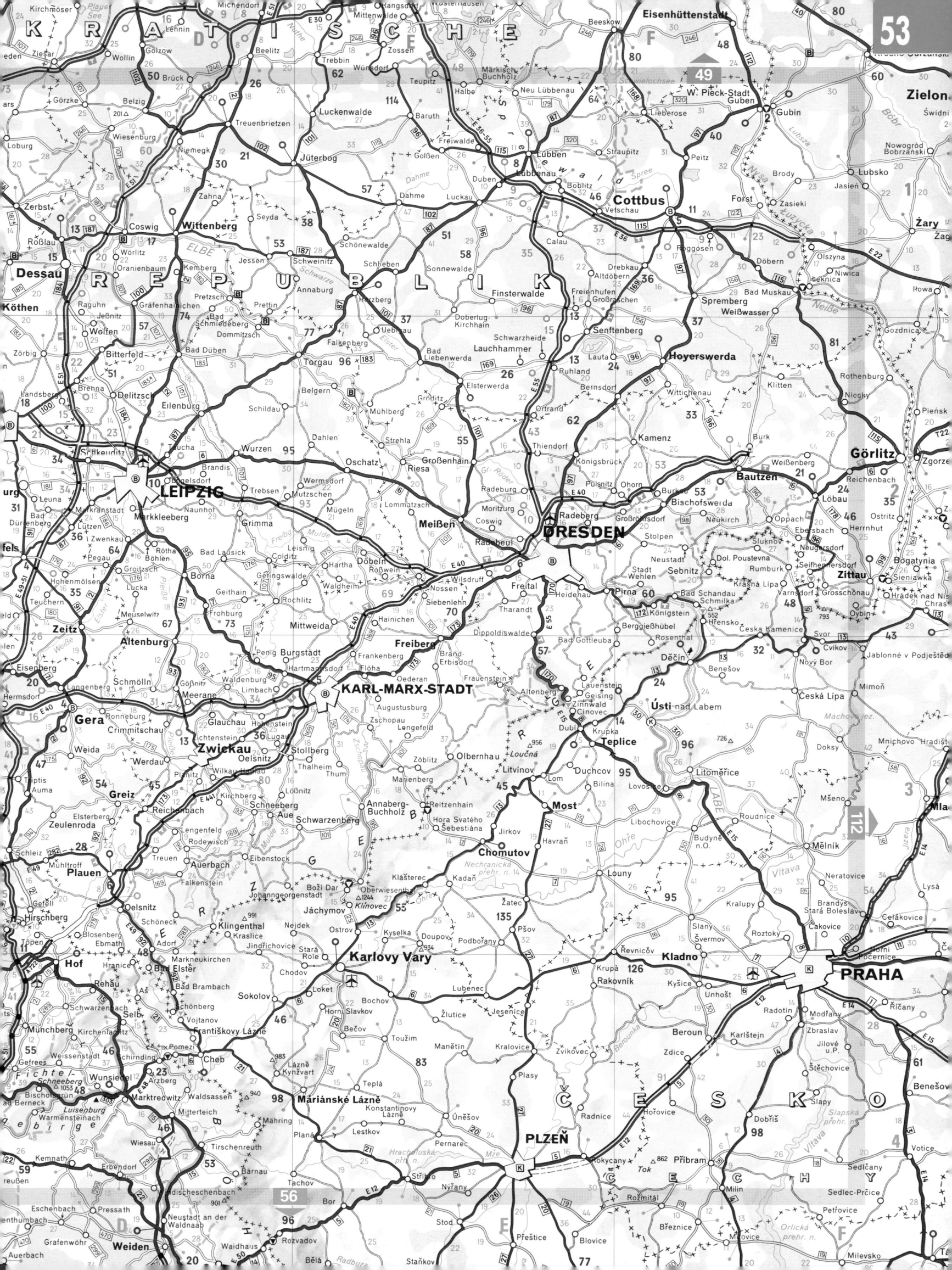

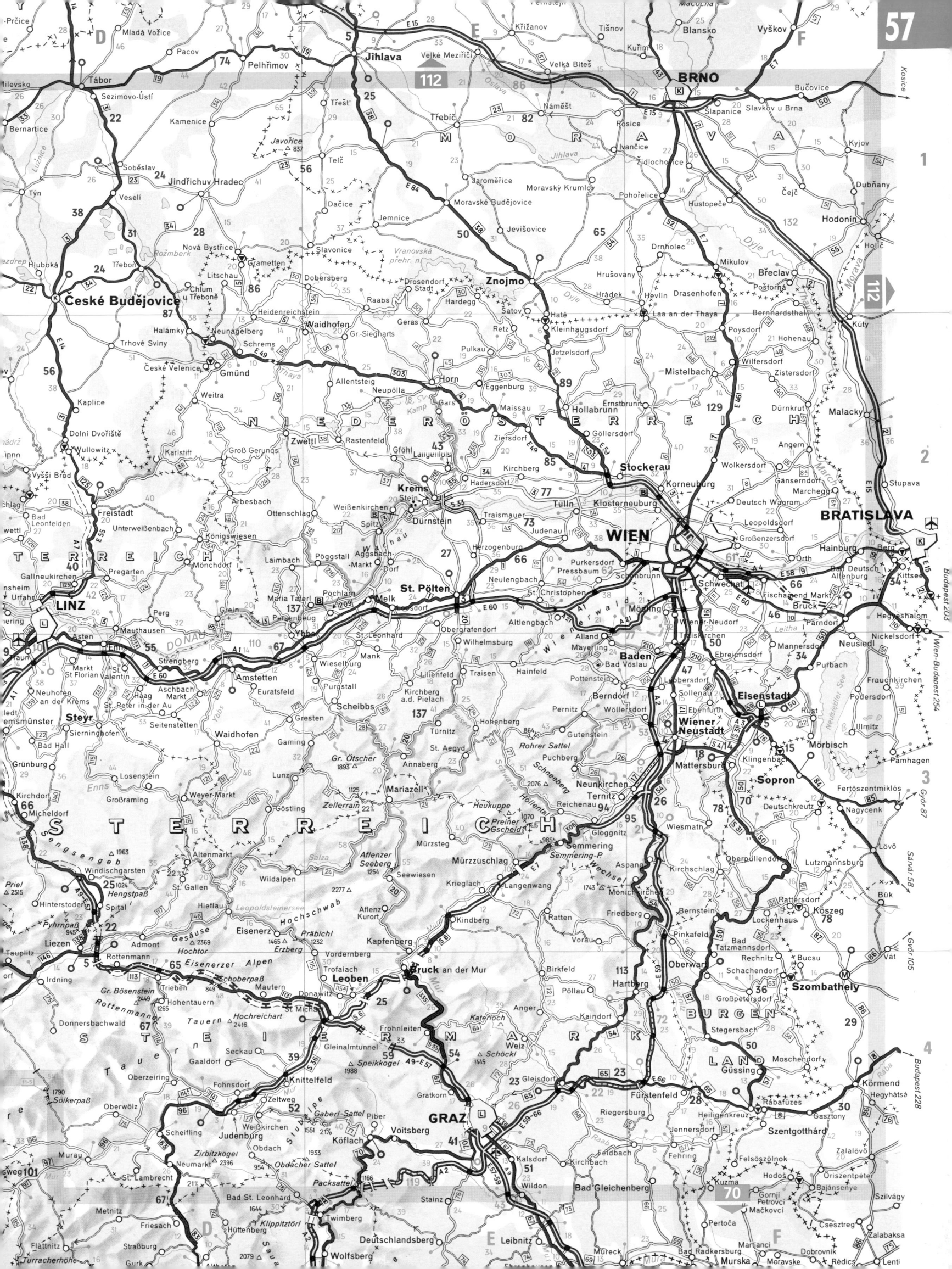

CORSE

Cap Corse

110 Rogliano
Pino
Pino D 180 Luri
D 80
Nónza D 90
1307
28
23 **Bastia**
S.t Florent D 81 Oletta
81
70 39 Oletta
Ste Pietro-di-Tenda D 62 D 82 N 193
Calvi I'lle-Rousse N 197 Belgodère Murato
N 197 D 71 Ponte-Leccia N 193 Vescovato
75 33 Ponte-Leccia 46 Golo
Muro N 197 Morosaglia 515 la Porta
163 81 Calenzana Asco N 193 N 198
HAUTE- 24 Piedicroce Cervione
Mte Cinto 2710 Scala di Sta Regina 1724 D 71
Calacuccia CORSE 48
Col de Vergio Corte
Golfe de Porto Porto 1477 2B Venaco N 200
les Calanche Evisa Mte Rotondo 2622 Vezzani
Piana D 84 Soccia Vizzavona Aléria
Col de Vizzavona 1163 D 343
Vico 1163 Ghisoni D 344
Cargèse CORSE- D 69 44 32
Sari-d'Orcino Bocognano 2352 Ghisonaccia
85 1289 Col de Verde
63 DU- Bastelica 140 N 198
Ajaccio N 193 Zicavo
N 196 Mte Incudine Solenzara
86 Sta Maria-Siché 2A 2136
Iles Sanguinaires Petreto-Bicchisano SUD Col de Bavella 1218
Aullène Zonza 100
Olmeto Levie 41
Propriano Ste Lucie-de-Tallano
D 69 Porto-Vecchio
Sartène 1339
54 N 196
N 198
Bonifacio

Arcipelago della Maddalena
Bocche di Bonifacio I. Maddalena
Sta Teresa Gallura La Maddalena
Palau I. Caprera

Castiglioncello
Riparbella
Solvay S 68 72
Cecina 9
Pomarance
Larderello
Marina di Castagneto-Donoratico
Sassetta
S. Vincenzo Suvereto Monterotondo Maritt.
Campiglia Maritt. Montioni 1060
Venturina Massa Maritt.
97 Ribolla
Piombino Follonica
Portoferràio Cavo
Marciana Marina Rio Marina Punta Ala
Porto Azzurro Castiglione della Pescaia
Marina di Campo Marina di Grosseto
Isola d'Elba Grosse

Arcipelago

Toscano

I. Pianosa

I. d. Giglio

I. di Montecristo

I. di Capraia

I. di Gorgona

Roma (inset)

⑩ LA GIUSTINIANA
OTTAVIA
Roma
0 3 km
MONTE MA
verso Autostrada A 12 72 km CIVITAVECCHIA
⑨
⑧ 26 km AEROPORTO DI FIUMICINO
A 12 78 km CIVITAVECCHIA
CORVIALE
⑦ 24 Km OSTIA ANTICA 28 Km LIDO DI ROMA ⑦

Isola Asinara
Golfo dell' Asinara
Stintino
Porto Torres
Platamona Lido
Castelsardo
Sedini
Martis Nulvi Sennori
Sorso

Arzachena
Porto Rotondo
Costa Smeralda
Baja Sardinia Porto Cervo
Golfo Aranci
19 Olbia
I. Tavolara
Luogosanto 61
Trinità d'Agultu e V.
S. Antonio
Aggius Calangianus
121 Tempio Pausania Telti Loiri
M. Limbara Monti
Padru 57
M. Nieddu
971

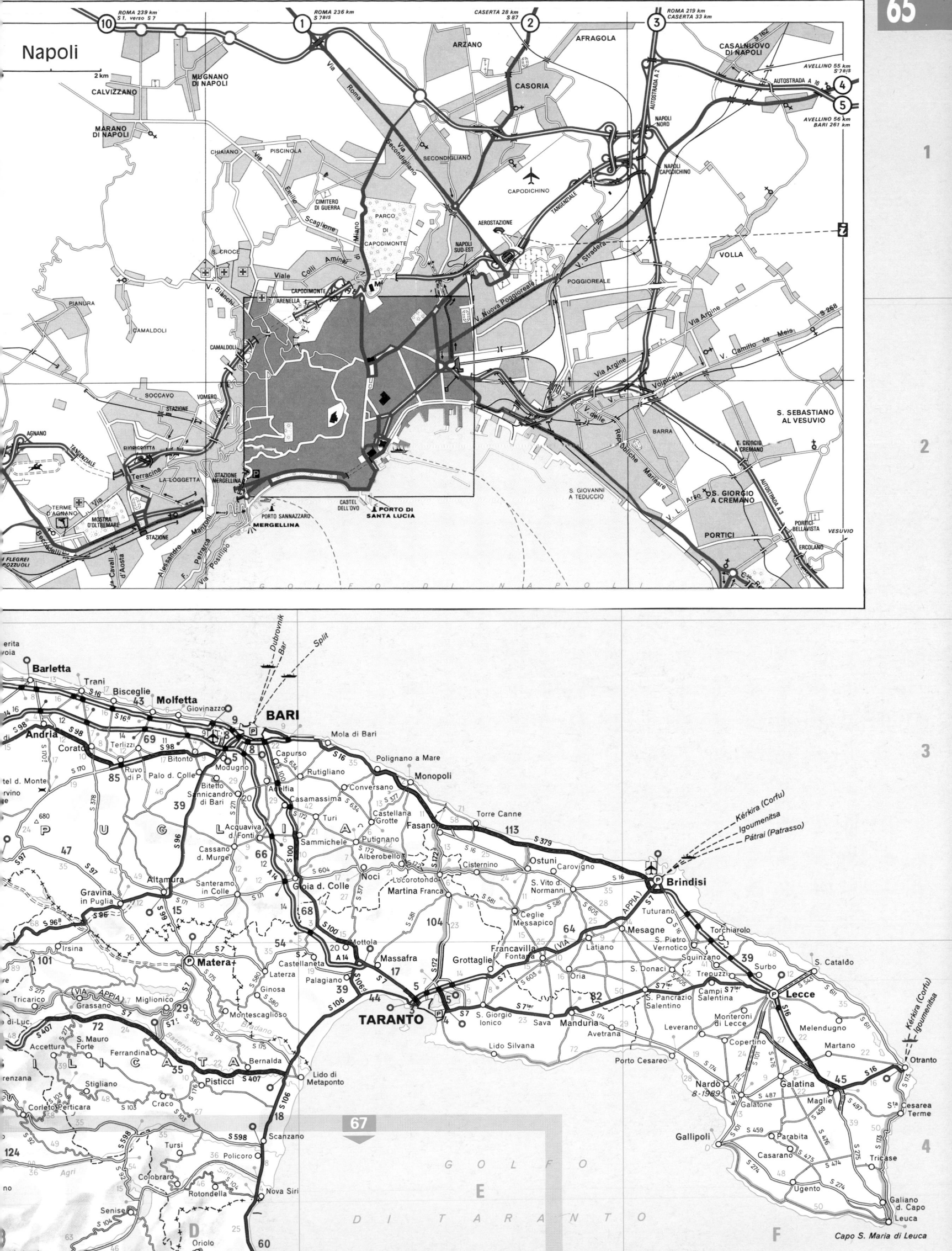

Napoli

2 km

MUGNANO
DI NAPOLI

CALVIZZANO

MARANO
DI NAPOLI

ARZANO

AFRAGOLA

CASALNUOVO
DI NAPOLI

CASORIA

AUTOSTRADA A 2

AUTOSTRADA A 16

NAPOLI
NORD

CHIAIANO

PISCINOLA

SECONDIGLIANO

NAPOLI
CAPODICHINO

TANGENZIALE

VOLLA

PIANURA

CAMALDOLI

CIMITERO
DI GUERRA

PARCO
DI
CAPODIMONTE

CAPODICHINO

AEROSTAZIONE

POGGIOREALE

S. SEBASTIANO
AL VESUVIO

S. CROCE

NAPOLI
SUD-EST

V. Nuova Poggioreale

V. Argine

S. GIORGIO
A CREMANO

SOCCAVO

VOMERO

STAZIONE

CAMALDOLI

ARENELLA

V. Blanchi

BARRA

S. GIOVANNI
A TEDUCCIO

OS. GIORGIO
A CREMANO

AGNANO

TANGENZIALE

FUORIGROTTA

TERRACINA

LA LOGGETTA

STAZIONE
MERGELLINA

PORTICI
BELLAVISTA

PORTICI

TERME
D'AGNANO

MOSTRA
D'OLTREMARE

STAZIONE

ERCOLANO

MERGELLINA

PORTO SANNAZZARO

CASTEL
DELL'OVO

PORTO DI
SANTA LUCIA

VESUVIO

I FLEGREI
POZZUOLI

G O L F O   D I   N A P O L I

1

2

Barletta

Trani

Biscegle

43 Molfetta

Giovinazzo

BARI

S 16

9

Andria

S 98

Corato

Terlizzi

69

S 98

Bitonto

Mola di Bari

S 16

Polignano a Mare

Monopoli

Ruvo di P.

Palo d. Colle

85

Modugno

Adelfia

Rutigliano

Conversano

S 378

Bitetto
Sannicandro
di Bari

39

Casamassima

Turi

Castellana
Grotte

Torre Canne

S 379

113

S 170

S 96

Acquaviva
d. Fonti

Sammichele

Putignano

Fasano

Cassano
d. Murge

66

Alberobello

Cisternino

Ostuni

Carovigno

47

S 97

Altamura

Noci

Locorotondo

S. Vito d.
Normanni

Brindisi

Gravina
in Puglia

Santeramo
in Colle

A 14

Gioia d. Colle

Martina Franca

S 581

APPIA

15

S 99

68

104

Ceglie
Messapico

Tuturano

S 605

Torchiarolo

Irsina

101

S 100

Mottola

54

Massafra

Grottaglie

Francavilla
Fontana

Mesagne

S. Pietro
Vernotico

S 7ter

Squinzano

Surbo

39

S. Cataldo

Matera

Castellaneta

17

Latiano

Oria

S. Donaci

Trepuzzi

Lecce

Laterza

Palagiano

5

Taranto

S. Giorgio
Ionico

Sava

Manduria

Leverano

Monteroni
di Lecce

Copertino

Ginosa

39

44

82

Campi
Salentina

Tricarico

Grassano

Miglionico

29

S 7

Montescaglioso

Avetrana

Melendugno

Martano

Otranto

72

S. Mauro
Forte

Accettura

Ferrandina

Bernalda

Lido Silvana

Porto Cesareo

Nardo

Galatina

45

S 16

35

Pisticci

S 407

Lido di
Metaponto

Galatone

Maglie

S.ta
Cesarea
Terme

Stigliano

Craco

67

Gallipoli

Parabita

Casarano

Tricase

124

Tursi

Policoro

Scanzano

G O L F O

Ugento

Corleto-Perticara

Senise

Rotondella

Nova Siri

D I   T A R A N T O

Galiano
d. Capo

Leuca

D

E

60

Oriolo

Capo S. Maria di Leuca

F

3

4

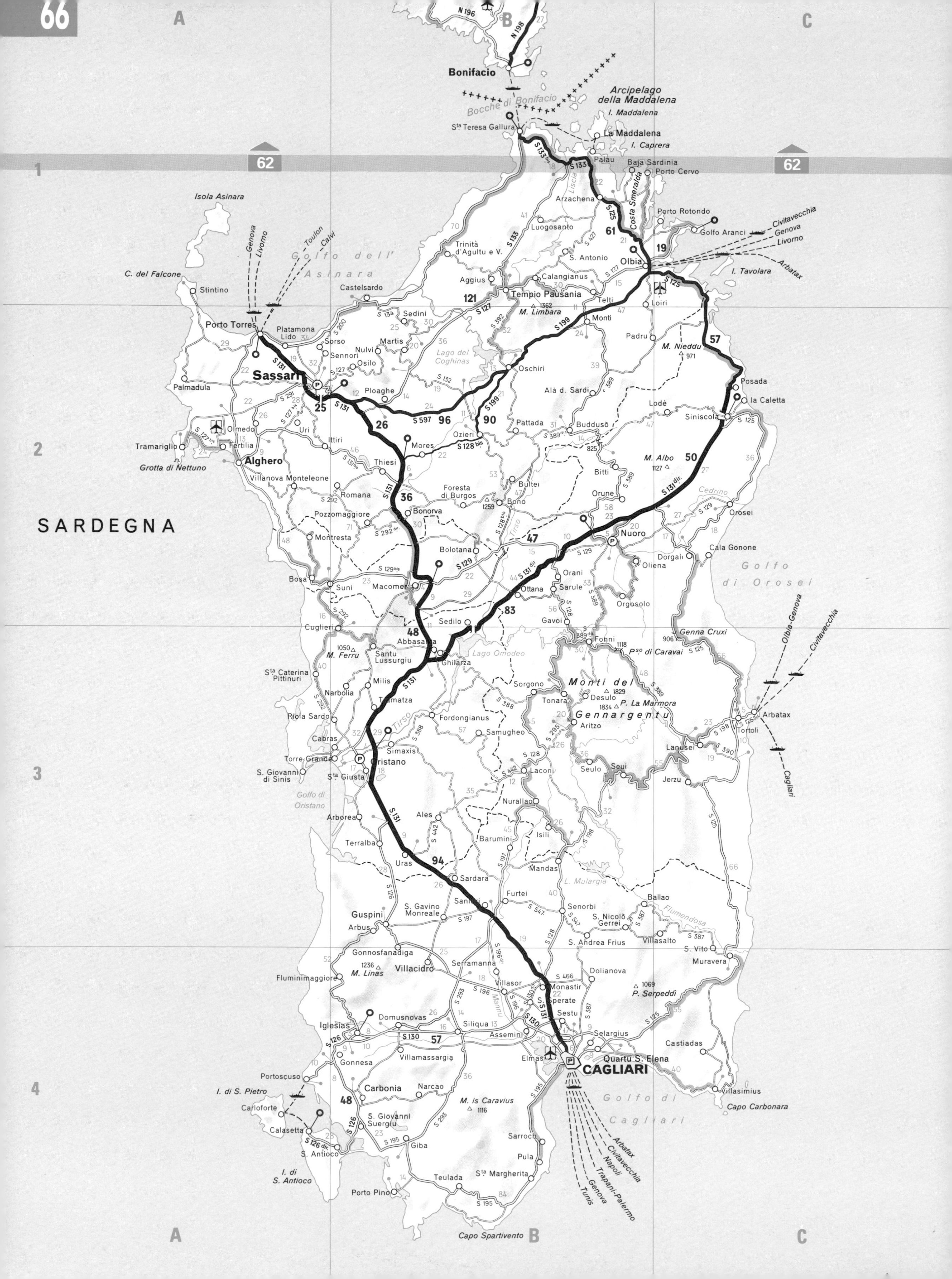

A | B | C

N 196

Bonifacio

N 198

62 | 62

Arcipelago della Maddalena

Bocche di Bonifacio

I. Maddalena

S.ta Teresa Gallura

La Maddalena
I. Caprera

Isola Asinara

Palau
Baja Sardinia
Porto Cervo

S 133

Liscia

Costa Smeralda

Arzachena

Golfo dell' Asinara

Trinità d'Agultu e V.

Luogosanto

Porto Rotondo

61

Golfo Aranci
Civitavecchia
Genova
Livorno

S 133

S.Antonio

Olbia

19

C. del Falcone

Castelsardo

Aggius

Calangianus

S 127

I. Tavolara

Stintino

Tempio Pausania

Telti

Loiri

Arbatax

S 125

Sedini

S 134

M. Limbara
1362

S 199

Monti

57

Martis

S 592

Padru

M. Nieddu
971

Porto Torres

Platamona Lido

Sorso

Nulvi

S 127

Oschiri

Alà d. Sardi

Posada
la Caletta

S 131

Sennori
Osilo

S 132

S 199

Lodè

Siniscola

Sassari

Ploaghe

25

26

S 597

96

90

Pattada

Buddusò

S 125

Palmadula

Uri

Ittiri

Ozieri

389 dir

M. Albo
1127

50

Olmedo

Mores

S 128 bis

825

Bitti

Fertilia

Thiesi

36

Orune

Cedrino

Alghero

Tramariglio

Villanova Monteleone

Romana

S 131

Foresta di Burgos

Bùltei

Bono

Orani

Orosei

Grotta di Nettuno

Pozzomaggiore

Bonorva

1259

Nuoro

Sarule

Cala Gonone

Montresta

S 292

47

Bolotana

S 129

S 131 dir

Ottana

Oliena

Dorgali

Golfo di Orosei

Bosa

Suni

Macomer

S 129

83

Gavoi

Orgosolo

SARDEGNA

Cuglieri

48

Sedilo

Ghilarza

Lago Omodeo

Fonni

Genna Cruxi

M. Ferru
1050

Abbasanta
Santu Lussurgiu

S 131

Sorgono

Monti del

P.so di Caravai

Olbia-Genova
Civitavecchia

S.ta Caterina Pittinuri

Milis

Tramatza

Fordongianus

Desulo
1829
1834 P. La Marmora

Gennargentu

Narbolia

Samugheo

Aritzo

Arbatax

Riola Sardo

Tirso

Tonara

S 198
Tortolì

Cabras

Simaxis

Oristano

S 388

Laconi

Seulo
Seui

Lanusei

Cagliari

Torre Grande

S.ta Giusta

Nurallao

Jerzu

S. Giovanni di Sinis

Golfo di Oristano

Arborea

Ales

Isili

Barumini

Terralba

94

Uras

Sardara

Furtei

Mandas

Senorbì

Ballao

Flumendosa

Guspini

Sanluri

S. Nicolò Gerrei

Villasalto

Arbus

S.Gavino Monreale

S. Andrea Frius

S. Vito

Gonnosfanadiga

Serramanna

Villasor

Dolianova

Muravera

M. Linas
1236

Villacidro

Villasor
Monastir

P. Serpeddi
1069

Fluminimaggiore

Siliqua

Serramanna

Sestu

Selargius

Castiadas

Domusnovas

57

S 130

Assemini

CAGLIARI

Quartu S. Elena

Iglesias

S 126

Villamassargia

Elmas

Villasimius

Portoscuso

Gonnesa

Narcao

48

Carbonia

M. is Caravius
1116

Golfo di Cagliari

Capo Carbonara

I. di S. Pietro

Carloforte

S. Giovanni Suergiu

Sarroch

Arbatax
Civitavecchia
Napoli
Genova
Trapani-Palermo
Tunis

Calasetta

S 126 dir

Giba

Pula

I. di S. Antioco

Teulada

S.ta Margherita

Porto Pino

S 195

Capo Spartivento

A B C

1

2

Isole
I. Filicudi
I. Alicudi

I. di Ustica

MARE TIRRENO

SICILIA

Cagliari
Genova
Livorno
Napoli

Ustica
Tunis

Capo Gallo
Mondello
M. Pellegrino
Sferracavallo
Punta Raisi 6 30
S 113   A 29
Cinisi   17   Capaci   **PALERMO**
Carini
S. Vito lo Capo   Torre d. Impiso   63   Monreale   606   Soluto
S. Stefano
di Camastra   153
Cefalù
26   27
S. Stefano
S 113
Golfo di   46   S 186   Bagheria   Casteldaccia
Castellammare   Misilmeri   24   S 113   Termini   A 20   14   Collesano   Castelbuono   Mistretta
Castellammare   Partinico   Piana   Imerese   A 19   Pº Carbonara   48
d. Golfo   29   30   d. Albanesi   S 121   Altavilla   Buonfornello   △1979   C. del Contrasto   Fe
Erice   S 187   Marineo   Trabia   14   S 120   Petralia   1107
Trapani   S 113   17   S 113   Alcamo   16   S. Cipirello   58   Caccamo   Villafrati   Montemaggiore   M   Caltavuturo   S 643   Gangi   Nicosia
I. di   Paceco   S 187   19   12   Belsito   42   38   S 120
Levanzo   Fulgatore   18   S 119   Rª Busambra   Alia   S 290
Isole Egadi   42   Sedesta   Roccapalumba   50   126   66   19   Leonforte
I-Maréttimo   Birgi   50   50   Calatafini   43   △1613   S 285   Resuttano   56   S 117
I. Favignana   50   11   41   A 29   Corleone   41   S 121   52   16   A 19
38   S 115   S 188   S 119   46   28   Lercara   126   Sta Caterina   Enna
Tunis   12   Salemi   57   Friddi   S 121   Villarosa   12
Pantelleria   S 188   S. Ninfa   Prizzi   126   Mussomeli   15   35   S 117   Valg
Marsala   Partanna   Sta Margherita   S 188   S 189   Serradifalco   S 122   Pietraperzia   Aido
19   di Belice   Chiusa Sclafani   Caltanissetta   33
Castelvetrano   5   S 188   S. Stefano   Montedoro   S 122   Barrafranca   Piazza Arm
S 115   22   A 29   24   Sambuca   Quisquina   Casteltermini   62   Mazzarino   S 191   Nis
Mazara d. Vallo   20   di Sicilia   Alessandria   S. Biagio Platani   58   Delia   Riesi   S 190
Campobello   Menfi   d. Rocca   93   Caltabellotta   83   Canicatti   Sommatino   Ravanusa   81
di Mazara   Selinunte   16   Ribera   Aragona   Favara   Naro   Campobello
Marinella   Sciacca   Raffadali   S 189   di Licata   Butera
Agrigento   8   72   Palma   S 115   Gela
Porto Empedocle   6   di Montechiaro   Licata
Lampedusa

3

MARE   **MEDITERRANEO**

4

Trapani

Pantelleria   Tracino
836
I. di Pantelleria

I. di Linosa

Isole
Pelagie

I. di Lampedusa   Porto Empedocle
Lampedusa

Gozo
Victoria   Nadur
Mgarr   Comino
Siracusa
Mellieha
Mosta   Sliema
MALTA   Rabat   **Valletta**
Vittoriosa
Dingli   249   Zejtun
Zurrieq   Birzebugga
Filfola

A   **B**   **C**

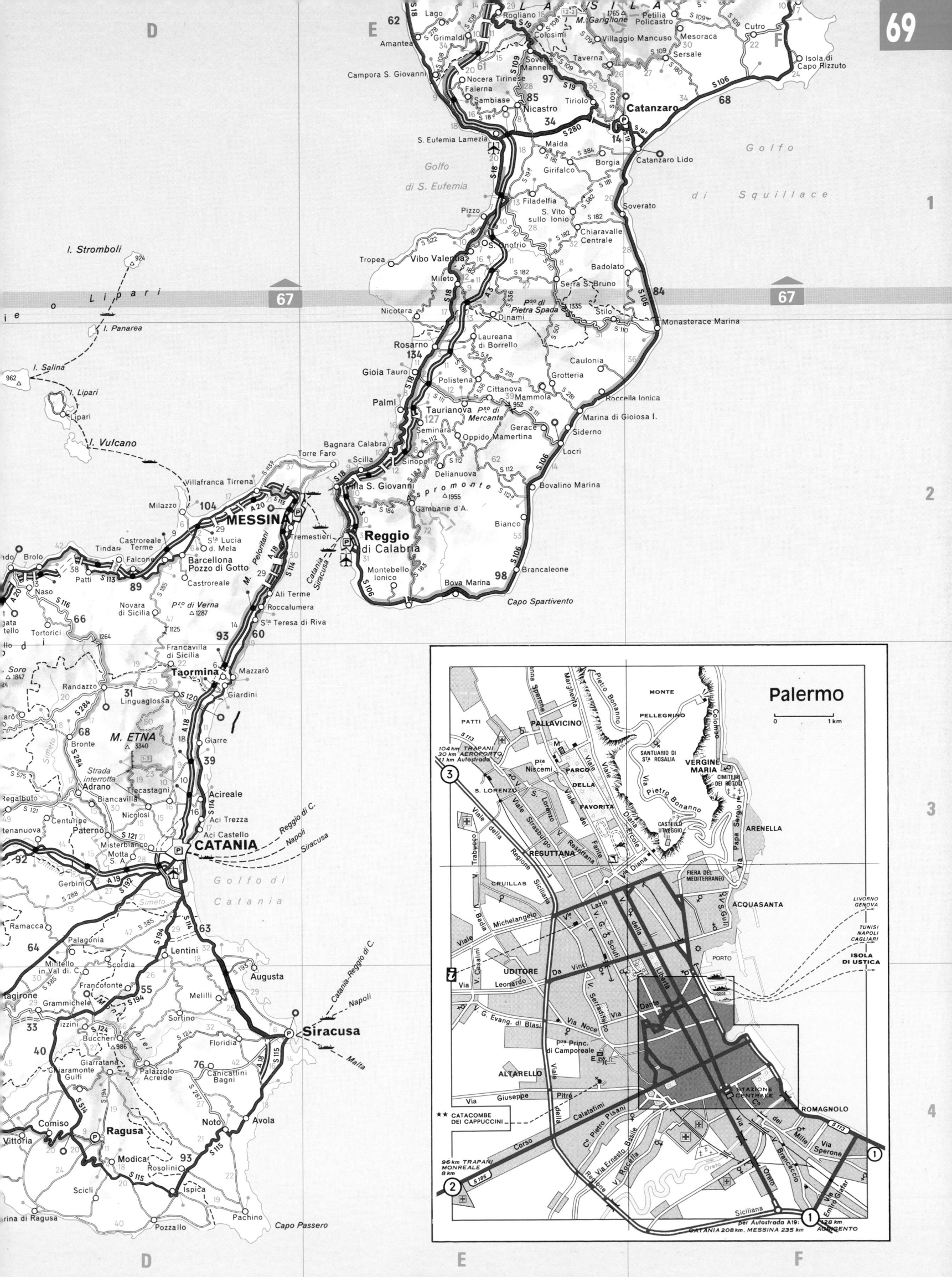

A | B | C

SARAJEVO
Semizovac, Vogošća, Podromanija, Romanija, M5, Rogatica, Pešurići, Višegrad, Višegradska Banja, Mokra Gora, Čajetina, Rožanstvo, Prilike, Ivanjica, Katići, Međurečje, Studenica

Ilidža, Hadžići, Hrasnica, Krupac, Pale, Mesići, Međeđa, Prača, Ustiprača, Dobrun, E 761 762, E 762, Lovag, Ljubiš, Tornik 1496, Jasenovo, 72, Uvac, Ušće, Biljanovac

Ivan Sedlo 967, Trebević nac. park, Jahorina 1913, Goražde, Rudo, Priboj, Banja, Kokin Brod, Nova Varoš, Zlatarsko jezero, Kladnica, Jankov kamen 1833, Plešin, Raška

Bjelašnica, Visočica 1974, Gornja Ljuta, Trnovo, 78, Dobro Polje, Ustikolina, Foča, Čajniče, Metaljka, Hercegov Goleša, Pljevlja, Prijepolje, Mileševo, Sjenica, Duga Poljana, Raždaginja, Novi Pazar

Ivan 967, Kalinovik, Jelašca, Ocrkavlje 1205, Brod, M18, Vikoč, Šuplja-Stijena, Gradac, Trlica 1360, Ljutići, Brodarevo, E 763, 59, Bare, Giljevo 1499, Žilinda 1616, Ugao, Tutin, Ribariće 113, Žubin

Glavatičevo 1002, Luka, Sopilja, Plužine, Fojnica, Nevesinje, Popov Most, Šćepan Polje, Dragaši, Kosanica, Đurđevića Tara, Pavino Polje, Tomaševo, Bijelo Polje, Bioča, Trpezi, Mehov Krš, 93

Zelengora, Sutjeska nac. park, Maglić 2386, Mratinje 2396, Vel. Vitao, Trsa, Žabljak 143, 103, Bistrica, Mojkovac, 29, Krstača 1755, Rožaje, 73, Vrela, Istok, 71

Bjelašnica, Gacko, Čemerno 1329, Plužine, Boričje 2522, Crno jez., Sinjajevina, 980, Nac. park Biogradsko, 2137, Ivangrad, 18, V. Jablanica 2400, Peć, M9

Hodovo, Berkovići, G. Lukavac, Korita 1026, Donja Bukovica, Šavnik, Boan, 2253, Babljak 1040, Kolašin, Matešević, Trepča, Andrijevica, Kučište, Rugovska klisura, Pečška

Radimlje, Stolac, Bijeljani, Krstac, Donja Brezna, Gvozd, Dragovića Polje, Jasenovo, Morača klisura, 117, Trešnjevik, 1572, Murino, Plav, Visoki Dečani 2656, Deravica, Barane, K

Blato, Žegulja, Plana, G. Dubočke 1721, Presjeka, Krnovo 1440, G. Morakovo, 115, E 65-80, Komovi 2484, Ljeva Rijeka, Gusinje, Junik, Skivjane, Đurakovac

Vranjak, Ljubinje, Bileća, Vidrovan, Rubeži, Nikšić, Radovče, Surdup 2182, Prokletije, M. Jezerce 2694, Valbonë, Mörina, 72, Đakovica

Dobromani, Staro Slano, Mosko, Vilusi, 107, Bijele Poljane, Bogetići, Gračanica, 2570, M. Radohinës, Korita, 2560, Ndrejaj, Bajram Curri, Zogaj

Zavala, Trebišnjica, Trebinje, Duži, Čičevo, Lastva, Grahovo, Ubli, Danilovgrad, Spuž, Bioče, Okol, Bogë

Slano, Trsteno, Orašac, Zaton, Uskoplje, Mlini, Jablan Do, Crkvice, Čevo, Lazarev Krst, Tuzi, Hani i Hotit, 2232, M. Krrabe

DUBROVNIK, Lokrum, Cavtat, Čilipi, Gruda, Igalo, Zelenika, Kamenari, Risan, Perast, Resna, Orasi, Titograd, 89, Gornji Kokoti, Golubovci, Plavnica, 55, Koplik, Drisht, Puke

Ancona, Bari, Kotor, 1749, Lepetane, Tivat, Rijeka Crnojevića, Žabljak, M2, Skadarsko jezero, Liqeni i Shkodrës, Shkodër, 152

Kêrkira (Corfou), Hercegnovi, Rose, Radovići, Budva, Bečići, Miločer, Sv. Stefan, Petrovac, Virpazar, Limljani, Livari, Sukobin, Murigan, Bushat, Vau i Dejës, Fushë Arrëz

91, Boka Kotorska, 42, Sutomore, 46, Stari Bar, Bar, Pečurice, Krute, Pulaj, Shëngjin, Lezhë, Mirdit

75, Kêrkira (Corfou) Igoumenitsa, Ulcinj, Sv. Nikola, Gjiri i Drinit, Drin, Mal Dejë, Rrëshen

Gjiri i Rodonit, Laç, 100, Skenderbeut, Ishëm, Kruje, Qaf'e Shtamës, Burrel, Klos

Gjiri i Lalzit, Durrës, Sukth, Shijak, Vorë, 22, 16, **TIRANË**, Mal i Dajt 1612

Gjiri i Durrësit, Kavajë, K. e Thanes 757, Bradashesh, Elbasan, 43

Peqin, Divjakë, Belsh, Çërrik, Rrogozhinë

SHQIPËRI

A | B | C

SOFIA

Niš · Pirot · Dimitrovgrad · Pernik · Leskovac · Prokuplje · Kuršumlija · Titova Mitrovica · Priština · Vranje · Kjustendil · Blagoevgrad · Prizren · Tetovo · SKOPJE · Kumanovo · Štip · Strumica · Gostivar · Titov Veles · Kavadarci · Gevgelija · Prilep · Struga · Ohrid · Bitola · Édessa · Flórina · Náoussa

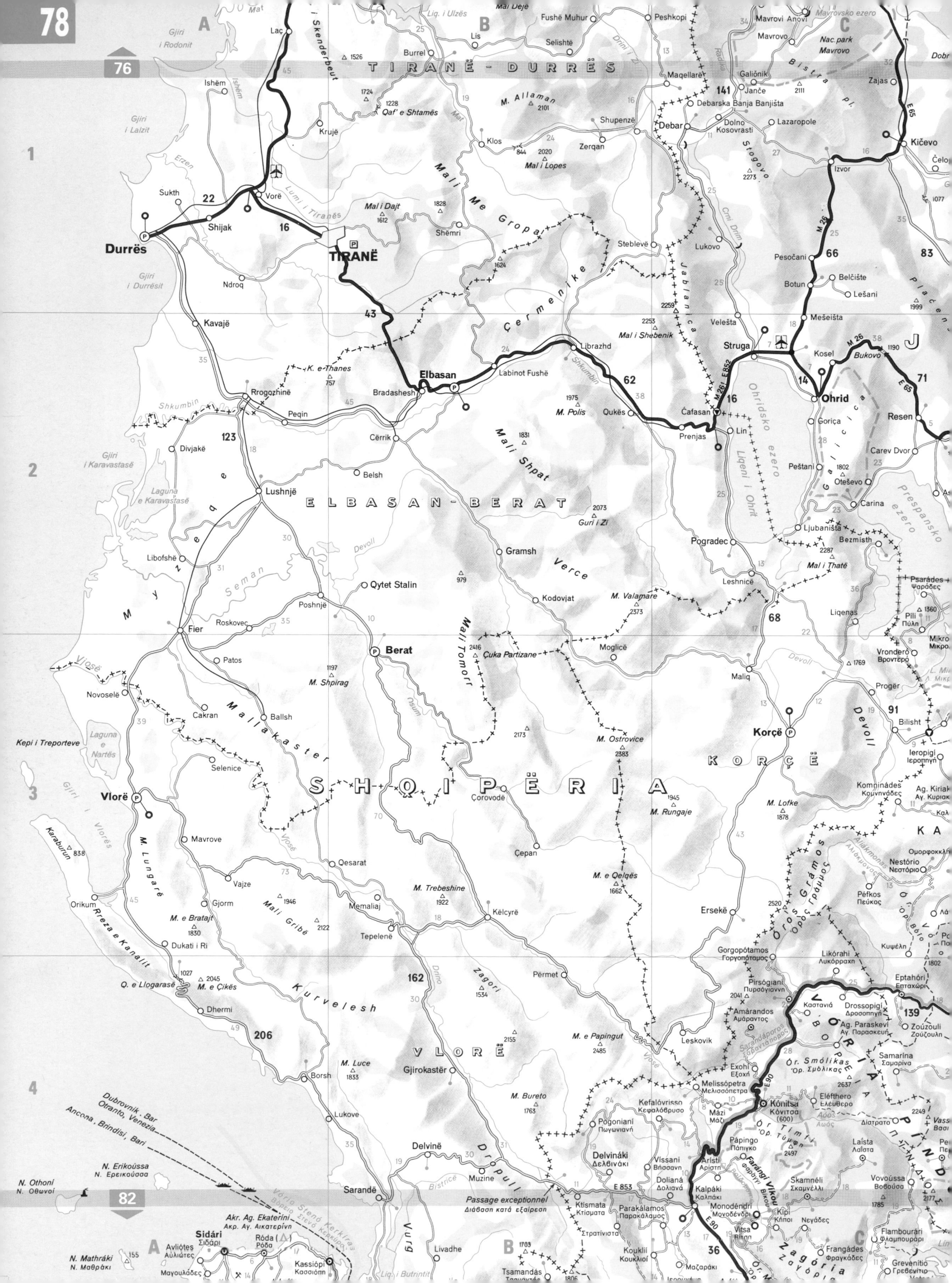

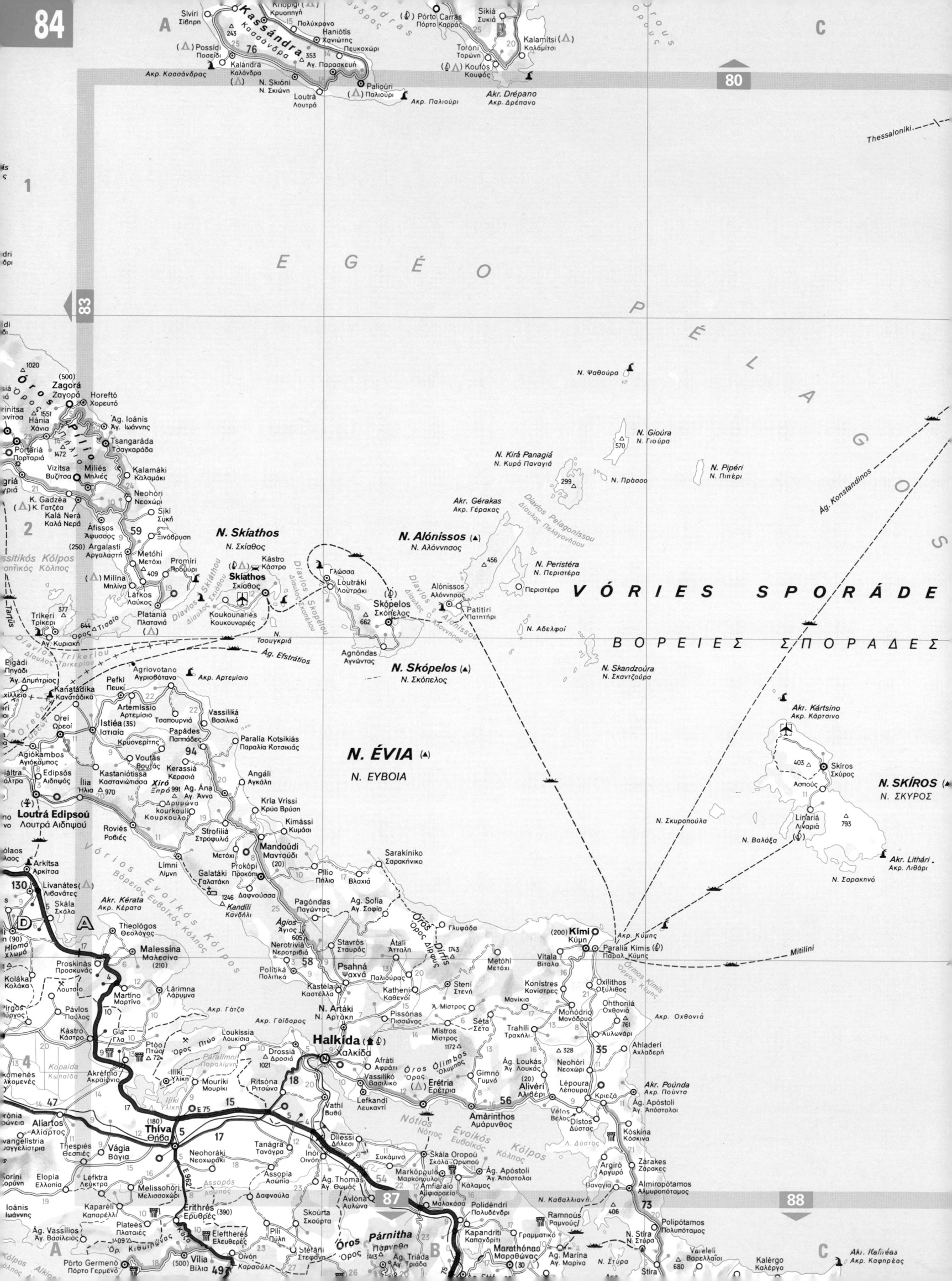

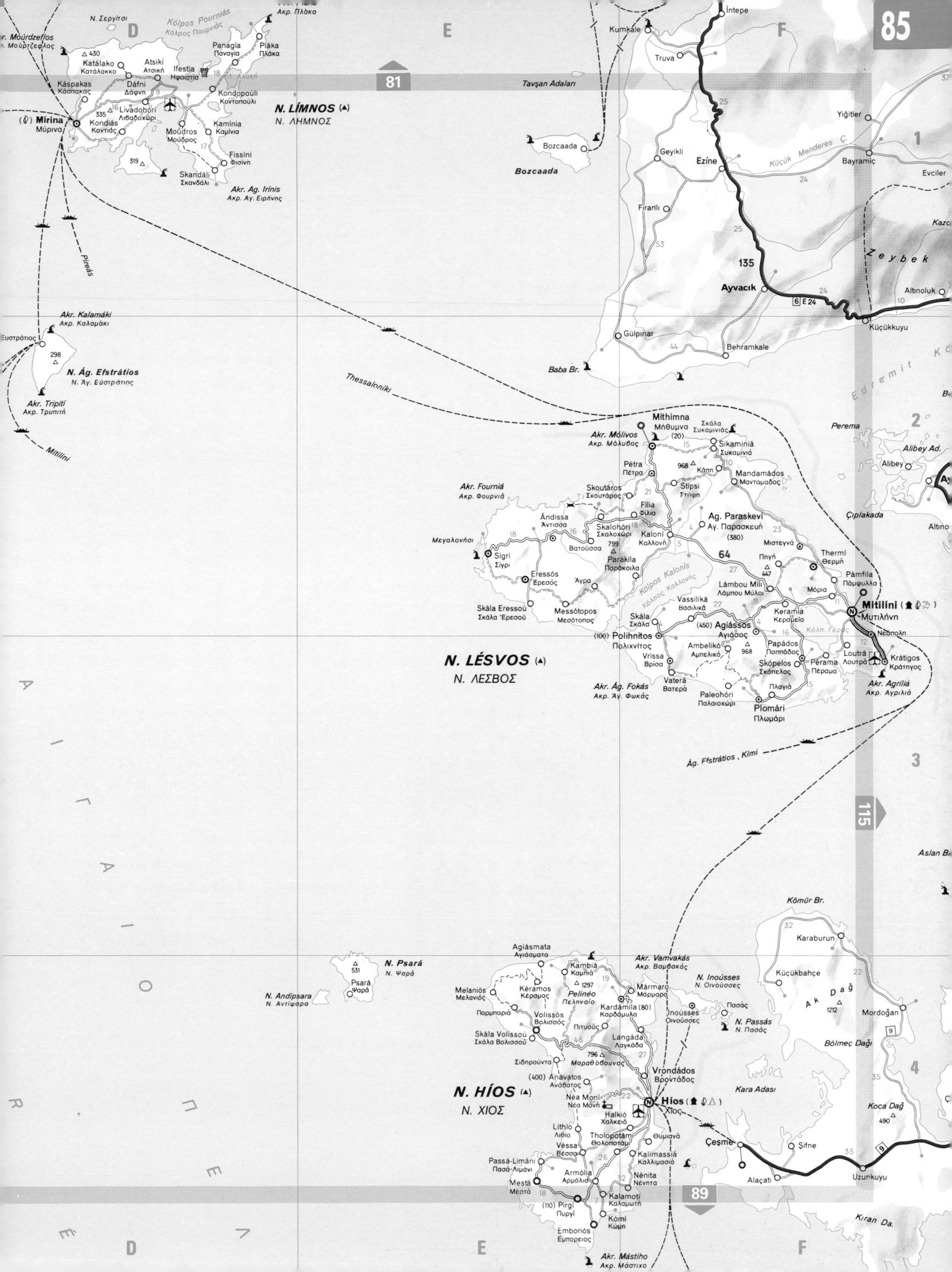

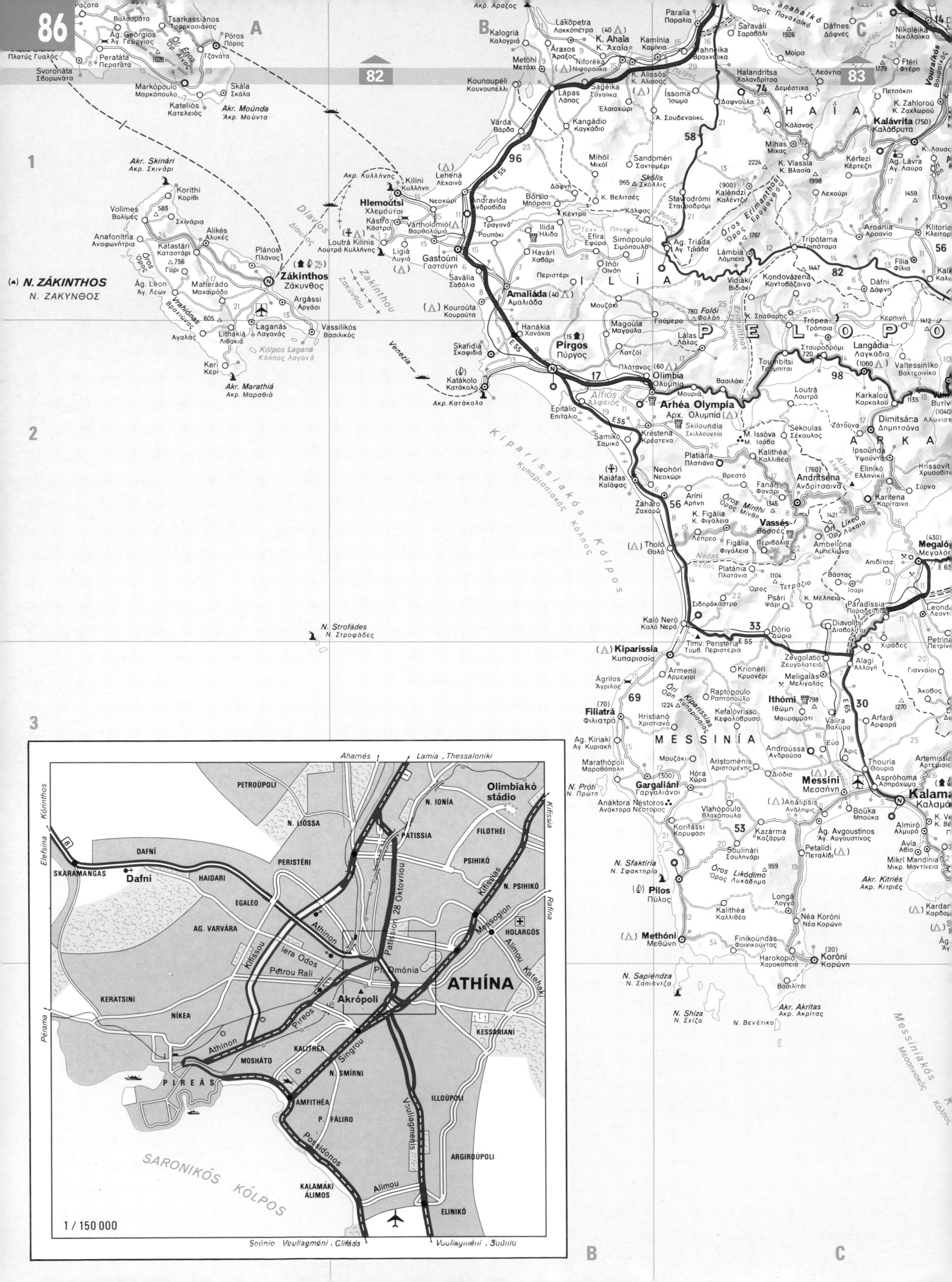

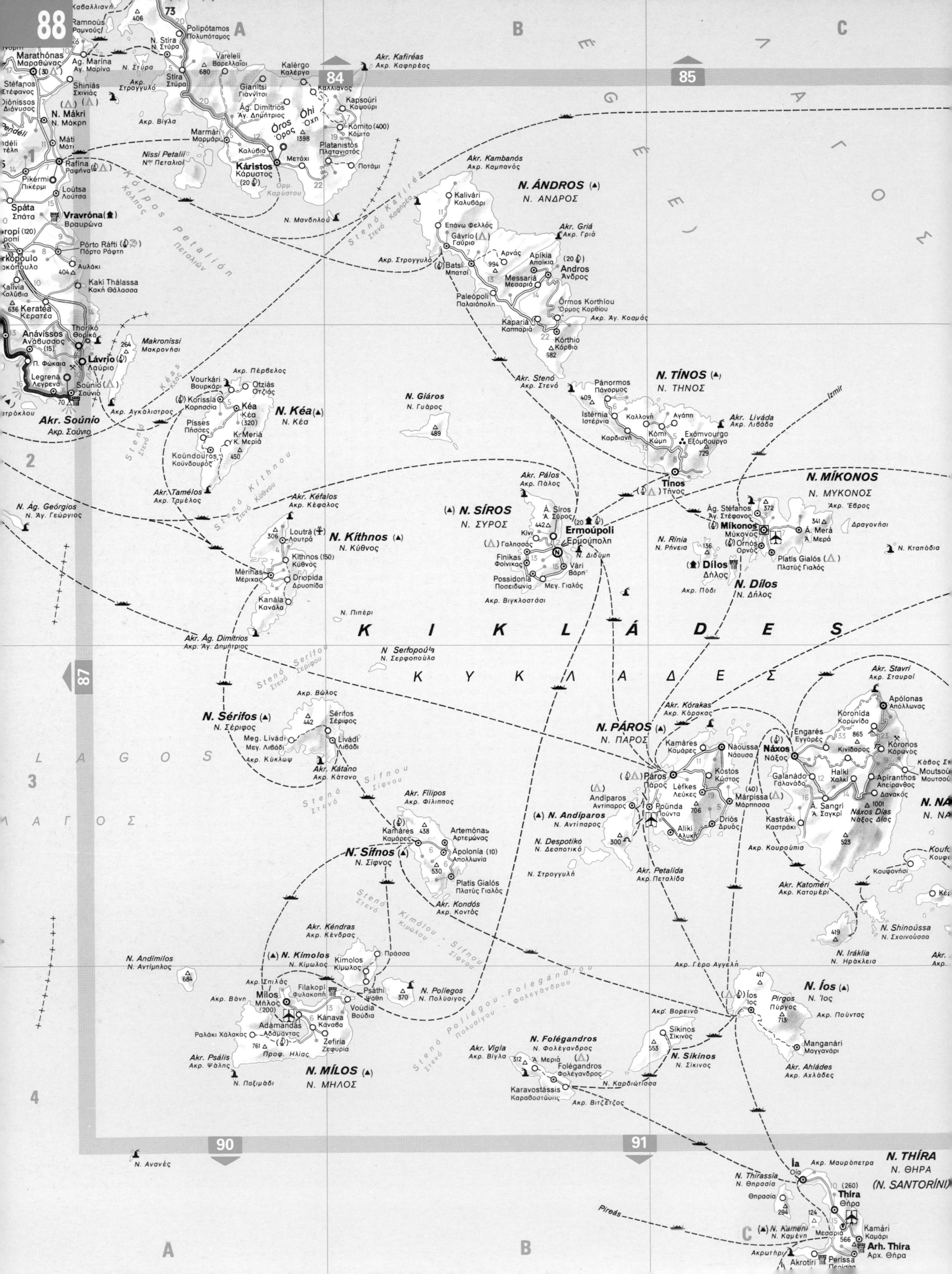

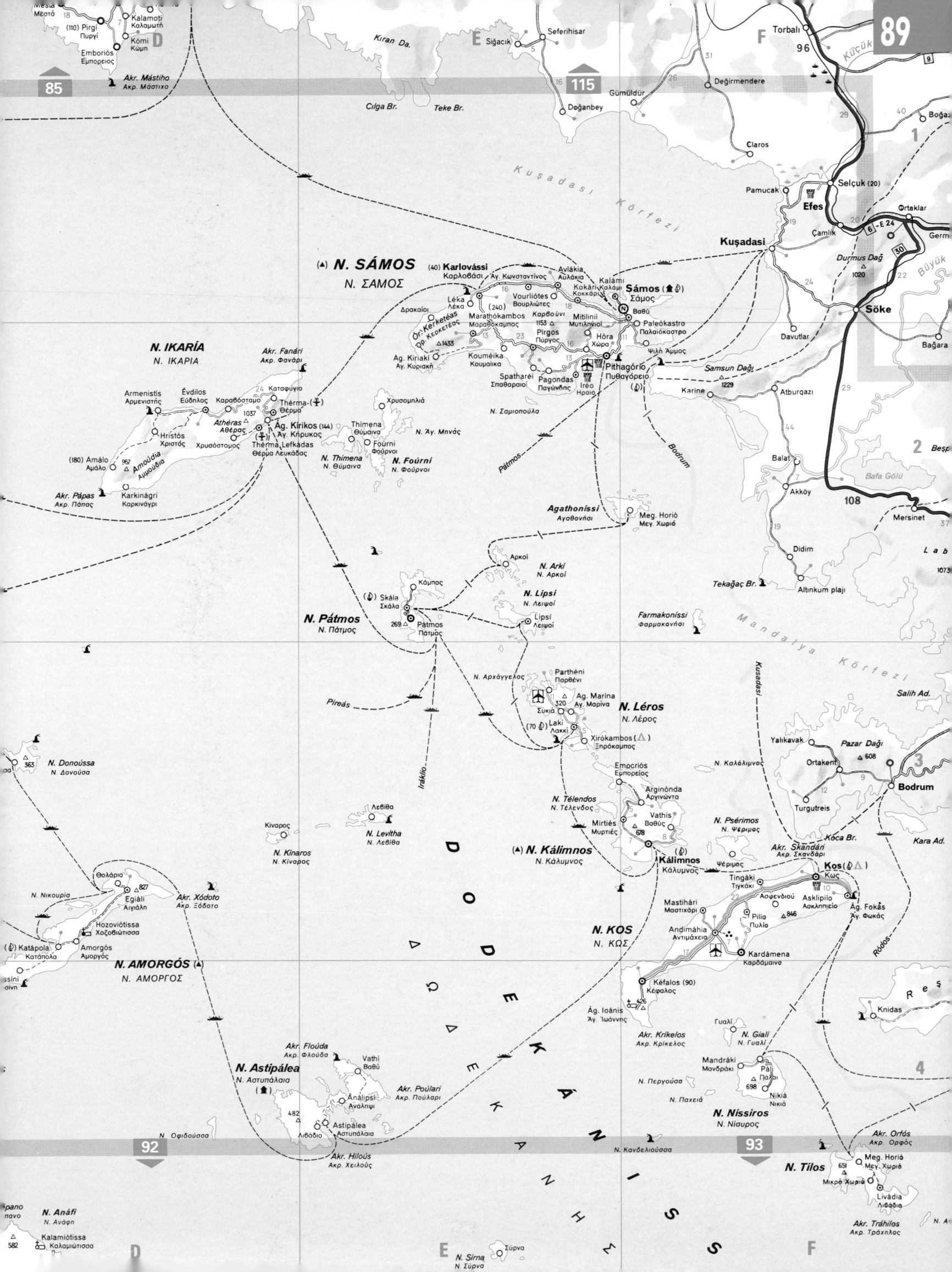

Monemvassía
Μονεμβασία

Tálanda
Τάλαντα

Nómia
Νόμια

716

Pandánassa
Πανταλάσσα

Áy. Apóstoli
Άγ. Απόστολοι

Víglafia
Βιγκλαφια

Elafónssos
Ελαφόνησος

Neápoli
Νεάπολη

Elafoníssi
Ελαφόνησοι

772

Óros Krithína
Όρος Κρίθινα

Á. Kastánia
Ά. Καστάνια

Ó. Áy. Andréas
Ό. Άγ. Ανδρέας

Velanídia
Βελανίδια

Kólpos Epidávrou Limirás
Κόλπος Επιδαύρου Λιμηράς

Akr. Maléas
Ακρ. Μαλέας

Porthmós
Πορθμός

Akr. Spathí
Ακρ. Σπαθί

Karavás
Καραβάς

Ag. Pelagía
Αγ. Πελαγία

Aroniádika
Αρωνιάδικα

Potamós
Ποταμός

Frilingiániká
Φριλιγκιάνικα

Milopótamos
Μυλοπόταμος

507

389

Avlémonas
Αβλέμονας

HIRA (▲)
ΗΡΑ

Kíthira
Κύθηρα

Kapsáli
Καψάλι

Livádi
Λιβάδι

Akr. Kapélo
Ακρ. Καπέλλο

Akr. Kefáli
Ακρ. Κεφάλι

Potamós
Ποταμός

Galaniná
Γαλανιανά

N. Andikíthira
Ν. Αντικύθηρα

378

Akr. Apolitáres
Ακρ. Απολυτάρες

Kastéli

Raláki Hálakas
Ραλάκι Χάλακας

Adámantas
Αδάμαντας

Zefíria
Ζεφυρία

Akr. Psális
Ακρ. Ψάλης

761

Prof. Ilías
Προφ. Ηλίας

N. MÍLOS (▲)
Ν. ΜΗΛΟΣ

N. Paximádi
Ν. Παξιμάδι

N. Ananés
Ν. Ανανές

K R I T I K Ó   P É L A G

(M E I

Potamós
Ποταμός

Akr. Spánda
Ακρ. Σπάντα

Diktinéon
Δικτυναίον

Akr. Voúxa
Ακρ. Βούξα

748

Gonía
Γωνία

Rodopós
Ροδωπός

Kolimvári
Κολυμβάρι

Kólpos Haníon
Κόλπος Χανίων

Stavrós
Σταυρός

Hers. Akrotíri (▲)
Χερσ. Ακρωτήρι

Falássarna
Φαλάσσαρνα

762

Kastéli
Καστέλλι

Taurvonítes
Ταυρωνίτης

Plataniás
Πλατανιάς

Haniá
Χανιά

Kounoupidianá
Κουνουπιδιανά

Perivólitsa
Περβολίτσα

Plátanos
Πλάτανος

E 65

Kaloudianá
Καλουδιανά

Máleme
Μάλεμε

Ag. Marína
Αγ. Μαρίνα

7

Soúda
Σούδα

Stérnes
Στέρνες

Órmos Soúdas
Όρμος Σούδας

Akr. Drápano
Ακρ. Δράπανο

Polirínia
Πολυρρηνία

Topólia
Τοπόλια

Voukoliés
Βουκολιές

Manoliópoulo
Μανολιόπουλο

Alikianós
Αλικιανός

Fournés
Φουρνές

Mourniés
Μουρνιές

14

Maláda
Μαλάδα

Kalíves
Καλύβες

Órmos Almiroú
Όρμος Αλμυρού

Kámbos
Κάμπος

1071

Kakópetros
Κακόπετρος

N. Roúma
Ν. Ρούμα

35

Láki
Λάκκοι

36
22

Thériso
Θέρισο

Áptera
Άπτερα

Ramní
Ραμνή

Vámos
Βάμος

13

Kefalás
Κεφαλάς

Réthimno
Ρέθυμνο

Perivólia
Περιβόλια

Platané
Πλατανέ

Élos
Έλος

Strovlés
Στρουβλές

1331

Kándanos
Κάνδανος

Xilóskalo
Ξυλόσκαλο

Omalós
Ομαλός

HANIÁ

2453
Páhnes
Πάχνες

2218

Vrisses
Βρύσες

Georgioúpoli (▲)
Γεωργιούπολη

E 75

Prínes
Πρινές

Prassiés
Πρασιές

23

21

RÉTHIMN
ΡΕΘΙΜΝ

Hrissoskalítissa
Χρυσοσκαλίτισσα

Sklavopoúla
Σκλαβοπούλα

iVoútas
Βούτας

Ródováni
Ροδοβάνι

18

Soúgia
Σούγια

Ag. Roúmeli
Αγ. Ρούμελη

Lefká Óri
Λευκά Όρη

Farángi Samariás
Φαράγγι Σαμαριάς

Anópoli
Ανώπολη

Embáneros
Εμπάνερος

Kournás
Κουρνάς

Askífou
Ασκίφου

Argiroúpoli
Αργυρούπολη

1512

Miriokéfala
Μυριοκέφαλα

Angouselianá
Αγκουσελιανά

Sélia
Σέλια

Sellía
Σελλία

984

Spíli
Σπήλι

Akr. Kriós
Ακρ. Κριός

Paleohóra
Παλαιοχώρα

Sfakiá (80)
Σφακιά

Patsianós
Πατσιανός

Á. Rodákino
Ά. Ροδάκινο

38

Ásfendo
Άσφενδο

Asómatos
Ασώματος

16

Frangokástelo
Φραγκοκάστελλο

Plakiás
Πλακιάς

Préveli
Πρέβελη

Kissoú Kám
Κισσού Κάμ

N. Gavdopoúla
Ν. Γαυδοπούλα

N. Paximád
Ν. Παξιμάδ

N. Gávdos
Ν. Γαύδος

368

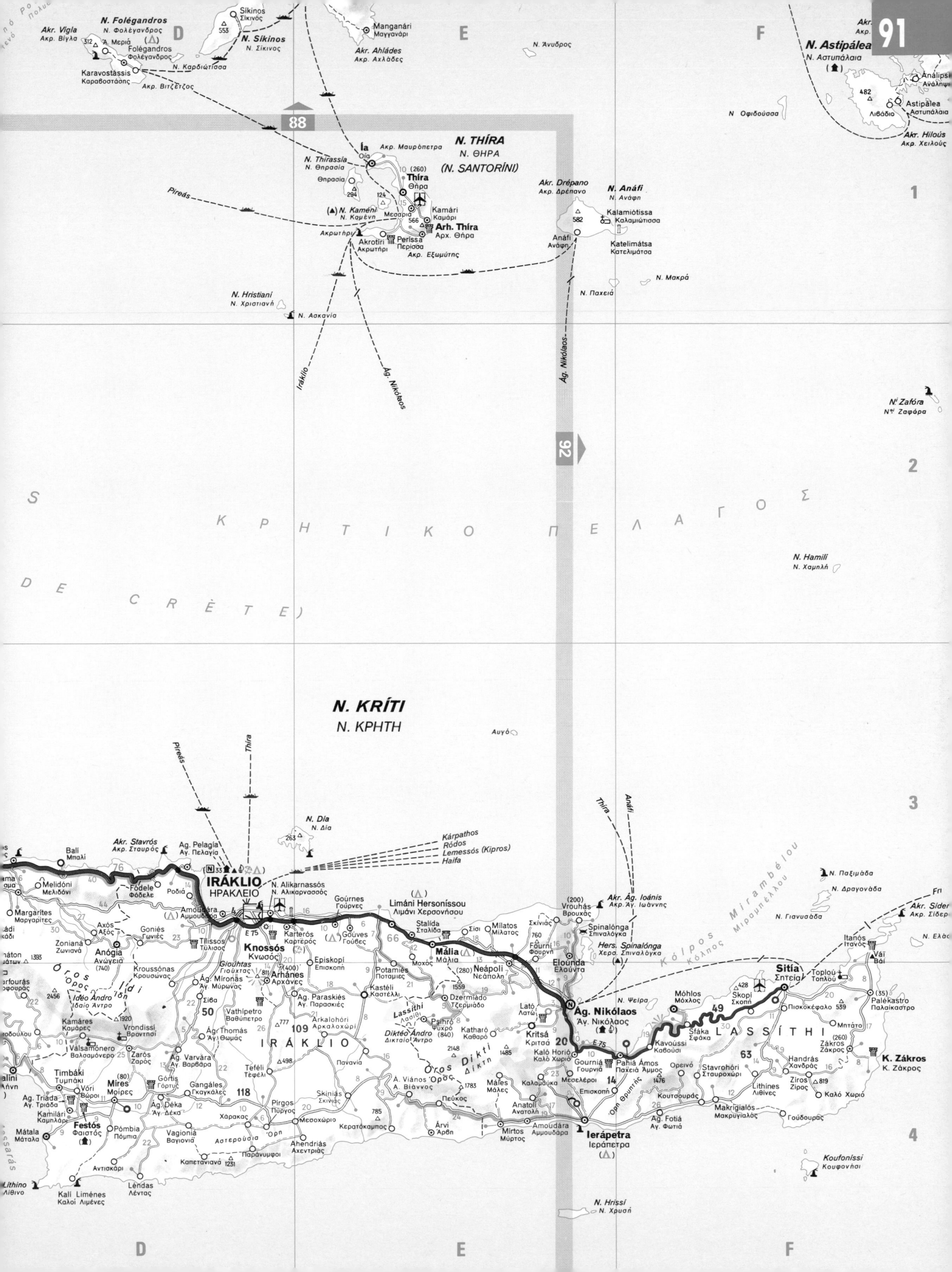

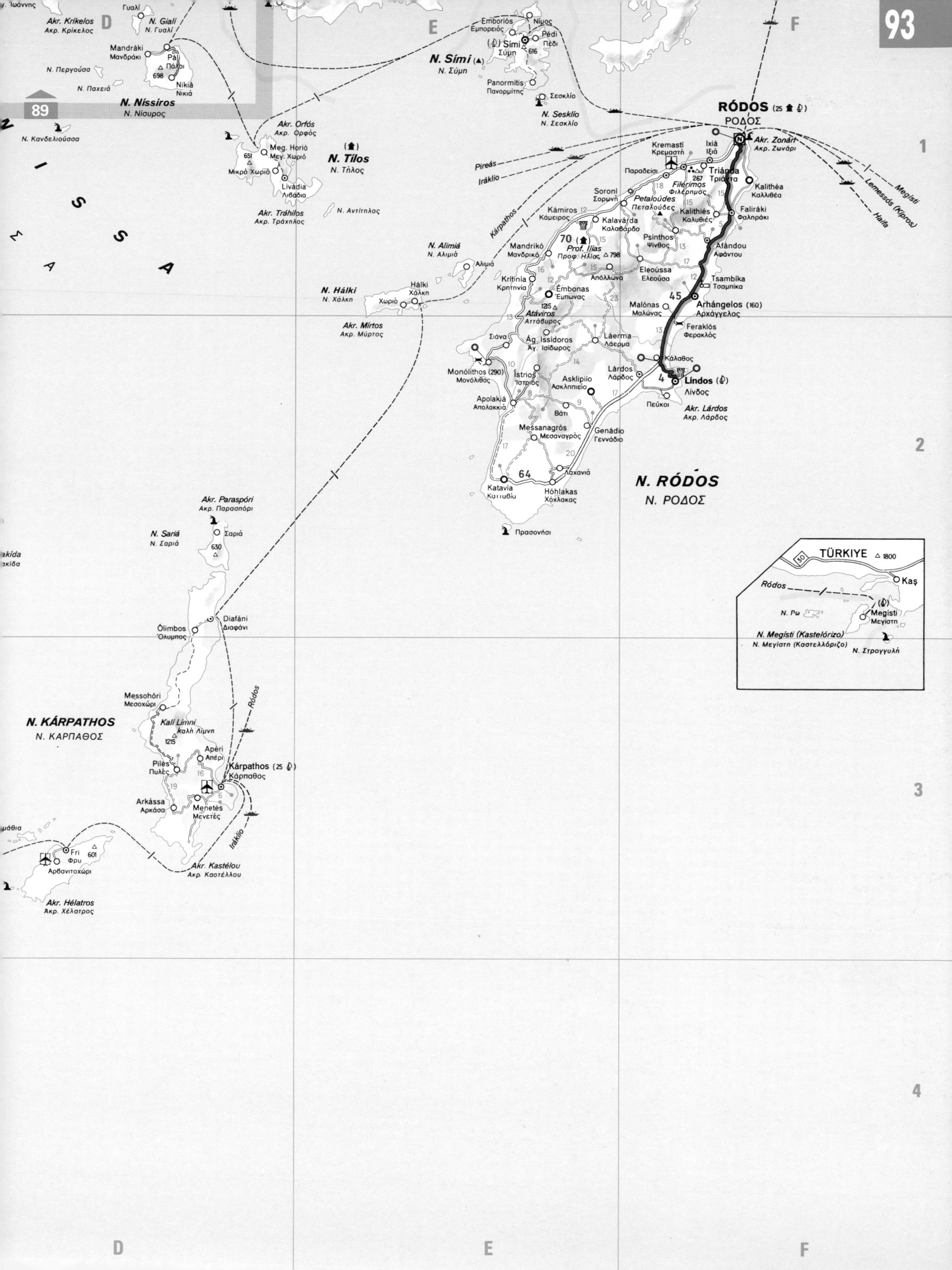

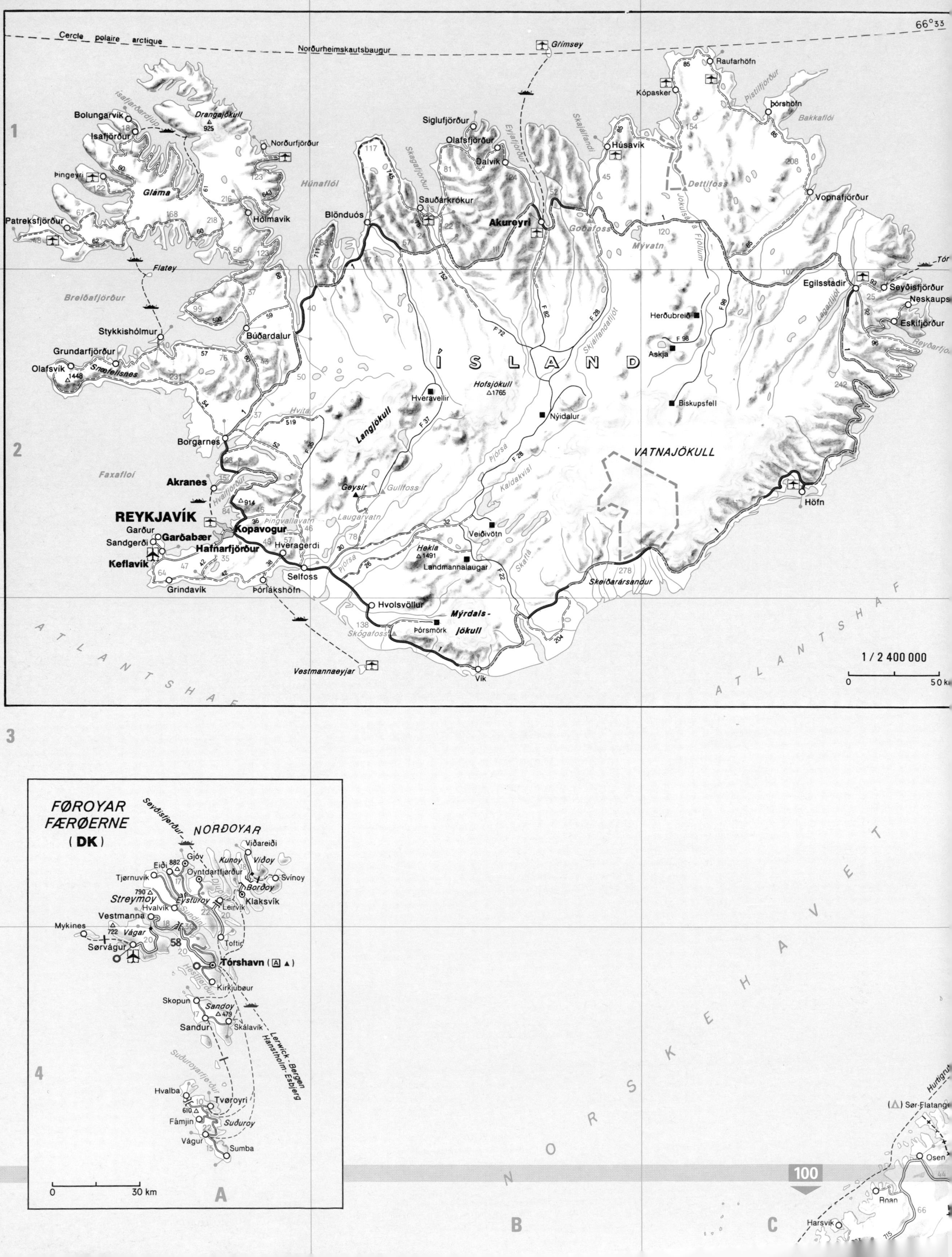

A　　　　B　　　　C

Cercle polaire arctique
Norðurheimskautsbaugur
66°33

Grímsey

1

Bolungarvík
Ísafjörður
Norðurfjörður
Drangajökull
925
Raufarhöfn
85
Kópasker
þórshöfn
Bakkaflói
þingeyri
Gláma
Siglufjörður
Húsavík
154
Olafsfjörður
Dalvík
Hólmavík
Blönduós
Saudárkrókur
Akureyri
Dettifoss
208
Vopnafjörður
Patreksfjörður
Hünaflói
Myvatn

Flatey
Breiðafjörður
Egilsstadir
Seyðisfjörður
Neskaupst.
Stykkishólmur
I S L A N D
Herðubreið
Eskifjörður
Grundarfjörður
Askja
F 98
Ólafsvík
1448
Snæfellsnes
Búðardalur
Biskupsfell

2

Faxaflói
Hveravellir
Hofsjökull
1765
Nýidalur
VATNAJÖKULL
Borgarnes
Langjökull
F 37
Akranes
914
Geysir
Gullfoss
Höfn
REYKJAVÍK
Garður
Kopavogur
þingvallavatn
Laugarvatn
Veiðivötn
Sandgerði
Garðabær
Hveragerdi
Hafnarfjörður
Hekla
1491
Landmannalaugar
Keflavík
Selfoss
Grindavík
þórlákshöfn
Hvolsvöllur
Skeiðarársandur
278
Mýrdals-
jökull
Skógafoss
þórsmörk
204
ATLANTSHAF
Vestmannaeyjar
Vík

1 / 2 400 000
0　　　50 km

3

**FØROYAR
FÆRØERNE
(DK)**

Seyðisfjörður
NORÐOYAR
Viðareiði
Eiði
882
Gjóv
Kunoy
Viðoy
Tjørnuvík
Oyntdartfjørður
Svinoy
790
Borðoy
Streymoy
Eysturoy
Klaksvík
Vestmanna
Hvalvík
Leirvik
Mykines
722
Vágar
Sørvágur
58
Tórshavn (Ⓐ ▲)
Kirkjubøur
Skopun
Sandoy
479
Sandur
Skálavík
Lerwik - Bergen
Hanstholm - Esbjerg

4

Hvalba
Tvøroyri
610
Suðuroy
Fámjin
Vágur
Sumba

0　　30 km

N O R S K E H A V E T

100

A　　　　B　　　　C

Osen
Rønan
Harsvik

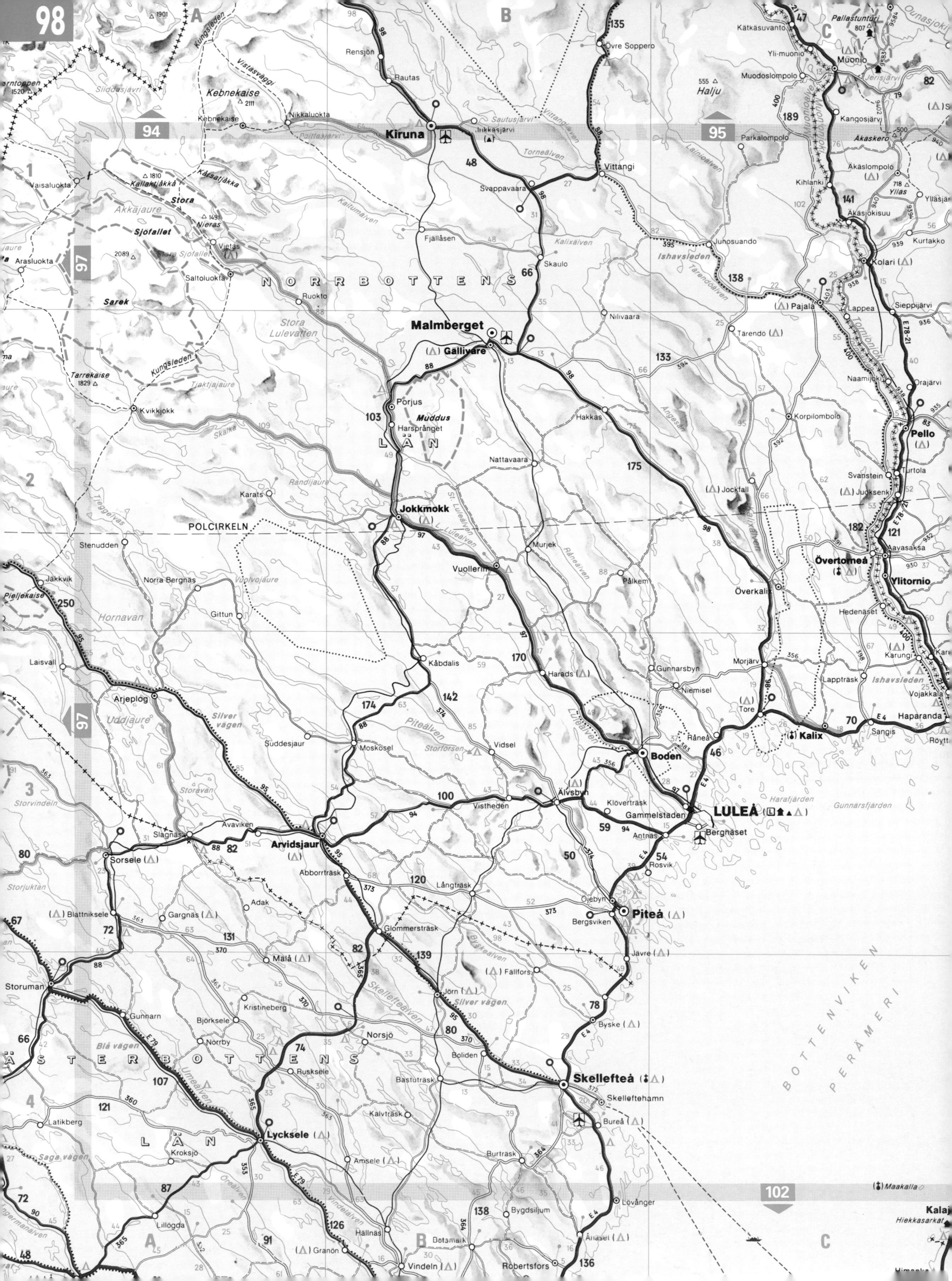

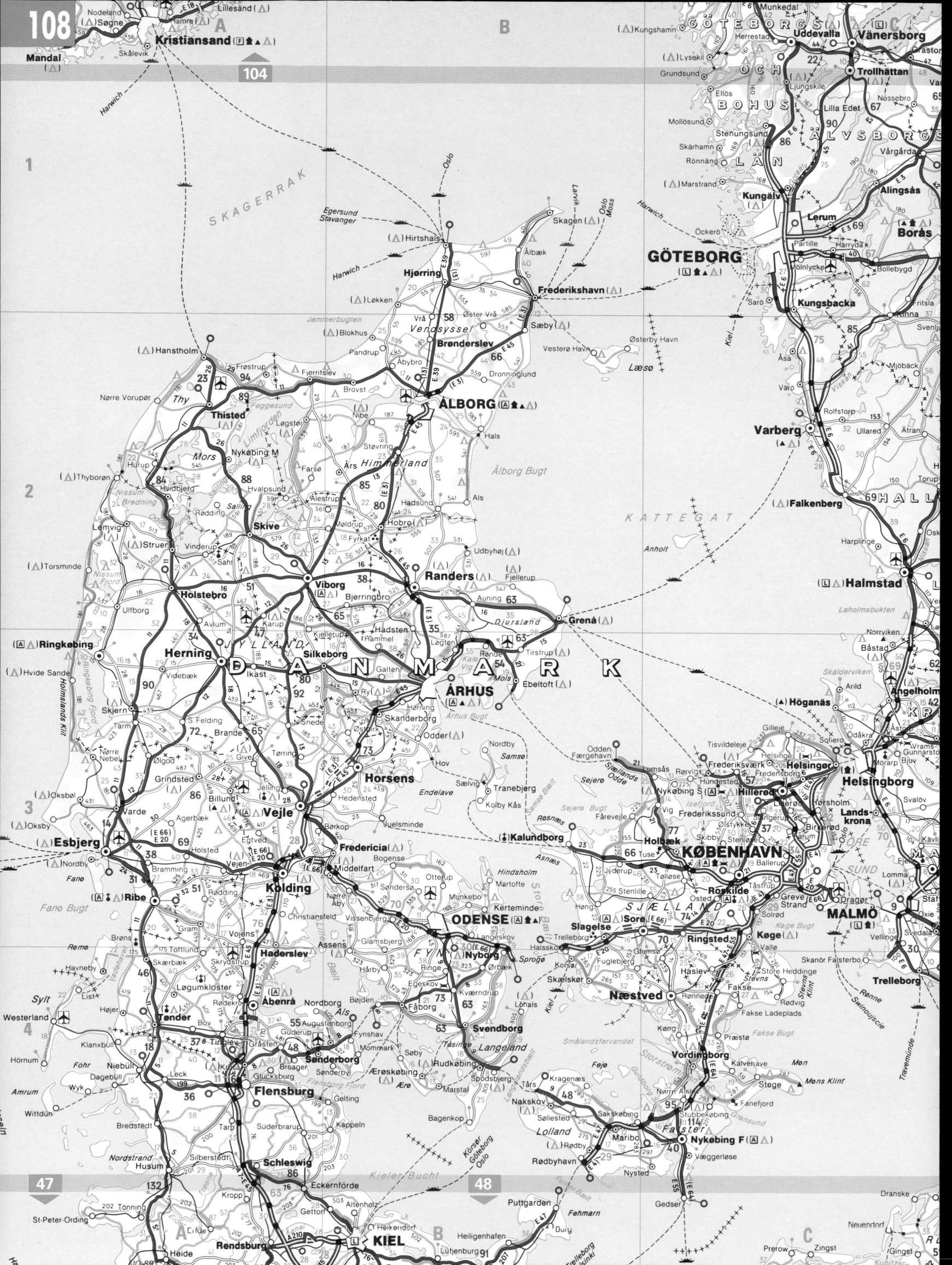

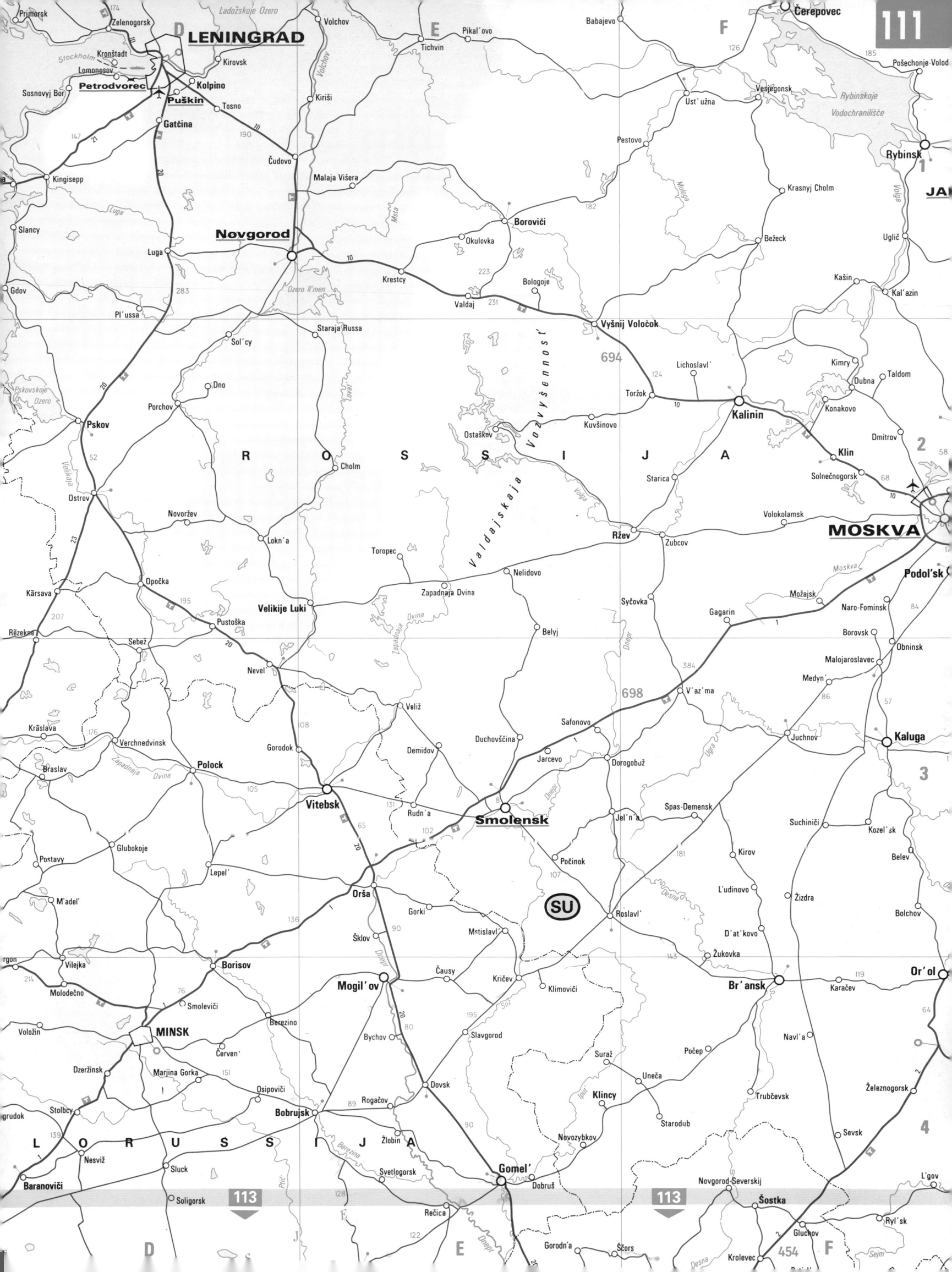

(F) Lorsqu'un nom figure plusieurs fois dans l'index, une précision est ajoutée entre parenthèses pour permettre de l'identifier plus facilement: pays, région ou ville la plus proche, élément géographique d'après les abréviations ci-dessous.

(GB) Where there are two or more identical place names, the name of the distinguishing country or region or nearest large town is given in brackets; geographical features are indicated by the abbreviations below.

(D) Tritt ein Name mehrfach im Register auf, wird er durch eine in Klammern gesetzte nähere Bestimmung genauer definiert. Sie finden folgende Zusätze: Land, Region oder nächstgelegene Stadt, geographische Gegebenheiten, ggf. abgekürzt.

(NL) Bij namen die meermalen in het register voorkomen, staat tussen haakjes een aanduiding ter verklaring: het land, de streek, de dichtstbijgelegen stad of een geografisch gegeven (zie de afkortingen hieronder).

(E) Cuando un mismo nombre figura varias veces en el índice, para poder localizarlo con facilidad, se añade entre paréntesis el país, la región o la ciudad más cercana; los accidentes geográficos se indican con las abreviaturas siguientes.

(I) Quando un nome figura più volte nell'indice, una precisazione viene aggiunta tra parentesi per permettere d'identificarlo più facilmente: nazione, regione o città la più vicina, elemento geografico come da abbreviazioni qui di seguito.

Abbr.	Meaning	Abbr.	Meaning	Abbr.	Meaning
Ákr	Ákra, Akrotirion	Liq	Liquen	Pk	Park
B	Bay, Baie, Bucht, Bahía, Baia, Bukt(en), Bugt, Bukhta	Meg	Méga, Megál, -a, -i, -o	Pl	Planina
Bgem	Barragem	Mikr	Mikr-í, -ón	Pque	Parque
C	Cape, Cap, Cabo, Capo	Mgne(s)	Montagne(s)	Prov	Province
Co	County	M, Mte(s)	Maj, Maj'e, Monte(s), Mont(s)	Pso	Passo
Ch	Chaîne	Mt(s), *Mt(s)*	Mount(s), Mountain(s), Mont(s)	Pt(e)	Point(e)
Chan	Channel	Mti	Monti, Muntii	Rib	Ribeirão
Dépt	Département	Nac	Nacional(e)	R, *R*	River, Rivière, Rio, Ria, Rijeka
Emb	Embalse	Nat	National	Reg	Region, Région
Ez	Ezero	Naz	Nazionale	Res	Reservoir, Reservoire
G	Gulf, Golfe, Golfo	N	Nissí, Nissos	Sa	Sierra, Serra
Gges	Gorges	Ni	Nissiá, Nissi	Sd	Sound, Sund
I(s), *I(s)*	Isles(s), Island(s), Ile(s), Ilha(s), Isla(s), Isola(e)	Os	Ostrov(a)	St	Saint, Sankt, Sint
Jez	Jezoro, Jezioro	Ot	Otok(i), Otoci	Ste(s)	Sainte(s)
K	Kanal, Kanaal	Oz	Ozero(a)	Teh L	Tehnití Límni
L, *L*	Lake, Loch, Lough, Llyn, Lac, Laguna, Lago, Límni	P	Pass	V	Valley, Vale, Vallée, Val, Valle, Vall
		Pal	Paleós, á, ó		
		Pen	Peninsula, Penisola		

A

Aachen	51 D3	Abanilla	45 D2	Abcoude	16 C2	Aberhonddu	8 C1	Aboyne	3 E4
Aalen	55 E2	Abano Terme	61 D1	Abejar	36 B3	Aberlady	5 D2	Abrantes	38 B3
Aalsmeer	16 C2	Abbadia San Salvatore	63 D1	Abejuela	41 E3	Aberpennar	8 C2	Abreschviller	21 E4
Aalst	50 B3	Abbasanta	66 B3	Abela	42 A1	Aberporth	8 B1	Abriès	31 E2
Aalten	17 D3	Abbazia di Casamari	63 F3	Abelvær	97 D4	Abersoch	6 A3	Abruzzo	63 F2
Aalter	50 B3	Abbazia di Fossanova	63 F3	Abenberg	55 E2	Abertawe	8 C2	Abruzzo, Parco Nazionale d'	64 A2
Äänekoski	103 D2	Abbazia di Montecassino	64 A3	Abenójar	39 F4	Aberteifi	8 B1	Abstadt-Tailfingen	55 D3
Aapajärvi	95 F4	Abbazia San Clemente a Casauria	64 A2	Åbenrå	108 A4	Abertillery	9 D2	Abtenau	59 E1
Aarau	27 F2	Abbeville	19 E2	Abensberg	55 F2	Aber-Wrac'h, l'	22 A2	Åby	105 F4
Aarberg	27 E2	Abbeyfeale	14 B3	Aberaeron	8 C1	Aberystwyth	8 C1	Åbybro	108 B2
Aarburg	27 F2	Abbeyleix	12 C4	Aberdar	8 C2	Abetone	60 C3	A Caniza	34 A3
Aare	58 A3	Abbey Town	5 D4	Aberdare	8 C2	Abiego	37 E3	Accéglio	31 E2
Aargau	27 F2	Abbiategrasso	60 A1	Aberdaron	6 A3	Abingdon	9 E2	Accettura	65 D4
Aarlen	21 D2	Abborrträsk	98 B3	Aberdaugleddau	8 B2	Abington	5 D3	Acciaroli	67 D1
Aarschot	50 C3	Abbots Bromley	6 C3	Aberdeen	3 E4	Abisko	94 B3	Accous	37 D1
Aavasaksa	98 C2	Abbotsbury	9 D3	Aberdovey	6 A3	Abisko (Nat park)	94 B4	Accrington	6 C2
Abades	40 A1			Aberfeldy	4 C1	Abla	44 B3	Acebo	39 D2
Abadiño	36 B1			Aberfoyle	4 C2	Åblis	19 E4	Acedo	36 B2
A Baiuca	34 A1			Abergavenny	9 D2	Åbo	107 D2		
				Abergele	6 B2	Abondance	27 E3		
				Abergwaun	8 B1	Abony	112 B4		

Acehuche	39 D3	Afjord	100 C1
Acerno	64 B4	Åfjorden	104 A1
Acerra	64 B4	Aflenzer Seeberg	57 E3
Aceuchal	39 D4	Aflenz Kurort	57 E3
Ache	59 E1	Afráti	84 B4
Achenkirch	59 D1	A Garda	34 A3
Achenpaß	56 A4	Agathoníssi	89 E2
Achensee	59 D1	Agay	31 E4
Achern	54 C3	Agazzano	60 B2
Acheux	19 F2	Agde	30 A4
Achill I	12 A2	Agdenes	100 C1
Achim	17 F1	Agen	28 C3
Achnacroish	4 B1	Àger	37 F3
Achnasheen	2 C3	Ager	56 C3
A'Chràlaig	2 C4	Ageranós	87 D4
Aci Castello	69 D3	Agerbæk	108 A3
Acıpayam	115 F4	Agger	17 E4
Acireale	69 D3	Aggius	66 B1
Aci Trezza	69 D3	Aggsbach-Dorf	57 E2
Acle	7 F3	Aggsbach-Markt	57 E2
A Coruña	34 B1	Agiá	83 F1
Acqualagna	61 E4	Agiá, Akr	83 F4
Acquapendente	63 D1	Agía Ána (Évia)	84 A3
Acquasanta Terme	63 F1	Agía Ána (Viotía)	83 F4
Acquasparta	63 E1	Agía Efimía	82 B4
Acquaviva dei Fonti	65 D3	Agía Efthimía	83 E4
Acqui-Terme	60 A2	Agía Ekateríni, Akr	82 A1
Acri	67 E2	Agía Fotiá	91 F4
Ada	72 C1	Agía Galíni	91 D4
Adaja, R	39 F2	Agía Kiriakí (Makedonía)	78 C3
Adak	98 A3	Agía Kiriakí (Pelopónissos)	86 B3
Ádalsel	104 C2	Agía Kiriakí (Sámos)	89 E2
Adamandás	88 A4	Agía Lávra	86 C1
Adamclisi	115 E1	Agía Marína (Égina)	87 F2
Adamello	58 C3	Agía Marína (Kríti)	90 B3
Adamello Brenta, Parco Naturale	58 C3	Agía Marína (Léros)	89 E3
Adamello, Mont'	58 C3	Agía Marína (Stereá Eláda)	83 E3
Adamuz	43 F2	Agía Marína (Stereá Eláda)	88 A1
Adanero	39 F1	Agía Paraskeví (Lésvos)	85 F2
Adapazarı	115 F3	Agía Paraskeví (Makedonía)	80 C2
Adare	14 B3	Agía Paraskiés	91 E4
Adaševci	72 B3	Agía Pelagía (Kíthira)	90 A1
Adda	60 B2	Agía Pelagía (Kríti)	91 D3
Adelboden	27 E3	Agía Rouméli	90 B4
Adelfia	65 D3	Agíasma	80 C2
Adelsheim	55 D1	Agiásmata	85 E4
Ademuz	41 D3	Agía Sofía (Évia)	84 B3
Adenau	51 E4	Agía Sofía (Pelopónissos)	87 D2
Ádendro	79 F3	Agía Sotíra	87 E1
Adéres, Óros	87 E2	Agiássos	85 F2
Adiça, Sa da	42 C1	Agía Triáda (Kríti)	91 D4
Adige	61 D1	Agía Triáda (Makedonía)	79 F3
Adjud	113 E4	Agía Triáda (Pelopónissos)	86 C1
Admont	57 D3	Agía Triáda (Stereá Eláda)	87 F1
Adolfström	97 F3	Agía Varvára	91 D4
Adorf	53 D3	Agiófilo	83 D1
Adour	28 B4	Agiókambos (Évia)	83 F3
Adra	44 B4	Agiókambos (Thessalía)	83 F1
Adradas	36 B4	Agionóri	87 E2
Adrall	32 A3	Ágio Óros	80 C4
Adrano	69 D3	Agiopigí	83 D2
Adria	61 D2	Ágios	84 A3
Adriatic Sea	114 A3	Agía Triáda (Makedonía)	79 F3
Adzaneta	41 E3	Ágios Anárgiri (Pelopónissos)	87 D3
Aegean Sea	115 E4	Ágios Anárgiri (Thessalía)	83 E2
Aenona	74 C1	Ágios Andónios	80 A3
Aerinó	83 F2	Ágios Andréas (Arkadía)	87 D2
Ærø	108 B4		
Ærøskøbing	108 B4		
A Estrada	34 A2		
Aetópetra	82 B1		
Aetós (Kefaloniá)	82 B4		
Aetós (Makedonía)	79 D3		
Aetós (Stereá Eláda)	82 C3		
Äetsä	107 D2		
Afándou	93 F1		
Åfarnes	100 B2		
Aféa	87 F2		
Affi	60 C1		
Afiónas	82 A1		
Áfissos	83 F2		
Afitos	80 B4		

Ágios Andréas (Lakonía) 87 E4
Ágios Apóstoli (Évia) 84 B4
Ágios Apóstoli (Pelopónissos) 87 E4
Ágios Apóstoli (Stereá Eláda) 84 B4
Ágios Athanássios (Dráma) 80 C2
Ágios Athanássios (Péla) 79 D2
Ágios Avgoustínos 86 C3
Ágios Déka 91 D4
Ágios Dimítrios, Akr 88 A3
Ágios Dimítrios (Évia) 88 A1
Ágios Dimítrios (Lakonía) 87 D3
Ágios Dimítrios (Makedonía) 79 E4
Ágios Dimítrios (Messinía) 87 D4
Ágios Dimítrios (Stereá Eláda) 83 D3
Ágios Dionissios 79 E4
Ágios Efstrátios, N 85 D2
Ágios Fokás 89 F3
Ágios Fokás, Akr 85 F3
Ágios Geórgios (Évia) 83 F3
Ágios Geórgios, N 87 F2
Ágios Geórgios (Stereá Eláda) 83 D3
Ágios Geórgios (Zákinthos) 86 A1
Ágios Georgíou, Órmos 87 E3
Ágios Germanós 79 D2
Ágios Górdis 82 A1
Ágios Harálambos 81 E2
Ágios Ioánis, Akr 91 F3
Ágios Ioánis (Dodekánissa) 89 F4
Ágios Ioánis (Pelopónissos) 87 E2
Ágios Ioánis (Stereá Eláda) 83 F4
Ágios Ioánis (Thessalía) 83 F3
Ágios Ioánis (Thessalía) 83 F2
Ágios Iríni, Akr 85 D1
Ágios Issídoros 93 E2
Ágios Kírikos 89 D2
Ágios Konstandínos (Stereá Eláda) 83 F3
Ágios Konstandínos (Thessalía) 83 E2
Ágios Kosmás (Grevená) 79 D4
Ágios Kosmás (Kavála) 80 C2
Ágios Léon 86 A1
Ágios Loukás 84 B4
Ágios Mámas 80 A4
Ágios Márkos 80 A2
Ágios Mathéos 82 A2
Ágios Míronas 91 D4
Ágios Nikítas 82 B3
Ágios Nikólaos (Etolía-Akarnanía) 82 B3
Ágios Nikólaos (Fokída) 83 E4
Ágios Nikólaos (Fthiótida) 83 F3
Ágios Nikólaos (Hers.Methánon) 87 E2
Ágios Nikólaos (Ípiros) 82 B1
Ágios Nikólaos (Kríti) 91 E4
Ágios Nikólaos (Lakonía) 87 D3
Ágios Nikólaos (Makedonía) 80 B4
Ágios Nikólaos (Messinía) 86 C3
Ágios Pandeleímonos 79 D3
Ágios Pángalos, Akr 83 E4
Ágios Paraskeví (Ípiros) 78 C4
Ágios Paraskeví (Makedonía) 79 F2
Ágios Pávlos 80 A3
Ágios Pétros 87 D2
Ágios Pnévma 80 B2
Ágios Pródromos 80 A3
Ágios Sóstis 83 E3
Ágios Stéfanos (Kikládes) 88 C2
Ágios Stéfanos (Stereá Eláda) 87 F1
Ágios Theódori (Makedonía) 79 D4
Ágios Theódori (Pelopónissos) 87 E1
Ágios Theódori (Thessalía) 83 F3
Ágios Thomás (Kríti) 91 D4
Ágios Thomás (Stereá Eláda) 84 B4
Ágios Vassílios (Makedonía) 80 A3
Ágios Vassílios (Stereá Eláda) 84 A4
Ágios Vissários 83 E2
Agíou Órous, Kólpos 80 C4
Agira 68 C3
Agly 32 B2
Agnanda 82 C2
Agnanderó 83 D2
Agnandi 83 F3
Agnóndas 84 B3
Agnone 64 B2
Agnoúnda 87 E2
Agorá 80 C2
Agordo 59 D3
Agost 45 E1
Agout 29 D4
Agrafiótis 83 D2
Agramunt 37 F3
Agrate Br. 60 A1
Agreda 36 C3
Agreliá 83 D1
Agri 65 D4
Agriá 83 F2
Agrigento 68 B4
Agrília 82 C4
Agriliá, Akr 85 F3
Agrilos 86 B3
Agrínio 82 C3
Agriovótano 83 F3
Agropoli 64 B4
Agskaret 97 E2
Aguadulce (Almería) 44 B4
Aguadulce (Sevilla) 43 E3
Aguas Vivas, R 37 D4
Aguaviva 41 E2
A Gudiña 34 C3
Agudo 39 F4
Águeda 38 B1
Agueda, R 39 D2
Aguiar 42 B1
Aguiar da Beira 38 C1
Aguilafuente 40 A1
Aguilar 43 F2
Aguilar de Campóo 35 F2
Aguilar del Alfambra 41 E2
Aguilar, Emb de 35 F2
Águilas 44 C3
Ahaïa 86 C1
Aharnés 87 F1
Ahaus 17 E3
Åheim 100 A3
Ahelóos 82 C4
Ahendriás 91 E4
Ahérondas 82 B2
Ahigal 39 D2
Ahilio (Kérkira) 82 A1
Ahilio (Thessalía) 83 E2
Ahinós 80 B2
Ahjärvi 103 F3
Ahladerí 84 B4
Ahládes, Akr 88 C4
Ahladohóri 80 B1
Ahlainen 102 B3
Ahlbeck 49 E2
Ahlen 17 E3
Ahlhorn 17 F1
Ahrensbök 48 B2
Ahrensburg 48 B2
Ahrweiler 51 E4
Ähtäri 102 C2
Ähtärinjärvi 102 C2
Ähtävänjoki 102 C2
Ahtopol 115 E2
Ahun 25 E4
Åhus 109 D3
Ahvenanmaa 106 C3
Ahvenselkä 99 E1
Aichach 55 F3
Aidenbach 56 B2
Aidone 68 C3
Aigen 56 C2
Aigle 27 E3
Aigle, Bge de l' 29 E1
Aigle, l' 19 D4
Aignan 28 C4
Aignay-le-Duc 26 C2
Aigoual, Mt 29 F3
Aigre 24 C4
Aigrefeuille-d'Aunis 24 B4
Aigrefeuille-sur-Maine 24 B3
Aiguablava 32 C3
Aiguebelette 30 C1
Aiguebelle 31 D1
Aigueperse 26 A4
Aigues 30 C3
Aigues-Mortes 30 B4
Aigües Tortes, Parque Nac de 37 F2
Aiguilles 31 E2
Aiguillon 28 C3
Aiguillon, l' 24 B4
Aigurande 25 E4
Ailefroide 31 D2
Aillant 26 A1
Ailly-le-Haut-Clocher 19 E2
Ailly-sur-Noye 19 F2
Ailsa Craig 4 B3
Aimargues 30 B4
Aime 31 D1
Ain 27 D3
Ain (Dépt) 26 C4
Ainhoa 28 A4
Ainsa 37 E2
Ainsdale 6 B2
Ainzón 36 C3
Airaines 19 E2
Airasca 31 E2
Airdrie 4 C2
Aire *R* 7 D2
Aire 19 F1
Aire, I del 45 F2
Aire, Sa de 38 B3
Aire-sur-l'Adour 28 B4
Airisto 107 D3
Airolo 58 A3
Airvault 24 C3
Aisne 20 A3
Aisne (Dépt) 20 A2
Aitana 45 E1
Aiterhofen 56 B2
Aitrach 55 E3
Aitzgorri 36 B1
Aiud 112 C4
Aix-d'Angillon, les 26 A2
Aixe 29 D1
Aix-en-Othe 26 B1
Aix-en-Provence 30 C4
Aix, I d' 24 B4
Aix-les-Bains 27 D4
Aizenay 24 B3
Ajaccio 33 E4
Ajaureforsen 97 F3
Ajdanovac 77 D1
Ajdovščina 70 A2
Ajka 112 A4
Ajo 35 F1
Ajo, C de 36 A1
Ajos 99 D3
Ajtos 115 E2
Akarnaniká, Óri 82 C3
Äkäsjokisuu 95 D4
Äkäskero 95 D4
Äkäslompolo 95 D4
Akçakoca 115 F3
Aken 53 D1
Åkersberga 106 B3
Akershus 105 D3
Åkers styckebruk 106 B4
Akhisar 115 F4
Åkirkeby 109 D4
Akkajaure 94 B4
Akkerhaugen 104 C3
Akku 95 E3
Akranes 96 A2
Akráta 87 D1
Akrathos, Akr 80 C4
Akréfnio 83 F4
Åkrehamn 104 A3
Akrestrømmen 100 C3
Akrítas 79 D2
Akrítas, Akr 86 C4
Akrogiáli 80 B3
Akropótamos 80 B3
Akrotíri 91 E1
Akrovoúni 80 C2
Akti Apólona 87 F2
Akujärvi 95 F3
Akureyri 96 B1
Ål 104 C2
Ala 60 C1
Alà di Stura 31 E1
Alà d. Sardi 66 B2
Alaejos 35 E4
Alagí 86 C3
Alagna Valsesia 27 F4
Alagnon 29 F2
Alagón 37 D3
Alagón, R 39 D2
Alagonía 86 C3
Alaharma 102 C2
Ala-Honkajoki 102 B3
Alaior 45 F2
Alajärvi 102 C2
Alakylä 99 D1
Alalkomenés 83 F4
Alameda 43 F3
Alamillo 43 F1
Alanäs 101 F1
Aland 48 C3
Åland 106 C3
Alandroal 38 C4
Alange 39 D4
Alange, Emb de 39 D4
Alanís 43 E2
Alapitkä 103 E2
Alaraz 39 E1
Alarcón 40 C3
Alarcón, Emb de 40 C3
Alar del Rey 35 F3
Alaşehir 115 F4
Alassio 31 F3
Alastaro 107 D2
Alatoz 41 D4
Alatri 63 F3
Alavieska 102 C1
Ala-Vuokki 99 F4
Alavus 102 C2
Alba 31 F2
Alba Adriatica 64 A1
Albacete 40 C4
Albacken 101 F2
Alba de Tormes 39 E1
Ålbæk 108 B1
Albaida 45 E1
Albaida, Pto de 45 E1
Alba Iulia 114 C1
Albaladejo 44 B1
Albalate de Cinca 37 E3
Albalate del Arzobispo 37 D4
Albalate de las Nogueras 40 C2
Alban 29 E3
Albánchez 44 C3
Albano di Lucania 65 D4
Albano Laziale 63 E3
Albarca 37 F4
Albarella, I 61 D1
Albares 35 D2
Albarracín 41 D2
Albarracín, Sa de 41 D2
Albatana 45 D1
Albatera 45 D2
Albena 115 E2
Albenga 31 F3
Albens 27 D4
Alberche, R 39 F2
Alberga 105 F4
Albergaria-a-Velha 38 B1
Alberique 41 E4
Albernoa 42 B1
Alberobello 65 E3
Albersdorf 48 A2
Albert 19 F2
Albert Kanaal 50 C3
Albertville 27 D4
Albestroff 21 E3
Albi 29 E3
Albiano 31 F1
Albinia 63 D2
Albino 58 B4
Albisola Marina 60 A3
Albocácer 41 F2
Albolodúy 44 B3
Albolote 44 A3
Albo, M 66 C2
Alborea 41 D4
Ålborg 108 B2
Ålborg Bugt 108 B2
Albox 44 C3
Albstadt-Ebingen 55 D3
Albufeira 42 A3
Albujón 45 D2
Albulapass 58 B3
Albuñol 44 A4
Alburno, Mte 64 C4
Alburquerque 38 C3
Alby (F) 27 D4
Alby (S) 101 E3
Alcácer do Sál 42 A1
Alcáçovas 42 B1
Alcadozo 44 C1
Alcafozes 38 C2
Alcains 38 C2
Alcalá de Chivert 41 F2
Alcalá de Guadaira 43 D3
Alcalá de Henares 40 B2
Alcalá de la Selva 41 E2
Alcalá del Júcar 41 D4
Alcalá de los Gazules 43 D4
Alcalá del Río 43 D2
Alcalá la Real 44 A3
Alcamo 68 B3
Alcampel 37 E3
Alcanadre, R 37 E3
Alcanar 41 F2
Alcanede 38 A3
Alcanena 38 B3
Alcanhões 38 B3
Alcañices 34 C4
Alcañiz 37 E4
Alcántara 39 D3
Alcántara, Emb de 39 D3
Alcantarilha 42 A2
Alcantarilla 45 D2
Alcaracejos 43 E1
Alcaraz 44 B1
Alcaraz, Sa de 44 C1
Alcaria do Cume 42 B2
Alcaria Ruiva 42 B2
Alcarrache, R 42 C1
Alcarràs 37 E4
Alcaudete 43 F3
Alcaudete de la Jara 39 F3
Alcázar de San Juan 40 B4
Alceda 35 F2
Alcester 9 E1
Alcoba 39 F4
Alcobaça 38 A3
Alcoba de los Montes 39 F4
Alcobendas 40 B2
Alcoceber 41 F2
Alcochete 38 A4
Alcolea 43 F2
Alcolea de Cinca 37 E3
Alcolea del Pinar 36 B4
Alcolea del Río 43 E2
Alconchel 42 C1
Alcora 41 E3
Alcorisa 41 E2
Alcorlo, Emb de 40 B1
Alcoutim 42 B2
Alcover 37 F4
Alcoy 45 E1
Alcubierre 37 D3
Alcubierre, Sa de 37 D3
Alcubilla de Avellaneda 36 A3
Alcublas 41 E3
Alcudia 45 F2
Alcudia de Crespins 41 E4
Alcudia de Guadix 44 B3
Alcuéscar 39 D4
Aldeacentenera 39 E3
Aldeadávila, Emb de 34 C4
Aldea del Cano 39 D3
Aldea del Fresno 40 A2
Aldea del Rey 44 A1
Aldeanueva de Ebro 36 C3
Aldeanueva de la Vera 39 E2
Aldeanueva del Camino 39 E2
Aldeburgh 11 E1
Aldeia da Ponte 39 D2
Aldeia Nova de São Bento 42 C1
Alderney 18 A2
Aldershot 9 F3
Aldinci 77 E3
Aldocer 40 C2
Aledo 44 C2
Aleksandrija 113 F2
Aleksandrovac (Srbija) 73 D3
Aleksandrovac (Srbija) 77 D1
Aleksa Šantić 72 B1
Aleksinac 73 E4
Alençon 23 F3
Alenquer 38 A3
Alentejo 42 B1
Alepohóri (Pelopónissos) 87 D2
Alepohóri (Stereá Eláda) 87 E1
Aléria 33 F3
Alès 30 B3
Ales 66 B3
Aleşd 112 C4
Alessandria 60 A2
Alessandria d. Rocca 68 B3
Ålestrup 108 A2
Ålesund 100 A2
Aletschhorn 27 F3
Alexandria (GB) 4 C2
Alexándria (GR) 79 F3
Alexandria (RO) 115 D2
Alexandroúpoli 81 E2
Alf 51 E4
Alfajarín 37 D3
Alfambra (E) 41 D2
Alfambra (P) 42 A2
Alfambra, R 41 E2
Alfândega da Fé 34 C4
Alfaro 36 C3
Alfarrás 37 E3
Alfaz del Pi 45 E1
Alfedena 64 A2
Alfeizerão 38 A3
Alfeld (Bayern) 55 F1
Alfeld (Niedersachsen) 52 B1
Alfiós 86 B2
Alfonsine 61 D2
Alfonso XIII, Emb de 44 C2
Alford (Grampian) 3 E4
Alford (Lincs) 7 E3
Alfreton 7 D3
Alfta 101 F4
Algaida 45 F3
Algar 43 D4
Ålgård 104 A4
Algar de Palancia 41 E3
Algarinejo 43 F3
Algarrobo 43 F4
Algarve 42 B2
Algatocín 43 E4
Algeciras 43 D4
Algemesí 41 E4
Alghero 66 A2
Alginet 41 E4
Algodonales 43 E3
Algodor, R 40 A3
Algora 40 C1
Algorta 36 B1
Algoz 42 A2
Alhama de Almería 44 B3
Alhama de Aragón 36 C4
Alhama de Granada 43 F3
Alhama de Murcia 45 D2
Alhambra 40 B4
Alhamilla, Sa 44 B3
Alhaurín el Grande 43 E4
Alhóndiga 40 B2
Alia (E) 39 E3
Alia (I) 68 C3
Aliaga 41 E2
Aliaguilla 41 D3
Aliákmona, L 79 E4
Aliákmonas 79 D4
Aliartos 83 F4
Alibunar 73 D2
Alicante 45 E2
Alicudi, I 68 C2
Alicún de Ortega 44 B2
Alife 64 B3
Alijó 34 B4
Alikés 86 A1
Alikianós 90 B3
Alikí (Kikládes) 88 C3
Alikí (Thássos) 81 D3
Alimiá, N 93 E1
Alingsås 108 C1
Alinyà 32 A3
Aliseda 39 D3
Alise-Ste-Reine 26 B2
Aliste, R 35 D4
Alistráti 80 B2
Ali Terme 69 D2
Alivéri 84 B4
Aljezur 42 A2
Aljibe 43 D4
Aljucén 39 D4
Aljustrel 42 B1
Alkionídon, Kólpos 87 E1
Alkmaar 16 C2
Allaire 22 C4
Allaman, M 76 C4
Allanche 29 E2
Alland 57 E3
Allariz 34 B3
Alleen 104 B4
Alleghe 59 D3
Allègre 29 F2
Allen, L 12 C2
Allensbach 55 D4
Allentsteig 57 E2
Allepuz 41 E2
Aller 48 A4
Allersberg 55 F1
Allershausen 55 F3
Alleuze 29 F2
Allevard 31 D1
Allier (Dépt) 26 A3
Allier *R* 26 A3
Allinge-Sandvig 109 D4
Allo 36 C2
Alloa 5 D2
Allonnes 23 F4
Allos 31 D3
Allos, Col d' 31 D3
Alloza 41 E1
Allstedt 52 C2
Almacelles 37 E3
Almáchar 43 F3
Almada 38 A4
Almadén 39 F4
Almadén de la Plata 43 D2
Almadenejos 43 F1
Almagro 40 A4
Almajano 36 B3
Almansa 45 D1
Almansil 42 B3
Almanza 35 E2
Almanzora, R 44 B3
Almanzor, Pico 39 E2
Almaraz 39 E3
Almargen 43 E3
Almarza 36 B3
Almazán 36 B4
Almazora 41 E3
Almedinilla 43 F3
Almeida (E) 35 D4
Almeida (P) 39 D1
Almeirim 38 B3

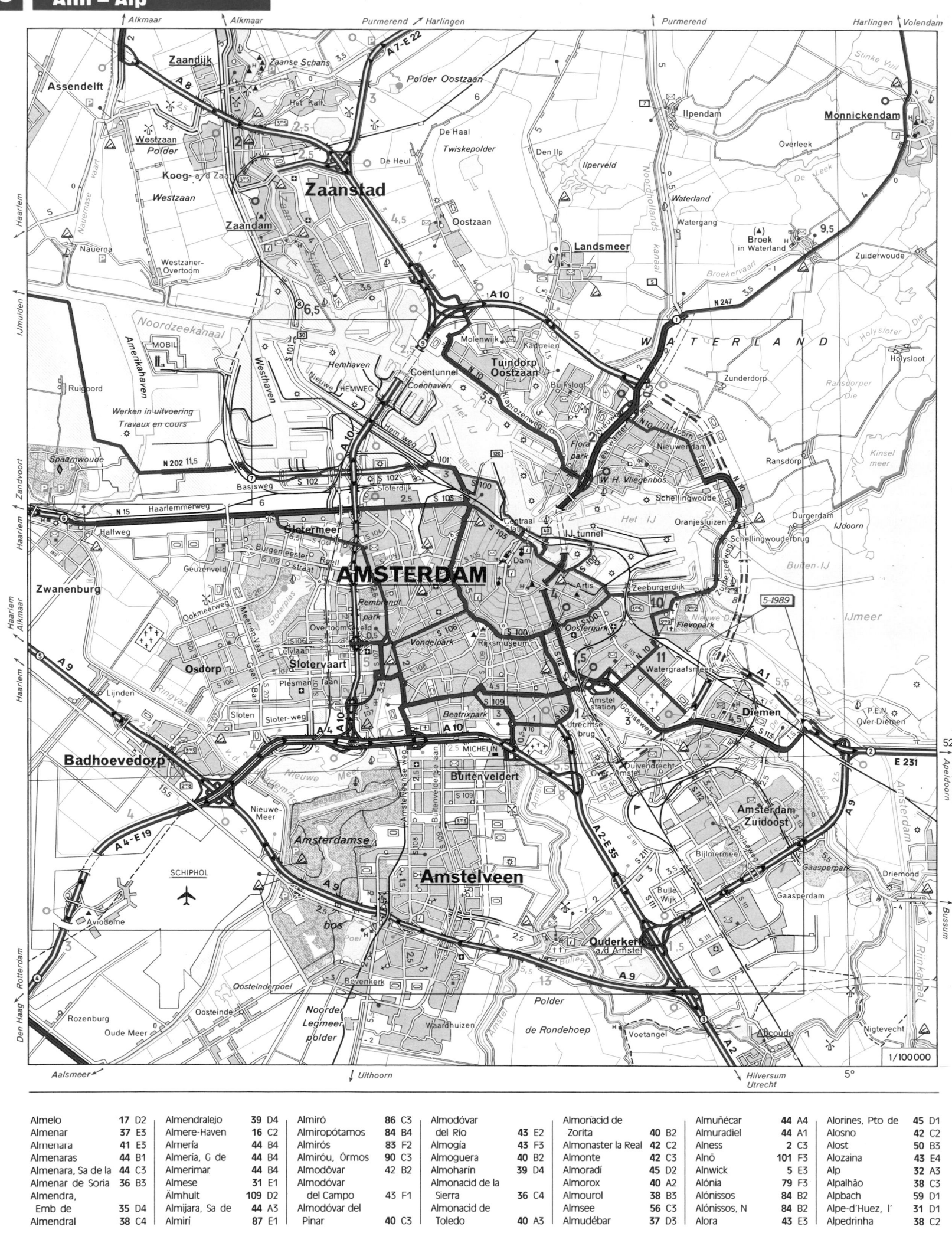

Almelo	17 D2	Almendralejo	39 D4	Almiró	86 C3	Almodóvar		Almonacid de		Almuñécar	44 A4	Alorines, Pto de	45 D1
Almenar	37 E3	Almere-Haven	16 C2	Almiropótamos	84 B4	del Río	43 E2	Zorita	40 B2	Almuradiel	44 A1	Alosno	42 C2
Almenara	41 E3	Almería	44 B4	Almirós	83 F2	Almogía	43 F3	Almonaster la Real	42 C2	Alness	2 C3	Alost	50 B3
Almenaras	44 B1	Almería, G de	44 B4	Almiróu, Órmos	90 C3	Almoguera	40 B2	Almonte	42 C3	Alnö	101 F3	Alozaina	43 E4
Almenara, Sa de la	44 C3	Almerimar	44 B4	Almodóvar	42 B2	Almoharín	39 D4	Almoradí	45 D2	Alnwick	5 E3	Alp	32 A3
Almenar de Soria	36 B3	Almese	31 E1	Almodóvar		Almonacid de la		Almorox	40 A2	Alónia	79 F3	Alpalhão	38 C3
Almendra,		Älmhult	109 D2	del Campo	43 F1	Sierra	36 C4	Almourol	38 B3	Alónissos	84 B2	Alpbach	59 D1
Emb de	35 D4	Almijara, Sa de	44 A3	Almodóvar del		Almonacid de		Almsee	56 C3	Alónissos, N	84 B2	Alpe-d'Huez, l'	31 D1
Almendral	38 C4	Almiri	87 E1	Pinar	40 C3	Toledo	40 A3	Almudébar	37 D3	Alora	43 E3	Alpedrinha	38 C2

Alpera 41 D4
Alpes-de-Haute-
Provence 31 D3
Alpes-Maritimes 31 E3
Alpe Veglia 58 A3
Alphen aan den
Rijn 16 C3
Alpi Apuane 60 B3
Alpiarça 38 B2
Alpignano 31 E1
Alpi Orobie 58 B3
Alpirsbach 54 C3
Alpua 99 D4
Alqueva 42 B1
Alqueva,
Bgem de 42 B1
Alquézar 37 E3
Als 108 B2
Als (Reg) 108 B4
Alsasua 36 B1
Alsdorf 17 D4
Alsen 101 E2
Alsfeld 52 A3
Alstahaug 97 D3
Alston 5 E4
Alta 95 D2
Altaelva 95 D2
Altafjorden 95 D2
Altamura 65 D3
Alta, Sa 41 D2
Altastenberg 17 F4
Altaussee 56 C3
Altavilla 68 B3
Altdöbern 53 E1
Altdorf (CH) 58 A2
Altdorf (D) 55 F1
Altea 45 E1
Altedo 61 D2
Altena 17 E4
Altenahr 51 E4
Altenau 52 B2
Altenberg 53 E3
Altenberge 17 E3
Altenburg 53 D3
Altenholz 48 A1
Altenhundem 17 F4
Altenkirchen (D) 51 E3
Altenkirchen (DDR) 49 D1
Altenmarkt (D) 56 B3
Altenmarkt
(Salzburg) 59 F1
Altenmarkt
(Steiermark) 57 D3
Altenstadt 55 E3
Altensteig 54 C3
Altentreptow 49 D2
Altenwalde 47 F2
Alte Oder 49 E3
Alter do Chão 38 C3
Altglashütten 54 C4
Altheim 56 C3
Althofen 70 B1
Altkirch 27 E1
Altlandsberg 49 E4
Altlengbach 57 E2
Altmühl 55 F2
Altmühlsee 55 E2
Altmünster 56 C3
Altnaharra 2 C2
Alto Campó 35 F2
Alto Cruz 36 C4
Alto de Allariz 34 B3
Alto de Barazar 36 B1
Alto de Covelo 34 C3
Alto de Estividas 34 B3
Alto de Fumaces 34 B3
Alto del Couso 34 B3
Alto del Portalé 37 E4
Alto del Rodicio 34 B3
Alto de
Santo Domingo 34 B2
Alto do Cañizo 34 C3
Alto Laza 37 D2
Altomira 40 B2
Alton 9 F3
Altopascio 60 C3
Alto Rabagão,
Bgem do 34 B3
Altorricon 37 E3
Altotero 36 A2
Altötting 56 B3
Altrincham 6 C2
Alt Ruppin 49 D3
Altshausen 55 D4

Altstätten 58 B2
Altura 41 E3
Altweilnau 51 F4
Alustante 41 D2
Alva 4 C2
Alvaiázere 38 B2
Alvalade 42 A1
Alvão, Sa de 34 B4
Alva, R 38 B2
Alvdal 100 C3
Älvdalen 101 E4
Alvelos, Sa de 38 B2
Alverca do
Ribatejo 38 A4
Alvesta 109 D2
Ålvik 104 B2
Alvito 42 B1
Alvito, Bgem do 42 B1
Älvkarleby 106 B2
Alvor 42 A2
Älvros 101 E3
Älvsborgs Län 108 C1
Älvsbyn 98 B3
Alyth 5 D1
Alytus 110 C4
Alz 56 B3
Alzenau 52 A4
Alzey 54 C1
Alzira 41 E4
Alzola 36 B1
Alzon 29 F3
Alzonne 32 B1
Amadora 38 A4
Åmål 105 E4
Amalfi 64 B4
Amaliáda 86 B1
Amaliápoli 83 F2
Amálo 89 D2
Amance 27 D1
Amancey 27 D2
Amandola 61 F4
Amantea 67 E3
Amárandos
(Ípiros) 78 C4
Amárandos
(Thessalía) 83 D2
Amarante 34 B4
Amareleja 42 C1
Amares 34 A4
Amárinthos 84 B4
Amatrice 63 F1
Amay 50 C4
Amaya 35 F3
Ambarès-et-
Lagrave 28 B2
Ambasaguas 35 E2
Ambazac 25 E4
Ambelákia
(Thessalía) 83 E1
Ambelákia (Thráki) 81 F1
Ambelía 83 E2
Ambelikó 85 F3
Ambelióna 86 C2
Ambelónas 83 E1
Amberg 55 F1
Ambérieu-en-
Bugey 26 C4
Ambert 29 F1
Ambès 28 B2
Ambierle 26 B4
Amble 5 E3
Ambleside 5 D4
Amblève 51 D4
Amboise 25 D2
Ambra 61 D4
Ambrières-les-
Vallées 18 C4
Ameixial 42 B2
Ameland 16 C1
Amelia 63 E2
Amélie-les-Bains-
Palalda 32 B3
Amelinghausen 48 B3
Amer 32 B3
A Merca 34 B3
Amerongen 16 C3
Amersfoort 16 C3
Amersham 9 F2
Amesbury 9 E3
A Mezquita 34 C3
Amfiaraío 84 B4
Amfíklia 83 E3
Amfilohía 82 C3

Amfípoli 80 B2
Ámfissa 83 E4
Amiata, Mont' 63 D1
Amiens 19 F2
Amigdaleónas 80 C2
Amigdaliá 83 E4
Amíndeo 79 D3
Ámli 104 B4
Ammanford 8 C2
Ämmänsaari 99 E3
Ammarfjället 97 F3
Ammarnäs 97 F3
Ammel 56 A4
Ammersattel 55 F4
Ammersee 56 A3
Amohóri 79 D3
Amoliani 80 B4
Amorbach 55 D1
Amorebieta 36 B1
Amorgós 89 D3
Amorgós, N 89 D3
Amório 81 F1
Åmot (Buskerud) 104 C3
Åmot (S) 105 F2
Åmot (Telemark) 104 B3
Åmotfors 105 D3
Amótopos 82 C2
Amoudára 91 D3
Amoudára 91 E4
Amoúdia 89 D2
Ampezzo 59 E3
Ampfing 56 B3
Amphion 27 D3
Amplepuis 26 B4
Amposta 41 F2
Ampthill 9 F2
Ampudia 35 E4
Ampuero 36 A1
Amriswil 58 B1
Amrum 47 F1
Amsele 98 B4
Amstelveen 16 C2
Amsterdam 16 C2
Amstetten 57 D5
Amungen 101 E4
Amurrio 36 B1
Amusco 35 F3
Amvrakía, L 82 C3
Amvrakikós
Kólpos 82 C3
Anadia 38 B1
Anáfi 91 E1
Anáfi, N 91 F1
Anafonítria 86 A1
Anagni 63 F3
Anáktora
Néstoros 86 B3
Análipsi 83 F4
Análipsi 92 C1
Análipsis 86 C3
Ananjev 113 E3
Anaráhi 79 D3
Anárgiri 79 D3
Anatolí (Ípiros) 82 C1
Anatolí (Kríti) 91 E4
Anatolí (Thessalía) 83 F1
Anatolikí Rodópi 81 D2
Anatolikó 79 D3
Anávatos 85 E4
Anávissos 87 F2
Anávra (Kardítsa) 83 E2
Anávra (Magnisía) 83 E3
An Cabhán 13 D3
Ancares, Sa de 34 C2
Ancenis 23 D4
Ancerville 20 C4
Anchuras 39 F3
An Clochán 12 A3
An Cóbh 14 C4
Ancona 61 F3
Ancy-le-Franc 26 B1
Anda 100 A3
Andalo 58 C3
Åndalsnes 100 B2
Andalucía 43 E2
Andarax, R 44 B3
Andartikó 79 D2

Andebu 104 C3
Andelot 26 C1
Andelys, les 19 E3
Andenes 94 A3
Andenne 50 C4
Anderlues 50 B4
Andermatt 58 A3
Andernach 51 E4
Andernos 28 A2
Anderstorp 109 D2
Andfjorden 94 B3
Andígonos 79 D3
Andíkira 83 E4
Andikíras, Kólpos 83 E4
Andikíthira, N 90 A2
Andimáhia 89 F3
Andímilos, N 88 A4
Andinítsa 83 E3
Andíparos 88 B3
Andíparos, N 88 B3
Andípaxi, N 82 B2
Andípsara, N 85 E4
Andírio 83 D4
Andíssa 85 E2
Andoain 36 C1
Andorno Micca 31 F1
Andorra 41 E1
Andorra la Vella 32 A2
Andosilla 36 C2
Andover 9 E3
Andøya 94 A3
Andratx 45 E3
Andravída 86 B1
Andretta 64 C3
Andríjevica 76 C2
Andrítsena 86 C2
Andros 88 B1
Ándros, N 88 B1
Androússa 86 C3
Andselv 94 B3
Andújar 43 F2
Anduze 30 B3
Aneby 109 D1
Ânes 100 B2
Anet 19 E4
Aneto, Pico de 37 E2
Angáli 84 A3
Ânge (Jämtlands
Län) 101 E2
Ånge (Väster-
norrlands Län) 101 E3
Angeja 38 B1
Ängelholm 108 C3
Angeli 95 E3
Angelohóri 79 E3
Angelókastro
(Pelopónissos) 87 E2
Angelókastro
(Stereá Eláda) 82 C4
Anger 57 E4
Angera 58 A4
Ångermanälven 101 F2
Angermünde 49 E3
Angern 57 F2
Angers 23 E4
Angerville 25 E1
Ängesån 98 C2
Anghiari 61 D4
Angístis,
Stathmós 80 B2
Angístri 87 E2
Angístri, N 87 E2
Angístro 80 B1
Angítis 80 B2
Angle 8 B2
Angles 25 D3
Anglès (E) 32 B3
Anglès (F) 32 B1
Anglesey, I of 6 A2
Anglesola 37 F3
Anglet 28 A4
Anglure 20 B4
Angoulême 28 C1
Angri 64 B4
Ångsö 106 C3
Angüés 37 E3
Anguiano 36 B2
Anguillara Veneta 61 D1
Angvik 100 B2

Aniene 63 F2
Ánixi 79 D4
Anizy-le-Château 20 A3
Anjalankoski 107 F2
Anjum 47 D3
Ankaran 70 A3
Ankarsrum 109 E1
Anklam 49 E2
Ankogel 59 E2
An Longfort 12 C3
An Muileann
gCearr 13 D3
Ånn 101 D2
Ånn L 101 D2
Annaberg 57 E3
Annaberg-
Buchholz 53 E3
Annaburg 53 E1
Annan 5 D3
Annan R 5 D3
Anndalsvågen 97 D3
Annecy 27 D4
Annemasse 27 D4
Annevoie-
Rouillon 50 C4
Annonay 30 B1
Annone Veneto 59 E4
Annot 31 D3
Annweiler 54 C2
Áno Drossini 81 E2
Anógia 87 D3
Anógia 91 D3
Áno Hóra 83 D4
Áno Kalendíni 82 C2
Áno Kaliníki 79 D2
Áno Kómi 79 E4
Áno Lefkími 82 A2
Áno Melás 79 D3
Áno Merá 88 C2
Anópoli 90 C4
Áno Polidéndri 83 F1
Áno Poróïa 80 A2
Áno Rodákino 90 C4
Áno Sangrí 88 C3
Áno Síros 88 B2
Añover de Tajo 40 A3
Áno Viános 91 E4
Áno Vrondoù 80 B2
Áno Zervohóri 79 E3
Ansbach 55 E1
Anse 26 C4
Ansedonia 63 D2
Ansião 38 B2
Ansnes 100 C1
Ansó 37 D2
Anstruther 5 D2
An tAonach 12 C4
Antas 44 C3
Antegnate 60 B1
Antemil 34 A1
Antequera 43 F3
Anterselva 59 D2
Ánthia 81 E2
Anthíli 83 E3
Anthís 80 B2
Antholz 59 D2
Anthótopos 83 E2
Antibes 31 E4
Antifer, Cap d' 19 D3
An tInbhear Mór 15 E3
Antnäs 98 C3
Antraigues 30 B2
Antrain 18 B4
Antrim 13 E2
Antrim (Co) 13 E2
Antrim Coast 13 E1
Antrim Mts 13 E1
Antrodoco 63 F2
Anttola 103 E3
Antwerpen 50 B3
Antwerpen (Prov) 50 B3
An Uaimh 13 D3
Anvers 50 B3
Anzano di Puglia 64 C3
Anzio 63 E3
Anzola d'Ossola 58 A4
Anzy-le-Duc 26 B4
Aoiz 36 C2
Aóos 78 C4
Aosta 27 E4
Aoste 27 E4
Apatin 72 B2
Apatovac 71 D2

Apecchio 61 E4
Apeldoorn 17 D2
Apen 47 E3
Apéri 93 D3
Aphrodisias 115 F4
Apidiá 87 D3
Apíkia 88 B1
Apíranthos 88 C3
Apolakiá 93 E2
Apolda 52 C3
Apolitáres, Akr 90 A2
Apólonas 88 C3
Apolonía
(Kikládes) 88 B3
Apolonía
(Makedonía) 80 B3
A Pontenova
Villaodriz 34 C1
Apóstoli 90 C4
Áppelbo 105 E2
Appenweier 54 C3
Appenzell 58 B2
Appiano 59 D3
Appingedam 47 D3
Appleby 5 D4
Aprica 58 C3
Apricena 64 C2
Aprilia 63 E3
Ápsalos 79 E2
Apt 30 C3
Áptera 90 C3
Aquileia 59 F3
Aquitaine, L' 25 E2
Arabba 59 D3
Aracena 42 C2
Aracena, Emb de 43 D2
Aracena, Sa de 42 C2
Aračinovo 77 E3
Arad 112 C4
Åradalsfjorden 104 B1
Arada, Sa de 38 B1
Aragón 37 D3
Aragona 68 B4
Aragón, R 36 C2
Arahneo, Óros 87 E2
Aráhova (Etolía-
Akarnanía) 83 D3
Aráhova (Viotía) 83 E4
Arákinthos, Óros 83 D4
A Ramallosa 34 A3
Aramits 37 D1
Aran I 12 C1
Aran Is 12 A4
Aranjuez 40 B3
Arantzazu 36 B1
Aran, Vall d' 37 F2
Ara, R 37 E2
Araquil, R 36 C2
Aras de Alpuente 41 D3
Arasluokta 97 F1
Áratos 81 E2
Aravaca 40 A2
Aravis, Col des 27 D4
Aravissós 79 E2
Áraxos 86 B1
Áraxos, Akr 86 B1
Arba, R 36 C3
Arbatax 66 C3
Arbeca 37 F4
Arbesbach 57 D2
Arboga 105 F3
Arbois 27 D3
Arbón, Emb de 34 C1
Arborea 66 B3
Arborio 31 F1
Arbrå 101 F4
Arbroath 5 E1
Arbresle, l' 26 B4
Arbúcies 32 B4
Arbus 66 B3
Arc 31 D1
Arcachon 28 A2
Arce 64 A3
Arcen 17 D3
Arc-en-Barrois 26 C1
Arcevia 61 E4
Archena 45 D2
Arches 27 D1

Archiac 28 B1
Archidona 43 F3
Arcidosso 63 D1
Arcipelago
Toscano 62 B1
Arcis 20 B4
Arciz 113 E4
Arco 58 C4
Arco de Baúlhe 34 B4
Arcos 35 F3
Arcos de Jalón 36 B4
Arcos de la
Frontera 43 D3
Arcos de
Valdevez 34 A3
Arcouest, Pte de l' 22 C2
Arcs, les (Savoie) 31 D1
Arcs, les (Var) 31 D4
Arcusa 37 E2
Arda 115 E3
Ardales 43 E3
Årdalstangen 104 B1
Ardánio 81 F2
Ardara 12 C1
Árdas 81 F1
Ardbeg 4 B2
Ardèche (Dépt) 30 B2
Ardèche R 30 B2
Ardèche,
Gges de l' 30 B3
Ardee 13 D3
Ardennes (Dépt) 20 B3
Ardennes,
Canal des 20 C3
Ardentes 25 E3
Ardentinny 4 C2
Ardes 29 F1
Ardez 58 B2
Ardglass 13 E2
Ardila, R 42 C1
Ardila, Rib de 42 C1
Ardisa 37 D3
Ardlussa 4 B2
Ardmore 14 C4
Ardrahan 12 B4
Ardres 19 E1
Ardrishaig 4 B2
Ardrossan 4 C2
Ards Pen 13 E2
Arduaine 4 B1
Ardvasar 2 B4
Åre 101 D2
Arenas de
Cabrales 35 E2
Arenas de Iguña 35 F2
Arenas de San
Juan 40 B4
Arenas de San
Pedro 39 F2
Arendal 104 C4
Arendonk 50 C3
Arendsee 48 C3
Arenos, Emb de 41 E3
Arenys de Mar 32 B4
Arenzano 60 A3
Areópoli 87 D4
Ares 28 A2
Ares (Galicia) 34 B1
Ares (Valencia) 41 E2
Ares, Col des 37 F2
Ares, Pto de 32 B3
Åreskutan 101 D2
Aréthoussa 80 B3
Aretí 80 A3
Arévalo 39 F1
Arez 38 C3
Arezzo 61 D4
Arfará 86 C3
Argalastí 83 F2
Argamasilla de
Alba 40 B4
Argamasilla de
Calatrava 44 A1
Arganda 40 B2
Arganil 38 B2
Argás 36 C2
Argássi 86 A2
Argelès 32 B2
Argelès-Gazost 37 E1
Argens 31 D4
Argenta 61 D2
Argentan 19 D4
Argentario, Mte 63 D2

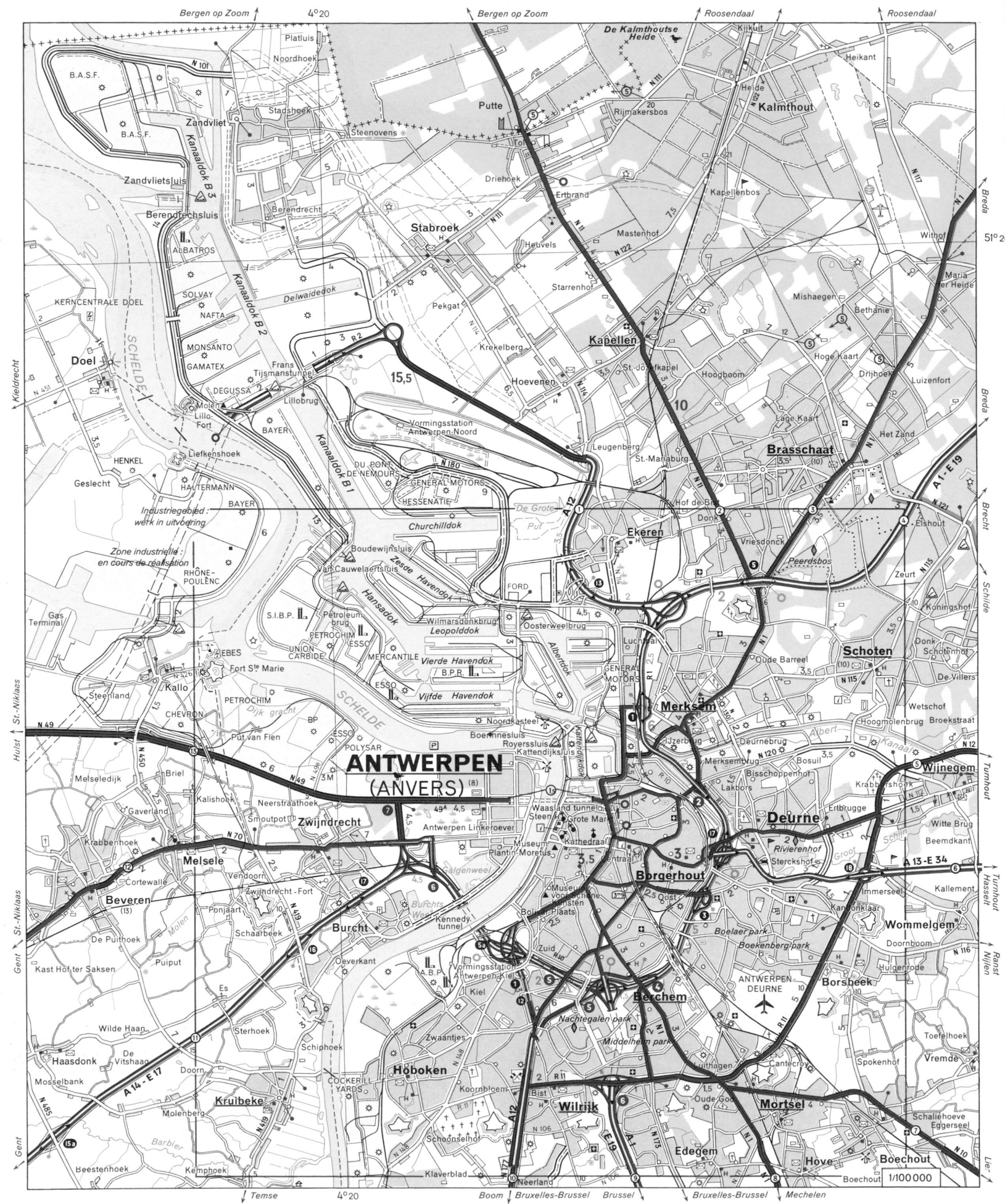

Name	Map	Ref
Argentat	29	D2
Argente	41	D2
Argentera	31	E3
Argentière	27	E4
Argentière-la-Bessée, l'	31	D2
Argentona	32	B4
Argenton-Château	24	C3
Argenton-sur-Creuse	25	E3
Argentré-du-Plessis	23	E3
Arginónda	89	F3
Argirádes	82	A2
Argiró	84	B4
Argiropoúlio	83	E1
Argiroúpoli	90	C3
Argithéa	83	D2
Argolída	87	E2
Argolikós Kólpos	87	E2
Árgos	87	D2
Árgos Orestikó	79	D3
Argos, R	44	C2
Argostóli	82	B4
Arguedas	36	C3
Argueil	19	E3
Arguellite	44	B1
Arguis	37	D2
Argyll	4	B1
Argyll Forest Park	4	C2
Arhánes	91	D4
Arhángelos (Makedonía)	79	E2
Arhángelos (Ródos)	93	F1
Arhéa Epídavros	87	E2
Arhéa Kleonés	87	D1
Arhéa Kórinthos	87	E1
Arhéa Neméa	87	D1
Arhéa Olympía	86	C2
Arhéa Thíra	91	E1
Århus	108	B3
Arianá	81	E2
Ariano Irpino	64	B3
Ariano nel Polesine	61	D2
Aridéa	79	E2
Ariège (Dépt)	32	A2
Ariège R	32	A2
Arija	35	F2
Arild	108	C3
Arilje	72	C4
Arinagour	2	B4
Aríni	86	C2
Ariño	37	D4
Arinthod	27	D3
Arisaig	2	B4
Arisaig, Sd of	2	B4
Arísti	78	C4
Aristoménis	86	C3
Arísvi	81	E2
Aritzo	66	B3
Arive	36	C2
Ariza	36	B4
Årjäng	105	D3
Arjeplog	98	A3
Arjona	44	A2
Arkádi	91	D3
Arkadía	86	C2
Arkaig, L	2	C4
Arkalohóri	91	E4
Arkássa	93	D3
Arkessíni	89	D3
Arki, N	89	E2
Arkítsa	83	F3
Arklow	15	E3
Arkona, Kap	49	D1
Arkoúdi, N	82	B4
Arlaban, Pto de	36	B1
Arlanc	29	F1
Arlanda	106	B3
Arlanza, R	36	A3
Arlanzón	36	A2
Arlanzón, R	35	F3
Arlbergpaß	58	B2
Arlberg-Straßentunnel	58	B2
Arlempdes	30	A2
Arles (Bouches-du-Rhône)	30	B4
Arles (Pyrénées-Orientales)	32	B3
Arlesheim	27	E2
Arlon	21	D2
Arlsleben	52	C2
Armação de Péra	42	A3
Armadale	5	D2
Arma di Taggia	31	F3
Armagh	13	D2
Armagh (Co)	13	D2
Armamar	34	B4
Arméni	90	C3
Armenií	86	C3
Armenistís	89	D2
Armentières	19	F1
Armilla	44	A3
Armólia	85	E4
Armunia	35	D3
Árna	87	D3
Arnac-Pompadour	29	D1
Arnay-le-Duc	26	R2
Arnéa	80	B3
Arneburg	48	C4
Arnedillo	36	B3
Arnedo	36	C3
Arnes	41	F2
Årnes	105	D3
Arnhem	17	D3
Arni	60	B3
Árnissa	79	E2
Arno	60	C4
Arnoldstein	59	F2
Arnon	25	F3
Arnøy	94	C2
Arnsberg	17	F3
Arnstadt	52	C3
Arnstein	52	B4
Aroania, Óri	86	C1
Aroche	42	C2
Aroche Mt	42	C1
Arogí	81	D2
Arolsen	52	A2
Arona	58	A4
Aroniádika	90	A1
Aronkylä	102	B3
Åros	104	C3
Arosa	58	B2
Arouca	38	B1
Arousa, I de	34	A2
Årøysund	104	C3
Arpajon	19	F4
Arpela	99	D3
Arquata del Tronto	63	F1
Arques (Pas-de-Calais)	19	F1
Arques (Seine-Maritime)	19	E2
Arquillos	44	A2
Arrabal	34	A3
Arrábida, Sa da	38	A4
Arracourt	21	D4
Arraiolos	38	B4
Arran	4	B2
Arras	19	F2
Arrasate-Mondragon	36	B1
Arreau	37	E2
Arrecife	42	C4
Arredondo	36	A1
Arrée, Mts d'	22	B2
Arrens	37	E2
Arrifana	38	C3
Arrigorriaga	36	B1
Arriondas	35	E1
Arrochar	4	C2
Arromanches	18	C3
Arronches	38	C4
Arroux	26	B3
Arrow, L	12	C2
Arroyo de la Luz	39	D3
Arroyo del Ojanco	44	B1
Arroyo de San Serván	39	D4
Arroyomolinos de León	43	D1
Arroyomolinos de Montánchez	39	D4
Arruda dos Vinhos	38	A3
Års	108	A2
Ars (Charente-Maritime)	24	B4
Ars (Moselle)	21	D3
Arsié	59	D3
Arsiero	59	D4
Arsunda	106	B2
Arsy	19	F3
Artà	45	F2
Árta	82	C2
Artajona	36	C2
Árta (Nomos)	82	C2
Arta Terme	59	E3
Arteaga, G de	36	B1
Artemíssia	86	C3
Artemíssio (Évia)	83	F3
Artemíssio (Pelopónissos)	87	D2
Artemónas	88	B3
Artena	63	F3
Artenay	25	E1
Artern	52	C2
Artesa de Segre	37	F3
Artessianó	83	D2
Arth (CH)	58	A2
Arth (D)	56	D2
Arthurstown	15	D4
Arties	37	F2
Artjärvi	107	F2
Artotína	83	D3
Artruix, C de	45	F2
Arucas	42	B4
Arudy	37	D1
Arundel	9	F3
Arve	27	E4
Árvi	91	E4
Arvidsjaur	98	A3
Årvik	100	A2
Arvika	105	E3
Árviksand	94	C2
Arzachena	66	B1
Arzacq-Arraziguet	28	B4
Arzano	22	B3
Arzano	75	E1
Arzberg	53	D4
Arzignano	60	C1
Árzos	81	F1
Arzúa	34	B2
As	50	C3
Aš	53	D4
Åsa	108	C2
Asamati	77	D4
Åsarna	101	E2
Åsarp	109	D1
Ascain	28	A4
Ascha	56	B2
Aschach	56	C2
Aschaffenburg	52	A4
Aschau	56	B3
Aschbach Markt	57	D3
Ascheberg (Nordrhein-Westfalen)	17	E3
Ascheberg (Schleswig-Holstein)	48	B2
Aschendorf	17	E1
Aschersleben	52	C2
Asciano	61	D4
Ascione, Colle d'	67	F3
Asco	33	F3
Ascó	37	E4
Ascoli Piceno	63	F1
Ascoli Satriano	64	C3
Ascona	58	A3
Ascot	9	F2
Åse	94	A3
Åseda	109	E2
Åsele	101	F1
Åsen	101	D1
Asenovgrad	115	D3
Åseral	104	B4
Asfáka	82	B1
Asfeld	20	B3
Åsgårdstrand	104	C3
Ashbourne (GB)	6	C3
Ashbourne (IRL)	13	D3
Ashburton	8	C4
Ashby de la Zouch	6	C3
Ashford	11	D3
Ashington	5	E3
Ashton-under-Lyne	6	C2
Asiago	59	D4
Asikkala	107	F2
Asín	37	D3
Asinara, G dell'	66	B1
Asinara, I	66	A1
Ask	105	D3
Askainen	107	D2
Askeaton	14	B3
Askersund	105	E4
Askífou	90	C3
Askim	105	D3
Áskio, Óros	79	D3
Askja	96	C2
Asklipiío (Dodekánissa)	89	F3
Asklipiío (Ródos)	93	E2
Áskola	107	F2
Askós	80	A3
Askøy	104	A2
Askvoll	104	A1
Asmunti	99	D3
Asnæs	108	B3
Asnen	109	D2
As Neves	34	A3
Asola	60	B1
Asolo	59	D4
Aspang	57	F3
Aspatria	5	D4
Aspe	45	D2
Aspe, Gave d'	37	D1
Asperg	55	D2
Aspet	37	F2
Aspin, Col d'	37	E2
As Ponte de Garcia Rodriguez	34	B1
Áspra Spítia	83	E4
Aspres	30	C2
Áspro	79	E3
Aspróhoma	86	C3
Asprókavos, Akr	82	A2
Aspromonte	67	E4
Asprópirgos	87	F1
Asproválta	80	B3
Asse	50	B3
Assemini	66	B4
Assen	17	D1
Assens	108	B3
Assergi	63	F2
Assíni	87	E2
Assisi	63	E1
Aßmannshausen	51	F4
Assómaton	91	D3
Assopía	84	A4
Assopós (Korinthía)	87	D1
Assopós (Lakonía)	87	E4
Assopós R	87	E1
Ássos (Ípiros)	82	B2
Ássos (Kefaloniá)	82	B4
Astaffort	28	C3
Astafjorden	94	B3
Astakída, N	93	D2
Astakós	82	C4
Asten	57	D3
Asti	31	F2
Astipálea	92	C1
Astipálea, N	92	C1
Astorga	35	D3
Åstorp	108	C3
Ástros	87	D2
Astudillo	35	F3
Asturias	34	C2
Asvestádes	81	F1
Asvestohóri	82	B1
Asvestópetra	79	D3
Atalaia	38	A3
Atalaia	83	F3
Atalaya de la Calzada	44	A1
Atalayassa	45	D4
Átali	84	B3
Ataquines	39	F1
Atarfe	44	A3
Atáviros	93	E2
Ateca	36	C4
Atella	64	C3
Atessa	64	B2
Ath	50	B4
Athamánon, Óri	82	C2
Athániio	82	B3
Athboy	13	D3
Athéras	89	D2
Athéras, Akr	82	B4
Atherstone	9	E1
Athína	87	F1
Áthira	79	F2
Athlone	12	C3
Áthos	80	C4
Athy	13	D4
Atienza	36	B4
Atikí-Piréas	87	F1
Atina	64	A3
Átokos, N	82	C4
Atouguia da Baleia	38	A3
Átran	108	C2
Átran R	108	C2
Atri	64	A1
Atsikí	85	D1
Attendorn	17	F4
Attersee	56	C3
Attersee L	56	C3
Attigliano	63	E2
Attigny	20	B3
Attleborough	11	D1
Attnang	56	C3
Åtvidaberg	109	E1
Au	55	F2
Aub	55	E1
Aubagne	30	C4
Aubange	21	D2
Aube	20	B4
Aube (Dépt)	20	B4
Aubenas	30	B2
Aubenton	20	B2
Auberive	26	C1
Aubeterre	28	C1
Aubigny (Cher)	25	F2
Aubigny (Pas-de-Calais)	19	F2
Aubin	29	E3
Aubisque, Col d'	37	E1
Aubonne	27	D3
Aubrac	29	F2
Aubrac, Mts d'	29	F2
Aubusson	25	F4
Auch	28	C4
Auchencairn	4	C3
Auchterarder	5	D1
Auchtermuchty	5	D1
Aude (Dépt)	32	B2
Aude R	32	B1
Audenge	28	A2
Audeux	27	D2
Audierne	22	A3
Audincourt	27	E2
Audlem	6	C3
Audruicq	19	F1
Audun-le-Roman	21	D3
Audun-le-Tiche	21	D3
Aue R	48	A4
Aue	53	D3
Auer	59	D3
Auerbach (D)	55	F1
Auerbach (DDR)	53	D3
Auffach	59	D1
Aughnacloy	13	D2
Aughrim	13	D4
Augsburg	55	F3
Augusta	69	D4
Augustenborg	108	B4
Augustów	110	C4
Augustusburg	53	E3
Aukan	100	B2
Aukra	100	B2
Aulanko	107	E2
Auletta	64	C4
Aulla	60	B3
Aullène	33	F4
Aulnay	24	C4
Aulne	22	B3
Aulnoye-Aymeries	20	B2
Ault	19	E2
Aulus-les-Bains	37	F2
Auma	53	D3
Aumale	19	E2
Aumetz	21	D3
Aumont-Aubrac	29	F2
Aunay-sur-Odon	18	C3
Auneau	19	E4
Auneuil	19	E3
Auning	108	B2
Aups	31	D4
Aura	107	D2
Aurajoki	107	D2
Auray	22	C4
Aurdal	104	C2
Aure	100	B2
Aure R	25	F3
Aurich	47	E3
Aurignac	37	F1
Aurillac	29	E2
Aurland	104	B2
Auron	31	E3
Auron R	25	F3
Auronzo di Cadore	59	E2
Auros	28	B3
Aursjøen	100	B3
Aursunden	101	D2
Ausonia	64	A3
Außernbrünst	56	C2
Ausso Corno	59	F3
Aust-Agder	104	B4
Austbygd	104	C3
Austvågøy	94	A3
Auterive	37	F1
Authie	19	F2
Autol	36	C3
Autrans	30	C1
Autrey	26	C2
Auttoinen	107	E1
Autun	26	B3
Auvézère	28	C2
Auvillar	28	C3
Auxerre	26	A1
Auxi-le-Château	19	E2
Auxonne	26	C2
Auzances	25	F4
Auzon	29	F1
Availles-Limouzine	25	D4
Avala	73	D3
Avaldsnes	104	A3
Avallon	26	B2
Avaloirs, Mt des	23	E3
Ávas	81	E2
Avaviken	98	A3
Åvdira	81	D2
A Veiga	34	C3
Aveiras de Cima	38	A3
Aveiro	38	B1
Aveiro, R de	38	B1
Avellino	64	B4
Aven Armand	29	F3
Aven d'Orgnac	30	B3
Averøya	100	B2
Aversa	64	B4
Avesnes	20	B2
Avesnes-le-Comte	19	F2
Avesta	105	F3
Avetrana	65	E4
Aveyron	29	D3
Aveyron (Dépt)	29	E3
Avezzano	63	F2
Avgerinós	79	D4
Avgó	82	C2
Avía	86	C3
Aviano	59	E3
Aviémonas	90	A2
Aviemore	3	D4
Aviés	79	E4
Avigliana	31	E1
Avigliano	64	C4
Avignon	30	B3
Ávila	39	F2
Ávila, Sa de	39	F2
Avilés	35	D1
Avintes	34	A4
Avión	34	B2
Avioth	20	C3
Avis	38	B4
Avisio	59	D3
Avize	20	B3
Avlákia	89	E1
Avlí	80	C2
Avlíotes	82	A1
Avlóna	84	B4
Avlum	108	A2
Avola	69	D4
Avon (Co)	9	D2
Avon R (Hants)	9	E1
Avon R (Warw)	9	E3
Avonmouth	9	D2
Avord	25	F3
Avoriaz	27	E4
Avranches	18	B4
Avre	19	D4
Avtovac	76	A2
Awe, L	4	B1
Axams	59	D2
Axat	32	B2
Axiohóri	79	F2
Axiós	79	F3
Axióupoli	79	F2
Ax-les-Thermes	32	A2
Axminster	9	D3
Axós	91	D3
Ay	20	B3
Ayamonte	42	B2
Aydın	115	F4
Ayedo	36	B3
Ayerbe	37	D3
Aylesbury	9	F2
Ayllón	36	A4
Ayllón, Sa de	36	A4
Aylsham	7	F3
Ayna	44	C1
Ayora	41	D4
Ayr	4	C3
Ayre, Pt of	6	A1
Ayvacık	115	E4
Ayvalık	115	E4
Aywaille	51	D4
Azáceta, Pto de	36	B2
Azaila	37	D4
Azambuja	38	A3
Azanja	73	D3
Azaruja	38	B4
Azay-le-Ferron	25	E3
Azay-le-Rideau	25	D2
Azinheira dos Barros	42	A1
Azkoitia	36	B1
Aznalcázar	43	D3
Aznalcóllar	43	D2
Azpeitia	36	B1
Azuaga	43	E1
Azuara	37	D4
Azuer, R	40	A4
Azuqueca de Henares	40	B2
Azután, Emb de	39	F3
Azzano Decimo	59	E3

B

Baad	58	B2
Baal	17	D4
Baamonde	34	B1
Baarle-Nassau	16	C4
Baarn	16	C2
Baba	77	E4
Babadag	113	E4
Babajevo	111	E1
Babelsberg	49	D4
Babenhausen (Bayern)	55	E3
Babenhausen (Hessen)	52	A4
Babina Greda	71	F3
Babin Kal	73	F4
Babin Most	77	D2
Babino Polje	75	F2
Babin Potok	70	C4
Babljak	76	B2
Babuna	77	E3
Babušnica	77	E1
Bač	72	B2
Bački Breg	72	B1
Bacau	113	D4
Baccarat	21	E4
Bæccegæhal'di	94	C2
Baceno	58	A3
Bacharach	51	E4
Bächistock	58	A2
Bachmač	113	F1
Bačina	73	E4
Bačka Palanka	72	B2
Bäckaskog	109	D3
Bačka Topola	72	B1
Backe	101	F1
Bäckebo	109	E2
Bäckefors	105	D4
Bački Breg	71	F1
Bački Brestovac	72	B2
Bački Monoštor	72	B2
Bački Petrovac	72	B2
Backnang	55	D2
Bačko Gradište	72	C2
Bačko Novo Selo	72	B2
Bačko Petrovo Selo	72	C1
Bačkovo	115	D3
Bacoli	64	A4
Bacqueville	19	D2
Baczyna	49	F3
Bad Aibling	56	B3
Badajoz	38	C4
Badalona	32	B4
Bad Aussee	56	C3
Bad Bentheim	17	E2
Bad Bergzabern	54	C2
Bad Berka	52	C3
Bad Berleburg	17	F4
Bad Berneck	53	D4
Bad Bertrich	51	E4
Bad Bevensen	48	B3
Bad Bibra	52	C2
Bad Blankenburg	52	C3
Bad Brambach	53	D4
Bad Bramstedt	48	A2
Bad Brückenau	52	B4
Bad Buchau	55	D3
Bad Camberg	51	F4
Bad Deutsch Altenburg	57	F2
Bad Doberan	48	C2
Bad Driburg	52	A2
Bad Düben	53	D2
Bad Dürkheim	54	C1
Bad Dürrenberg	53	D2
Bad Durrheim	54	C3
Bad Elster	53	D4
Bad Ems	51	E4
Baden (A)	57	F3
Baden (CH)	27	F2
Baden-Baden	54	C2
Bad Endorf	56	B3
Badenweiler	54	C4
Baden-Württemberg	55	D3
Baderna	70	A3
Bad Essen	17	F2
Bad Frankenhausen	52	C2
Bad Freienwalde	49	E3
Bad Friedrichshall	55	D2
Bad Gandersheim	52	B1
Badgastein	59	E2
Bad Gleichenberg	57	F4
Bad Godesberg	51	E3
Bad Goisern	56	C3
Bad Gottleuba	53	D3
Bad Griesbach	56	C2
Bad Grund	52	B2
Bad Hall	57	D3
Bad Harzburg	52	B1
Bad Herrenalb	54	C2
Bad Hersfeld	52	B3
Bad Hofgastein	56	C4
Bad Homburg	51	F4
Bad Honnef	51	E4
Bad Honnigen	51	E4
Badia Polesine	61	D2
Badia Tedalda	61	D3
Badija	75	E2
Bad Ischl	56	C3
Bad Iburg	17	F2
Bad Karlshafen	52	A2
Bad Kissingen	52	B4
Bad Kleinen	48	C2
Bad Kleinkirchheim	59	E2
Bad König	55	D1
Bad Königshofen	52	B4
Bad Kösen	52	C2
Bad Kreuznach	54	B1
Bad Krozingen	54	C3
Bad Laasphe	17	F4
Bad Langensalza	52	B3
Bad Lauchstädt	53	D2
Bad Lausick	53	D2
Bad Lauterberg	52	B2
Bad Leonfelden	57	D2
Bad Liebenstein	52	B3
Bad Liebenwerda	53	E2
Bad Liebenzell	54	C2
Bad Lippspringe	17	F3
Badljevina	71	D2
Bad Meinberg	52	A2
Bad Mergentheim	55	D1
Bad Mitterndorf	56	C4
Bad Münder	52	A1
Bad Münster am Stein-Ebernburg	54	B1
Bad Münstereifel	51	E4
Bad Muskau	53	F1
Bad Nauheim	52	A4
Bad Nenndorf	52	A1
Bad Neuenahr-Ahrweiler	51	E4
Bad Neustadt	52	B4
Bad Oeynhausen	17	F2
Badolato	67	F3
Badolatosa	43	F3
Badl		
Badonviller	21	E4
Bad Orb	52	A4
Badovinci	72	B3
Bad Peterstal-Griesbach	54	C3
Bad Pyrmont	52	A2
Bad Radkersburg	70	C1
Bad Ragaz	58	B2
Bad Rappenau	55	D2
Bad Reichenhall	56	B3
Bad Rippoldsau-Schapbach	54	C3
Bad Rothenfelde	17	F2
Bad Saarow-Pieskow	49	E4
Bad Sachsa	52	B2
Bad Säckingen	54	C4
Bad St Leonhard	57	D4
Bad Salzdetfurth	52	B1
Bad Salzschlirf	52	B3
Bad Salzuflen	17	F2
Bad Salzungen	52	B3
Bad Schallerbach	56	C3
Bad Schandau	53	F2
Bad Schmiedeberg	53	D1
Bad Schönborn	54	C2
Bad Schussenried	55	D3
Bad Schwälbach	51	F4
Bad Schwartau	48	B2
Bad Segeberg	48	B2
Bad Soden	51	F4
Bad Soden-Salmünster	52	A4
Bad Sooden-Allendorf	52	B2
Bad Sulza	52	C2
Bad Sülze	49	D2
Bad Tatzmannsdorf	57	F4
Bad Tennstedt	52	C2
Bad Tölz	56	A4
Badules	36	C3
Bad Urach	55	D3
Bad Vilbel	52	A4
Bad Vöslau	57	F3
Bad Waldsee	55	D4
Bad Wiessee	56	A4
Bad Wildungen	52	A3
Bad Wilsnack	48	C3
Bad Wimpfen	55	D2
Bad Windsheim	55	E1
Bad Wörishofen	55	E3
Bad Wurzach	55	E4
Bad Zwischenahn	47	E3
Bae Colwyn	6	B2
Baena	43	F2
Baeza	44	A2
Bagà	32	A3
Bâge-le-Châtel	26	C4
Bagenalstown	15	D3
Bagenkop	108	B4
Bagheria	68	B3
Bagnacavallo	61	D2
Bagnara Calabra	67	E4
Bagnères-de-Bigorre	37	E1
Bagnères-de-Luchon	37	E2
Bagni del Masino	58	B3
Bagni di Lucca	60	C3
Bagno a Ripoli	61	D3
Bagno di Romagna	61	D3
Bagnoles-de-l'Orne	18	C4
Bagnoli del Trigno	64	B2
Bagnolo Mella	60	B1
Bagnols-les-Bains	29	F3
Bagnols-sur-Cèze	30	B3
Bagnoregio	63	E1
Bagolino	58	C4
Bagrationovsk	110	B4
Bagrdan	73	E4
Baia Mare	112	C3
Baiano	64	B4
Baião	34	B4
Baiersbronn	54	C3
Baignes-Ste-Radegonde	28	B1
Baigneux-les-Juifs	26	C2
Baile Átha Cliath	13	E4
Baile Átha Luain	12	C3
Băile Herculane	114	C1
Bailén	44	A2
Băile Tuşnad	113	D4
Bailieborough	13	D3
Bailleul	19	F1
Bain-de-Bretagne	23	D3

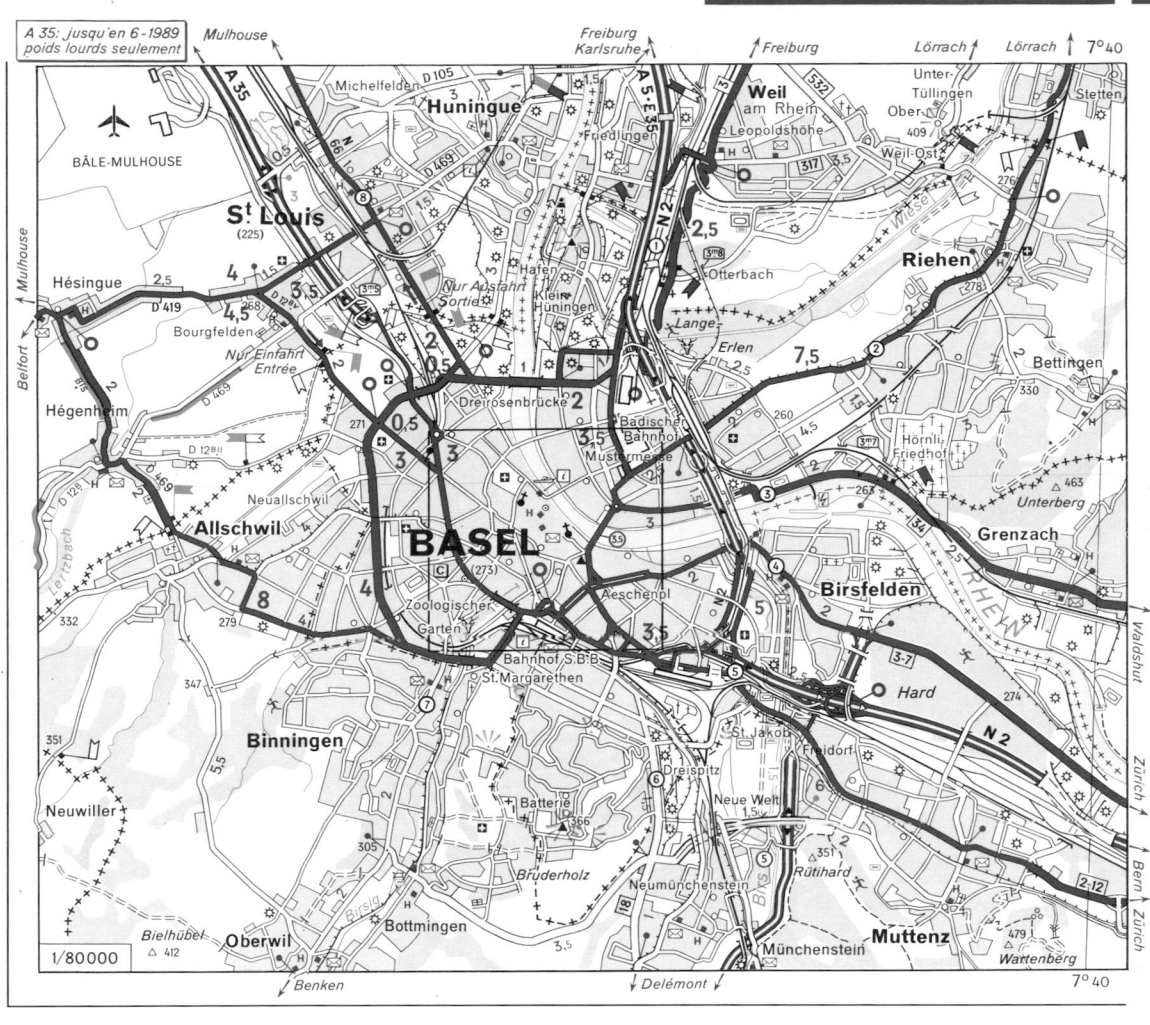

Bains-les-Bains 27 D1
Baio 34 A1
Baiono 34 A3
Bais 23 E3
Baîse 28 C3
Baîse-Darré 37 E1
Baja 114 B1
Baja Sardinia 66 B1
Bajgora 77 D1
Bajina Bašta 72 C4
Bajmok 72 B1
Bajram Curri 76 C2
Bajša 72 B1
Bajžë 76 B3
Bakar 70 B3
Bakarac 70 B3
Bakewell 6 C3
Bakio 36 B1
Bakkaflói 96 C1
Bakony 112 A4
Bakvattnet 101 E1
Bala 6 B3
Balaguer 37 F3
Balanegra 44 B4
Balaruc 30 A4
Balassagyarmat 112 B3
Balaton 112 A4
Balatonfüred 112 A4
Balatonkeresztúr 112 A4
Balazote 40 C4
Balbigny 26 B4
Balbriggan 13 E3
Balčik 115 E2
Balderschwang 55 E4
Baldock 9 F2
Baldo, Mte 58 C4
Bale 70 A4
Baleal 38 A3
Baleizão 42 B1
Balerma 44 B4
Balestrand 100 A3
Bali 91 D3
Balikesir 115 E4
Bålinge 106 B3
Balingen 55 D3
Balivanich 2 A1
Ballachulish 2 C4
Ballaghaderreen 12 C3
Ballangen 94 B3
Ballantrae 4 B3
Ballao 66 B3
Ballater 3 D4
Ballaugh 6 A1
Ballenstedt 52 C2
Balleroy 18 C3
Ballerup 108 C3
Ballina 12 B2
Ballinamore 12 C3
Ballinasloe 12 C3
Ballingarry 14 C3
Ballinrobe 12 B3
Ballintober 12 B3
Ballobar 37 E4
Ballon 23 F3
Ballon d'Alsace 27 E1
Ballstad 97 E1
Ballybay 13 D2
Ballybofey 12 C1
Ballybunnion 12 A4
Ballycastle 12 B2
Ballycastle 13 E1
Ballyclare 13 E2
Ballyconnell 12 C2
Ballycotton 14 C4
Ballycroy 12 B2
Ballyduff 14 B3
Ballyforan 12 C3
Ballygawley 13 D2
Ballyhaunis 12 B3
Ballyheige 14 A3
Ballyjamesduff 13 D3
Ballymahon 12 C3
Ballymena 13 E2
Ballymoe 12 C3
Ballymoney 13 E1
Ballymore 12 C3
Ballymote 12 C2
Ballynahinch 13 E2
Ballysadare 12 C2
Ballyshannon 12 C2
Ballyvaughan 12 B4
Balmaseda 36 A1
Balme 31 E1
Balmoral Castle 3 D4

Balneario de
  Panticosa 37 E2
Balsareny 32 A3
Balsfjorden 94 B2
Balsicas 45 D2
Balsorano 63 F2
Bålsta 106 B3
Balsthal 27 E2
Balta 113 E3
Baltanás 35 F4
Baltar 34 B3
Baltic Sea 110 B2
Baltijsk 110 B4
Baltinglass 13 D4
Baltrum 47 E3
Bambalió 82 C3
Bamberg 52 C4
Bambini 82 C3
Bamburgh 5 E1
Bampton 8 C3
Banagher 12 C4
Banat 114 C1
Banatska Palanka 73 D2
Banatska Topola 72 C1
Banatski
  Brestovac 73 D3
Banatski Dvor 72 C2
Danatski Karlovac 73 D2
Banatsko
  Aranđelovo 72 C1
  Karađorđevo 72 C2
Banatsko Novo
  Selo 73 D2
Banbridge 13 E2
Banbury 9 E1
Banchory 3 E4
Bande 34 B3
Bandak 104 B2
Bandirma 115 E3
Bandol 30 C4
Bandon 14 B4
Bandon R 14 B4
Bañeres 45 E1
Banff 3 E3
Bangor (IRL) 12 B2
Bangor (N Ire) 13 E2
Bangor (Wales) 6 A2
Bangsund 97 D4
Banie 49 E3
Banja (Srbija) 73 D3
Banja (Srbija) 76 B1
Banja Koviljača 72 B3
Banja Luka 71 E3
Banjani 72 C3
Banja Vručica 71 F3
Banjska 76 C1
Bankeryd 109 D1
Bann (N Ire) 13 D1
Bann (Wexford) 15 D3
Bannalec 22 B3
Banon 30 C3
Bañon 41 D2
Baños de Cerrato 35 F4
Baños de la Encina 44 A2
Baños de
  la Fuensanta 44 C2
Baños de Molgas 34 B3
Baños de
  Montemayor 39 E2
Baños de
  Fuensanta 35 E1
Banova Jaruga 71 D2
Banovići 71 F4
Banque de
  Fraiture 51 D4
Banque Michel 51 D4
Bansin 49 E2
Banská-Bystrica 112 B3
Banská-Štiavnica 112 B3
Bansko 77 F3
Bantry 14 B4
Bantry B 14 A4
Bañuela 43 F1
Banyalbufar 45 E2
Banyoles 32 B3
Banyuls 32 C3
Bao, Emb de 34 C3
Bapaume 19 F2
Bar (SU) 113 D3
Bar (YU) 76 B3
Baracaldo 36 B1
Barači 71 E4
Baradla 112 B3

Barahona 36 B4
Barajas 40 B2
Barajas de Melo 40 B3
Barajevo 73 D3
Baralla 34 C2
Barane 76 C2
Baranoviči 111 D4
Baraqueville 29 E3
Barasona, Emb de 37 E3
Barbadillo del
  Mercado 36 A3
Barban 70 A3
Barbarano
  Vicentino 61 D1
Barbarušince 77 E2
Barbastro 37 E3
Barbat 70 B4
Barbate de Franco 43 D4
Barbate, Emb de 43 D4
Barbazan 37 F2
Barberino
  di Mugello 60 C3
Barbezieux 28 B1
Barbizon 19 F4
Barbotan 28 B3
Barby 52 C1
Barca de Alva 39 D1
Barca, Emb de la 35 D1
Barcarrota 42 C1
Barcellona Pozzo di
  Gotto 69 D2
Barcelona 32 B4
Barcelonnette 31 D2
Barcelos 34 A4
Barcena, Emb de 34 C2
Barchfeld 52 B3
Barcis 59 E3
Barcones 36 B4
Barcs 114 A1
Bardal 101 D1
Bardejov 112 B3
Bardi 60 B2
Bardineto 31 F3
Bardolino 60 C1
Bardonecchia 31 D1
Bardu 94 B3
Bardufoss 94 B3

Bare 76 B1
Barèges 37 E2
Barentin 19 D3
Barenton 18 C4
Bares, Estaca de 34 B1
Barfleur 18 B2
Barfleur, Pte de 18 B2
Bargas 40 A3
Bargoed 9 D2
Bargteheide 48 B2
Bari 65 D3
Barić Draga 70 C4
Barisciano 63 F2
Barjac 30 B3
Barjols 31 D4
Barlby 7 D2
Bar, le 31 E3
Bar-le-Duc 20 C1
Barletta 65 D3
Barlinek 49 F3
Barlovento 42 A4
Barmouth 6 A3
Barmstedt 48 A2
Barna 12 B3
Barnard Castle 5 E4
Bärnau 53 D4
Barneveld 16 C3
Barneville 18 B3
Barnsley 7 D2
Barnstaple 8 C3
Barnstorf 17 F1
Barntrup 52 A1
Barovo 77 E3
Barqueiro 38 B2
Barr 21 E4
Barra 2 A4
Barracas 41 E4
Barrachina 41 D2
Barraco 39 F2
Barrafranca 68 C4
Barra Head 2 A4
Barrancos 42 C1
Barranco Velho 42 B2
Barranda 44 C2
Barra, Sd of 2 A4
Barrax 40 C4
Barrea 64 A2

Barre-des-
  Cévennes 29 F3
Barreiro 38 A4
Barrême 31 D3
Barrhead 4 C2
Barrhill 4 C3
Barri 9 D2
Barrow 13 D4
Barrow-
  in-Furness 6 B1
Barrow, R 15 D3
Barruecopardo 39 D1
Barruelo de
  Santullán 35 F2
Barry 9 D2
Barsinghausen 52 A1
Bar-sur-Aube 26 B1
Bar-sur-Seine 26 B1
Barth 49 D1
Barthe-de-Neste,
  la 37 E1
Barton-upon-
  Humber 7 D2
Barumini 66 B3
Baruth 53 E1
Barvas 2 B2
Barycz 112 A2
Barzio 58 B4
Bašaid 72 C1
Bàscara 32 B3
Baschi 63 E1
Basconcillos
  del Tozo 35 F2
Basel 27 E2
Baselga di Pinè 59 D3
Bas-en-Basset 30 B1
Basento 65 D4
Basildon 11 D2
Basilicata 65 D4
Basingstoke 9 E3
Baška 70 B3
Bæskades 95 D2
Baška Voda 75 E2
Baške Oštarije 70 C4
Baslow 6 C3
Basovizza 59 F4
Bas-Rhin 21 E4

Bassano del
  Grappa 59 D4
Bassée, la 19 F1
Bassella 37 F3
Bassens 28 B2
Bassum 17 F1
Båstad 108 C3
Bastasi 71 D4
Bastelica 33 F3
Bas'tevarri 95 D3
Bastia 33 F2
Bastide-de-
  Sérou, la 37 F2
Bastogne 20 C2
Bastunäsfjället 97 E4
Bastuträsk 98 B4
Bataille, Col de la 30 C2
Batajnica 72 C3
Batak 115 D3
Batalha 38 B3
Batea 41 F1
Bath 9 D2
Bathgate 5 D2
Bâtie-Neuve, la 31 D2
Batina 72 B1
Batlava 77 D1
Batočina 73 D3
Båtsfjord 95 F1
Batsí 88 B1
Battaglia Terme 61 D1
Battenberg 17 F4
Battice 51 D3
Battipaglia 64 B4
Battle 11 D3
Batz (Finistère) 22 B2
Batz (Loire-
  Atlantique) 24 A2
Baud 22 C3
Baugé 23 E4
Baugy 26 A2
Baule, la 24 A2
Baume, Cirque de 27 D3
Baume-les-
  Dames 27 D2
Baumholder 54 B1
Bauska 110 C3
Bautzen 53 F2

Baux, les 30 B3
Bavanište 73 D2
Bavay 20 B1
Bavella, Col de 33 F4
Båven 106 B4
Baveno 58 A4
Bawtry 7 D2
Bayard, Col 31 D2
Bayerisch
  Eisenstein 56 C1
Bayerischer Wald 56 B2
Bayern 55 F2
Bayeux 18 C3
Bayhirivagh 2 A4
Bayındır 115 F4
Bayon 21 D4
Bayonne 28 A4
Bayreuth 52 C4
Bayrischzell 56 B4
Baza 44 B3
Bazas 28 B3
Baza, Sa de 44 B3
Bazoches-sur-
  Hoëne 19 D4
Bazzano 60 C2
Beachy Head 10 C3
Beaconsfield 9 F2
Béal an Átha 12 B2
Béal Átha
  na Sluaighe 12 C3
Beaminster 9 D3
Beanntraí 14 B4
Beara 14 A4
Beariz 34 B2
Beas 42 C2
Beasain 36 C1
Beas de Segura 44 B2
Beattock 5 D3
Beaucaire 30 B3
Beaucaire 30 B3
Beaufort (Jura) 26 C3
Beaufort (Savoie) 27 E4
Beaufort-en-
  Vallée 23 E4
Beaugency 25 E2
Beaujeu 26 C4
Beaulieu (Alpes-
  Maritime) 31 E3

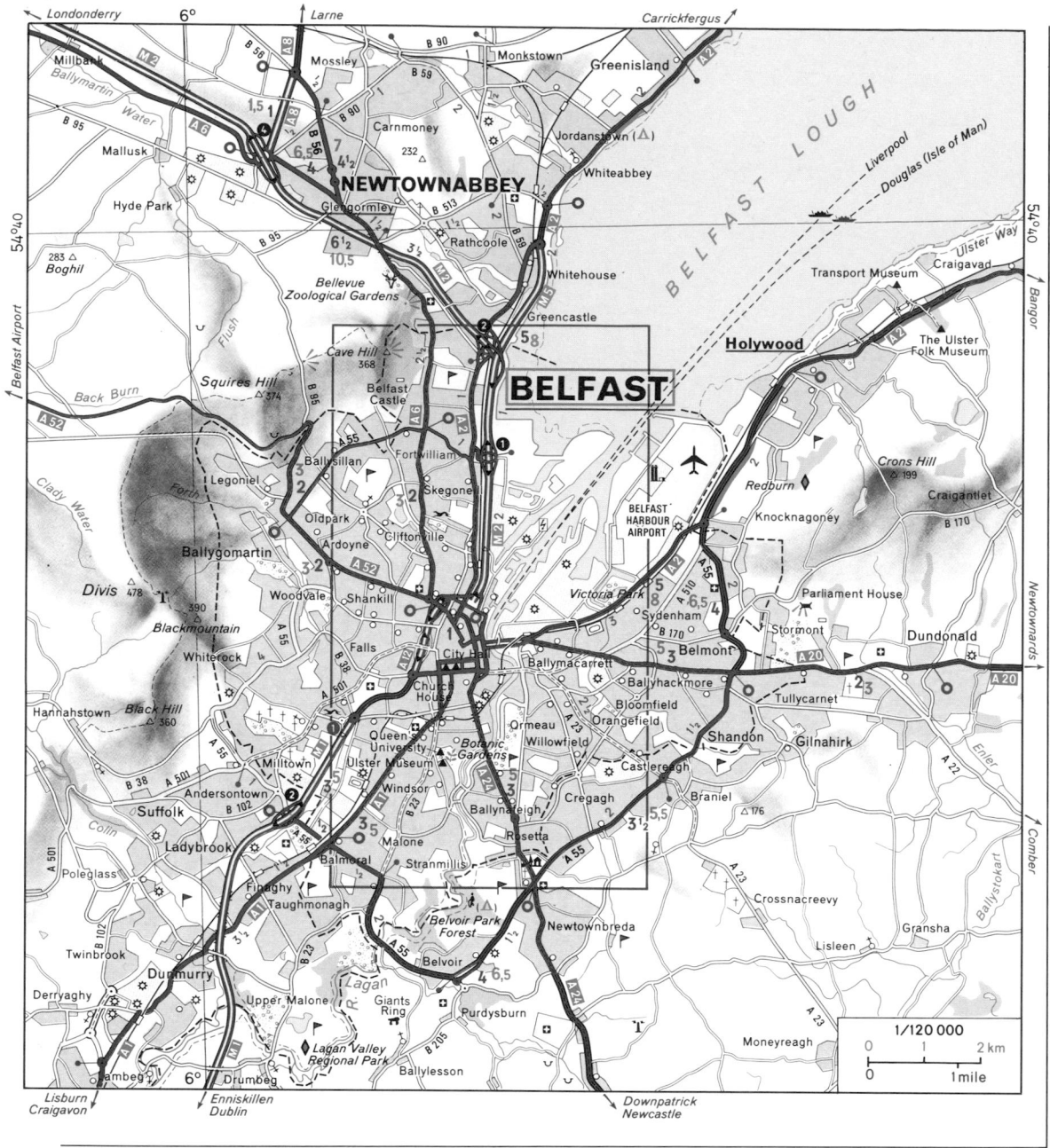

Map of Belfast area. Scale 1/120 000.

Bellême	23 F3		Benifaió	41 E4
Bellencombre	19 E2		Beninar, Emb de	44 B3
Bellerive	26 A4		Benissa	45 E1
Belleville	26 C4		Benítses	82 A1
Belley	27 D4		Ben Klibreck	2 C2
Bellinzona	58 A3		Benkovac	74 C1
Bell-lloc d'Urgell	37 F3		Ben Lawers	4 C1
Bello	41 D1		Ben Lomond	4 C1
Bellpuig	37 F4		Ben Macdui	3 D4
Belluno	59 E3		Ben More	
Bellver	45 E3		(Grampian)	4 C1
Bellver de			Ben More (Mull)	4 B1
Cerdanya	32 A3		Ben More Assynt	2 C2
Bélmez	43 E1		Benneckenstein	52 B2
Belmont (F)	26 B4		Ben Nevis	2 C4
Belmont (GB)	3 F1		Bénodet	22 B3
Belmonte			Benquerencia	
(Asturias)	35 D1		de la Serena	43 E1
Belmonte (Castilla-la-			Bensberg	17 E4
Mancha)	40 C3		Bensersiel	47 E3
Belmonte (P)	38 C2		Bensheim	54 C1
Belmont-sur-			Bentley	7 D2
Rance	32 B1		Ben Vorlich	4 C1
Belmullet	12 A2		Ben Wyvis	2 C3
Belo Brdo	76 C1		Bény-Bocage, le	18 C3
Belogradčik	114 C2		Beočin	72 C2
Belo jez	72 C2		Beograd	73 D3
Beloljin	77 D1		Bérarde, la	31 D2
Beloœil	50 B4		Berat	114 C3
Belo Polje	76 C2		Berbegal	37 E3
Belopolje	113 F1		Berberana	36 B1
Belorado	36 A2		Berbería, C de	45 D4
Belorussija	111 D4		Berceto	60 B3
Belpech	32 A2		Berching	55 F2
Belper	6 C3		Berchtesgaden	56 C4
Belsay	5 E3		Berck-Plage	19 E1
Belsh	76 C4		Berdičev	113 E2
Beltinci	70 C1		Beregovo	112 C3
Belturbet	13 D2		Bereguardo	60 A2
Belušić	73 E4		Bere I	14 A4
Belvedere			Berek	71 D2
Marittimo	67 E2		Bere Regis	9 D3
Belver	37 E3		Beret	37 F2
Belvès	28 C2		Berettyóújfalu	112 C4
Belvis de la Jara	39 F3		Berezina	111 D4
Belyj	111 E2		Berezino	111 D4
Belz	22 C4		Berg (A)	57 F2
Belzig	53 D1		Berg (Nordland)	97 D3
Bembézar,			Berg (S)	101 E2
Emb de	43 E2		Berg (Troms)	94 B2
Bembézar, R	43 E2		Berga (DDR)	52 C2
Bembibre	35 D2		Berga (E)	32 A3
Bemposta	38 B3		Bergama	115 E4
Bemposta,			Bergamo	60 B1
Bgem da	34 C4		Bergara	36 B1
Benabarre	37 E3		Bergby	106 B2
Benaguacil	41 E3		Bergedorf	48 B3
Benahadux	44 B3		Bergen (B)	50 B4
Ben Alder	2 C4		Bergen (DDR)	49 D1
Benalmádena	43 F4		Bergen (N)	104 A2
Benalúa			Bergen	
de las Villas	44 A3		(Niedersachsen)	48 A4
Benamargosa	43 F3		Bergen	
Benamaurel	44 B2		(Niedersachsen)	48 B3
Benamejí	43 F3		Bergen (NL)	16 C2
Benamocarra	43 F4		Bergen aan Zee	16 C2
Benaoján	43 E4		Bergen op Zoom	16 B4
Ben Armine	3 D2		Bergerac	28 C2
Benasal	41 E2		Berggießhübel	53 F2
Benasque	37 E2		Berghamn	
Benavente (E)	35 D3		fjärden	107 D3
Benavente (P)	38 A4		Bergheim	17 D4
Benavides	35 D3		Bergisch Gladbach	17 E4
Benbecula	2 A3		Bergnäset	98 C3
Ben Chonzie	4 C1		Bergneustadt	17 E4
Ben Cruachan	4 B1		Bergö	102 B2
Bendery	113 E4		Berg-	
Bendorf	51 E4		Rudolphstein	53 D3
Benediktbeuern	56 A4		Bergsjö	101 F3
Benešov			Bergsviken	98 B3
(Severočeský)	53 F3		Bergues	19 F1
Benešov			Bergum	47 D3
(Středočeský)	53 F4		Bergün	58 B3
Bénévent-			Beringel	42 B1
l'Abbaye	25 E4		Beringen	50 C3
Benevento	64 B3		Berja	44 B4
Benfeld	21 E4		Berka	52 B3
Benfleet	11 D2		Berkåk	100 C2
Bengtsfors	105 D4		Berkel	17 D2
Ben Hope	2 C2		Berkhamsted	9 F2
Beničanci	71 E2		Berkheim	55 E3
Benicarló	41 F2		Berkhof	48 A4
Benicasim	41 F3		Berkovica	114 C2
Benidorm	45 E1		Berkovići	75 F2

Beaulieu		Bebington	6 B2	Beerfelden	55 D1	Béjar, Pto de	39 E2	Belforte all'Isauro	61 E3
(Corrèze)	29 D2	Bebra	52 B3	Beeskow	49 E4	Békés	112 C4	Belgern	53 E2
Beaulieu (GB)	9 E3	Beccles	11 E1	Beetzendorf	48 B4	Békéscsaba	112 C4	België	16 B3
Beaumaris	6 A2	Beccedas	39 E2	Bégard	22 C2	Bel	41 F2	Belgique	50 B3
Beaumesnil	19 D3	Beceite	41 F2	Begejci	72 C2	Bělá	56 B1	Belgodère	33 F3
Beaumetz-lès-		Bečej	72 C2	Begejski kanal	72 C2	Bélâbre	25 E3	Belgorod-Dnes-	
Loges	19 F2	Becerreá	34 C2	Beg-Meil	22 B3	Bela Crkva (Srbija)	72 C3	trovskij	113 F4
Beaumont (B)	50 B4	Bec-Hellouin, le	19 D3	Begna	104 C2	Bela Crkva		Belice	68 B3
Beaumont		Bécherel	23 D3	Begov Han	71 F4	(Vojvodina)	73 D2	Belin-Béliet	28 B3
(Dordogne)	28 C2	Bechet	115 D2	Bégude-de-Mazenc,		Belaja Cerkov'	113 E2	Beli Drim	76 C2
Beaumont		Bechhofen	55 E2	la	30 C2	Belalcázar	43 E1	Beli Manastir	71 F2
(Manche)	18 B2	Bečići	76 B3	Begues	32 A4	Belanovce	77 E2	Belin-Béliet	28 B3
Beaumont		Becilla de		Begur	32 C3	Belanovica	73 D3	Beli Potok	73 F4
(Val d'Oise)	19 F3	Valderaduey	35 E3	Behalúa de Guadix	44 B3	Bela Palanka	77 E1	Belišće	71 F2
Beaumont-de-		Beckenried	58 A2	Behobia	28 A4	Belasica	77 F3	Beli Timok	73 F4
Lomagne	28 C3	Beckington	9 D3	Behringersmühle	52 C4	Belcaire	32 A2	Beljakovce	77 E2
Beaumont-le-		Beckum	17 F3	Beiarn	97 E2	Belchen	54 C4	Beljanica	73 E3
Roger	19 D3	Bečov	53 E4	Beilen	17 D1	Belchite	37 D4	Beljina	73 D3
Beaumont-sur-		Bedale	6 C1	Beilingries	55 F2	Belčište	77 D4	Bellac	25 D4
Sarthe	23 F3	Bédarieux	30 A4	Beinn a'Ghlò	3 D4	Belcoo	12 C2	Bellagio	58 B4
Beaune	26 C2	Beddgelert	6 A3	Beinn an Oir	4 B2	Bel'cy	113 E4	Bellano	58 B4
Beaune-la-		Bedekesa	47 F3	Beinn Bheigeir	4 B2	Belec	70 C2	Bellaria	61 E3
Rolande	25 F1	Bederkesa	47 F3	Beinn Dearg	2 C3	Belecke	17 F3	Bellcaire d'Urgell	37 F3
Beaupréau	24 C2	Bedford	9 F1	Beira Alta	38 B1	Belegiš	72 C2	Belledonne,	
Beauraing	50 C4	Bedfordshire	9 F1	Beira Baixa	38 C2	Belej	70 B4	Chaîne de	31 D1
Beaurepaire	30 C1	Bedlington	5 E3	Beira Litoral	38 B1	Beleña, Emb de	40 B1	Belleek	12 C2
Beaurepaire-en-		Bedmar	44 A2	Beira Litoral	38 B1	Belesar, Emb de	34 B2	Bellegarde (Ain)	27 D4
Bresse	26 C3	Bedrija	70 C1	Bcisfjord	94 B3	Belev	111 F3	Bellegarde (Gard)	30 B3
Beausset, le	31 D4	Bedonia	60 B3	Beith	4 C2	Bele Vode	76 C1	Bellegarde (Loiret)	25 F1
Beauvais	19 E3	Bedum	47 D3	Beitostølen	104 C1	Beli		Bellegarde-en-	
Beauvoir (Deux-		Bedwas	9 D2	Beitstadfjorden	101 D1	Belfast	13 E2	Marche	25 E4
Sèvres)	24 C4	Bedworth	9 E1	Beiuș	112 C4	Belfast L	13 E2	Belle-Ile	22 B4
Beauvoir (Vendée)	24 A3	Beeford	7 E2	Beja	42 B1	Belford	5 E3	Belle-Isle-en-Terre	22 B2
		Beelitz	49 D4	Béjar	39 E2	Belfort	27 E2		

Berlin

Berkshire 9 E2
Berlaimont 20 A2
Berlanga 43 D1
Berlanga de Duero 36 B4
Berlebeck 17 F3
Berlenga, I 38 A3
Berlevåg 95 F1
Berlin (Ost) 49 E4
Berlin (West) 49 D4
Bermejales, Emb 43 F3
Bermeja, Sa 43 E3
Bermeo 36 B1
Bermillo 35 D4
Bern 27 E2
Bernalda 65 D4
Bernardsthal 57 F1
Bernartice 57 D1
Bernau (Baden-Württemberg) 54 C4
Bernau (Bayern) 56 B3
Bernau (DDR) 49 E4
Bernaville 19 F2
Bernay 19 D3
Bernburg 52 C1
Berndorf 57 E3
Berne 47 F3
Bernesga, R 35 D2
Bernina, Piz 58 B3
Bernina, Pso del 58 B3
Bernkastel-Kues 54 B1
Bernsdorf 53 F2
Bernstein 57 F3
Beroun 53 F4
Berounka 53 F4
Berovo 77 F3
Der'oza 112 C1
Ber'ozovka 113 F3
Berra 61 D2
Berre 30 C4
Berre, Etang de 30 C4
Beršad' 113 E3
Bersenbrück 17 E2
Bertamirans 34 A2
Bertinoro 61 D3
Bertrix 20 C2
Berwang 58 C1
Berwick-upon-Tweed 5 E2
Berwyn 6 B3
Berzocana 39 E3
Berzosa 39 D1
Besalú 32 B3
Besançon 27 D2
Besande 35 E2
Besaya, R 35 F2
Besbre 26 B3
Besigheim 55 D2
Beška 72 C2
Besna Kobila 77 E2
Besse 29 E1
Bessèges 30 B3
Besse-sur-Issole 31 D4
Bessines 25 E4
Betancuria 42 C4
Betanzos 34 B1
Betelu 36 C1
Bétera 41 E3
Beteta 40 C2
Bétharram, Grottes de 37 E1
Bethesda 6 A2
Béthune 19 F1
Béthune R 19 E2
Bettna 106 A4
Bettola 60 B2
Bettolle 61 D4
Bettyhill 3 D2
Betws-y-Coed 6 A3
Betz 19 F3
Betzdorf 51 F3
Beuil 31 E3
Beura 58 A4
Beuron 55 D3
Beuvray, Mont 26 B3
Beuvron 25 E2
Beuzeville 19 D3
Bevagna 63 E1
Beveren-Waas 50 B3
Beverley 7 D2
Beverstedt 47 F3
Beverungen 52 A2
Beverwijk 16 C2
Bewdley 9 D1

Bex 27 E3
Bexhill 11 D3
Beynac 29 D2
Beynat 29 D2
Bežanija 72 C3
Bezau 58 A3
Bézards, les 26 A1
Bezas 41 D2
Bezdan 72 B1
Bezdrep 57 D1
Bežeck 111 F1
Béziers 30 A4
Bezmisht 77 D4
Béznar 44 A3
Biała Podlaska 112 C1
Białowieska 112 C1
Białystok 112 C1
Biancavilla 69 D3
Bianco 67 E4
Bianco, M 27 E4
Biandrate 31 F1
Biar 45 D1
Biarritz 28 A4
Biasca 58 A3
Bibbiena 61 D4
Biberach 54 C3
Biberach an der Riß 55 E3
Bibione 59 F4
Bibinje 74 C1
Bibury 9 E2

Bicaj 76 C3
Bicaz 113 D4
Bicester 9 E2
Bichl 56 A4
Bidache 28 A4
Bidart 28 A4
Bidasoa, R 36 C1
Biddendon 11 D3
Bidean nam Bian 4 C1
Bideford 8 C3
Biedenkopf 17 F4
Biel 27 E2
Bielefeld 17 F2
Bielerhöhe 58 B2
Biella 31 F1
Bielsa 37 E2
Bielsa, Tunnel de 37 E2
Bielsko-Biała 112 B3
Bielsk Podlaski 112 C1
Bienne R 27 D3
Bienne 27 E2
Bientina 60 C4
Bienvenida 43 D1
Bierné 23 E4
Bierre 26 B2
Biesbosch 16 C3
Biescas 37 D2
Biese 48 C4

Biesenthal 49 E3
Bietigheim-Bissingen 55 D2
Biferno 64 B2
Biga 115 E3
Biggar 5 D2
Biggleswade 9 F1
Bignasco 58 A3
Bihać 70 C3
Bihorului, M 112 C4
Bijele Poljane 76 B2
Bijeljani 75 F2
Bijeljina 72 B3
Bijelo Brdo 71 F2
Bijelolasica 70 B3
Bijelo Polje 76 B2
Bilbao 36 B1
Bileća 76 A2
Bilecik 115 F3
Bilećko jez 76 A2
Biłgoraj 112 C2
Bilina 53 E3
Biljača 77 E2
Biljanovac 76 C1
Bilje 71 F2
Billerbeck 17 E3
Billericay 11 D2
Billingham 5 E4
Billingshurst 10 C3
Billom 29 F1

Billund 108 A3
Bilo 77 E1
Bilogora 71 D2
Bilto 94 C2
Bilzen 50 C3
Binaced 37 E3
Binača Morava 77 D2
Binasco 60 A1
Binche 50 B4
Binéfar 37 E3
Bingen 51 F4
Bingham 7 D3
Bingley 6 C2
Bingsjö 101 E4
Binic 22 C2
Binz 49 D1
Bioča 76 C2
Bioče 76 B2
Biograd 74 C1
Biogradsko, nac park 76 B2
Biokovo 75 E2
Bionaz 27 E4
Biot, le 27 E3
Birchington 11 D2
Birgi 68 A3
Biri 105 D2
Birkebeiner veien 104 C1
Birkeland 104 B4

Birkenfeld 54 B1
Birkenhead 6 B2
Birkenwerder 49 D4
Birkerød 108 C3
Birkfeld 57 E4
Birmingham 9 E1
Bîrlad 113 E4
Birnau 55 D4
Birr 12 C4
Biržai 110 C3
Birzebbuga 68 B4
Bisaccia 64 C3
Biscarrosse 28 A3
Biscarrosse-Plage 28 A3
Bischofsgrün 53 D4
Bischofsheim 52 B4
Bischofshofen 59 E1
Bischofswerda 53 F2
Bischofswiesen 56 C4
Bischofszell 58 A1
Bischwiller 21 F4
Bisenti 63 F1
Biševo 75 D2
Bishop Auckland 5 E4
Bishop's Castle 9 D1
Bishop's Stortford 10 C2
Bisignano 67 E2
Bisko 75 D1
Biskupfell 96 C2

Bismark 48 C4
Bismo 100 B3
Bispgården 101 F2
Bispingen 48 A3
Bistar 77 E2
Bistra pl 77 D3
Bistrica (Crna Gora) 76 B2
Bistrica (Srbija) 76 B1
Bistrica ob S. 70 C2
Bistričak 71 E4
Bistrița 113 D4
Bistrița R 113 D4
Bitburg 54 A1
Bitche 21 E3
Bitetto 65 D3
Bitola 77 E4
Bitonto 65 D3
Bitovnja 75 E2
Bitterfeld 53 D2
Bitti 66 B2
Bizákos 82 C3
Bizau 58 B2
Bizovac 71 F2
Bjala 115 D2
Bjarkøy 94 B3
Bjästa 102 A2
Bjelašnica 75 F1
Bjelašnica 76 A2
Bjelovar 71 D2

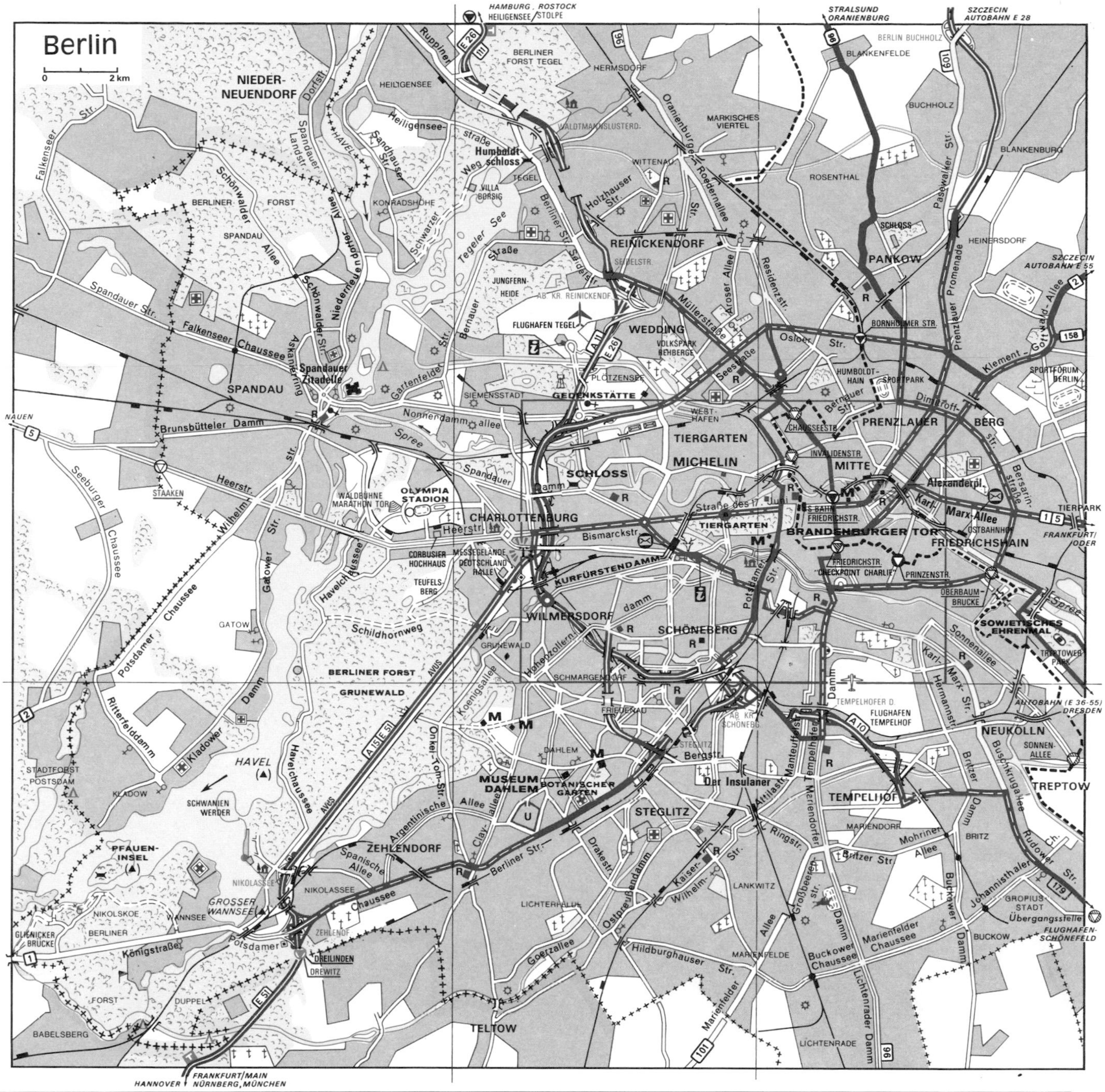

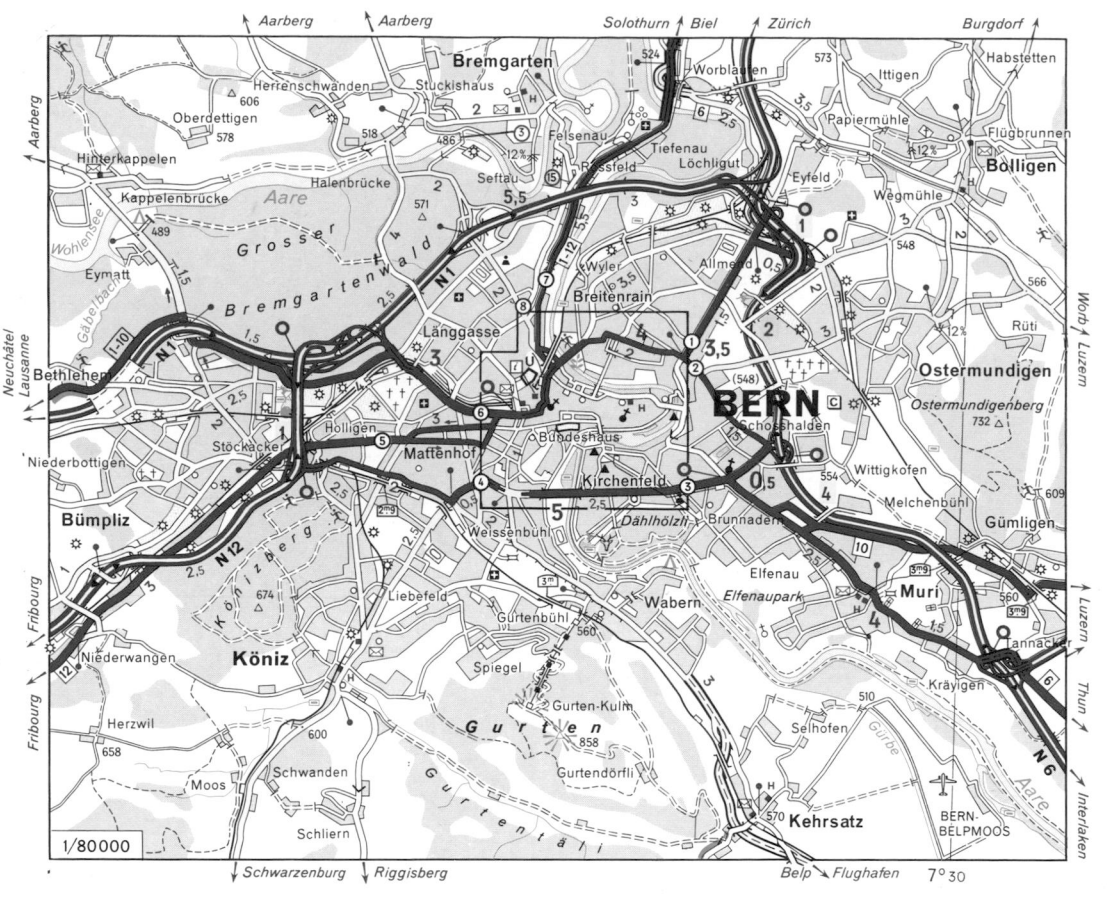

Aarberg Aarberg Solothurn Biel Zürich Burgdorf

1/80000

Schwarzenburg Riggisberg Belp Flughafen 7°30

Bolsena	63 D1	Borgo San	
Bolsena, L di	63 D2	Dalmazzo	31 E2
Bolsward	16 C1	Borgo	
Boltaña	37 E2	San Lorenzo	61 D3
Boltenhagen	48 B2	Borgosesia	58 A4
Bolton	6 C2	Borgo Tufico	61 E4
Bolungarvík	96 A1	Borgo Val di Taro	60 B3
Bolus Head	14 A4	Borgo Valsugana	59 D3
Bolzano	59 D3	Borgsjö	101 F3
Bombarral	38 A3	Borgund	104 B1
Bomenzien	48 C3	Borgvattnet	101 F2
Bom Jesus	34 A4	Boričje	76 B2
Bømlo	104 A3	Borisov	111 D4
Bonaigua,		Borispol'	113 E2
Pto de la	37 F2	Borja (E)	36 C3
Boñar	35 E2	Borja (YU)	71 E4
Bonar Bridge	2 C3	Borken	17 E3
Bonares	42 C2	Borkenes	94 A3
Bonassola	60 B3	Børkop	108 B3
Bondeno	60 C2	Borkum	47 D3
Bondone, Mte	58 C3	Borlänge	105 F2
Bonefro	64 B2	Bormes-les-	
Bo'-Ness	5 D2	Mimosas	31 D4
Bonete	45 D1	Bormida	60 A2
Bonette,		Bormio	58 C3
Col de la	31 D3	Born	48 C1
Bonhomme,		Borna	53 D2
Col du	27 E1	Bornes	34 C4
Bonifacio	33 F4	Bornes, Sa de	34 C4
Bonn	51 E3	Bornholm	109 D4
Bonnåsjøen	97 F1	Bornhöved	48 B2
Bonnat	25 E4	Börnicke	49 D4
Bonndorf	54 C4	Bornos	43 D3
Bonnétable	23 F3	Bornos, Emb de	43 D3
Bonneuil-		Boroughbridge	7 D1
Matours	25 D3	Borovec	115 D3
Bonneval		Boroviči	111 E1
(Eure-et-Loir)	25 E1	Borovnica	70 B2
Bonneval (Savoie)	31 E1	Borovo	72 B2
Bonneville	27 D4	Borovsk	111 F2
Bonneville, la	19 E4	Borre	104 C3
Bonnières	19 E3	Borriol	41 E3
Bonnieux	30 C3	Borris	15 D3
Bono	66 B2	Borrisokane	12 C4
Bonorva	66 B2	Borşa	113 D3
Bønsnes	104 C3	Børselv	95 E1
Boo	106 B4	Børselva	95 E2
Boom	50 B3	Børselvfjellet	95 E2
Boos	19 E3	Bórsio	86 B1
Bootle	6 B2	Bort-les-Orgues	29 E1
Bopfingen	55 E2	Börtnan	101 E2
Boppard	51 E4	Borzna	113 F1
Bor (CS)	53 E4	Borzonasca	60 A3
Bor (YU)	73 E3	Bosa	66 A2
Boračko jez	75 F1	Bosanci	70 C3
Borås	108 C1	Bosanska Dubica	71 D3
Borba	38 C4	Bosanska Gradiška	71 E3
Borbollón,		Bosanska	
Emb de	39 D2	Kostajnica	71 D3
Borbona	63 F1	Bosanska Krupa	71 D3
Borča	72 C3	Bosanska Rača	72 B3
Borci	75 F1	Bosanski Brod	71 E3
Bordeaux	28 B2	Bosanski Kobaš	71 E3
Bordeira	42 A2	Bosanski Novi	71 D3
Bordères-Louron	37 E2	Bosanski	
Border Forest Park,		Petrovac	71 D4
The	5 D3	Bosanski Šamac	71 F3
Borders Region	5 D3	Bosansko	
Bordesholm	48 A2	Grahovo	71 D4
Bordighera	31 E3	Bosansko Petrovo	
Borðoy	96 A3	Selo	71 F3
Bore	60 B2	Bosco	61 E4
Borello	61 D3	Bosco	
Borensberg	105 F4	Chiesanuova	59 D4
Boréon, le	31 E3	Bosilegrad	77 E2
Borga	107 F2	Bosiljevo	70 C3
Borgafjäll	97 E4	Bosjökloster	109 D3
Borga-fjällen	97 E4	Boskoop	16 C3
Borgarnes	96 A2	Bosna	71 F4
Børgefjell	97 E3	Bosna	
Børgefjellet	97 E3	i Hercegovina	71 E4
Borger	17 D1	Bošnjace	77 E1
Börger	17 E1	Bošnjaci	72 B3
Borghetto	63 E2	Bossòst	37 F2
Borghetto S.S.	31 F3	Bostan	75 E2
Borgholm	109 E2	Boštanj	70 B2
Borgholzhausen	17 F2	Boston	7 E3
Borghorst	17 F2	Bosut	72 B2
Borgia	67 F3	Botev	115 D2
Borgomanero	58 A4	Botevgrad	115 D2
Borgone	31 E1	Bothel	5 D4
Borgonovo Val		Boticas	34 B4
Tidone	60 B2	Botley	9 E3
Borgorose	63 F2	Botngård	100 C

Bjerkreim	104 A4	Blanca	45 D2	Bleymard, le	29 F3	Böckstein	59 E2	Böhlen	53 D2
Bjerkvik	94 B3	Blanc, C	45 E3	Blidinje jez	75 E1	Bockum-Hövel	17 E3	Böhme	48 A4
Bjerringbro	108 B2	Blanc, le	25 D3	Blieskastel	54 B2	Bocognano	33 F3	Böhmenkirch	55 E2
Bjørkelangen	105 D3	Blanc, Mont	27 E4	Bligny	26 C2	Boda	101 E4	Böhmer Wald	56 B1
Bjørketorp	109 E3	Blanco, R	43 E3	Blinisht	76 C3	Böda	109 F2	Bohmte	17 F2
Bjørkfjället	97 F3	Blandford Forum	9 D3	Blinja	71 D3	Bodafors	109 D2	Böhönye	114 A1
Björkliden	94 B3	Blanes	32 B4	Bloemendaal	16 B2	Bodđani	72 B2	Boiano	64 B3
Björklinge	106 B3	Blangy	19 E2	Blois	25 E2	Bode	52 C1	Boiro	34 A2
Björköby	102 B2	Blangy-le-		Blokhus	108 B2	Bodegraven	16 C3	Bois-d'Amont	27 D3
Bjorli	100 B3	Château	19 D3	Blomberg	52 A1	Boden	98 B3	Boitzenburg	49 E3
Björna	102 A2	Blankenberge	50 A3	Blönduós	96 B1	Bodenmais	56 B1	Bóixols	37 F3
Bjørnafjorden	104 A2	Blankenburg	52 C2	Blonville	19 D3	Bodensee	58 B1	Boizenburg	48 B3
Björneborg	107 D1	Blankenheim	51 D4	Bloody Foreland		Bodenteich	48 B4	Bojana	76 B3
Bjørnevatn	95 F2	Blankernhain	52 C3	Head	12 C1	Bodenwerder	52 A1	Bøjden	108 B4
Bjørntoppen	97 F1	Blanquefort	28 B2	Blosenberg	53 D3	Bodenwöhr	56 B1	Bojnik	77 D1
Björsäter	109 E1	Blanquilla	44 B2	Bloška Polica	70 B2	Bodman-		Boka Kotorska	76 A3
Bjurholm	102 A1	Blansko	57 F1	Blovice	56 C1	Radolfzell	55 D4	Bøkfjorden	95 F2
Bjursås	101 E4	Blanzac	28 C1	Bludenz	58 B2	Bodmin	8 B4	Bokn	104 A3
Bjuv	108 C3	Blanzy	26 B3	Blue Stack Mts	12 C2	Bodø	97 E1	Boknafjorden	104 A3
Blace	77 D1	Blåøret	100 C3	Blumberg (D)	54 C4	Boecillo	35 E4	Bol	75 E2
Blackburn	6 C2	Blarney	14 B4	Blumberg (DDR)	49 E4	Boëge	27 D4	Bøla	101 D1
Black Head	12 B4	Blatná	56 C1	Blyth	5 E3	Boën	26 B4	Bølbec	19 D3
Black Isle	2 C3	Blatnica	71 E4	Bø (Telemark)	104 C3	Boeza	35 D2	Bolchov	111 F3
Black Mt	8 C2	Blato	75 E1	Bø (Vesterålen)	94 A3	Boffalora	60 A1	Bolera, Emb de la	44 B2
Black Mts	9 D2	Blattniksele	98 A3	Boadella, Emb de	32 B3	Bogarra	44 C1	Bolesławiec	112 A2
Blackpool	6 B2	Blaubeuren	55 D3	Boal	34 C1	Bogatić	72 C3	Boleszkowice	49 E3
Black Sea	115 F2	Blaufelden	55 E2	Boan	76 B2	Bogdanci	77 F3	Bolgrad	113 E4
Blacksod B	12 A2	Blaustein	55 E3	Boara Pisani	61 D1	Bogdaniec	49 F3	Boliden	98 B4
Blackstairs Mts	15 D3	Blavet	22 C3	Bobbio	60 A2	Bogë	76 C2	Boliqueime	42 B2
Blackwater	15 D3	Blaye	28 B2	Bobigny	19 F4	Bogen (D)	56 B2	Boljanići	76 B1
Blackwaterfoot	4 B2	Blaževo	77 D1	Bobingen	55 F3	Bogen (N)	94 B3	Boljevac	73 E4
Blackwater, R	14 C4	Bleckede	48 B3	Böblingen	55 D2	Bogense	108 B3	Boljevci	72 C3
Blackwater Res	2 C4	Bled	70 A2	Boblitz	53 E1	Bogetići	76 B2	Boljkovci	73 D4
Blaenau Ffestiniog	6 A3	Blefjell	104 C3	Boborás	34 B2	Bognanco	27 F4	Boljuni	75 F2
Blaenavon	9 D2	Bleiburg	70 B1	Bobova	72 C4	Bognes	94 A4	Bolkesjø	104 C3
Blåfjellhatten	101 E1	Bleicherode	52 B2	Bobrinec	113 F3	Bognor Regis	9 F3	Bollebygd	108 C1
Blagaj	75 F2	Bleik	94 A3	Bobrovica	113 E2	Bogodol	75 F1	Bollène	30 B3
Blagnac	29 D4	Bleiloch-Talsperre	53 D3	Bobrujsk	111 E2	Bogojevo	72 B2	Bollstabruk	101 F4
Blagoevgrad	115 D3	Blekinge Län	109 D3	Bočac	71 E4	Bogomila	77 E3	Bollullos de	
Blåhammaren	101 D2	Blendija	73 E4	Bocairent	45 E1	Bogomolje	75 E2	la Mitación	43 D2
Blåhø	100 C2	Bléneau	26 A2	Bocca Trabaria	61 E4	Bogorodika	77 F4	Bollullos par	
Blain	23 D4	Blenheim Palace	9 E2	Bocche di		Bogovina	73 E4	del Condado	42 C2
Blainville	21 D4	Blénod	21 D3	Bonifacio	33 F4	Bogøy	97 E1	Bolmen	109 D2
Blair Atholl	3 D4	Bléone	31 D3	Bocco, Pso del	60 B3	Boguslav	113 E2	Bolnäos	
Blairgowrie	5 D1	Blérancourt	19 F3	Boceguillas	36 A4	Bogutovac	73 D4	de Calatrava	40 A4
Blå Jungfrun	109 E2	Bléré	25 D2	Bocholt	17 D3	Bohain-en-Verman-		Bologna	60 C2
Blakeney	7 F3	Blesle	29 F1	Bochov	53 E4	dois	20 A2	Bologne	26 C1
Blakstad	104 B4	Bletchley	9 F2	Bochum	17 E3	Boherboy	14 B3	Bologoje	111 E1
Blåmannsisen	97 E2	Bletterans	26 C3	Bockel	48 A3	Bohinjska Bistrica	70 A2	Bolos	40 B2
Blåmont	21 E4	Blexen	47 F3	Bockenem	52 B1	Bohinjsko jez	70 A2	Bolotana	66 B2

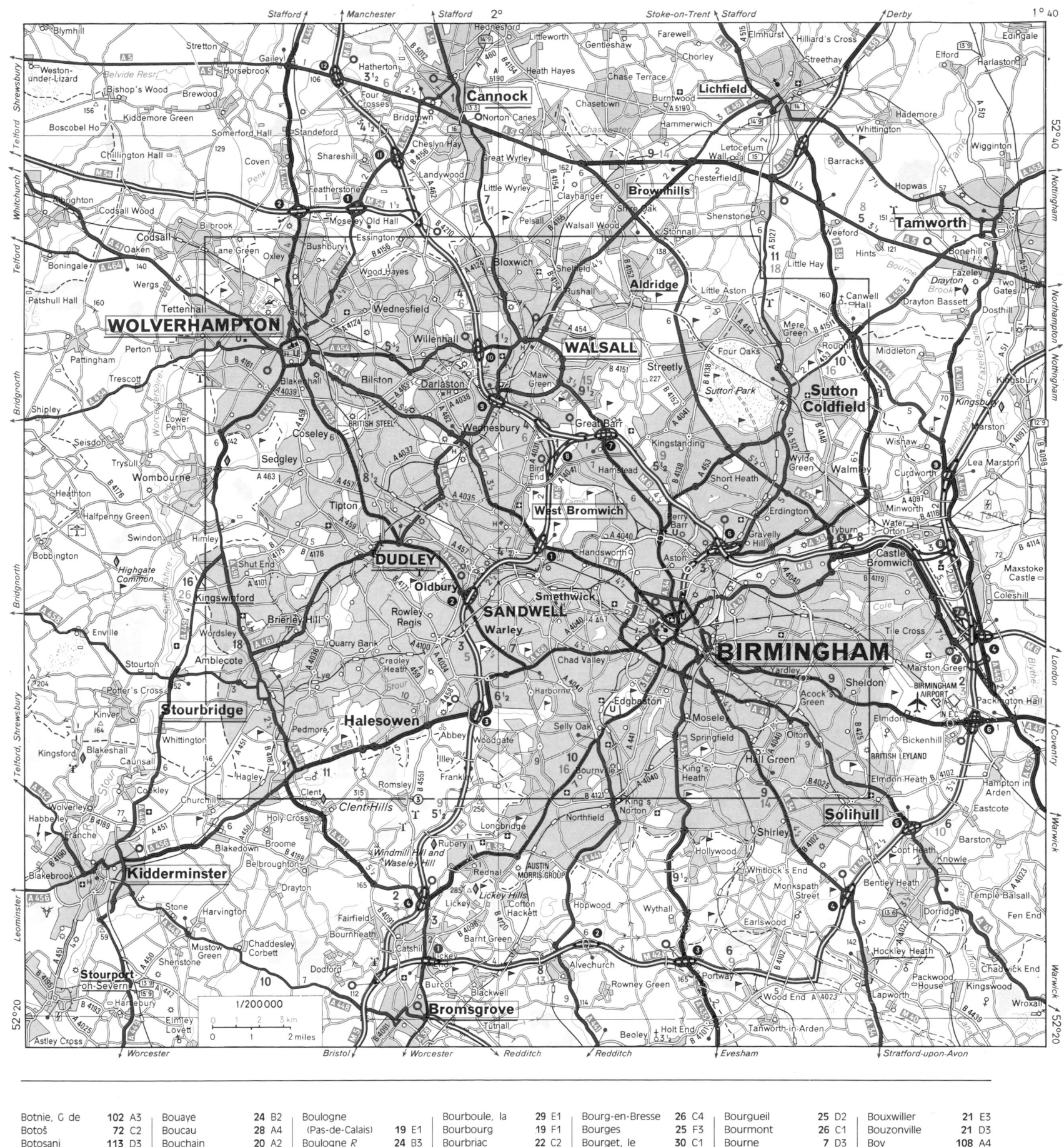

Botnie, G de	102 A3	Bouaye	24 B2	Boulogne		Bourboule, la	29 E1	Bourg-en-Bresse	26 C4	Bourgueil	25 D2	Bouxwiller	21 E3
Botoš	72 C2	Boucau	28 A4	(Pas-de-Calais)	19 E1	Bourbourg	19 F1	Bourges	25 F3	Bourmont	26 C1	Bouzonville	21 D3
Botoşani	113 D3	Bouchain	20 A2	Boulogne R	24 B3	Bourbriac	22 C2	Bourget, le	30 C1	Bourne	7 D3	Bov	108 A4
Botrange	51 D4	Bouches-		Bouloire	23 F3	Bourdeaux	30 C2	Bourg-Lastic	29 E1	Bourne,		Bovalino Marina	67 F4
Botsmark	102 A1	du-Rhône	30 B4	Boulou, le	32 B2	Bourdeilles	28 C1	Bourg-Madame	32 A3	Gges de la	30 C2	Bova Marina	67 E4
Botte Donato,		Boudry	27 E2	Boumort	37 F3	Bourg	28 B2	Bourgneuf		Bournemouth	9 E3	Bovan	73 E4
Mte	67 F2	Bouillon	20 C2	Bourbon-		Bourg-Achard	19 D3	-en-Retz	24 B3	Bourniá, Akr	87 E3	Bóveda	34 B2
Bottenhavet	102 A3	Bouilly	26 B1	Lancy	26 B3	Bourganeuf	25 E4	Bourgogne	26 C2	Bousquet-d'Orb,		Bovec	70 A2
Bottniska Viken		Boúka	86 C3	Bourbon-		Bourg-Argental	30 B1	Bourgoin-Jallieu	30 C1	le	30 A4	Bøverdal	100 B3
Pohjanlahti	102 A3	Boulay-Moselle	21 D3	l'Archambault	26 A3	Bourg-de-Péage	30 C2	Bourg-St-Andéol	30 B3	Boussac	25 F4	Boves	19 F2
Bottrop	17 E3	Boulogne		Bourbonne-		Bourg-de-Visa	28 C3	Bourg-St-Maurice	31 D1	Boussens	37 F1	Boves	31 E3
Botun	77 D4	(Haute-Garonne)	37 F1	les-Bains	27 D1	Bourg-d'Oisans, le	31 D2	Bourgtheroulde	19 D3	Boutonne	24 C4	Bovey Tracy	8 C3

Bologna

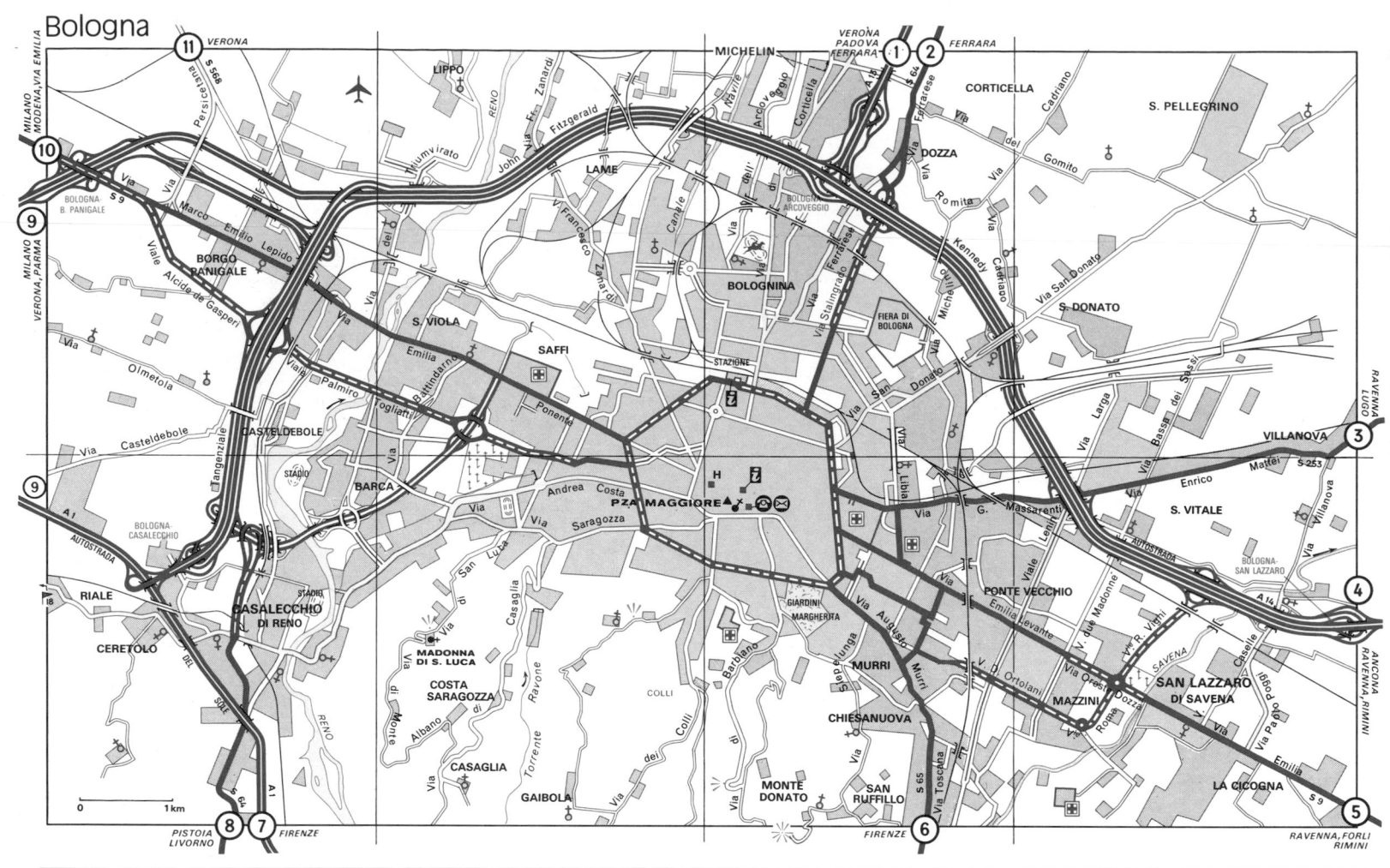

Place	Pg	Grid
Bovolone	60	C1
Bowes	5	E4
Bowness	6	B1
Bowness-on-Solway	5	D3
Boxholm	109	E1
Boxmeer	17	D3
Boxtel	16	C3
Boyle	12	C2
Boyne	13	D3
Božaj	76	B3
Božava	74	C1
Bozdoğan	115	F4
Bozel	31	D1
Bozen	59	D3
Božica	77	E2
Boži Dar	53	E3
Bozouls	29	E3
Bozüyük	115	F3
Bozzolo	60	C2
Bra	31	F2
Brabant	50	B3
Brač	75	E2
Bracadale	2	B3
Bracadale, L	2	B3
Bracciano	63	E2
Bracciano, L di	63	E2
Bračevci	71	F2
Bracieux	25	D2
Bräcke	101	E2
Brackenheim	55	D2
Brackley	9	E2
Brackwede	17	F3
Brad	112	C4
Bradano	65	D4
Bradashesh	76	C4
Bradford	6	C2
Bradford-on-Avon	9	D2
Bradina	75	F1
Brading	9	E3
Bradwell-on-Sea	11	D2
Braemar	3	D4
Braga	34	A4
Bragança	34	A3
Braguia, Pto de	35	F2
Braies, L di	59	D2
Brăila	113	E4
Braine	20	A3
Braine-le-Comte	50	B4
Braintree	11	D2
Brake	47	F3
Brakel	52	A2
Bräkne-Hoby	109	D3
Brallo di Pregola	60	A2
Brálos	83	E3
Bramming	108	A3
Brampton	5	D3
Bramsche	17	E2
Brancaleone	67	E4
Brancion	26	C4
Brand	58	B2
Brandbu	105	D2
Brande	108	A3
Brandenburg	49	D4
Brand-Erbisdorf	53	E3
Brander, Pass of	4	C1
Brandis	53	D2
Brändö	107	D2
Brandon	11	D1
Brandon Head	14	A3
Brandon Mt	14	A3
Brandýs Stará Boleslav	53	F3
Braničevo	73	E3
Braniewo	110	B4
Branne	28	B2
Braño Caballo	35	D2
Brañosera	35	F2
Br'ansk	111	E4
Brantôme	28	C1
Braskereidfoss	105	D2
Braslav	111	D3
Brașov	113	D4
Brasschaat	50	B3
Bratislava	112	A3
Brattvåg	100	A2
Bratunac	72	B4
Braubach	51	E4
Braunau	56	C3
Braunfels	51	F4
Braunlage	52	B2
Braunsbedra	53	D2
Braunschweig	52	B1
Braunton	8	C3
Braus, Col de	31	E3
Bravães	34	A3
Bravuogn	58	B3
Bray (IRL)	13	E4
Bray (Seine-et-Marne)	20	A4
Bray (Somme)	19	F2
Bray-Dunes	19	F1
Brazatortas	43	F1
Brbinj	74	C1
Brčko	72	B3
Brda	110	A4
Brdđani	73	D4
Brea	36	C4
Brécey	18	B4
Brechin	3	E4
Brecht	50	C3
Břeclav	57	F1
Brecon	8	C1
Brecon Beacons Nat Pk	8	C2
Breda (E)	32	B4
Breda (NL)	16	C3
Bredbyn	102	A2
Bredelar	17	F3
Bredstedt	47	F1
Bree	50	C3
Bregalnica	77	F3
Breganze	59	D4
Bregenz	58	B1
Bréhal	18	B4
Bréhat, I de	22	C2
Breidafjörður	96	A2
Breil-sur-Roya	31	E3
Breisach	54	B4
Breitengüßbach	52	C4
Breitungen	52	B3
Breivikbotn	95	D1
Breivikeidet	94	C2
Brekke	104	A1
Brekken	101	D2
Brekkvasselv	97	D4
Brekstad	100	C1
Bremanger Landet	100	A3
Bremen	47	F3
Bremerhaven	47	F3
Bremervörde	47	F3
Bremsnes	100	B2
Breña, Emb de la	43	E2
Brenes	43	D2
Brenna	53	D2
Brenner	59	D2
Brennilis	22	B3
Breno	58	C4
Brénod	26	C4
Brentwood	10	C2
Brescia	60	B1
Breskens	16	B4
Bresle	19	E2
Bresles	19	F3
Bressanone	59	D2
Bressuire	24	C3
Brest (F)	22	A2
Brest (SU)	112	C1
Brest R	23	D4
Brestanica	70	C2
Brestova	70	B3
Brestovac (Hrvatska)	71	E2
Brestovac (Srbija)	73	E3
Brestovac (Srbija)	77	D1
Brestovac (Srbija)	77	E1
Brestovačka Banja	73	E3
Bretenoux	29	D2
Breteuil (Eure)	19	D4
Breteuil (Oise)	19	F3
Bretten	54	C2
Breuil-Cervinia	27	F4
Brevik	104	C4
Breza	71	E4
Brežđe	72	C2
Brežice	70	C2
Breznica	70	C2
Breznica	26	A2
Brezno	112	B3
Brezolles	19	E4
Brezovica	77	D2
Brezovo Polje (Bosna i Hercegovina)	72	B3
Brezovo Polje (Hrvatska)	71	E2
Briançon	31	D2
Briare	26	A2
Bribirske Mostine	75	D1
Bricquebec	18	B3
Brides	31	D1
Bridgend (Scotland)	4	A2
Bridgend (Wales)	8	C2
Bridge of Allan	4	C1
Bridgnorth	9	D1
Bridgwater	9	D3
Bridlington	7	E1
Bridport	9	D3
Briec	22	B3
Brie-Comte-Robert	19	F4
Brielle	16	B3
Brienne-le-Château	20	B4
Brienon	26	A1
Brienz	27	F3
Brienza	64	C4
Briey	21	D3
Brig	27	F3
Brigg	7	D2
Brighouse	6	C2
Brightlingsea	11	D2
Brighton	10	C3
Brignogan	22	A2
Brignoles	31	D4
Brihuega	40	B2
Brijuni	70	A4
Briksdal	100	A3
Brilon	17	F3
Brimnes	104	B2
Brinches	42	B1
Brindisi	65	F3
Brinon	26	A2
Brionne	19	D3
Brioude	29	F1
Brioux	24	C4
Briouze	18	C4
Brisighella	61	D3
Brissac-Quincé	24	C2
Brissago	58	A3
Bristol	9	D2
Bristol Chan	8	C2
Brive-la-Gaillarde	29	D2
Briviesca	36	A2
Brixen	59	D2
Brixham	8	C4
Brixlegg	59	D1
Brka	72	B3
Brna	75	E2
Brnaze	75	D1
Brno	57	F1
Bro (Gotlands Län)	109	F4
Bro (Stockholms Län)	106	B3
Broad B	2	B2
Broadford (GB)	2	B3
Broadford (IRL)	12	B4
Broad Haven	12	B2
Broad Law	5	D3
Broadstairs	11	D3
Broadway	9	E1
Broager	108	A4
Broby	109	D3
Brocken	52	B2
Brod (Bosna i Hercegovina)	76	A1
Brod (Makedonija)	77	D3
Brodarevo	76	B1
Brodica	73	E3
Brodick	4	B2
Brod na Kupi	70	B3
Brodnica	112	B3
Brody (PL)	53	F1
Brody (SU)	113	D2
Broglie	19	D3
Brohl-Lützing	51	E4
Brolo	69	D2
Bromarv	107	D3
Brombachsee	55	E2
Brome	48	B4
Bromölla	109	D3
Bromsgrove	9	E1
Bromyard	9	D1
Bronchales	41	D2
Brønderslev	108	B2
Broni	60	A2
Brønnøysund	97	D3
Brøns	108	A3
Bronte	69	D3
Bronzani Majdan	71	E3
Broom, L	2	C2
Broons	22	C3
Brora	3	D3
Brösarp	109	D3
Brossac	28	B1
Brøstadbotn	94	B3
Brøttum	105	D2
Brotas	38	B4
Broto	37	E2
Brotton	5	F4
Brøttum	105	D2
Brou (Eure-et-Loir)	25	E3
Brouage	24	B4
Brough	5	E4
Brough Head	3	D1
Broughshane	13	E1
Broughton-in-Furness	6	B1
Brouis, Col de	31	E3
Brovst	108	B2
Brownhills	9	E1
Brozas	39	D3
Bruay-en-Artois	19	F1
Bruay-sur-l'Escaut	20	A1
Bruchsal	54	C2
Bruck (D)	56	B1
Bruck (Niederösterreich)	57	F2
Bruck (Salzburg)	59	E1
Bruck an der Mur	57	E2
Brückl	70	B1
Bruckmühl	56	B3
Bruel	48	C2
Brués	34	B2
Bruges	50	A3
Brugg	27	F2
Brügge	17	E4
Brugge	50	A3

Bonn

Brühl	17 E4	Bruton	9 D3	Bucine	61 D4	Budrio	61 D2	Bujaraloz	37 E4	Buñol	41 E4	Burgess Hill	10 C3
Brújula, Pto de la	36 A2	Bruvno	70 C4	Bučje	73 F4	Budva	76 B3	Buje	70 A3	Bunratty Castle	12 B4	Burggrub	52 C4
Bruksvallarna	101 D2	Bruxelles	50 B3	Bückeburg	52 A1	Budyně nad		Bujeo, Pto del	43 D4	Buntingford	9 F2	Burghasungen	52 A2
Brûlon	23 E3	Bruyères	27 D1	Buckfastleigh	8 C4	Ohře	53 F3	Bukinje	71 F3	Buñuel	36 C3	Burghausen	56 B3
Brumath	21 E4	Brvenik	76 C1	Buckhaven	5 D2	Buenache		Bukova Gora	75 E1	Buonabitacolo	67 D1	Burgjoß	52 B4
Brummen	17 D3	Bryne	104 A4	Buckie	3 D3	de Alarcón	40 C3	Bukovi	72 C4	Buonalbergo	64 B3	Burgkunstadt	52 C4
Brumunddal	105 D2	Brynmawr	9 D2	Buckingham	9 F2	Buen Amor	39 E1	Bukovo	77 D4	Buonconvento	61 D4	Burglengenfeld	55 F1
Bruneck	59 D2	Brzan	73 D3	Buckinghamshire	9 F2	Buenavista		Bülach	58 A1	Buonfornello	68 C3	Burgohondo	39 F2
Brunete	40 A2	Brza Palanka	73 F3	Buckovička		de Valdavia	35 E3	Buldan	115 F4	Burbach	51 F3	Burgos	35 F3
Brunflo	101 E2	Brzeće	77 D1	Banja	73 D3	Buendía	40 C2	Bulgnéville	27 D1	Burbáguena	41 D1	Burgsinn	52 B4
Brunico	59 D2	Brzeg	112 A2	Buckow	49 E4	Buendia, Emb de	40 C2	Bullas	44 C2	Búrdalo, R	39 E4	Burgstädt	53 E3
Brünigpass	27 F3	Buarcos	38 B2	Bückwitz	49 D3	Buet, Mt	27 E4	Bulle	27 E3	Bure	7 F3	Burg Stargard	49 D2
Bruniquel	29 D3	Buavåg	104 A3	Bučovice	57 F1	Bueu	34 A2	Büllingen	51 D4	Bureå	98 B4	Burgsvik	109 F4
Brunkeberg	104 B3	Bubry	22 C3	Bucovina	113 D3	Bugo	112 C1	Bully	19 F1	Burela	34 C1	Burgsviken	109 F4
Brunnen	58 A2	Bučač	113 D3	București	115 D1	Bugeat	29 D1	Bultei	66 B2	Burguete	36 C1	
Brunsbüttel	47 F2	Buçaco	38 B2	Bud	100 B2	Bugojno	71 E4	Buna	75 F2	Buren	47 D3	Burgui	37 D2
Brunssum	17 D4	Buccheri	69 D4	Budapest	112 B4	Bugøynes	95 F2	Bunclody	15 D3	Burfjord	95 D2	Burguillo,
Bruntál	112 A3	Bucchianico	64 A2	Buðardalur	96 A2	Bugue, le	28 C2	Buncrana	13 D1	Burford	9 E2	Emb de	39 F2
Bruravik	104 B2	Bucelas	38 A4	Buddon Ness	5 D1	Bühl	54 C3	Bünde	17 F2	Burg (D)	48 B1	Burguillos
Brus	77 D1	Buchan Ness	3 E3	Budduso	66 B2	Builth Wells	9 D1	Bunde	47 E3	Burg (DDR)	48 C4	del Cerro	43 D1
Brusand	104 A4	Büchen	48 B3	Bude	8 B3	Buin, Piz	58 B2	Bun Dobhráin	12 C2	Burgas	115 E2	Burhaniye	115 E4
Brušane	70 C4	Buchen	55 D1	Büdelsdorf	48 A2	Buis-les-		Bundoran	12 C2	Burgau	55 E3	Burhave	47 F3
Brusasco	31 F1	Buchenwald	52 C3	Büdingen	52 A4	Baronnies	30 C3	Bunë	76 B3	Burgbernheim	55 E1	Burie	28 B1
Brusnik	73 F3	Buchholz	48 A3	Budimlić Japra	71 D3	Buitrago		Bunessan	4 B1	Burgdorf (CH)	27 E2	Burjassot	41 E4
Brussel	50 B3	Buchloe	55 E3	Budinščina	70 C2	del Lozoya	40 B1	Bungay	11 D1	Burgdorf (D)	48 B4	Burk	53 F2
Brusson	27 F4	Buchs	58 B2	Budleigh		Bujalance	43 F2	Bunić	70 C4	Bürgel	52 C3	Burkau	53 F2
Brüssow	49 E2	Buchy	19 E3	Salterton	8 C4	Bujanovac	77 E2	Bunmahon	14 C4	Burgenland	57 F4	Burnham	9 D3

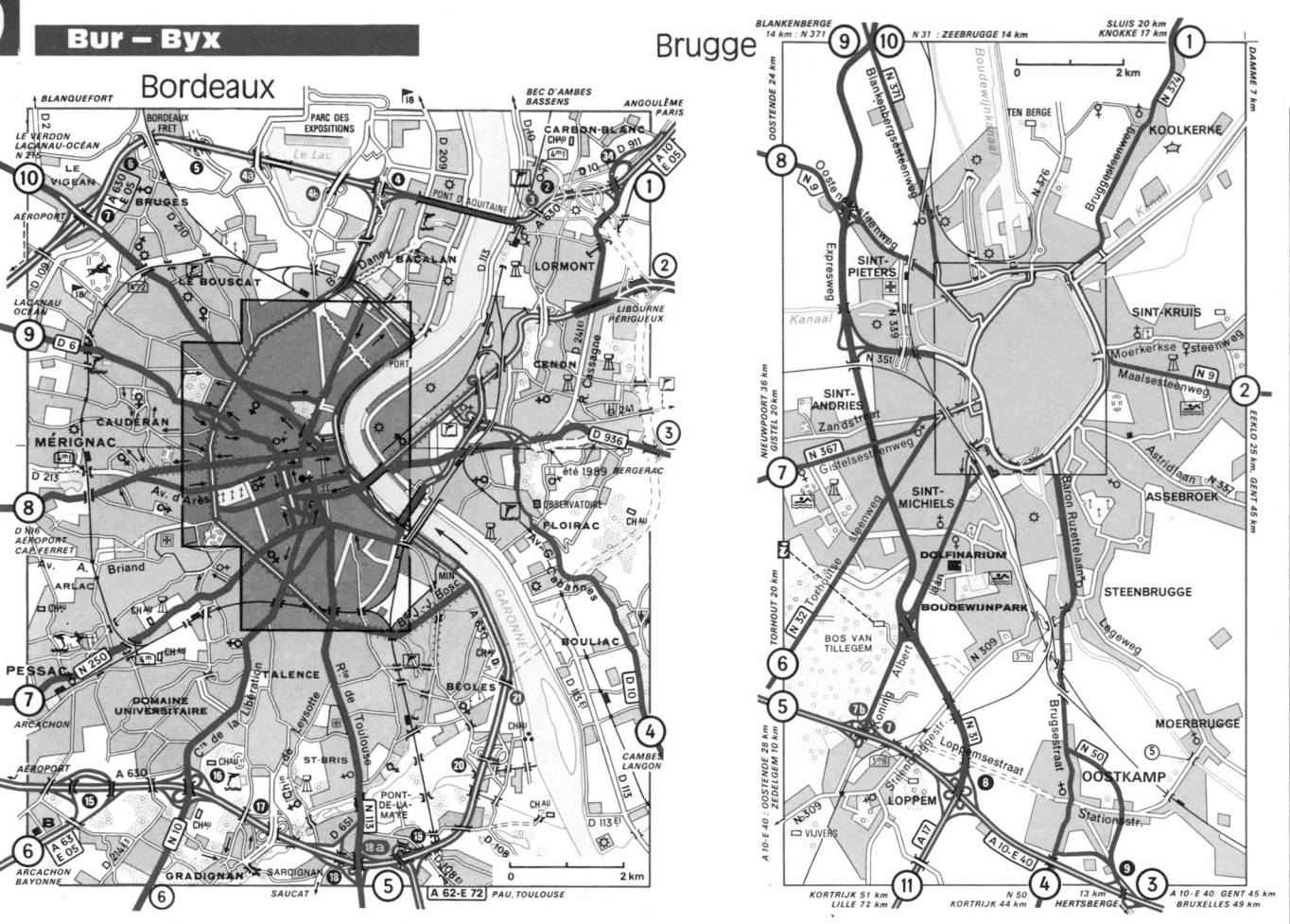

Bordeaux

Brugge

BUDAPEST

1 / 200 000

Burnham-		
on-Crouch	11	D2
Burnley	6	C2
Burntisland	5	D2
Buronzo	31	F1
Burrel	76	C3
Burriana	41	E3
Burrow Head	4	C4
Burry Port	8	C2
Bursa	115	F3
Burscheid	17	E4
Bürstadt	54	C1
Burton-upon-Trent	6	C3
Burträsk	98	B4
Burwick	3	E1
Bury	6	C2
Buryn'	113	F1
Bury St Edmunds	11	D1
Busalla	60	A3
Busambra, Rca	68	B3
Busca	31	E2
Buševa pl	77	D3
Buševec	70	C2
Bushat	76	C3
Bushmills	13	E1
Buskerud	104	C2
Buško Blato	75	D1
Busko-Zdrój	112	B2
Busovača	71	F4
Bussang	27	E1
Busseto	60	B2
Bussière-Badil	28	C1
Bussolengo	60	C1
Bussum	16	C2
Busto Arsizio	60	A1
Busto de Bureba	36	A2
Büsum	47	F2
Bute	4	B2
Butera	68	C2
Buthrotum	114	C4
Buttermere	5	D4
Buttevant	14	B3
Butt of Lewis	2	B2
Buttstädt	52	C2
Butzbach	51	F4
Bützow	48	C2
Buxtehude	48	A3
Buxton	6	C3
Buxy	26	C3
Buzançais	25	E3
Buzancy	20	C3
Buzău	113	E4
Buzău R	113	E4
Buzet	70	A3
Bužim	70	C3
Bychov	111	E4
Bydgoszcz	112	A1
Bygdeå	102	B1
Bygdin	100	B3
Bygdin L	100	B3
Bygdsiljum	102	B1
Bygland	104	B4
Byglandsfjord	104	B4
Byglandsfjord L	104	B4
Bykle	104	B3
Bykleheiene	104	B3
Byrkjelo	100	A3
Byske	98	B4
Byskeälven	98	B4
Bytom	112	B2
Bytów	110	A4
Byxelkrok	109	E2

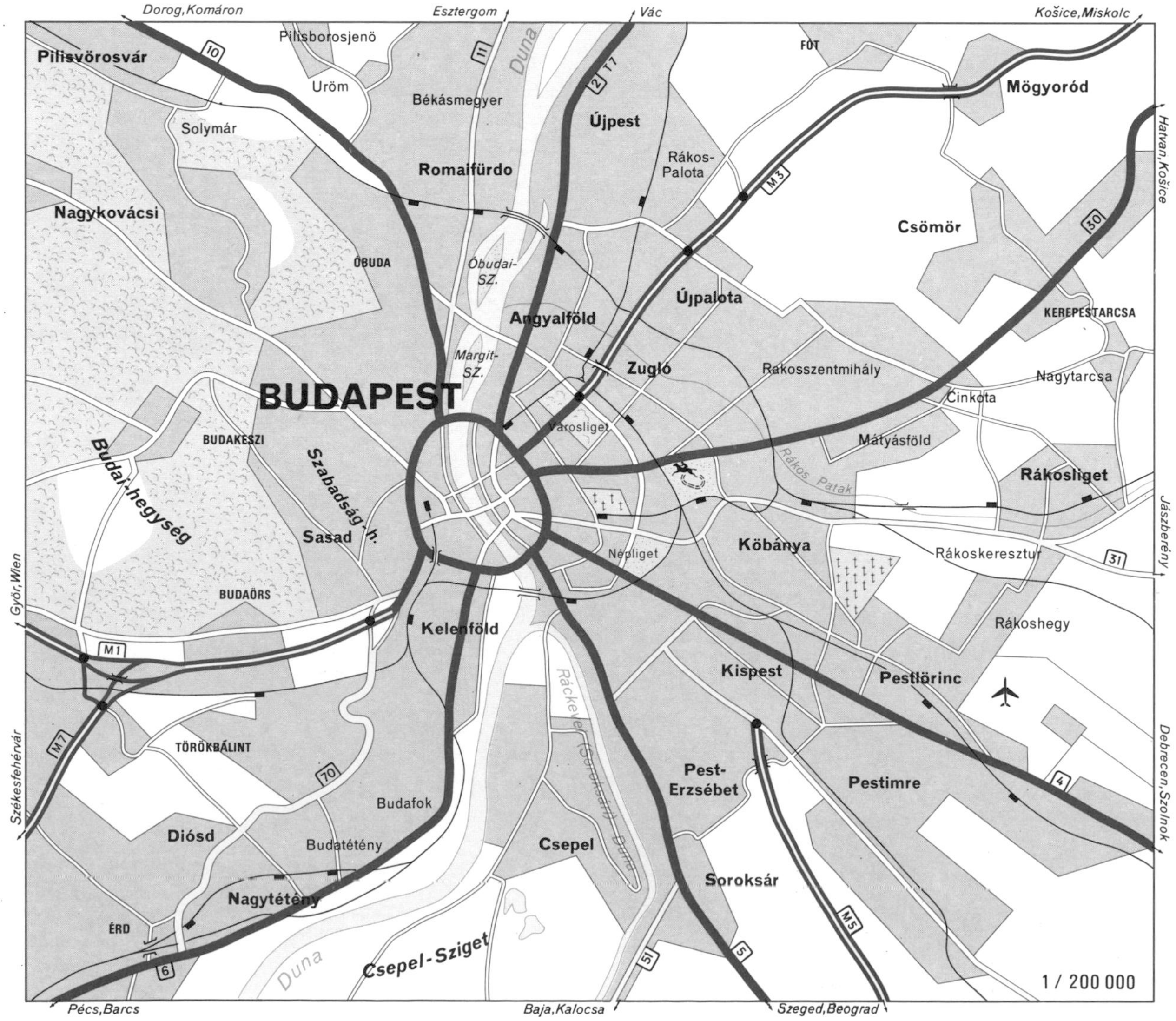

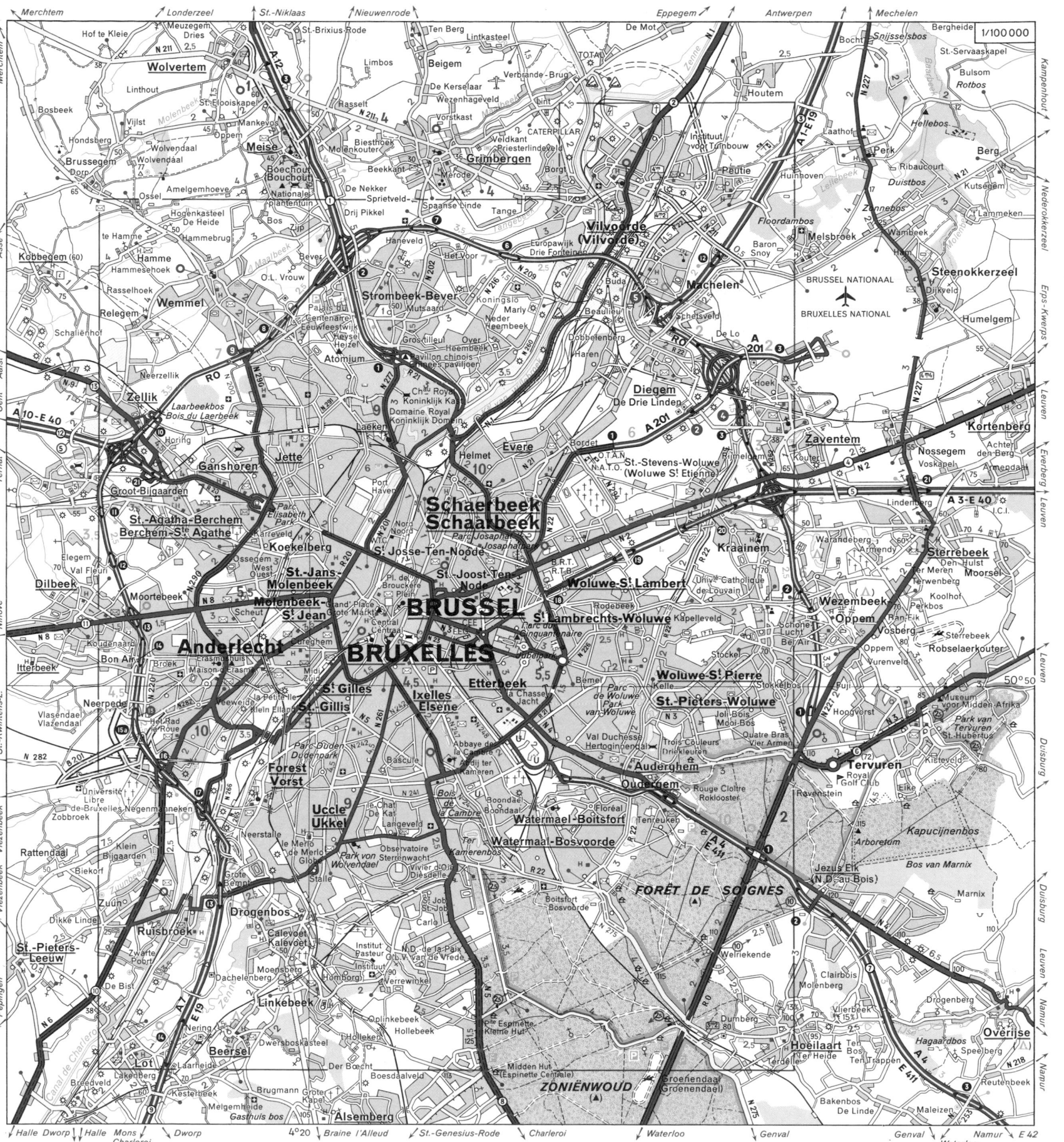

C

Cabañaquinta 35 D2
Cabañas 44 B2
Cabanes 41 F3
Cabannes, les 32 A2
Čabar 70 B3
Cabeceiras 34 B4
Cabeço de Vide 38 C3
Cabella Ligure 60 A2
Cabeza del Buey 39 E4
Cabezas Rubias 42 C2
Cabezo Gordo 42 C2
Cabezón 35 E4
Cabezón de la Sal 35 F2
Cabezuela del Valle 39 E2
Cabo de Gata 44 C4
Cabourg 18 C3
Cabra 43 F2
Cabra del Santo Cristo 44 A2
Cabras 66 A3
Cabre, Col de 30 C2
Cabreira, Sa da 34 B4
Cabreiros 34 B1
Cabrejas, Pto de 40 C3
Cabrejas, Sa de 36 A3
Cabréra 36 C4
Cabrera, I de 45 F3
Cabrera, Sa de la 34 C3
Cabrerets 29 D3
Cabriel, R 41 D3
Cabril, Bgem do 38 B2
Cabrillas 39 E1
Cabrito, Pto del 43 D4
Cabuérniga 35 F2
Čabulja 75 E1
Cacabelos 34 C2
Čačak 73 D4
Caccamo 68 B3
Cacela 42 B3
Cáceres 39 D3
Cachafeiro 34 A2
Cachopo 42 B2
Čačinci 71 E2
Cadabo 34 C2
Cadalso de los Vidrios 40 A2
Cadaqués 32 C3
Cadarache 30 C3
Cadaval 38 A3
Čadđavica 71 E4
Čadca 112 B3
Cadelbosco di Sopra 60 C2
Cadenabbia 58 B4
Cadena, Pto de la 45 D2
Cadenberge 47 F2
Cadenet 30 C3
Cader Idris 6 A3
Cádiar 44 A3
Cadillac 28 B2
Cadipietra 59 D2
Cadi, Serra del 32 A3
Cádiz 43 D4
Cádiz, B de 43 D4
Cádiz, G de 42 C3
Cadouin 28 C2
Čadyr-Lunga 113 E4
Caen 18 C3
Caerdydd 9 D2
Caerfyrddin 8 C2
Caergybi 6 A2
Caernarfon 6 A3
Caernarfon B 6 A3
Caerphilly 9 D2
Caersws 9 D1
Cafasan 77 D4
Cagli 61 E4
Cagliari 66 B4
Cagliari, G di 66 B4
Čaglin 71 E2
Cagnano Varano 64 C2
Cagnes 31 E3
Caha Mts 14 A4
Caher 14 C3
Cahersiveen 14 A4
Cahore Pt 15 E3
Cahors 29 D3
Caia, Bgem do 38 C4
Caianello 64 A3
Caión 34 A1
Cairn Gorm 3 D4
Cairngorm Mts 3 D4
Cairnryan 4 B3
Cairo Montenotte 31 F2
Caiseal 14 C3
Caisleán an Bharraigh 12 B3
Caistor 7 D2
Caivano 64 B4
Cajarc 29 D3
Čajetina 72 C4
Čajniče 76 B1
Čakor 76 C2
Čakovec 70 C1
Čakovice 53 F3
Çal 115 F4
Calabor 34 C3
Calabria 67 E2
Calaceite 41 F1
Calacuccia 33 F3
Cala d'Or 45 F3
Cala, Emb de la 43 D2
Calaf 37 F3
Calafat 114 C2
Calafell 37 F4
Calafort Ros Láir 15 D4
Cala Gonone 66 C2
Calahonda 44 A4
Calahorra 36 C2
Calais 19 E1
Calamocha 41 D1
Calañas 42 C2
Calanche, les 33 E3
Calanda 41 E1
Calanda, Emb de 41 E2
Calangianus 66 B1
Cala'n Porter 45 F2
Calar Alto 44 B3
Călărași 115 E1
Cala Ratjada 45 F2
Calasetta 66 A4
Calasparra 44 C2
Calatafimi 68 B3
Calatañazor 36 B3
Calatayud 36 C4
Calatorao 36 C4
Calau 53 E1
Calazzo 64 B3
Calbe 52 C1
Calcena 36 C3
Caldaro 59 D3
Caldarola 61 F4
Caldas da Rainha 38 A3
Caldas das Taipas 34 A4
Caldas de Reis 34 A2
Caldas de Vizela 34 A4
Caldeirão, Sa do 42 B2
Caldelas 34 A3
Caldera de Taburiente, Pque Nac de la 42 A4
Calderina 40 A4
Caldes de Boí 37 F2
Caldes de Malavella 32 B3
Caldes de Montbui 32 A4
Caldirola 60 A2
Caledonian Canal 2 C4
Calella (Palamós) 32 C3
Calella (Pinedo de Mar) 32 B4
Calenzana 33 F3
Calera de León 43 D1
Calera y Chozas 39 F3
Caleruega 36 A3
Caletta, la 66 C2
Càlig 41 F2
Călimănești 115 D1
Călimani, M 113 D4
Calitri 64 C3
Calizzano 31 F3
Callac 22 B3
Callan 15 D3
Callander 4 C1
Calla, Pso della 61 D3
Callington 8 C4
Callosa de Ensarrià 45 E1
Callosa de Segura 45 D2
Calmazzo 61 E3
Calmbach 54 C2
Calne 9 E2
Calolziocorte 58 B4
Calonge 32 B3
Calpe 45 E1
Caltabellotta 68 B3
Caltagirone 69 D4
Caltanissetta 68 C3
Caltavuturo 68 C3
Caluso 31 E1
Calvados 18 C3
Calvi 33 E3
Calvitero 39 E2
Calvörde 48 C4
Calw 54 C2
Calzada de Calatrava 44 A1
Calzada de Valdunciel 39 E1
Cam 9 F1
Camacho, Pto 44 A3
Camaiore 60 C3
Camaldoli 61 D3
Camaleño 35 E2
Camarasa 37 F3
Camarasa, Emb de 37 F3
Camarat, Cap 31 D4
Camarena 40 A2
Camarès 32 B1
Camaret 22 A3
Camarillas 41 E2
Camarillas, Emb de 44 C1
Camariñas 34 A1
Camarzana 35 D3
Camas 43 D2
Cambados 34 A2
Cambas 38 C2
Camberley 9 F2
Cambil 44 A2
Cambo-les-Bains 28 A4
Camborne 8 B4
Cambrai 20 A2
Cambre 34 B1
Cambremer 19 D3
Cambrian Mts 8 C1
Cambridge 10 C1
Cambridgeshire 10 C1
Cambrils de Mar 37 F4
Camburg 52 C3
Camelford 8 B3
Camerino 61 E4
Camigliatello Silano 67 E2
Caminha 34 A3
Caminomorisco 39 D2
Caminreal 41 D2
Camogli 60 A3
Campagna 64 C4
Campagne-lès-Hesdin 19 E2
Campan 37 E1
Campana 67 F2
Campanario 39 E4
Campania 64 B4
Campaspero 35 F4
Campbeltown 4 B3
Campello 45 E1
Campi Bisenzio 60 C3
Campiglia Marittima 62 C1
Campilhas, Bgem de 42 A1
Campillo de Altobuey 41 D3
Campillo de Aragón 36 C4
Campillo de Arenas 44 A2
Campillo de Llerena 43 D1
Campillos 43 E3
Campione 58 A4
Campi Salentina 65 F4
Campitello M 64 B3
Campli 63 F1
Campo 37 E2
Campobasso 64 B3
Campobello di Licata 68 C4
Campobello di Mazara 68 A3
Campo Carlo Magno 58 C3
Campo de Beisteros 38 B1
Campo de Caso 35 E2
Campo de Criptana 40 B4
Campo di Fiori 58 A4
Campo di Giove 64 A2
Campodonico 61 E4
Campoformido 59 F3
Campogalliano 60 C2
Campo Imperatore 63 F1
Campo Ligure 60 A3
Campo Maior 38 C4
Campomanes 35 D2
Campomarino 64 B2
Campora San Giovanni 67 E3
Camporredondo, Emb de 35 E2
Camporrobles 41 D3
Campos 45 F3
Camposampiero 59 D4
Campos, Canal de 35 E4
Campotosto, L di 63 F1
Campo Tures 59 D2
Camprodon 32 B3
Camucia 61 D4
Camuñas 40 B3
Cañada de Benatanduz 41 E2
Cañadas, Pto 43 D1
Çanakkale 115 E3
Çanakkale Boğazı 115 E3
Canal du Nord 19 F2
Canal du Rhône au Rhin 27 E2
Canales de la Sierra 36 A3
Canals 41 E4
Canal San Bovo 59 D3
Cañamero 39 E3
Canarias, Is 42 B4
Canas de Senhorim 38 C1
Cañaveral 39 D3
Cañaveral de León 43 D2
Cañaveras 40 C2
Canazei 59 D3
Cancale 18 B4
Cancárix 45 D1
Canche 19 E1
Cancon 28 C2
Candanchu 37 D2
Candas 35 D1
Candasnos 37 E4
Candé 23 E4
Candeeiros, Sa dos 38 A3
Candela 64 C3
Candelaria, Sa 39 E2
Candelario 39 E2
Candelaro 64 C2
Candeleda 39 F2
Candes 25 D2
Canelles, Emb de 37 F3
Canelli 31 F2
Canero 35 D1
Canet de Mar 32 B4
Cañete 41 D3
Cañete de las Torres 43 F2
Cañete la Real 43 E3
Canet-Plage 32 B2
Canfranc-Estación 37 D2
Cangas 34 A3
Cangas de Narcea 34 C2
Cangas de Onís 35 E1
Canha 38 B4
Canicatti 68 C4
Canicattini Bagni 69 D4
Canigou, Pic du 32 B2
Cañigral 41 D3
Caniles 44 B3
Canin, M 59 F3
Canino 63 D2
Canis 18 B3
Cañizál 39 E1
Canjáyar 44 B3
Canna 2 B4
Cannero Riviera 58 A4
Cannes 31 E4
Canneto 60 C4
Cannich 2 C3
Cannobio 58 A4
Cannock 9 E1
Canonbie 5 D3
Canosa di Puglia 64 C3
Canourgue, la 29 F3
Cansano 64 A2
Cansiglio 59 E3
Cantabria 35 F2
Cantal (Dépt) 29 E2
Cantal, Mts du 29 E2
Cantalapiedra 39 F1
Cantalejo 40 A1
Cantalpino 39 E1
Cantanhede 38 B2
Cantavieja 41 E2
Čantavir 72 B1
Canterbury 11 D3
Cantillana 43 D2
Cantoira 31 E1
Cantoral 35 E2
Cantoria 44 C3
Cantù 60 A1
Canvey I 11 D2
Cany-Barville 19 D2
Caorle 59 E4
Caorso 60 B2
Capaccio 64 C4
Capaci 68 B3
Capalbio 63 D2
Capannelle, Pso delle 63 F1
Caparde 72 B4
Caparroso 36 C2
Capbreton 28 A4
Cap Corse 33 F2
Cap-d'Agde, le 30 A4
Cap d'Antibes 31 E4
Capdenac-Gare 29 E2
Capel Curig 6 A3
Capelle, la 20 B2
Capendu 32 B2
Capestang 30 A4
Capestrano 64 A2
Capileira 44 A3
Capistrello 63 F2
Čapljina 75 F2
Capmany 32 B3
Cappelle sul Tavo 64 A1
Cappoquin 14 C4
Capracotta 64 A2
Capraia, I di 62 B1
Caprera, I 66 B1
Capri 64 B4
Capriati a Volturno 64 A3
Capri,I di 64 B4
Captieux 28 B3
Capua 64 B3
Capurso 65 D3
Capvern 37 E1
Caracal 115 D2
Caracuel 40 A4
Caragh, L 14 A4
Caraman 29 D4
Caramanico Terme 64 A2
Caramulo 38 B1
Caramulo, Sa do 38 B1
Caransebeș 114 C1
Carantec 22 B2
Caravaca de la Cruz 44 C2
Caravai, Pso di 66 B3
Caravius, M. is 66 B4
Carbajales de Alba 35 D4
Carballiño 34 B2
Carballo 34 A1
Carbayo 35 D2
Carbonara, C 66 C4
Carbonara, Pzo 68 C3
Carbon-Blanc 28 B2
Carboneras 44 C3
Carboneras de Guadazaón 41 D3
Carbonero el Mayor 40 A1
Carbonia 66 B4
Carbonin 59 E2
Carbonne 37 F1
Carcaboso 39 D2
Carcabuey 43 F3
Carcaixent 41 E4
Carcans 28 A2
Carcans-Plage 28 A2
Carcare 31 F2
Carcassonne 32 B1
Carcastillo 36 C2
Carcès 31 D4
Carche 45 D1
Čardak 71 F4
Çardak 115 F4
Cardedeu 32 B4
Cardeña 43 F1
Cardener, R 32 A4
Cardenete 41 D3
Cardiff 9 D2
Cardigan 8 B1
Cardigan B 8 B1
Cardona 32 A3
Carei 112 C3
Carentan 18 B3
Cares, R 35 E2
Carevdar 71 D2
Carev Dvor 77 D4
Cargèse 33 E3
Carhaix-Plouguer 22 B3
Caria 38 C2
Cariati 67 F2
Caričin Grad 77 D1
Carignan 20 C2
Carignano 31 E2
Carina 77 D4
Cariñena 36 C4
Carini 68 B3
Cariño 34 B1
Carinola 64 A3
Carisio 31 F1
Carlet 41 E4
Carling 21 D3
Carlingford 13 E3
Carlingford L 13 E3
Carlisle 5 D3
Carlit, Pic 32 A2
Carloforte 66 A4
Carlow 13 D4
Carlow (Co) 13 D4
Carloway 2 B2
Carluke 4 C2
Carmagnola 31 E2
Carmarthen 8 C2
Carmarthen B 8 B2
Carmaux 29 E3
Carmona 43 E2
Carna 12 A3
Carnac 22 C4
Carnaio, Pso del 61 D3
Carn Ban 2 C4
Carndonagh 13 D1
Carnedd Llewelyn 6 A3
Carn Eige 2 C3
Carneros, Pto de los 39 F4
Carnew 15 D3
Carnforth 6 B1
Carnia 59 F3
Carnia (Reg) 59 E3
Carnlough 13 E1
Carnon 30 B4
Carnota 34 A2
Carnoustie 5 D1
Carnsore Pt 15 D4
Carnwath 5 D2
Caroch 41 D4
Carolles 18 B4
Carovigno 65 E3
Carpaneto Piacentino 60 B2
Carpații Meridionali 114 C1
Carpenedolo 60 B1
Carpentras 30 C3
Carpi 60 C2
Carpignano Sesia 58 A4
Carpineti 60 C3
Carpineto Romano 63 F3
Carpinone 64 A3
Carquefou 24 B2
Carqueiranne 31 D4
Carracedelo 34 C2
Carradale 4 B2
Carraig na Siúire 14 C3
Carral 34 B1
Carrantuohill 14 A4
Carranza 36 A1
Carrara 60 B3
Carrascal 41 E2
Carrascosa del Campo 40 C3
Carrascoy 45 D2
Carrasqueta, Pto de la 45 E1
Carrazeda de Ansiães 34 B4
Carrazedo de Montenegro 34 B4
Carrbridge 3 D4
Carregado 38 A3
Carregal do Sal 38 B2
Carreña de Cabrales 35 E1
Carrickfergus 13 E2
Carrickmacross 13 D3
Carrick-on-Shannon 12 C3
Carrick-on-Suir 14 C3
Carrigart 12 C1
Carrio 34 B1
Carrión de Calatrava 40 A4
Carrión de los Condes 35 E3
Carrión, R 35 E3
Carrizo de la Ribera 35 D2
Carro 30 C4
Carrouges 18 C4
Carrù 31 F2
Carry-le-Rouet 30 C4
Carsoli 63 F2
Cartagena 45 D3
Cártama 43 F4
Cartaxo 38 A3
Cartaya 42 C2
Carter Bar 5 D3
Carteret 18 B3
Carvajal 43 F4
Carviçais 39 D1
Carvin 19 F1
Carvoeira 42 A3
Carvoeiro, C 38 A3
Casabermeja 43 F3
Casa Branca (Alentejo) 42 A1
Casa Branca (Ribatejo) 38 B4
Casacalenda 64 B2
Casalárreina 36 B2
Casalbordino 64 B2
Casalbuttano 60 B1
Casal di Principe 64 A4
Casalecchio di Reno 60 C2
Casale Monferrato 31 F1
Casale sul Sile 59 E4
Casalmaggiore 60 B2
Casalpusterlengo 60 B2
Casamassima 65 D3
Casamicciola Terme 64 A4
Casa Nuevas 44 C2
Casarabonela 43 E3
Casarano 65 F4
Casar de Cáceres 39 D3
Casares 43 E4
Casares de las Hurdes 39 D2
Casariche 43 E3
Casarsa 59 E3
Casas de Don Pedro 39 E4
Casas de Fernando Alonso 40 C4
Casas de Juan Núñez 41 D4
Casas del Puerto 45 D1
Casas de Luján 40 B3
Casas de Miravete 39 E3
Casas Ibáñez 41 D4
Casasimarro 40 C4
Casatejada 39 E3
Casavieja 39 F2
Cascais 38 A4
Cascante 36 C3
Cascia 63 E1
Casciana Terme 60 C4
Cascina 60 C4
Casei Gerola 60 A2
Caselle in Pittari 67 D1
Caselle Torinese 31 E1
Caserío del Puente 35 D3
Caserta 64 B3

Casetas 37 D3
Cas-gwent 9 D2
Cashel 14 C3
Casicas del Río Segura 44 B2
Casillas 39 D2
Casina 60 C2
Casinos 41 E3
Casnewydd 9 D2
Casoio 34 C3
Casola in Lunigiana 60 B3
Casoli 64 A2
Casoria 64 B4
Caspe 37 E4
Cassà de la Selva 32 B3
Cassagnes-Begonhès 29 E3
Cassano allo Ionio 67 E2
Cassano delle Murge 65 D3
Cassel 19 F1
Cassino 64 A3
Cassis 30 C4
Castalla 45 D1
Castanet-Tolosan 29 D4
Castanheira de Pêra 38 B2
Castaños, Pto de los 39 D3
Castasegna 58 B3
Casteggio 60 A2
Castejón 36 C3
Castejón de Monègros 37 E4
Castejón de Sos 37 E2
Castejón de Valdejasa 37 D3
Castelbuono 68 C3
Casteldaccia 68 B3
Casteldelfino 31 E2
Castel del Monte (Abruzzo) 63 F2
Castel del Monte (Puglia) 65 D3
Castel del Rio 61 D3
Castel di Sangro 64 A2
Castelfidardo 61 F4
Castelfiorentino 60 C4
Castelfranco Emilia 60 C2
Castelfranco in Miscano 64 B3
Castelfranco Veneto 59 D4
Castel Gandolfo 63 E3
Casteljaloux 28 B3
Castellabate 67 D1
Castellamare di Stabbia 64 B4
Castellammare d. Golfo 48 B3
Castellammare, G di 68 B3
Castellamonte 31 E1
Castellana Grotte 65 E3
Castellane 31 D3
Castellaneta 65 E4
Castellar de la Muela 41 D2
Castellar del Vallès 32 A4
Castellar de Santiago 44 B1
Castellar de Santisteban 44 B2
Castell' Arquato 60 B2
Castelldans 37 F4
Castelldefels 32 A4
Castell de Ferro 44 A4
Castelleone 60 B1
Castellfollit de la Roca 32 B3
Castellina in Chianti 61 D4
Castell-nedd 8 C2
Castelló de la Plana 41 F3
Castello del Lago 64 B3
Castelló d'Empúries 32 B3
Castellolí 32 A4
Castellón de la Plana 41 F3
Castellón de Rugat 45 E1
Castellote 41 E2
Castello Tesino 59 D3
Castellterçol 32 A4
Castelluccio 63 F1
Castel Madama 63 F2
Castelmassa 60 C2
Castelmauro 64 B2
Castelmoron 28 C3
Castelnaudary 32 A1
Castelnau-de-Médoc 28 B2
Castelnau-de-Montmiral 29 D3
Castelnau-Magnoac 37 E1
Castelnau-Montratier 29 D3
Castelnau-Rivière-Basse 28 B4
Castelnovo ne' Monti 60 B3
Castelnuovo Berardenga 61 D4
Castelnuovo Bocca d'Adda 60 B2
Castelnuovo della Daunia 64 B3
Castelnuovo di Garfagnana 60 C3
Castelnuovo di Porto 63 E2
Castelnuovo Scrivia 60 A2
Castelo Branco 38 C2
Castelo de Bode, Bgem do 38 B3
Castelo de Paiva 34 A4
Castelo de Vide 38 C3
Castelraimondo 61 E4
Castelrotto 59 D3
Castel San Giovanni 60 A2
Castel San Lorenzo 64 C4
Castel San Pietro Terme 61 D3
Castelsardo 66 B1
Castelsarrasin 29 D3
Castelserás 41 E1
Casteltermini 68 B3
Castelvecchio Subequo 63 F2
Castelvetrano 68 A3
Castel Volturno 64 A4
Castets 28 A3
Castiadas 66 C4
Castiglioncello 60 C4
Castiglione d'Adda 60 B2
Castiglione dei Pepoli 60 C3
Castiglione del Lago 61 D4
Castiglione della Pescaia 62 C1
Castiglione delle Stiviere 60 C1
Castiglione in Teverina 63 E1
Castiglione Messer Marino 64 B2
Castiglione Olona 60 A1
Castiglion Fiorentino 61 D4
Castilblanco 39 F4
Castilblanco de los Arroyos 43 D2
Castilla, Canal de 35 E4
Castilla-La Mancha 40 A4
Castilla-León 35 F4
Castilla, Mar de 40 C2
Castilleja del Campo 43 D2
Castilléjar 44 B2
Castillejo 39 E1
Castillejo de Martin Viejo 39 D1
Castillo de Loarre 37 D2
Castillo de Locubín 43 F2
Castillon, Bge de 31 D3
Castillon-en-Couserans 37 F2
Castillon-la-Bataille 28 B2
Castillonnès 28 C2
Castillo, Pto del 44 A3
Castillo y Elejabeitia 36 B1
Castilruiz 36 C3
Castions di Strada 59 F3
Castlebar 12 B3
Castlebay 2 A4
Castlebellingham 13 D3
Castleblayney 13 D3
Castlecomer 13 D4
Castledawson 13 D2
Castlederg 13 D2
Castledermot 13 D4
Castle Douglas 4 C3
Castleford 7 D2
Castleisland 14 B3
Castlemaine 14 A3
Castlepollard 13 D3
Castlerea 12 C3
Castlerock 13 D1
Castleton 6 C2
Castletownbere 14 A4
Castletown (I of Man) 6 A1
Castletown (Scotland) 3 D2
Castlewellan 13 E2
Castocalbón 35 D3
Castrejón 39 F1
Castrejón, Emb de 40 A3
Castres 32 B1
Castries 30 B4
Castril 44 B2
Castrillo de la Reina 36 A3
Castrillo de Villavega 35 F3
Castro 34 B2
Castro Caldelas 34 B3
Castrocaro Terme 61 D3
Castrocontrigo 35 D3
Castro Daire 38 C1
Castro del Río 43 F2
Castrogeriz 35 F3
Castro Laboreiro 34 B3
Castro Marim 42 B2
Castromonte 35 E4
Castronuevo 35 D4
Castronuño 35 E4
Castropol 34 C1
Castrop-Rauxel 17 E3
Castroreale 69 D2
Castroreale Terme 69 D2
Castrotierra 35 E3
Castro Urdiales 36 A1
Castroverde 34 C2
Castro Verde 42 B2
Castroverde de Campos 35 E3
Castrovillari 67 E2
Castuera 39 E4
Cataluña 32 A3
Catalunya 37 F3
Catania 69 D3
Catania, G di 69 D3
Catanzaro 67 F3
Catanzaro Lido 67 F3
Catarroja 41 E4
Cateau, le 20 A2
Catelet, le 20 A2
Catenanuova 69 D3
Catež 70 C2
Cathair na Mart 12 B3
Čatići 71 F4
Catignano 64 A2
Catoira 34 A2
Catoute 35 D2
Catral 45 D2
Catria, Mte 61 E4
Cattenom 21 D3
Cattolica 61 E3
Catus 29 D2
Caudebec 19 D3
Caudete 45 D1
Caudiel 41 E3
Caudry 20 A2
Caulnes 23 D3
Caulonia 67 F4
Caumont-l'Eventé 18 C3
Caunes 32 B1
Caussade 29 D3
Čausy 111 E4
Cauterets 37 E2
Cava de' Tirreni 64 B4
Cávado, R 34 A4
Cavaglià 31 F1
Cavaillon 30 C3
Cavalaire 31 D4
Cavalerie, la 29 F3
Cavalese 59 D3
Cavalière 31 D4
Cavan 13 D3
Cavan (Co) 13 D3
Cavarzere 61 D1
Cavazzo 59 E3
Çavdarhisar 115 F4
Cavero, Pto de 36 C4
Cavezzo 60 C2
Cavo 62 C1
Cavo, Mte 63 E3
Cavour 31 E2
Cavtat 76 A3
Caya 38 C4
Cayeux 19 E2
Caylar, le 29 F3
Caylus 29 D3
Cayolle, Col de la 31 E3
Cayres 29 F2
Cazalla de la Sierra 43 D2
Cazals 29 D2
Cazaubon 28 B3
Cazaux 28 A2
Cazères 37 F1
Cazin 70 C3
Čazma 71 D2
Cazorla 44 B2
Cazorla, Sa de 44 B2
Cea 34 B2
Ceanannus Mor 13 D3
Cea, R 35 E3
Ceatharlach 13 D4
Cebolla 39 F3
Cebollera 36 B3
Cebreros 40 A2
Ceccano 63 F3
Cece 112 B4
Cechy 53 F4
Cecina 60 C4
Cecina *R* 60 C4
Cecita, L di 67 F2
Ceclavín 39 D3
Cedeira 34 B1
Cedillo, Bgem de 38 C3
Cedrillas 41 E2
Cedrino 66 C2
Cedynia 49 E3
Cefalù 68 C3
Cega, R 40 A1
Cegléd 112 B4
Ceglie Messapico 65 E3
Čegrane 77 D3
Cehegín 44 C2
Čehotina 76 A1
Ceira, R 38 C2
Čejč 57 F1
Celákovice 53 F3
Celano 63 F2
Celanova 34 B3
Celavevo 72 B2
Čelebić 75 D1
Čelebići 76 B1
Celemín, Emb de 43 D4
Čelić 72 B3
Čelinac Donji 71 E3
Celje 70 B2
Cella 41 D2
Celle 48 B4
Celle Ligure 60 A3
Celles 24 C4
Čelopeci 77 D3
Celorico 34 B4
Celorico da Beira 38 C1
Čemerna pl 73 D4
Čemernica 71 E4
Čemerno 76 A2
Cenajo, Emb del 44 C1
Cencenighe 59 D3
Cenicero 36 B2
Čenta 72 C2
Centelles 32 B4
Cento 60 C2
Cento Croci, Pso 60 B3
Central Region 4 C1
Centre, Canal du 26 B3
Centuripe 69 D3
Cepagatti 64 A2
Čepin 71 F2
Ceppo 63 F1
Ceprano 63 F3
Cer 72 C3
Čeralije 71 E2
Cerbère 32 C3
Cercal (Alentejo) 42 A1
Cercal (Estremadura) 38 A3
Cercedilla 40 A2
Cerchiara di Calabria 67 E2
Cerchov 56 B1
Cerdedo 34 A2
Cerdeira 39 D2
Cère 29 E2
Cerea 60 C1
Cereda, Pso di 59 D3
Čerepovec 111 F1
Ceres 31 E1
Ceresole Reale 31 E1
Céret 32 B3
Cerezo de Abajo 36 A4
Cerezo de Riotirón 36 A2
Cerignola 64 C3
Cérilly 26 A3
Cerisiers 26 A1
Cerisy-la-Salle 18 B3
Cerizay 24 C3
Čerkassy 113 F2
Cerknica 70 B2
Cerkniško jez 70 B2
Cerkno 70 A2
Cerler 37 E2
Černá 56 C2
Cerna 71 F2
Cernache de Bonjardim 38 B2
Čern'achovsk 110 B4
Cernadilla, Emb de 34 C3
Cernavodă 115 E1
Cernay 27 E1
Černigov 113 E1
Cernik 71 E3
Cernobbio 58 B4
Černobyl' 113 E1
Černomorskoje 113 F4
Černovcy 113 D3
Cerreto, Pso del 60 B3
Cerreto Sannita 64 B3
Cerrigydrudion 6 B3
Čerrik 76 C4
Certaldo 60 C4
Certosa di Pavia 60 A2
Cervales 39 E3
Cervaro 64 C3
Cervati, Mte 67 D1
Cervatos 35 F2
Cervatos de la Cueza 35 E3
Červen 111 D4
Cervera 37 F3
Cervera de la Cañada 36 C4
Cervera del Río Alhama 36 C3
Cervera de Pisuerga 35 F2
Cerveteri 63 E2
Cervia 61 E3
Cervialto, Mte 64 C4
Cervignano del Friuli 59 F3
Cervinara 64 B3
Cervino 27 E4
Cervione 33 F3
Cervo 34 C1
Červonograd 112 C2
Cesana Torinese 31 D2
Cesarica 70 C4
Cesarò 69 D3
Cesena 61 D3
Cesenatico 61 E3
Cēsis 110 C2
Česka Kamenice 53 F2
Česká Lípa 53 F3
České Budějovice 57 D1
České Velenice 57 D2
Český Krumlov 57 D2
Česma 71 D2
Çeşme 115 E4
Cespedosa 39 E2
Cessalto 59 E4
Cetina (E) 36 C4
Cetina *R* (YU) 75 D1
Cetinje 76 B3
Cetraro 67 E2
Ceutí 45 D2
Ceva 31 F2
Cevedale, Mte 58 C3
Cévennes, Parc Nat des 29 F3
Cevico de la Torre 35 F4
Čevo 76 B2
Ceyrat 29 F1
Ceyzériat 26 C4
Cèze 30 B3
Chabanais 25 D4
Chabeuil 30 C2
Chablis 26 B1
Chabris 25 E2
Chagny 26 C3
Chailland 23 E3
Chaillé 24 B3
Chaise-Dieu, la 29 F1
Chalabre 32 A2
Chalais 28 C1
Chalamont 26 C4
Chalampé 27 E1
Chalindrey 26 C1
Challans 24 B3
Challes 31 D1
Chalonnes 24 C2
Châlons-sur-Marne 20 B3
Chalon-sur-Saône 26 C3
Châlus 28 C1
Cham 56 B1
Chambéry 31 D1
Chambley 21 D3
Chambly 19 F3
Chambon, Bge du 31 D2
Chambon-Feugerolles, le 30 B1
Chambon-sur-Lac 29 E1
Chambon-sur-Lignon, le 30 B2
Chambon-sur-Voueize 25 F4
Chambord 25 E2
Chambre, la 31 D1
Chamonix 27 E4
Champagnac-de-Belair 28 C1
Champagne-Mouton 25 D4
Champagnole 27 D3
Champdeniers 24 C3
Champeaux 23 D3
Champéry 27 E4
Champex 27 E4
Champlitte 26 C2
Champlon, Bre.de 50 C4
Champoluc 27 F4
Champorcher 31 E1
Champs-sur-Tarentaine 29 E1
Champtoceaux 24 B2
Chamrousse 31 D1
Chamusca 38 B3
Chanac 29 F3
Chanas 30 B1
Chança, R 42 C2
Chantada 34 B2
Chantelle 26 A4
Chantemerle 31 D2
Chantilly 19 F3
Chantonnay 24 B3
Chanza, Emb del 42 B2
Chaource 26 B1
Chapel-en-le-Frith 6 C2
Chapelle-d'Angillon, la 25 F2
Chapelle-de-Guinchay, la 26 C4
Chapelle-en-Valgaudemar, la 31 D2
Chapelle-en-Vercors, la 30 C2
Chapinería 40 A2
Charbonnières 26 C4
Charco Redondo, Emb de 43 D4
Chard 9 D3
Charente 28 B1
Charente (Dépt) 28 C1
Charente-Maritime 24 B4
Charenton-du-Cher 25 F3
Charité, la 26 A2
Charleroi 50 B4
Charlestown 12 B3
Charleville 14 B3
Charleville-Mézières 20 C2
Charlieu 26 B4
Charlottenberg 105 D3
Charly 20 A3
Charmes 21 D4
Charny (Meuse) 20 C3
Charny (Yonne) 26 A1
Charolles 26 B3
Chârost 25 E3
Charquemont 27 E2
Charroux 25 D4
Chartre, la 23 F4
Chartres 19 E4
Chãs 38 B1
Chasseneuil 28 C1
Chasseral la Neuveville 27 E2
Chasseron, le 27 D3
Châtaigneraie, la 24 C3
Château-Arnoux 31 D3
Châteaubourg 23 D3
Châteaubriant 23 D4
Château-Chinon 26 B2
Château-de-Bonaguil 29 D2
Château de Ventadour 29 E1
Château d'Oex 27 E3
Château-du-Loir 23 F4
Châteaudun 25 E1
Châteaugiron 23 D3
Château-Gontier 23 E4
Château-Landon 25 F1
Château-la-Vallière 25 D2
Château, le 24 B4
Châteaulin 22 B3
Châteaumeillant 25 F3
Châteauneuf (Charente) 28 B1
Châteauneuf (Ille-et-Vilaine) 18 B4
Châteauneuf-de-Randon 29 F2
Châteauneuf-du-Faou 22 B3
Châteauneuf-du-Pape 30 B3
Châteauneuf-en-Thymerais 19 E4
Châteauneuf-la-Forêt 29 D1
Châteauneuf-les-Bains 26 A4
Châteauneuf-sur-Cher 25 F3
Châteauneuf-sur-Loire 25 F1
Châteauneuf-sur-Sarthe 23 E4
Châteauponsac 25 E4
Château-Porcien 20 B3
Château-Queyras 31 D2
Château-Regnault 20 C2
Châteaurenard (Loiret) 25 F1
Châteaurenard (Vaucluse) 30 B3
Château-Renault 25 D2
Châteauroux 25 E3
Château-Salins 21 D4
Château-Thierry 20 A3
Châteauvillain 26 C1
Châtel 27 E3
Châtelaillon-Plage 24 B4
Châtelard, le 27 D4
Châtelaudren 22 C2
Châteldon 26 A4
Châtelet 50 C4
Châtelet, le (Cher) 25 F3
Châtelet, le (Seine-et-Marne) 19 F4
Châtelguyon 26 A4

Châtellerault 25 D3
Châtel-Montagne 26 B4
Châtel-St-Denis 27 E3
Châtel-sur-Moselle 21 D4
Châtelus-Malvaleix 25 E4
Châtenois 27 D1
Chatham 11 D2
Châtillon 27 F4
Châtillon-Coligny 26 A1
Châtillon-en-Bazois 26 B2
Châtillon-en-Diois 30 C2
Châtillon-sur-Chalaronne 26 C4
Châtillon-sur-Indre 25 E3
Châtillon-sur-Loire 26 A2
Châtillon-sur-Marne 20 B3
Châtillon-sur-Seine 26 B1
Châtre, la 25 E3
Chatsworth House 6 C3
Chatteris 9 F1
Chaudes-Aigues 29 F2
Chauffailles 26 B4
Chaufour 19 E4
Chaulnes 19 F2
Chaumergy 26 C3
Chaumont-en-Vexin 19 E3
Chaumont (Haute-Marne) 26 C1
Chaumont (Loir-et-Cher) 25 E2
Chauny 20 A2
Chausey, I 18 B4
Chaussin 26 C3
Chauvigny 25 D3
Chaux-de Fonds, la 27 E2
Chaves 34 B3
Chazelles 30 B1
Cheb 53 D4
Cheddar Gorge 9 D3
Chef-Boutonne 24 C4
Cheles 42 C1
Chełm 112 C2
Chełmno 112 A1
Chelmsford 11 D2
Cheltenham 9 E2
Chelva 41 D3
Chemillé 24 C2
Chemin 26 C3
Chénérailles 25 F4
Chenonceaux 25 E2
Chepstow 9 D2
Cher 25 F3
Cher (Dépt) 25 F2
Chera 41 D3
Cherbourg 18 B2
Chéroy 26 A1
Cherson 113 F3
Chert 41 F2
Cheshire 6 C2
Cheshunt 9 F2
Chesne, le 20 C3
Cheste 41 E4
Chester 6 B3
Chesterfield 7 D3
Chester-le-Street 5 E4
Chevagnes 26 A3
Chevillon 20 C4
Cheviot Hills, The 5 E3
Cheviot, The 5 E3
Chèvre, Cap de la 22 A3
Chevreuse 19 E4
Cheylard, le 30 B2
Chèze, la 22 C3
Chiampo 59 D4
Chianciano Terme 63 D1
Chianti 61 D4
Chiaramonte Gulfi 69 D4
Chiaravalle 61 F3
Chiaravalle Centrale 67 F3
Chiari 60 B1
Chiasso 58 A4
Chiavari 60 A3
Chiavenna 58 B3
Chichester 9 F3
Chiclana de la Frontera 43 D4
Chieming 56 B3
Chiemsee 56 B3
Chieri 31 E1
Chiers 20 C3
Chiesa in Valmalenco 58 B3
Chiesina Uzz 60 C3
Chieti 64 A2
Chiltern Hills 9 F2
Chimay 50 B4
Chimorra 43 E1
Chinchilla de Monte Aragón 41 D4
Chinchón 40 B2
Chinon 25 D2
Chioggia 61 D1
Chioula, Col de 32 A2
Chipiona 42 C3
Chippenham 9 E2
Chipping Campden 9 E1
Chipping Norton 9 E2
Chipping Sodbury 9 D2
Chirivel 44 C2
Chişineu-Criş 112 C4
Chisone 31 E2
Chiusa 59 D2
Chiusa di Pesio 31 E2
Chiusa Sclafani 68 B3
Chiusatorte 59 F3
Chiusi 63 D1
Chiva 41 E4
Chivasso 31 F1
Chlum u Třeboně 57 D1
Chmel'nickij 113 D2
Chmel'nik 113 E2
Chociwel 49 F2
Chodov 53 E4
Chojna 49 E3
Chojnice 110 A4
Chojniki 113 E1
Cholet 24 C3
Chollerford 5 E3
Cholm 111 E2
Chomutov 53 E3
Chorges 31 D2
Chorley 6 C2
Chorol 113 F2
Choszczno 49 F3
Chotin 113 D3
Chouto 38 B3
Chrastava 53 F2
Christchurch 9 E3
Christiansfeld 108 A3
Christiansø 109 D4
Chur 58 B2
Church Stretton 9 D1
Chust 112 C3
Ciamarella 31 E1
Cians, Gorges du 31 E3
Cičarija 70 A3
Čičavica 77 D2
Cicciano 64 B4
Čičevac 73 E4
Čičevo 76 A2
Cidacos, R 36 B3
Cidade Nova de Santo André 42 A1
Cidones 36 B3
Ciechanów 112 B1
Ciechocinek 112 B1
Ciempozuelos 40 B2
Cíes, Is 34 A3
Cieszyn 112 B3
Cieza 45 D2
Cifuentes 40 C2
Cigliano 31 F1
Cigüela R 40 B3
Cijara, Emb de 39 F4
Cijevna 76 B3
Cilavegna 60 A1
Čilipi 76 A3
Cill Airne 14 B4
Cillas 36 C4
Cill Chainnigh 15 D3
Cilleros 39 D2
Cilleruelo de Bezana 35 F2
Cill Mhantáin 13 E4
Cima Brenta 58 C3
Cima d'Asta 59 D3
Cimadolmo 59 E4
Cima Presanella 58 C3
Čimišlija 113 E4
Cimone, Mte 60 C3
Cîmpeni 112 C4
Cîmpina 115 D1
Cîmpulung 115 D1
Cîmpulung Moldovenesc 113 D3
Cinca, R 37 E3
Cincar 75 E1
Cinctorres 41 E2
Ciney 50 C4
Cinfães 34 A4
Cingoli 61 F4
Cinigiano 63 D1
Cinisi 68 B3
Cinovec 53 E3
Cinque Terre 60 B3
Cintegabelle 32 A1
Cinto, M 33 F3
Cintruénigo 36 C3
Ciórraga 36 B1
Ciotat, la 30 C4
Čiovo 75 D2
Cirencester 9 E2
Cirey 21 E4
Ciria 36 C3
Ciriè 31 E1
Cirò 67 F2
Cirò Marina 67 F2
Čirpan 115 D2
Cisa, Pso della 60 B3
Cisneros 35 E3
Čista 74 C1
Cista Provo 75 E1
Cisterna di Latina 63 F3
Cisternino 65 E3
Cistierna 35 E2
Čitluk (Mostar) 75 F2
Čitluk (Posušje) 75 E1
Cittadella 59 D4
Città del Pieve 63 D1
Città di Castello 61 E4
Cittaducale 63 F2
Cittanova 67 E4
Cittareale 63 F1
Città Sant' Angelo 64 A1
Ciudad Encantada 40 C3
Ciudad Real 40 A4
Ciudad Rodrigo 39 D1
Ciutadella de Menorca 45 F1
Cividale del Friuli 59 F3
Civita Castellana 63 E2
Civitanova Marche 61 F4
Civitavecchia 63 D2
Civitella del Tronto 63 F1
Civitella Roveto 63 F2
Civray 25 D4
Çivril 115 F4
Clacton-on-Sea 11 D2
Clain 25 D4
Clairvaux-les-Lacs 27 D3
Clamecy 26 A2
Claonaig 4 B2
Clapham 6 C1
Clara 12 C4
Clare 11 D1
Clare 12 B3
Clare (Co) 12 B4
Clare I 12 A3
Claremorris 12 B3
Claudy 13 D1
Clausthal-Zellerfeld 52 B2
Claut 59 E3
Claviere 31 D2
Clavin, Pto de 39 D3
Clay Cross 6 C3
Claye-Souilly 19 F4
Clayette, la 26 B4
Clear I 14 A4
Clécy 18 C4
Clefmont 26 C1
Cléguérec 22 C3
Clelles 30 C2
Clères 19 E3
Clermont 19 F3
Clermont-en-Argonne 20 C3
Clermont-Ferrand 29 F1
Clermont-l'Hérault 30 A4
Clervaux 21 D2
Cléry 25 E2
Cles 58 C3
Clevedon 9 D2
Cleveland Hills 7 D1
Cleveleys 6 B2
Clew B 12 B3
Clifden 12 A3
Clisham 2 B2
Clisson 24 B2
Clitheroe 6 C2
Cloghan 12 C4
Clogheen 14 C3
Clogherhead 13 E3
Clogher Head 14 A3
Clogh Mills 13 E1
Clonakilty 14 B4
Clonbur 12 B3
Clondalkin 13 D4
Clones 13 D2
Clonfert 12 C4
Clonmacnoise 12 C4
Clonmel 14 C3
Cloppenburg 17 E1
Clovelly 8 B3
Cloyes 25 E1
Cluain Meala 14 C3
Cluj-Napoca 112 C4
Clun 9 D1
Cluny 26 C3
Clusaz, la 27 D4
Cluse de Pontarlier 27 D3
Cluses 27 E4
Clusone 58 B4
Clwyd 6 B3
Clyde 4 C2
Clydebank 4 C2
Clyde, Firth of 4 B2
Coachford 14 B4
Coalisland 13 D2
Coalville 9 E1
Coaña 34 C1
Côa, R 39 D2
Coatbridge 4 C2
Cobeña 40 B2
Cobh 14 C4
Coburg 52 C4
Coca 40 A1
Coca, Pso di 58 B3
Cocentaina 45 E1
Cochem 51 E4
Cockburnspath 5 E2
Cockermouth 5 D4
Codevigo 61 D1
Codigoro 61 D2
Codogno 60 B2
Codos 36 C4
Codroipo 59 E3
Coesfeld 17 E3
Coevorden 17 D2
Cofrentes 41 D4
Coghinas, L del 66 B2
Cognac 28 B1
Cogne 31 E1
Cogolin 31 D4
Cogolludo 40 B1
Coigach 2 C2
Coimbra 38 B2
Coin 43 E4
Coina 38 A4
Čoka 72 C1
Col 70 A2
Colares 38 A4
Cölbe 17 F4
Colchester 11 D2
Coldbackie 2 C2
Colditz 53 D2
Coldstream 5 E2
Coleford 9 D2
Coleraine 13 D1
Colfiorito 63 E1
Colico 58 B3
Coligny 26 C3
Colindres 36 A1
Colintraive 4 B2
Coll 2 A4
Collado Bajo 41 D2
Coll de Nargó 37 F3
Collecchio 60 B2
Colle di Val d'Elsa 60 C4
Colleferro 63 F3
Colle Isarco 59 D2
Colle Salvetti 60 C4
Colle Sannita 64 B3
Collesano 68 C3
Colli a Volturno 64 A3
Collina, Pso della 60 C3
Collinée 22 C3
Colline Metallifere 60 C4
Collio 58 C4
Collioure 32 B2
Collobrières 31 D4
Collodi 60 C3
Collonges 27 D4
Collonges-la-Rouge 29 D2
Colmar 27 E1
Colmars 31 D3
Colmenar 43 F3
Colmenar de Oreja 40 B3
Colmenar Viejo 40 A2
Colnabaichin 3 D4
Colne 6 C2
Colobraro 65 D4
Cologna Veneta 60 C1
Cologne 28 C4
Colombey-les-Belles 21 D4
Colombey-les-Deux-Eglises 26 C1
Colombière, Col de la 27 D4
Colombres 35 F1
Colomera 44 A3
Colonsay 4 A2
Colorno 60 B2
Colosimi 67 F3
Columbretes, I 41 F3
Colunga 35 E1
Colwyn Bay 6 B2
Comacchio 61 D2
Comănești 113 D4
Coma-ruga 37 F4
Combarro 34 A2
Combeaufontaine 27 D1
Combe Laval 30 C2
Combe Martin 8 C3
Comber 13 E2
Combloux 27 E4
Combourg 18 B4
Combronde 26 A4
Comeglians 59 E2
Comeragh Mts 14 C3
Comillas 35 F1
Comines 19 F1
Comino 68 B4
Comiso 69 D4
Commentry 26 A4
Commercy 20 C4
Como 58 B4
Como, L di 58 B3
Cómpeta 43 F3
Compiègne 19 F3
Comporta 38 A4
Comps-sur-Artuby 31 D3
Comunanza 63 F1
Concarneau 22 B3
Conches 19 D4
Concordia sulla Secchia 60 C2
Condat 29 E1
Condé 20 A1
Conde, Emb del 43 E3
Condé-en-Brie 20 A3
Condeixa-a-Nova 38 B2
Condé-sur-Noireau 18 C4
Condom 28 C3
Condrieu 30 B1
Conegliano 59 E3
Conejeros, Pto de los 38 C4
Conflans 21 D3
Confolens 25 D4
Cong 12 B3
Congleton 6 C3
Congost de Tresponts 32 A3
Congosto de Valdavia 35 E2
Congresbury 9 D2
Conil de la Frontera 43 D4
Conisbrough 7 D2
Coniston 5 D4
Conlie 23 F3
Conliège 26 C3
Connaught 12 B3
Connel 4 B1
Connemara 12 A3
Connerré 23 F3
Conn, L 12 B2
Čonoplja 72 B1
Conques 29 E2
Conquet, le 22 A2
Conquista 43 F1
Conselice 61 D2
Conselve 61 D1
Consett 5 E4
Constância 38 B3
Constanța 115 E1
Constantina 43 E2
Consuegra 40 A3
Consuma 61 D3
Contamines, les 27 E4
Contarina 61 D2
Conthey 27 E3
Contigliano 63 E2
Contin 2 C3
Contrasto, C del 68 C3
Contraviesa, Sa de la 44 B4
Contreras, Emb de 41 D3
Contres 25 E2
Contrexéville 27 D1
Contursi 64 C4
Conty 19 F2
Convento de Calatrava 44 A1
Conversano 65 E3
Conwy 6 A2
Cookstown 13 D2
Cootehill 13 D3
Čop 112 C3
Cope 45 D3
Cope, C 45 D3
Copertino 65 F4
Copparo 61 D2
Corabia 115 D2
Cora Droma Rúisc 12 C3
Corato 65 D3
Coray 22 B3
Corbeil-Essonnes 19 F4
Corbie 19 F2
Corbigny 26 B2
Corbola 61 D2
Corbones, R 43 E2
Corbridge 5 E3
Corby 9 F1
Corcaigh 14 B4
Corcieux 27 E1
Córcoles, R 40 C4
Corconte 35 F2
Corcubión 34 A1
Cordes 29 D3
Córdoba 43 F2
Cordobilla de Lácara 39 D4
Cordobilla, Emb de 43 F3
Corduente 40 C2
Corella 36 C3
Coreses 35 D4
Corfe Castle 9 E3
Corgo 34 B2
Cori 63 F3
Coria 39 D2
Coria del Río 43 D3
Corias 34 C2
Corigliano Calabro 67 F2
Corinaldo 61 E3
Coripe 43 E3
Cork 14 B4
Cork (Co) 14 B4
Corlay 22 C3
Corleone 68 B3
Corleto Perticara 65 D4
Çorlu 115 E3
Cormatin 26 C3
Cormeilles 19 D3
Cormery 25 D2
Cormons 59 F3
Cornago 36 C3
Cornellana 35 D1
Corniche des Cévennes 29 F3
Corniglio 60 B3
Cornimont 27 E1
Cornuda 59 D4
Cornus 29 F3
Cornwall 8 B4
Corps 31 D2
Corraes 34 C3
Corral de Almaguer 40 B3
Corral de Cantos 39 F3
Corralejo 42 C4
Corrales 35 D4
Corran 2 C4
Corraun 12 B2
Corredoiras 34 B2
Correggio 60 C2
Corrèze 29 D1
Corrèze (Dépt) 29 D1
Corrèze R 29 D2
Corrib, L 12 B3
Corridonia 61 F4
Corrofin 12 B4
Corse 33 E2
Corse-du-Sud 33 F3
Corsham 9 D2
Čortanovci 72 C2
Corte 33 F3
Corte de Peleas 39 D4
Cortegada 34 B3
Cortegana 42 C2
Cortemaggiore 60 B2
Cortemilia 31 F2
Corteolona 60 A2
Cortes de Aragón 41 E1
Cortes de Baza 44 B2
Cortes de la Frontera 43 E4
Cortijos Nuevos 44 B2
Cortina d'Ampezzo 59 E3
Čortkov 113 D3
Cortona 61 D4
Coruche 38 B4
Corvara in Badia 59 D3
Corvera 45 D2
Corvera Toranzo 35 F2
Corwen 6 B3
Cosenza 67 E2
Cosham 9 E3
Cosne 26 A2
Cosne-d'Allier 26 A3
Cossato 31 F1
Cossé-le-Vivien 23 E3
Cosson 25 E2
Cossonay 27 D3
Costa Blanca 45 E2
Costa Brava 32 C3
Costa da Caparica 38 A4
Costa del Sol 44 A4
Costa de Santo André 42 A1
Costalunga, Pso di 59 D3
Costa Smeralda 66 B1
Costa Vasca 36 B1
Costa Verde 35 D1
Costigliole d'Asti 31 F2
Coswig (Dresden) 53 E2
Coswig (Halle) 53 D1
Côte-d'Or (Dépt) 26 C2
Côtes-du-Nord 22 C3
Côte-St-André, la 30 C1
Cotignac 31 D4
Cottbus 53 F1
Coubet, Collado de 32 B3
Coubre, Pointe de la 28 A1
Couches 26 B3
Couço 38 B4
Coucy-le-Château-Auffrique 20 A3
Couesnon 23 D3
Couhé 25 D4
Couilly 19 F4
Couiza 32 B2
Coulanges 26 A2
Coulanges-la-Vineuse 26 A2
Coulommiers 19 F4
Coulon 24 C4
Coulonges 24 C3
Coupar Angus 5 D1
Couptrain 18 C4
Courchevel 31 D1
Cour-Cheverny 25 E2
Courçon 24 C4

Courmayeur 27 E4	Crailsheim 55 E2	Creuse (Dépt) 25 E4	Crni Guber 72 C4	Crotoy, le 19 E2	Cueva de Nerja 44 A4	Cumbres Mayores 42 C1
Couronne, la 28 C1	Craiova 115 D2	Creußen 53 D4	Crni Lug (Bosna i	Crowborough 10 C3	Cueva Foradada, Emb	Cumbria 5 D4
Courpière 29 F1	Cranborne 9 E3	Creusot, le 26 B3	Hercegovina) 75 D1	Crowland 9 F1	de 41 E1	Cumbrian Mts 5 D4
Cours 26 B4	Crans 27 E3	Creutzwald 21 D3	Crni Lug (Hrvatska) 70 B3	Crowle 7 D2	Cueva, Sa do 35 E1	Cumiana 31 E2
Coursan 32 B1	Craon 23 E3	Creuzburg 52 B3	Crni Timok 73 E4	Croyde 8 C3	Cuevas de	Čumić 73 D3
Coursegoules 31 E3	Craonne 20 B3	Crevacuore 58 A4	Crni vrh Mt (Bosna	Croydon 9 F2	Altamira 35 F1	Cumnock 4 C3
Courseulles 18 C3	Craponne 29 F1	Crevalcore 60 C2	i Hercegovina) 71 D4	Crozant 25 E4	Cuevas de Artà 45 F3	Cunault 24 C2
Courson-les-	Crathes Castle 3 E4	Crèveccœur-	Črni vrh Mt	Crozon 22 A3	Cuevas de	Cuneo 31 E2
Carrières 26 A2	Crati 67 E2	le-Grand 19 E3	(Slovenija) 70 B1	Cruden Bay 3 E3	Canalobre 45 E1	Cunlhat 29 F1
Courtenay 26 A1	Crato 38 C3	Crevillente 45 D2	Crni vrh Mt	Crudgington 6 C3	Cuevas del Aguila 39 F2	Čunski 70 B4
Courthézon 30 C3	Craughwell 12 B4	Crewe 6 C3	(Srbija) 76 B1	Crumlin 13 E2	Cuevas del	Cuorgné 31 E1
Courtine, la 29 E1	Crau, la 31 D4	Crewkerne 9 D3	Črni vrh	Cruseilles 27 D4	Amanzora 44 C3	Cupar 5 D1
Courtomer 19 D4	Craven Arms 9 D1	Crianlarich 4 C1	(Slovenija) 70 A2	Crussol 30 B2	Cuevas del	Cupello 64 B2
Courtown 15 E3	Crawinkel 52 C3	Criccieth 6 A3	Crnivec 70 B2	Cruz 40 B3	Becerro 43 E3	Cupramontana 61 E4
Courtrai 50 A3	Crawley 10 C3	Crickhowell 9 D2	Crnjelovo Donje 72 B3	Cruzamento de	Cuevas del Campo 44 B2	Cuprija 73 E4
Courville 19 E4	Creag Meagaidh 2 C4	Cricklade 9 E2	Črnkovci 71 F2	Pegões 38 A4	Cuevas del Drac 45 F3	Cure 26 B2
Cousin 26 B2	Creagorry 2 A3	Crieff 4 C1	Crno jez 76 B2	Cruz da Légua 38 A3	Cuevas del Valle 39 F2	Cure, la 27 D3
Coussey 20 C4	Crécy 20 A2	Criel 19 E2	Črnomelj 70 B3	Cruz de Tejeda 42 β4	Cuevas de	Curia 38 B1
Coutainville 18 B3	Crécy-en-	Crikvenica 70 B3	Croagh Patrick 12 B3	Crven Grm 75 E2	San Clemente 35 F3	Currane, L 14 A4
Coutances 18 B3	Ponthieu 19 E2	Crimmitschau 53 D3	Croce dello Scrivano,	Crvenka 72 B2	Cuevas de	Curtea de Argeş 115 D1
Coutras 28 B2	Crécy-la-Chapelle 19 F4	Crinan 4 B2	Pso 64 C4	Crymmych 8 B1	San Marcos 43 F3	Curtis 34 B1
Couvertoirade, la 29 F3	Crediton 8 C3	Criquetot-	Croce Domini,	Csongrád 112 B4	Cuevas de	Čurug 72 C2
Couvin 50 C4	Creegh 12 B4	l'Esneval 19 D3	Pso di 58 C4	Csorna 112 A4	Valporquero 35 D2	C'urupinsk 113 F3
Couze 25 E4	Creeslough 12 C1	Crissolo 31 E2	Crocello, Pso di 64 C4	Cuacos 39 E2	Cuevas de	Cusano Mutri 64 B3
Cova da Iria 38 B3	Creglingen 55 E1	Crişu Alb 112 C4	Crocq 25 F4	Cualedro 34 B3	Vinromá 41 F2	Cushendall 13 E1
Covadonga 35 E1	Creil 19 F3	Crişu Negru 112 C4	Croisic, le 24 A2	Cuba 42 B1	Cuglieri 66 A3	Cushendun 13 E1
Covadonga, Pque	Crema 60 B1	Crişu Repede 112 C4	Croisière, la 25 E4	Cubel 36 C4	Cuijk 17 D3	Cusna, Mte 60 C3
Nac de la Sa de 35 E2	Crémieu 26 C4	Crivitz 48 C2	Croix de Fer,	Cucalón, Sa de 41 D1	Cuillin Sd 2 B4	Cusset 26 A4
Covarrubias 36 A3	Cremona 60 B2	Crkvice 76 A2	Col de la 31 D1	Cuckfield 10 C3	Cuillins, The 2 B3	Cutro 67 F3
Coventry 9 E1	Créon 28 B2	Crmljan 76 C2	Croix Haute,	Cudillero 35 D1	Cuiseaux 26 C3	Cuxhaven 47 F2
Covilhã 38 C2	Crepaja 73 D2	Črmošnjice 70 B2	Col de la 30 C2	Čudovo 111 D1	Cuisery 26 C3	Cvikov 53 F3
Cowbridge 8 C2	Crépy-en-Valois 19 F3	Črna 70 B1	Croix-Valmer, la 31 D4	Čudskoje Ozero 110 C1	Culan 25 F3	Čvrsnica 75 E1
Cowdenbeath 5 D2	Cres 70 B4	Crna Bara (Srbija) 72 B3	Crolly 12 C1	Cuéllar 35 F4	Culdaff 13 D1	Čvrstec 71 D2
Cowes 9 E3	Cres I 70 B4	Crna Bara	Cromarty 3 D3	Cuenca 40 C3	Culebra, Sa de la 34 C3	Cwmbrân 9 D2
Cowfold 10 C3	Crescentino 31 F1	(Vojvodina) 72 C1	Cromer 7 F3	Cuenca, Serr de 40 C3	Culemborg 16 C3	Cybinka 49 F4
Cozes 28 B1	Crespino 61 D2	Crnac (Hrvatska) 71 E2	Crook 5 E4	Cuenca, Serr de 40 C3	Cúllar Baza 44 B2	Cysoing 20 A1
Craco 65 D4	Crespo 30 C2	Crnac (Srbija) 76 C1	Croom 14 B3	Cuerda 41 D3	Cullen 3 E3	Czarnków 112 A1
Craigavon 13 E2	Cresta 58 B3	Crna Gora 76 B2	Cross Fell 5 D4	Cuerda del Pozo,	Cullera 41 E4	Czersk 110 A4
Craigellachie 3 D3	Cresta del Gallo 45 D2	Crna gora 77 E2	Cross Hands 8 C2	Emb de la 36 B3	Cullompton 8 C3	Częstochowa 112 B2
Craighouse 4 B2	Créteil 19 F4	Crna reka 77 E4	Crosshaven 14 C4	Cuers 31 D4	Culoz 27 D4	Człuchów 112 A1
Craigievar Castle 3 E4	Crêtes, Route des 27 E1	Crna Trava 77 E1	Crossmaglen 13 D3	Cuerva 40 A3	Culross 5 D2	
Craignure 4 B1	Creully 18 C3	Crnča 72 B4	Crossmolina 12 B2	Cueva de la Pileta 43 E4	Cumbernauld 4 C2	
Crail 5 D2	Creuse 25 E4	Crni Drim 77 D4	Crotone 67 F3	Cueva de la Vieja 41 D4	Cumbre Alta 39 F3	

D

	Daimuz 41 E4	Damgan 22 C4	Dasburg 51 D4	Dečani 76 C2	Delianuova 67 E4	Denizli 115 F4
	Dajt, Mal i 76 C4	Damianó 79 F2	Dasing 55 F3	Decazeville 29 E2	Deliblato 73 D2	Denkendorf 55 F2
Dabar 70 C3	Đakovica 76 C2	Dammartin-en-	Dassel 52 B2	Děčín 53 F3	Deliblatska	Dennington 11 D1
Dąbie 49 E2	Dakovo 71 F2	Goële 19 F3	Dassohóri 81 D2	Decize 26 A3	Peščara 73 D2	Denny 4 C2
Dabie, Jez 49 E2	Đala 72 C1	Damme 17 F2	Dassow 48 B2	Dedemsvaart 17 D2	Deliceto 64 C3	Den Oever 16 C1
Dabilje 77 F3	Dalälven 106 A3	Damnjane 76 C2	D'at'kovo 111 F3	Dee (Scotland) 3 D4	Delimedde 76 C1	Dent de Vaulion 27 D3
Dabo 21 E4	Dalane 104 A4	Dampierre 27 D2	Datteln 17 E3	Dee (Wales/Eng) 6 B3	Delitzsch 53 D2	De Panne 50 A3
Dachau 55 F3	Dalbeattie 4 C3	Dampierre-sur-	Daugava 110 C3	Degaña 34 C2	Delle 27 E2	Đeravica 76 C2
Dachsteingruppe 59 F1	Dalbosjön 105 E4	Salon 27 D2	Daugavpils 110 C3	Degebe, R 38 B4	Dellen, N 101 F3	Derby 6 C3
Dačice 57 E1	Dalby 109 D3	Damville 19 E4	Daun 51 E4	Degerfjärden 102 A2	Dellen, S 101 F3	Derbyshire 6 C3
Dadiá 81 F2	Dale (Hordaland) 104 A2	Damvillers 20 C3	Dava 3 D3	Degerfors 105 E4	Delme 21 D3	Der Chantecoq,
Dáfnes 86 C1	Dale (Sogn og	Dangé 25 D3	Davat 77 D4	Degerndorf 56 B4	Delmenhorst 47 F3	L du 20 C4
Dáfni (Limnos) 85 D1	Fjordane) 104 A1	Danilovgrad 76 B2	Daventry 9 E1	Deggendorf 56 B2	Delnice 70 B3	Đerdap, H.E. 73 F2
Dáfni (Makedonía) 80 C4	Dalen 104 B3	Dannemarie 27 E2	Davia 87 D2	Dego 31 F2	Delsbo 101 F3	Đerdap, Klisura 73 E3
Dáfni	Dalhem 109 F4	Dannenberg 48 B3	Davidovac 73 F2	Degracias 38 B2	Delta Dunării 113 E4	Derekoy 115 E2
(Pelopónissos) 86 C1	Dalías 44 B4	Dão, R 38 C1	Dávlia 83 F4	De Haan 50 A3	Delvin 13 D3	Derenburg 52 C1
Dáfni (Stereá	Daliburgh 2 A3	Daoulas 22 A3	Davor 71 E3	Dehesa de	Delvináki 82 B1	Derg, L (Clare) 12 C4
Eláda) 83 D4	Dalj 72 B2	Darda 71 F2	Davos 58 B2	Montejo 35 F2	Demanda, Sa de la 36 B2	Derg, L (Donegal) 12 C2
Dafní (Stereá	Dalkeith 5 D2	Dardesheim 52 C1	Dawlish 8 C3	Deià 45 E2	Demer 50 C3	Der Grabow 49 D1
Eláda) 87 F1	Dalkey 13 E4	Darfo Boario	Dax 28 A4	Deidesheim 54 C1	Demidov 111 E3	Dermatás, Akr 83 F1
Dáfnio 87 D3	Dalmally 4 C1	Terme 58 C4	Deädnu 95 E2	Deinze 50 B3	Demirci 115 F4	Dermbach 52 B3
Dafnónas	Dalmellington 4 C3	Dargilan,	Deal 11 D3	Deiva Marina 60 B3	Demir Kapija 77 F3	Derneburg 52 B1
(Stereá Eláda) 83 D3	Dalmine 60 B1	Grotte de 29 F3	Deauville 19 D3	Dej 112 C4	Demmin 49 D2	Derravaragh, L 13 D3
Dafnónas (Thráki) 80 C2	Dalry 4 C2	Dargun 49 D2	Deba 36 B1	Dejë, Mal 76 C3	Demoiselles,	Derrynasaggart
Dafnotí 82 C2	Dalsbruk 107 D3	Darlington 5 E4	Debar 77 D3	Deje 105 E3	Grotte des 29 F3	Mts 14 B4
Dafnoúdi, Akr 82 B4	Dalsfjorden 104 A1	Darłowo 110 A4	Debarska Banja	Delčevo 77 F2	Demonía 87 E4	Derryveagh Mts 12 C1
Dagali 104 C2	Dalsjöfors 109 D1	Darmstadt 54 C1	Banjišta 77 D3	Delden 17 D2	Denain 20 A1	Deruta 63 E1
Dagebüll 47 F1	Dals Långed 105 D4	Darney 27 D1	Debeli Lug 73 E3	Deleitosa 39 E3	Denbigh 6 B3	Dervaig 4 B1
Dagenham 10 C2	Dalton 6 B1	Daroca 36 C4	Debeli vrh 70 B2	Delémont 27 E2	Den Burg 16 C1	Derval 23 D4
Dahlen 53 E2	Daluis, Gorges de 31 E3	Darque 34 A3	Debeljača 72 C2	Deleitosa 39 E3	Dendermonde 50 B3	Dervéni 87 D1
Dahlenburg 48 B3	Dalvík 96 B1	Darß 48 C1	Dębica 112 B2	Deléria 83 E1	Dendre 50 B4	Derventa 71 E3
Dahme (D) 48 B2	Dalwhinnie 2 C4	Dartford 10 C2	Dęblin 112 C2	Delet Teili 106 C3	Dendrohóri 79 D3	Dervíziana 82 B2
Dahme (DDR) 53 E1	Damaskiniá 79 D3	Dartmoor Nat Pk 8 C3	Dębno 49 F3	Delfi 83 E4	Denekamp 17 E2	Derwent (Derbys) 6 C3
Dahme R 53 E1	Damássi 83 E1	Dartmouth 8 C4	Debrc 72 C3	Delft 16 B3	Den Haag 16 B3	Derwent (Durham) 5 E4
Dahn 54 B2	Damazan 28 C3	Daruvar 71 E2	Debrecen 112 C4	Delfzijl 47 D3	Den Helder 16 C1	Derwent (Yorks) 7 D1
Daimiel 40 A4	Damelevières 21 D4	Darwen 6 C2	Delia 68 C4	Denia 45 E1	Derwent Water 5 D4

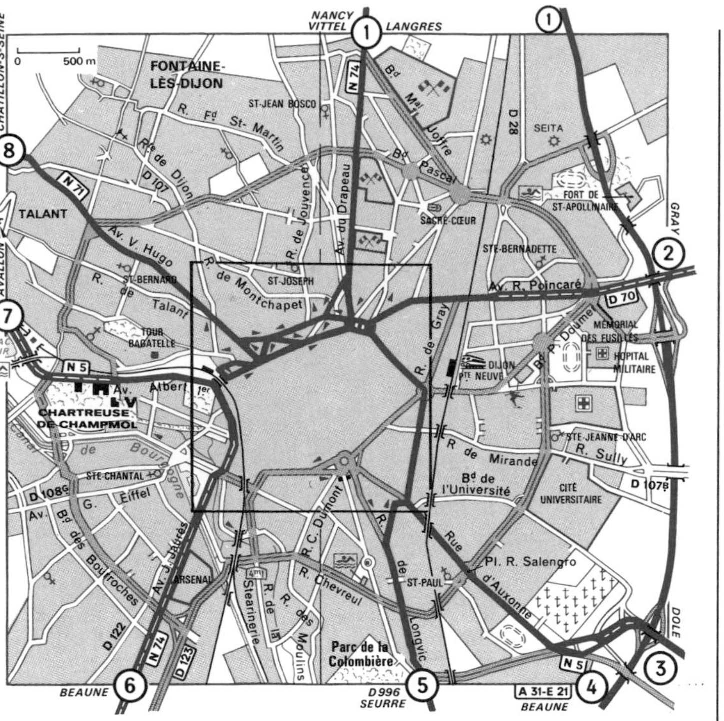
NANCY VITTEL
LANGRES
TROYES CHÂTILLON-S-SEINE
A 38 : MOULINS AVALLON
GRAY
DOLE
BEAUNE
D 996 SEURRE
A 31-E 21 BEAUNE
500 m
FONTAINE-LÈS-DIJON
TALANT
ST-JEAN BOSCO
SEITA
FORT DE ST-APOLLINAIRE
SACRÉ-CŒUR
ST-BERNADETTE
ST-JOSEPH
TOUR BARATELLE
MÉMORIAL DES FUSILLÉS
HÔPITAL MILITAIRE
DIJON PTE NEUVE
CHARTREUSE DE CHAMPMOL
STE-JEANNE-D'ARC
STE-CHANTAL
CITÉ UNIVERSITAIRE
Bd de l'Université
Pl. R. Salengro
ST-PAUL
ARSENAL
Parc de la Colombière
Av. R. Poincaré
R. de Mirande
R. Sully
Av. du Drapeau
Bd Pascal
N 71
N 74
N 5
D 70
D 107
D 108
D 122
D 123
D 107B
D 28
Av. V. Hugo
Av. Albert 1er
Bd des Bourroches
Av. J. Jaurès
Rue d'Auxonne
R. Chevreul
R. des Moulins
R. de Stalingrad

Dijon

Desborough 9 F1
Descartes 25 D3
Desenzano 60 B1
Desertas 42 A3
Desfiladero de Despeñaperros 44 A1
Desfiladero de la Hermida 35 F2
Desfiladero de los Beyos 35 E2
Desfiladero del Teverga 35 D2
Desfina 83 E4
Desimirovac 73 D4
Desio 60 A1
Deskáti 83 D1
Desna 111 F3
Despotikó, N 88 B3
Despotovac 73 E3
Despotovo 72 B2
Dessau 53 D1
Destriana 35 D3
Desulo 66 B3
Desvres 19 E1
Deta 114 C1
Đetinja 72 C4
Detmold 52 A1
Dettelbach 55 E1
Dettifoss 96 C1
Deurne 17 D3
Deutsche Alpenstraße 55 E4
Deutsche Bucht 47 E2
Deutschkreutz 57 F3
Deutschlandsberg 70 B1
Deutsch-Wagram 57 F2
Deux-Alpes, les 31 D2
Deux-Sèvres 24 C3
Deva 114 C1
Deve Bair 77 E2
Deventer 17 D2
Deveron 3 E3
Devetak 72 B4
Devil's Bridge 8 C1
Devil's Elbow 3 D4
Devizes 9 E2
Devnja 115 E2
Dewsbury 6 C2
Deza 36 C4
Diablerets, les 27 E3
Diablerets, les *Mt* 27 E3
Diafáni 93 D2
Diakoftó 86 C1
Diamante 67 E2
Día, N 91 E3
Diano Marina 31 F3
Diápora Nissiá 87 E1
Diavatá 79 F3
Díavlos Alonissou 84 B2
Díavlos Oreón 83 F3
Díavlos Pelagonissou 84 B2
Díavlos Skiáthou 84 A2
Díavlos Skopélou 84 A2
Díavlos Trikeríou 83 F3
Díavlos Zákinthou 86 A1
Diavolítsi 86 C3
Diavolo, Pso del 64 A2
Diavolórema 81 E2
Dibbersen 48 A3
Dicmo 75 D1
Dicomano 61 D3
Dídima 87 E2
Dídimo, Óros 87 E2
Didimótiho 81 F1
Die 30 C2
Dieburg 52 A4
Diedorf 52 B2
Diego Alvaro 39 E2
Diekirch 21 D2
Diemel 52 A2
Diemelstadt 52 A2
Diepholz 17 F2
Dieppe 19 E2
Dierdorf 51 E4
Dieren 17 D3
Diesdorf 48 B4
Dießen 56 A3
Diest 50 C3
Dietenheim 55 E3
Dietfurt 55 F2
Dietikon 27 F2
Dietmannsried 55 E4
Dieulefit 30 C2
Dieulouard 21 D4
Dieuze 21 D4
Diez 51 F4
Diezma 44 A3
Differdange 21 D3
Digerkampen 100 B3
Digermulen 94 A4
Dignano 59 E3
Digne 31 D3
Digoin 26 B3
Dijle 50 C3
Dijon 26 C2
Dikanäs 97 F3
Díkea 81 F1
Díkela 81 E2
Diksmuide 50 A3
Diktéo Ándro 91 E4
Diktinéon 90 B3
Díkti, Óros 91 E4
Dílessi 84 B4
Dilináta 82 B4
Dilj 71 E2
Dillenburg 51 F3
Dillingen (Bayern) 55 E2
Dillingen (Saarland) 54 A2
Dílofos 81 F1
Dílos 88 C2
Dílos, N 88 C2
Dímena 87 E2
Dímitra 83 E1
Dimitrítsi 80 B2
Dimitrovgrad (BG) 115 D3
Dimitrovgrad (YU) 77 F1
Dimitsána 86 C2
Dinami 67 E4
Dinan 18 B4
Dinant 50 C4
Dinar 115 F4
Dinara *Mt* 75 D1
Dinara (Reg) 75 D1
Dinard 18 B4
Dinbych 6 B3
Dinbych-y-pysgod 8 B2
Dingelstädt 52 B2
Dingle 14 A3
Dingle 105 D4
Dingle (Reg) 14 A3
Dingle B 14 A3
Dingli 68 B4
Dinglingen 54 C3
Dingolfing 56 B2
Dingwall 2 C3
Dinjiška 70 C4
Dinkelsbühl 55 E2
Dinklage 17 F2
Dinslaken 17 D3
Dío 79 F4
Diónissos 87 F1
Dióriga Korínthou 87 E1
Dipótama 80 C1
Dippoldiswalde 53 E2
Diráhio 86 C3
Dírfis, Óros 84 B3
Disentis 58 A3
Disgrazia, Mte 58 B3
Dispílio 79 D3
Diss 11 D1
Dissen 17 F2
Dístomo 83 E4
Dístos 84 B4
Ditikí Rodópi 80 C1
Dittaino 69 D3
Ditzingen 55 D2
Divača 70 A3
Divaráta 82 B4
Divčibare 72 C4
Dives 18 C3
Dives *R* 18 C3
Divič 72 B4
Divjakë 76 C4
Divljana 77 E1
Divonne 27 D3
Divor, Bgem do 38 B4
Divor, Rib de 38 B4
Divoúnia, Ni 92 C2
Dívri 83 E3
Divuša 71 D3
Djupini 96 A3
Djupvik 94 C2
Djurås 105 F2
Djursland 108 B2
Dmitrov 111 F2
Dnepr 111 E3
Dneprodzeržinskoje Vodochranilišče 113 F2
Dneprovskij Liman 113 F3
Dnestr 112 C3
Dnestrovskij Liman 113 F4
Dno 111 D2
Dobanovci 72 C3
Dobbiaco 59 E2
Dobel 54 C2
Dobele 110 C3
Döbeln 53 E2
Doberlug-Kirchhain 53 E1
Döbern 53 F1
Dobersberg 57 E1
Dobieszczyn 49 E2
Doboj 71 F3
Dobošnica 71 F3
Dobra (PL) 49 F2
Dobra (YU) 73 E3
Dobra *R* 70 C3
Dobra Voda 73 D4
Dobra Voda *Mt* 77 D3
Dobrašinci 77 F3
Dobratsch 59 F2
Dobrčane 77 D2
Döbriach 59 F2
Dobrica 73 D2
Dobričevo 73 D2
Dobri Do 77 D1
Dobrinj 70 B3
Dobříš 53 F4
Dobrljin 71 D3
Dobrna 70 B1
Dobromani 75 F2
Dobro Polje 76 A1
Dobrovnik 70 C1
Dobrun 72 C4
Dobruš 111 E4
Dobruševo 77 E4
Dobrzany 49 F2
Dobšiná 112 B3
Docksta 102 A2
Doc Penfro 8 B2
Dodekánissa 89 E3
Dodóni 82 B1
Doesburg 17 D3
Doetinchem 17 D3
Doganović 77 D2
Dogliani 31 F2
Doïráni 79 F2
Doïránis, L 79 F2
Doiras, Emb de 34 C1
Dojransko Ez 77 F3
Dokanj 72 B3
Dokka 104 C2
Dokkum 47 D3
Dokós, N 87 E3
Doksy 53 F3
Dolac 76 C2
Dol-de-Bretagne 18 B4
Dole 26 C2
Dôle, la 27 D3
Dølemo 104 B4
Dolenci 77 D4
Dolenja Vas 70 B2
Dolenjske Toplice 70 B2
Dolga Vas 71 D1
Dolgellau 6 A3
Dolianá 78 C4
Dolianova 66 B4
Dolíhi 79 E4
Dolina 112 C3
Doljani 71 D4
Doljevac 77 D1
Dolla 12 C4
Döllach 59 E2
Dollar 5 D2
Dolle 48 C4
Dolní Dvořiště 57 D2
Dolno Kosovrasti 77 D3
Dolo 61 D1
Dolomiti 59 D3
Dolores 45 D2
Dolovo 73 D2
Dol Poustevna 53 F2
Domaševo 75 F2
Domažlice 56 B1
Dombås 100 B3
Dombasle 21 D4
Dombóvár 114 B1
Domburg 16 B3
Domène 30 C1
Doméniko 83 E1
Domèvre-en-Haye 21 D4
Domfront 18 C4
Dömitz 48 C3
Domme 29 D2
Dommitzsch 53 D2
Domnista 83 D3
Domodossola 58 A4
Domokós 83 E2
Dompaire 27 D1
Dompierre 26 B3
Domrémy 20 C4
Domusnovas 66 B4
Domžale 70 B2
Don (England) 7 D2
Don (Scotland) 3 E4
Donaghadee 13 E2
Doña María Ocaña 44 B3
Doña Mencía 43 F2
Doñana, Parque Nac de 43 D3
Donau 56 C2
Donaueschingen 54 C4
Donauwörth 55 E2
Donawitz 57 E4
Don Benito 39 E4
Doncaster 7 D2
Donegal 12 C2
Donegal B 12 C2
Donegal (Co) 12 C1
Dongen 16 C3
Donges 23 D4
Donington 7 E3
Donja Bebrina 71 F3
Donja Brela 75 E2
Donja Brezna 76 B2
Donja Bukovica 76 B2
Donja Kamenica 72 C3
Donja Šatornja 73 D3
Donje Crniljevo 72 C3
Donje Dragovlje 77 E1
Donje Ljupče 77 D2
Donji Andrijevci 71 F3
Donji Barbeš 77 E1
Donji Kanzanci 75 D1
Donji Lapac 71 D4
Donji Malovan 75 E1
Donji Miholjac 71 E2
Donji Milanovac 73 E3
Donji Ruzani 75 D1
Donji Seget 75 D2
Donji Vakuf 71 E4
Donji Vijačani 71 E3
Donji Zemunik 74 C1
Donjon, le 26 B3
Dønna 97 D3
Donnemarie-Dontilly 20 A4
Donnersbachwald 57 D4
Dønnes 97 D2
Donon 21 E4
Donon, Col du 21 E4
Donostia-San Sebastián 36 C1
Donoússa, N 89 D3
Donzenac 29 D2
Donzère 30 B2
Donzy 26 A2
Doorn 16 C3
Doornik 50 A4
Dora Baltéa 27 E4
Dora Riparia 31 E1
Dorat, le 25 D4
Đorče Petrov 77 D3
Dorchester 9 D3
Dordives 25 F1
Dordogne 29 E1
Dordogne (Dépt) 28 C2
Dordogne *R* 28 B2
Dordrecht 16 C3
Dore 29 F1
Dorfen 56 B3
Dorfmark 48 A4
Dorgali 66 C2
Dório 86 C3
Dorkáda 80 A2
Dorking 10 C3
Dormagen 17 E4
Dormans 20 A3
Dornbirn 58 B2
Dornburg 52 C3
Dorndorf 52 B3
Dornes 26 A3
Dornie 2 B3
Dornoch 3 D3
Dornoch Firth 3 D3
Dornstetten 54 C3
Dornum 47 E3
Dorog 112 B4
Dorogobuž 111 E3
Dorohoi 113 D3
Dorotea 101 F1
Dörpstedt 48 A1
Dorset 9 D3
Dorsten 17 E3
Dortan 27 D3
Dortmund 17 E3
Dortmund-Ems-Kanal 17 E2
Dorum 47 F3
Dörzbach 55 D1
Dosbarrios 40 B3
Dos Hermanas 43 D3
Dosse 49 D3
Douai 19 F2
Douarnenez 22 A3
Doubs 26 C3
Doubs (Dépt) 27 D2
Doucier 27 D3
Doudeville 19 D2
Doué 24 C2
Douglas (I of Man) 6 A1
Douglas (Scotland) 4 C2
Doukáto, Akr 82 B3
Doulaincourt 20 C4
Doulevant-le-Château 20 C4
Doullens 19 F2
Doulus Head 14 A4
Doune 4 C2
Doupov 53 E3
Dourdan 19 E4
Dourgne 32 A1
Douro 34 A4
Douro, R 34 A4
Douvaine 27 D3
Douve 18 B3
Douvres 18 C3
Dover 11 D3
Dover, Str of 11 D3
Dovre 100 C3
Dovrefjell 100 C3
Dovsk 111 E4
Down 13 E2
Downham Market 10 C1
Downpatrick 13 E2
Dowra 12 C2
Doxarás 83 E2
Doxáto 80 C2
Dozulé 19 D3
Drac 30 C2
Dračevo 77 E3
Drachten 17 D1
Drag 94 A4
Dragalovci 71 E3
Dragaš 77 D3
Drăgăşani 115 D1
Dragaši 76 B1
Draginac 72 C3
Draginje 72 C3
Dragočaj 71 E3
Dragocvet 73 D4
Dragoevo 77 E3
Dragoman 114 C2
Dragonera, I 45 E3
Dragoni 64 B3
Dragør 108 C3
Dragoš 77 E4
Dragotiná 82 A2
Dragović 71 E2
Dragovića Polje 76 B2
Dragozetići 70 B3
Dragsfjärd 107 D3
Dragsvik 100 A3
Draguignan 31 D4
Dráma 80 C2
Dráma (Nomos) 80 C1
Drammen 104 C3
Drammen selva 104 C3
Drangajökull 96 A1
Drangedal 104 C3
Dranske 49 D1
Drápano, Akr 90 C3
Drasenhofen 57 F1
Drau 59 F2
Dráva 71 E2
Dravograd 70 B1
Drawno 49 F2
Drawsko Pomorskie 112 A1
Draženov 56 B1
Draževac 72 C3
Drebkau 53 F1
Drenewydd 9 D1
Drenovac 77 E2
Drenovci 72 B3
Drenovo 77 E3
Drenthe 17 D1
Drépano (Makedonía) 79 E3
Drépano (Pelopónissos) 87 E2
Drépano, Akr (Anáfi) 91 E1
Drépano, Akr (Makedonía) 80 B4
Dresden 53 E2
Dreux 19 E4
Drežnik-Grad 70 C3
Driebergen 16 C3
Driebes 40 B2
Driméa 83 E3
Drimós 79 F3
Drin 76 C3
Drina 76 A1
Drini i Zi 77 D3
Drinit, Gjiri i 76 B3
Drinjača 72 B4
Drinjača *R* 72 B4
Drinovci 75 E2
Driopída 88 A2
Driós 88 C3
Drisht 76 C3
Driva 100 B2
Drlače 72 C4
Drnholec 57 F1
Drniš 75 D1
Drnje 71 D1
Drnovo 70 C2
Drøbak 105 D3
Drobeta-Turnu Severin 114 C1
Drochtersen 48 A2
Drogheda 13 D3
Drogobyč 112 C3
Droichead Átha 13 D3
Droichead Nua 13 D4
Droitwich 9 E1
Drokija 113 E3
Dromcolliher 14 B3
Drôme (Dépt) 30 C2
Drôme *R* 30 C2
Dromore (Down) 13 E2
Dromore (Tyrone) 13 D2
Dronero 31 E2
Dronfield 7 D2
Drongaráti 82 B4
Dronne 28 C1
Dronninglund 108 B2
Dronten 16 C2
Drosendorf Stadt 57 E1
Drossáto 79 F2
Drosseró 79 E2
Drossiá 84 A4
Drossohóri 83 E4
Drossopigí (Árta) 82 C2
Drossopigí (Ioánina) 78 C4
Drossopigí (Makedonía) 79 D3
Drottningholm 106 B4
Droué 25 E1
Drulingen 21 E3

DUBLIN / BAILE ÁTHA CLIATH

1/120 000

Drumkeeran	12 C2	Dubrave Donje	72 B3	Dulovo	115 E2		
Drummore	4 B4	Dubravica	73 D3	Dumbarton	4 C2		
Drumnadrochit	2 C3	Dubrovnik	76 A2	Dumbria	34 A1		
Drumochter,		Ducey	18 B4	Dumfries	4 C3		
Pass of	2 C4	Ducherow	49 E2	Dumfries and			
Drumshanbo	12 C2	Duchkov	53 E3	Galloway	4 C3		
Drusenheim	21 F4	Duchovščina	111 E3	Dun	20 C3		
Druskininkai	110 C4	Duclair	19 D3	Dunaföldvár	112 B4		
Druten	16 C3	Dudelange	21 D3	Dunajevcy	113 D3		
Drvenik (Hrvatska)	75 D2	Duderstadt	52 B2	Dunárea	113 E4		
Drvenik (Hrvatska)	75 E2	Dudley	9 E1	Dunaújváros	112 B4		
Dryburgh	5 D3	Dudweiler	54 B2	Dunav	72 B2		
Drymen	4 C2	Dueñas	35 E4	Dunav	114 D2		
Duben	53 E1	Duero, R	35 D4	Dunbar	5 E2		
Dubi	53 E3	Duesund	104 A1	Dunblane	4 C2		
Dubica	71 D3	Dufftown	3 D3	Duncansby Head	3 E2		
Dublin	13 E4	Duga Poljana	76 C1	Dundalk	13 D3		
Dublin (Co)	13 D4	Duga Resa	70 C3	Dundalk B	13 E3		
Dubna	111 F2	Dugi Otok	74 C1	Dun Dealgan	13 D3		
Dubňany	57 F1	Dugi Rat	75 D2	Dundee	5 D1		
Dubno	113 D2	Dugo Selo	70 C2	Dundonnell	2 C3		
Dubona	73 D3	Duingt	27 D4	Dundrum B	13 E2		
Dubossary	113 E3	Duino	59 F3	Dunfanaghy	12 C1		
Duboštica	71 F4	Duisburg	17 D3	Dunfermline	5 D2		
Dubovac	73 D2	Dukagjin	76 C2	Dungannon	13 D2		
Dubovsko	71 D4	Dukat	77 E2	Dún Garbhán	14 C4		
Dubráva		Duleek	13 D3	Dungarvan	14 C4		
(Hrvatska)	71 D2	Dulje	77 D2	Dungarvan			
Dubrava (Pelješac)	75 D2	Dülken	17 D4	Harbour	14 C4		
Dubrava Stara	71 E3	Dülmen	17 E3	Dungeness	11 D3		
Dubrave	71 F3	Dulnain Bridge	3 D4	Dungiven	13 D1		

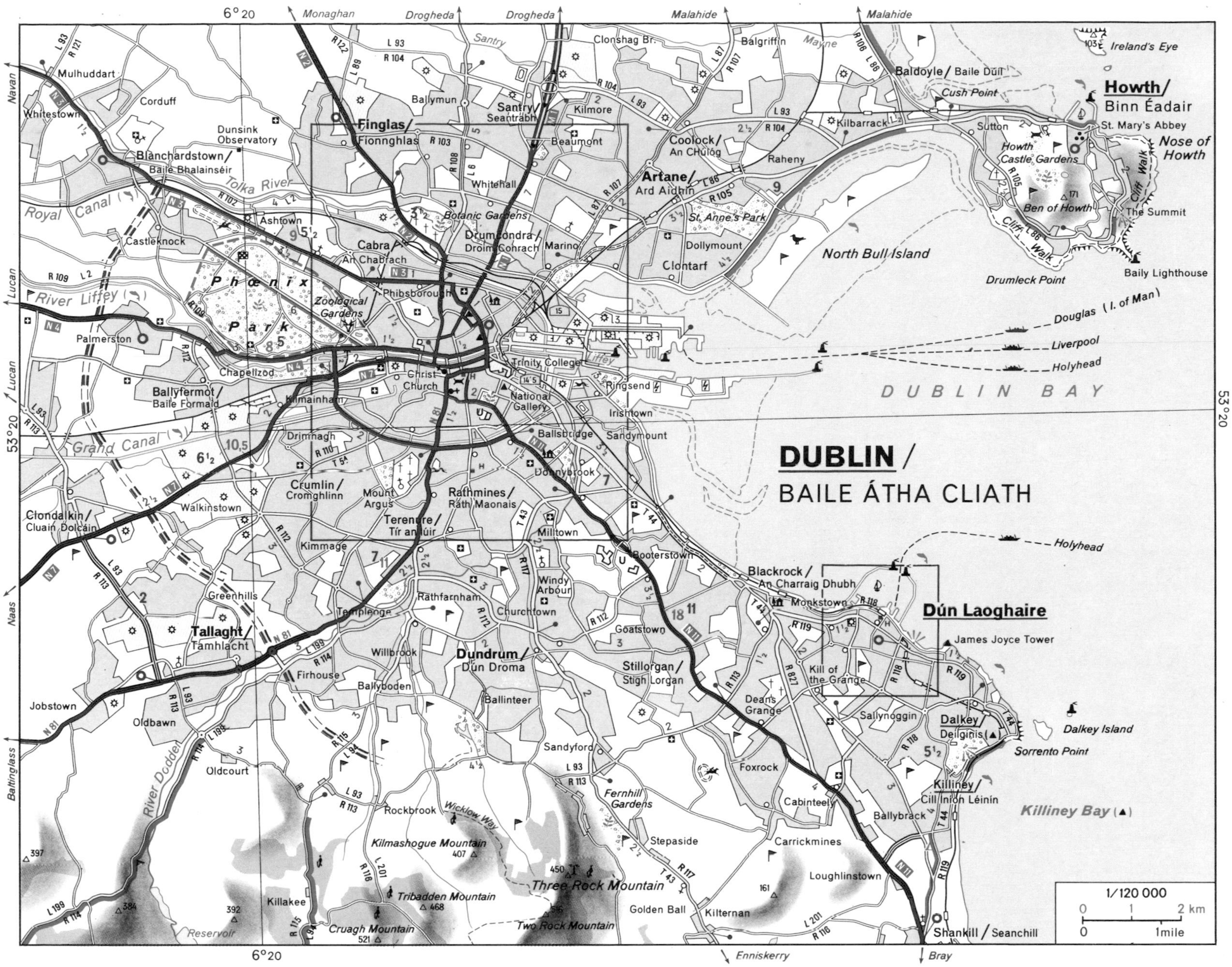

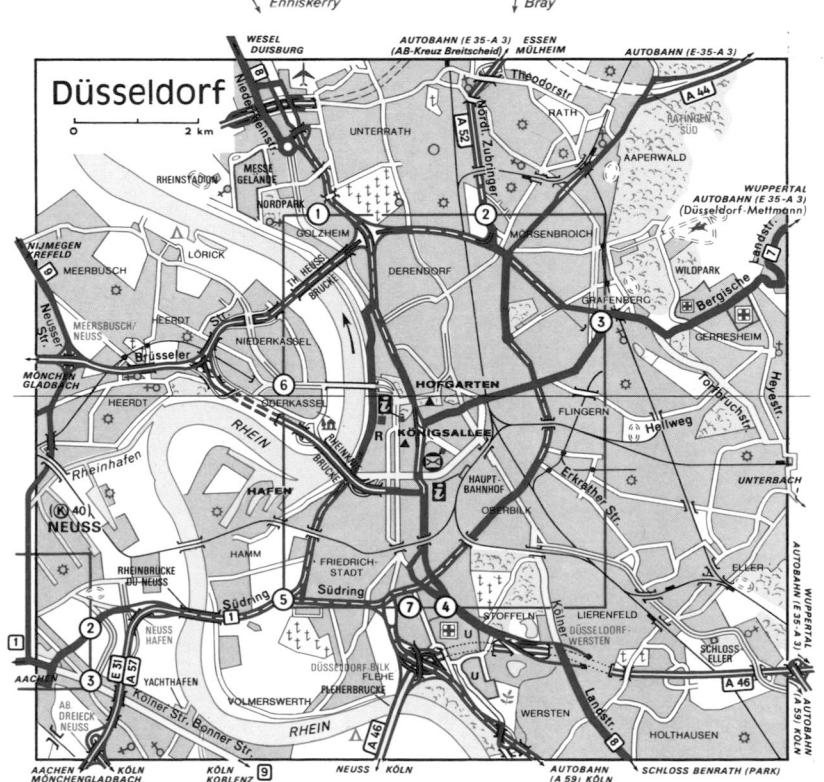

Düsseldorf

Dunglow	12 C1	Dún na nGall	12 C2	Đuolbbadasgai'sa	95 E1	Đurđevića Tara	76 B1	Dürnstein	57 E2	Duved	101 D2	Dyrøya	94 B3
Dunje	77 E4	Dunnet	3 D2	Đurakovac	76 C2	Durdevik	72 B4	Durrës	76 C4	Duvno	75 E1	Džami tepe	77 F3
Dunkeld	5 D1	Dunnet Head	3 D2	Durance	30 C3	Düren	51 D3	Durrësit, Gjiri i	76 C4	Duži (Bosna		Džanići	75 F1
Dunkerque	19 F1	Dunoon	4 C2	Durango	36 B1	Durham	5 E4	Durrow	12 C4	i Hercegovina)	75 F2	Džep	77 E1
Dún Laoghaire	13 E4	Duns	5 E2	Duran, Pso	59 D3	Durham (Co)	5 E4	Dursey I	14 A4	Duži (Bosna		Dzermiádo	91 E4
Dun-le-Palestel	25 E4	Dunshaughlin	13 D3	Duratón, R	40 A1	Durlach	54 C2	Dursley	9 D2	i Hercegovina)	76 A2	Dzeržinsk	111 D4
Dunmanus B	14 A4	Dunstable	9 F2	Durban-Corbières	32 B2	Durlas	14 C3	Durtal	23 E4	Dverberg	94 A3	Dzierżoniów	112 A2
Dunmanway	14 B4	Dunster	8 C3	Durbuy	50 C4	Durmanec	70 C2	Duruelo de la		Dvor	71 D3	Dziwnw	49 E1
Dunmore	12 B3	Dun-sur-Auron	25 F3	Dúrcal	44 A3	Durmitor	76 B2	Sierra	36 B3	Dyfed	8 C1	Džumajlija	77 E3
Dunmore East	15 D4	Dunvegan	2 B3	Durness	2 C2	Dusina	75 F1	Dyje	57 E1	Dźwirzyno	49 E1
Dunnamanagh	13 D1	Dunvegan Head	2 B3	Đurđđevac	71 D2	Dürnkrut	57 F2	Düsseldorf	17 E4	Dyrnes	100 B1	

E

		Eberbach	55 D1	Echternach	21 D2	Eder	52 A3	Efxinoúpoli	83 F2	Eisenhüttenstadt	49 F4	El Cubo de Tierra del
		Ebermannstadt	52 C4	Écija	43 E2	Eder-Stausee	52 A3	Egadi, Is	68 A3	Eisenkappel	70 A1	Vino	39 E1
Eaglescliffe	5 E4	Ebern	52 C4	Ečka	72 C2	Édessa	79 E3	Ega, R	36 C2	Eisenstadt	57 F3	El Cuervo	43 D3
Eani	79 D4	Eberndorf	70 B1	Eckartsberga	52 C2	Edewecht	47 E3	Egeln	52 C1	Eisfeld	52 C3	Elda	45 D1
Earith	10 C1	Ebersbach	53 F2	Eckernförde	48 A1	Edgeworthstown	12 C3	Egéo Pélagos	84 A1	Eišiškes	110 C4	Elde	48 C3
Earlston	5 D2	Ebersberg	56 B3	Eckerö	106 C3	Edinburgh	5 D2	Eger	112 B3	Eisleben	52 C2	Eldena	48 C3
Earn	5 D1	Eberstein	70 B1	Ecommoy	23 F4	Edipsós	83 F3	Egersund	104 A4	Eislingen	55 D2	Elefsína	87 F1
Easingwold	7 D1	Eberswalde	49 E3	Ecos	19 E3	Edirne	115 E3	Egeskov	108 B4	Eisriesenwelt-		Eleftherés
Easky	12 B2	Ebmath	53 D3	Ecouché	18 C4	Edland	104 B3	Egestorf	48 A3	Höhle	59 E1	(Makedonía)	80 C2
Eastbourne	10 C3	Eboli	64 C4	Ecrins, les	31 D2	Edolo	58 C3	Egg	58 B1	Eitorf	51 E3	Eleftherés
East Dereham	7 F3	Ebrach	52 C4	Ecrins, Massif des	31 D2	Edremit	115 E4	Eggenburg	57 E2	Eivissa	45 D4	(Stereá Eláda)	87 E1
Easter Ross	2 C3	Ebreichsdorf	57 F3	Ecrins,		Edsåsdalen	101 D2	Eggenfelden	56 B2	Ejea de los		Eleftherés
East Grinstead	10 C3	Ebreuil	26 A4	Parc Nat des	31 D2	Edsbro	106 B3	Eggesin	49 E2	Caballeros	37 D3	(Thessalía)	83 E1
East Kilbride	4 C2	Ebro, Emb del	35 F2	Ecueillé	25 E3	Edsbyn	101 E3	Eggum	94 A3	Ejulve	41 E2	Eléfthero	78 C4
Eastleigh	9 E3	Ebro, R	37 D4	Ed	105 D4	Edsele	101 F2	Eghezée	50 C4	Ekára	83 E2	Eleftherohóri	79 D4
East Linton	5 D2	Ebstorf	48 B3	Eda glasbruk	105 D3	Eeklo	50 B3	Egiáli	89 D3	Ekenäs	107 E3	Eleftheroúpoli	80 C2
East Retford	7 D2	Eccleshall	6 C3	Edam	16 C2	Eelde	47 D3	Egie	87 D4	Ekshärad	105 E3	El Ejido	44 B4
East Sussex	10 C3	Eceabat	115 E3	Edane	105 E3	Eemshaven	47 D3	Egilsstadir	96 C2	Eksjö	109 D1	Elemir	72 C2
Eaux-Bonnes	37 D2	Echallens	27 D3	Eday	3 E1	Eferding	56 C2	Égina	87 E2	Elafohóri	81 F1	Elena	115 D2
Eauze	28 B3	Echarmeaux, les	26 B4	Eddrachillis B	2 C1	Efes	115 E4	Égina, N	87 E2	Elafónissi	87 E4	Eleófito	82 C3
Ebbw Vale	9 D2	Echarri-Aranaz	36 C2	Ede	16 C3	Efira	86 B1	Egínio	79 F3	Elafos	82 B2	Eleohóri	80 C3
Ebeleben	52 C2	Echegárate,		Edelény	112 B3	Efkarpía		Égio	83 E4	El Algar	45 D2	Eleohória	80 A3
Ebeltoft	108 B3	Pto de	36 B1	Edelweißspitze	59 E2	(Makedonía)	79 F2	Égira	87 D1	El Almendro	42 C2	Eleónas	83 E4
Eben	59 F1	Echelles, les	30 C1	Eden	5 D4	Efkarpía		Egletons	29 D1	El Aquián	44 B4	Eleoússa	93 F1
Ebenfurth	57 F3	Echt	17 D4	Edenderry	13 D4	(Makedonía)	80 B2	Eglinton	13 D1	El Arahal	43 E3	El Escorial	40 A2
Ebensee	56 C3	Echte	52 B2	Edenkoben	54 C2	Eforie	115 E1	Egloffstein	55 F1	El Arenal	45 E3	El Espinar	40 A2
								Egmond aan Zee	16 C2	Elassóna	83 E1	El Figueró	32 B4
								Egósthena	87 E1	El Atazar, Emb de	40 B1	El Formigal	37 D2
								Egremont	5 D4	Eláti (Makedonía)	79 E4	Elgå	100 D3
								Egtved	108 A3	Eláti (Thessalía)	83 D2	Elgin	3 D3
								Egüés	36 C2	Eláti Mt	82 B3	Elgóibar	36 B1
								Eguzon	25 E3	Elátia	83 F3	Elgol	2 B4
								Ehinádes Nissiá	82 C4	Elatohóri	79 E3	El Grado	37 E3
								Ehingen	55 D3	Elatoú	83 D4	El Grado, Emb de	37 E3
								Ehinos	81 D2	Elatóvrissi	83 D3	El Grao	41 E4
								Ehra-Lessien	48 B4	Elba, Isola d'	62 C4	El Grau	41 F3
								Ehrang-Pfalzel	54 A1	El Barco de Ávila	39 E2	Elhovo	115 E2
								Ehrenberg	52 B3	Elbasan	76 C4	El Hoyo de Pinares	40 A2
								Ehrenhausen	70 C1	Elbe	48 B3	Eliá	87 D4
								Ehrwald	58 C1	Elbe-Lübeck-Kanal	48 B2	Elie	5 D2
								Eibar	36 B1	El Berrón	35 D1	Elikónas, Óros	83 F4
								Eibenstock	53 D3	Elbe-Seitenkanal	48 B4	Elimäki	107 F2
								Eibiswald	70 B1	Elbeuf	19 D3	Eliniká	86 C2
								Eichstätt	55 F2	Elbigenalp	58 C1	Elinohóri	81 F1
								Eide	100 B2	Elbingerode	52 C2	Elizondo	36 C1
								Eider	48 A2	Elblag	110 B4	Elk	110 C4
								Eidfjord	104 B2	El Bodón	39 D2	Ellesmere	6 B3
								Eidfjorden	104 B2	El Bonillo	40 C4	Ellesmere Port	6 B2
								Eiði	96 A3	El Bosque	43 E3	Ellingen	55 E2
								Eidkjosen	94 B2	Elburg	17 D2	Ellon	3 E4
								Eidsborg	104 B3	El Burgo	43 E3	Ellös	108 C1
								Eidsbugarden	100 B3	El Burgo de Osma	36 A3	Ellrich	52 B2
								Eidsdal	100 B2	El Burgo Ranero	35 E3	Ellwangen	55 E2
								Eidsfjorden	94 A3	El Cabaco	39 E2	El Madroño	42 C2
								Eidsfoss	104 C3	El Caló	45 D4	El Maestrazgo	41 E2
								Eidsvåg	100 B2	El Campo de		Elmas	66 B4
								Eidsvoll	105 D2	Peñaranda	39 F1	El Masnou	32 B4
								Eigg	2 B4	El Carpio	43 F2	El Molar	40 B2
								Eikelandsosen	104 A2	El Carpio de Tajo	39 F3	El Molinillo	40 A3
								Eiken	104 B3	El Casar de		El Moral	44 C2
								Eikeren	104 C3	Talamanca	40 B2	Elmshorn	48 A2
								Eikesdal	100 B2	El Castillo de las		Elne	32 B2
								Eilean Donan Castle	2 B3	Guardas	43 D2	Elnesvågen	100 B2
								Eilenburg	53 D2	El Centenillo	44 A1	Elóna	87 D3
								Eilsleben	52 C1	El Cerro de		Elopía	83 F4
								Einbeck	52 B2	Andévalo	42 C2	Elorn	22 B2
								Eindhoven	16 C4	Elche	45 D2	Élos (Kríti)	90 B3
								Einsiedeln	58 A2	Elche de la Sierra	44 C1	Élos
								Eisenach	52 B3	El Coronil	43 D3	(Pelopónnisos)	87 D4
								Eisenberg	53 D3	El Cubillo	41 D3	Eloúnda	91 E3
								Eisenerz	57 D3	El Cubo de		Eloyes	27 D1
								Eisenerzer Alpen	57 D4	Don Sancho	39 D1	El Pardo	40 A2

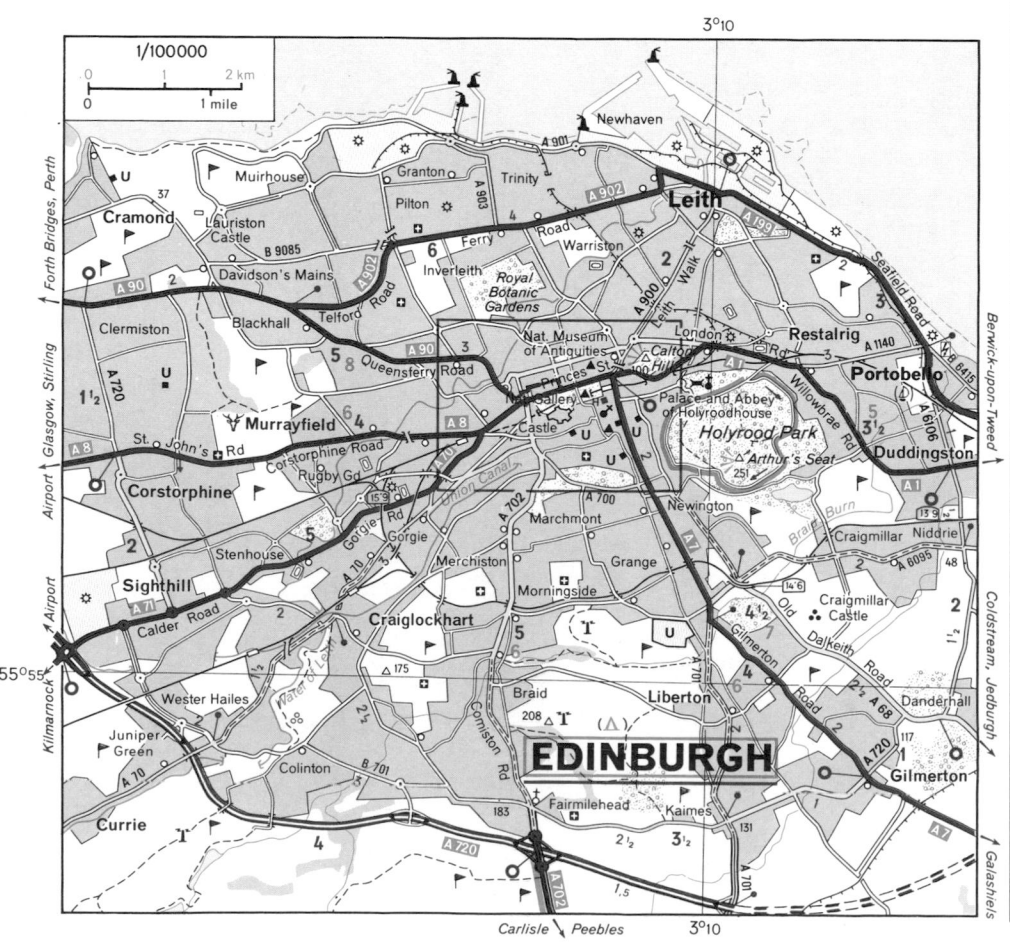

El Paular 40 A1
El Pedernoso 40 B3
El Pedroso 43 D2
El Perelló (Catalunya) 41 F2
El Perelló (Valencia) 41 E4
Elphin 12 C3
El Picazo 40 C4
El Pinell de Brai 41 F1
El Pobo de Dueñas 41 D2
El Pont d'Armentera 37 F4
El Portal 43 D4
El Port de la Selva 32 C3
El Port de Llança 32 B3
El Prat de Llobregat 32 A4
El Puente 36 A1
El Puente del Arzobispo 39 F3
El Puerto de Sagunto 41 E3
El Puerto de Santa María 43 D4
El Real de la Jara 43 D2
El Real de San Vicente 39 F2
El Remolcador, Pto 41 E3
El Robledo 39 F4
El Rocío 42 C3
El Romeral 40 B3
El Rompido 42 C3
El Ronquillo 43 D2
El Royo 36 B3
El Rubio 43 E3
Elsa 60 C4
El Saler 41 E4
El Salobral 40 C4
El Saucejo 43 E3
Elsdorf 17 D4
Elserdorf 55 F2
El Serrat 32 A2
Elsfleth 47 F3
Elsterberg 53 D3
Elsterwerda 53 E2
El Tiemblo 40 A2
Eltisley 9 F1
Eltmann 52 C4
El Toboso 40 B3
El Torcal 43 F3
Eltz 51 E4
El Vado, Emb de 40 B1
Elvanfoot 4 C3
Elvas 38 C4
Elvekrok 100 B3
El Vellón, Emb de 40 A2
Elven 22 C4
El Vendrell 37 F4
Elverum 105 D2
El Vicario, Emb de 40 A4
El Villar de Arnedo 36 C2
El Viso 43 D2
El Viso del Alcor 43 D2
Elx 45 D2
Ely 10 C1
Elygsfors 109 E2
Elzach 54 C3
Elze 52 B1
Emån 109 E2
Embessós 82 C3
Embid 41 D1
Embid de Ariza 36 C4
Émbonas 93 E1
Emboriós (Híos) 89 D1
Emboriós (Sími) 93 E1
Embrun 31 D2
Emden 47 E3
Emet 115 F4
Emilia-Romagna 60 C3
Emlichheim 17 E2
Emmaboda 109 E2
Emmeloord 16 C2
Emmen 17 E1
Emmendingen 54 C3
Emmerich 17 D3
Emocriós 89 F3
Em. Papás 80 B2
Empoli 60 C4
Empúries 32 C3
Ems 17 E1
Emsdetten 17 E2

Ems-Jade-Kanal 47 E3
Emskirchen 55 E1
Enafors 101 D2
Enäjärvi 103 E4
Enånger 101 F4
Encamp 32 A2
Encausse 37 E1
Encinas de Abajo 39 E1
Encinasola 42 C1
Encinedo 34 C3
Endelave 108 B3
Endrinal 39 E2
Enego 59 D3
Enfesta 34 A2
Eng 59 D1
Engadin 58 B3
Engarés 88 C3
Engelberg 27 F3
Engelhartszell 56 C2
Engeløya 97 E1
Engelsdorf 53 D2
Engelskirchen 17 E4
Engen 58 A1
Enger 17 F2
Engerdal 101 D3
Enghien 50 B3
England 9 F1
English Channel 10 A4
Engstingen 55 D3
Enguera 41 E4
Enguidanos 41 D3
Enhammarsfjärden 101 F4
Enipéas 83 E2
Enkhuizen 16 C2
Enköping 106 B3
Enna 68 C3
Enneberg 59 D3
Ennell, L 12 C3
Ennepetal 17 E4
Ennezat 26 A4
Ennis 12 B4
Enniscorthy 15 D3
Enniskerry 13 D4
Enniskillen 13 D2
Ennistimon 12 B4
Enns 57 D3
Enns R 57 D3
Eno 103 F2
Enol, L 35 E2
Enonkoski 103 F3
Enontekiö 95 D3
Énos, Óros 86 A1
Enschede 17 E2
Ensisheim 27 E1
Entlebuch 27 F2
Entraygues-sur-Truyère 29 E2
Entredichos 40 C3
Entre-os-Rios 34 A4
Entrepeñas, Emb de 40 C2
Entrevaux 31 E3
Entrèves 27 E4
Entroncamento 38 B3
Envalira, Pto de 32 A2
Envermeu 19 E2
Enviken 101 E4
Enz 54 C2
Enza 60 B2
Enzklösterle 54 C2
Eochaill 14 C4
Eo, R 34 C1
Epanomí 79 F3
Epe 17 D2
Epernay 20 B3
Epernon 19 E4
Epidávrou, Kólpos 87 E2
Epidávrou Limirás, Kólpos 87 E4
Épila 36 C3
Epinac 26 B3
Epinal 27 D1
Epine, l' 20 B3
Episkopí (Kríti) 90 C3
Episkopí (Kríti) 91 E3
Episkopí (Makedonía) 79 E3
Épiskopí (Pelopónissos) 87 E3
Epitálio 86 B2
Eppan 59 D3
Epping 10 C2

Eppingen 55 D2
Epsom 10 C3
Eptahóri 78 C4
Eptálofos 83 E3
Epte 19 E3
Epworth 7 D2
Eraclea 59 E4
Eraclea-Mare 59 E4
Eräjärvi 103 D3
Erásmio, N. 81 D2
Eratiní 83 E4
Eratinó 80 C2
Erátira 79 D3
Erba 58 B4
Erbach 55 D1
Erbalunga 33 F2
Erbendorf 53 D4
Ercina, L de la 35 E2
Ercolano 64 B4
Érd 112 B4
Erdek 115 E3
Erdevik 72 B2
Erding 56 A3
Erdre 23 D4
Erdut 72 B2
Eresma, R 40 A1
Eressós 85 E2
Erétria 84 B4
Erezée 50 C4
Erfde 48 A2
Erft 17 D4
Erftstadt 51 E3
Erfurt 52 C3
Erges, R 39 D2
Ergoldsbach 56 B2
Eriboll, L 2 C2
Erice 68 A3
Ericeira 38 A3
Ericht, L 2 C1
Eriksberg 106 A4
Eriksmåle 109 E2
Erillas 43 E1
Erímanthos 86 C2
Erímanthos, Óros 86 C1
Eripol, Pto del 37 E3
Erithrés 87 E1
Erkelenz 17 D4
Erkner 49 E4
Erla 37 D3
Erlangen 55 F1
Erlsbach 59 E2
Ermenonville 19 F3
Ermidas-Aldeia 42 A1
Ermióni 87 E2
Ermoúpoli 88 B2
Ermsleben 52 C2
Erndtebrück 17 F4
Erne 13 D3
Ernée 23 E3
Erne, R 12 C2
Ernestinovo 71 F2
Ernstbrunn 57 F2
Erquy 22 C2
Errazu 36 C1
Errigal Mt 12 C1
Erris Head 12 A2
Erskine Bridge 4 C2
Erstein 21 E4
Ervenik 75 D1
Ervidel 42 B1
Ervy 26 B1
Erwitte 17 F3
Erzberg 57 D3
Erzen 76 C4
Erzgebirge 53 E3
Esbjerg 108 A3
Esblada 37 F4
Esbo 107 E3
Escabas, R 40 C2
Escairón 34 B2
Escalada 35 F2
Escalante 36 A1
Escaldes, les 32 A2
Escalona 40 A2
Escalonilla 40 A3
Escalos de Cima 38 C2
Escandón, Pto de 41 D2
Esca, R 37 D2
Escarène, l' 31 E3
Escároz 37 D2
Escatrón 37 D4
Escaut (B) 50 B3
Escaut (F) 20 A2

Esch (D) 51 F4
Esch (L) 21 D2
Eschede 48 B4
Eschenbach 53 D4
Eschershausen 52 B1
Eschwege 52 B2
Eschweiler 51 D3
Escombreras 45 D3
Escorihuela 41 E2
Escudo, Pto del 35 F2
Escúllar 44 B3
Escurial 39 E4
Esera, R 37 E2
Esgueva 35 F4
Esguevillas de Esgueva 35 F4
Esher 9 F2
Esino 61 E4
Esk 5 D3
Eskifjörður 96 C2
Eskilstuna 106 A4
Eskisehir 115 F3
Eskoriatza 36 B1
Esla, R 35 D4
Eslarn 56 B1
Eslohe 17 F4
Eslöv 109 D3
Espa 105 D2
Espadañedo 34 C3
Espadán, Sa de 41 E3
Espalion 29 E3
Esparreguera 32 A4
Espedal 100 C3
Espejo 43 F2
Espelette 28 A4
Espelkamp 17 F2
Espenschied 51 F4
Esperó, Pta 45 F2
Espichel, C 38 A4
Espiel 43 E1
Espigüete 35 E2
Espinama 35 E2
Espinho 34 A4
Espinilla 35 F2
Espinosa de Cerrato 35 F4
Espinosa de los Monteros 36 A1
Espoo 107 E3
Esporles 45 E3
Esposende 34 A4
Espot 37 F2

Espuña, Sa de 44 C2
Esquedas 37 D3
Esquivias 40 A2
Essarts, les 24 B3
Esse 102 C1
Essen (Niedersachsen) 17 E2
Essen (Nordrhein-Westfalen) 17 E3
Essenbach 56 B2
Essex 11 D2
Essími 81 E2
Esslingen 55 D2
Essonne 25 F1
Essoyes 26 B1
Est, Canal de l' 27 D1
Estaca, Pto de la 42 A4
Estacas de Trueba, Pto de las 35 F2
Estadilla 37 E3
Estagel 32 B2
Estaires 19 F1
Estarreja 38 B1
Estats, Pic d' 37 F2
Estavayer 27 E3
Este 61 D1
Estella 36 C2
Estepa 35 E2
Estepona 43 E4
Esteras de Medina 36 B4
Esterel 31 E4
Esternay 20 A4
Esterri d'Àneu 37 F2
Estissac 26 B1
Estói 42 B3
Estonija 110 C2
Estoril 38 A4
Estrela, Sa da 38 C2
Estrella 44 A1

Estremadura 38 A3
Estremoz 38 C4
Estret de Collegats 37 F3
Estrées-St-Denis 19 F3
Esztergom 112 B4
Etables 22 C2
Etain 20 C3
Etampes 19 F4
Etaples 19 E1
Etel 22 B4
Etelhem 109 F4
Etive, L 4 B1
Etna, M 69 D3
Etne 104 A3
Etolía-Akarnanía 82 C3
Etolikó 82 C4
Etrépagny 19 E3
Etretat 19 D2
Ettelbruck 21 D2
Etten 16 C3
Ettenheim 54 C3
Ettington 9 E1
Ettlingen 54 C2
Eugénie-les-Bains 28 B4
Eume, Emb del 34 B1
Eume, R 34 B1
Eupen 51 D4
Eura 107 D2
Eurajoki 107 D2
Euratsfeld 57 D3
Eure 19 E4
Eure (Dépt) 19 E3
Eure-et-Loir 25 E1
Europabrücke 59 D2
Europoort 16 B3
Euskadi 36 B2
Euskirchen 51 E3
Eußenhausen 52 B3
Eutin 48 B2

Evangelismós 83 E1
Evangelistria 83 F4
Evaux-les-Bains 25 F4
Évdilos 89 D2
Evendorf 48 B3
Evenes 94 B3
Evenskjær 94 B3
Evergem 50 B3
Everöd 109 D3
Evertsberg 101 E4
Evesham 9 E1
Évia, N 84 B3
Evijärvi 102 C2
Evinohóri 83 D4
Évinos 83 D3
Evisa 33 F3
Evje 104 B4
Évlalo 81 D2
Evolène 27 E4
Évora 38 B4
Évoramonte 38 B4
Evran 18 C3
Evrecy 18 C3
Evreux 19 E3
Evritania 83 D2
Evron 23 E3
Evropós 79 F2
Évros 81 F2
Évros R 81 F2
Evrostina 87 D1
Evrótas 87 D3
Evry 19 F4
Évzoni 79 F2
Exaplátanos 79 E2
Éxarhos 83 F4
Excideuil 29 D1
Exe 8 C3

Essen

(Map of Essen with labelled districts and roads, including: STERKRADE BOTTROP, AUTOBAHN (E 34-A 2): HANNOVER, AUTOBAHN (A 42): DUISBURG GLADBECK, GELSENKIRCHEN, DELLWIG, BERGEBORBECK, VOGELHEIM, ALTENESSEN, STOPPENBERG, GERSCHEDE, BORBECK-MITTE, SCHLOSS BORBECK, STERKRADE OBERHAUSEN, BOCHOLD, MÜNSTER, DORTMUND BOCHUM, FRÖLLENDORF, SCHÖNEBECK, ALTENDORF, FROHNHAUSEN, DUISBURG OBERHAUSEN, STEELER STR, HUTTROP, MUSEUM FOLKWANG, FULERUM, HOLSTERHAUSEN, MARGARETHENHÖHE, GRUGAHALLE, GRUGA-PARK, RÜTTENSCHEID, ESSEN SÜD, STADION, BERGERHAUSEN, HEISINGEN, AUTOBAHN (E 35-A 3): DÜSSELDORF KÖLN, HAARZOPF, SCHLOSS SCHELLENBERG, STADTWALD, WUPPERTAL, RELLINGHAUSEN, SCHELLENBERGER WALD, STADT-WALD, RUINE ISENBURG, MEISENBURGSTR, BREDENEY, VILLA HÜGEL, BALDENEYSEE, DÜSSELDORF, WERDEN, Hardenbergufer, KETTWIG, WUPPERTAL SOLINGEN, scale 0 – 2 km)

F

FIRENZE
PIANTA D'INSIEME

Flevoland 16 C2
Flexenpaß 58 B2
Flims Waldhaus 58 B2
Flint 6 B2
Flisa 105 D2
Flix 37 E4
Flixecourt 19 F2
Flize 20 C2
Floda 105 F2
Flogny 26 B1
Flöha 53 E3
Flomohóri 87 E4
Flora 77 F3
Florac 29 F3
Flor da Rosa 38 C3
Florennes 50 C4
Florensac 30 A4
Florenville 20 C2
Florešty 113 E3
Floriáda 82 C2
Floridia 69 D4
Flórina 79 D2
Flórina (Nomos) 79 D3
Florø 104 A1
Flörsheim-
  Dalsheim 54 C1
Flötningen 101 D3
Floúda, Akr 92 C1
Floúnda 91 E3
Flüelapass 58 B2
Flüelen 58 A2
Flühli 27 F3
Flumendosa 66 C3
Flumen, R 37 D3
Flumet 27 D4
Fluminimaggiore 66 A4
Flums 58 B2
Fluvià, R 32 B3
Foča 76 A1
Foça 115 E4
Foce Verde 63 F3
Fochabers 3 D3
Fockbek 48 A2
Focşani 113 E4
Fódele 91 D3
Foggia 64 C3
Föglö 106 C3
Fohnsdorf 57 D4
Föhr 47 F1
Foiano della
  Chiana 61 D4
Foinaven 2 C2
Foix 32 A2
Fojnica (Bosna
  i Hercegovina) 75 F1
Fojnica (Bosna
  i Hercegovina) 75 F2
Foki 83 E4
Fokstuhø 100 C3
Folda 97 E1
Foldereid 97 D4
Foldfjorden 97 D4
Foleá 80 C2
Folégandros 91 D1
Folégandros, N 91 D1
Følen 104 A3
Folgaria 59 D4
Folgefonna 104 B2
Folgoët, le 22 A2
Folgoso de la
  Ribera 35 D2
Foligno 63 E1
Folkestad 100 A3
Folkestone 11 D3
Follafoss. 101 D1
Folldal 100 C3
Follebu 104 C1
Follina. 59 E3
Föllinge 101 E1
Follonica 62 C1
Folmava 56 B1
Folói 86 C2
Fombellida 35 F4
Fond-de-France,
  le 31 D1
Fondevila 34 B3
Fondi 63 F3
Fondo 59 D3
Fonfría (Aragón) 37 D4
Fonfría
  (Castilla-León) 35 D4
Fongen 101 D2
Fonn 100 A3
Fonni 66 B3

Fonollosa 32 A4
Fonsagrada 34 C2
Fontaine 27 E1
Fontainebleau 19 F4
Fontaine-de-
  Vaucluse 30 C3
Fontaine-
  Française 26 C2
Fontaine-Henry 18 C3
Fontaine-le-Dun 19 D2
Fontanigorda 60 A3
Fonte Longa 34 B4
Fontenay 26 B2
Fontenay-
  le-Comte 24 C3
Fontenay-
  Trésigny 19 F4
Fontevraud-
  l'Abbaye 25 D2
Fontfroide,
  Abbaye de 32 B2
Fontgombault 25 D3
Fontibre 35 F2
Fontiveros 39 F1
Fontoy 21 D3
Font-Romeu 32 A2
Fontvieille 30 B4
Fonz 37 E3
Fonzaso 59 D3
Foppolo 58 B3
Forata, Emb de 41 E4
Forbach 21 E3
Forca Canapine 63 F1
Forca Caruso 64 A2
Forca d'Acero 64 A2
Forcall 41 E2
Forcalquier 30 C3
Forcarei 34 A2
Forchheim 55 F1
Forclaz, Col de la 27 E4
Forcola di
  Mte Rest 59 E3
Førde 100 A3
Førdefjorden 104 A1
Förderstedt 52 C1
Fordingbridge 9 E3
Fordongianus 66 B3
Foreland 9 F3
Forenza 64 C3
Foresta di Burgos 66 B2
Føresvik 104 A3
Forêt d'Orient,
  Lac de la 26 B1
Forez, Monts du 29 F1
Forfar 5 D1
Forges-les-Eaux 19 E3
Forggensee 55 F4
Forio 64 A4
Forli 61 D3
Forli del Sannio 64 A2
Forlimpopoli 61 D3
Formazza 58 A3
Formby 6 B2
Formentera 45 D4
Formentor, C 45 F2
Formerie 19 E3
Formia 64 A3
Formigine 60 C2
Fornaci di Barga 60 C3
Fornells 45 F1
Forni Avoltri 59 E2
Forni di Sopra 59 E3
Forno di Zoldo 59 E3
Fornos de
  Algodres 38 C1
Fornovo di Taro 60 B2
Forøy 97 E2
Forøyar 96 A3
Forres 3 D1
Forsa 101 F3
Forserum 109 D1
Forshaga 105 E3
Forsnes 100 B1
Forssa 107 E2
Forst 53 F1
Fort Augustus 2 C4
Forte dei Marmi 60 B3
Forth 55 F1
Forth R 4 C2
Forth Bridges 5 D2
Forth, Firth of 5 D2
Fort-Mahon 19 E2
Fortore 64 B2
Fortrose 3 D3

Fortuna 45 D2
Fortuneswell 9 D4
Fort William 2 C4
Forvik 97 D3
Fos (Ariège) 37 F2
Fos (Bouches-du-
  Rhône) 30 C4
Foscagno, Pso di 58 C3
Fosnavåg 100 A2
Fossacesia 64 B2
Fossano 31 E2
Fossat, le 37 F1
Fossbakken 94 B3
Fosses 50 C4
Fossli 104 B3
Fossombrone 61 E3
Fotiná 79 E4
Fotolivos 80 B2
Fouesnant 22 B3
Foug 21 D4
Fougères 23 D3
Fougerolles 27 D4
Foula 3 E2
Foulness Pt 11 D2
Fouras 24 B4
Fourchamboult 26 A2
Fourfourás 91 D4
Foúrka 83 E3

Fourmies 20 B2
Fourná 83 D3
Fournels 29 F2
Fournés 90 B3
Foúrni
  (Dodekánissa) 89 E2
Foúrni (Kríti) 91 E3
Foúrni
  (Pelopónissos) 87 E2
Fourniá, Akr 85 E2
Foúrni, N 89 E2
Fours 26 B3
Fousseret, le 37 F1
Foústani 79 E2
Fowey 8 B4
Foxford 12 B2
Foyers 2 C4
Foyle, L 13 D1
Foyle, R 13 D1
Foz 34 C1
Foz do Arelho 38 A3
Foz do Douro 34 A4
Foz Giraldo 38 C2
Frabosa Soprana 31 F3
Fraddon 8 B4
Fraga 37 E4
Frailes 44 A3
Fraize 27 E1
Fram 70 C1

Frammersbach 52 B4
Fræna 100 B2
Francavilla al Mare 64 A1
Francavilla di
  Sicilia 69 D3
Francavilla
  Fontana 65 E4
Francavilla in
  Sinni 65 D4
Francker 16 C1
Francofonte 69 D4
Francolí, R 37 F4
Francorchamps 51 D4
Frändefors 105 D4
Frangádes 82 C1
Frangista 83 D3
Frangokástelo 90 C4
Frangy 27 D4
Frankenberg (D) 52 A3
Frankenberg
  (DDR) 53 E3
Frankenburg 56 C3
Frankenmarkt 56 C3
Frankenstein 54 C1
Frankenthal 54 C1
Frankfurt
  am Main 52 A4
Frankfurt
  an der Oder 49 F4

Fränk Rezat 55 E2
Fränk Saale 52 B4
Františkovy Lázně 53 D4
Franzburg 49 D1
Franz-Josephs-
  Höhe 59 E2
Frascati 63 E3
Frascineto 67 E2
Frasdorf 56 B3
Fraserburgh 3 E3
Frasno, Pto del 36 C4
Fratel 38 C3
Fratta Polesine 61 D2
Frauenfeld 58 A1
Frauenkirchen 57 F3
Frauenstein 53 E2
Frechen 17 E4
Freckenhorst 17 F3
Fredensborg 108 C3
Fredericia 108 B3
Frederikshavn 108 B1
Frederikssund 108 C3
Frederiksværk 108 C3
Fredrika 102 A1
Fredriksberg 105 D3
Fredrikstad 105 D3

Fregene 63 E3
Fréhel, Cap 22 C2
Frei 100 B2
Freiberg 53 E3
Freiberger Mulde 53 D2
Freiburg (Baden-
  Württemberg) 54 C4
Freiburg
  (Niedersachsen) 48 A2
Freienhufen 53 E1
Freilassing 56 C3
Freilingen 51 F4
Freising 55 F3
Freistadt 57 D2
Freital 53 E2
Freiwalde 53 E1
Freixedas 38 C1
Freixido 34 C3
Freixo de Espada à
  Cinta 39 D1
Fréjus, Tunnel du 31 D1
Frenchpark 12 C3
Frêne, Col du 31 D1
Freren 17 E2
Freshford 12 C4
Freshwater 9 E3
Fresnay-sur-
  Sarthe 23 F3

Frankfurt

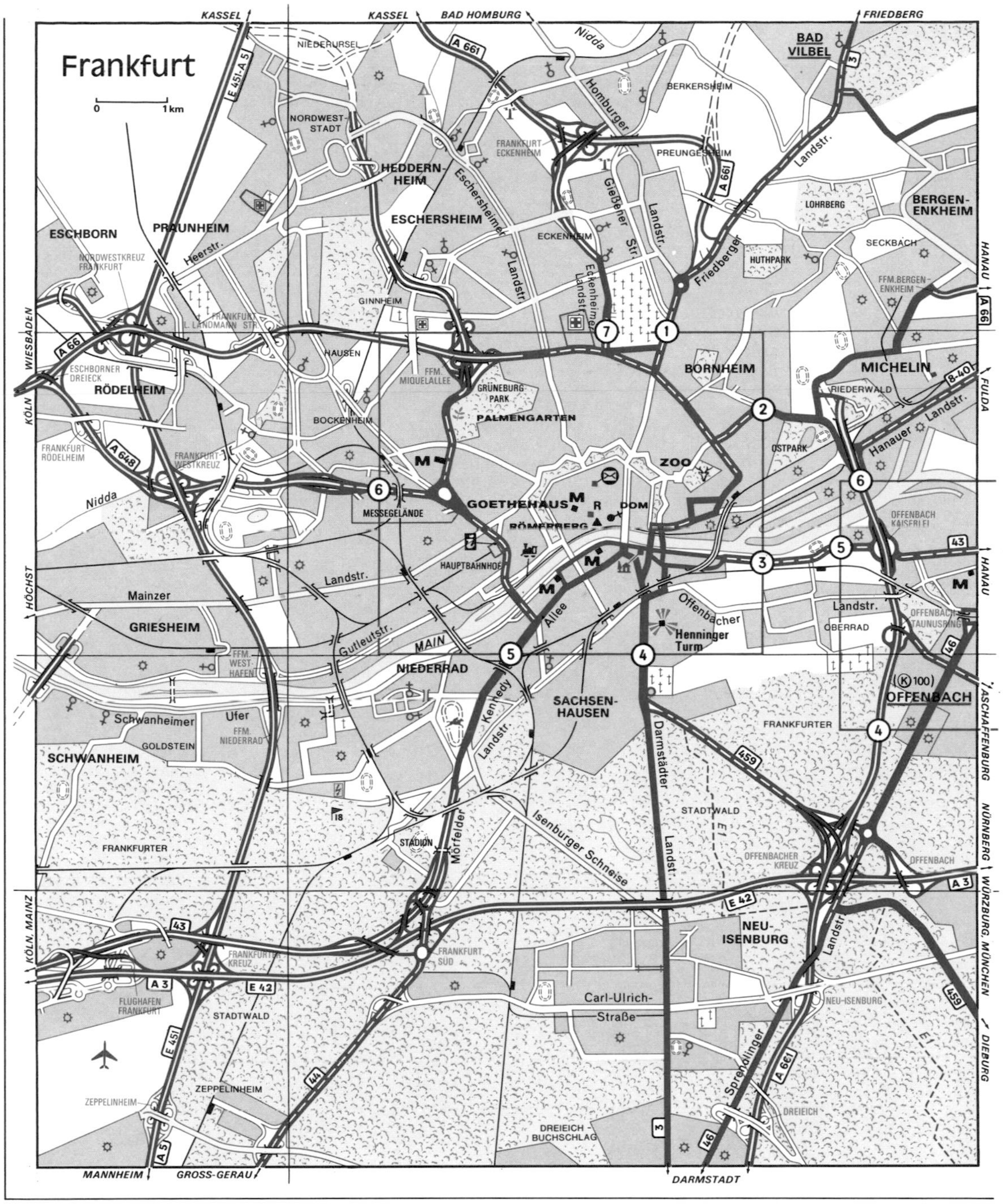

0   1 km

Fresne-St-Mamès	27 D2	Friedrichroda	52 B3	Froissy	19 F3
Fresnes-en-		Friedrichshafen	55 D4	Froitzheim	51 D3
Woëvre	20 C3	Friedrichskoog	47 F2	Frome	9 D3
Fresno Alhándiga	39 E1	Friedrichsort	48 A1	Fromentine	24 A3
Fresvikbreen	104 B1	Friedrichstadt	47 F1	Frómista	35 F3
Freudenberg (Baden-		Friedrichsthal	54 B2	Fronteira	38 C4
Württemberg)	55 D1	Friesach	57 D4	Frontenay-Rohan-	
Freudenberg (Nord-		Friesack	49 D4	Rohan	24 C4
rhein-Westfalen)	17 F4	Friesland	16 C1	Frontenhausen	56 B2
Freudenstadt	54 C3	Friesoythe	17 E1	Frontera	42 A4
Frévent	19 F2	Frigiliana	44 A4	Frontignan	30 A4
Freyburg	52 C2	Frihetsli	94 C3	Fronton	29 D3
Freyenstein	48 C3	Friis veien	100 C3	Frosinone	63 F3
Freyung	56 C2	Frikes	82 B4	Frosolone	64 B3
Fri	93 D3	Frilingiánika	90 A1	Frösön	101 E2
Frias	36 A2	Frinton-on-Sea	11 D2	Frosta	100 C1
Frías de Albarracín	41 D2	Friol	34 B2	Frostavallen	109 D3
Fribourg	27 E3	Fristad	109 D1	Frøstrup	108 A2
Fridingen	55 D3	Fritsla	108 C1	Frouard	21 D4
Friedberg (A)	57 F3	Fritzlar	52 A3	Froússa	82 C2
Friedberg		Friuli-Venezia		Frövi	105 F3
(Bayern)	55 F3	Giulia	59 E3	Frøya	100 B1
Friedberg		Frizington	5 D1	Frøyfjorden	100 B1
(Hessen)	52 A4	Frodsham	6 B2	Frøysjøen	100 A3
Friedeburg	47 E3	Frogner	105 D3	Fruges	19 F1
Friedersdorf	49 E4	Frohavet	100 C1	Fruška	72 b2
Friedland (D)	52 B2	Frohburg	53 D2	Frutigen	27 E3
Friedland (DDR)	49 D2	Frohnleiten	57 E4	Frýdek-Místek	112 B3

Fteliá	80 C2	Fuglebjerg	108 B4
Ftéri (Makedonía)	79 E4	Fugløysundet	94 C2
Ftéri		Fulda	52 B3
(Pelopónissos)	86 C1	Fulda R	52 B3
Fthiótida	83 E3	Fulgatore	68 A3
Fucecchio	60 C4	Fulpmes	59 D2
Fuencaliente (Castilla-		Fulufjället	101 D4
la-Mancha)	43 F1	Fumay	20 B2
Fuencaliente		Fumel	28 C3
(Is Canarias)	42 A4	Funäsdalen	101 D2
Fuendejalón	36 C3	Funchal	42 A3
Fuendetodos	37 D4	Fundão	38 C2
Fuengirola	43 F4	Funes	59 D2
Fuenlabrada	40 A2	Fuorn, Pso dal	58 C3
Fuenlabrada de		Furadouro	38 B1
los Montes	39 F4	Furci	64 B2
Fuenmayor	36 B2	Furkapass	58 A3
Fuensalida	40 A3	Furnace	4 B2
Fuensanta de		Furnás	45 D3
Martos	43 F2	Fürstenau	17 E2
Fuensanta,		Fürstenberg	49 D3
Emb de la	44 C1	Fürstenfeld	57 F4
Fuente-Alamo	45 D1	Fürstenfeldbruck	55 F3
Fuente Alamo	45 D2	Fürstenlager	54 C1
Fuentecén	35 F4	Fürstenwalde	49 E4
Fuente de Cantos	43 D1	Fürstenwerder	49 E3
Fuente del		Fürstenzell	56 C2
Maestre	43 D1	Furtei	66 B3

Fuente de Pedro		Fürth	55 E1
Naharro	40 B3	Furth	56 B1
Fuente de Piedra	43 E3	Furtwangen	54 C3
Fuente el Fresno	40 A4	Furudal	101 E4
Fuenteguinaldo	39 D2	Furuflaten	94 C2
Fuente la Higuera	45 D1	Fuscaldo	67 E2
Fuentelapeña	39 E1	Fusch	59 E1
Fuente Obéjuna	43 E1	Fuschl	56 C3
Fuente Palmera	43 E2	Fuseta	42 B3
Fuentepinilla	36 B3	Fushë Arrez	76 C3
Fuentesauco	39 E1	Fushë Muhur	76 C3
Fuentes de		Fusignano	61 D2
Andalucía	43 E2	Füssen	55 E4
Fuentes de		Fustiñana	36 C3
Ayódar	41 E3	Futa, Pso della	60 C3
Fuentes de Ebro	37 D4	Futog	72 C2
Fuentes de León	43 D1	Futrikelv	94 B2
Fuentes de Nava	35 E3	Fyn	108 B4
Fuentes de Oñoro	39 D1	Fyne, L	4 B2
Fuentes de Ropel	35 D3	Fynshav	108 B4
Fuentes de		Fyresdal	104 B3
Valdepero	35 F3	Fyresvatn	104 B3
Fuentidueña	35 F4	Fyrkat	108 B2
Fuentidueña			
de Tajo	40 B3		
Fuerte del Rey	44 A2		
Fuerteventura	42 C4		
Fügen	59 D1		

G

		Gaberl-Sattel	57 E4	Gabrovka	70 B2	Gad'ač	113 F1
		Gabia la Grande	44 A3	Gabrovo	115 D2	Gäddede	97 E4
Gaaldorf	57 D4	Gabicce Mare	61 E3	Gacé	19 D4	Gadebusch	48 B2
Gabarret	28 B3	Gabriel y Galán,		Gacilly, la	23 D4	Gádor	44 B3
Gabela	75 F2	Emb de	39 E2	Gacko	76 A2	Gádor, Sa de	44 B3

Gadžin Han	77 E1	Gallargues	30 B3
Gãești	115 D1	Gállego, R	37 D3
Gaeta	64 C3	Galley Head	14 B4
Gaeta, Golfo di	64 A3	Galliate	60 A1
Gagarin	111 F2	Gallipoli	65 F4
Gaggenau	54 C2	Gällivare	98 B2
Gagnef	105 F2	Gallneukirchen	57 D2
Gail	59 E2	Gällö	101 E2
Gailbergsattel	59 E2	Gallo, C	68 B2
Gaildorf	55 D2	Gallocanta, L de	41 D1
Gailey	9 E1	Gallo, R	41 D2
Gaillac	29 D3	Galloway Forest	
Gaillimh	12 B3	Park	4 C3
Gaillon	19 E3	Gallspach	56 C3
Gainsborough	7 D2	Gallur	36 C3
Gairloch	2 B3	Gälöfjärden	106 B4
Gaj	73 D2	Galston	4 C2
Gajdobra	72 B2	Galten	108 B3
Gajsin	113 E3	Galtür	58 C2
Gajvoron	113 E3	Galty Mts	14 C3
Gakovo	72 B1	Galveias	38 B3
Galan	37 E1	Gálvez	40 A3
Galanádo	88 C3	Galway	12 B3
Galaniá	90 A2	Galway (Co)	12 B3
Galanta	112 A3	Galway B	12 B4
Galapagar	40 A2	Gamaches	19 E2
Galarinós	80 A3	Gambarie	
Galaroza	42 C2	d'Aspromonte	67 E4
Galashiels	5 D2	Gaming	57 D3
Galatádes	79 E3	Gamleby	109 E1
Galatáki	84 A3	Gammelstaden	98 C3
Galatás		Gammertingen	55 D3
(Argolída)	87 E2	Gampenjoch	58 C3
Galatás		Gams	58 B2
(Korinthía)	87 D1	Gamvik	95 E1
Galați	113 E4	Gamzigrad	73 E4
Galatina	65 F4	Ganacker	56 B2
Galatini	79 D3	Gand	50 B3
Galátista	80 A3	Gándara	34 B1
Galatone	65 F4	Ganderkesee	17 F1
Galaxídi	83 E4	Gandesa	41 F1
Galdakao	36 B1	Gandía	41 E4
Galdhøpiggen	100 B3	Gandino	58 B4
Galeata	61 D3	Gandria	58 A4
Galegos	38 C3	Gangáles	91 D4
Galende	34 C3	Ganges	29 F3
Galera	44 B2	Gangi	68 C3
Galiano del		Gangkofen	56 B2
Capo	65 F4	Gannat	26 A4
Galibier, Col du	31 D1	Gänserndorf	57 F2
Galicia	34 B2	Gañuelas	45 D2
Galičica	77 D4	Gap	31 D2
Galičnik	77 D3	Garabit, Viaduc de	29 F2
Galikós	79 F3	Garajonay	42 A4
Galipsós	80 B2	Garajonay (Parque	
Galisteo	39 D2	Nac)	42 A4
Galiz, Pto de	43 D4	Gara, L	12 C3
Gallarate	60 A1	Garching	56 B3
Gallardon	19 E4	Garcia	37 E4

Garcia de Sola,		
Emb de	39 F4
Garciaz	39 E3
Gard (Dépt)	30 B3
Gard R	30 B3
Garda	60 C1
Garda, L di	58 C4
Garðabær	96 A2
Gardanne	30 C4
Cårdby	109 E2
Garde	109 F4
Garde-Freinet, la	31 D4
Gardelegen	48 C4
Gardermoen	105 D3
Gardiken	97 F3
Gardíki	83 D3
Garding	47 F2
Gardjönäs	97 F3
Gärdnäs	101 E1
Gardone Riviera	60 C1
Gardone Val		
Trompia	60 B1
Gärdslösa	109 E2
Gardunha, Sa da	38 C2
Garður	96 A2
Garešnica	71 D2
Garessio	31 F3
Garforth	7 D2
Gargaliáni	86 B3
Gargano,		
Promontorio del	64 C2
Garganta	44 B2
Garganta del		
Chorro	43 E3
Garganta del		
Escalar	37 E2
Garganta la Olla	39 E2
Gargantas	40 C2
Gargantas del Sil	34 B2
Gargellen	58 B2
Gargilesse	25 E3
Gargnano	58 C4
Gargnäs	98 A3
Garigliano	64 A3
Gariglione, Mte	67 F3
Garlasco	60 A2
Garlin	28 B4
Garlstorf	48 B3
Garmisch-Parten-		
kirchen	55 F4
Garona, R	37 F2
Garonne	28 B2
Garpenberg	105 F3
Garphyttan	105 F4
Garraf	32 A4
Garrafe de Torío	35 D2
Garray	36 B3
Garrel	17 E1
Garrovillas	39 D3

Gent

Garrucha	44 C3	Gebese	52 C2	
Gars	57 E2	Gebze	115 F3	
Gartempe	25 E4	Gedern	52 A4	
Gartow	48 C3	Gediz	115 F4	
Gartz	49 E3	Gediz R	115 E4	
Garvagh	13 D1	Gedser	108 C4	
Garvão	42 A2	Geel	50 C3	
Garve	2 C3	Geertruidenberg	16 C3	
Garynahine	2 B2	Geesthacht	48 B3	
Garz	49 D1	Gefell	53 D3	
Gaschurn	58 B2	Géfira	79 F3	
Gassino Torinese	31 E1	Gefiria	83 E2	
Gastoúni	86 B1	Gefrees	53 D4	
Gata		Gehren	52 C3	
(Extremadura)	39 D2	Geilenkirchen	17 D4	
Gata (Valencia)	45 E1	Geilo	104 C2	
Gata, C de	44 C4	Geiranger	100 B3	
Gata, Sa de	39 D2	Geirangerfjorden		
Gatčina	111 D1		100 B3	
Gatehouse of Fleet	4 C3	Geisa	52 B3	
Gateshead	5 E3	Geiselhöring	56 B2	
Gattinara	31 F1	Geisenfeld	55 F2	
Gattorna	60 A3	Geisenhausen	56 B2	
Gatwick Airport	10 C3	Geising	53 E3	
Gaucín	43 E4	Geisingen	54 C4	
Gauja	110 C2	Geislingen	55 E2	
Gaula	100 C2	Geismar	52 B2	
Gauldalen	100 C2	Geisnes	97 D4	
Gaulstad	101 D1	Geithain	53 D2	
Gauting	56 A3	Gela	68 C4	
Gavà	32 A4	Gelderland	17 D2	
Gavardo	60 B1	Geldern	17 D3	
Gavarnie	37 E2	Geldrop	16 C4	
Gavarnie,		Geleen	17 D4	
Cirque de	37 E2	Gelibolu	115 E3	
Gavdopoúla, N	90 B4	Gelnhausen	52 A4	
Gávdos, N	90 C4	Gelsa	37 D4	
Gave d'Oloron	28 A4	Gelsdorf	51 E4	
Gavi	60 A2	Gelsenkirchen	17 E3	
Gavião	38 B3	Gelting	48 A1	
Gavia, Pso di	58 C3	Gembloux	50 C4	
Gavirate	58 A4	Gemeaux	26 C2	
Gävle	106 B2	Gémenos	30 C4	
Gävleborgs Län	101 E3	Gemert	17 D3	
Gävlebukten	106 B2	Gemlik	115 F3	
Gavoi	66 B2	Gemona del		
Gavray	18 B4	Friuli	59 F3	
Gávrio	88 B1	Gémozac	28 B1	
Gåvsta	106 B3	Gemünd	51 D4	
Gåxsjö	101 E1	Gemünden		
Gazzuolo	60 C2	(Bayern)	52 B4	
Gdańsk	110 A4	Gemünden		
Gdov	111 D1	(Hessen)	52 A3	
Gdynia	110 A4	Gemünden		
Geaune	28 B4	(Rheinland-Pfalz)	54 B1	

Genádio	93 E2	Generalísimo		Generalski Stol	70 C3	Génolhac	29 F3	Gerabronn	55 E2
Gençay	25 D4	Emb del	41 D3	General-Toševo	115 E2	Genova	60 A3	Gerace	67 F4
				Generoso, Mte	58 A4	Genova, Golfo di	60 A4	Gerakári (Kriti)	90 C4
				Genève	27 D4	Genova, Val di	58 C3	Gerakári	
				Genil, R	43 E2	Gent	50 B3	(Makedonía)	79 F2
				Genisséa	81 D2	Genthin	49 D4	Gerakaroú	80 A3
				Génissiat,		Gentioux	29 D1	Gerakás	87 E4
				Barrage de	27 D4	Genzano di		Gérakas, Akr	84 B2
				Genk	50 C3	Lucania	64 C3	Geráki	87 D3
				Genlis	26 C2	Genzano di Roma	63 E3	Gerakiní	80 B4
				Genna Cruxi	66 C3	Georgiani	79 E3	Gerakovoúni	83 F3
				Gennargentu,		Georgioúpoli	90 C4	Geránia	87 E1
				Mti del	66 B3	Georgítsi	87 D3	Gérardmer	27 E1
				Gennep	17 D3	Gera	53 D3	Geras	57 E2
				Gennes	24 C2	Geraardsbergen	50 B3	Gerbéviller	21 D4

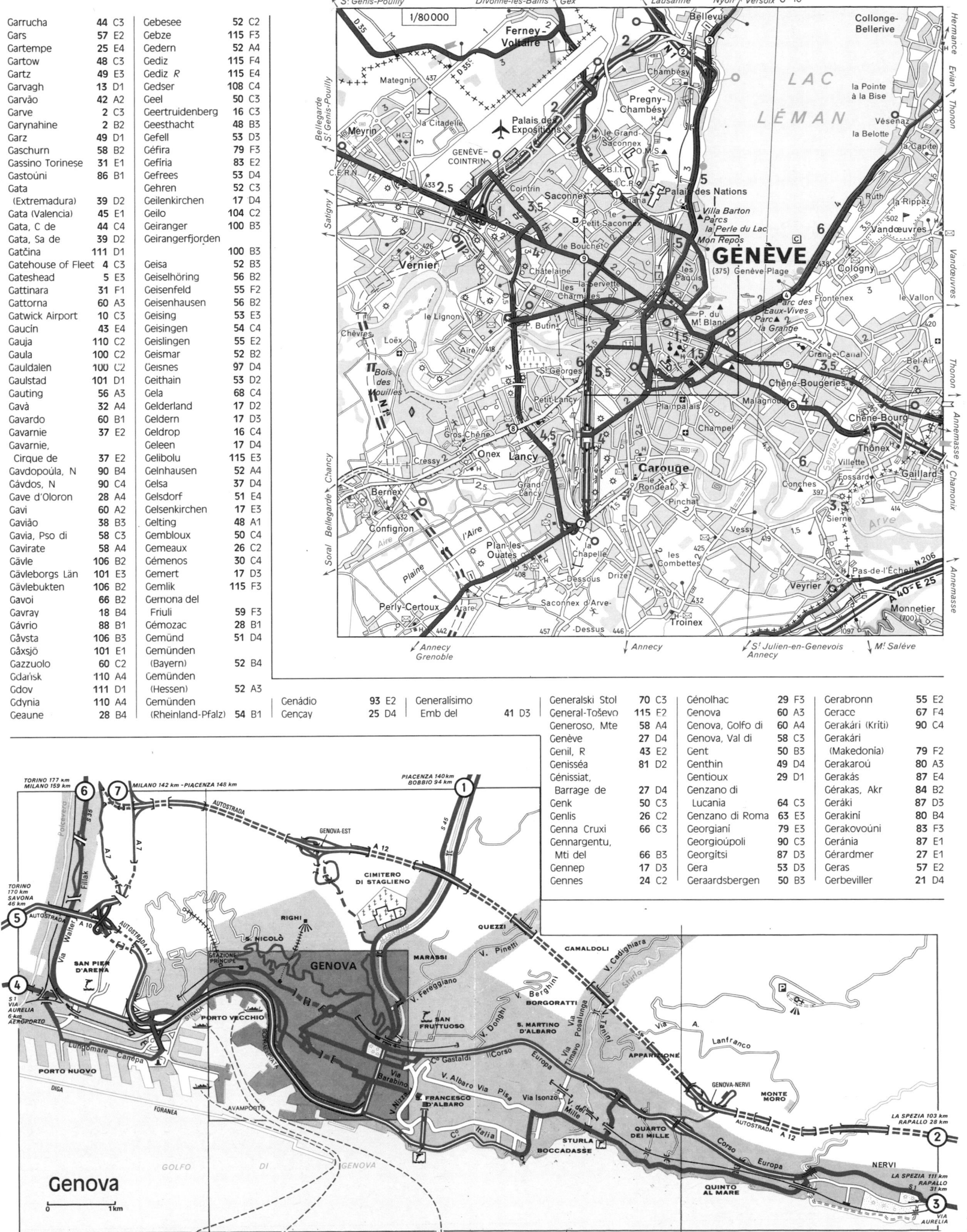

Genova

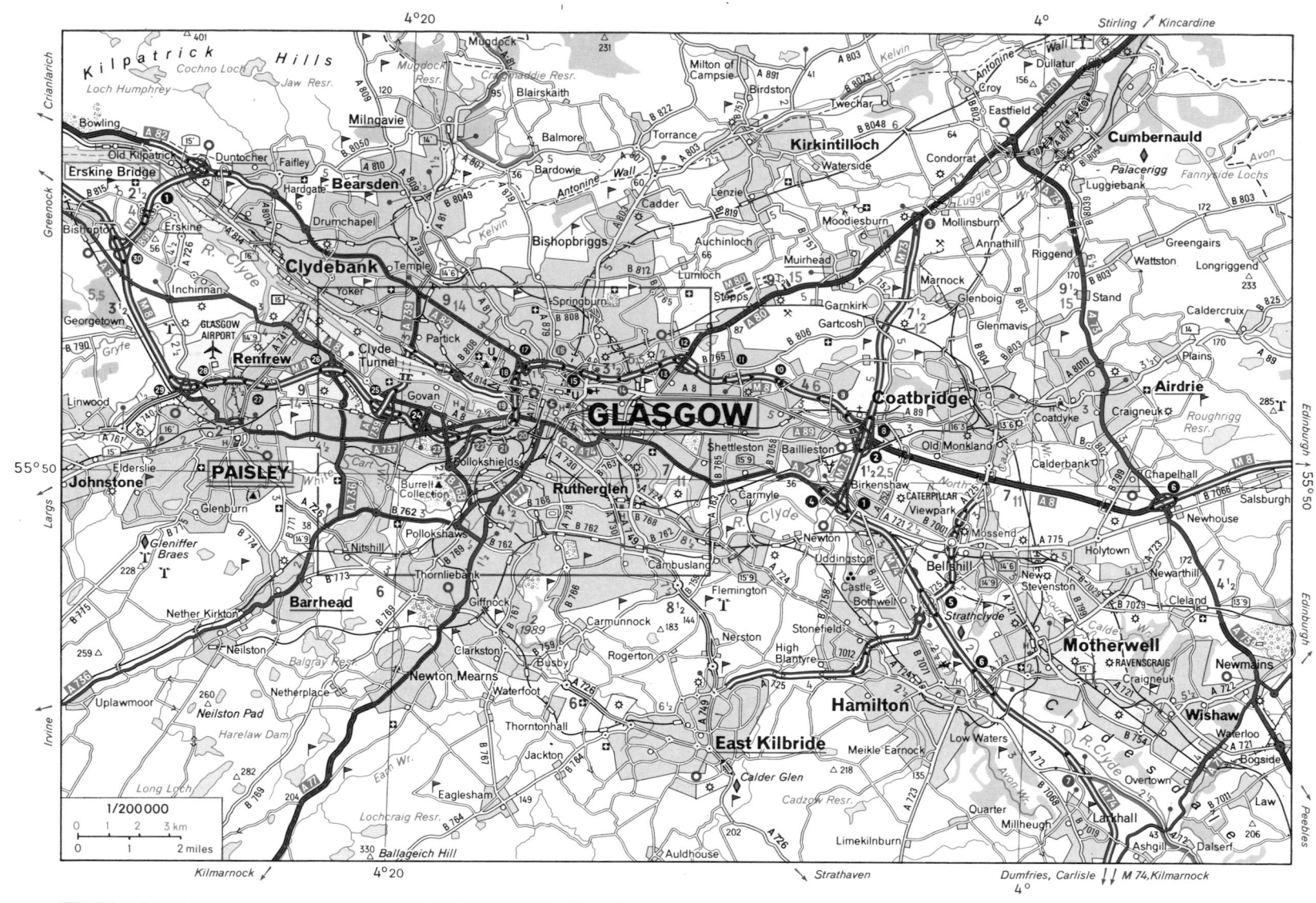

Name	Pg	Grid
Gerbier de Jonc	30	B2
Gerbini	69	D3
Gerbstedt	52	C2
Gerena	43	D2
Gerês	34	B3
Gerês, Sa do	34	B3
Geretsried	56	A3
Gérgal	44	B3
Geringswalde	53	E2
Gerlitzen	59	F2
Gerlos	59	D2
Gerlospaß	59	D1
Gérmas	79	D3
Germering	55	F3
Germersheim	54	C2
Gernika-Lumo	36	B1
Gernrode	52	C2
Gernsbach	54	C2
Gernsheim	54	C1
Gerola Alta	58	B3
Geroliménas	87	D4
Gerolstein	51	D4
Gerolzhofen	52	B4
Gerona	32	B3
Geroplátanos	80	B3
Gerovo	70	B3
Gerri de la Sal	37	F3
Gers	28	C3
Gers (Dépt)	28	C4
Gersau	58	A2
Gersfeld	52	B4
Gerstetten	55	E2
Gersthofen	55	E3
Gerswalde	49	E3
Gesäuse	57	D3
Gescher	17	E3
Geseke	17	F3
Gesualdo	64	B3
Geta	106	C2
Getafe	40	A2
Gets, les	27	E4
Gettorf	48	A1
Gevelsberg	17	E4
Gevgelija	77	F4
Gévora, R	38	C4
Gevrey-Chambertin	26	C2
Gex	27	D3
Geysir	96	B2
Geyve	115	F3
Gföhl	57	E2
Ghedi	60	B1
Gheorghe Gheorghiu-Dej	113	D4
Gheorgheni	113	D4
Ghilarza	66	B3
Ghisonaccia	33	F3
Ghisoni	33	F3
Giali, N	89	F4
Giáltra	83	F3
Gianitsá	79	E3
Gianitsi	84	C4
Giannádes	82	A1
Giannutri I di	63	D2
Gianoúli	81	F2
Giant's Causeway	13	E1
Giardini	69	D3
Giáros, N	88	B2
Giarratana	69	D4
Giarre	69	D3
Giat	29	E1
Giaveno	31	E1
Giba	66	B4
Gibostad	94	B2
Gibraleón	42	C2
Gibraltar	43	E4
Gideå	102	A2
Gideälven	102	A2
Gieboldehausen	52	B2
Gien	26	A2
Giengen	55	E2
Giens	31	D4
Gießen	51	F3
Giethoorn	17	D2
Gifhorn	48	B4
Gigha I	4	B2
Giglio, I del	62	C2
Giglio Porto	62	C2
Gignac	30	A4
Gijón	35	D1
Gilching	56	A3
Gilford	13	E2
Giljevo	76	C1
Gille	108	A3
Gilleje	108	C3
Gillhov	101	E2
Gillingham (Dorset)	9	D3
Gillingham (Kent)	11	D2
Gill, L	12	C2
Gilze	16	C3
Gimenells	37	E3
Gimnó	84	B4
Gimo	106	B3
Gimont	28	C4
Ginosa	65	D4
Ginzling	59	D2
Giogo di Scarperia	61	D3
Gioia del Colle	65	E3
Gioia Tauro	67	E4
Gióna, Óros	83	E3
Gioúhtas	91	D4
Gioúra, N	84	B4
Giovinazzo	65	D3
Giovi, Pso dei	60	A3
Girifalco	67	F3
Giromagny	27	E1
Girona	32	B3
Gironde	28	B1
Gironde (Dépt)	28	B2
Gironella	32	A3
Girvan	4	C3
Gisburn	6	C2
Gislaved	109	D2
Gisors	19	E3
Gistel	50	A3
Gissi	64	B2
Githio	87	D4
Gittun	98	A2
Giugliano in Campo	64	B4
Giulianova	64	A1
Giurgiu	115	D2
Give	108	A3
Givors	30	B1
Givry	26	C3
Givry-en-Argonne	20	C3
Gizéla	81	D2
Giżycko	110	B4
Gjalicë, M	77	D3
Gjendesheim	100	B3
Gjermundshavn	104	A2
Gjesvær	95	D1
Gjirokastër	114	C4
Gjøra	105	D2
Gjøv	96	A3
Gjøvik	105	D2
Gjuhezës, Kepi i	114	B4
Gla	83	F4
Gladbeck	17	E3
Gladenbach	17	F4
Gladstad	97	D3
Glafsfjorden	105	E3
Gláma	96	A1
Glamis	5	D1
Glamis Castle	5	D1
Glamoč	71	E4
Glamorgan	8	C2
Glamsbjerg	108	B3
Glan	54	B1
Glandon, Col du	31	D1
Glandorf	17	F2
Glan-Münchweiler	54	B1
Glanshammar	105	F4
Glarus	58	A2
Glasgow	4	C2
Glas Maol	3	D4
Glastonbury	9	D3
Glauchau	53	D3
Glava	105	D3
Glavatičevo	75	F1
Glavičice	72	B3
Glavnik	77	D1
Gledić	73	D3
Gledićske pl	73	D4
Gleinalmtunnel	57	E4
Gleisdorf	57	E4
Glen Albyn	2	C4
Glenamoy	12	B2
Glénan, I de	22	B4
Glenariff	13	E1
Glenarm	13	E1
Glenbeigh	14	A4
Glen Carron	2	C3
Glen Coe	4	C1
Glencolumbkille	12	C1
Glendalough	13	D4
Glenelg	2	B4
Glenfinnan	2	B4
Glengarriff	14	A4
Glenluce	4	C3
Glen More	2	C4
Glen More Forest Park	3	D4
Glennamaddy	12	C3
Glenrothes	5	D2
Glenties	12	C1
Glifa	83	F3
Glifáda (Atikí-Piréas)	87	F1
Glifáda (Fokída)	83	D4
Gliki	82	B2
Glikóvrissi	87	D4
Glina	70	C3
Glittertind	100	B3
Gliwice	112	B2
Globino	113	F2
Globočica	77	D2
Gloggnitz	57	E3
Głogów	112	A2
Glomfjord	97	E2
Glomma	105	D3
Glommersträsk	98	B3
Gloppet	102	B2
Glossop	6	C2
Gloucester	9	D2
Gloucestershire	9	D2
Głubczyce	112	A2
Glubokoje	111	D3
Głuchołazy	112	A2
Gluchov	113	F1
Glücksburg	48	A1
Glückstadt	48	A2
Glumsø	108	C4
Glušci	72	C3
Glyn Ebwy	9	D2
Gmund (D)	56	A4
Gmünd (Kärnten)	59	F2
Gmünd (Nieder-österreich)	57	E2
Gmunden	56	C3
Gnarp	101	F3
Gnesta	106	B4
Gnjilane	77	D2
Gnoien	49	D2
Gnosjö	109	D2
Goat Fell	4	B2
Goce Delčev	115	D3
Goch	17	D3
Godafoss	96	B1
Godalming	9	F3
Godby	106	C3
Godelheim	52	A2
Goderville	19	D3
Godmanchester	9	F1
Gödöllő	112	B4
Godovič	70	A2
Goduš	72	B3
Goeree	16	B3
Goes	16	B3
Göggingen	55	F3
Göhren	49	D1
Goirle	16	C3
Góis	38	B2
Goito	60	C1
Gokčanica	73	D4
Gokçe	115	E3
Gol	104	C2
Gola	71	D1
Golada	34	B2
Golaja Pristan'	113	F3
Golczewo	49	F2
Goldbach	52	A4
Goldberg	48	C2
Goldenstedt	17	F1
Golega	38	B3
Golema reka	77	D3
Golemo Selo	77	E2
Goleniów	49	F2
Goleš	77	E2
Golfe-Juan	31	E4
Golfo Aranci	66	C1
Goli	70	B3
Golija (Crna Gora)	76	A2
Golija (Srbija)	76	C1
Goljak	77	D2
Goljaki, M.	70	A2

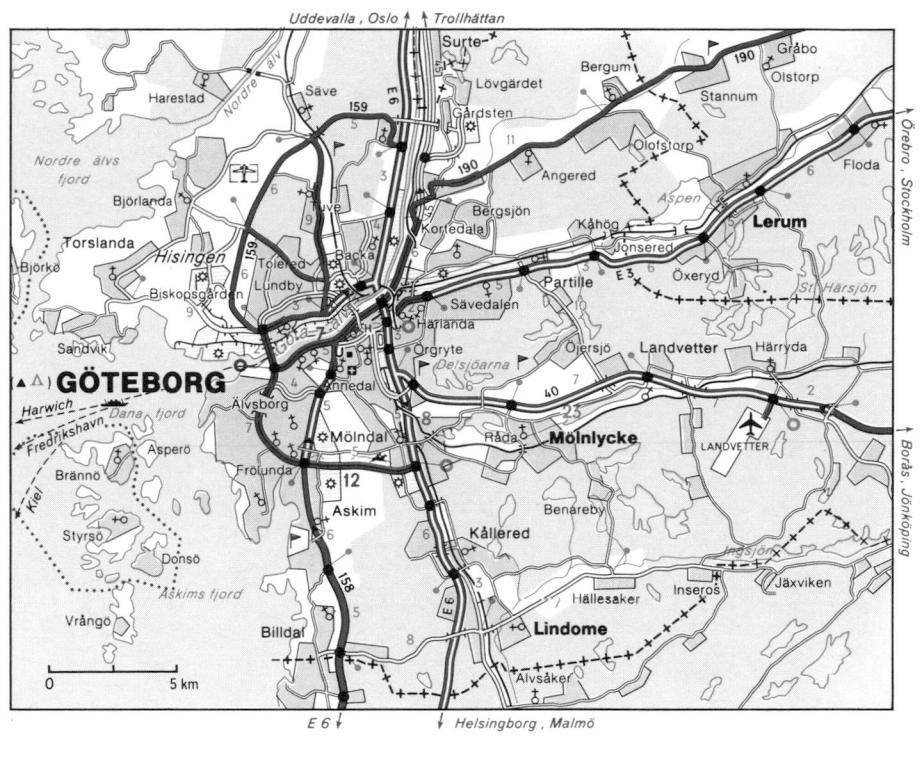

Goljam Perelik 115 D3
Göllersdorf 57 E2
Golling 59 E1
Golo 33 F3
Golpejas 39 E1
Golßen 53 E1
Golspie 3 D3
Golubac 73 E3
Golubovci 76 B3
Golubovec 70 C2
Golzow 49 D4
Gómara 36 B3
Gomáti 80 B3
Gombrèn 32 A3
Gomecello 39 E1
Gomel' 111 E4
Comera 42 A4
Gómfi 83 D2
Gommern 52 C1
Goncelin 31 D1
Gondomar 34 A4
Gondomar (E) 34 A3
Gondrecourt 20 C4
Gönen 115 E3
Góni 83 E1
Goniá 90 B3
Goniés 91 D3
Gonnesa 66 B4
Gonnosfanadiga 66 B4
Goole 7 D2
Goor 17 D2
Goppenstein 27 F3
Göppingen 55 D2
Gora 70 C3
Goražde 76 A1
Gördalen 101 D3
Gordes 30 C3
Gorenja Vas 70 A2
Gorey (GB) 18 B3
Gorey (IRL) 15 D3
Gorgona, I di 60 B4
Gorgonzola 60 A1
Gorgopótamos 78 C4
Gorica (Bosna i Hercegovina) 75 E2
Gorica (Makedonija) 77 D4
Goričan 71 D1
Gorice 70 B3
Gorinchem 16 C3
Goritsá 87 D3
Gorizia 59 F3
Gorjanci 70 C2
Gorki 111 E3
Gorleston-on-Sea 7 F4
Gorlice 112 B3
Görlitz 53 F2
Gorna Orjahovica 115 D2
Gornja Dobrinja 72 C4
Gornja Grabovica 75 F1
Gornja Kamenica 73 F4
Gornja Klina 77 D2
Gornja Ljubovidđa 72 C4
Gornja Ljuta 75 F1
Gornja Ploča 70 C4
Gornja Radgona 70 C1
Gornja Sabanta 73 D4
Gornja Sanica 71 D4
Gornja Slatina 71 F3
Gornja Toplica 72 C4
Gornja Toponica 73 E4
Gornja Tuzla 72 B3
Gornje Dubočke 76 A2
Gornje Ratkovo 71 E4
Gornje Selo 75 D2
Gornji Grad 70 B2
Gornji Kokoti 76 B3
Gornji Kosinj 70 C4
Gornji Lapac 71 D4
Gornji Lukavac 76 A2
Gornji Milanovac 73 D4
Gornji Petrovci 70 C1
Gornji Podgradci 71 D3
Gornji Rajić 71 E3
Gornji Stepoš 73 E4
Gornji Vakuf 75 E1
Gornji Zabar 71 F3
Gorno Orizari 77 E3
Goro 61 D2
Gorodišče 113 F2
Gorodn'a 111 E4
Gorodok (Belorussija) 111 D3

Gorodok (Ukraina) 112 C2
Gorredijk 17 D1
Gorron 23 E3
Gort 12 B4
Corteen 12 C3
Gortin 13 D2
Córtis 91 D4
Cortmore 12 B3
Gorumna I 12 B3
Coryn' 113 D2
Góry Świętokrzyskie 112 B2
Görzke 53 D1
Gorzów Wielkopolski 49 F3
Gosaldo 59 D3
Gosau 59 F1
Gosausee 59 F1
Göschenen 58 A3
Gościno 49 F1
Gosforth 5 D4
Gößl 56 C3
Goslar 52 B1
Gößnitz 53 D3
Gospić 70 C4
Gospoddinci 72 C2
Gosport 9 E3
Gossau 58 B2
Gosselies 50 B4
Gossensass 59 D2
Gössweinstein 52 C4
Gostivar 77 D3
Göstling 57 D3
Gostyń 112 A2
Götaälv 108 C1
Göta Kanal 105 E4
Göteborg 108 C1
Göteborgs och Bohus Län 108 C1
Götene 105 E4
Gotha 52 C3
Gothem 109 F4
Gotland 109 F4
Gotlands Län 109 F4
Gotska Sandön 106 C4
Göttingen 52 B2
Gottwaldov 112 A3
Götzis 58 B2
Gouarec 22 C3
Gouda 16 C3
Gouménissa 79 F2
Goumois 27 E2
Goúra 87 D1
Gourdon 29 D2
Gourin 22 B3
Gournay-en-Bray 19 E3
Goúrnes 91 E3
Gourniá 91 E4
Gourock 4 C2
Gouveia 38 C2
Goúves 91 E3
Gouviá 82 A1
Gouzon 25 F4
Goveddari 75 E2
Goverla 113 D2
Gowienica 49 F2
Göynük 115 F3
Gozd 70 A1
Gozo 68 B4
Gozzano 58 A4
Graal-Müritz 48 C1
Graben-Neudorf 54 C2
Grabenstätt 56 B3
Grabovac 75 E2
Grabovci 72 C3
Grabow 48 C3
Gračac 70 C4
Gračanica (Bosna i Hercegovina) 71 F3
Gračanica (Crna Gora) 76 B2
Gračanica (Kosovo) 77 D2
Gračanica (Srbija) 72 C4
Graçay 25 E2
Grächen 27 F4
Gradac (Crna Gora) 76 B1
Gradac (Hrvatska) 75 E2
Gradac (Srbija) 76 C1
Gradačac 71 F3
Gradara 61 E3
Gradče, Ez 77 F2
Gradec 71 D2

Gradefes 35 E2
Gradeška pl 77 F3
Gradina 77 F1
Gradisca d'Isonzo 59 F3
Gradište (Hrvatska) 71 E2
Gradište (Makedonija) 77 E2
Grado (E) 35 D1
Grado (I) 59 F4
Gradsko 77 E3
Gradskovo 73 F3
Grafelfing 56 A3
Grafenau 56 C2
Gräfenberg 55 F1
Gräfenhainichen 53 D1
Grafenwöhr 55 F1
Grafing 56 B3
Gragnano 64 B4
Grahovo (Bosna i Hercegovina) 76 A2
Grahovo (Slovenija) 70 A2
Graiguenamanagh 15 D3
Grain 11 D2
Grainau 55 F1
Grajewo 110 C4
Gram 108 A3
Gramat 29 D2
Gramatikó 83 E2
Gramatikoú 83 D4
Graméni 80 B2
Graméno 82 B1
Grametten 57 D1
Grammichele 69 D4
Grámos, Óros 78 C3
Grampian 3 E4
Grampian Mts 4 C1
Gramsh 77 D4
Gramzow 49 E3
Gran 105 D2
Granada 44 A3
Granadella 37 E4
Granadilla de Abona 42 B4
Granard 12 C3
Gran Canaria 42 B4
Grancey-le-Château 26 C2
Grandas 34 C1
Grand Ballon 27 E1
Grand Bois, Col du 30 B1
Grand-Bornand, le 27 D4
Grand-Bourg 25 E4
Grandcamp-Maisy 18 C3
Grand Canal d'Alsace 27 E1
Grand Canyon du Verdon 31 D3
Grand-Champ 22 C4
Grand-Colombier 30 C1
Grand-Combe, la 30 B3
Grand Combin 27 E4
Grand-Couronne 19 D3
Grand-Croix 30 B1
Grande Casse 31 D1
Grande de Europa, Punta 43 E4
Grande Dixence, Bge de la 27 E4
Grande-Motte, la 30 B4
Grande Sassière 31 E1
Grandes Rousses 31 D1
Grand-Fougeray 23 D4
Grand-Lemps, le 30 C1
Grand Lieu, L de 24 B3
Grand-Lucé, le 23 F4
Grand Morin 20 A4
Grândola 42 A1
Grandpré 20 C3
Grand-Pressigny, le 25 D3
Grand Rhône 30 B4
Grandrieu 29 F2
Grand-Serre, le 30 C1
Grands Goulets 30 C2
Grandval, Bge de 29 F2
Grandvilliers 19 E3
Grañén 37 D3
Grängärde 105 F3
Grangemouth 5 D2
Grange-Over-Sands 6 B1
Grängesberg 105 F3

Granges-sur-Vologne 27 E1
Granier, Col du 30 C1
Granítis 80 B1
Granítsa 83 D2
Granja (Alentejo) 42 C1
Granja (Douro) 34 A4
Granja de Torrehermosa 43 E1
Granja, Pto de la 43 D1
Gränna 109 D1
Granollers 32 A4
Granön 102 A1
Gran Paradiso 31 E1
Gran San Bernardo, Colle del 27 E4
Gran San Bernardo, Traforo del 27 E4
Gran Sasso d'Italia 63 F1
Gransee 49 D3
Gran Tarajal 42 C4
Grantham 7 D3
Grantown-on-Spey 3 D3
Granville 18 B4
Granvin 104 B2
Grappa, Mte 59 D3
Grasleben 52 C1
Grasmere 5 D4
Grassano 65 D4
Grasse 31 E3
Gråsten 108 A4
Gråstorp 108 C1
Gratangen 94 B3
Gratiní 81 E2
Gratkorn 57 E4
Graubünden 58 B2
Grau-du-Roi, le 30 B4
Graulhet 29 D4
Graus 37 E3
Gravalos 36 C3
Gravdal 97 E1
Grave 17 D3
Gravedona 58 B3
Grave, la 31 D1
Gravelines 19 F1
Gravellona-Toce 58 A4
Grave, Pointe de 28 A1
Gravesend 11 D2
Graviá 83 E3
Gravina in Puglia 65 D3
Gravona 33 F3
Gravoúna 80 C2
Gray 26 C2
Grays Thurrock 10 C2
Graz 57 E4
Grazalema 43 E3
Grazzanise 64 A3

Grdelica 77 E1
Great Blasket I. 14 A3
Great Driffield 7 D1
Great Dunmow 11 D2
Great Grimsby 7 E2
Great Malvern 9 D1
Great Ormes Head 6 A2
Great Ouse 7 E3
Great Torrington 8 C3
Great Yarmouth 7 F4
Grebbestad 105 D4
Greccio 63 E2
Greding 55 F2
Gredos 39 F2
Gredos, Sa de 39 F2
Greenhead 5 D3
Greenlaw 5 E2
Greenock 4 C2
Greenodd 6 B1
Greggio 31 F1
Gregolimano 83 F3
Greifenburg 59 E2
Greiffenberg 49 E3
Greifswald 49 D1
Greifswalder Bodden 49 D1
Grein 57 D2
Greiz 53 D3
Grenå 108 B2
Grenade (Haute-Garonne) 29 D4
Grenade (Landes) 28 B4
Grenchen 27 E2
Grenoble 30 C1
Grense Jakobselv 95 F2
Gréoux-les-Bains 31 D3
Gressåmoen 101 E1
Gresse 30 C2
Gressoney-la-Trinite 27 F4
Gressoney-St-Jean 27 F4
Gresten 57 D3
Grésy 31 D1
Greußen 52 C2
Greve 61 D4
Greven 17 E2
Grevená 79 D4
Grevená (Nomos) 79 D4
Grevenbroich 17 D4
Grevenbrück 17 F4
Grevenítio 82 C1
Grevesmühlen 48 B2
Greve Strand 108 C3
Greyabbey 13 E2

Greystones 13 E4
Grez-en-Bouère 23 E3
Grezzana 60 C1
Grgur 70 B4
Griá, Akr 88 B1
Grianan of Aileach 13 D1
Griebenow 49 D2
Gries 59 D2
Gries im Sellrain 58 C2
Grieskirchen 56 C3
Griffen 70 B1
Grignan 30 B2
Grigno 59 D3
Grignols 28 B3
Grimaldi 67 E3
Grimaud 31 D4
Grimma 53 D2
Grimmen 49 D2
Grimone, Col de 30 C2
Grimsbu 100 C3
Grimselpass 27 F3
Grimsey 96 B1
Grimstad 104 B4
Grindaheim 104 C2
Grindavík 96 A2
Grindelwald 27 F3
Grindsted 108 A3
Grintavec 70 B2
Griñón 40 A2
Grisignano 61 D1
Gris Nez, Cap 19 E1
Grisolles 29 D3
Grisslehamn 106 B3
Gríva 79 E2
Grizáno 83 D1
Grk 71 F3
Grljan 73 F3
Grmec 71 D4
Grøa 100 B2
Gröbming 59 F1
Grocka 73 D3
Gröditz 53 E2
Grodno 110 C4
Groenlo 17 D3
Gröer Arber 56 B1
Groitzsch 53 D2
Groix 22 B4
Groix, I de 22 B4
Grömitz 48 B2
Gronau 17 E2
Grönenbach 55 E4
Grong 97 D4
Grönhögen 109 E3
Gröningen 52 C1

Grönskåra 109 E2
Grønsund 108 C4
Gropello Cairoli 60 A2
Großbreitenbach 52 C3
Großburgwedel 48 A4
Groscavallo 31 E1
Großenbrode 48 B1
Großenhain 53 E2
Großenzersdorf 57 F2
Groß Gerungs 57 D2
Großglockner 59 E2
Großglockner Hochalpenstraße 59 E2
Großhabersdorf 55 E1
Grosio 58 C3
Grosne 26 C3
Groß Ötscher 57 E3
Großpetersdorf 57 F4
Großraming 57 D3
Großraschen 53 E1
Groß Reken 17 E3
Großröhrsdorf 53 E2
Groß Rosennock 59 F2
Gross Beerberg 52 C3
Gross Bösenstein 57 D4
Groß-Schönebeck 49 E3
Grosse Pierre 27 E1
Grosse Röder 53 E2
Grosser Plöner See 48 B2
Grosseto 62 C1
Gross Feldberg 51 F4
Gross-Gerau 54 C1
Groß Siegharts 57 E2
Gross Priel 57 D3
Gross Rachel 56 C2
Grossschönau 53 F2
Gross-Umstadt 55 D1
Grostenquin 21 D3
Grosuplje 70 B2
Großvenediger 59 E2
Großweil 56 A4
Grötlingbo 109 F4
Grøtsundet 94 C2
Grotta di Nettuno 66 A2
Grottaglie 65 E4
Grottaminarda 64 B3
Grottammare 61 F4
Grotte di Pertosa 64 C4
Grotteria 67 F4
Grouin, Pte du 18 B4
Grove 34 A2
Grövelsjön 101 D3
Grovfjord 94 B3
Grubišno Polje 71 D2
Gruda 76 A3

Name	Page	Grid
Grude	75	E2
Grudziądz	112	B1
Gruinard B	2	C3
Gruissan	32	B2
Grums	105	E3
Grünau	56	C3
Grünberg	52	A3
Grünburg	57	D3
Grundarfjörður	96	A2
Grundforsen	101	D4
Grundlsee	56	C3
Grundlsee L	56	C3
Grundsund	108	C1
Grundtjärn	101	F2
Grünstadt	54	C1
Grünwald	56	A3
Grupčin	77	D3
Gruyères	27	E3
Gruža	73	D4
Gruža R	73	D4
Grycksbo	105	F2
Gryfice	49	F2
Gryfino	49	E3
Gryllefjord	94	B2
Grythyttan	105	E3
Grytøya	94	B3
Grza	73	E4
Gschütt, Paß	59	F1
Gstaad	27	E3
Gstadt	56	B3
Guadahortuna	44	A2
Guadaira, R	43	E3
Guadajira, R	39	D4
Guadajoz, R	43	F2
Guadalajara	40	B2
Guadalaviar	41	D2
Guadalaviar, R	41	D2
Guadalcacín, Emb de	43	D3
Guadalcanal	43	D1
Guadalén, Emb de	44	A1
Guadalén, R	44	B1
Guadalest	45	E1
Guadalete, R	43	D4
Guadalfeo, R	44	A4
Guadalhorce, R	43	E4
Guadalimar, R (Andalucia)	43	D3
Guadalimar, R (Andalucia)	44	B2
Guadalmellato, Emb de	43	F2
Guadalmena, Emb de	44	B1
Guadalmena, R	44	B1
Guadalmez, R	43	F1
Guadalope, R	41	E2
Guadalquivir, R	43	D3
Guadal, R	44	B2
Guadalteba-Guadalhorce, Emb del	43	E3
Guadalupe	39	E3
Guadalupe, Sa de	39	E3
Guadarrama	40	A2
Guadarrama, Pto de	40	A2
Guadarrama, R	40	A2
Guadarrama, Sa de	40	A1
Guadarranque, Emb del	43	E4
Guadasuar	41	E4
Guadazaón, R	40	C3
Guadiamar, R	43	D3
Guadiana Menor, R	44	B2
Guadiana, R	39	F4
Guadiaro	43	E4
Guadiaro, R	43	E4
Guadiato, R	43	E2
Guadiela, R	40	C2
Guadix	44	B3
Guajaraz, Emb de	40	A3
Gualdo Tadino	61	E4
Guara, Sa de	37	E3
Guarda	38	C1
Guardamar del Segura	45	D2
Guardiagrele	64	A2
Guardia Sanframondi	64	B3
Guardias Viejas	44	B4
Guardo	35	E2
Guareña	39	D4
Guarrizas, R	44	A1
Guarromán	44	A2
Guastalla	60	C2
Gubbio	61	E4
Guben	53	F1
Guberevac	73	D4
Gubin	53	F1
Guča	73	D4
Guca Gora	71	E4
Gúdar, Sa de	41	E2
Gudavac	71	D3
Gudbrandsdalen	100	C3
Guderup	108	A4
Gudhjem	109	D4
Gudingen	109	E1
Gudow	48	B3
Gudvangen	104	B2
Guebwiller	27	E1
Guémené-Penfao	23	D4
Güeñes	36	B1
Guer	23	D3
Guérande	22	C4
Guerche-de-Bretagne, la	23	D3
Guerche, la	26	A3
Guéret	25	E4
Guérigny	26	A2
Guerlédan, L de	22	C3
Guernsey	18	A3
Guéthary	28	A4
Gueugnon	26	B3
Güglingen	55	D2
Guglionesi	64	B2
Guía	42	B4
Guía de Isora	42	A4
Guichen	23	D3
Guidonia	63	E2
Guignes	19	F4
Guijo de Granadilla	39	D2
Guijuelo	39	E2
Guildford	9	F3
Guillaumes	31	E3
Guillena	43	D2
Guillestre	31	D2
Guillon	26	B2
Guilvinec	22	A3
Güimar	42	B4
Guimarães	34	A4
Guimiliau	22	B2
Guînes	19	E1
Guingamp	22	C2
Guipavas	22	A2
Guisborough	5	F4
Guiscard	19	F3
Guise	20	A2
Guissona	37	F3
Guist	7	F3
Guitiriz	34	B1
Guitres	28	B2
Gujan-Mestras	28	A2
Gulbene	110	C2
Guldborg Sund	108	C4
Gullesfjorden	94	A3
Gullfoss	96	B2
Gullkrona fjärd	107	D3
Gullspång	105	E4
Gumiel de Hizán	36	A3
Gummersbach	17	E4
Gundelfingen	55	E3
Gundelsheim	55	D2
Gunnarn	97	F4
Gunnarsbyn	98	B3
Gunnärsfjärden	98	C3
Gunnarskog	105	E3
Gunten	27	F3
Günterode	52	B2
Guntin de Pallares	34	B2
Gunzenhausen	55	E2
Gurk	70	A1
Gurk R	59	F2
Gurrea de Gállego	37	D3
Gusev	110	B4
Gusinje	76	C2
Guspini	66	B3
Güssing	57	F4
Güsten	52	C1
Güstrow	48	C3
Gutcher	3	F1
Gutenstein	57	E3
Gütersloh	17	F3
Gutulia	100	D3
Gützkow	49	D2
Guyhirn	10	C1
Gvardejsk	110	B4
Gvarv	104	C3
Gvozd	76	B2
Gweebarra B	12	C1
Gwent	9	D2
Gwynedd	6	A3
Gy	27	D2
Gyöngyös	112	B4
Győr	112	A4
Gysinge	106	A3
Gyula	112	C4

H

Name	Page	Grid
Haag (A)	57	D3
Haag (D)	56	B3
Haag am Hausruck	56	C3
Haaksbergen	17	D2
Haamstede	16	B3
Haapajärvi	103	D1
Haapajärvi L	103	D1
Haapakoski	103	E2
Haapamäki (Keski-Suomen Lääni)	102	C3
Haapamäki (Oulun Lääni)	103	D1
Haapavesi	103	D1
Haapsalu	110	B2
Haar	56	A3
Haaren	17	F3
Haarlem	16	B2
Habay	20	C2
Habo	109	D1
Habsheim	27	E1
Hachenburg	51	F3
Hachmühlen	52	A1
Hackås	101	E2
Hadamar	51	F4
Haddington	5	D2
Hadersdorf	57	E2
Haderslev	108	A4
Hadleigh	11	D2
Hadmersleben	52	C1
Hadrian's Wall	5	E3
Hadselfjorden	94	A3
Hadsten	108	B2
Hadsund	108	B2
Hadžići	75	F1
Hafnarfjörður	96	A2
Haganj	71	D2
Hægebostad	104	B4
Hagen (Niedersachsen)	47	F3
Hagen (Nordrhein-Westfalen)	17	E4
Hagenow	48	B3
Hagetmau	28	B4
Hagfors	105	E3
Häggdånger	101	F3
Haggenås	101	E2
Hagondange	21	D3
Hague, Cap de la	18	B2
Haguenau	21	E3
Hahn	47	F3
Hahnbach	55	F1
Haigerloch	55	D3
Hailsham	10	C3
Hailuoto	99	D4
Hainaut	99	D4
Hainburg	57	F2
Hainfeld	57	E3
Hainichen	53	E2
Hajdúböszörmény	112	C4
Hajdučica	73	D2
Hajdúszoboszló	112	C4
Hajla	76	C2
Hajnówka	112	C1
Hakarp	109	D1
Hakkas	98	B2
Häkkilä	103	D2
Halámky	57	D2
Halandritsa	86	C1
Halbe	53	E1
Halberstadt	52	C1
Halden	105	D4
Haldensleben	48	C4
Halesowen	9	E1
Halesworth	11	E1
Halhjem	104	A2
Halifax	6	C2
Halikko	107	E2
Halju	95	D4
Halkeró	80	C2
Hálki (Dodekánissa)	93	E1

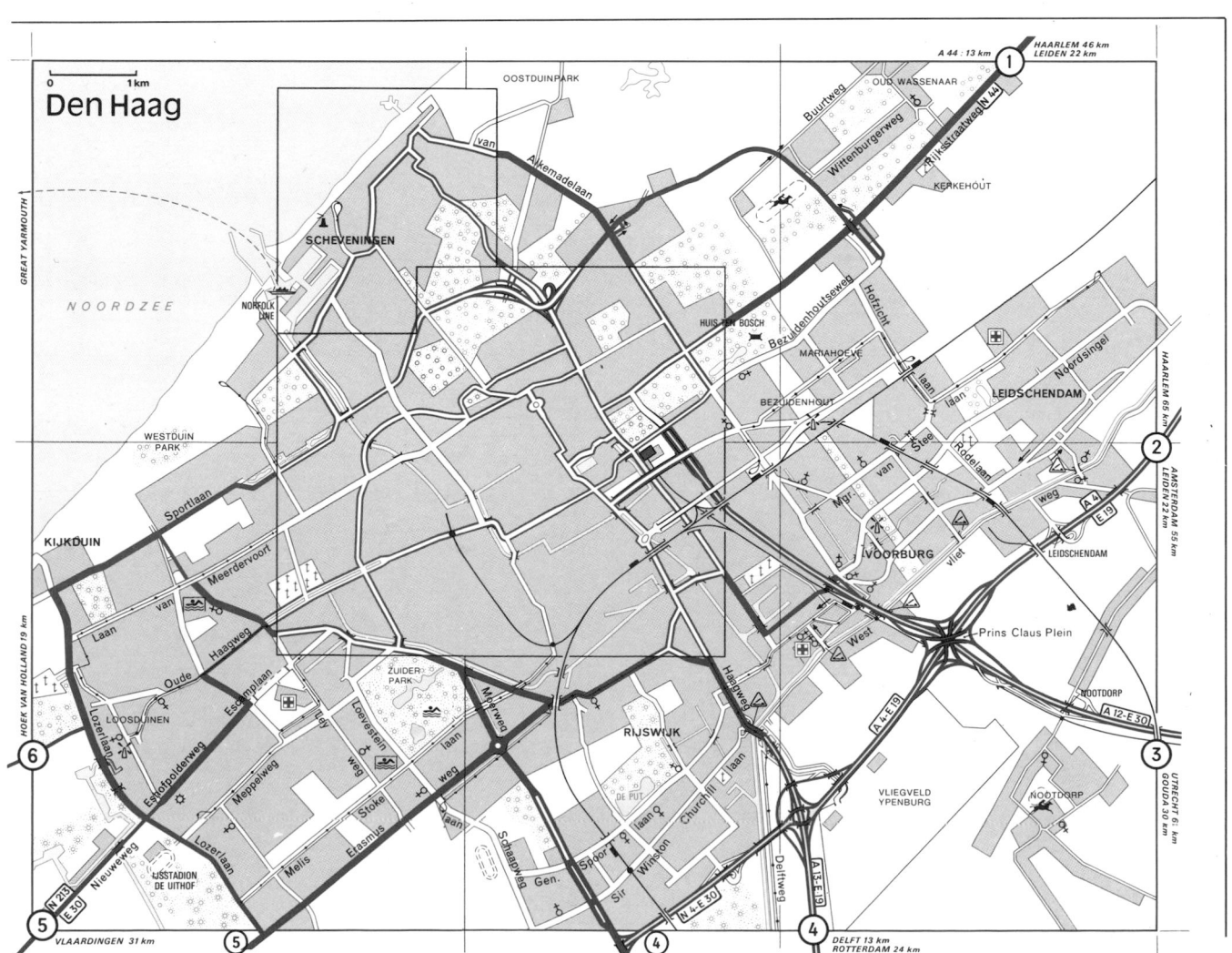

Den Haag

Name	Ref		Name	Ref		Name	Ref
Halki (Kikládes)	88 C3		Haniá (Nomos)	90 B3		Hasle	109 D4
Hálki (Thessalía)	83 E1		Hánia (Thessalía)	83 F2		Haslemere	9 F3
Halkiádes	83 E2		Hani i Hotit	76 B3		Haslev	108 C4
Halkída	84 B4		Hanion, Kólpos	90 B3		Hasparren	28 A4
Halkidikí	80 B3		Haniótis	80 B4		Hassela	101 F3
Hálki, N	93 E1		Hankamäki	103 E1		Hasselfelde	52 C2
Halkidóna	79 F3		Hankasalmen as	103 D3		Hasselt	50 C3
Halkió	85 F4		Hankasalmi	103 D3		Hássia, Óri	83 D1
Halkio	87 D1		Hankensbüttel	48 B4		Hässleholm	109 D3
Halkodóni, Óros	83 E2		Hanko	107 E3		Hastière	50 C4
Hallands Län	108 C2		Hannover	48 A4		Hastings	11 D3
Halle (B)	50 B3		Hannut	50 C4		Hasvik	95 D1
Halle (D)	17 F2		Hanöbukten	109 D3		Hatě	57 E1
Halle (DDR)	53 D2		Hansnes	94 C2		Hateg	114 C1
Hällefors	105 E3		Han-sur-Lesse	50 C4		Hatfield	9 F2
Hälleforsnäs	105 E4		Hanstedt	48 A3		Hatherleigh	8 C3
Hallein	56 C3		Hanstholm	108 A2		Hattem	17 D2
Hällekis	105 E4		Haparanda	98 C3		Hattfjelldal	97 E3
Hallenberg	17 F4		Harads	98 B3		Hattingen	17 E3
Hallencourt	19 E2		Harafjärden	98 C3		Hattula	107 E2
Halle-Neustadt	53 D2		Haraldshaugen	104 A3		Hattuvaara (Lieksa)	103 F1
Hällesjö	101 F2		Haranes	97 D4		Hattuvaara (Ilomantsi)	103 F2
Hällevadsholm	105 D4		Haravgí	79 E3		Hatvan	112 B4
Halligen	47 F1		Harburg (Bayern)	55 E2		Hatvik	104 A2
Hallingdal	104 C2		Harburg (Hamburg)	48 A3		Hatzí	82 C2
Hallingskarvet	104 B2		Hårby	108 B4		Haubourdin	19 F1
Hall in Tirol	59 D1		Hardangerfjorden	104 A2		Hauge	104 A4
Hällnäs	102 A1		Hardangerjøkulen	104 B2		Haugesund	104 A3
Hallsberg	105 A4		Hardangervidda	104 B2		Hauho	107 E2
Hallstadt	52 C4		Hardbakke	104 A1		Haukelifjell	104 B2
Hallstahammar	105 F3		Hardegg	57 E1		Haukeligrend	104 B3
Hallstatt	59 F1		Hardegsen	52 B2		Haukipudas	99 D3
Hallstavik	106 B3		Hardelot	19 E1		Haukivesi	103 E3
Halluin	19 F1		Hardenberg	17 D2		Haukivuori	103 E3
Halmstad	108 C2		Harderwijk	16 C2		Haunstetten	55 F3
Hals	108 B2		Hardheim	55 D1		Haus	59 F1
Halsa	100 B2		Hardwick Hall	7 D3		Hausach	54 C3
Halsafjorden	100 B2		Hareid	100 A2		Hausham	56 A4
Hälsingtuna	101 F3		Harelbeke	50 A3		Hausjärvi	107 E2
Halsskov	108 B3		Haren (D)	17 E1		Hautajärvi	99 E2
Halstead	11 D2		Haren (NL)	47 D3		Hautecombe	27 D4
Halsteren	16 B3		Harewood	6 C2		Haute-Corse	33 F3
Halsua	102 C2		Haria	42 C3		Hautefort	29 D1
Haltdålen	101 D2		Haringvlietdam	16 B3		Haute-Garonne	29 D4
Haltern	17 E3		Haritoméni	80 B2		Haute-Loire	29 F2
Halti-Haldi	94 C3		Härjångsfjällen	101 D2			
Halver	17 E4		Harjavalta	107 D2			
Ham	19 F2		Harjunpää	107 D1			
Hamar	105 D2		Hårkan	101 E2			
Hamarøy	94 A4		Härkmeri	102 B3			
Hamburg	48 A3		Harlech	6 A3			
Hambye	18 B4		Harlesiel	47 E3			
Hamdorf	48 A2		Harleston	11 D1			
Hämeenkyrö	102 C3		Harlingen	16 C1			
Hämeen Lääni	102 C3		Harlow	10 C2			
Hämeenlinna	107 E2		Harmånger	101 F3			
Hämelerwald	52 B1		Harmanli	115 E3			
Hameln	52 A1		Härnösand	101 F3			
Hamersleben	52 C1		Haro	36 B2			
Hamili, N	92 C2		Harokopió	86 C4			
Hamilton	4 C2		Haroldswick	3 F1			
Hamina	103 F4		Haroué	21 D4			
Hamm	17 E3		Harøyfjorden	100 A2			
Hammarland	106 C3		Harpenden	9 F2			
Hammarstrand	101 F2		Harplinge	108 C2			
Hammaslahti	103 F2		Harpstedt	17 F1			
Hammel	108 B3		Harris	2 A2			
Hammelburg	52 B4		Harrislee	47 F1			
Hammerdal	101 E2		Harris, Sd of	2 A3			
Hammerfest	95 D1		Harrogate	6 C1			
Hammershus	109 D4		Härryda	108 C1			
Hamneidet	94 C2		Harsefeld	48 A3			
Hamningberg	95 F1		Harsprånget	98 B2			
Hamoir	50 C4		Harstad	94 B3			
Hampshire	9 E3		Harsvik	96 C4			
Hamra	101 E3		Hartberg	57 F4			
Hamra (Reg)	101 E3		Hårteigen	104 B2			
Hamre	104 B4		Hartha	53 E2			
Hamzali	77 E3		Hartkjölen	101 E1			
Hamzići	75 F2		Hartland Pt	8 B3			
Hanákia	86 B2		Hartlepool	5 F4			
Hanau	52 A4		Hartmannsdorf	53 E2			
Handrás	91 F4		Hartola	103 D3			
Hanerau-Hademarschen	48 A2		Harwich	11 D2			
Hangö	107 E3		Harz	52 B2			
Hangon läntinenselkä	107 D3		Harzgerode	52 C2			
Hangö västra fjärd	107 D3		Hase	17 E2			
Haniá (Haniá)	90 B3		Haselünne	17 E2			
Hánia (Lakonía)	87 D3		Haßfurt	52 C4			
			Haskovo	115 D3			
			Haslach (A)	56 C2			
			Haslach (D)	54 C3			

Name	Ref		Name	Ref		Name	Ref
Haute-Marne	26 C1		Hedal	104 C2		Hekla	96 B2
Hautes-Alpes	31 D2		Heddal	104 C3		Hekuravë, Maj'e	76 C2
Haute-Saône	27 D1		Hédé	23 D3		Helagsfjället	101 D2
Haute-Savoie	27 D4		Hede	101 E3		Hélatros, Akr	93 D3
Haute-Vienne (Dépt)	29 D1		Hedemora	105 F3		Heldburg	52 C4
Hauteville-Lompnes	27 D4		Hedenäset	98 C2		Heldrungen	52 C2
Hautmont	20 B2		Hedensted	108 B3		Helechal	43 E1
Haut-Rhin (Dept)	27 E1		Hedesundafjärdarna	106 B3		Helensburgh	4 C2
Havant	9 F3		Hedeviken	101 E3		Helgå (N)	101 D1
Havári	86 B1		Hedmark	104 C1		Helgaå (S)	109 D3
Havdalsfjället	97 E4		Hedon	7 E2		Helgasjön	109 D3
Havdáta	82 B4		Heemstede	16 C2		Helgoland	47 E2
Havel	49 D4		Heerde	17 D2		Helland	3 D2
Havelange	50 C4		Heerenveen	17 D1		Hella	104 B1
Havelberg	48 C3		Heerlen	51 D3		Hellemofjorden	97 F1
Haverfordwest	8 B2		Heeze	16 C4		Hellendoorn	17 D2
Haverhill	11 D1		Hegge	104 C1		Hellesylt	100 A3
Haverö	101 E3		Hegra	101 D2		Hellevoetsluis	16 B3
Havneby	108 A4		Heia	94 C3		Hellin	44 C1
Havøysund	95 D1		Heide	47 F2		Hellvik	104 A4
Havran	53 E3		Heidelberg	54 C1		Helmbrechts	53 D4
Havre, Le	19 D3		Heidenau	53 E2		Helme	52 C2
Hawes	6 C1		Heidenheim	55 E2		Helmond	17 D3
Hawick	5 D3		Heidenreichstein	57 D1		Helmsdale	3 D2
Hawkhurst	11 D3		Heikendorf	48 A1		Helmsley	7 D1
Hayange	21 D3		Heikkila	99 F2		Helmstadt	55 D1
Haye-du-Puits, la	18 B3		Heilbronn	55 D2		Helmstedt	52 C1
Haye-Pesnel, la	18 B4		Heiligenberg	55 D4		Helpter Berge	49 E2
Hayle	8 A4		Heiligenblut	59 E2		Helsa	52 B2
Hay-on-Wye	9 D1		Heiligenkirchen	17 F3		Helsingborg	108 C3
Haywards Heath	10 C3		Heiligenkreuz	57 F4		Helsinge	108 C3
Hazebrouck	19 F1		Heiligenstadt	52 B2		Helsingfors	107 F3
Headcorn	11 D3		Heimari	103 E3		Helsingør	108 C3
Headford	12 B3		Heimdal	100 C2		Helsinki	107 F3
Heanor	7 D3		Heimertingen	55 E3		Helston	8 B4
Héas	37 E2		Heinävaara	103 F2		Helvetinjärvi	102 C3
Heathfield	10 C3		Heinävesi	103 E3		Helvick Head	14 C4
Heathrow Airport	9 F2		Heinola	107 F1		Hemau	55 F2
Hebrides, Outer	2 A2		Heinolan mlk	107 F1		Hemavan	97 E3
Hebrides, Sea of the	2 A3		Heinsberg	17 D4		Hemel Hempstead	9 F2
Heby	106 B3		Heist	50 A3		Hemer	17 E3
Hechingen	55 D3		Heist-op-den-Berg	50 C5		Hemme	100 C2
Hecho	37 D2		Hejde	109 F4		Hemmoor	48 A2
Hechtel	50 C3					Hemnefjorden	100 C1
Hecklingen	52 C1					Hemnes	105 D3
						Hemnesberget	97 E2
						Hemsedal	104 C2
						Hemsedal V	104 C2

Name	Ref
Henares, R	40 B2
Hendaye	28 A4
Hengelo	17 D2
Hengersberg	56 B2
Hengstpaß	57 D3
Hénin-Beaumont	19 F1
Henley	9 E1
Henley-on-Thames	9 F2
Henneberg	52 B3
Hennebont	22 B3
Hennef	51 E3
Hennigsdorf	49 D4
Henrichemont	25 F2
Henstedt-Ulzburg	48 A2
Henstridge	9 D3
Heraclea	77 E4
Hérault	29 F4
Hérault (Dépt)	30 A4
Herbault	25 D2
Herbertingen	55 D3
Herbiers, les	24 B3
Herbignac	22 C4
Herbolzheim	54 C3
Herborn	51 F3
Herbrechtingen	55 E2
Herbstein	52 A3
Herceg Novi	76 A3
Hercegovac	71 D2
Hercegovi Goleša	76 B1
Herðubreið	96 C2
Hereford	9 D1
Hereford and Worcester	9 D1
Herencia	40 B4
Herentals	50 C3
Herford	17 F2
Héricourt	27 E2
Heringsdorf	49 E2
Herisau	58 B2
Hérisson	26 A3
Hérisson, Cascades du	27 D3
Herk	50 C3
Herleshausen	52 B3
Hermagor	59 F2

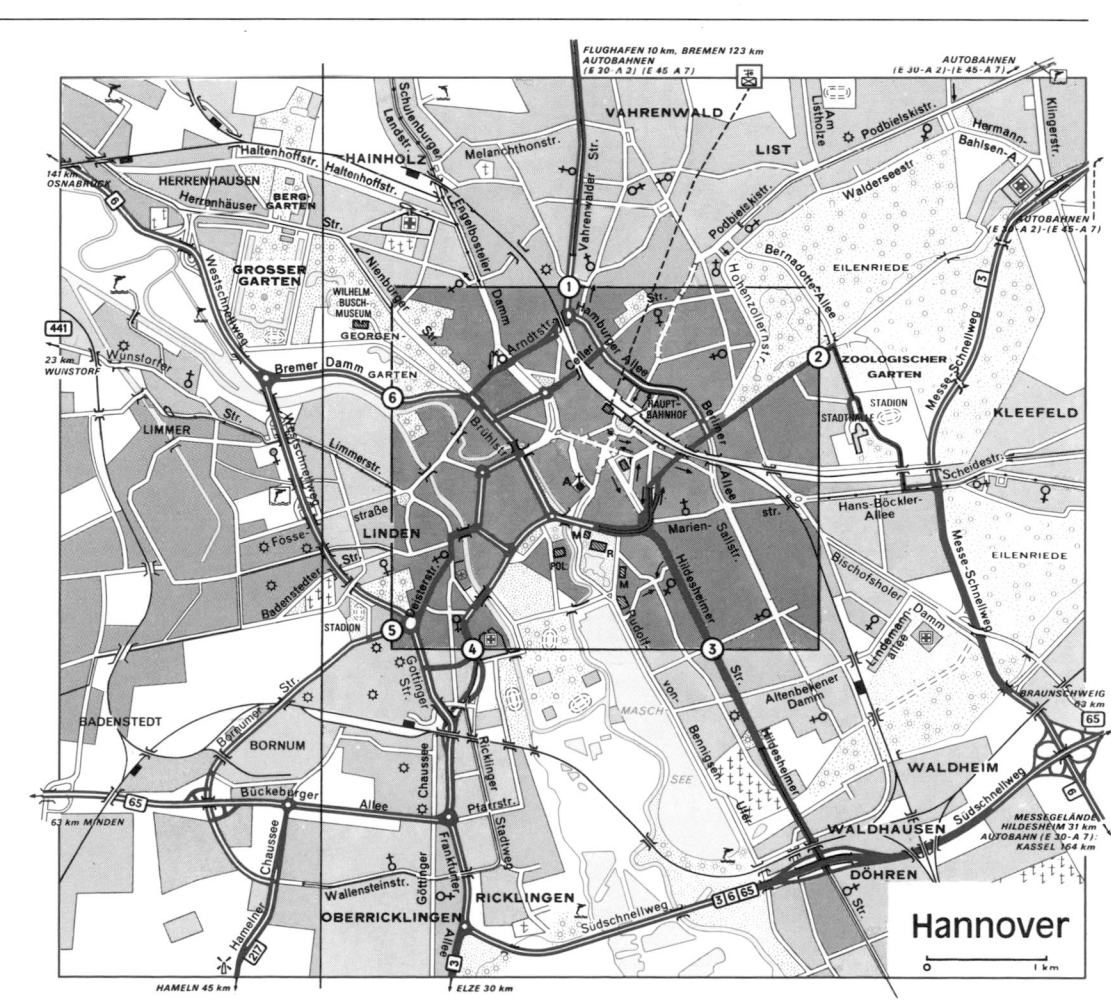

Hannover

Herma Ness 3 F1
Hermannsburg 48 B4
Hermansverk 104 B1
Hermenault, l' 24 C3
Herment 29 E1
Hermeskeil 54 B1
Hermigua 42 A4
Hermsdorf 53 D3
Hernani 36 C1
Hernansancho 39 F1
Herne 17 E3
Herne Bay 11 D3
Herning 108 A3
Heroldsberg 55 F1
Herónia 83 F4
Herøy 100 A2
Herrala 107 F2
Herre 104 C3
Herrenberg 55 D3
Herrenchiemsee 56 B3
Herrera (Andalucía) 43 E3
Herrera (Aragón) 37 D4
Herrera *Mt* 37 D4
Herrera de Alcántara 38 C3
Herrera del Duque 39 F4
Herrera de Pisuerga 35 F3
Herrera, Pto de 36 B2
Herreruela 39 D3
Herrestad 108 C1
Herrieden 55 E2
Herrljunga 109 D1
Herrnburg 48 B2
Herrnhut 53 F2
Herrsching 56 A3
Herrskog 102 A2
Hersbruck 55 F1
Herselt 50 C3
Hérso 79 F2
Hersónissos Akrotíri 90 C3
Hersónissos Methánon 87 E2
Hersónissos Spinalónga 91 E3
Herstal 51 D3
Herten 17 E3
Hertford 9 F2
Hertfordshire 9 F2
Hervás 39 E2
Herzberg (D) 52 B2
Herzberg (DDR) 53 E1
Herzogenaurach 55 E1
Herzogenburg 57 E2
Herzsprung 49 D3
Hesdin 19 E2
Hesel 47 E3
Hessen 52 A3
Hesseng 95 F2
Hessisch-Lichtenau 52 B2
Hessisch Oldendorf 52 A1
Hestfjørður 96 A4
Hetekylä 99 E3
Hetin 72 C1
Hettange 21 D3
Hettstedt 52 C2
Heubach 55 E2
Heuchin 19 F1
Heukuppe 57 E3
Hevlin 57 F1
Hexham 5 E3
Heyrieux 30 C1
Heysham 6 B1
Hiddensee 49 D1
Hieflau 57 D3
Hiekkasarkät 102 C1
Hierbas 41 E3
Hierro 42 A4
Hiersac 28 C1
Hietaniemi 95 F4
Higham Ferrers 9 F1
Highland 2 C3
High Peak 6 C2
High Willhays 8 C3
High Wycombe 9 F2
Higuera de Arjona 44 A2
Higuera de la Serena 43 E1
Higuera de la Sierra 43 D2
Higuera de Vargas 42 C1
Higuera la Real 42 C1
Higueruela 41 D4
Hiidenportti 103 E1
Hiiumaa 110 B1
Híjar 37 D4
Hilchenbach 17 F4
Hildburghausen 52 C3
Hilden 17 E4
Hilders 52 B3
Hildesheim 52 B1
Hiliomódi 87 E1
Hillegom 16 B2
Hillerød 108 C3
Hillesøy 94 B2
Hillswick 3 F1
Hiloús, Akr 92 C1
Hilpoltstein 55 F2
Hiltula 103 E3
Hilvarenbeek 16 C4
Hilversum 16 C2
Himanka 102 C1
Himaros 80 A2
Himmerland 108 B2
Hinckley 9 E1
Hindelang 55 E4
Hindhead 9 F3
Hindsholm 108 B3
Hinnøya 94 A3
Hinodejo 36 B3
Hinojares 44 B2
Hinojosa de Duero 39 D1
Hinojosa del Duque 43 E1
Hinterrhein 58 B3
Hintersee (D) 56 B4
Hintersee (DDR) 49 E2
Hinterstoder 57 D3
Hintertux 59 D2
Hinterweidenthal 54 B2
Hios 85 F4
Hios, N 85 E4
Hirschau 55 F1
Hirschberg 53 D3
Hirschegg 58 B2
Hirsingue 27 E2
Hirson 20 B2
Hirşova 115 E1
Hirtshals 108 B1
Hirvasvaara 99 E2
Hirvensalmi 103 E3
Hirvilahti 103 E2
Hirwaun 8 C2
Hisarja 115 D2
Histria 115 E1
Hitchin 9 F2
Hitra 100 C1
Hitzacker 48 B3
Hjälmaren 105 F4
Hjartdal 104 C3
Hjellestad 104 A2
Hjelmeland 104 A3
Hjelmsøya 95 D1
Hjo 109 D1
Hjørring 108 B1
Hjørundfjorden 100 A2
Hlebine 71 D1
Hlemoútsi 86 B1
Hlomó, Óros 83 F3
Hluboká 57 D1
Hobro 108 B2
Höchberg 55 D1
Hochdorf 27 F2
Hochfeiler 59 D2
Hochfelden 21 E4
Hochgolling 59 F1
Hochgrabe 59 E2
Hochosterwitz 70 B1
Hochreichart 57 D4
Hochschober 59 E2
Hochschwab 57 D3
Hochspeyer 54 C1
Höchst 55 D1
Höchstadt 55 E1
Höchstädt 55 E2
Hochtannbergpaß 58 B2
Hochtor (Osttirol) 59 E2
Hochtor (Steiermark) 57 D3
Hockenheim 54 C2
Hoddesdon 9 F2
Hodenhagen 48 A4
Hœdic 22 C4
Hódmezővásárhely 114 B1
Hodnet 6 B3
Hodonín 57 F1
Hodoš 70 C1
Hodovo 75 F2
Hoedekenskerke 16 B4
Hoek van Holland 16 B3
Hoemsbu 100 B2
Hof 53 D4
Hofgeismar 52 A2
Hofheim 52 B4
Hofles 97 D4
Höfn 96 C2
Hofolding 56 A3
Hofors 105 F2
Hofsjökull 96 B2
Höganäs 108 C3
Høgebru 100 A3
Höglekardalen 101 E2
Högsäter 105 D4
Högsby 109 E2
Høgset 100 B2
Hohe Acht 51 E4
Hohenau 57 F2
Hohenberg 57 E3
Hohenems 58 B2
Hohengandern 52 B2
Hohenlimburg 17 E4
Hohenlinden 56 B3
Hohenlockstedt 48 A2
Hohenmölsen 53 D2
Hohenpeißenberg 56 A4
Hohenseeden 48 C4
Hohenstein 53 D3
Hohentauern 57 D4
Hohenwestedt 48 A2
Hohenzollern 55 D3
Hoher Zinken 56 C3
Hohe Tauern 59 E2
Hohe Tauern, Nat Pk 59 E2
Hóhlakas 93 E2
Hohneck 27 E1
Hohwachter Bucht 48 B1
Hohwald, le 21 E4
Højer 108 A4
Hokksund 104 C3
Hol 104 C2
Holbæk 108 C3
Holbeach 7 E3
Holdorf 17 F2
Holíč 57 F1
Höljäkkä 103 E1
Höljes 101 D4
Hollabrunn 57 E2
Høllen 104 B4
Hollenstedt 48 A3
Höllental 57 E3
Holles 97 D4
Hollfeld 52 C4
Hollingsholm 100 B2
Hollola 107 F2
Hollum 16 C1
Hollywood 13 D4
Holm (N) 97 D3
Holm (S) 101 F2
Hólmavík 96 A1
Holmec 70 B1
Holmen 105 D2
Holmestrand 104 C3
Holmfirth 6 C2
Holmön 102 B1
Holmsjön 101 E3
Holmslands Klit 108 A3
Holmsund 102 B1
Holomóndas, Óros 80 B3
Holstebro 108 A2
Holsted 108 A3
Holsworthy 8 C3
Holt 7 F3
Holwerd 47 D3
Holycross Abbey 14 C3
Holyhead 6 A2
Holy I (Anglesey) 6 A2
Holy I (Northumberland) 5 E2
Holywell 6 B2
Holywood 13 E2
Holzappel 51 F4
Holzgau 58 C2
Holzkirchen 56 A3
Holzleitner Sattel 58 C2
Holzminden 52 A2
Homberg (Hessen) 52 A3
Homberg (Nordrhein-Westfalen) 17 D3
Homburg 54 B2
Hommelstø 97 D3
Hommelvik 100 C2
Hommersåk 104 A3
Homoljske planine 73 E3
Hondarribia Fuenterrabia 36 C1
Hondón de las Nieves 45 D2
Hönebach 52 B3
Hønefoss 104 C3
Honfleur 19 D3
Høng 108 B3
Hónikas 87 D2
Honiton 9 D3
Honkajoki 102 B3
Honningsvåg 95 E1
Honrubia 40 C3
Honrubia de la Cuesta 36 A3
Hontalbilla 40 A1
Hontoria del Pinar 36 A3
Hooge 47 F1
Hoogeveen 17 D2
Hoogezand 47 D3
Hoogstraten 50 C2
Hook Head 15 D4
Höör 109 D3
Hoorn 16 C2
Hopetoun House 5 D2
Hopfgarten 59 D1
Hopperstad 104 B1
Hóra (Dodekánissa) 89 E2
Hóra (Pelopónissos) 86 C3
Hora Svatého Šebestiána 53 E3
Horažďovice 56 C1
Horb 54 C3
Hörby 109 D3
Horcajo de los Montes 39 F4
Horcajo de Santiago 40 B3
Horcajo de Trevélez 44 A3
Horcajo-Medianero 39 E2
Horche 40 B2
Hordaland 104 B2
Horden 5 E4
Horeftó 83 F2
Horezu 115 D1
Horgen 58 A2
Horgoš 72 C1
Horley 10 C3
Horn (A) 57 E2
Horn (Baden-Württemberg) 55 D4
Horn (N) 97 D3
Horn (Nordrhein-Westfalen) 52 A2
Hornachos 43 D1
Hornachuelos 43 E2
Hornavan 98 A2
Hornberg 54 C3
Hornburg 52 B1
Horncastle 7 E3
Horndal 106 A3
Horneburg 48 A3
Hörnefors 102 A2
Hörnerkirchen 48 A2
Hornet 100 C2
Hornindal 100 A3
Hornindalsvatn 100 A3
Hørning 108 B3
Horni Počernice 53 F3
Hornisgrinde 54 C3
Horni Slavkov 53 E4
Hornos 44 B2
Hornoy 19 E2
Hornsea 7 E2
Hörnum 47 F1
Hořovice 53 F4
Horsens 108 B3
Horsham 10 C3
Hørsholm 108 C3
Horšovký Týn 56 B1
Horst 48 B3
Horstmar 17 E2
Hortafjorden 97 D3
Horten 104 C3
Hortezuela 36 B4
Hortiátis 80 A3
Hospental 58 A3
Hospital 14 C3
Hospital de Órbigo 35 D3
Hossa 99 F3
Hossegor 28 A4
Hostalric 32 B4
Hotagen 101 E1
Hotagen *L* 101 E1
Hotton 50 C4
Houat 22 C4
Houches, les 27 E4
Houdain 19 F1
Houdan 19 E4
Houeillès 28 B3
Houffalize 51 D4
Houghton-le-Spring 5 E4
Houlgate 18 C3
Houmnikó 80 B2
Hoúni 83 D3
Hourtin 28 A2
Houtskår 107 D3
Hov 108 B3
Hovärken 101 D3
Hovden 104 B3
Hove 10 C3
Hovet 104 B2
Hovmantorp 109 E2
Høvringen 100 C3
Howden 7 D2
Howth 13 E4
Höxter 52 A2
Hoy 3 D1
Hoya 17 F1
Høyanger 100 A3
Hoyerswerda 53 F2
Hoylake 6 B2
Høylandet 97 D4
Hoym 52 C1
Hoyos 39 D2
Höytiäinen 103 F2
Hoz de Beteta 40 C2
Hozoviótissa 89 D3
Hracholuská přehr nádrž 53 E4
Hradec-Králove 112 A2
Hrádek 57 E1
Hrádek nad Nisou 53 F2
Hranice (Severomoravský) 112 A3
Hranice (Západočeský) 53 D4
Hrasnica 75 F1
Hrastnik 70 B2
Hrastovlje 70 A3
Hřensko 53 F2
Hríssafa 87 D3
Hrissí, N 91 E4
Hrissó 80 B2
Hrissoskalítissa 90 B3
Hrissoúpoli 80 C2
Hrissovítsi 86 C2
Hristiani, N 91 D1
Hristianó 86 C3
Hristós 89 D2
Hrómio 79 D4
Hrtkovci 72 C3
Hrušovany 57 F1
Hrvace 75 D1
Hrvatska 70 C2
Hückeswagen 17 E4
Hucknall 7 D3
Hucqueliers 19 E1
Huddersfield 6 C2
Hude 47 F3
Hudiksvall 101 F3
Huebra, R 39 E1
Huedin 112 C4
Huélago 44 A3
Huélamo 40 C2
Huelgoat 22 B3
Huelma 44 A2
Huelva 42 C2
Huelva, Riv. de 43 D2
Huércal-Overa 44 C3
Huérguina 41 D3
Huerta del Rey 36 A3
Huerta de Valdecarábanos 40 A3
Huertahernando 40 C2
Huerto 37 E3
Huerva, R 37 D4
Huesa 44 B2
Huesca 37 D3
Huéscar 44 B2
Huesna, Emb de 43 D2
Huete 40 B3
Huétor-Santillán 44 A3
Huétor-Tájar 43 F3
Hüfingen 54 C4
Huftarøy 104 A2
Huisne 23 F3
Huittinen 107 D2
Huizen 16 C2
Hulst 16 B4
Hultsfred 109 E2
Humada 35 F3
Humanes 40 B1
Humber Bridge 7 D2
Humber, R 7 E2
Humberside 7 D2
Humberside (Airport) 7 D2
Humenné 112 C3
Humppila 107 E2
Hundested 108 C3
Hundorp 100 C3
Hunedoara 114 C1
Hünfeld 52 B3
Hungerford 9 E2
Hunnebostrand 105 D4
Húnsflói 96 A1
Hunspach 21 F3
Hunsrück 54 B1
Hunstanton 7 E3
Hunte 17 F1
Huntingdon 9 F1
Huntly 3 E3
Hurdal 105 D2
Huriel 25 F4
Hurones, Emb de los 43 D3
Hurskaala 103 E3
Hürth 17 E4
Hurum 104 C1
Hurup 108 A2
Húsavík 96 B1
Husavik 104 A2
Husbands Bosworth 9 F1
Hushinish 2 A2
Huşi 113 E4
Huskvarna 109 D1
Husnes 104 A2
Hustadvika 100 B2
Hustopeče 57 F1
Husum (D) 47 F1
Husum (S) 102 A2
Hutovo 75 F2
Hutovo Blato 75 F2
Hüttenberg 57 D4
Hüttschlag 59 E1
Huttula 103 D3
Huttwil 27 F2
Huy 50 C4
Hvalba 96 A4
Hvalfjörður 96 A2
Hvalpsund 108 A2
Hvalvík 96 A3
Hvar 75 D2
Hvar *I* 75 E2
Hvarski kan 75 D2
Hveragerði 96 A2
Hveravellir 96 B2
Hvidbjerg 108 A2
Hvide Sande 108 A3
Hvítá 96 A2
Hvittingfoss 104 C3
Hvitträsk 107 E3
Hvolsvöllur 96 B3
Hwlffordd 8 B2
Hyde 6 C2
Hyen 100 A3
Hyères 31 D4
Hyères, Iles d' 31 D4
Hylsfjorden 104 A3
Hyltebruk 108 C2
Hyrynsalmi 99 E4
Hythe 11 D3
Hyvinkää 107 E2
Hyypiö 99 D2

I

Ía	91	E1
Ialomiţa	115	E1
Iaşi	113	E3
Iasmos	81	D2
Ibañeta, Pto	36	C1
Ibar	73	D4
Ibbenbüren	17	E2
Ibestad	94	B3
Ibi	45	E1
Ibias, R	34	C2
Ibiza	45	D4
Ibiza I	45	D3
Iblei, Mti	69	D4
Ičn'a	113	F1
Icod de los Vinos	42	A4
Idanha a Nova	38	C2
Idar-Oberstein	54	B1
Idéo Ándro	91	D4
Ídi, Óros	91	D4
Idoméni	79	F2
Iddoš	72	C1
Ídra	87	F2
Ídra, N	87	F3
Ídras, Kólpos	87	E2
Idre	101	D3
Idrigill Pt	2	B3
Idrija	70	A2
Idrijca	70	A2
Idro	58	C4
Idstein	51	F4
Ielsi	64	B3
Ieper	50	A3
Ierápetra	91	E4
Ierissós	80	B3
Ieropigí	78	C3
If, Château d'	30	C4
Ifestía	85	D1
Ifjord	95	E1
Ifjordfjellet	95	E1
Igalo	76	A3
Iga Vas	70	B2
Iggesund	101	F3
Iglesias	66	B4
Igls	59	D2
Igoumenítsa	82	B2
Igrane	75	E2
Igualada	37	F4
Ihtiman	115	D2
Ii	99	D3
Iijarvi	95	E2
Iijoki	99	D3
Iisalmi	103	E1
Iisvesi	103	E2
IJmuiden	16	B2
IJssel	17	D3
IJsselmeer	16	C2
IJsselmuiden	17	D2
IJzendijke	16	B4
IJzer	50	A3
Ikaalinen	102	C3
Ikaría, N	89	D2
Ikast	108	A3
Ilandža	73	D2
Ilanz	58	B3
Ilche	37	E3
Ilchester	9	D3
Ile-Bouchard, l'	25	D3
Ile-Rousse, l'	33	F2
Ilfracombe	8	C3
Ílhavo	38	B1
Ília	83	F3
Ilia	86	B1
Il'ičevsk	113	F4
Ilida	86	B1
Ilidza	75	F1
Ilijas	71	F4
Ilíki	84	A4
Ilíki, L	84	A4
Iliókastro	87	E2
Ilirska Bistrica	70	B3
Ilkeston	7	D1
Ilkley	6	C2
Illana	40	B2
Illano	34	C1

Illar	44	B3
Ille	23	D3
Ille et Rance, Canal d'	23	D3
Ille-et-Vilaine	23	D3
Illertissen	55	E3
Iller	55	E4
Illescas	40	A2
Ille-sur-Têt	32	B2
Illiers	25	E1
Illingen	55	D2
Illmitz	57	F3
Illora	44	A3
Illueca	36	C4
Ilm	52	C3
Ilmajoki	102	C2
Ilmenau (D)	48	B3
Ilmenau (DDR)	52	C3
Il'men, Ozero	111	D1
Ilminster	9	D3
Ilok	72	B2
Ilomantsi	103	F2
Ilova	71	D2
Ilovik	70	B4
Ilsenburg	52	B1
Ilsfeld	55	D2
Imathía	79	E3
Imatra	103	F4
Ímeros	81	E2
Imitós	87	F1
Immenstaad	55	D4
Immenstadt	55	E4
Immingham	7	E2
Immingham Dock	7	E2
Imola	61	D3
Imotski	75	E1
Imperia	31	F3
Imphy	26	A3
Impruneta	61	D4
Imst	58	C2
Ina	49	F3
Inari	95	E3
Inarijärvi	95	E3
Inarijoki	95	E3
Inca	45	F2
Inchnadamph	2	C2
Inchtree	2	C4
Incisa in Val d'Arno	61	D4
Incudine, M	33	F4
Indal	101	F3
Indalsälven	101	E3
Indija	72	C2
Indre	25	D2
Indre (Dépt)	25	E3
Indre-et-Loire	25	D2
Infiesto	35	E1
Ingå	107	E3
Ingelmunster	50	A3
Ingleton	6	C1
Ingolstadt	55	F2
Ingrandes	23	E4
Ingul	113	F3
Ingulec	113	F3
Ingulec R	113	F3
Ingwiller	21	E3
Iniesta	41	D4
Iniö	107	D2
Iniön aukko	107	D2
Inis	12	B4
Inis Córthaidh	15	D3
Inishbofin	12	A3
Inishcrone	12	B2
Inisheer	12	B4
Inishkea	12	A2
Inishmaan	12	B4
Inishmore	12	B4
Inishmurray	12	C2
Inishowen	13	D1
Inishowen Head	13	D1
Inishshark	12	A3
Inishtrahull	13	D1
Inishturk	12	A3
Inkee	99	E3
Inkoo	107	E3

Inn (CH)	58	B3
Inn (D)	56	B3
Innbygda	104	C1
Inndyr	97	E2
Innellan	4	B2
Innerleithen	5	D2
Inner Sd	2	B3
Innfield	13	D3
Innhavet	97	F1
Innichen	59	E2
Inning	56	A3
Innsbruck	59	D2
Innset	94	B3
Innvik	100	A3
Inói (Pelopónnissos)	86	B1
Inói (Stereá Eláda)	84	A4
Inoússes	85	F4
Inoússes, N	85	F4
Inowrocław	112	A1
Ins	27	E2
Ínsko	49	F2
Interlaken	27	F3
Întorsura Buzăuli	113	D4
Inveraray	4	B1
Inverbervie	3	E4
Invergarry	2	C4
Invergordon	3	D3
Inverkeithing	5	D2
Invermoriston	2	C4
Inverness	2	C3
Inverurie	3	E4
Inzell	56	B3
Ioánina	82	C1
Ioánina (Nomos)	82	B1
Ioanínon, L	82	C1
Iona	4	A1
Iónia Nissiá	82	A2
Íos	88	C4
Íos, N	88	C4
Ipáti	83	E3
Ipéria	83	E2
Iphofen	55	E1
Ípiros	82	B2
Ipsilí Ráhi	80	C2
Ípsos	82	A1
Ipsoúnda	86	C2
Ipswich	11	D2
Iput	111	E4
Iráklia (Makedonía)	80	A2
Iráklia (Stereá Eláda)	83	E3
Iráklia, N	88	C3
Iráklio	91	D3
Iráklio (Nomos)	91	D4
Irati, R	36	C2
Irbes Šaurums	110	B2
Irdning	57	D4
Iregua, R	36	B2
Iréo (Argolída)	87	D2
Iréo (Dodekánissa)	89	E2
Iréo (Korinthía)	87	E1
Iréo, Akr	87	E1
Íria	87	E2
Irig	72	C2
Irish Sea	13	F3
Iriški venac	72	C2
Irixoa	34	B1
Irnijärvi	99	E3
Iron-Bridge	9	D1
Irschenberg	56	B3
Irsina	65	D4
Irún	36	C1
Irurzun	36	C2
Irvine	4	C2
Irvinestow	12	C2
Irxleben	52	C1
Isaba	37	D2
Isaccea	113	E4
Ísafjarðardjúp	96	A1
Ísafjörður	96	A1
Ísala	115	E3
Isane	100	A3

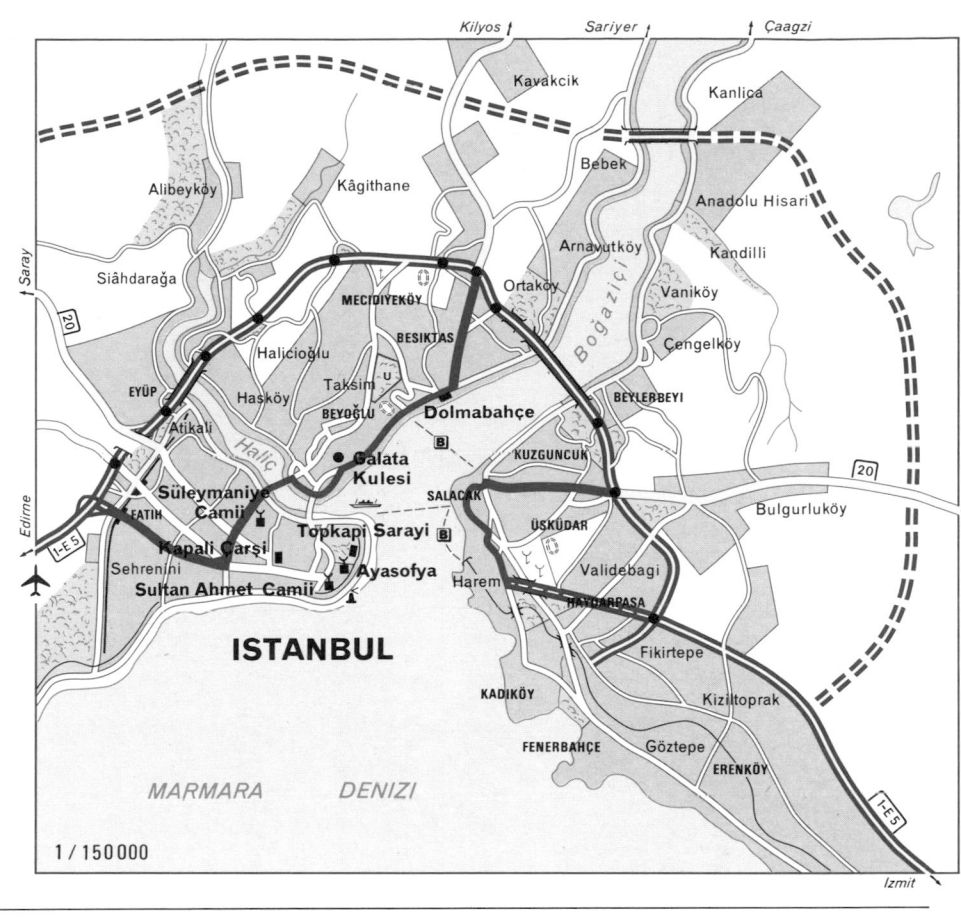

1 / 150 000

Isar	56	B2
Isarco	59	D2
Isbister	3	F1
Iscar	35	E4
Ischgl	58	C2
Ischia	64	A4
Ischia, I d'	64	A4
Ise	105	D3
Isefjord	108	C3
Iselle	58	A3
Iselsberg	59	E2
Iseo	60	B1
Iseo, L d'	58	B4
Iseran, Col de l'	31	E1
Isère (Dépt)	30	C1
Isère (R)	30	C1
Iserlohn	17	E3
Isernia	64	A3
Isfjellet	94	C2
Isfjorden	100	B2
Ishavsleden	94	C3
Ishëm	76	C4
Ishëm R	76	C4
Isigny	18	C3
Isili	66	B3
Iskår	115	D2
Is'kuras	95	E2
Isla	3	D4
Isla	36	A1
Isla Cristina	42	A3
Isla Mayor	43	D3
Island Magee	13	E2
Islay	4	A2
Isle	28	C2
Isle-Adam, l'	19	F3
Isle-de-Noé, l'	28	C4
Isle-en-Dodon, l'	37	F1
Isle-Jourdain, l' (Gers)	28	C4
Isle-Jourdain, l' (Vienne)	25	D4
Isle of Man	6	A1

Isle of Portland	9	D4
Isle of Whithorn	4	C4
Isle of Wight	9	E4
Isleornsay	2	B4
Isles of Scilly	8	A4
Isle-sur-la-Sorgue, l'	30	C3
Isle-sur-le-Doubs, l'	27	D2
Isle-sur-Serein, l'	26	C2
Ismaning	55	F3
Isnäs	107	F2
Isny	55	E4
Iso-Evo	107	E2
Isojärvi	103	D3
Isojoki	102	B3
Isokylä	99	E2
Isokyrö	102	B2
Isola	31	E3
Isola del Gran Sasso d'Italia	63	F1
Isola della Scala	60	C1
Isola del Liri	64	A3
Isola di Capo Rizzuto	67	F3
Isona	37	F3
Isonzo	59	F3
Isorella	60	B1
Ispica	69	D4
Issambres, les	31	D4
Issel	17	D3
Issigeac	28	C2
Issoire	29	F1
Issóva, M.	86	C2
Íssoma	86	C1
Issoudun	25	E3
Is-sur-Tille	26	C2
Issy-l'Evêque	26	B3
Ist	74	B1
Istán	43	E4
İstanbul	115	F3

Istarske Toplice	70	A3
Istérnia	88	B2
Istha	52	A2
Isthmía	87	E1
Istibanja	77	F2
Istiéa	83	F3
Istindan	94	B3
Istok	76	C2
Istres	30	C4
Ístrios	93	E2
Isturits et d'Oxocelhaya, Grottes d'	28	A4
Itä-Aure	102	C3
Itäinen Suomenlahti	107	F2
Itanós	91	F3
Itéa (Flórina)	79	D2
Itéa (Grevená)	79	D4
Itéa (Stereá Eláda)	83	E4
Itéa (Thessalía)	83	E2
Itéas, Kólpos	83	E4
Itháki	82	B4
Itháki, N	82	B4
Ithómi	86	C3
Iti	83	E3
Ítilo	87	D4
Íti, Óros	83	E3
Iton	19	E3
Itri	64	A3
Itta	52	B3
Ittiri	66	A2
Itz	52	C4
Ivačevići	112	C1
Ivajlovgrad	115	E3
Ivalo	95	E3
Ivalojoki Ävvil	95	E3
Ivančiće	57	F1
Ivančići	71	F4
Ivančna Gorica	70	B2
Ivanec	70	C1

Ivangrad	76	C2
Ivanić Grad	71	D2
Ivanjica	73	D4
Ivanjska	71	E3
Ivankovo	71	F2
Ivano-Frankovsk	113	D3
Ivanščica	70	C2
Ivan Sedlo	75	F1
Ivanska	71	D2
Iveland	104	B4
Iveragh	14	A4
Ívira	80	B2
Íviron	80	C4
Ivrea	31	F1
Ivry-la-Bataille	19	E4
Ixiá	93	F1
Ixworth	11	D1
Iž	74	C1
Izeda	34	C4
Izegem	50	A3
Izernore	26	C4
Izlake	70	B2
Izmail	113	E4
İzmir	115	E4
İzmit	115	F3
Iznájar	43	F3
Iznájar, Emb de	43	F3
Iznallos	44	A3
İznik	115	F3
İznik Gölü	115	F3
Izoard, Col d'	31	D2
Izola	70	A3
Iz Veli	74	C1
Izvor (Makedonija)	77	D4
Izvor (Makedonija)	77	E3
Izvor (Srbija)	73	E4

J

Jaala 107 F2
Jaäsjärvi 103 D3
Jabalón, R 44 A1
Jabbeke 50 A3
Jablanac 70 B4
Jablan Do 76 A2
Jablanica 75 F1
Jablanica (Reg) 77 D4
Jablanica *R* 77 D1
Jablaničko jez 75 F1
Jablonec nad Nisou 112 A2
Jablonné v Podještědí 53 F3
Jabugo 42 C2
Jabuka (Bosna i Hercegovina) 76 A1
Jabuka (Srbija) 76 B1
Jabuka (Vojvodina) 73 D2
Jabuka, I 74 C2
Jabukovac (Hrvatska) 71 D3
Jabukovac (Srbija) 73 F3
Jabukovik 77 E1
Jaca 37 D2
Jáchymov 53 E3
Jadar (Bosna i Hercegovina) 72 C4
Jadar (Srbija) 72 B3
Jäder 106 A3
Jaderberg 47 F3
Jadovik 76 B1
Jadovnik 71 D4
Jadranska Lešnica 72 B3
Jadransko More 74 B2
Jadraque 40 B1
Jaén 44 A2
Jagodnjac 71 F2
Jagotin 113 F2
Jagst 55 E2
Jagsthausen 55 D2
Jahorina 76 A1
Jahorina (Reg) 76 A1
Jajce 71 E4
Jäkkvik 97 F2
Jakobselv 95 F2
Jakobstad 102 C1
Jakšić 71 E2
Jakupica 77 E3
Jalasjärvi 102 C3
Jaligny 26 A3
Jalón, R 36 C3
Jalovik Izvor 73 F4
Jambol 115 E2
Jamena 72 B3
Jämijärvi 102 C3
Jäminkipohja 102 C3
Jämjö 109 E3
Jammerbugten 108 A2
Jamnička Kiselica 70 C2
Jämsä 103 D3
Jämsänkoski 103 D3
Jämtlands Län 101 E2
Janakkala 107 E2
Janče 77 D3
Jandía, Pta de 42 C4
Jándula, Emb del 44 A1
Jandula, R 44 A1
Jänisselkä 103 F2
Janja 72 B3
Janjevo 77 D2
Janjina 75 E2
Jankov kamen 76 C1
Jañona 39 D2
Jantra 115 D2
Janville 25 E1
Janzé 23 D3
Japetić 70 C2
Jäppilä 103 E2
Jaraba 36 C4
Jarafuel 41 D4
Jaraicejo 39 E3
Jaráiz 39 E2
Jarak 72 C3
Jarama, R 40 B2
Jarandilla de la Vera 39 E2
Järbo 106 A2
Jarcevo 111 E3
Jard 24 B3
Jæren 104 A4
Jaren 105 D2
Jargeau 25 E1
Jarkovac 73 D2
Jarmen 49 D2
Jarmenovci 73 D3
Jarnac 28 B1
Jarnages 25 E4
Järna (Kopparbergs Län) 105 E2
Järna (Stockholms Län) 106 B4
Jarny 21 D3
Jarocin 112 A2
Jaroměřice 57 E1
Jarosław 112 C2
Järpen 101 E2
Jarrow 5 E3
Jarvelä 107 F2
Järvenpää 107 E2
Järvsö 101 F3
Jaša Tomić 73 D2
Jasenak 70 B3
Jasenica (Bosna i Hercegovina) 71 D3
Jasenica (Srbija) 73 D3
Jasenovac 71 D3
Jasenovo (Crna Gora) 76 B2
Jasenovo (Srbija) 76 B1
Jasenovo (Vojvodina) 73 D2
Jasień 53 F1
Jasika 73 E4
Jasikovo 73 E3
Jasło 112 C3
Jasmund 49 D1
Jastrebarsko 70 C2
Jastrowie 112 A1
Jászberény 112 B4
Jau, Col de 32 B2
Jaufenpass 59 D2
Jaunay-Clan 25 D3
Jaunpass 27 E3
Jausiers 31 D2
Javalambre 41 D3
Javalambre, Sa de 41 E3
Javalón 41 D2
Javea 45 E1
Jävenitz 48 C4
Javie, la 31 D3
Javor 76 C1
Javořice 57 D1
Javornjača 71 D4
Javorov 112 C2
Jävre 98 B4
Javron 23 E3
Jedburgh 5 D3
Jedincy 113 D3
Jędrzejów 112 B2
Jeesiö 95 E4
Jeetze 48 B3
Jegun 28 C4
Jegunovce 77 D3
Jēkabpils 110 C3
Jektevik 104 A2
Jelah 71 E3
Jelašca 76 A1
Jelenia Góra 112 A2
Jelenje 70 B3
Jelgava 110 C3
Jelling 108 A3
Jel'n'a 111 E3
Jelsa (N) 104 A3
Jelsa (YU) 75 E2
Jemnice 57 E1
Jena 52 C3
Jenbach 59 D1
Jengejetneme 97 E4
Jennersdorf 57 F4
Jeppo 102 C2
Jerez de la Frontera 43 D3
Jerez de los Caballeros 42 C1
Jérica 41 E3
Jerichow 49 D4
Jerisjärvi 95 D4
Jerpoint Abbey 15 D3
Jersey 18 A3
Jerte 39 E2
Jerte, R 39 E2
Jerxheim 52 B1
Jerzu 66 C3
Jesenice (CS) 53 E4
Jesenice (YU) 70 A1
Jeseník 112 A2
Jesi 61 F4
Jeßnitz 53 D2
Jesolo 59 E4
Jessen 53 D1
Jessheim 105 D3
Jetzelsdorf 57 E2
Jeumont 20 B1
Jevenstedt 48 A2
Jever 47 E3
Jevišovice 57 E1
Jevnaker 105 D2
Jezerane 70 C3
Jezerce 77 D2
Jezercë, M 76 C2
Jezero 71 E4
Jezero Šćit 75 E1
Jezersko 70 B1
Ježevica 72 C4
Jičín 112 A2
Jiekkevarre 94 C2
Jihlava 57 E1
Jihlava *R* 57 E1
Jijona 45 E1
Jiloca, R 41 D2
Jilové u Prahy 53 F4
Jimbolia 114 C1
Jimena 44 A2
Jimena de la Frontera 43 E4
Jindřichovice 53 D3
Jindřichuv Hradec 57 D1
Jirkov 53 E3
Jiu 115 D2
Jizera 53 F3
Joachimsthal 49 E3
Jockfall 98 C2
Jódar 44 A2
Jodoigne 50 C3
Joensuu 103 F2
Jõgeva 110 C1
Johanngeorgenstadt 53 D3
John o'Groats 3 D2
Johnstone 4 C2
Johovac 71 F3
Joigny 26 A1
Joinville 20 C4
Jokela 107 E2
Jokijärvi 99 E3
Jokikylä 99 E4
Jokioinen 107 E2
Jokkmokk 98 B2
Jökulsá-á Fjöllum 96 C1
Joloskylä 99 D3
Jølstravatnet 100 A3
Jomala 106 C3
Jönåker 106 A4
Jondal 104 B2
Jongunjärvi 99 E3
Joniškis 110 C3
Jönköping 109 D1
Jönköpings Län 109 D2
Jonzac 28 B1
Jordbro 106 B4
Jordbruksveien 95 D2
Jormlien 97 E4
Jörn 98 B4
Joroinen 103 E3
Jørpeland 104 A3
Jørstadmoen 105 D2
Jošanica 73 E4
Jošanička Banja 76 C1
Jošavka 71 E3
Josenfjorden 104 A3
Josipdol 70 C3
Josipovac 71 F2
Josselin 22 C3
Jostedalsbreen 100 A3
Jotunheimen 100 B3
Jou, Coll de 32 A3
Joué 25 D2
Jougne 27 D3
Joutjärvi 107 F2
Joutsa 103 D3
Joutseno 103 E4
Joutsijärvi 99 E2
Joyeuse 30 B2
Juankoski 103 E2
Juan-les-Pins 31 E4
Júcar, R 41 E4
Jüchen 17 D4
Juchnov 111 F3
Judaberg 104 A3
Judenau 57 E2
Judenburg 57 D4
Judio 43 F1
Juelsminde 108 B3
Jugenheim 54 C1
Jugon 22 C3
Jugorje 70 B2
Juillac 29 D1
Juist 47 E3
Jukkasjärvi 94 C4
Jülich 17 D4
Julierpass 58 B3
Jullouville 18 B4
Jumaliskylä 99 F4
Jumeaux 29 F1
Jumièges 19 D3
Jumilhac-le-Grand 29 D1
Jumilla 45 D1
Jumilla, Pto de 45 D1
Juminen 103 E1
Jumisko 99 E2
Juneda 37 F4
Jungfrau 27 F3
Junik 76 C2
Juniville 20 B3
Junkeren 97 E2
Junosuando 95 D4
Junsele 101 F2
Juntusranta 99 F3
Juojärvi 103 E2
Juoksenki 98 C2
Juorkuna 99 E4
Jura 4 B2
Jura (Canton) 27 E2
Jura (Dépt) 27 D3
Jura, Sd of 4 B2
Jurbarkas 110 C3
Jurjevo 70 B4
Jūrmala 110 C2
Jurmofjärden 107 D3
Jurmu 99 E3
Juromenha 38 C4
Jurva 102 B2
Jussey 27 D1
Justel 34 D3
Jüterbog 53 E1
Juuka 103 E2
Juupajoki 103 D3
Juurusvesi 103 E2
Juva (Mikkelin Lääni) 103 E3
Juva (Turun ja Porin Lääni) 107 D2
Juvigny-le-Tertre 18 C4
Juvigny-sous-Andaine 18 C4
Juvola 103 E3
Juzennecourt 26 C1
Južna Morava 73 E4
Južnyj Bug 113 E2
Jyderup 108 B3
Jylland 108 A3
Jyrkkä 103 E1
Jyväskylä 103 D3

K

Kaamanen 95 E3
Kaamaskoki 95 E2
Kaaresuvanto 95 D3
Kaarina 107 D2
Kaatsheuvel 16 C3
Kaavi 103 E2
Kaavinjärvi 103 E2
Kåbdalis 98 B3
Kablart 72 C4
Kać 72 C2
Kačanik 77 D2
Kačarevo 73 D2
Kačikol 77 D2
Kadaň 53 E3
Kadi Bogaz 73 F4
Kadrifakovo 77 E3
Kafiréas, Akr 84 C4
Kafiréa, Stenó 88 B1
Kåfjord 95 E1
Kåfjorden 94 C2
Kaga 106 A4
Kagarlyk 113 E2
Kagul 113 E4
Kahla 52 C3
Kaiáfas 86 B2
Kailbach 55 D1
Kaimaktsalán 79 E2
Kainasto 102 B3
Kaindorf 57 E4
Kaipola 103 D3
Kairala 95 F4
Kaisergebirge 59 D1
Kaiserslautern 54 B1
Kaisheim 55 E2
Kaitumälven 94 C4
Kaiudđerovo 73 E2
Kajaani 99 E4
Kakan 74 C1
Kakanj 71 F4
Kaki Thálassa 88 A1
Kaki Vígla 87 F1
Kakslauttanen 95 E3
Kalajoki 102 C1
Kalajoki *R* 102 C1
Kalak 95 E1
Kalamáki (Lárissa) 83 F2
Kalamáki (Magnissía) 84 A2
Kalamáki, Akr 85 D2
Kalamáta 86 C3
Kalambáka 83 D1
Kalambáki 80 C2
Kalámi 89 E1
Kalamiótissa 91 F1
Kalamítsi (Makedonía) 80 B4
Kalamítsi (Stereá Eláda) 82 B3
Kálamos, N 82 C3
Kalamotí 85 F4
Kalamotó 80 A3
Kalándra 80 A4
Kalá Nerá 83 F2
Kalá Nissiá 87 E1
Kalanti 107 D2
Kalapódi 83 F3
Kalaraš 113 E3
Kälarne 101 F2
Kalavárda 93 E1
Kalávrita 86 C1
Kal'azin 111 F1
Kalbe 48 C4
Kalce 70 A2
Kaldakvisl 96 B2
Kaléndzi (Ípiros) 82 C2
Kaléndzi (Pelopónissos) 86 C1
Kalenić 73 D4
Kalérgo 84 C4
Kalesija 72 B3
Kali 74 C1
Kaliakoúda 83 D3
Kaliáni 87 D1
Kalídromo, Óros 83 E3
Kalífitos 80 C2
Kalí Liménes 91 D4
Kalí Límni 93 D3
Kalimassiá 85 F4
Kalimenci, Ez 77 F2
Kálimnos 89 F3
Kálimnos, N 89 E3
Kalinin 111 F2
Kaliningrad 110 B4
Kalinkoviči 113 E1
Kalinovik 75 F1
Kalipéfki 79 E4
Kalirráhi 79 D4
Kalithéa (Dodekánissa) 93 F1
Kalithéa (Ília) 86 C2
Kalithéa (Makedonía) 80 B2
Kalithéa (Messinía) 86 C3
Kalithéa (Stereá Eláda) 83 D3
Kalithéa (Thessalía) 83 D2
Kalithiés 93 F1
Kalíthiro 83 D2
Kalivári 88 B1
Kalíves (Kríti) 90 C3
Kalíves (Thássos) 80 C3
Kalívia (Ahaïa) 86 C1
Kalívia (Atikí-Piréas) 87 F1
Kalívia (Etolía-Akarnanía) 82 C3
Kalívia (Korinthía) 87 D1
Kalívia Varikoú 79 F4
Kalix 98 C3
Kalixälven 98 C2
Kaljord 94 A3
Kalkar 17 D3
Kalkkinen 107 F1
Kall 101 D2
Kallaktjåkkå 94 B4
Kallavesi 103 E2
Kållby 102 C1
Källby 105 E4
Kallinge 109 E3
Kallio 102 C3
Kalliojoki 99 F4
Kallislahti 103 E3
Kallmünz 55 F2
Kallsjön 101 D1
Kalmar 109 E2
Kalmar Län 109 E2
Kalmar sund 109 E2
Kalmit 54 C2
Kalna 73 F4
Kalnik 71 D2
Kalnik *Mt* 71 D2
Kalocsa 112 B4
Kalogerikoú 87 D2
Kalogriá 86 B1
Kalohóri 83 D1
Kaló Horió 91 E4
Kalókastro 80 A2
Kaló Neró 86 C3
Kaloni (Lésvos) 85 F2
Kaloni (Pelopónissos) 87 E2
Kalonís, Kólpos 85 F2
Kaloskopí 83 E3
Kalotássi, Akr 89 D4
Kalø Vig 108 B3
Kalpáki 78 C4
Kals 59 E2
Kalsdorf 57 E4
Kaltbrunn 58 A2
Kaltenkirchen 48 A2
Kaltennordheim 52 B3
Kaltern 59 D3
Kaltezés 87 D2
Kaluga 111 F3
Kalundborg 108 B3
Kaluš 112 C3
Kalvåg 104 A1
Kalvehave 108 C4
Kälviä 102 C1
Kalvola 107 E2
Kalvträsk 98 B4
Kamáres (Kríti) 91 D4
Kamarés (Páros) 88 C3
Kamáres (Pelopónissos) 83 D4
Kamáres (Sífnos) 88 B3
Kamári 91 E1
Kamariótissa 81 E3
Kambanós, Akr 88 B1
Kambiá 85 E4
Kámbos (Kríti) 90 B3
Kámbos (Pelopónissos) 86 C3
Kámbos (Stereá Eláda) 83 D4
Kamčija 115 E2
Kamen 17 E3
Kamenari 76 A3
Kaména Voúria 83 F3
Kamenec-Podol'skij 113 D3
Kamenica 77 F2
Kamenice 57 D1
Kaméni, N 91 E1
Kamenjak, Rt 70 A4
Kamenka 113 F2
Kamensko (Hrvatska) 71 E2
Kamensko (Hrvatska) 75 E1
Kamenz 53 F2
Kamień Pomorski 49 E2
Kamieński, Zalew 49 E2
Kamilári 91 D4
Kamínia 86 B1
Kámiros 93 E1
Kamnik 70 B2
Kamp 57 E2
Kamp-Bornhofen 51 E4
Kampen (D) 47 F1
Kampen (NL) 17 D2
Kamp-Lintfort 17 D3
Kanal 70 A2
Kanála 88 A2
Kanal Dunav-Tisa-Dunav 73 D2
Kanália 55 D4
Kanatádika 83 F3
Kánava 88 A4
Kándanos 90 B3
Kandel 54 C2
Kandel *Mt* 54 C3
Kandern 54 C4
Kandersteg 27 F3
Kándia 87 E2
Kandíla (Pelopónissos) 87 D2
Kandíla (Stereá Eláda) 82 C3
Kandíli 84 A3
Kandíra 115 F3
Kandrše 70 B2
Kanestraum 100 B2
Kanev 113 F2
Kanfanar 70 A3
Kangádio 86 B1
Kangasala 107 E1
Kangaslampi 103 E2
Kangasniemi 103 D3
Kangosjärvi 95 D4
Kanjiža 72 C1
Kankaanpää 102 C3
Kannonkoski 103 D2
Kannus 102 C1
Kannusjärvi 103 E4

Kanturk 14 B3
Kaona 73 D4
Kaonik (Bosna i Hercegovina) 71 F4
Kaonik (Srbija) 73 E4
Kapandríti 87 F1
Kaparéli 83 F4
Kapariá 88 B2
Kapele, Vrh 70 C3
Kapellskär 106 C3
Kapélo, Akr 90 A2
Kapfenberg 57 E3
Kaplice 57 D2
Kaposvár 114 B1
Kapp 105 D2
Kappel 51 E4
Kappeln 48 A1
Kappelshamnsviken 109 F3
Kaprije 74 C1
Kaprun 59 E1
Kapsáli 90 A2
Kápsas 87 D2
Kapsoúri 88 B1
Kapsukas 110 C4
Kapuvár 112 A4
Karabiga 115 E3
Karaburun 115 F4
Karačev 111 F4
Karadeniz Boğazı 115 F3
Karan 72 C4
Karasjåkka 95 E2
Karasjok 95 E2
Karasu 115 F3
Karats 98 A2
Karavás 90 A1
Karavómilos 83 F3
Karavónissia 92 C2
Karavostássis 91 D1
Kårböle 101 E3
Karcag 112 B4
Kardámena 89 F3
Kardámila 85 E4
Kardamíli 86 C3
Kardeljevo 75 E2
Kärdla 110 B1
Karditsa 55 D4
Karditsa (Nomos) 55 D4
Kârdžali 115 D3
Karerpass 59 D3
Karesuando 95 D3
Karfás 85 F4
Karhukangas 99 D4
Karhula 103 F4
Karhunkierros 99 F2
Karhutunturi 95 F4
Kariá (Pelopónissos) 87 D2
Kariá (Stereá Eláda) 83 F3
Kariés (Makedonía) 80 C4
Kariés (Pelopónissos) 87 D3
Karigasniemi 95 E2
Karijoki 102 B3
Karinainen 107 D2
Kariótisa 79 E3
Karis 107 E3
Káristos 88 A1
Karítena 86 C2
Karjaa 107 E3
Karjalohja 107 E3
Karkaloú 86 C2
Karkinágri 89 D2
Karkku 107 D1
Kärkölä 107 E2
Karleby 102 C1
Karlevi 109 E3
Karlino 49 F1
Karl-Marx-Stadt 53 E3
Karlobag 70 C4
Karlovac 70 C3
Karlovássi 89 E1
Karlovo 115 D2
Karlovy Vary 53 E4
Karlsborg 105 E4
Karlsburg 49 D2
Karlsfeld 55 F3
Karlshamn 109 D3
Karlshuld 55 F2
Karlskoga 105 E4
Karlskrona 109 E3
Karlsøy 94 C2
Karlsruhe 54 C2
Karlstad 105 E3
Karlstadt 52 B4
Karlštejn 53 F4
Karlstift 57 D2
Karmøy 104 A3
Karnezéika 87 E2
Karnobat 115 E2
Kärnten 59 F2
Karolinerleden 101 E2
Karow 48 C2
Kärpankylä 99 F2
Kárpathos 93 D3
Kárpathos, N 93 D3
Karpenissi 83 D3
Karperi 80 A2
Karperó 79 D4
Kärsämäki 103 D1
Kårsatjåkka 94 B4
Kārsava 111 D2
Karstädt 48 C3
Karstula 103 D2
Kartal 115 F3
Kartéri (Ípiros) 82 B2
Kartéri (Pelopónissos) 87 D1
Karterós 91 D3
Kártsino, Akr 84 C3
Karttula 103 E2
Kartuzy 110 A4
Karungi 98 C3
Karunki 98 C3
Karup 108 A2
Karvala 102 C2
Kärväskylä 103 D2
Karvia 102 C3
Karviná 112 B3
Karvoskylä 103 D1
Karvounári 82 B2
Karwendelgebirge 59 D1
Kašalj 76 C1
Kašin 111 F1
Kašina 70 C2
Kaskinen 102 B3
Kasko 102 B3
Káspakas 85 D1
Kašperské Hory 56 C1
Kassándra 80 B4
Kassándras, Kólpos 80 B4
Kassándria 80 A4
Kassel 52 A2
Kassiópi 82 A1
Kassópi 82 B2
Kássos, N 93 D3
Kastaniá (Makedonía) 79 E3
Kastaniá (Pelopónissos) 87 D1
Kastaniá (Thessalía) 82 C1
Kastaniá (Thessalía) 83 D2
Kastaniés 81 F1
Kastaniótissa 83 F3
Kastéla 84 B4
Kastelhoms 106 C3
Kastéli (Kriti) 90 B3
Kastéli (Kriti) 91 E4
Kastellaun 51 E4
Kastelórizo 93 F2
Kastélou, Akr 93 D3
Kastelruth 59 D3
Kaštel Stari 75 D1
Kaštel Žegarski 75 D1
Kasterlee 50 C3
Kastl 55 F1
Kastorf 48 B2
Kastóri 87 D3
Kastoriá 79 D3
Kastoriá (Nomos) 78 C3
Kastoriás, L 79 D3
Kastós, N 82 C4
Kastráki (Kiklådes) 88 C3
Kastráki (Stereá Eláda) 82 C3
Kastráki (Thessalía) 83 D1
Kastrakíou, Teh L 82 C3
Kastrí (Pelopónissos) 87 D2
Kastrí (Stereá Eláda) 83 E3
Kastrí (Thessalía) 83 F1
Kástro (Pelopónissos) 86 B1
Kástro (Skíathos) 84 A2
Kástro (Stereá Eláda) 83 F4
Kastrossikiá 82 B2
Katafígio 79 E4
Katáfito 80 B1
Katáfourko 82 C3
Katahás 79 F3
Katákolo 86 B2
Katálako 85 D1
Kátano, Akr 88 A3
Katápola 89 D3
Katára 82 C1
Katastári 86 A1
Katavía 93 E2
Katelimátsa 91 F1
Kateliós 86 A1
Katerini 79 F4
Katerloch 57 E4
Katharó 91 E4
Katheni 84 B4
Katići 76 C1
Kätkäsuvanto 95 D4
Katlanovo 77 E3
Katlanovska Banja 77 E3
Katlenburg-Duhm 52 B2
Káto Ahaïa 86 B1
Káto Alissós 86 B1
Káto Asséa 87 D2
Káto Doliana 87 D2
Káto Figália 86 C2
Káto Gadzéa 83 F2
Katohí 82 C4
Káto Kamíla 80 B2
Káto Klinés 79 D2
Káto Makrinoú 83 D4
Katoméri, Akr 88 C3
Káto Moussounítsa 83 E3
Káto Nevrokópi 80 B1
Káto Ólimbos 83 E1
Káto Tithoréa 83 E4
Katoúna (Lefkáda) 82 B3
Katoúna (Stereá Eláda) 82 C3
Káto Vassilikí 83 D4
Káto Vérga 86 C3
Káto Vérmio 79 E3
Káto Vlassía 86 C1
Katowice 112 B2
Káto Zahloroú 86 C1
Káto Zákros 91 F4
Katrineholm 106 A4
Katschberg 59 F2
Katschberg-Tunnel 59 F2
Kattegat 108 C2
Katwijk aan Zee 16 B2
Kaub 51 F4
Kaufbeuren 55 E3
Kauhajärvi 102 C2
Kauhajoki 102 B3
Kauhaneva-Pohjankangas 102 C3
Kauhava 102 C2
Kaukonen 95 E4
Kaunas 110 C3
Kaupanger 104 B1
Kaušany 113 E4
Kaustinen 102 C2
Kautokeino 95 D3
Kautokeinoelva 95 D3
Kauttua 107 D2
Kavadarci 77 E3
Kavajë 76 C4
Kavála 80 C2
Kavála (Nomos) 80 C2
Kaválas, Kólpos 80 C2
Kavarna 115 E2
Kavíli 81 F1
Kävlinge 108 C3
Kávos 82 A2
Kavoússi 91 F4
Käylä 99 E2
Kaysersberg 27 E1
Kazan 73 E2
Kažani 77 E4
Kazanlăk 115 D2
Kazárma 86 C3
Kazatin 113 E2
Kazimierz Dolny 112 C2
Kazincbarcika 112 B3
Kdyně 56 B1
Kéa 88 A2
Keadew 12 C2
Keady 13 D2
Keähkkiljohka 95 D3
Keal, L na 4 B1
Kéa Meriá 88 A2
Kéa, N 88 A2
Kéas, Stenó 88 A2
Kebnekaise 94 B4
Kebnekaise *Mt* 94 B4
Kebock Head 2 B2
Kecskemét 112 B4
Kėdainiai 110 C3
Kédros 83 D2
Kędzierzyn-Koźle 112 B2
Keel 12 A2
Keerbergen 50 C3
Kefalári 87 D2
Kefálas, Akr 80 C3
Kefáli, Akr 90 A2
Kefaloniá, N 82 B4
Kéfalos 89 F4
Kéfalos, Akr 88 A2
Kefalóvrisso (Ípiros) 78 C4
Kefalóvrisso (Pelopónissos) 86 C3
Kefalóvrisso (Stereá Eláda) 82 C4
Kefalóvrisso (Thessalía) 83 D1
Keflavík 96 A2
Kehl 54 C3
Kehlstein 56 C4
Kehrókambos 80 C2
Kéhros 81 E2
Keighley 6 C2
Keimaneigh, Pass of 14 B4
Keitele 103 D2
Keitele *L* 103 D2
Keith 3 D3
Kéla 79 D2
Kelankylä 99 E3
Kelberg 51 E4
Kelbra 52 C2
Këlcyrë 114 C4
Kelebija 72 B1
Kelefá 87 D4
Kelheim 55 F2
Kellinghusen 48 A2
Kellojärvi 99 F4
Kellokoski 107 E2
Kells 13 D3
Kelso 5 E2
Kelujärvi 95 E4
Kemberg 53 D1
Kembs 27 E1
Kemi 99 D3
Kemihaara 95 F4
Kemijärvi 99 E2
Kemijärvi *L* 99 E2
Kemijoki 99 D2
Keminmaa 99 D3
Kemiö 107 D3
Kemnath 53 D4
Kempele 99 D4
Kempen 17 D4
Kempenich 51 E4
Kempten 55 E4
Kendal 6 B1
Kéndras, Akr 88 B3
Kendrikó 79 F2
Kenilworth 9 E1
Kenmare 14 A4
Kenmare River 14 A4
Kennacraig 4 B2
Kenoúrgio 83 D3
Kent 11 D3
Kentallen 4 B1
Kenzingen 54 C3
Keramía 85 F2
Keramídi 83 F2
Keramítsa 82 B1
Kéramos 85 E4
Keramotí 81 D2
Kerassiá (Évia) 84 A3
Kerassiá (Thessalía) 83 F2
Kerassiés 79 E2
Kerassohóri 83 D3
Kerassóna 82 C2
Kérata, Akr 83 F3
Keratéa 87 F2
Kerava 107 E2
Kerdília, N. 80 B3
Kérěs 72 C1
Kerí 86 A2
Kerimäki 103 F3
Kerken 17 D3
Kerketéas, Óros 89 E1
Kerkétio, Óri 83 D2
Kerkíni, Óros 80 A1
Kerkínis, L 80 A2
Kérkira 82 A1
Kérkira, N 82 A1
Kerkonkoski 103 D2
Kerkrade 51 D3
Kernascléden 22 B3
Kéros, N 88 C3
Kerpen 17 D4
Kerrera 4 B1
Kerry 14 B3
Kerry Head 14 A3
Kerteminde 108 B3
Kértezi 86 C1
Kerzers 27 E2
Kesälahti 103 F3
Keşan 115 E3
Kesch, Piz 58 B3
Kesh 12 C2
Keski-Suomen Lääni 103 D2
Kessariani 87 F1
Kestilä 99 D4
Keswick 5 D4
Keszthely 112 A4
Kętrzyn 110 B4
Kettering 9 F1
Kettletoft 3 E1
Kettwig 17 E4
Ketzin 49 D4
Keukenhof 16 B2
Keurusselkä 103 D3
Keuruu 102 C3
Kevelaer 17 D3
Kevo 95 E2
Kevo (Nat Pk) 95 E2
Key, L 12 C3
Keynsham 9 D2
Kežmarok 112 B3
Kiani 81 F1
Kiantajärvi 99 F3
Kiáto 87 D1
Kiberg 95 F1
Kičevo 77 D3
Kidderminster 9 D1
Kidlington 9 E2
Kidsgrove 6 C3
Kidwelly 8 C2
Kiefersfelden 56 B4
Kiekinkoski 99 F4
Kiel 48 A1
Kielce 112 B2
Kielder Reservoir 5 E3
Kieler Bucht 48 A1
Kiental 27 F3
Kierinki 99 D1
Kietz 49 F4
Kifissiá 87 F1
Kifissos 83 F4
Kifjord 95 E1
Kihlanki 95 D4
Kihniö 102 C3
Kihti Skiftet 107 D3
Kiihtelysvaara 103 F2
Kiikala 107 E2
Kiikka 107 D2
Kiikoinen 107 D1
Kiimanen 99 E4
Kiiminginjoki 99 D3
Kiiminki 99 D3
Kiiskilä 102 C1
Kiistala 95 E4
Kijev 113 E2
Kijevo (Hrvatska) 75 D1
Kijevo (Kosovo) 77 D2
Kijevskoje Vodochranilišče 113 E2
Kikinda 72 C1
Kiklådes 88 B2
Kil 105 E3
Kila 79 D3
Kiláda (Makedonía) 79 E3
Kiláda (Pelopónissos) 87 E2
Kilafors 101 F4
Kilbaha 12 A4
Kilbeggan 12 C4
Kilbirnie 4 C2
Kilboghamn 97 E2
Kilbotn 94 B3
Kilbrannan Sd 4 B2
Kilchoan 2 B4
Kilcock 13 D4
Kilcormac 12 C4
Kilcreggan 4 C2
Kilcullen 13 D4
Kildare 13 D4
Kildare (Co) 13 D4
Kildorrery 14 C3
Kilfenora 12 B4
Kilgarvan 14 B4
Kilija 113 E4
Kilingi-Nõmme 110 C2
Kilini 86 B1
Kilini, Óros 87 D1
Kilkee 12 A4
Kilkeel 13 E3
Kilkenny 15 D3
Kilkenny (Co) 15 D3
Kilkhampton 8 B3
Kilkieran B 12 A3
Kilkis 79 F2
Kilkís (Nomos) 79 F2
Killadysert 12 B4
Killala B 12 B2
Killaloe 12 B4
Killarney 14 B4
Killary Harbour 12 A3
Killashandra 12 C3
Killenaule 14 C3
Killimer 12 B4
Killin 4 C1
Killinkoski 102 C3
Killorglin 14 A3
Killybegs 12 C2
Killyleagh 13 E2
Kilmaing 12 B3
Kilmallock 14 B3
Kilmarnock 4 C2
Kilmartin 4 B2
Kilmore Quay 15 D4
Kilmurry 12 B4
Kilninver 4 B1
Kilnsea 7 E2
Kilpisjärvi 94 C3
Kilpisjärvi *L* 94 C3
Kilrea 13 D1
Kilronan 12 B4
Kilrush 12 B4
Kilsyth 4 C2
Kiltamagh 12 B3
Kiltealy 15 D3
Kilwinning 4 C2
Kilyos 115 F3
Kimássi 84 A3
Kiméria 81 D2
Kimi 84 B3
Kímina 79 F3
Kimis, Órmos 84 B4
Kimisseos Theotókou 87 D2
Kimito 107 D3
Kímolos 88 B4
Kímolos, N 88 B4
Kimólou Sífnou, Stenó 88 B3
Kimry 111 F2
Kimstad 105 F4
Kínaros, N 89 D3
Kinbrace 3 D2
Kincardine 5 D2
Kindberg 57 E3
Kindelbrück 52 C2
Kinéta 87 E1
Kingisepp 111 D1
Kingissepp 110 B2
Kingsbridge 8 C4
Kingscourt 13 D3
King's Lynn 7 E3
Kingston 9 F2
Kingston-upon-Hull 7 E2
Kingswear 8 C4
Kington 9 D1
Kingussie 3 D4
Kinira 81 D3
Kinlochbervie 2 C2
Kinlochewe 2 C3
Kinloch Rannoch 4 C1
Kinna 108 C1
Kinnairds Head 3 E3
Kinnasniemi 103 F2
Kinnegad 13 D3
Kinnitty 12 C4
Kinnula 103 D2
Kinross 5 D2
Kinsale 14 B4
Kinsarvik 104 B2
Kintaus 103 D3
Kintore 3 E4
Kintyre 4 B2
Kinvarra 12 B4
Kinzig 54 C3
Kióni 82 B4
Kiparíssi 87 E3
Kiparissía 86 C3
Kiparissiakós Kólpos 86 B2
Kiparissías, Óri 86 C3
Kipárissos 83 E2
Kípi (Ípiros) 78 C4
Kípi (Thráki) 81 F2
Kipinä 99 D3
Kípos, Akr 81 E3
Kipourío 79 D4
Kippure 13 D4
Kipséli 83 E2
Kir 76 C3
Kirá Panagiá, N 84 B2
Kirchbach 57 E4
Kirchberg (D) 54 B1
Kirchberg (DDR) 53 D3
Kirchberg (Nieder österreich) 57 E2
Kirchberg (Tirol) 59 E1
Kirchberg an der Pielach 57 E3
Kirchdorf 57 D3
Kirchenlamitz 53 D4
Kirchenthumbach 53 D4
Kirchhain 52 A3
Kirchheim (Baden-Württemberg) 55 D2
Kirchheim (Hessen) 52 B3
Kirchheimbolanden 54 C1
Kirchheim unter Teck 55 D2
Kirchhundem 17 F4
Kirchlengern 17 F2
Kirchmöser 49 D4
Kirchschlag 57 F3
Kiriakí 81 F1
Kiriáki 83 F4
Kiriši 111 E1
Kırkağaç 115 E4
Kirkby Lonsdale 6 C1
Kirkby Stephen 5 E4
Kirkcaldy 5 D2
Kirkcolm 4 B3
Kirkcudbright 4 C3
Kirkenær 105 D2
Kirkenes 95 F2
Kirkeøy 105 D4
Kirkestinden 94 B3
Kirkham 6 B2
Kirki 81 E2
Kirkintilloch 4 C2
Kirkjubøur 96 A4
Kirkkonummi 107 E3
Kırklareli 115 E3
Kirkonmaanselkä 103 F4
Kirkwall 3 E1
Kirn 54 B1
Kirov 111 F3
Kirovograd 113 F2
Kirovsk 111 D1
Kirriemuir 5 D1
Kirtorf 52 A3
Kiruna 94 C4
Kisa 109 E1
Kisac 72 C2
Kiseljak (Loznica) 72 B3
Kiseljak (Sarajevo) 75 F1
Kiseljak (Tuzla) 71 F3
Kišin'ov 113 E3
Kisko 107 E3
Kiskőrös 112 B4
Kiskunfélegyháza 112 B4
Kiskunhalas 114 B1
Kißlegg 55 E4

Kjerringvik	101 D1	Knittelfeld	57 D4	Kómi (Híos)	89 D1
Kjølifjell	101 D2	Knivskjellodden	95 D1	Komílio	82 B3
Kjøllefjord	95 E1	Knivsta	106 B3	Komin	70 C2
Kjøpsvik	94 B4	Knjaževac	73 F4	Kómito	88 B1
Kjustendil	114 C3	Knockmealdown Mts	14 C3	Komiža	75 D2
Klæbu	100 C2	Knokke-Heist	50 A3	Komló	114 B1
Kladanj	72 B4	Knole House	10 C3	Komninádes	78 C3
Kladnica	76 C1	Knossós	91 D3	Komniná (Makedonía)	79 D3
Kladnice	75 D1	Knutsford	6 C2	Komniná (Thráki)	81 D2
Kladno	53 F4	Koarvikodds	95 E3	Komorane	77 D2
Kladovo	73 F2	Kobarid	70 A2	Komotiní	81 E2
Klagenfurt	70 A1	Kobbfjorden	95 D1	Komovi	76 B2
Klaipėda	110 B3	Kobel'aki	113 F2	Komrat	113 E4
Klaksvik	96 A3	København	108 C3	Komulanköngäs	99 E4
Klana	70 B3	Kobern-Gondorf	51 E4	Konak	73 D2
Klanac	70 C4	Kobišnica	73 F3	Konakovo	111 F2
Klanxbüll	47 F1	Koblenz	51 E4	Končanica	71 D2
Klarälven	105 E2	Koca D	115 F3	Kondiás	85 D1
Klašnice	71 E3	Kočani	77 F2	Kondopoúli	85 D1
Klässbol	105 E3	Koceljevo	72 C3	Kondós, Akr	88 B3
Klášterec	53 E3	Kočerin	75 E2	Kondovázena	86 C1
Klasvík	96 A3	Kočevje	70 B2	Kondrić	71 F2
Klatovy	56 C1	Kočevski rog	70 B2	Konečka pl	77 E3
Klaukkala	107 E2	Kochel	56 A4	Køng	108 C4
Klausen	59 D2	Kocher	55 E2	Köngernheim	54 C1
Klausenpass	58 A2	Kodiksami	107 D2	Konginkangas	103 D2
Klazienaveen	17 E2	Kodisjoki	107 D2	Kongsberg	104 C3
Kleinhaugsdorf	57 E2	Köflach	57 E4	Kongselva	94 A3
Kleinheubach	55 D1	Køge	108 C3	Kongsfjord	95 F1
Kleinwalsertal	55 E4	Køge Bugt	108 C3	Kongsvinger	105 D3
Klekovača	71 D4	Kohtla-Järve	110 C1	Kœnigsbourg	27 E1
Klenike	77 E2	Koikkala	103 E3	Königsbrück	53 E2
Klenovica	70 B3	Koirakoski	103 E1	Königsbrunn	55 F3
Kleppe	104 A3	Koitajoki	103 F2	Königsee	52 C3
Kleppestø	104 A2	Koltelainen	95 E4	Königsfeld	54 C3
Kleve	17 D3	Koitere	103 F2	Königslutter	52 B1
Kličevac	73 D2	Koivujärvi	103 D1	Königsschlösser	55 F4
Klimovici	111 E4	Koivusuo	103 F2	Königssee	56 C4
Klimpfjäll	97 E4	Kokála	87 D4	Königssee L	56 C4
Klin	111 F2	Kökar	106 C3	Königstein (D)	51 F4
Klina	76 C2	Kokári	89 E1	Königstein (DDR)	53 F2
Klinča Selo	70 C2	Kökarsfjärden	106 C3	Königswiesen	57 D2
Klincy	111 E4	Kokemäenjoki	107 D1	Königswinter	51 E3
Klingenbach	57 F3	Kokcmäki	107 D2	Königs-Wusterhausen	49 E4
Klingenthal	53 D3	Kokin Brod	76 B1	Konin	112 A1
Klinovec	53 E3	Kókino Neró	83 F1	Koniskós	83 D1
Klintehamn	109 F4	Kokkola	102 C1	Konístres	84 B4
Klippan	108 C3	Koksijde-Bad	50 A3	Kónitsa	78 C4
Klippen	97 E3	Kola	71 E3	Konj	75 E1
Klippitztörl	57 D4	Koláka	83 F4	Konjevrate	75 D1
Klis	75 D1	Kolari (SF)	98 C1	Konjic	75 F1
Klissoúra	79 D3	Kolari (YU)	73 D3	Konjsko	76 A2
Klisura (Makedonija)	77 F3	Kolåsen	101 D1	Konjuh	71 F4
Klisura (Srbija)	77 E1	Kolašin	76 B2	Konkämäälven	94 C3
Klitoría	86 C1	Kolbäck	105 F3	Können	52 C2
Klitten	53 F2	Kołbacz	49 F2	Konnevesi	103 D2
Klixbüll	47 F1	Kołbaskowo	49 E2	Konnevesi L	103 D2
Kljajićevo	72 B2	Kolbermoor	56 B3	Könönpelto	103 E3
Ključ	71 D4	Kolby Kås	108 B3	Konopište	77 E3
Kłodzko	112 A2	Kolding	108 A3	Konotop	113 F1
Kløfta	105 D3	Kolho	103 D3	Konsko	77 F4
Klokkarvik	104 A2	Koli	103 F2	Konsmo	104 B4
Klokočevac	73 F3	Kolima	103 D2	Konstantinovy Lázně	53 E4
Klos	76 C4	Kolimvári	90 B3	Konstanz	55 D4
Kloštar	71 D2	Kolin	112 A3	Kontich	50 B3
Kloštar Ivanić	71 D2	Kolindrós	79 F3	Kontiolahti	103 F2
Klösterle	58 B2	Kolínes	87 D3	Kontiomäki	99 E4
Klosterneuburg	57 F2	Kolka	110 B2	Konttajärvi	98 C2
Klosters	58 B2	Kolkanlahti	103 D2	Konz	54 A1
Kloten	58 A2	Kolkasrags	110 B2	Kopaida	83 F4
Klötze	48 C4	Kölleda	52 C2	Kopáni	82 C2
Klöverträsk	98 B3	Kolmården	106 A4	Kopanós	79 E3
Klövsjö	101 E3	Koloveč	56 B1	Kopaonik	77 D1
Kluczbork	112 A2	Kolovrat	76 B1	Koparnes	100 A2
Klupe	71 E3	Kolpino	111 D1	Kópasker	96 C1
Klütz	48 B2	Kolsva	105 F3	Kopavogur	96 A2
Knapdale	4 B2	Kolubara	72 C3	Köpenick	49 E4
Knappogue Castle	12 B4	Kolvereid	97 D4	Koper	70 A3
Knäred	109 D2	Kolvik	95 D2	Kopervik	104 A3
Knaresborough	6 C1	Kómanos	79 D3	Köping	105 F3
Knarvik	104 A2	Komar	71 E4	Köpingsvik	109 E2
Kneginec	71 D1	Komárno	112 B4	Koplik	76 B3
Kneža	115 D2	Kómbóti	82 C2	Köpmanholmen	102 A2
Knežak	70 B3	Koméno	82 C3	Koporiće	77 D1
Kneževi Vinogradi	71 F2	Kómi (Kikládes)	88 B2	Koppang	100 C3
Kneževo	71 F2			Kopparberg	105 F3
Knežica	71 D3			Kopparbergs Län	105 E2
Knežina	72 B4			Kopparleden	101 E2
Knić	73 D4			Kopperby	48 A1
Knidi	79 D4			Kopperveien	100 D3
Knighton	9 D1			Koprivna	71 F3
Knight's Town	14 A4				
Knin	75 D1				

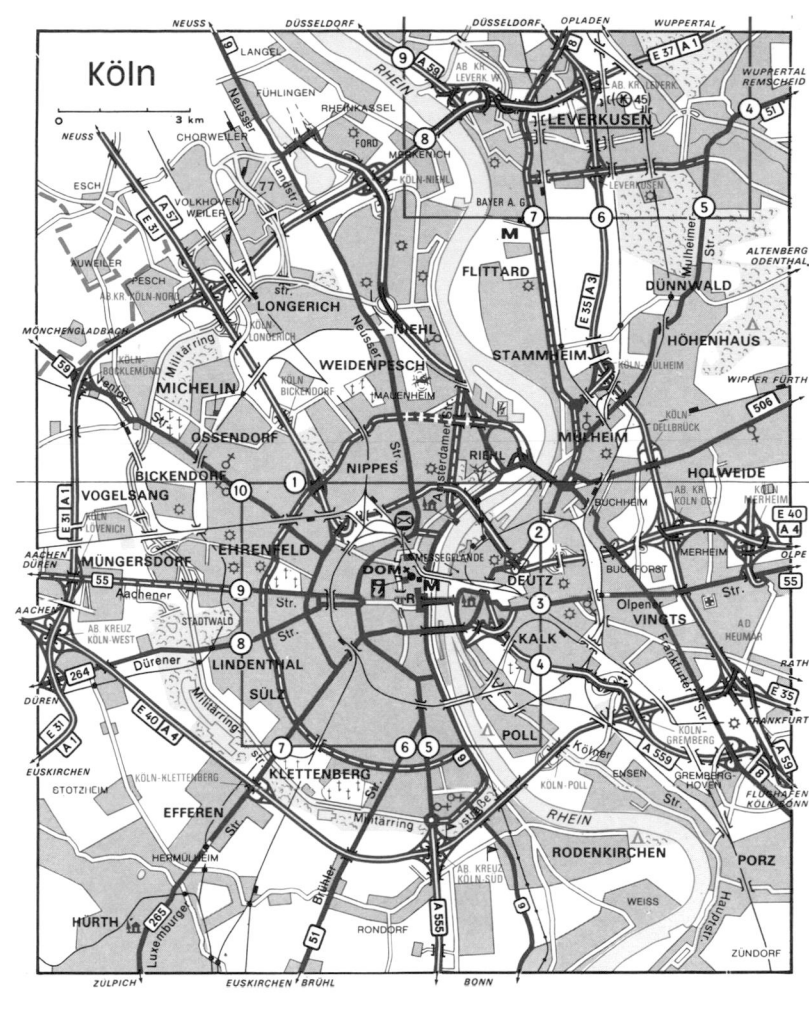

Koprivnica (Bosna i Hercegovina)	71 D1	Kornofoléa	81 F2	Koška	71 F2	Kotorsko	71 F3
Koprivnica (Srbija)	73 F3	Kornwestheim	55 D2	Koskenkorva	102 B2	Kotor Varoš	71 E4
Korab	77 D3	Koromacno	70 B4	Koskenpää	103 D3	Kotovsk (Moldavija)	113 E4
Kórakas, Akr	88 C3	Koróna	79 F2	Koski (Hämeen Lääni)	107 E2	Kotovsk (Ukraina)	113 E3
Koralpe	70 B1	Króni	86 C4	Koski (Turun ja Porin Läni)	107 D2	Kotraža	73 D4
Korana	70 C3	Korónia	83 F1	Kóskina	84 B4	Kótronas	87 D4
Korbach	52 A2	Korónia, L	80 A3	Koskue	102 C3	Kotroniá	81 F2
Korbevac	77 E2	Koronída	88 C3	Kosmaj	73 D3	Kötschach-Mauthen	59 E2
Korbovo	73 F2	Koronissía	82 C3	Kosmás	87 D3	Köttsjön	101 F2
Korçë	114 C3	Korónos	88 C3	Kósmio	81 E2	Kötzting	56 B1
Korčula	75 E2	Koronoúda	80 A2	Kosovo	77 D2	Koufália	79 F3
Korčula I	75 E2	Koropí	87 F1	Kosovo Polje	77 D2	Koufoníssi (Kikládes)	88 C3
Korčulanski kan	75 E2	Körös	112 B4	Kosovska Kamenica	77 D2	Koufoníssi (Kríti)	91 F4
Korensko sedlo	70 A1	Kos, N	89 F3	Kössen	59 E1	Koufós	80 B4
Kórfos	87 E2	Korosten´	113 E2	Kósta	87 E3	Kouklií	82 B1
Korgåsen	95 F2	Korostyšev	113 E2	Kostajnica	71 D3	Koukounariés	84 A2
Korgen	97 E3	Korouoma	99 E2	Kostanjevac	70 C2	Koúla	81 D1
Koria	107 F2	Korpilahti	103 D3	Kostanjevica	70 C2	Kouméika	89 E2
Korifássi	86 C3	Korpilombolo	98 C2	Kostenec	115 D3	Koúndouros	88 A2
Koríkio Ándro	83 E4	Korpo	107 D3	Köster	105 D4	Kounoupéli	86 B1
Kórimvos	81 F1	Korppoo	107 D3	Kostolac	73 D3	Koura	102 C2
Korini	83 F4	Korsberga	109 E2	Kostonjärvi	99 E3	Koúrenda	82 B1
Korinós	79 F4	Korsfjorden	104 A2	Kostopol'	113 D2	Kourkoulí	84 A3
Korinthía	87 D1	Korsholm	102 B2	Kóstos	88 C3	Kournás	90 C3
Korinthiakós Kólpos	87 D1	Korsnäs	102 B2	Kostrzyn	49 F4	Kouroúta	86 B2
Kórinthos	87 E1	Korsør	108 B4	Kosturino	77 F3	Koutselió	82 C1
Korissía	88 A3	Korsun-Ševčenkovskij	113 F2	Kosula	103 E2	Koutsó	81 D2
Korissós	79 D3	Kortesjärvi	102 C2	Koszalin	110 A4	Koutsóhero	83 E1
Korita (Bosna i Hercegovina)	76 A2	Kórthio	88 B2	Kőszeg	112 A4	Kouvola	107 F2
Korita (Crna Gora)	76 B2	Kortrijk	50 A3	Kotala (Keski-Suomen Lääni)	103 D2	Kovačica	72 C2
Korita (Mljet)	75 E2	Kortteenperä	99 D2	Kotala (Lapin Lääni)	99 E1	Kovel'	112 C2
Koríthi	86 A1	Korvala	99 D2	Kotel	115 E2	Kovero	103 F2
Koritnik	76 C1	Korvaluoma	102 C3	Köthen	53 D1	Kovin	73 D3
Koritnik, M.	77 D3	Korvatunturi	95 F3	Kotka	103 F4	Köyliö	107 D2
Korkeakangas	103 F3	Kos	89 F3	Kotor	76 B3	Kozáni	79 D3
Korkeakoski	103 D2	Kosančić	77 D1	Kotoriba	71 D1	Kozáni	79 D3
Körmend	112 A4	Kosanica	76 B1			Kozara	71 D3
Kornat	74 C1	Kościan	112 A2			Kozarac (Bosna i Hercegovina)	71 D3
Kornati	74 C1	Kościerzyna	110 A4			Kozarac (Hrvatska)	71 F2
Korneuburg	57 F2	Kosel	77 D4				
		Koserow	49 E1				
		Košice	112 C3				
		Kosjerić	72 C4				

154
Koz – La M

Koželʼsk 111 F3
Kozica 75 E2
Kozina 70 A3
Kozjak 77 E4
Kozluk 72 B3
Kožuf 77 F4
Kragenæs 108 B4
Kragerø 104 C4
Kragujevac 73 D4
Krajišnik 73 D2
Krajkovac 77 D1
Krajn 76 C3
Krajnik Dln 49 E3
Krakhella 104 A1
Krakow 48 C2
Kraków 112 B2
Kraljeva Sutjeska 71 F4
Kraljevica 70 B3
Kraljevo 73 D4
Kralovice 53 E4
Kralupy 53 F3
Kramfors 101 F2
Kranenburg 17 D3
Krani 77 E4
Kraniá Elassónas 79 E4
Kraniá (Makedonía) 79 D4
Kraniá (Thessalía) 82 C1
Kranichfeld 52 C3
Kranídi 87 E2
Kranj 70 A2
Kranjska Gora 70 A1
Krapina 70 C2
Krapinske Toplice 70 C2
Krašić 70 C2
Krāslava 111 D3
Kraslice 53 D3
Krasná Lípa 53 F2
Kraśnik 112 C2
Krasno Polje 70 C4
Krasnyj Cholm 111 F1
Krasnystaw 112 C2
Kráthio 87 D1
Krátigos 85 F3
Kratovo 77 E2
Kratovska-Stena 72 C4
Krauchenwies 55 D3
Krautheim 55 D1
Kravarsko 70 C2
Krefeld 17 D4
Kremastí (Pelopónissos) 87 E3
Kremastí (Ródos) 93 F1
Kremastón, Teh L 83 D3
Kremenčug 113 F2
Kremenčugskoje Vodochranilišče 113 F2
Kremenec 113 D2
Kremídi, Akr 87 E4
Kremmen 49 D3
Kremna 72 C4
Kremnica 112 B3
Krems 57 E2
Kremsmünster 57 D3
Krepoljin 73 E3
Kreševo 75 F1
Krestcy 111 E1
Kréstena 86 B2
Kreuth 56 A4
Kreuzbergpass 59 E2
Kreuzlingen 58 A1
Kreuztal 17 F4
Kría Vríssi (Évia) 84 A3
Kría Vríssi (Makedonía) 79 E3
Kričev 111 E4
Krieglach 57 E3
Kriens 27 F2
Kríkelo 83 D3
Kríkelos 82 C3
Kríkelos, Akr 89 F4
Krimml 59 D2
Krimmler Wasserfälle 59 D2
Krimpen 16 C3
Krinídes 80 C2
Krionéri (Makedonía) 80 A2
Krionéri (Pelopónissos) 86 C3
Krionéri (Pelopónissos) 87 D1
Kriopigí 80 B4
Kriós, Akr 90 B4
Kristalopigí 78 C3
Kristdala 109 E2
Kristiansand 104 B4
Kristianstad 109 D3
Kristianstads Län 109 D3
Kristiansund 100 B2
Kristiinankaupunki 102 B3
Kristineberg 98 A4
Kristinehamn 105 E4
Kristinehov 109 D3
Kristinestad 102 B3
Krithéa 79 F2
Krithína, Óros 87 E4
Kritikó Pélagos 90 B2
Kriti, N 91 E3
Kritinía 93 E1
Kritsá 91 E4
Kriva Feja 77 E2
Krivaja (Bosna i Hercegovina) 71 F4
Krivaja (Vojvodina) 72 B1
Kriva Palanka 77 E2
Kriva reka 77 E2
Krivogaštani 77 E4
Krivoj Rog 113 F3
Krivolak 77 E3
Křižanov 57 E1
Križevci 71 D2
Krk 70 B3
Krk *I* 70 B3
Krka 70 B2
Krka *R* 75 D1
Krkonoše 112 A2
Krmčine 74 C1
Krn 70 A2
Krnjača 72 C3
Krnjak 70 C3
Krnjeuša 71 D4
Krnjevo 73 D3
Krnov 112 A3
Krnovo 76 B2
Krøderen 104 C2
Krokeés 87 D3
Krokeide 104 A2
Krokek 106 A4
Krokílio 83 D4
Krokom 101 E2
Krókos 79 E4
Kroksjö 98 A4
Krolevec 113 F1
Kröller Müller 17 D3
Kroměříž 112 A3
Kronach 52 C4
Kronobergs Län 109 D2
Kronoby 102 C1
Kronshagen 48 A1
Kronštadt 111 D1
Kröpelin 48 C2
Kropp 48 A1
Kroppenstedt 52 C1
Krosno 112 C3
Krosno Odrzańskie 53 F1
Krotoszyn 112 A2
Kroussónas 91 D4
Krovili, Pal 81 E2
Krrabe, M 76 C3
Krško 70 C2
Krstac 76 A2
Krstača 76 C2
Krstinja 70 C3
Kruë i Fushës 76 C3
Kruiningen 16 B4
Krujë 76 C4
Krumbach 55 E3
Krumpendorf 70 A1
Krün 55 F4
Krupà 53 E4
Krupac (Bosna i Hercegovina) 75 F1
Krupac (Crna Gora) 76 B2
Krupac (Srbija) 77 E1
Krupaja 73 E3
Krupa na Vrbasu 71 E4
Krupanj 72 C3
Krupište 77 E3
Krupka 53 E3
Kruså 108 A4
Kruščica 71 E4
Kruščica, Jezero 70 C4
Krušedol Selo 72 C2
Kruševac 73 E4
Kruševica 73 D3
Kruševo 77 E4
Krute 76 B3
Kruunupyy 102 C1
Krvavec 70 B2
Krynica 112 B3
Krzeszyce 49 F4
Ktenías, Óros 87 D2
Ktísmata 82 B1
Kubitzer Bodden 49 D1
Küblis 58 B2
Kučaj 73 E4
Kučevište 77 D2
Kučevo 73 E3
Kuchl 59 E1
Kučina Kosa 71 D4
Kućište 75 E2
Kućište 76 C2
Kudowa-Zdrój 112 A2
Kufstein 59 D1
Kühlungsborn 48 C2
Kuhmalahti 103 D3
Kuhmo 99 F4
Kuhmoinen 103 D3
Kuivajärvi 99 F4
Kuivajoki 99 D3
Kuivalahti 107 D2
Kuivaniemi 99 D3
Kuivasjärvi 102 C3
Kuivi 95 E2
Kuk 70 C4
Kukavica 77 E1
Kukës 76 C3
Kukkia 107 E1
Kukko 102 C2
Kukujevci 72 B2
Kukulje 71 E3
Kula (BG) 114 C2
Kula (TR) 115 F4
Kula (YU) 72 B2
Kuldīga 110 B3
Kulennoinen 103 F3
Kulen Vakuf 71 D4
Kulina 73 E4
Kulju 107 E1
Kulkjica 74 C1
Kullaa 107 D1
Kulm 27 F2
Kulmbach 52 C4
Kuloharju 99 E2
Külsheim 55 D1
Kultakero 99 E1
Kultsjön 97 E4
Kum 70 B2
Kumane 72 C2
Kumanovo 77 E2
Kumla 105 F4
Kumlinge 106 C3
Kummavuopio 94 C3
Kummerower See 49 D2
Kumputunturi 95 E4
Kumrovec 70 C2
Kungälv 108 C1
Kungsbacka 108 C1
Kungshamn 105 D4
Kungsör 105 F3
Kunoy 96 A3
Kunrau 48 B4
Kunszentmárton 112 B4
Künzelsau 55 D2
Kuolimo 103 E4
Kuolio 99 E3
Kuopio 103 E2
Kuopion Lääni 103 E2
Kuorboaivi 95 E2
Kuorevesi 103 D3
Kuortane 102 C2
Kuortovare 94 C4
Kuortti 103 D3
Kupa 70 B3
Kupa 70 C3
Kupferzell 55 D2
Kupinova Glava 73 E3
Kupinovo 72 C3
Kupres 75 E1
Kupreška vrata 75 E1
Kurfar 59 D3
Kurikka 102 B2
Kuřim 57 F1
Kuršėnai 110 C3
Kuršskij Zaliv 110 B3
Kursu 99 E2
Kuršumlija 77 D1
Kuršumlijska Banja 77 D1
Kurtakko 95 D4
Kuru 102 C3
Kusadak 73 D3
Kuşadasi 115 E4
Kusel 54 B1
Küsnacht 58 A2
Küssnacht 58 A2
Kustavi 107 D2
Küstenkanal 17 E1
Kütahya 115 F3
Kutina 71 D2
Kutjevo 71 E2
Kutná Hora 112 A3
Kutno 112 B1
Kuttanen 95 D3
Kuttura 95 E3
Kúty 57 F2
Kuumu 99 F4
Kuusamo 99 E2
Kuusamojärvi 99 F2
Kuusankoski 107 F2
Kuusjärvi 103 E2
Kuusjoki 107 E2
Kuvšinovo 111 E2
Kuzma 70 C1
Kuzmin 72 B3
Kvæfjord 94 A3
Kvaløy 94 B2
Kvaløya 95 D1
Kvalsund 95 D1
Kvalvøg 100 B2
Kvam 100 C3
Kvænangen 94 C2
Kvænangsbotn 95 D2
Kvanndal 104 B2
Kvanne 100 B2
Kværndrup 108 B4
Kvarner 70 B4
Kvarnerič 70 B4
Kvernes 100 B2
Kvevlax 102 B2
Kvikkjokk 98 A2
Kvikne 100 C2
Kvina 104 B4
Kvinesdal 104 B4
Kvinesdal *V* 104 B4
Kvisvik 100 B2
Kviteseid 104 B3
Kvitnes 100 B2
Kvitsøy 104 A3
Kwidzyn 110 B4
Kyjov 57 F1
Kyläinpää 102 B2
Kylänlahti 103 F1
Kyleakin 2 B3
Kyle of Lochalsh 2 B3
Kyle of Tongue 2 C2
Kylerhea 2 B3
Kylestrome 2 C2
Kyll 51 D4
Kyllburg 51 D4
Kylmäkoski 107 E2
Kylmälä 99 D4
Kymen Lääni 103 F4
Kynsivesi 103 D3
Kyritz 49 D3
Kyrksæterøra 100 C2
Kyrkslätt 107 E3
Kyrönjoki 102 C2
Kyrösjärvi 102 C3
Kyselka 53 E3
Kyšice 53 F4
Kyyjärvi 102 C2
Kyyvesi 103 E3

L

Laa an der Thaya 57 F2
La Adrada 39 F2
Laage 48 C2
Laakajärvi 103 E1
La Alberca 39 E2
La Alberca de Záncara 40 C3
La Alberguería de Argañán 39 D2
La Albuera 38 C4
La Albufera 41 E4
La Alcarria 40 C2
La Algaba 43 D2
La Almarcha 40 C3
La Almunia de Doña Godina 36 C4
La Antillas 42 C3
La Azohia 45 D3
Labacolla 34 A2
La Baells, Emb de 32 A3
Labajos 40 A1
La Bañeza 35 D3
La Barca de la Florida 43 D3
Labasheeda 12 B4
Labastida 36 B2
Labastide-Clairence 28 A4
Labastide-Murat 29 D2
Labastide-Rouairoux 32 B1
Labe 53 F3
Labin 70 A3
Labinot Fushë 76 C4
La Bisbal de Falset 37 E4
La Bisbal d'Empordà 32 B3
Laboe 48 A1
Labouheyre 28 A3
Labouret, Col du 31 D3
La Bóveda de Toro 35 D4
La Brède 28 B2
Labrit 28 B3
Labruguière 32 B1
Labudnjača 72 B2
Laç 76 C4
La Cabrera 40 B1
Lacalahorra 44 B3
La Campana 43 E2
Lacanau 28 A2
Lacanau-Océan 28 A2
Lacapelle-Marival 29 D2
Laćarak 72 B3
La Carlota 43 E2
La Carolina 44 A1
Lacaune 32 B1
Lacaune, Mts de 32 B1
La Cava 41 F2
La Cazada de Oropesa 39 E3
Lacedonia 64 C3
Läckö 105 E4
Lac Léman 27 E3
La Codosera 38 C3
Laconi 66 B3
La Coronada 39 E4
La Coruña 34 B1
Lacq 28 B4
La Cumbre 39 E3
La Espina 35 D1
Ladbergen 17 E2
Ládi 81 F1
Ladispoli 63 E2
Ladoeiro 38 C3
Ladožskoje Ozero 111 D1
Láerma 93 E2
La Felguera 35 D1
Laferté 27 D1
Laffrey 30 C2
Láfka 87 D1
Láfkos 83 F2
Lafnitz 57 F4
La Franca, 35 E1
Lafrançaise 29 D3
La Fregeneda 39 D1
La Frontera 40 C2
La Fuente de San Esteban 39 D1
Lagan 109 D2
Lagan *R* 109 D2
Laganá, Kólpos 86 A2
Laganás 86 A2
Lagarfljót 96 C2
La Garganta 34 C1
La Garriga 32 B4
Lagartera 39 E3
Lagastrello, Pso di 60 B3
Lage 17 F3
Lagen 100 C3
Lågen (Buskerud) 104 C3
Lågen (Oppland) 100 C3
Laggan 2 C4
Laggan, L 2 C4
Laginá (Makedonía) 79 F3
Laginá (Thráki) 81 F2
La Gineta 40 C4
Lagnieu 26 C4
Lagny 19 F4
Lago 67 E3
Lagoa 42 A2
Lagoaça 34 C4
Lagonegro 65 D4
Lagonissi 87 F2
Lagos 42 A2
Lágos 81 D2
Łagów 49 F4
La Granjuela 43 E1
Lagrasse 32 B2
Laguardia 36 B2
La Guardia 40 B3
La Guardia de Jaén 44 A2
Laguarres 37 E3
Laguarta 37 E2
Laguiole 29 E2
Laguna de Duero 35 E4
Lahanás 80 A2
La Hermida 35 E2
La Herradura 44 A4
Lahinch 12 B4
Lahn 17 F4
Lahnstein 51 E4
Laholm 108 C2
Laholmsbukten 108 C2
La Horcajada 39 E2
La Horra 35 F4
Lahr 54 C3
Lahti 107 F2
Laichingen 55 D3
Laide 2 B3
La Iglesuela del Cid 41 E2
Laignes 26 B1
Laigueglia 31 F3
Laihia 102 B2
Laïliás 80 B2
Laimbach 57 D2
Laimoluokta 94 C3
Lainate 60 A1
Lainioälven 95 D4
Lairg 2 C2
Laissac 29 E3
Laïsta 78 C4
Laisvall 97 F3
Laitikkala 107 E2
Laitila 107 D2
La Jana 41 F2
Lajkovac 72 C3
La Jonquera 32 B3
Laká 82 A2
Lakavica 77 E3
Lake District Nat Pk 5 D4
Laki 89 E3
Láki 90 B3
Lákmos, Óri 82 C1
Lákoma 81 E3
Lákones 82 A1
Lakonía 87 D3
Lakonikós Kólpos 87 D4
Lakópetra 86 B1
Laksefjorden 95 E1
Lakselv 95 D2
Laktaši 71 E3
La Laguna 42 B4
La Lantejuela 43 E3
Lálas 86 C2
Lalbenque 29 D3
L'Alcudia 41 E4
L'Aldea 41 F2
Lalín 34 B2
Lalinac 73 F4
Lalinde 28 C2
La Línea de la Concepción 43 E4
Laliótis 87 D1
Lalm 100 C3
La Losa 44 B2
Lalouvesc 30 B1
Lalueza 37 E3
La Luisiana 43 E2
Lalzit, Gjiri i 76 C4
Lam 56 B1
Lama dei Peligni 64 A2
La Magdalena 35 D2
Lamalou 30 A4
La Manche 10 A4
La Manga del Mar Menor 45 D2
Lamarche 27 D1
La Marmora, P 66 B3
Lamarque 28 B2
Lamastre 30 B2
Lambach 56 C3
Lamballe 22 C3
Lambesc 30 C4
Lámbia 86 C1
Lambíri 83 D4
Lámbou Míli 85 F2
Lambrecht 54 C2
Lamego 34 B4
La Mesa Roldán 44 C3
Lamía 83 E3
Lamlash 4 B2
Lammermuir Hills 5 D2
Lammhult 109 D2
Lammi 107 E2
La Molina 32 A3
Lamotte-Beuvron 25 E2
Lampaul 22 A2
Lampedusa 68 A4
Lampedusa, I di 68 A4
Lampertheim 54 C1
Lampeter 8 C1
L'Ampolla 41 F2
Lamstedt 47 F3
La Mudarra 35 E4

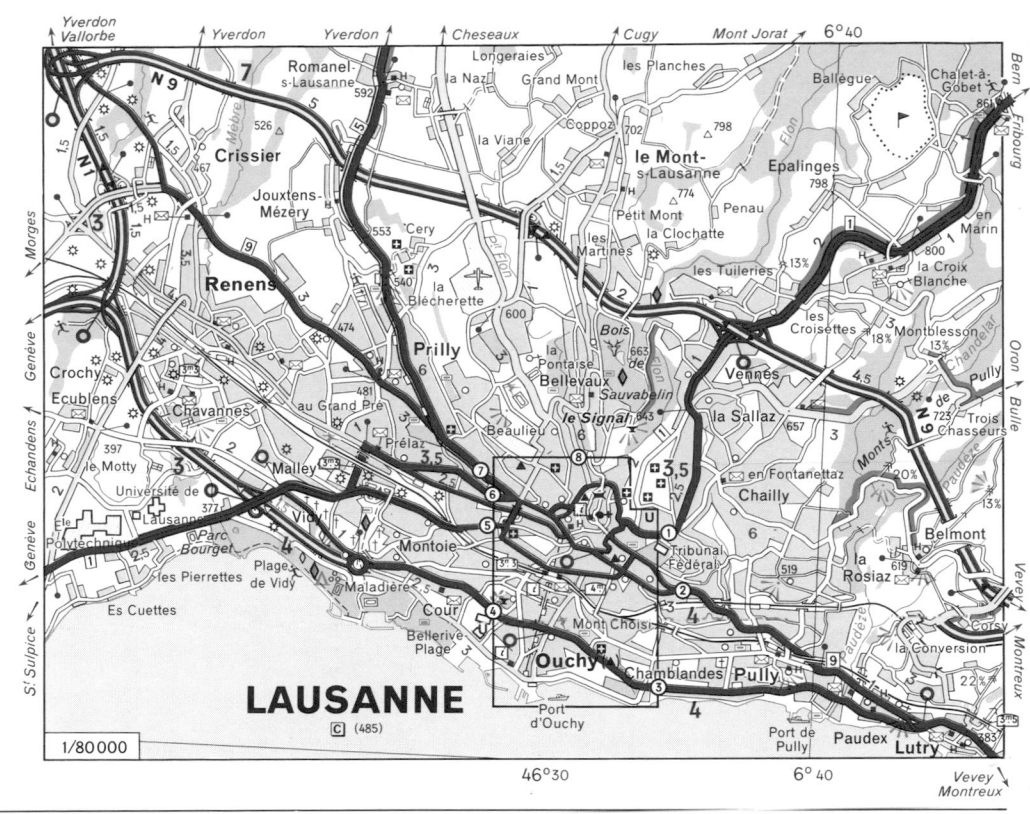

LAUSANNE
1/80 000
© (485)
46°30 6°40

La Muela 37 D4
Lamure 26 B4
Lana 58 C3
Lanaja 37 D3
Lanaken 51 D3
Lanark 4 C2
La Nava de Ricomalillo 39 F3
La Nava de Santiago 39 D4
Lancashire 6 B2
Lancaster 6 B1
Lanchester 5 E4
Lanciano 64 A2
Landau (Bayern) 56 B2
Landau (Rheinland-Pfalz) 54 C2
Landeck 58 C2
Landerneau 22 B2
Landes 28 B3
Landes de Lanvaux 22 C3
Landete 41 D3
Landévennec 22 A3
Landivisiau 22 B2
Landivy 18 C4
Landmannalaugar 96 B2
Landquart 58 B2
Landrecies 20 A2
Landriano 60 A1
Landsberg 53 D2
Landsberg 56 A3
Land's End 8 A4
Landshut 56 B2
Landskapet Åland 106 C2
Landskrona 108 C3
Landstuhl 54 B2
Landverk 101 D2
Lanersbach 59 D2
Lanesborough 12 C3
Langáda (Híos) 85 F4
Langáda (Pelopónnissos) 87 D4
Langadás 79 F3
Langadás 87 D3
Langa de Duero 36 A3
Langádia 86 C2
Langadíkia 80 A3
Langangen 104 C2
Langeac 29 F2
Langeais 25 D2
Langeland 108 B4
Langelandsbælt 108 B4
Langelmäki 103 D3
Langelmävesi 103 D3
Langelsheim 52 B1
Langenargen 55 D4
Langenau 55 E3
Langenberg 53 D3
Langenbruck 55 F2
Langenburg 55 D2
Langeneß 47 F1
Langenfeld 17 E4
Langenfeld 58 C2
Langenhagen 48 A4
Langenhahn 51 F3
Langen (Hessen) 52 A4
Langen (Niedersachsen) 47 F3
Langenlois 57 E2
Langenthal 27 F2
Langenwang 57 E3
Langenzenn 55 E1
Langeoog 47 E3
Långeserud 105 E3
Langeskov 108 B3
Langesund 104 C4
Langevåg 100 A2
Langevåg 100 A2
Långfjället 101 D3
Langfjord 95 D2
Langfjorden 95 E1
Langfjordjøkelen 94 C2
Langforden 100 B2
Langhirano 60 B2
Langholm 5 D3
Langjökull 96 B2
Langnau 27 F2
Langogne 29 F2
Langon 28 B2
Langøya 94 A3
Langport 9 D3
Langres 26 C1

Langrune 18 C3
Långsele 101 F2
Långshyttan 105 F2
Långträsk 98 B3
Lanjarón 44 A3
Lanke 49 E3
Länkipohja 103 D3
Lanmeur 22 B2
Lannemezan 37 E1
Lannilis 22 A2
Lannion 22 B2
Lanouaille 29 D1
Lans-en-Vercors 30 C1
Lanslebourg 31 E1
Lanta 29 D4
Lantosque 31 E3
La Nuez de Arriba 35 F3
Lanusei 66 C3
Lanvollon 22 C2
Lanzahita 39 F2
Lanzarote 42 C3
Lanzo Tonnese 31 E1
Laois 12 C4
La Oliva (Is Canarias) 42 C4
La Oliva (Navarra) 36 C2
Laon 20 A3
La Orotava 42 B4
La Paca 44 C2
La Palma 42 A4
La Palma del Condado 42 C2
La Panadella 37 F4
Lápas 86 B1
Lapa, Sa da 38 C1
Laperdiguera 37 E3
La Pinilla 36 A4
Lapinjärvi 107 F2
Lapin Lääni 95 E4
Lapinlahti 103 E2
La Platja d'Aro 32 B4
La Plaza 35 D2
Lapleau 29 E1
Laplume 28 C3
La Pobla 41 E4
La Pobla de Lillet 32 A3
La Pobla de Massaluca 37 E4
La Pobla de Segur 37 F3
La Pobla de Vallbona 41 E3
Lapoutroie 27 E1
Lapovo 73 D3
Lappajärvi 102 C2
Lappajärvi L 102 C2
Lappalaisten-Kesätuvat 95 D3
Lappea 98 C2
Lappeenranta 103 F4
Lappfjärd 102 B3
Lappfors 102 C2
Lappi 107 D2
Lappoå 102 C2
Lappohja 107 E3
Lappträsk 98 C3
Lappträsk 107 F2
Lappvesi 106 C3
Lapua 102 C2
Lapuanjoki 102 C2
La Puebla de Almoradiel 40 B3
La Puebla de Cazalla 43 E3
La Puebla de Híjar 37 D4
La Puebla de los Infantes 43 E2
La Puebla del Río 43 D3
La Puebla de Montalbán 39 F3
La Puebla de Valverde 41 D2
La Pueblanueva 39 F3
La Puerta de Segura 44 B1
Lapväärtti 102 B3
L'Aquila 63 F2
La Rábida 42 C3
La Rábita 44 B4
Laracha 34 A1
Laragh 13 D4
Laragne-Montéglin 30 C3
La Rambla 43 F2

Lärbro 109 F3
Larche (Alpes-de-Haute-Provence) 31 E2
Larche (Corrèze) 29 D2
Larche, Col de 31 E2
Lærdalsøyri 104 B1
Lardarello 60 C4
Lárdos 93 F2
Lárdos, Akr 93 F2
Laredo 36 A1
Laren 16 C2
Largentière 30 B2
Largs 4 C2
Lárimna 84 A4
La Rinconada 43 D3
Larino 64 B2
La Rioja 36 B2
Lárissa 83 E1
Lárissa (Nomos) 83 E2
Larmor 22 B4
Larne 13 E2
La Robla 35 D2
La Roca 32 B4
La Roca de la Sierra 39 D4
Larochette 21 D2
La Roda (Andalucía) 43 E3
La Roda (Castilla-la-Mancha) 40 C4
Laroles 44 B3
Laroquebrou 29 E2
Laroque-d'Olmes 32 A2
Laroque-Timbaut 28 C3
Larouco 34 B3
Larraga 36 C2
Larrau, Pto de 37 D2
Larsmo 102 C1
Laruns 37 D2
Larv 109 D1
Larvik 104 C4
Lasalle 29 F3
Las Alpujarras 44 A3
Las Arenas 36 B1
Lasarte 36 C1
Las Batuecas 39 E2
Las Cabezas de San Juan 43 D3
Las Cabrillas, Pto de 41 E2
Las Caldas de Besaya 35 F2
Las Campanas 36 C2
Lascaux, Grotte de 29 D2
La Seca 35 E4

La Selva del Camp 37 F4
La Sénia 41 F2
La Seu d'Urgell 32 A3
Las Huelgas Reales 35 F3
Lasinjski Sjeničak 70 C3
Laško 70 B2
Las Mesas 40 B4
Las Mestas 39 E2
Las Minas 44 C1
Las Navas de la Concepción 43 E3
Las Navas del Marqués 40 A2
Las Negras 44 C4
Læsø 108 B2
La Solana 40 B4
Las Pajanosas 43 D2
Las Palmas de Gran Canaria 42 B4
Las Pedroñeras 40 C4
Las Pedrosas 37 D3
La Spezia 60 B3
Las Portas, Emb de 34 B3
Las Rozas 40 A2
Lassan 49 E2
Lassay 23 E3
Lassigny 19 F3
Lassíthi 91 E4
Lassíthi (Nomos) 91 F4
Lastovo 75 E3
Lastovo I 75 E3
Lastovski kan 75 E2
Lastra a Signa 60 C3
Lastres 35 E1
Lastrup 17 E1
Lastva 76 A2
Lašva 71 F4
Lás Veguillas 39 E1
Las Ventas con Peña Aguilera 40 A3
Las Vertientes 44 B3
Las Viñas 43 F2
Lätäseno 95 D3
Laterza 65 D4
Lathen 17 E1
Latheron 3 D2
Latiano 65 E3
Latikberg 97 F4
Latina 63 F3
Latisana 59 E3
Lató 91 E4
La Torre del Valle 35 D3
Latour-de-France 32 B2
Latronico 65 D4

Latronquière 29 E2
Latvija 110 C3
Lauchhammer 53 E2
Lauder 5 D2
Lauenau 52 A1
Lauenburg 48 B3
Lauenstein 53 E3
Lauf 55 F1
Laufen (CH) 27 E2
Laufen (D) 56 B3
Laufenburg 54 C4
Lauffen 55 D2
Laugarvatn 96 B2
Lauhanvuori 102 B3
Lauingen 55 E2
Laujar de Andarax 44 B3
Laukaa 103 D3
Lauksundskaret
Launceston 8 B3
La Unión 45 D3
Laupheim 55 E3
Lauragh 14 A4
Laureana di Borrello 67 E4
Laurencekirk 3 E4
Laurenzana 65 D4
Lauria 67 E1
Laurière 25 E4
Lausanne 27 D3
Lauta 53 E2
Lautaret, Col du 31 D2
Lautenthal 52 B1
Lauter 54 C2
Lauterbach 52 B3
Lauterbourg 21 F3
Lauterbrunnen 27 F3
Lauterecken 54 B1
Lautrec 32 A1
Lauttakylä 107 D2
Lauvstad 100 A2
Lauvvik 104 A3
Lauzerte 29 D3
Lauzet-Ubaye, le 31 D2
Lauzun 28 C2
Lavagna 60 B3
Laval 23 E3
Lavamünd 70 B1
Lavandou, le 31 D4
Lavangen 94 B3
Lavant 70 B1
Lávara 81 F2
Lavardac 28 C3
La Vecilla 35 E2
La Vellés 39 E1
Lavello 64 C3

Lavelsloh 17 F2
Lavenham 11 D1
Laveno 58 A4
Lavéra 30 C4
La Verna 61 D3
Lavia 102 C3
Laviano 64 C4
Lavik 104 A1
La Villa de Don Fadrique 40 B3
Lavinio Lido di Enea 63 E3
La Virgen del Camino 35 D2
Lavis 59 D3
Lavit 28 C3
Låvong 97 E3
Lavour 29 D4
Lavoûte-Chilhac 29 F2
Lavre 38 B4
Lávrio 88 A2
Lavvuoai'vi 95 D3
Laxá 105 E4
Laxe 34 A1
Laxford Bridge 2 C2
Laxo 3 F1
La Yesa 41 D3
Layos 40 A3
Laza 34 B3
Lazarevac 72 C3
Lazarev Krst 76 B2
Lazarevo 72 C2
Lazaropole 77 D3
Lazio 63 E2
Lazise 60 C1
Lázně Kynžvart 53 D4
Laznica 73 E3
Leadenham 7 D1
Leamington Spa, Royal 9 E1
Leane, L 14 B4
Leba 110 A4
Lebach 54 B2
Lebane 77 E1
Lebedin 113 F1
Lebesby 95 E1
Lębork 110 A4
Lebrija 43 D3
Lebus 49 E4
Lecce 65 F4
Lecco 58 B4
Lécera 37 D4
Lecévica 75 D1

Léchère, la 31 D1
Lechlade 9 E2
Leciñena 37 D3
Leck 47 F1
Lecques, les 30 C4
Lectoure 28 C3
Lecumberri 36 C1
Ledaña 41 D4
Ledanca 40 B1
Ledbury 9 D1
Ledesma 39 E1
Lédignan 30 B3
Ledmore 2 C2
Lee 14 B4
Leeds 6 C2
Leek 6 C3
Leenane 12 B3
Leer 47 E3
Leerdam 16 C3
Leese 48 A4
Leeuwarden 16 C1
Lefkáda 82 B3
Lefkáda, N 82 B3
Lefkádia 79 E3
Lefkadíti 83 E3
Lefkandí 84 B4
Lefká Óri 90 B3
Lefkára 79 E4
Léfkes 88 C3
Lefkími 81 F2
Lefkími, Akr 82 A2
Lefkógia 80 B1
Lefkopigí 79 D4
Léfktra 83 F4
Legan 48 A2
Leganés 40 A2
Legé 24 B3
Legnago 60 C1
Legnano 60 A1
Legnica 112 A2
Legrad 71 D1
Legrená 87 F2
Léguevin 29 D4
Legutiano 36 B1
Lehená 86 B1
Lehesten 52 B3
Lehnin 49 D4
Léhovo 79 D3
Lehrberg 55 E1
Lehre 52 B1
Lehrte 52 B1
Lehtimäki 102 C2
Lehtovaara (Lapin Lääni) 99 D1
Lehtovaara (Oulun Lääni) 103 E1

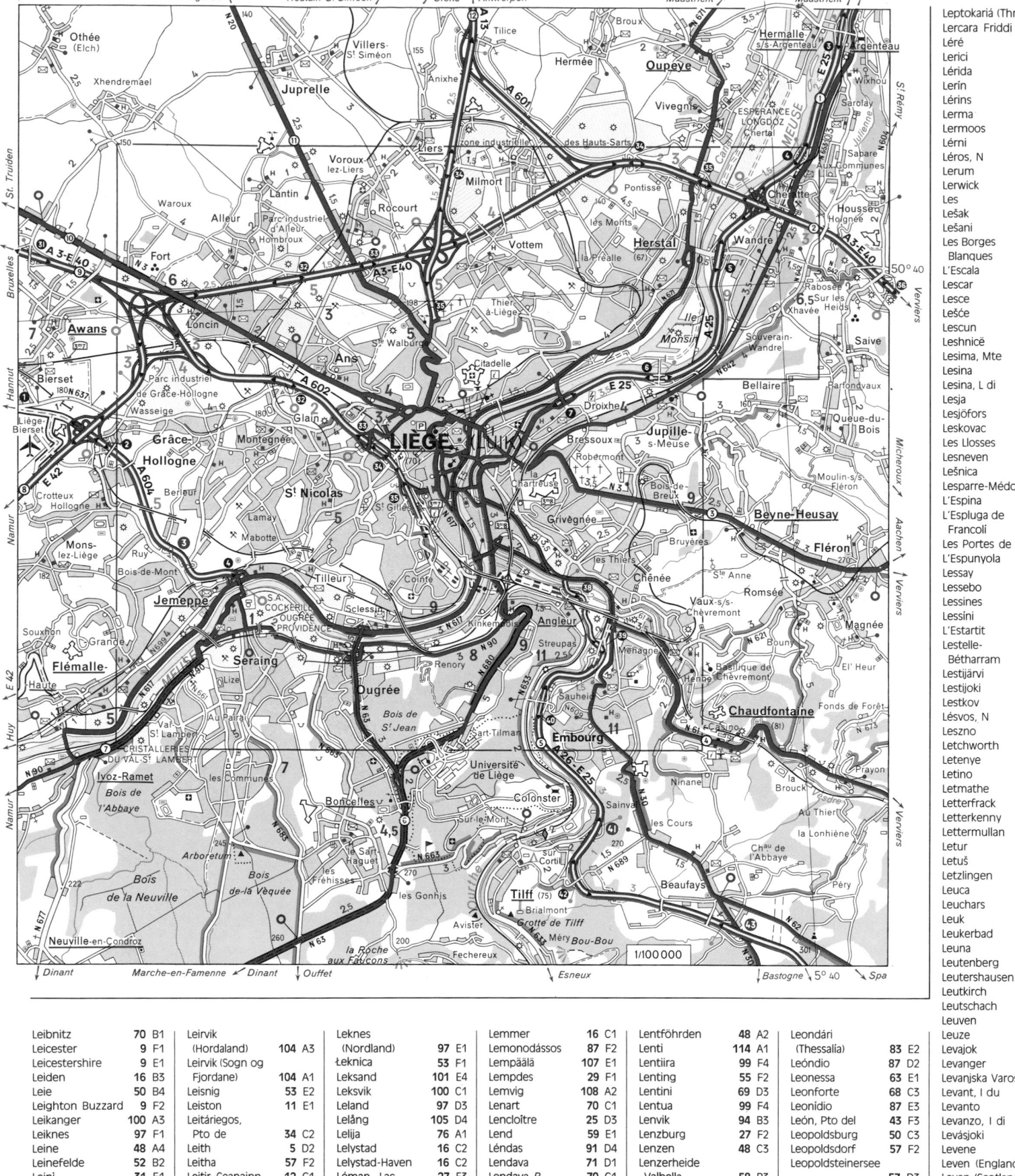

Leptokariá (Thráki)	81	E2
Lercara Friddi	68	B3
Léré	26	A2
Lerici	60	B3
Lérida	37	E4
Lerín	36	C1
Lérins	31	E4
Lerma	35	F3
Lermoos	58	C1
Lérni	87	D2
Léros, N	89	E3
Lerum	108	C1
Lerwick	3	F2
Les	37	F2
Lešak	76	C1
Lešani	77	D4
Les Borges Blanques	37	F4
L'Escala	32	C3
Lescar	28	B4
Lesce	70	A2
Lešće	70	C3
Lescun	37	D2
Leshnicë	77	D4
Lesima, Mte	60	A2
Lesina	64	C2
Lesina, L di	64	C2
Lesja	100	B3
Lesjöfors	105	E3
Leskovac	77	E1
Les Llosses	32	A3
Lesneven	22	B2
Lešnica	72	B3
Lesparre-Médoc	28	A1
L'Espina	41	F2
L'Espluga de Francolí	37	F4
Les Portes de Fer	73	E3
L'Espunyola	32	A3
Lessay	18	B3
Lessebo	109	E2
Lessines	50	B3
Lessini	82	C4
L'Estartit	32	C3
Lestelle-Bétharram	37	C2
Lestijärvi	102	C2
Lestijoki	102	C1
Lestkov	53	E4
Lésvos, N	85	F2
Leszno	112	A2
Letchworth	9	F2
Letenye	114	A1
Letino	64	A3
Letmathe	17	E4
Letterfrack	12	A3
Letterkenny	12	C1
Lettermullan	12	A3
Letur	44	C1
Letuš	70	B1
Letzlingen	48	C4
Leuca	65	F4
Leuchars	5	D1
Leuk	27	F3
Leukerbad	27	E3
Leuna	53	D2
Leutenberg	52	C3
Leutershausen	55	E1
Leutkirch	55	E4
Leutschach	70	B1
Leuven	50	C3
Leuze	50	B4
Levajok	95	E2
Levanger	101	D1
Levanjska Varoš	71	F2
Levant, I du	31	D4
Levanto	60	B3
Levanzo, I di	68	A3
Levásjoki	102	B3
Levene	108	C1
Leven (England)	7	D2
Leven (Scotland)	5	D2
Levens	31	E3
Leverano	65	F4
Leverburgh	2	A3
Leverkusen	17	E4
Levet	25	F3
Levi	95	E4
Levice	112	B3
Levico Terme	59	D3
Lévídi	87	D2
Levie	33	F4
Levier	27	D3
Levítha, N	89	E3

Leibnitz	70	B1	Leirvik (Hordaland)	104	A3	Leknes (Nordland)	97	E1	Lemmer	16	C1
Leicester	9	F1	Leirvik (Sogn og Fjordane)	104	A1	Łeknica	53	F1	Lemonodássos	87	F2
Leicestershire	9	E1	Leisnig	53	E2	Leksand	101	E4	Lempäälä	107	E1
Leiden	16	B3	Leiston	11	E1	Leksvik	100	C1	Lempdes	29	F1
Leie	50	B4	Leitáriegos, Pto de	34	C2	Leland	97	D3	Lemvig	108	A2
Leighton Buzzard	9	F2	Leith	5	D2	Lelång	105	D4	Lemvik	69	D3
Leikanger	100	A3	Leitha	57	F2	Lelija	76	A1	Lenart	70	C1
Leiknes	97	F1	Leitir Ceanainn	12	C1	Lelystad	16	C2	Lenčloître	25	D3
Leine	48	A4	Leitrim	12	C1	Lelystad-Haven	16	C2	Lend	59	E1
Leinefelde	52	B2	Leitzkau	52	C1	Léman, Lac	27	E3	Léndas	91	D4
Leini	31	E1	Leivonmäki	103	D3	Le Mans	23	F3	Lendava	71	D1
Leipheim	55	E3	Leiza	36	C1	Lembach	21	E3	Lendava R	70	C1
Leipzig	53	D2	Lek	16	C3	Lembeye	28	B4	Lendinara	61	D2
Leira (Møre og Romsdal)	100	B2	Léka	89	E1	Lemförde	17	F2	Lengefeld	53	E3
Leira (Oppland)	104	C2	Leka	97	D3	Lemgo	17	F2	Lengenfeld	53	D3
Leirbotn	95	D2	Lekáni	80	C2	Lemgow	48	C3	Lengerich	17	E2
Leiria	38	B2	Lekeitio	36	B1	Lemi	103	E4	Lenggries	56	A4
Leiro	34	B2	Lekenik	71	D2	Lemland	106	C3	Lenhovda	109	E2
Leirpollskogen	95	F1	Leknes (Møre og Romsdal)	100	A2	Lemmenjoki	95	E3	Leningrad	111	D1
Leirvåg	104	A1				Lemmenjoki (Nat Pk)	95	E3	Lenk	27	E3
Leirvik (Færøerne)	96	A3				Lemmenjoki R	95	E3	Lenne	17	F4

Lennestadt	17	F4	Lentföhrden	48	A2
Lens	19	F2	Lenti	114	A1
Lensahn	48	B2	Lentiira	99	F4
			Lenting	55	F2
			Lentini	69	D3
			Lentua	99	F4
			Lenvik	94	B3
			Lenzburg	27	F2
			Lenzen	48	C3
			Lenzerheide Valbella	58	B3
			Lenzkirch	54	C4
			Leoben	57	E4
			Leobersdorf	57	F3
			Leogang	59	E1
			Leominster	9	D1
			Léon	28	A3
			León	35	D2
			León, Mtes de	35	D2
			Leonberg	55	D2
			Léoncel	30	C2
			Leondári (Pelopónnisos)	86	C2

Leondári (Thessalía)	83	E2
Leóndio	87	D2
Leonessa	63	E1
Leonforte	68	C3
Leonídio	87	D2
León, Pto del	43	F3
Leopoldsburg	50	C3
Leopoldsdorf	57	F2
Leopoldsteinersee	57	D3
Leovo	113	E4
Lepel'	111	D3
Lepenoú	80	C3
Lepenski vir	73	E3
Lepetane	76	B3
Lepoglava	70	C1
Leposavić	77	D1
Lépoura	84	B4
Leppäjärvi	95	D3
Leppävirta	103	E2
Leptokariá (Makedonía)	79	F4

Levoča	112 B3	Ligny-le-Châtel	26 B1
Levroux	25 E3	Ligourió	87 E2
Lévy, Cap	18 B2	Ligueil	25 D3
Lewes	10 C3	Liguria	60 A3
Lewis	2 B2	Liháda	83 F3
Leyburn	6 C1	Liikasenvaara	99 E2
Leyland	6 B2	Lijeva Rijeka	76 B2
Leyre	37 D2	Lijevi Dubravčak	71 D2
Leysdown-on-Sea	11 D2	Lika	70 C4
Leysin	27 E3		
Lézardrieux	22 C2	Limáni Hersoníssou	91 E3
Lézat	37 F1	Limáni Litohórou	79 F4
Lezay	24 C4	Lima, R	34 A3
Lezhë	76 C3	Limavady	13 D1
Lézignan-Corbières	32 B2	Limbach	53 D3
Ležimir	72 C2	Limbara, M	66 B2
Lezoux	29 F1	Limburg (B)	50 C3
Lezuza	40 C4	Limburg (D)	51 F4
L'gov	111 F4		
L'Hospitalet de l'Infant	37 F4	Linas, M	66 B4
Liabygda	100 B2	Lincoln	7 D3
Liákoura	83 E4	Lincolnshire	7 D3
Lianokládi	83 E3	Lindås	104 A2
Liathach	2 C3	Lindau	55 D4
Liberec	112 A2	Linden	52 C4
Libochovice	53 F3	Lindenberg	55 E4
Libourne	28 B2	Linderhof	55 F4
Librazhd	77 D4	Lindesberg	105 F3
Librilla	45 D2		
Licata	68 C4		
Licciana Nardi	60 B3		
Lich	52 A4		
Lichfield	9 E1		
Lichoslavl'	111 F2		
Lichtenberg	53 D3		
Lichtenfels	52 C4		
Lichtenstein	53 D3		
Lichtenvoorde	17 D3		
Lička Jesenica	70 C4		
Lički Osik	70 C4		
Ličko Lešće	70 C4		
Lida	110 C4		
Liddel Water	5 D3		
Liden	101 F2		
Lidhult	109 D2		
Lidingö	106 A2		
Lidköping	105 E4		
Lido degli Estensi	61 D2		
Lido delle Nazioni	61 D2		
Lido di Camaiore	60 B3		
Lido di Classe	61 E3		
Lido di Jesolo	59 E4		
Lido di Metaponto	65 E4		
Lido di Ostia	63 E3		
Lido di Savio	61 E3		
Lido di Spina	61 D2		
Lido di Venezia	61 D1		
Lidoríki	83 E4		
Lido Silvana	65 E4		
Lidzbark Warmiński	110 B4		
Liebenwalde	49 D3		
Lieberose	53 F1		

Lille

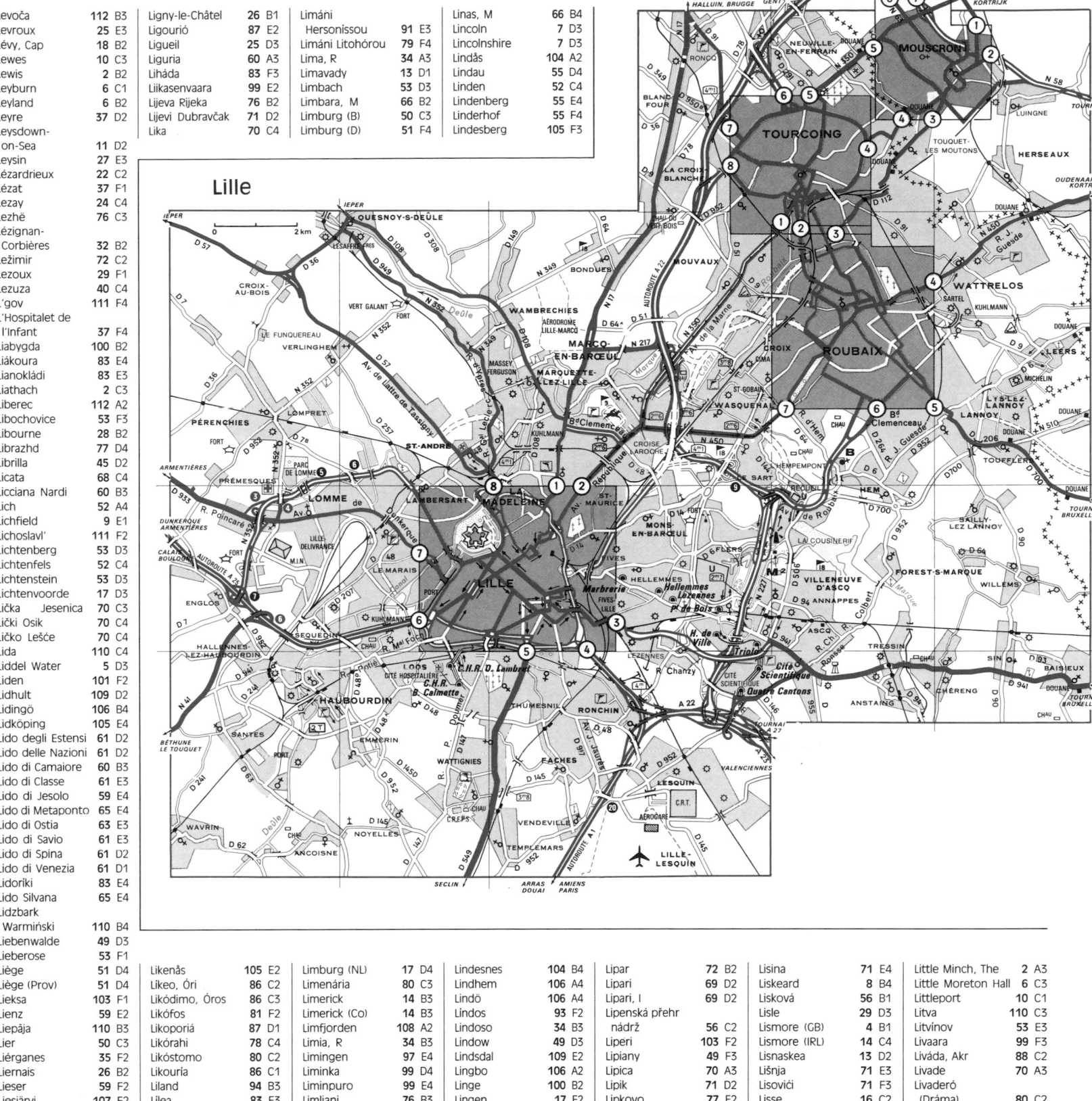

Liège	51 D4	Likenås	105 E2	Limburg (NL)	17 D4	Lindesnes	104 B4	Lipar	72 B2	Lisina	71 E4	Little Minch, The	2 A3
Liège (Prov)	51 D4	Líkeo, Óri	86 C2	Limenária	80 C3	Lindhem	106 A4	Lipari	69 D2	Liskeard	8 B4	Little Moreton Hall	6 C3
Lieksa	103 F1	Likódimo, Óros	86 C3	Limerick	14 B3	Lindö	106 A4	Lipari, I	69 D2	Lisková	56 B1	Littleport	10 C1
Lienz	59 E2	Likófos	81 F2	Limerick (Co)	14 B3	Líndos	93 F2	Lipenská přehr nádrž	56 C2	Lisle	29 D3	Litva	110 C3
Liepāja	110 B3	Likoporiá	87 D1	Limfjorden	108 A2	Lindoso	34 B3	Lipiany	49 F3	Lismore (GB)	4 B1	Litvínov	53 E3
Lier	50 C3	Likórahi	78 C4	Limia, R	34 B3	Lindow	49 D3	Lipica	70 A3	Lismore (IRL)	14 C4	Livaara	99 F3
Liérganes	35 F2	Likóstomo	80 C2	Limingen	97 E4	Lindsdal	109 E2	Lipik	71 D2	Lisnaskea	13 D2	Livade	70 A3
Liernais	26 B2	Likoúria	86 C1	Liminka	99 D4	Lingbo	106 A2	Lipkovo	77 E2	Lišnja	71 E3	Livaderó (Dráma)	80 C2
Lieser	59 F2	Liland	94 B3	Liminpuro	99 E4	Linge	100 B2	Lipljan	77 D2	Lisovići	71 E3	Livaderó (Kozáni)	79 E4
Liesjärvi	107 E3	Lílea	83 E3	Limljani	76 B3	Lingen	17 E2	Lipno	57 D2	Lisse	16 C2	Livádi (Kíthira)	90 A2
Liestal	27 E2	Lilienfeld	57 E3	Limnes	87 E2	Linguaglossa	69 D3	Lipova	112 C4	List	47 F1	Livádi (Makedonía)	80 A3
Lieto	107 D2	Liljendal	107 F2	Límni	84 A3	Linken	49 E2	Lipovac	72 B3	Listafjorden	104 A4	Livádi (Sérifos)	88 A3
Liétor	44 C1	Lilla Edet	108 C1	Limniá	80 C2	Linköping	106 A4	Lippe	17 E3	Lištica	75 E2	Livádi (Thessalía)	79 E4
Lieurey	19 D3	Lillby	102 C2	Limnítsa	83 D3	Linlithgow	5 D2	Lippstadt	17 F3	Listowel	14 B3	Livádi (Makedonía)	80 A2
Lievestuore	103 D3	Lille	19 F1	Limnos, N	85 D1	Linnansaari	103 E3	Lipsí	89 E2	Lit	101 E2	Livadiá	83 F4
Liévin	19 F1	Lille Bælt	108 A3	Limoges	29 D1	Linnhe, L	4 B1	Lipsí, N	89 E2	Lit-et-Mixe	28 A3	Livádi (Tílos)	89 F4
Liezen	57 D3	Lillebonne	19 D3	Limone Piemonte	31 E3	Linsell	101 E3	Liptovský Mikuláš	112 B3	Lithakiá	86 A2	Livadítis	80 C1
Liffey	13 D4	Lillehammer	105 D2	Limonest	26 C4	Linslade	9 F2	Liqenas	77 D4	Lithári, Akr	84 C3	Livadohóri	85 D1
Liffol-le-Grand	20 C4	Lillerød	108 C3	Limours	19 E4	Linthal	58 A2	Lírkia	87 D2	Lithines	91 F4	Livanátes	83 F4
Lifford	13 D1	Lillers	19 F1	Limoux	32 B2	Linyola	37 F3	Lis	76 C3	Líthino, Akr	91 D4	Livari	76 B3
Liffré	23 D3	Lillesand	104 B4	Lin	77 D4	Linz	51 E4	Lisac	71 E4	Lithio	85 E4	Livarot	19 D4
Lifjell	104 C3	Lillestrøm	105 D3	Linares	44 A2	Linz	57 D2	Lisboa	38 A4	Liti	79 F3	Livenza	59 E4
Ligiá	86 B1	Lillhärdal	101 E3	Linares del Arroyo, Emb de	36 A3	Lion	18 C3	Lisburn	13 D2	Litija	70 B2		
Lignano Sabbiadoro	59 F4	Lillo	40 B3	Linares de Mora	41 E2	Lion-d'Angers, le	23 E4	Liscia	66 B1	Litóhoro	79 F4		
Ligné	23 D4	Lillögda	102 A1	Linares de Riofrio	39 E2	Lioni	64 C4	Lisdoonvarna	12 B4	Litoměřice	53 F3		
Lignières	25 F3	Lillholmsjön	101 E1	Linariá	84 C3	Lióprasso	83 D1	Lisieux	19 D3	Litomyšl	112 A3		
Ligny-en-Barrois	20 C4	Lim	76 B1			Lioran, le	29 E2			Litschau	57 D1		
		Lima	101 D4							Littlehampton	10 C3		

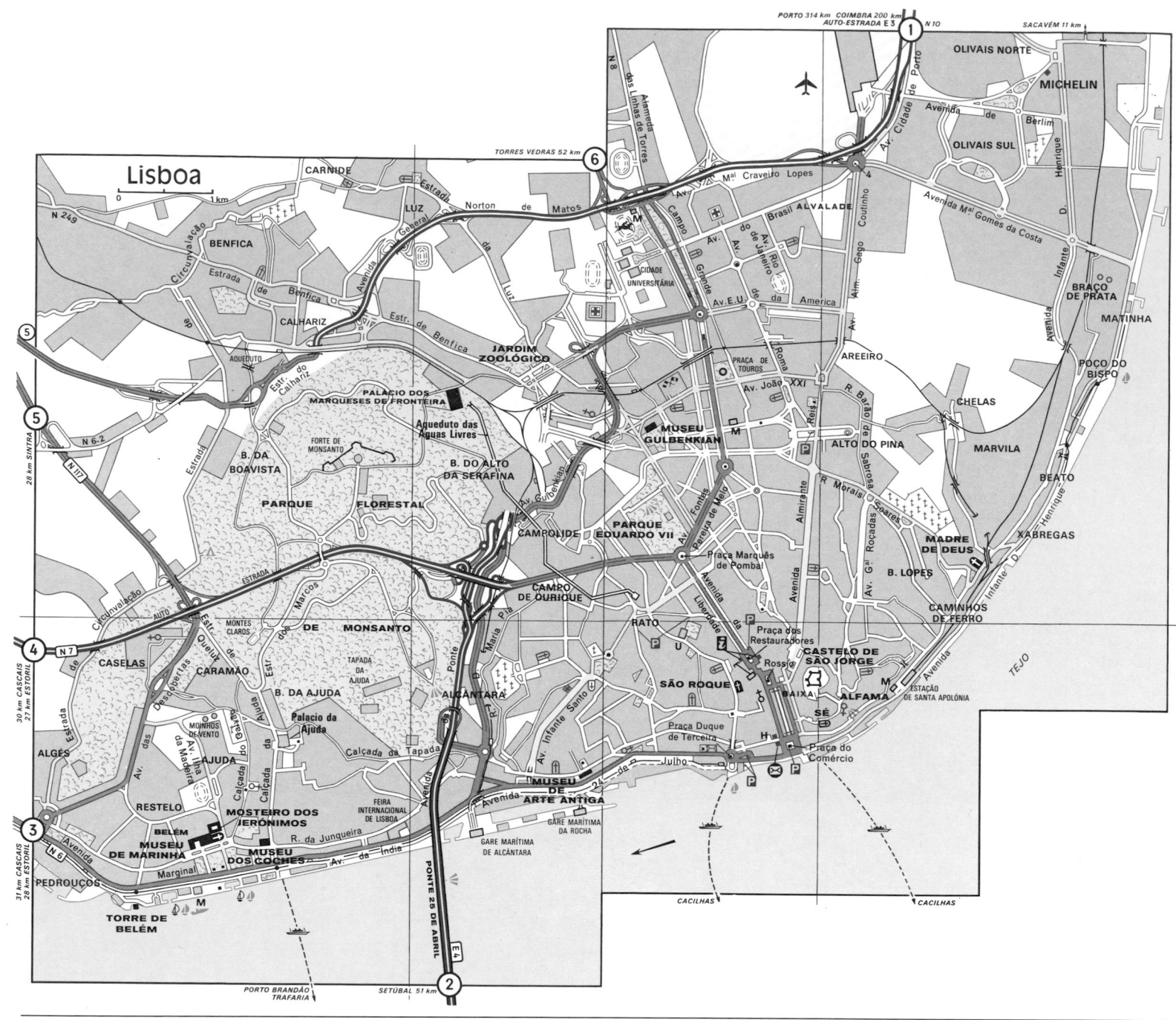

Lisboa

Liverá	79 D3	Ljubišnja	76 B1	Llandysul	8 C1	Lloret de Mar	32 B4	Lochranza	4 B2	Lofthus	104 B2	Loire (Dépt)	29 F1
Liverdun	21 D4	Ljubljana	70 B2	Llanelli	8 C2	Llucmajor	45 F3	Lochvica	113 F2	Loftus	5 F4	Loire-Atlantique	23 D4
Livernon	29 D2	Ljubno	70 B1	Llanerchymedd	6 A2	Llynclys	6 B3	Lochy, L	2 C4	Log	70 A2	Loir-et-Cher	25 D2
Liverpool	6 B2	Ljubojno	77 E4	Llanes	35 E1	Lnáre	56 C1	Lockenhaus	57 F3	Logarska dolina	70 B1	Loiret	25 E1
Liverpool B	6 B2	Ljubostinja	73 D4	Llanfairfechan	6 A2	Loanhead	5 D2	Lockerbie	5 D3	Logatec, D.	70 A2	Loiri	66 B1
Livigno	58 C3	Ljuboten	77 D2	Llanfair-ym-Muallt	9 D1	Loano	31 F3	Löcknitz	49 E2	Logroño	36 B2	Loiron	23 E3
Livingston	5 D2	Ljubovija	72 C4	Llanfyllin	6 B3	Löbau	53 F2	Locle, le	27 E2	Logrosán	39 E3	Loitz	49 D2
Livno	75 E1	Ljubuša	75 E1	Llangadog	8 C2	Löbejün	53 D2	Locmariaquer	22 C4	Løgstør	108 A2	Loja	43 F3
Livo	99 E3	Ljubuški	75 E2	Llangefni	6 A2	Lobenstein	52 C3	Locminé	22 C3	Løgten	108 B3	Lojsta	109 F4
Livojärvi	99 E2	Ljugarn	109 F4	Llangollen	6 B3	Łobez	49 F2	Locorotondo	65 E3	Løgumkloster	108 A4	Lokalahti	107 D2
Livojoki	99 E3	Ljungan	101 F3	Llangurig	8 C1	Löbnitz	49 D1	Locquirec	22 B2	Lohals	108 B4	Lokan Tekojärvi	95 F4
Livold	70 B3	Ljungby	109 D2	Llanidloes	8 C1	Lobo	36 A4	Locri	67 F4	Lohberg	56 B1	Løken	105 D3
Livorno	60 C4	Ljungbyhed	109 D3	Llano, Pto	39 E3	Lobón	39 D4	Locronan	22 B3	Lohilahti	103 E3	Lokeren	50 B3
Livorno Ferraris	31 F1	Ljungdalen	101 D2	Llanrhystud	53 D1	Loburg	53 D1	Loctudy	22 B3	Lohiniva	99 D1	Loket	53 E4
Livron	30 B2	Ljungsbro	105 E2	Llanrwst	6 A3	Locana	31 E1	Lodè	66 C2	Lohja	107 E3	Lokka	95 F4
Lixoúri	82 B4	Ljungskile	108 C1	Llanwrtyd-Wells	8 C1	Locarno	58 A3	Lodève	30 A4	Lohjanjärvi	107 E3	Løkken (N)	100 C2
Lizard	8 A4	Ljusdal	101 F3	Llanymyddfri	8 C1	Lochaline	4 B1	Lodi	60 B1	Lohne	17 F2	Løkken (S)	108 B1
Lizard Pt	8 B4	Ljusnan	101 E3	Llarga	41 E4	Lochboisdale	2 A3	Løding	97 E1	Löhne	17 F2	Lokn'a	111 D2
Lizy	19 F3	Ljusne	101 F3	Llavorsi	37 F3	Lochcarron	2 B3	Lødingen	94 A3	Lohr	52 B4	Lokrum	76 A2
Lizzano in		Ljutići	76 B1	Lleida	37 F4	Lochearnhead	4 C1	Lodosa	36 C2	Lohtaja	102 C1	Lokve (Hrvatska)	70 B3
Belvedere	60 C3	Ljutoglav	77 D2	Llera	43 D1	Lochem	17 D2	Łódź	112 B2	Loiano		Lokve (Slovenija)	70 A2
Ljeskove Vode	71 E3	Ljutomer	70 C1	Llerena	43 D1	Loches	25 D3	Loeches	40 B2	Rioveggio	60 C3	Lokve (Vojvodina)	73 D2
Ljig	72 C3	Llagostera	32 B3	Lles	32 A3	Loch Garman	15 D3	Loen	100 A3	Loibltunnel	70 A1	Lolland	108 B4
Ljubaništa	77 D4	Llanberis	6 A3	Llessui	37 F2	Lochgelly	5 D2	Løfallstrand	104 A2	Loimaa	107 E2	L'Ollería	45 E1
Ljubata, D.	77 E2	Llanca	32 C3	Lleyn Pen	6 A3	Lochgilphead	4 B2	Lofário	81 E2	Loimaan kunta	107 D2	Lom (BG)	115 D2
Ljubelj	70 A1	Llandeilo	8 C2	Lliria	41 E3	Lochinver	2 C2	Lofer	59 E1	Loimijoki	107 D2	Lom (CS)	53 E3
Ljubija	71 D3	Llandovery	8 C1	Llívia	32 A2	Lochmaben	5 D3	Löffingen	54 C4	Loing	26 A2	Lom (N)	100 B3
Ljubinje	75 F2	Llandrindod Wells	9 D1	Llobregat, R	32 A3	Lochmaddy	2 A3	Lofoten	97 E1	Loir	25 E1	Loma Negra	36 C3
Ljubiš	72 C4	Llandudno	6 A2	Llodio	36 B1	Loch Ness	2 C3	Lofsdalen	101 D3	Loire	23 E4	Lomazzo	60 A1

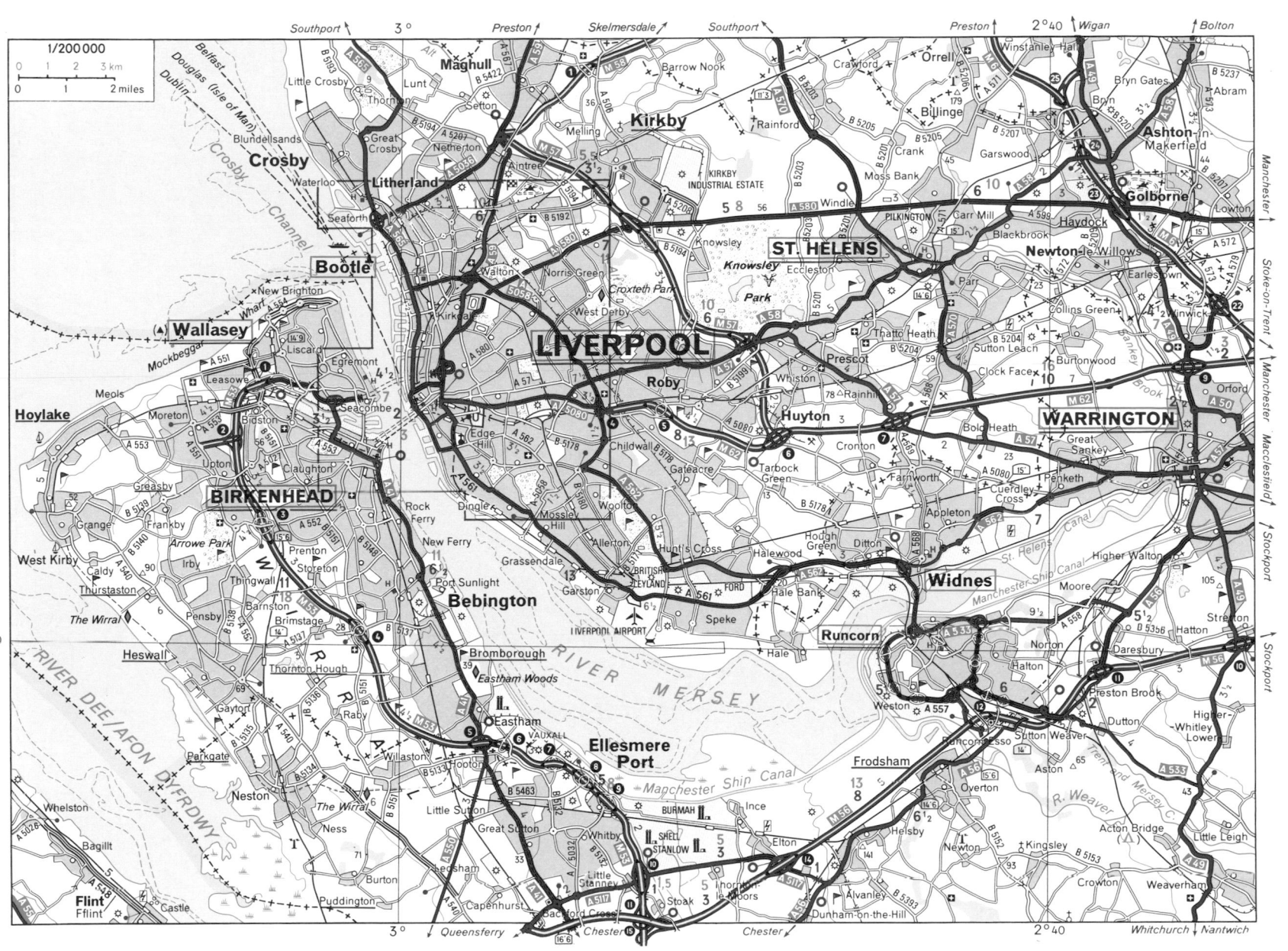

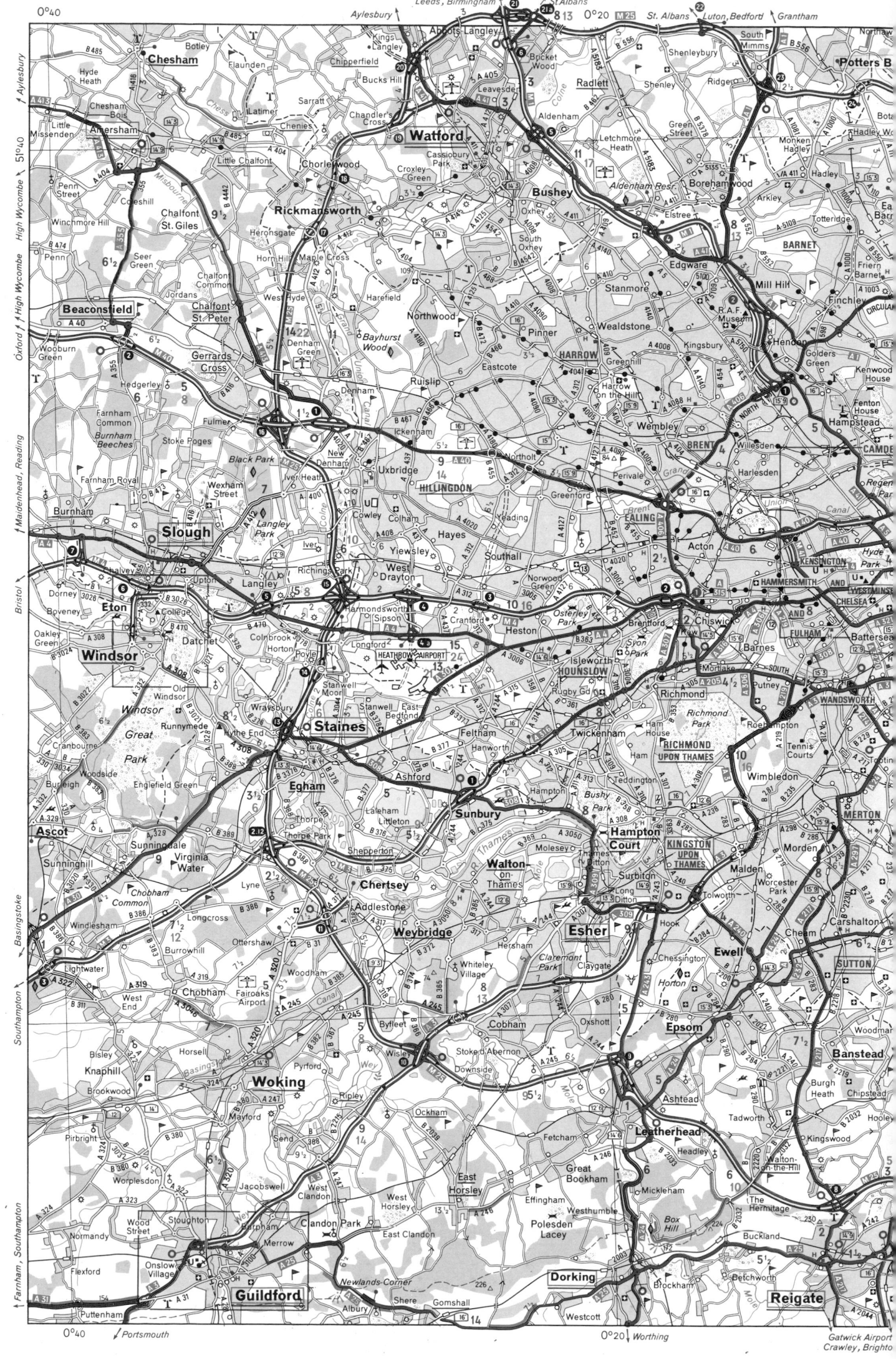

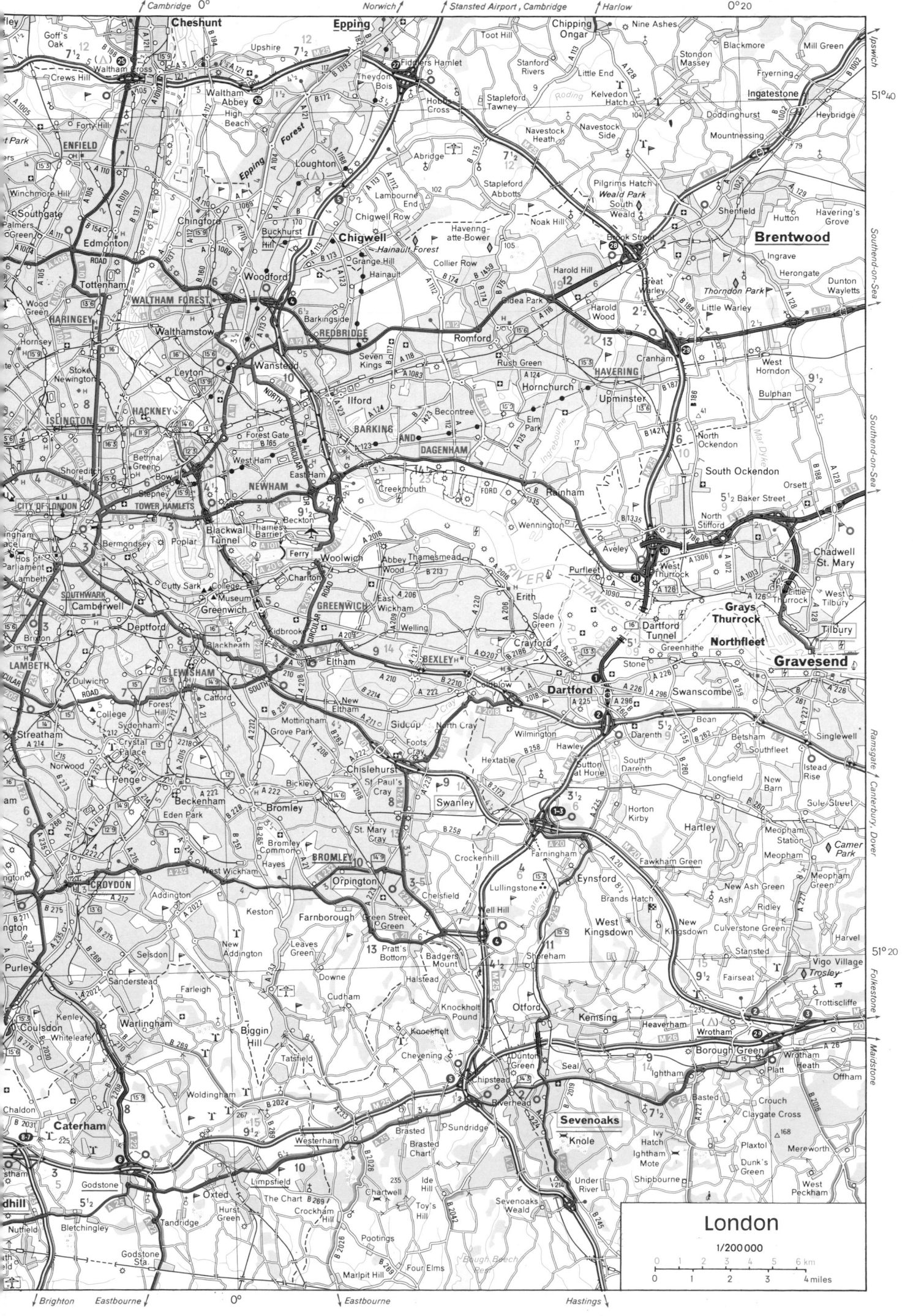

London
1/200 000

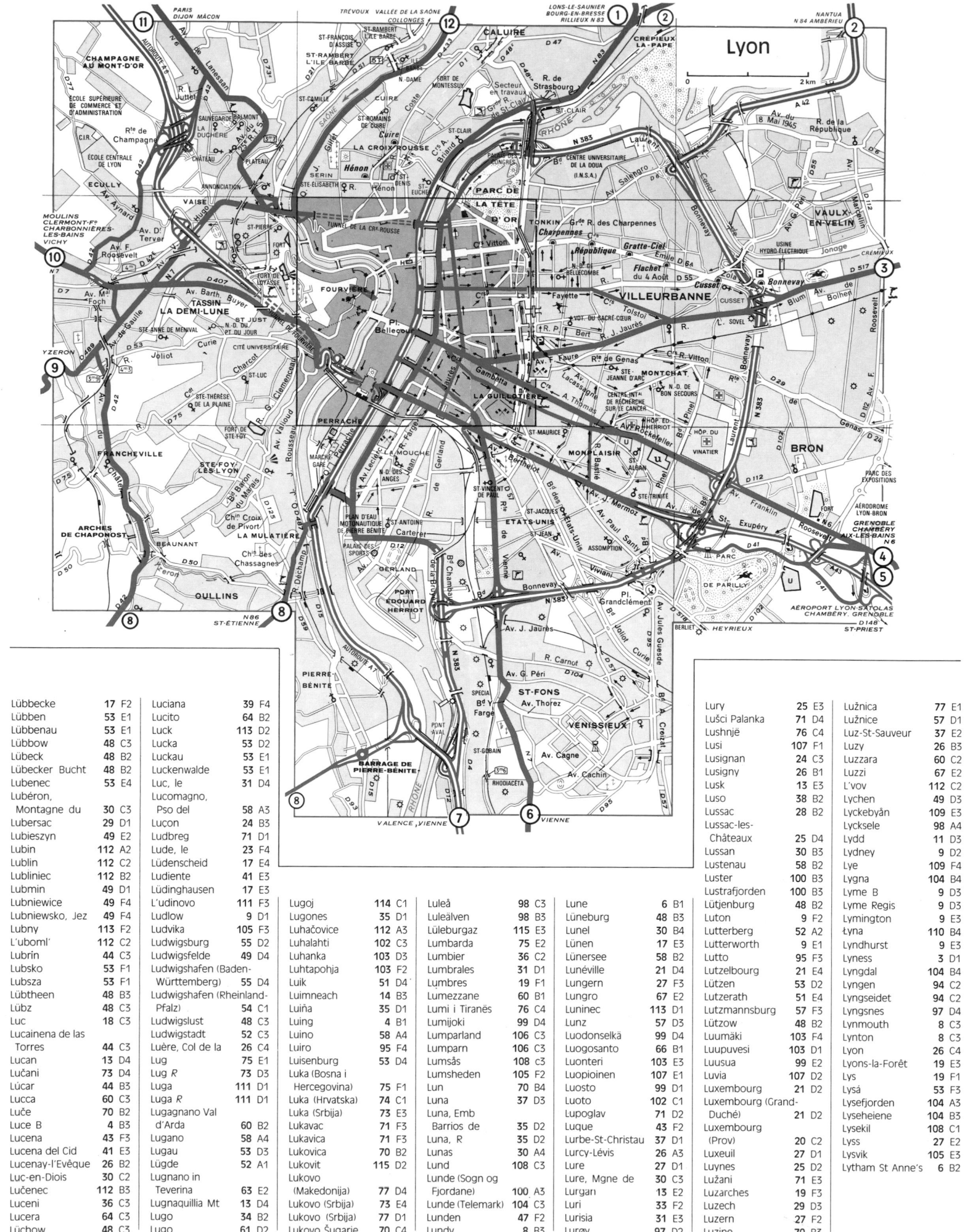

Lyon

Lübbecke	17 F2		Luciana	39 F4
Lübben	53 E1		Lucito	64 B2
Lübbenau	53 E1		Luck	113 D2
Lübbow	48 C3		Lucka	53 D2
Lübeck	48 B2		Luckau	53 E1
Lübecker Bucht	48 B2		Luckenwalde	53 E1
Lubenec	53 E4		Luc, le	31 D4
Lubéron, Montagne du	30 C3		Lucomagno, Pso del	58 A3
Lubersac	29 D1		Luçon	24 B3
Lubieszyn	49 E2		Ludbreg	71 D1
Lubin	112 A2		Lude, le	23 F4
Lublin	112 C2		Lüdenscheid	17 E4
Lubliniec	112 B2		Ludiente	41 E3
Lubmin	49 D1		Lüdinghausen	17 E3
Lubniewice	49 F4		L'udinovo	111 F3
Lubniewsko, Jez	49 F4		Ludlow	9 D1
Lubny	113 F2		Ludvika	105 F3
L'uboml'	112 C2		Ludwigsburg	55 D2
Lubrin	44 C3		Ludwigsfelde	49 D3
Lubsko	53 F1		Ludwigshafen (Baden-Württemberg)	55 D4
Lubsza	53 F1		Ludwigshafen (Rheinland-Pfalz)	54 C1
Lübtheen	48 B3		Ludwigslust	48 C3
Lübz	48 C3		Ludwigstadt	52 C3
Luc	18 C3		Luère, Col de la	26 C4
Lucainena de las Torres	44 C3		Lug	75 E1
Lucan	13 D4		Lug R	73 D3
Lučani	73 D4		Luga	111 D1
Lúcar	44 B3		Luga R	111 D1
Lucca	60 C3		Lugagnano Val d'Arda	60 B2
Luče	70 B2		Lugano	58 A4
Luce B	4 B3		Lugau	53 D3
Lucena	43 F1		Lugnano in Teverina	63 E2
Lucena del Cid	41 E3		Lugnaquillia Mt	13 D4
Lucenay-l'Evêque	26 B2		Lugo	34 B2
Luc-en-Diois	30 C2		Lugo	61 D2
Lučenec	112 B3			
Luceni	36 C3			
Lucera	64 C3			
Lüchow	48 C3			

Lugoj	114 C1		Luleå	98 C3
Lugones	35 D1		Luleälven	98 B3
Luhačovice	112 A3		Lüleburgaz	115 E3
Luhalahti	102 C3		Lumbarda	75 E2
Luhanka	103 D3		Lumbier	36 C2
Luhtapohja	103 F2		Lumbrales	31 D1
Luik	51 D4		Lumbres	19 F1
Luimneach	14 B3		Lumezzane	60 B1
Luiña	35 D1		Lumijoki	99 D4
Luing	4 B1		Lumi i Tiranës	76 C4
Luino	58 A4		Lumparland	106 C3
Luiro	95 F4		Lumparn	106 C3
Luisenburg	53 D4		Lumsås	108 C3
Luka (Bosna i Hercegovina)	75 F1		Lumsheden	105 F2
Luka (Hrvatska)	74 C1		Lun	70 B4
Luka (Srbija)	73 E3		Luna	37 D3
Lukavac	71 F3		Luna, Emb Barrios de	35 D2
Lukavica	71 F3		Luna, R	35 D2
Lukovica	70 B2		Lunas	30 A4
Lukovit	115 D2		Lund	108 C3
Lukovo (Makedonija)	77 D4		Lunde (Sogn og Fjordane)	100 A3
Lukovo (Srbija)	73 E4		Lunde (Telemark)	104 C3
Lukovo (Srbija)	77 D1		Lunden	47 F2
Lukovo Šugarje	70 C4		Lundy	8 B3

Lune	6 B1		Lury	25 E3
Lüneburg	48 B3		Lušci Palanka	71 D4
Lunel	30 B4		Lushnjë	76 C4
Lünen	17 E3		Lusi	107 F1
Lünersee	58 B2		Lusignan	24 C3
Lunéville	21 D4		Lusigny	26 B1
Lungern	27 F3		Lusk	13 E3
Lungro	67 E2		Luso	38 B2
Luninec	113 D1		Lussac	28 B2
Lunz	57 D3		Lussac-les-Châteaux	25 D4
Luodonselkä	99 D4		Lussan	30 B3
Luogosanto	66 B1		Lustenau	58 B2
Luonteri	103 E3		Luster	100 B3
Luopioinen	107 E1		Lustrafjorden	100 B3
Luosto	99 D1		Lütjenburg	48 B2
Luoto	102 C1		Luton	9 F2
Lupoglav	71 D2		Lutterberg	52 A2
Luque	43 F2		Lutterworth	9 E1
Lurbe-St-Christau	37 D1		Lutto	95 F3
Lurcy-Lévis	26 A3		Lutzelbourg	21 E4
Lure	27 D1		Lützen	53 D2
Lure, Mgne de	30 C3		Lutzerath	51 E4
Lurgan	13 D2		Lutzmannsburg	57 F3
Luri	33 F2		Lützow	48 B2
Lurisia	31 E3		Luumäki	103 F4
Lurøy	97 D2		Luupuvesi	103 D1
			Luusua	99 E2
			Luvia	107 D2
			Luxembourg	21 D2
			Luxembourg (Grand-Duché)	21 D2
			Luxembourg (Prov)	20 C2
			Luxeuil	27 D1
			Luynes	25 D2
			Lužani	71 E3
			Luzarches	19 F3
			Luzech	29 D3
			Luzern	27 F2
			Luzine	70 B3

Lužnica	77 E1
Lužnice	57 D1
Luz-St-Sauveur	37 E2
Luzy	26 B3
Luzzara	60 C2
Luzzi	67 E2
L'vov	112 C2
Lychen	49 D3
Lyckebyån	109 E3
Lycksele	98 A4
Lydd	11 D3
Lydney	9 D2
Lye	109 F4
Lygna	104 B4
Lyme B	9 D3
Lyme Regis	9 D3
Lymington	9 E3
Łyna	110 B4
Lyndhurst	9 E3
Lyness	3 C1
Lyngdal	104 B4
Lyngen	94 C2
Lyngseidet	94 C2
Lyngsnes	97 C3
Lynmouth	8 C3
Lynton	8 C3
Lyon	26 C4
Lyons-la-Forêt	19 E3
Lys	19 F1
Lysá	53 F3
Lysefjorden	104 A3
Lyseheiene	104 B3
Lysekil	108 C1
Lyss	27 E2
Lysvik	105 F3
Lytham St Anne's	6 B2

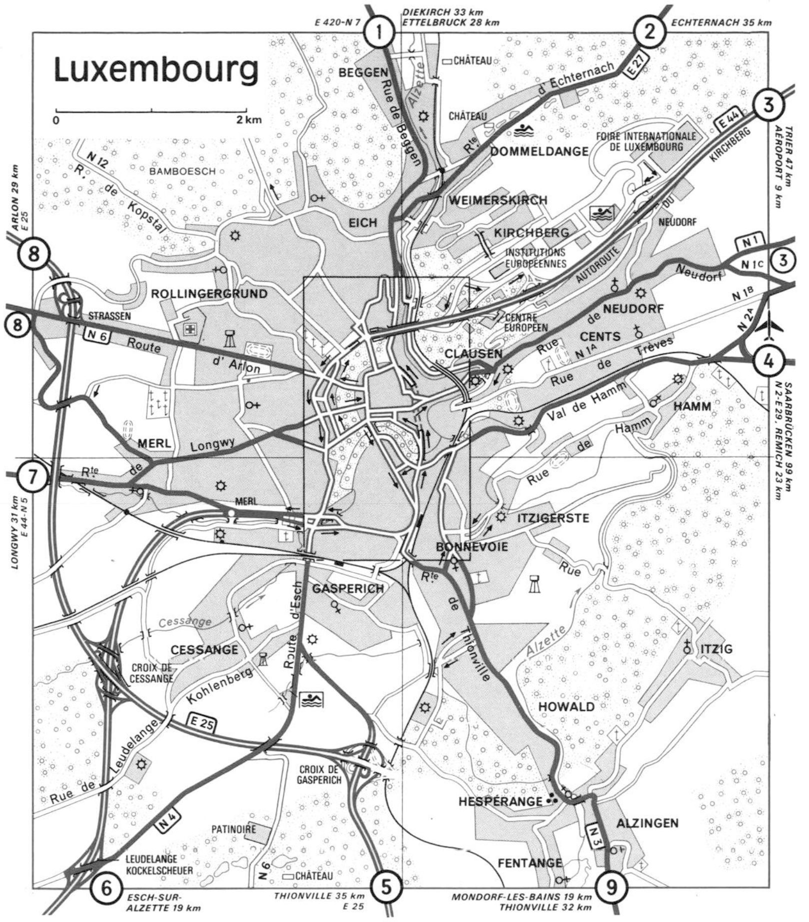
Luxembourg
0
2 km
DIEKIRCH 33 km
ETTELBRUCK 28 km
E 420-N 7
ECHTERNACH 35 km
TRIER 47 km
AÉROPORT 9 km
SAARBRÜCKEN 99 km
N 2-E 29 · REMICH 23 km
MONDORF-LES-BAINS 19 km
THIONVILLE 32 km
THIONVILLE 35 km
E 25
ESCH-SUR-ALZETTE 19 km
LONGWY 31 km
E 44-N 5
ARLON 29 km
E 25
BEGGEN
DOMMELDANGE
WEIMERSKIRCH
EICH
KIRCHBERG
INSTITUTIONS EUROPÉENNES
FOIRE INTERNATIONALE DE LUXEMBOURG
NEUDORF
BAMBOESCH
ROLLINGERGRUND
STRASSEN
CENTRE EUROPÉEN
CLAUSEN
CENTS
HAMM
MERL
ITZIGERSTE
BONNEVOIE
GASPERICH
CESSANGE
CROIX DE CESSANGE
HOWALD
ITZIG
CROIX DE GASPERICH
HESPERANGE
ALZINGEN
PATINOIRE
FENTANGE
LEUDELANGE KOCKELSCHEUER
CHÂTEAU
Rue de Beggen
Route d'Arlon
Val de Hamm
Rue de Trèves
Rte de Thionville
Route d'Esch
Rue de Leudelange
Kohlenberg
Alzette
Cessange
Autoroute
Neudorf
Longwy
1
2
3
4
5
6
7
8
9

M

Maakalla 102 C1
Maalanti 102 B2
Maam Cross 12 B3
Maaninka 103 E2
Maaninkavaara 99 E2
Maanselkä 103 E1
Maarestatunturit 95 E3
Maarianhamina 106 C3
Maarianvaara 103 E2
Maas 16 C3
Maaseik 51 D3
Maasmechelen 51 D3
Maassluis 16 B3
Maastricht 51 D3
Määttälänvaara 99 F2
Mablethorpe 7 E2
Macael 44 C3
Maçâo 38 B3
Macclesfield 6 C3
Macduff 3 E3
Maceda 34 B3
Macedo de Cavaleiros 34 C4
Macelj 70 C1
Macerata 61 F4
Macerata Feltria 61 E3
Macgillycuddy's Reeks 14 A4
Machault 20 B3
Machecoul 24 B3
Machero 39 F4
Machichaco, C 36 B1
Machine, la 26 A3
Máchovo jez 53 F3
Machrihanish 4 B3
Machynlleth 6 A3
Mackendorf 52 C1
Mackenrode 52 B2
Mačkovci 70 C1
Macocha 57 F1
Macomer 66 B2
Mâcon 26 C4
Macotera 39 F1
Macroom 14 B4
Macugnaga 27 F4
Mačvanska Mitrovica 72 C3
Mačvanski Pričinović 72 C3
Madara 115 E2
Maddalena, Arc della 66 B1
Maddalena, Colle della 31 E2
Maddalena, I 66 B1
Maddalena La 66 B1
Maddaloni 64 B3
Madeira, Arquipélago da 42 A3
Madeira, I da 42 A3
M'adel' 111 D3
Madeleine, Col de la 31 D1
Madero, Pto del 36 C3
Maderuelo 36 A3
Madesimo 58 B3
Madine, Lac de 20 C3
Madon 21 D4
Madona 110 C2
Madonie Nebrodi 68 C3
Madonna di Campiglio 58 C3
Madrid 40 A2
Madrid (Prov) 40 A2
Madridejos 40 B3
Madrigal de las Altas Torres 39 F1
Madrigal de la Vera 39 E2
Madrigalejo 39 E4
Madrona 40 A1
Madrona, Sa 44 A1
Madroñera 39 E3
Maël-Carhaix 22 B3
Maella 37 E4
Maesteg 8 C2
Mafra 38 A3
Magacela 39 E4
Magallón 36 C3
Magaña 36 B3
Magaz 35 F3
Magdalena, Pto de la 35 D2
Magdeburg 52 C1
Magenta 60 A1
Magerøya 95 E1
Maggia 58 A3
Maggiore, L 58 A4
Maghera 13 D1
Magherafelt 13 D2
Mágina 44 A2
Magione 61 E4
Maglaj 71 F3
Magliano di Marsi 63 F2
Magliano in Toscana 63 D2
Magliano Sabina 63 E2
Maglić 73 D4
Maglić *Mt* 76 A1
Maglie 65 F4
Magnac-Laval 25 E4
Magnissía 83 E2
Magnor 105 D3
Magny-en-Vexin 19 E3
Magoúla 86 B2
Magro, R 41 D4
Magura 77 D2
Maherádo 86 A1
Mahlu 103 D2
Mahón 45 F2
Mahora 41 D4
Mahovo 71 D2
Mähring 53 D4
Maia 34 A4
Maials 37 E4
Maîche 27 E2
Maida 67 F3
Maidenhead 9 F2
Maidstone 11 D3
Maiella, la 64 A2
Maienfeld 58 B2
Maignelay 19 F3
Maigue 14 B3
Maillezais 24 C4
Mailly-le-Camp 20 B4
Main 55 D1
Mainar 36 C4
Mainburg 55 F2
Maine-et-Loire 23 E4
Mainistir na Búille 12 C3
Mainland (Orkney) 3 D1
Mainland (Shetland) 3 F2
Maintenon 19 E4
Mainz 51 F4
Maira 31 E2
Mairena del Alcor 43 D2
Maisach 55 F3
Maison-Neuve 26 B1
Maisons-Blanches, les 25 D4
Maissau 57 E2
Maizières 21 D3
Maja 70 C3
Majales, Pto de los 40 A4
Majdanpek 73 E3
Majevica 72 B3
Majšperk 70 C1
Makarska 75 E2
Makce 73 E3
Makedonía 79 F2
Makedonija 77 E3
Makedonija 77 F3
Makedonski Brod 77 D3
Makljen 75 E1
Makó 114 B1
Makovo 77 E4
Makrakómi 83 E3
Mákri 81 E2
Makríamos 80 C3
Makrígialos 79 F3
Makrigialós 91 F4
Makrihóri (Makedonía) 80 C2
Makrihóri (Thessalía) 83 E1
Makrinítsa 83 F2
Makrinóros 82 C3
Makriplágio 80 C2
Makrirráhi 83 E3
Makrívrahos, Akr 81 E3
Makrohóri 79 E3
Makronissi 88 A2
Maksniemi 99 D3
Mala 14 B4
Malå 98 A4
Mala Bosna 72 B1
Malacky 57 F2
Maladeta 37 E2
Malaga 43 F4
Malagón 40 A4
Malahide 13 E4
Malaja Višera 111 E1
Malaja Viska 113 F2
Mala Kapela 70 C3
Mala Krsna 73 D3
Malalbergo 61 D2
Malámata 83 D4
Malandrino 83 E4
Malangen 94 B2
Mälaren 106 B3
Mala Subotica 71 D1
Malaucène 30 C3
Malax 102 B2
Malbork 110 B4
Malbuisson 27 D3
Malcata, Sa de 39 D2
Malcesine 58 C4
Malchin 49 D2
Malchiner See 49 D2
Malchow 49 D2
Maldegem 50 B3
Maldon 11 D2
Malè 58 C3
Maléas, Akr 87 E4
Máleme 90 B3
Malène, la 29 F3
Malente Gremsmühlen 48 B2
Male Pijace 72 C1
Máles 91 E4
Malesherbes 25 F1
Malessína 83 F3
Malestroit 22 C3
Malgomaj 97 F4
Malgrat de Mar 32 B4
Mália 91 E3
Malicorne 23 E4
Mali Haian 70 C4
Mali Iđđos 72 B2
Mali kanal 72 B2
Mali Lošinj 70 B4
Malin 113 E2
Malines 50 B3
Malin Head 13 D1
Malinska 70 B3
Mali Požerevac 73 D3
Mališevo 77 D2
Mäiskylä 103 D1
Malit, Maj'e 76 C3
Mali Zvornik 72 B4
Maljen 72 C4
Malko Târnovo 115 E2
Mallaig 2 B4
Mållejus 95 D2
Mallén 36 C3
Mallersdorf-Pfaffenberg 56 B2
Malles Venosta 58 C2
Mallnitz 59 E2
Mallorca- 45 E2
Mallow 14 B4
Mallwyd 6 A3
Malm 101 D1
Malmberget 98 B2
Malmédy 51 D4
Malmesbury 9 E2
Malmköping 106 A4
Malmö 108 C3
Malmöhus Län 109 D3
Malmslätt 106 A4
Malo 59 D4
Maloja 58 B3
Malojaroslavec 111 F3
Malo Konjari 77 E4
Malo-les-Bains 19 F1
Malónas 93 F1
Malori 64 B4
Måløy 100 A3
Malpartida de Cáceres 39 D3
Malpartida de Plasencia 39 E2
Malpica (E) 34 A1
Malpica (P) 38 C3
Mals 58 C2
Målselv 94 B3
Målselva 94 B3
Målsnes 94 B3
Malsta 101 F3
Malta 59 F2
Malta/ 68 B4
Maltby 7 D2
Maltiotunturi 95 F4
Malton 7 D1
Maluenda 36 C4
Malung 105 E2
Malungsfors 101 D4
Malveira 38 A4
Malvik 100 C2
Malzieu-Ville, le 29 F2
Mamaia 115 E1
Mamarrosa 38 B1
Mamers 23 F3
Mammola 67 F4
Mamonovo 110 B4
Mampodre 35 E2
Mamry, Jez 110 B4
Manacor 45 F3
Manacore 64 C2
Manamansalo 99 E4
Manasija 73 E3
Mancha Real 44 A2
Manche 18 B3
Manchester 6 C2
Manching 55 F2
Manciano 63 D2
Mandal 104 B4
Mandal selva 104 B4
Mandamádos 85 F2
Mandas 66 B3
Mandela 63 F2
Mandelieu 31 E4
Manderscheid 51 E4
Mandínia 87 D2
Mandoúdi 84 A3
Mandráki 89 F4
Mándra (Stereá Eláda) 87 F1
Mándra (Thráki) 81 F2
Mandre 70 B4
Mandrikó 93 E1
Mandrioli, Pso dei 61 D3
Manduria 65 E4
Måne 104 C3
Manerbio 60 B1
Manětín 53 E4
Manfredonia 64 C2
Manfredonia, G di 64 C2
Mangalia 115 E2
Mángana 81 D2
Manganári 88 C4
Manger 104 A2
Mangerton Mt 14 B4
Mangrt, Planica 59 F2
Mangualde 38 C1
Maniago 59 E3
Manilva 43 E4
Man, I of 6 A1
Máni (Pelopónissos) 87 D4
Máni (Thráki) 81 F1
Manisa 115 E4
Manises 41 E4
Manjača 71 E4
Mank 57 E3
Månkarbo 106 B3
Manlleu 32 B3
Mannersdorf 57 F3
Mannheim 54 C1
Mannu 66 B4
Manojlovac slap 75 D1
Manojlovce 77 E1
Manoppello 64 A2
Manorhamilton 12 C2
Manosque 30 C3
Manresa 32 A4
Manschnow 49 F4
Mansfeld 52 C2
Mansfield 7 D3
Mansilla de las Mulas 35 E3
Mansilla, Emb de 36 B3
Mansle 25 D4
Manteigas 38 C2
Mantes 19 E4
Mantiel 40 C2
Mäntlahti 103 F4
Mantorp 109 E1
Mantova 60 C2
Mäntsälä 107 F2
Mänttä 103 D3
Mäntyharju 103 E3
Mäntyjärvi 99 E2
Mäntyluoto 102 B3
Manzanal, Pto del 35 D2
Manzanares 40 B4
Manzanares el Real 40 A2
Manzaneda 34 C3
Manzanera 41 E3
Manzat 26 A4
Manziana 63 E2
Maó 45 F2
Maqellarë 77 D3
Maqueda 40 A2
Maramureș 112 C3
Maranchón 40 C1
Maranchón, Pto de 40 C1
Maranello 60 C2
Maranhão, Bgem do 38 B4
Marano 59 F3
Marano di Napoli 64 B4
Marano, L di 59 F4
Marans 24 B4
Marão, Sa do 34 B4
Marássia 81 F1
Maratea 67 E2
Marateca 38 A4
Marathéa 83 D2
Marathiá, Akr 86 A2
Marathiás 83 D4
Marathókambos 89 E1
Marathónas 87 F1
Marathópoli 86 B3
Márathos 83 F2
Marbach 55 D2
Mårbacka 105 E3
Marbella 43 E4
Marburg 17 F4
Marby 101 E2
Marčana 70 A4
March (A) 57 F2
March (GB) 10 C1
Marchamalo 40 B2
Marchaux 27 D2
Marche 61 E4
Marche-en-Famenne 50 C4
Marchegg 57 F2
Marchena 43 E3
Marchenoir 25 E1
Marchiennes 20 A1
Marciac 28 C4
Marciana Marina 62 C1
Marcianise 64 B3
Marcigny 26 B4
Marcilla 36 C2
Marcillac-Vallon 29 E3
Marcillat-en-Combraille 25 F4
Marcilly-le-Hayer 20 B4
Marckolsheim 27 E1
Marco de Canaveses 34 A4
Marcoule 30 B3
Mære 101 D1
Maree, L 2 C3
Mare Ligure 60 A4
Marene 31 E2
Marennes 28 A1
Marentes 34 C2
Marèttimo, I- 68 A3
Mareuil (Dordogne) 28 C1
Mareuil (Vendée) 24 B3
Margarítes 91 D3
Margaríti 82 B2
Margate 11 D2
Margherita di Savoia 65 D3
Marguerittes 30 B3
María 44 C2
María Cristina, Emb de 41 E3
Mariannelund 109 E1
Mariánské Lázně 53 E4
Maria Saal 70 A1
Maria Taferl 57 E2
Mariazell 57 E3
Maribo 108 B4
Maribor 70 C1
Mariborsko Pohorje 70 C1
Marica 115 D3
Mariefred 106 B4
Mariehamn 106 C3
Marienberg 53 E3
Marienborn 52 C1
Marienburg 51 E4
Marienstedt 48 B3
Mariestad 105 E4
Marignane 30 C4
Marigny 18 B3
Marigny-le-Châtel 20 B4
Marija Bistrica 70 C2
Marikirk 3 E4
Marin 34 A2
Marina 75 D2
Marina di Camerota 67 D2
Marina di Campo 62 C2
Marina di Carrara 60 B3

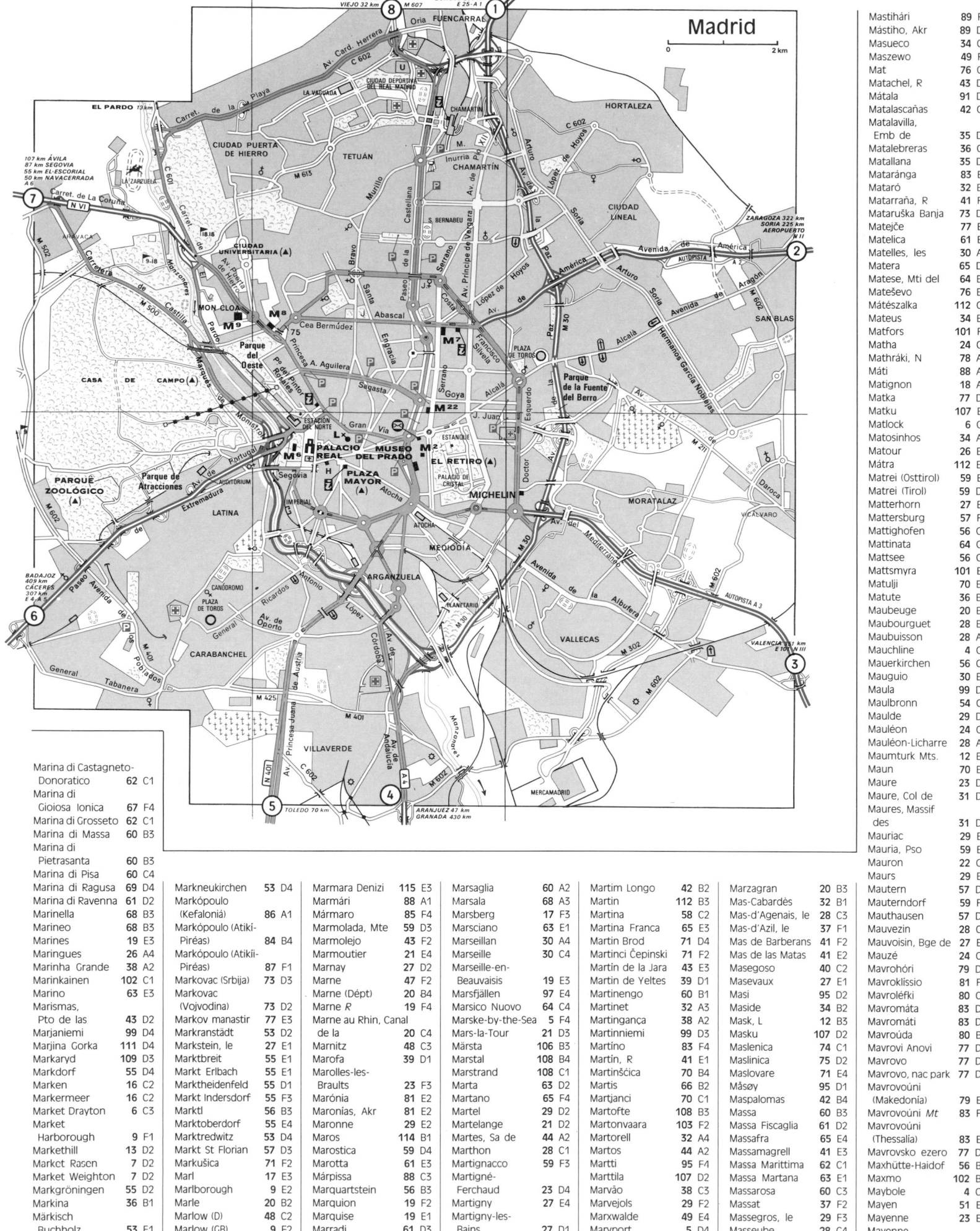

Madrid

0   2 km

Mastihári	89	F3
Mástiho, Akr	89	D1
Masueco	34	C4
Maszewo	49	F2
Mat	76	C3
Matachel, R	43	D1
Mátala	91	D4
Matalascañas	42	C3
Matalavilla, Emb de	35	D2
Matalebreras	36	C2
Matallana	35	D2
Mataránga	83	E2
Mataró	32	B4
Matarraña, R	41	F2
Mataruška Banja	73	D4
Matejče	77	E2
Matelica	61	E4
Matelles, les	30	A4
Matera	65	D4
Matese, Mti del	64	B3
Mateševo	76	B2
Mátészalka	112	C3
Mateus	34	B4
Matfors	101	F3
Matha	24	C4
Mathráki, N	78	A4
Máti	88	A1
Matignon	18	A4
Matka	77	D3
Matku	107	E2
Matlock	6	C3
Matosinhos	34	A4
Matour	26	B4
Mátra	112	B3
Matrei (Osttirol)	59	E2
Matrei (Tirol)	59	D2
Matterhorn	27	E4
Mattersburg	57	F3
Mattighofen	56	C1
Mattinata	64	C2
Mattsee	56	C3
Mattsmyra	101	E4
Matulji	70	B3
Matute	36	B3
Maubeuge	20	B1
Maubourguet	28	B4
Maubuisson	28	A2
Mauchline	4	C2
Mauerkirchen	56	C3
Mauguio	30	B4
Maula	99	D3
Maulbronn	54	C2
Maulde	29	D1
Mauléon	24	C3
Mauléon-Licharre	28	A4
Maumturk Mts.	12	B3
Maun	70	B4
Maure	23	D3
Maure, Col de	31	D3
Maures, Massif des	31	D4
Mauriac	29	E2
Mauria, Pso	59	E3
Mauron	22	C3
Maurs	29	E2
Mautern	57	D4
Mauterndorf	59	F1
Mauthausen	57	D2
Mauvezin	28	C4
Mauvoisin, Bge de	27	E4
Mauzé	24	C4
Mavrohóri	79	D4
Mavroklíssio	81	F1
Mavroléfki	80	C2
Mavromáta	83	D3
Mavromáti	83	D2
Mavroúda	80	B3
Mavrovi Anovi	77	D3
Mavrovo	77	D3
Mavrovo, nac park	77	D3
Mavrovoúni (Makedonía)	79	D3
Mavrovoúni *Mt*	83	E2
Mavrovoúni (Thessalía)	83	E2
Mavrovsko ezero	77	D3
Maxhütte-Haidof	56	B1
Maxmo	102	B2
Maybole	4	C3
Mayen	51	E4
Mayenne	23	E3
Mayenne (Dépt)	23	E3

Marina di Castagneto-Donoratico	62	C1
Marina di Gioiosa Ionica	67	F4
Marina di Grosseto	62	C1
Marina di Massa	60	B3
Marina di Pietrasanta	60	B3
Marina di Pisa	60	C4
Marina di Ragusa	69	D4
Marina di Ravenna	61	D2
Marinella	68	B3
Marineo	68	B3
Marines	19	E3
Maringues	26	A4
Marinha Grande	38	A2
Marinkainen	102	C1
Marino	63	E3
Marismas, Pto de las	43	D2
Marjaniemi	99	D4
Marjina Gorka	111	D4
Markaryd	109	D3
Markdorf	55	D4
Marken	16	C2
Markermeer	16	C2
Market Drayton	6	C3
Market Harborough	9	F1
Markethill	13	D2
Market Rasen	7	D2
Market Weighton	7	D2
Markgröningen	55	D2
Markina	36	B1
Märkisch Buchholz	53	E1
Markkleeberg	53	D2

Markneukirchen	53	D4
Markópoulo (Kefaloniá)	86	A1
Markópoulo (Atikí-Piréas)	84	B4
Markópoulo (Atikí-Piréas)	87	F1
Markovac (Srbija)	73	D3
Markovac (Vojvodina)	73	D2
Markov manastir	77	E3
Markranstädt	53	D2
Markstein, le	27	E1
Marktbreit	55	E1
Markt Erlbach	55	E1
Marktheidenfeld	55	D1
Markt Indersdorf	55	F3
Marktl	56	B3
Marktoberdorf	55	E4
Marktredwitz	53	D4
Markt St Florian	57	D3
Markušica	71	F2
Marl	17	E3
Marlborough	9	E2
Marle	20	B2
Marlow (D)	48	C2
Marlow (GB)	9	F2
Marmande	28	C3

Marmara Denizi	115	E3
Marmári	88	A1
Mármaro	85	F4
Marmolada, Mte	59	D3
Marmolejo	43	F2
Marmoutier	21	E4
Marnay	27	D2
Marne	47	F2
Marne (Dépt)	20	B4
Marne *R*	19	F4
Marne au Rhin, Canal de la	20	C4
Marnitz	48	C3
Marofa	39	D1
Marólia	81	E2
Maronías, Akr	81	E2
Maronne	29	E2
Maros	114	B1
Marostica	59	D4
Marotta	61	E3
Márpissa	88	C3
Marquartstein	56	B3
Marquion	19	F2
Marquise	19	E1
Marradi	61	D3
Marraskoski	99	D2

Marsaglia	60	A2
Marsala	68	A3
Marsberg	17	F3
Marsciano	63	E1
Marseillan	30	A4
Marseille	30	C4
Marseille-en-Beauvaisis	19	E3
Marsfjällen	97	E4
Marsico Nuovo	64	C4
Marske-by-the-Sea	5	F4
Mars-la-Tour	21	D3
Märsta	106	B3
Marstal	108	B4
Marstrand	108	C1
Marta	63	D2
Martano	65	F4
Martel	29	E2
Martelange	21	D2
Martes, Sa de	44	A2
Marthon	28	C1
Martignacco	59	F3
Martigné-Ferchaud	23	D4
Martigny	27	E4
Martigny-les-Bains	27	D1
Martigues	30	C4

Martim Longo	42	B2
Martin	112	B3
Martina	58	C2
Martina Franca	65	E3
Martinci Čepinski	71	F2
Martín de la Jara	43	E3
Martin de Yeltes	39	D1
Martinengo	60	B1
Martinet	32	A3
Martinniemi	99	D3
Martíno	83	F4
Martín, R	41	E1
Martinšćica	70	B4
Martis	66	B2
Martjanci	70	C1
Martofte	108	B3
Martonvaara	103	F2
Martorell	32	A4
Martos	44	A2
Martti	95	F4
Marttila	107	D2
Marvão	38	C3
Marvejols	29	F2
Marwalde	49	E4
Maryport	5	D4
Mary, Puy	29	E2

Marzagran	20	B3
Mas-Cabardès	32	B1
Mas-d'Agenais, le	28	C3
Mas-d'Azil, le	37	F1
Mas de Barberans	41	F2
Mas de las Matas	41	E2
Masegoso	40	C2
Masevaux	27	E1
Masi	95	D2
Maside	34	B2
Mask, L	12	B3
Masku	107	D2
Maslenica	74	C1
Maslinica	75	D2
Maslovare	71	E4
Måsøy	95	D1
Maspalomas	42	B4
Massa	60	B3
Massa Fiscaglia	61	D2
Massafra	65	E4
Massamagrell	41	E3
Massa Marittima	62	C1
Massa Martana	63	E1
Massarosa	60	C3
Massat	37	F2
Massegros, le	29	F3
Masseube	28	C4
Massiac	29	F1

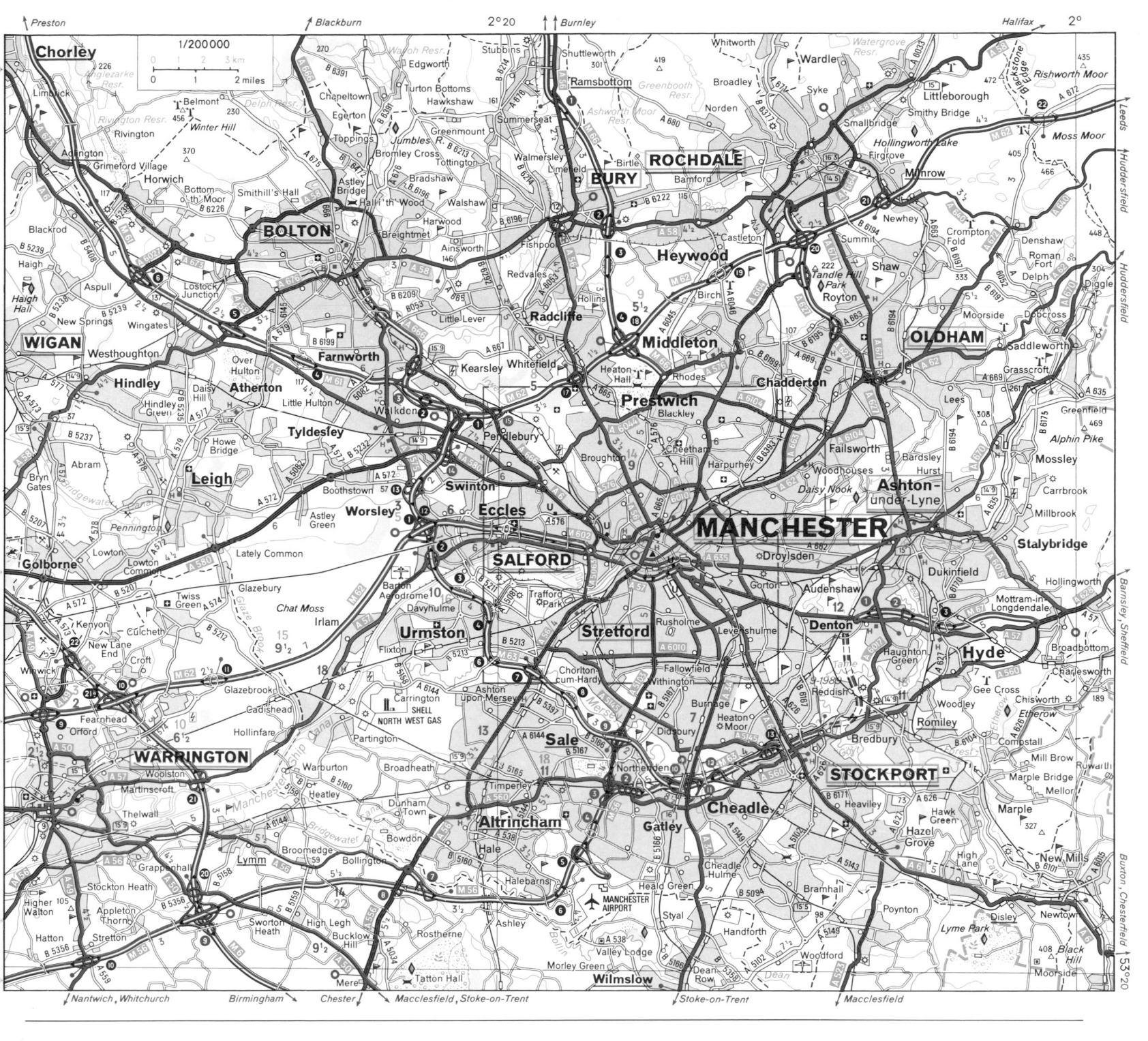

Mayenne R	23 E3	Mazières-en-		Medena Selišta	71 E4	Medvednica	70 C2	Megaló Horió		Meiningen	52 B3	Melfi	64 C3
Mayerling	57 E3	Gâtine	24 C3	Mediano, Emb de	37 E2	Medveja	70 B3	(Agathoníssi)	89 F2	Meira	34 C1	Melfjorden	97 E2
Mayet	23 F4	Mazorra, Pto de la	36 A2	Mediaş	113 D4	Medvida	74 C1	Megaló Horió		Meira, Sa de	34 C1	Melgaço	34 B3
Mayet-de-Montagne,		Mazury	110 B4	Medicina	61 D2	Medvode	70 B2	(Tílos)	89 F4	Meiringen	27 F3	Melgar de Abajo	35 E3
le	26 B4	Mazzarino	68 C4	Medina Azahara	43 E2	Medyn'	111 F3	Megísti	93 F2	Meißen	53 E2	Melgar de
Maynooth	13 D4	Mazzarò	69 D3	Medinaceli	36 B4	Medžitlija	77 E4	Megísti, N	93 F2	Meisenheim	54 B1	Fernamental	35 F3
Mayo	12 B2	Mealhada	38 B2	Medina del		Meerane	53 D3	Megístis Lávras	80 C4	Meitingen	55 E3	Melhus	100 C2
Mayor, C	35 F1	Meath	13 D3	Campo	35 E4	Meersburg	55 D4	Meg. Livádi	88 A3	Mel	59 E3	Melía	83 E2
Mayorga	35 E3	Meaux	19 F4	Medina de Pomar	36 A1	Mées, les	31 D3	Meg. Panagía	80 B3	Melalahti	99 E4	Melide	34 B2
Mayrhofen	59 D2	Mechelen	50 B3	Medina de		Mefjordbotn	94 B2	Meg. Vólvi	80 B3	Melámbes	91 D4	Melides	42 A1
Maza, Barrié		Meckenbeuren	55 D4	Ríoseco	35 E4	Mefjordvær	94 B2	Mehamn	95 E1	Melaniós	85 E4	Melidóni	91 D3
Emb de la	34 A2	Mecklenburger B	48 C1	Medina-Sidonia	43 D4	Méga Dério	81 F2	Mehedeby	106 B2	Melánthio	78 C3	Meligalás	86 C3
Mazagón	42 C3	Meda	38 C1	Médous,		Mega Horió (Stereá		Mehov Krš	76 C2	Melátes	82 C2	Melíki	79 E3
Mazamet	32 B1	Medđa	73 D2	Grotte de	37 D1	Eláda)	83 D3	Mehun	25 F2	Melbeck	48 B3	Melilli	69 D4
Mazara d. Vallo	68 A3	Medak	70 C4	Megalohóri	83 D1	Meigle	5 D1	Meijel	17 D4	Melbu	94 A3	Mélisey	27 D1
Mazarakiá	82 B2	Mede	60 A2	Medoussa	81 D1	Megalópoli	86 C2	Meije, la	31 D2	Meldal	100 C2	Mélissa	81 D2
Mazarete	40 C1	Medebach	17 F4	Medugorje	75 F2	Meganíssi	82 B3	Meilen	58 A2	Meldola	61 D3	Mélissa, Akr	82 B4
Mazarrón	45 D3	Medđedđa	76 B1	Medulin	70 A4	Megaplátanos	83 E1	Meillant	25 F3	Meldorf	47 F2	Melissáni	82 B4
Mazarrón, G de	45 D3	Medelim	38 C2	Medđumajdan	71 D3	Mégara	87 E1	Meimoa	38 C2	Melegnano	60 A1	Melíssi	87 D1
Mažeikiai	110 B3	Medellín	39 E4	Meduna	59 E3	Megárhi	83 D1	Mêle, le	19 D4	Melenci	72 C2	Melissohóri	84 A4
Mazères	32 A1	Medel, Piz	58 A3	Meduno	59 E3	Meddurečje	76 C1	Mélida	36 C3	Melendugno	65 F4	Melissópetra	78 C4
Mázi	78 C4	Medemblik	16 C2	Medvedđa	77 D1	Megève	27 E4	Meinerzhagen	17 E4	Melendugno	65 F4	Melissourgós	80 B3

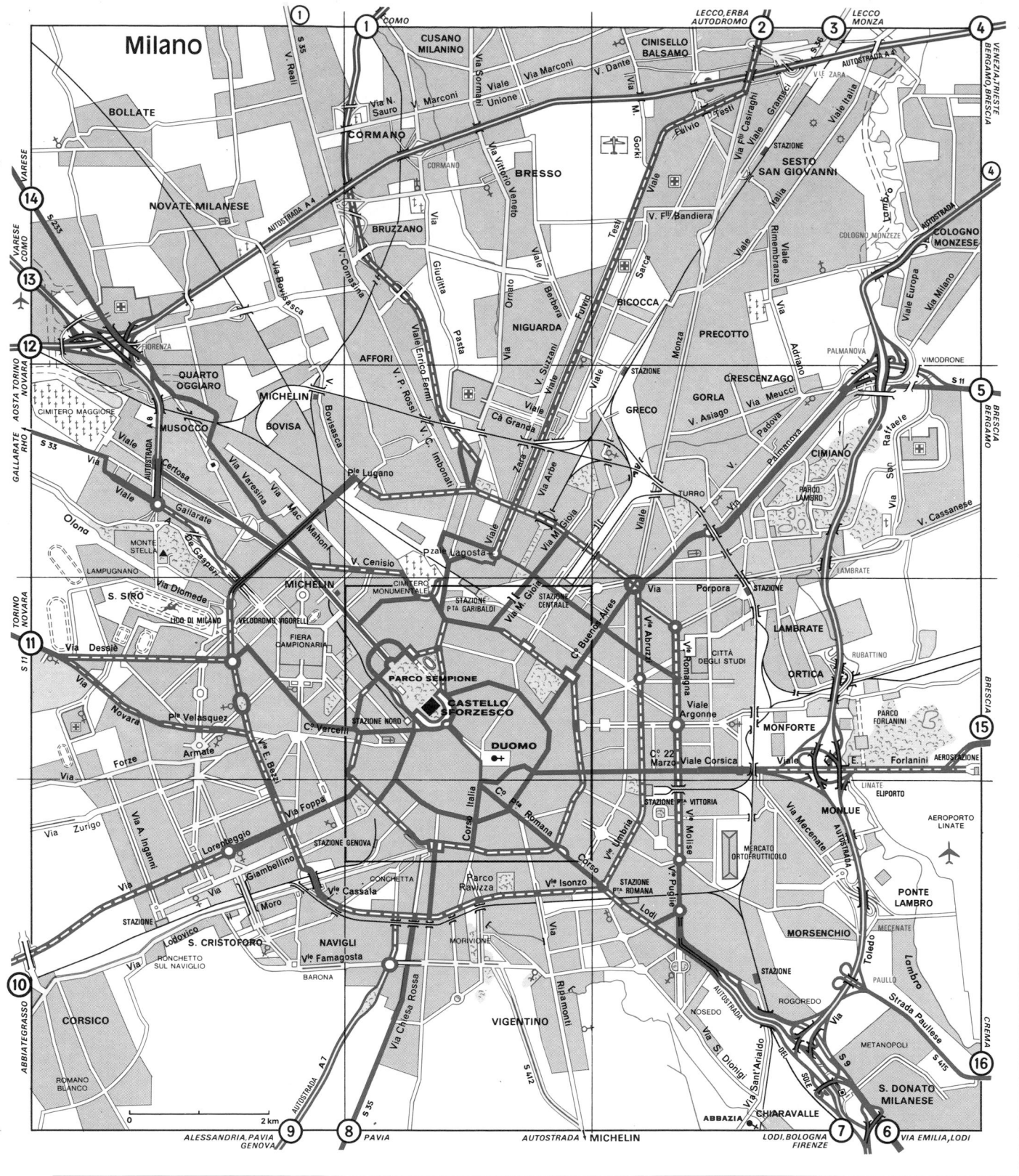

Milano

Méréville	25	F1
Mergozzo	58	A4
Méribel	31	D1
Mérida	39	D4
Mérignac	28	B2
Mérihas	88	A2
Merijärvi	99	D4
Merikarvia	102	B3
Mering	55	F3
Merkendorf	55	D3
Merklingen	55	D3
Merlerault, le	19	D4
Mer Noir	115	F1
Merošina	77	D1
Merrenkurkku	102	B2
Merrick	4	C3
Mers	19	E2
Mersch	21	D2
Merseburg	53	D2
Merthyr Tydfil	8	C2
Mértola	42	B2
Méru	19	F3
Méry	20	B4
Merville (Calvados)	18	C3
Merville (Pas-de-Calais)	19	F1
Merzig	54	A2
Mesagne	65	F3
Mesão Frio	34	B4
Meschede	17	F3
Mescherin	49	E3
Meschers	28	A1
Meßdorf	48	C4
Mešeišta	77	D4
Mesići	76	A1
Mesihovina	75	E1
Meßkirch	55	D3
Meslay	23	E3
Mesocco	58	B3
Mesola	61	D2
Mesón do Vento	34	B1
Mesoraca	67	F3
Mespelbrunn	52	A4
Messanagrós	93	E2
Messarás, Órmos	91	D4
Messariá	88	B1
Messei	18	C4
Méssi	81	D2
Messiméri	79	F3
Messimvría	81	E2
Messina	69	D2
Messíni	86	C3
Messinía	86	C3
Messiniakós Kólpos	86	C4
Messlingen	101	D2
Messohóra	82	C2
Messohóri (Kárpathos)	93	D3
Messohóri (Thessalía)	83	E1
Messolóngi	82	C4
Messongí	82	A2
Messopótamo	82	B2
Messótopos	85	E2
Meßstetten	55	D3
Mestá	85	E4
Mesta	115	D3
Mestanza	44	A1
Mésti	81	E2
Mestlin	48	C2
Mestre	61	D1
Mesvres	26	B3
Metajna	70	C4
Meta, la	64	A2
Metalika	76	B1
Metalikó	79	F2
Metalió	83	E3
Metamórfossi (Halkidikí)	80	B4
Metamórfossi (Kilkís)	79	F2
Metangítsi	80	B4
Metanopoli	60	A1
Metauro	61	E3
Metaxádes	81	F1
Metéora	83	D1
Méthana	87	E2
Methil	5	D2
Methóni (Makedonía)	79	F3
Methóni (Pelopónissos)	86	C3
Metković	75	F2

Melíti	279	D2	Mellrichstadt	52	B4	Membrilla	40	B4	Mendrisio	58	A4	Menor, Mar	45	D2
Melito di Porto Salvo	67	E4	Mellum	47	F3	Membrio	38	C3	Menée, Col de	30	C2	Mens	30	C2
Melívia (Thessalía)	83	F1	Melnica	73	E3	Memmingen	55	E3	Menen	50	A3	Mentana	63	E2
Melívia (Thráki)	81	D1	Melnice	70	B3	Mena	113	F1	Menesjärvi	95	E3	Menthon	27	D4
Melk	57	E2	Mělník	53	F3	Menaggio	58	B4	Menetés	93	D3	Menton	31	E3
Melksham	9	E2	Mělník	53	F4	Menai Bridge	6	A2	Ménez-Hom	22	B3	Méntrida	40	A2
Mellan Fryken	105	E3	Melogno, Colle di	31	F3	Ménalo, Óros	86	C3	Menfi	68	B3	Menuires, les	31	D1
Mellansel	102	A2	Meløy	97	E2	Menasalbas	40	A3	Mengamuñoz	39	F2	Meppel	17	D2
Melle (D)	17	F2	Meløyfjorden	97	E2	Menat	26	A4	Menga, Pto de	39	F2	Meppen	17	D2
Melle (F)	24	C4	Melpers	52	B3	Mencal	44	B3	Mengara	61	E4	Mequinenza	37	E4
Mellerstair	5	D2	Melrose	5	D2	Mendavia	36	B2	Mengen	55	D3	Mequinenza, Emb de	37	F4
Mellerud	105	D4	Melsungen	52	A3	Mende	29	F3	Mengeš	70	B2	Mer Adriatique	74	B2
Mellieha	68	B4	Meltaus	99	D2	Mendelpass	59	D3	Mengíbar	44	A2	Meråker	101	D2
Mellifont Abbey	13	D3	Melton Mowbray	7	D3	Menden	17	E3	Menídi	82	C2	Meran	59	D2
Mellilä	107	D2	Meltosjärvi	99	D2	Mendenítsa	83	E3	Ménigoute	24	C3	Merano	59	D2
Mellin	48	B4	Melun	19	F4	Menderes, B	115	F4	Meníkio, Óros	80	B2	Merate	60	A1
Mellingen	52	C3	Melvich	3	D2	Mendola, Pso della	59	D3	Mennetou	25	E2	Mercadal	45	F1
			Melvin, L	12	C2				Menorca	45	F1			
												Menor, Mar	45	D2
												Mercante, Pso di	67	E4
												Mercantour, Parc Nat du	31	E3
												Mercatale (Marche)	61	E3
												Mercatale (Toscana)	61	D4
												Mercatino Conca	61	E3
												Mercator San Severino	64	B4
												Mercato Saraceno	61	D3
												Merćez	77	D1
												Mercœur	29	D2
												Mer de Crète	90	C2
												Merdrignac	22	C3
												Mer du Nord	16	A2
												Mere	9	D3
												Mer Égée	85	D4

Metlika 70 C2
Metnitz 57 D4
Metóhi (Ahaïa) 86 B1
Metóhi (Argolída) 87 E2
Metóhi (Évia) 84 B3
Metóhi (Thessalía) 83 F2
Metsákyla 99 E3
Metsäkylä 103 F4
Metsämaa 107 E2
Métsovo 82 C1
Mettingen 17 E2
Mettlach 54 A1
Mettmann 17 E4
Metz 21 D3
Metzervisse 21 D3
Metzingen 55 D3
Meulan 19 E3
Meung 25 E2
Meursault 26 C3
Meurthe-et-Moselle 21 D4
Meuse 20 C3
Meuse (Dépt) 20 C3
Meuselwitz 53 D2
Mevagissey 8 B4
Meximieux 26 C4
Meyenburg 48 C3
Meymac 29 E1
Meyrand, Col de 30 B2
Meyrueis 29 F3
Meyzieu 26 C4
Mezas 39 D2
Mezdra 115 D2
Mèze 30 A4
Mézel 31 D3
Mézenc, Mt 30 B2
Mežgorje 112 C3
Mežica 70 B1
Mézidon 18 C3
Mézières 25 D4
Mézières-en-Brenne 25 E3
Mézin 28 C3
Mezöberény 112 C4
Mezökövesd 112 B4
Mezötúr 112 B4
Mezquita de Jarque 41 E2
Mezzano 59 D3
Mezzolombardo 58 C3
Mgarr 68 B4
Miajadas 39 E4
Miastko 110 A4
Michalovce 112 C3
Micheldorf 57 D3
Michelstadt 55 D1
Michendorf 49 D4
Mičurin 115 E2
Middelburg 16 B3
Middelfart 108 B3
Middelharnis 16 B3
Middelkerke-Bad 50 A3
Middlesbrough 5 F4
Middleton-in-Teesdale 5 E4
Middlewich 6 C3
Midhurst 9 F3
Midi, Canal du 32 B1
Midi de Bigorre, Pic du 37 E2
Midi d'Ossau, Pic du 37 D2
Midleton 14 C4
Midouze 28 B3
Midsund 100 B2
Mid Yell 3 F1
Miedes 36 C4
Miedwie, Jez 49 F3
Międzychód 112 A1
Międzylesie 112 A2
Międzyrzec Podlaski 112 C1
Międzyzdroje 49 E2
Miehikkälä 103 F4
Miekojärvi 98 C2
Miélan 28 C4
Mielec 112 B2
Mielno 49 F1
Mieluskylä 103 D1
Miera, R 35 F2
Miercurea-Ciuc 113 D4
Mieres 35 D2

Miesbach 56 B3
Mieszkowice 49 E3
Mietoinen 107 D2
Miettila 103 F3
Migennes 26 A1
Migliarino 61 D2
Miglionico 65 D4
Miguel Esteban 40 B3
Miguelturra 40 A4
Mihajlovac (Srbija) 73 D3
Mihajlovac (Srbija) 73 F3
Mihajlovgrad 115 D2
Míhas 86 C1
Mihói 86 B1
Mijas 43 E4
Mijoux 27 D3
Míki 81 D2
Mikínes 87 D2
Mikkeli 103 E3
Mikkelin Läär 103 E3
Mikkelvik 94 B2
Mikleuš 71 E2
Míkonos 88 C2
Míkonos, N 88 C2
Mikrí Mandínia 86 C3
Mikrí Préspa, L 78 C3
Mikró Horió 83 D3
Mikrókambos 79 F2
Mikroklissoúra 80 B1
Mikrolímni 78 C3
Mikromiliá 80 C1
Mikrón Dério 81 F1
Mikron Eleftherohóri 79 E4
Mikrópoli 80 B2
Mikulov 57 F1
Milagro 36 C2
Milano 60 A1
Milano Marittimo 61 E3
Mílatos 91 E3
Milazzo 69 D2
Mileševo (Srbija) 76 B1
Mileševo (Vojvodina) 72 C1
Milestone 14 C3
Miletíci 70 C4
Mileto 67 E3
Miletto, Mte 64 B3
Milevsko 57 D1
Milford (GB) 9 F3
Milford (IRL) 13 D1
Milford Haven 8 B2
Milhão 34 C3
Míli 87 D2
Miliá (Makedonía) 79 D4
Miliá (Pelopónnissos) 87 D2
Miliá (Thráki) 81 F1
Milići 72 B4
Miliés 83 F2
Milín 53 F4
Milína 83 F2
Milis 66 B3
Militello in Val di C. 69 D3
Miljevina 76 A1
Millas 32 B2
Millau 29 F3
Millesimo 31 F2
Millevaches, Plateau de 29 D1
Millom 6 B1
Millport 4 C2
Millstatt 59 F2
Millstreet 14 B4
Milltown Malbay 12 B4
Milly 19 F4
Milmarcos 36 C4
Milmersdorf 49 E3
Milna 75 D2
Miločer 76 B3
Milohnić 70 B3
Milopótamos 90 A1
Milos 88 A4
Miloševa Kula 73 E3
Mílos, N 88 A4
Miltach 56 B1
Miltenberg 55 D1
Milton Keynes 9 F2
Milutinovac 73 F2
Mimizan 28 A3
Mimizan-Plage 28 A3
Mimoň 53 F3
Mína 87 D4

Mina de São Domingos 42 B2
Minas de Riotinto 42 C2
Minaya 40 C4
Minch, The 2 B2
Mincio 60 C1
Mindelheim 55 E3
Minden 17 F2
Mindin 24 A2
Minehead 8 C3
Minerbe 60 C1
Minerbio 61 D2
Minervino Murge 65 D3
Minglanilla 41 D3
Mingorria 39 F1
Mínguez, Pto 41 D2
Mingulay 2 A4
Minho 34 A3
Minićevo 73 F4
Minilla, Emb de la 43 D2
Ministra, Sierra 36 B4
Minkió 107 E2
Miño, R 34 B2
Minsk 111 D4
Mińsk Mazowiecki 112 B1
Minsterley 9 D1
Minthi, Óros 86 C2
Mintlaw 3 E3
Miokovićevo 71 E2
Mionica 72 C3
Mionnay 26 C4
Mira (E) 41 D3
Mira (I) 61 D1
Mira (P) 38 B1
Mirabella Imbaccari 68 C4
Mira de Aire 38 B3
Mirador de Coto Rondo 34 A2
Mirador del Fito 35 E1
Miraflores 35 F3
Miraflores de la Sierra 40 A1
Miramar (F) 31 E4
Miramar (P) 34 A4
Miramare 61 E3
Miramas 30 C4
Mirambeau 28 B1
Miramont-de-Guyenne 28 C2
Miranda de Ebro 36 B2
Miranda del Castañar 39 E2
Miranda do Corvo 38 B2
Miranda do Douro 34 C4
Mirande 28 C4
Mirandela 34 C4
Mirandola 60 C2
Mirano 61 D1
Mira, R 42 A2
Mirador de Llesba 35 E2
Miravalles 34 C2
Miravci 77 F3
Miravete, Pto de 39 E3
Mirditë 76 C3
Mirebeau (Côte-d'Or) 26 C2
Mirebeau (Vienne) 25 D3
Mirecourt 27 D1
Mirepoix 32 A2
Míres 91 D4
Mirgorod 113 F2
Miribel 26 C4
Mírina 85 D1
Mirna 70 B2
Mirna R 70 A3
Miroč 73 E3
Mironovka 113 E2
Miroševce 77 E1
Mirotice 56 C1
Mirovice 56 C1
Mirow 49 D3
Mirsíni 87 D4
Mirtiés 89 E3
Mirtóo Pélagos 87 E3
Mírtos 91 E4
Mírtos, Akr 93 E2
Mírtou, Kólpos 82 B4
Mirueña 39 F1
Mišar 72 C3
Misi 99 D2

Misilmeri 68 B3
Miskolc 112 B3
Mislinja 70 B1
Mistelbach 57 F2
Misterbianco 69 D3
Mistrás 87 D3
Mistretta 68 C3
Místros 84 B4
Misurina 59 E2
Mitchelstown 14 C3
Mittelland-Kanal 17 F2
Míthimna 85 F2
Mítikas 82 C3
Mítikas Mt 79 E4
Mitilíni 85 F2
Mitilíni 89 E1
Mitrašinci 77 F3
Mitrópoli 83 D2
Mitsikéli, Óros 82 B1
Mittelberg (Tirol) 58 C2
Mittelberg (Vorarlberg) 58 B2
Mittenwald 55 F4
Mittenwalde 49 E4
Mittersill 59 E1
Mitterteich 53 D4
Mittweida 53 E2
Mizen Head 14 A4
Mjällån 101 F2
Mjällom 102 A2
Mjöbäck 108 C2
Mjölby 109 E1
Mjøndalen 104 C3
Mjøsa 105 D2
Mladá Boleslav 112 A2
Mladá Vožice 57 D1
Mladenovac 73 D3
Mlado Nagoričane 77 E2
Mladost, Ez 77 E2
Mlava 73 E3
Mława 112 B1
Mlini 76 A2
Mliniše 71 D4
Mljet 75 E2
Mljetski Kanal 75 F2
Mnichovo Hradiště 53 F3
Moalven 102 A2
Moaña 34 A3
Moate 12 C3
Mocejón 40 A3
Möckern 52 C1
Möckmühl 55 D2
Moclin 44 A3
Modane 31 D1
Modbury 8 C4
Modena 60 C2
Módi 83 E3
Modica 69 D4
Modigliana 61 D3
Mödling 57 F2
Modračko jez 71 F3
Modran 71 E3
Modřany 53 F4
Modrava 56 C1
Modriča 71 F3
Modrište 77 D3
Modugno 65 D3
Moëlan 22 B3
Moelv 105 D2
Moen 94 B3
Moena 59 D3
Moers 17 D3
Moesa 58 B3
Moffat 5 D3
Mogadouro 34 C4
Mogadouro, Sa do 34 C4
Mogente 45 D1
Mogila 77 E4
Mogil'ov 111 E4
Mogil'ov-Podol'skij 113 E3
Moglia 60 C2
Mogliano Veneto 59 E4
Mogón 44 B2
Mogorrit 41 D2
Moguer 42 C2
Mohács 114 B1
Moher, Cliffs of 12 B4
Mohill 12 C3

Moholm 105 E4
Moi 104 A4
Moià 32 A4
Moie 61 E4
Moimenta 34 C3
Moimenta da Beira 38 C1
Moirans 30 C1
Moirans-en-Montagne 27 D3
Moisdon 23 D4
Moisiovaara 99 F4
Moisling 48 B2
Moissac 29 D3
Moita 38 A4
Mojácar 44 C3
Mojados 35 E4
Mojkovac 76 B2
Mojón Pardo, Pto de 36 B3
Mojstrana 70 A1
Mokra Gora 72 C4
Mokra Gora Mts 76 C3
Mokrin 72 C1
Mokronog 70 B2
Mokro Polje 75 D1
Mol (B) 50 C3
Mol (YU) 72 C1
Mola di Bari 65 E3
Molái 87 D4
Molat 74 B1
Molat I 74 B1
Molatón 41 D4
Mold 6 B3
Moldavija 113 E3
Molde 100 B2
Moldefjorden 100 B2
Moldova Nouă 114 C1
Moldoveanu 113 D4
Moldrup 108 B2
Moledo do Minho 34 A3
Molène 22 A2
Molétai 110 C3
Molfetta 65 D3
Molières 29 D3
Molina de Aragón 40 C2
Molina de Segura 45 D2
Molinella 61 D2
Molinicos 44 C1

Molins de Rei 32 A4
Molise 64 B2
Moliterno 65 D4
Molitg-les-Bains 32 B2
Molkom 105 E3
Mólivos, Akr 85 F2
Möllbrücke 59 F2
Mollerussa 37 F3
Molliens-Vidame 19 E2
Mollina 43 F3
Mölln 48 B2
Mollösund 108 C1
Molnlycke 108 C1
Molodečno 111 D4
Mologa 111 F1
Mólos 83 E3
Molpe 102 B2
Mols 108 B3
Molsheim 21 E4
Molve 71 D1
Molveno 58 C3
Mombeltrán 39 F2
Mombuey 35 D3
Mommark 108 B4
Momo 60 A1
Møn 108 C4
Monach, Sd of 2 A3
Monadhliath Mts 2 C4
Monä fjärd 102 B2
Monaghan 13 D2
Monaghan (Co) 13 D2
Monasterace Marina 67 F4
Monasterboice 13 D3
Monasterevin 13 D3
Monasterio de Rodilla 36 A2
Monastier, le 30 B2
Monastir 66 B4
Monastiráki (Steréa Eláda) 82 C3
Monastiráki (Thráki) 81 F1
Monastíri Doukáto 81 E1
Monastiri, N 83 E2
Monbazillac 28 C2
Moncalieri 31 E2
Moncalvo 31 F1
Moncão 34 A3
Moncarapacho 42 B3

Moncayo, Sa de 36 C3
Mönchdorf 57 D2
Mönchengladbach 17 D4
Monchique 42 A2
Monchique, Sa de 42 A2
Monclar-de-Quercy 29 D3
Moncófar 41 E3
Moncontour (Côtes-du-Nord) 22 C3
Moncontour (Vienne) 24 C3
Moncoutant 24 C3
Monda 43 E4
Mondariz 34 A3
Mondavio 61 E3
Mondego, Cabo 38 A2
Mondego, R 38 B2
Mondéjar 40 B2
Mondello 68 B2
Mondim 34 B4
Mondolfo 61 E3
Mondoñedo 34 C1
Mondorf 21 D3
Mondoubleau 23 F3
Mondovì 31 F2
Mondragón 36 B1
Mondragone 64 A3
Mondsee 56 C3
Monein 28 B4
Monemvassía 87 E4
Monesi 31 E3
Monesterio 43 D1
Monestier-de-Clermont 30 C2
Monestiés 29 E3
Monétier, le 31 D2
Moneygall 12 C4
Moneymore 13 D2
Monfalcone 59 F3
Monflanquin 28 C2
Monforte 38 C4
Monforte de Lemos 34 B2

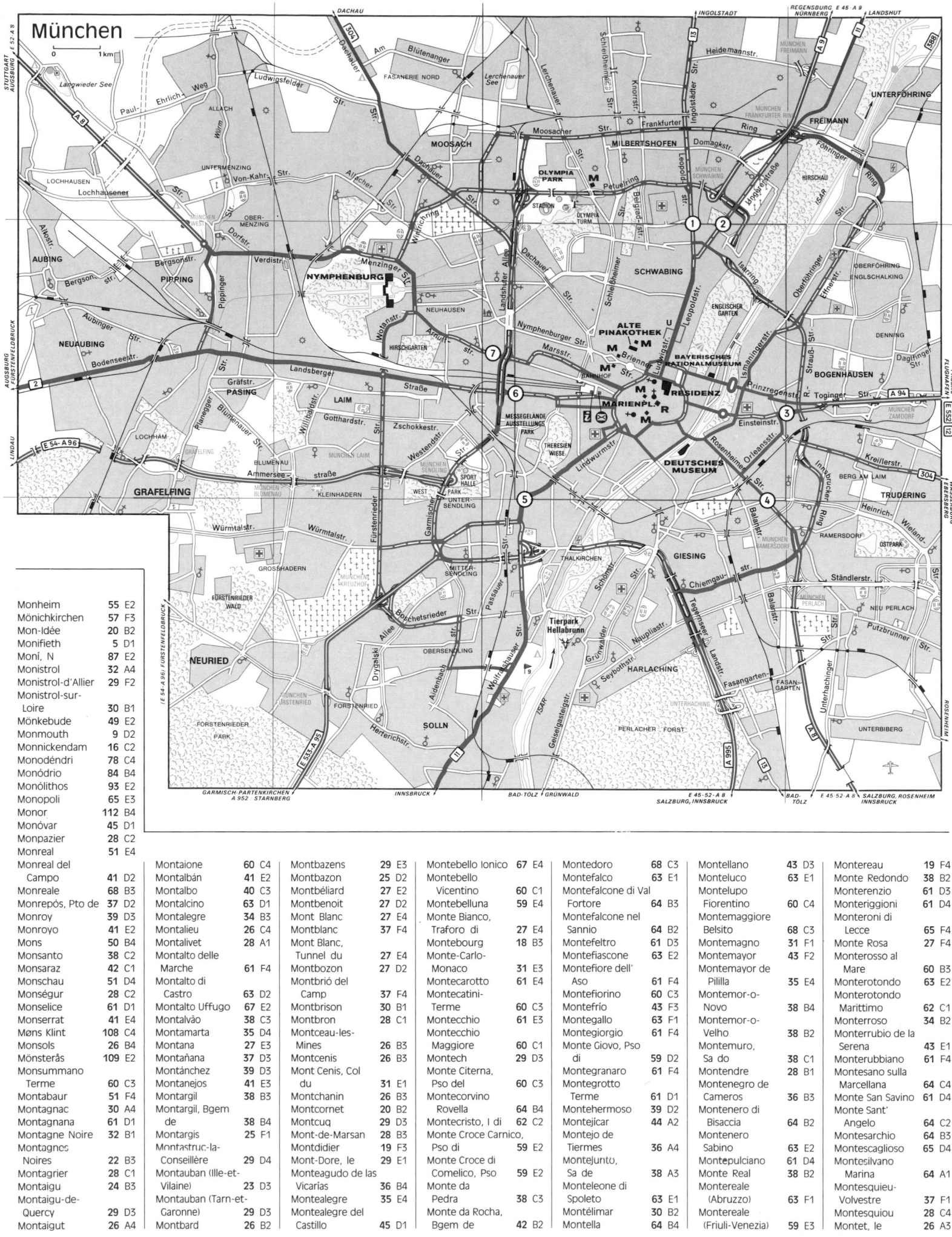

München

Monheim	55	E2
Mönichkirchen	57	F3
Mon-Idée	20	B2
Monifieth	5	D1
Moní, N	87	E2
Monistrol	32	A4
Monistrol-d'Allier	29	F2
Monistrol-sur-Loire	30	B1
Mönkebude	49	E2
Monmouth	9	D2
Monnickendam	16	C2
Monodéndri	78	C4
Monódrio	84	B4
Monólithos	93	E2
Monopoli	65	E3
Monor	112	B4
Monóvar	45	D1
Monpazier	28	C2
Monreal	51	E4
Monreal del Campo	41	D2
Monreale	68	B3
Monrepós, Pto de	37	D2
Monroy	39	D3
Monroyo	41	E2
Mons	50	B4
Monsanto	38	C2
Monsaraz	42	C1
Monschau	51	D4
Monségur	28	C2
Monselice	61	D1
Monserrat	41	E4
Møns Klint	108	C4
Monsols	26	B4
Mönsterås	109	E2
Monsummano Terme	60	C3
Montabaur	51	F4
Montagnac	30	A4
Montagnana	61	D1
Montagne Noire	32	B1
Montagnes Noires	22	B3
Montagrier	28	C1
Montaigu	24	B3
Montaigu-de-Quercy	29	D3
Montaigut	26	A4

Montaione	60	C4
Montalbán	41	D2
Montalbo	40	C3
Montalcino	63	D1
Montalegre	34	B3
Montalieu	26	C4
Montalivet	28	A1
Montalto delle Marche	61	F4
Montalto di Castro	63	D2
Montalto Uffugo	67	E2
Montalvão	38	C3
Montamarta	35	D4
Montana	27	E3
Montañana	37	D3
Montánchez	39	D3
Montanejos	41	E3
Montargil	38	B3
Montargil, Bgem de	38	B4
Montargis	25	F1
Montastruc-la-Conseillère	29	D4
Montauban (Ille-et-Vilaine)	23	D3
Montauban (Tarn-et-Garonne)	29	D3
Montbard	26	B2

Montbazens	29	E3
Montbazon	25	D2
Montbéliard	27	E2
Montbenoit	27	D2
Mont Blanc	27	E4
Montblanc	37	F4
Mont Blanc, Tunnel du	27	E4
Montbozon	27	D2
Montbrió del Camp	37	F4
Montbrison	30	B1
Montbron	28	C1
Montceau-les-Mines	26	B3
Montcenis	26	B3
Mont Cenis, Col du	31	E1
Montchanin	26	B3
Montcornet	20	B2
Montcuq	29	D3
Mont-de-Marsan	28	B3
Montdidier	19	F3
Mont-Dore, le	29	E1
Monteagudo de las Vicarías	36	B4
Montealegre	35	E4
Montealegre del Castillo	45	D1

Montebello Ionico	67	E4
Montebello Vicentino	60	C1
Montebelluna	59	E4
Monte Bianco, Traforo di	27	E4
Montebourg	18	B3
Monte-Carlo-Monaco	31	E3
Montecarotto	61	E4
Montecatini-Terme	60	C3
Montecchio	61	E3
Montecchio Maggiore	60	C1
Montech	29	D3
Monte Citerna, Pso del	60	C3
Montecorvino Rovella	64	B4
Montecristo, I di	62	C2
Monte Croce Carnico, Pso di	59	E2
Monte Croce di Comelico, Pso	59	E2
Monte da Pedra	38	C3
Monte da Rocha, Bgem de	42	B2

Montedoro	68	C3
Montefalco	63	E1
Montefalcone di Val Fortore	64	B3
Montefalcone nel Sannio	64	B2
Montefeltro	61	D3
Montefiascone	63	E2
Montefiore dell' Aso	61	F4
Montefiorino	60	C3
Montefrío	43	F3
Montegallo	63	F1
Montegiorgio	61	F4
Monte Giovo, Pso di	59	D2
Montegranaro	61	F4
Montegrotto Terme	61	D1
Montehermoso	39	D2
Montejicar	44	A2
Montejo de Tiermes	36	A4
Montejunto, Sa de	38	A3
Monteleone di Spoleto	63	E1
Montélimar	30	B2
Montella	64	B4

Montellano	43	D3
Monteluco	63	E1
Montelupo Fiorentino	60	C4
Montemaggiore Belsito	68	C3
Montemagno	31	F1
Montemayor	43	F2
Montemayor de Pililla	35	E4
Montemor-o-Novo	38	B4
Montemor-o-Velho	38	B2
Montemuro, Sa do	38	C1
Montendre	28	B1
Montenegro de Cameros	36	B3
Montenero di Bisaccia	64	B2
Montenero Sabino	63	E2
Montepulciano	61	D4
Monte Real	38	B2
Montereale (Abruzzo)	63	F1
Montereale (Friuli-Venezia)	59	E3

Montereau	19	F4
Monte Redondo	38	B2
Monterenzio	61	D3
Monteriggioni	61	D4
Monteroni di Lecce	65	F4
Monte Rosa	27	F4
Monterosso al Mare	60	B3
Monterotondo	63	E2
Monterotondo Marittimo	62	C1
Monterroso	34	B2
Monterrubio de la Serena	43	E1
Monterubbiano	61	F4
Montesano sulla Marcellana	64	C4
Monte San Savino	61	D4
Monte Sant' Angelo	64	C2
Montesarchio	64	B3
Montescaglioso	65	D4
Montesilvano Marina	64	A1
Montesquieu-Volvestre	37	F1
Montesquiou	28	C4
Montet, le	26	A3

Montets, Col des	27	E4
Montevarchi	61	D4
Monteviejo, Pto de	35	E2
Montfaucon-en-Velay	30	B1
Montfaucon (Maine-et-Loire)	24	B2
Montfaucon (Meuse)	20	C3
Montfort	23	D3
Montfort-en-Chalosse	28	B4
Montfort-l'Amaury	19	E4
Montfort-sur-Risle	19	D3
Montgaillard	32	A2
Montgenèvre	31	D2
Montgenèvre, Col de	31	D2
Montgiscard	29	D4
Montgomery	9	D1
Montguyon	28	B1
Monthermé	20	C2
Monthey	27	E4
Monthois	20	C3
Monthureux	27	D1
Monti	66	B2
Montichiari	60	B1
Monticiano	61	D4
Montiel	44	B1
Montier-en-Der	20	C4
Montignac	29	D2
Montigny-le-Roi	26	C1
Montigny-sur-Aube	26	C1
Montijo (E)	39	D4
Montijo (P)	38	A4
Montilla	43	F2
Montioni	62	C1
Montivilliers	19	D3
Montjean	23	E4
Montlhéry	19	f4
Montlieu	28	B1
Montlouis	25	D2
Mont Louis	32	A3
Montluçon	25	F4
Montluel	26	C4
Montmarault	26	A4
Montmartin	18	B3
Montmédy	20	C3
Montmélian	31	D1
Montmirail (Marne)	20	A4
Montmirail (Sarthe)	23	F3
Montmirey-le-Château	26	C2
Montmoreau	28	C1
Montmorillon	25	D4
Montmort	20	B3
Montoggio	60	A3
Montoire	23	F4
Montoito	38	C4
Montone	61	D3
Montorio al Vomano	63	F1
Montoro	43	F2
Montòro, Emb de	43	F1
Montpellier	30	A4
Montpellier-le-Vieux, Chaos de	29	F3
Montpezat-de-Quercy	29	D3
Montpezat-sous-Bauzon	30	B2
Montpon-Ménestérol	28	C2
Montpont	26	C3
Montréal (Aude)	32	A2
Montréal (Gers)	28	C3
Montréal-la-Cluse	26	C4
Montredon-Labessonnie	32	B1
Montréjeau	37	E1
Montrésor	25	E2
Montresta	66	A2
Montreuil	19	E1
Montreuil-Bellay	24	C2
Montreux	27	E3
Montrevault	24	B2
Montrevel	26	C3
Montrichard	25	E2
Mont-roig del Camp	37	F4
Montrond-les-Bains	30	B1
Montrose	5	E1
Mont-St-Michel, le	18	B4
Mont-St-Vincent	26	B3
Montsalvy	29	E2
Montsant, Sa del	37	F4
Montsauche	26	B2
Montsec, Serra de	37	F3
Montseny	32	B4
Montseny, Sa de	32	B4
Montserrat	32	A4
Mont-sous-Vaudrey	26	C3
Monts-sur-Guesnes	25	D3
Montsûrs	23	E3
Montuenga	39	F1
Montuiri	45	F3
Monviso	31	E2
Monza	60	A1
Monzón	37	E3
Monzón de Campos	35	F3
Moordorf	47	E3
Moorfoot Hills	5	D2
Moosburg	56	B2
Mór	112	B4
Mora (E)	40	A3
Mora (P)	38	B4
Mora (S)	101	E4
Morača	76	B2
Morača R	76	B2
Morača klisura	76	B2
Móra d'Ebre	37	E4
Mora de Rubielos	41	E2
Moraira	45	E1
Moraira, Pta de	45	E1
Morais	34	C4
Moraïtika	82	A2
Morakovo, G.	76	B2
Móra la Nova	41	F1
Moral de Calatrava	40	A4
Moraleda de Zafayona	44	A3
Moraleja	39	D2
Moraleja de Sayago	39	E1
Morales de Rey	35	D3
Morales de Toro	35	E4
Morano Calabro	67	E2
Mora, Pto de la	44	A3
Morar, L	2	B4
Mörarp	108	C3
Morasverdes	39	D2
Morata de Jalón	36	C4
Morata de Tajuña	40	B2
Moratalla	44	C2
Morata, Pto de	36	C4
Morava	57	E1
Morava R	112	A3
Moravče	70	B2
Moravci	70	C1
Moravica	73	D4
Moravské Budějovice	57	E1
Moravske Toplice	70	C1
Moravský Krumlov	57	E1
Moray Firth	3	D3
Morbach	54	B1
Morbegno	58	B3
Morbihan	22	C3
Mörbisch	57	F3
Mörbylånga	109	E3
Morcenx	28	A3
Morciano di Romagna	61	E3
Morcone	64	B3
Morcote	58	A4
Morcuera, Pto de la	40	A1
Mordelles	23	D3
Morecambe	6	B1
Morecambe Bay	6	B1
Moreda	44	A3
Morée	25	E1
Moreleja del Vino	35	D4
Morella	41	E2
Møre og Romsdal	100	B2
Mores	66	B2
Morestel	30	C1
Moret	19	F4
Moreton	9	E2
Moretonhampstead	8	C3
Moreuil	19	F2
Morez	27	D3
Morfasso	60	B2
Mórfio	82	B2
Morgat	22	A3
Morges	27	D3
Morgex	27	E4
Morgins, Pas de	27	E4
Morhange	21	D3
Mori	58	C4
Morina	76	C2
Moritzurg	53	E2
Morjärv	98	C3
Morlaàs	37	E1
Morlaix	22	B2
Mormanno	67	E2
Mormant	19	F4
Mormoiron	30	C3
Mornant	30	B1
Mórnou, Teh L	83	E4
Morón de Almazán	36	B4
Morón de la Frontera	43	E3
Morosaglia	33	F3
Morović	72	B3
Morpeth	5	E3
Morrón	44	B3
Mörrum	109	D3
Mors	108	A2
Morsbach	17	E4
Mörsil	101	E2
Morsleben	52	C1
Mortagne	28	B1
Mortagne-au-Perche	19	D4
Mortagne-sur-Sèvre	24	C3
Mortágua	38	B2
Mortain	18	C4
Mortara	60	A2
Morteau	27	D2
Mortrée	19	D4
Morven	3	D2
Moryń	49	E3
Morzine	27	E4
Morzyczyn	49	F2
Mosbach	55	D2
Mosby	104	B4
Mošćenice	70	B3
Mošćenička Draga	70	B3
Moschendorf	57	F4
Mosel	51	E4
Moselle (Dépt)	21	D3
Moselle R	27	D4
Moshokariá	83	E3
Moshopótamos	79	E3
Mosjøen	97	E3
Moskenesøya	97	E1
Moskenstraumen	97	E1
Mosko	76	A2
Moskosel	98	B3
Moskva	111	F2
Moskva R	111	F2
Moslavačka gora	71	D2
Mosonmagyaróvár	112	A4
Mosor	75	E2
Mosqueruela	41	E2
Moss	105	D3
Mossala	107	D3
Mossat	3	D4
Mosses, Col des	27	E3
Mössingen	55	D3
Most (CS)	53	E3
Most (YU)	70	A2
Mosta	68	B4
Mostar	75	F2
Mosteiro	34	A2
Mosterhamn	104	A3
Mostiska	112	C2
Móstoles	40	A2
Mostonga	72	B2
Mostrim	12	C3
Mosty	110	C4
Mosvik	101	D1
Mota del Cuervo	40	B3
Mota del Marqués	35	E4
Motajica	71	E3
Motala	105	F4
Motala S	106	A4
Mothe-Achard, la	24	B3
Motherwell	4	C2
Mothe-St-Héray, la	24	C4
Motilla del Palancar	40	C3
Motovun	70	A3
Motril	44	A4
Motta di Livenza	59	F4
Motta S.A.	69	D3
Motta Visconti	60	A1
Motte-Chalancon, la	30	C2
Motte, la	31	D3
Mottola	65	E4
Mouchard	27	D3
Moudon	27	E3
Moúdros	85	D1
Mouhijärvi	107	D1
Mouilleron-en-Pareds	24	C3
Moulins	26	A3
Moulins-Engilbert	26	B3
Moulins-la-Marche	19	D4
Moult	18	C3
Moúnda, Akr	86	A1
Mountain Ash	8	C2
Mount Bellew	12	C3
Mountmellick	13	D4
Mountrath	12	C4
Mount's B	8	B4
Mountsoúna	88	C3
Moura	42	B1
Mourão	42	C1
Mourenx	28	B4
Mouríki	84	A4
Mourmelon-le-Grand	20	B3
Mourne	13	D2
Mourne Mts	13	E3
Mourniés	90	B3
Mourujärvi	99	E2
Mouscron	50	A3
Moustiers-Ste-Marie	31	D3
Mouthe	27	D3
Mouthier	27	D2
Mouthoumet	32	B2
Moutier	27	E2
Moutiers	31	D1
Moutiers-les-Mauxfaits	24	B3
Mouzákéi	82	C1
Mouzáki	83	D2
Mouzon	20	C2
Moville	13	D1
Moy	12	B2
Moyenneville	19	E2
Moyeuvre	21	D3
Moyuela	37	D4
Možajsk	111	F2
Mozirje	70	B1
Mozyr'	113	E1
Mrągowo	110	B4
Mrakovica	71	D3
Mramorak	73	D2
Mratinje	76	A1
Mrazovac	70	C3
Mrčajevci	73	D4
Mrežičko	77	E4
Mrkonjić Grad	71	E4
Mrkopalj	70	B3
Mrzeżyno	49	F1
Mšeno	53	F3
Msta	111	E1
Mstislavl'	111	E3
Mú	42	B2
Muć	75	D1
Muccia	61	E4
Much	17	E4
Mücheln	52	C2
Much Wenlock	9	D1
Mucientes	35	E4
Muck	2	B4
Muckle Roe	3	F1
Muckross House	14	B4
Mudanya	115	F3
Mudau	55	D1
Muddus	98	B2
Muel	37	D4
Muelas del Pan	35	D4
Muff	13	D1
Muge	38	B3
Mügeln	53	E2
Muggia	59	F4
Mugron	28	B4
Mugueimes	34	B3
Mühlbach	59	E1
Mühlberg	53	E2
Mühldorf	56	B3
Mühlen-Eichsen	48	B2
Mühlhausen	52	B2
Mühltroff	53	D3
Muhniemi	107	F2
Muhos	99	D4
Muhu	110	B2
Muineachán	13	D2
Muine Bheag	15	D3
Muirkirk	4	C3
Muir of Ord	2	C3
Mukačevo	112	C3
Mukos	77	E3
Mula	45	D2
Mülacker	54	C2
Mula, R	45	D2
Mulargia, L	66	B3
Mulhacén	44	A3
Mülheim	17	E3
Mulhouse	27	E1
Mull	4	B1
Müllheim	54	C4
Mullingar	13	D3
Mull of Galloway	4	B4
Mull of Kintyre	4	B3
Mull of Oa	4	A2
Müllrose	49	F4
Mull, Sd of	4	B1
Mullsjö	109	D1
Mulrany	12	B2
Multia	103	D3
Mumbles, The	8	C2
Muñana	39	F2
Münchberg	53	D4
Müncheberg	49	E4
München	56	A3
Münchhausen	17	F4
Münden	52	B2
Mundesley	7	F3
Mundford	11	D1
Mundo, R	44	C1
Munera	40	C4
Mungia	36	B1
Muñico	39	F2
Muniesa	37	D4
Munkebo	108	B3
Munkedal	105	D4
Munkfors	105	E3
Münnerstadt	52	B4
Muñogalindo	39	F2
Munsala	102	B2
Munsfjället	101	E1
Münsingen (CH)	27	E3
Münsingen (D)	55	D3
Munster (F)	27	E1
Münster (CH)	27	F3
Münster (Niedersachsen)	48	B3
Münster (Nordrhein-Westfalen)	17	E3
Münstertal	54	C4
Münzenberg	52	A4
Münzkirchen	56	C2
Muodoslompolo	95	D4
Muojärvi	99	F2
Muonio	95	D4
Muonioälven	95	D4
Muotkatonturit	95	E2
Mur	57	E4
Mura	70	C1
Muraglione, Pso del	61	D3
Murano	61	D1
Murat	29	E2
Murato	33	F3
Murat-sur-Vèbre	32	B1
Murau	57	D4
Muravera	66	C4
Murca	34	B4
Murchante	36	C3
Murcia	45	D2
Murcia (Reg)	44	C2
Mur-de-Barrez	29	E2
Mur-de-Bretagne	22	C3
Mureck	57	E4
Mure, la	30	C2
Mureş	112	C4
Muret	29	D4
Murg	54	C2
Murguía	36	B1
Muri	27	F2
Murias de Paredes	35	D2
Murino	76	C2
Muriqan	76	B3
Müritz See	49	D3
Murjek	98	B2
Murnau	56	A4
Muro	33	F4
Muro de Alcoy	45	E1
Murol	29	E1
Murole	102	C3
Muro Lucano	64	C4
Muros	34	A2
Mürren	27	F3
Murrhardt	55	D2
Murska Sobota	70	C1
Mursko Središče	70	C1
Murten	27	E3
Murter	74	C1
Murter I	74	C1
Murtosa	38	B1
Murtovaara	99	F3
Murvica	74	C1
Murviel	30	A4
Mürz	57	E3
Mürzsteg	57	E3
Mürzzuschlag	57	E3
Musala	115	D3
Mussalo	103	F4
Musselburgh	5	D2
Musselkanaal	17	E1
Mussidan	28	C2
Mussomeli	68	C3
Mussy	26	B1
Mustair	58	C3
Mustasaari	102	B2
Mustèr	58	A3
Mustion as	107	E3
Mustvee	110	C1
Muta	70	B1
Mutala	102	C3
Mutterstadt	54	C1
Mutzschen	53	E2
Muurame	103	D3
Muurasjärvi	103	D1
Muuratjärvi	103	D3
Muurla	107	E2
Muurola	99	D2
Muuruvesi	103	E2
Muxía	34	A1
Muy, le	31	D4
Muzillac	22	C4
Muzzana del Turgnano	59	F3
Mweelrea Mts.	12	B3
Myckegensjö	101	F2
Mykines	96	A3
Myllykoski	107	F2
Myllykylä	102	C3
Myllymäki	102	C2
Mynämäki	107	D2
Mýrdalsjökull	96	B3
Myre	94	A3
Myrlandshaugen	94	B3
Myrskylä	107	F2
Myrviken	101	E2
Mysen	105	D3
Mysingen	106	B4
Mýsla	49	F3
Myślibórskie, Jez	49	F3
Myślibórz	49	F3
Mývatn	96	B1
Mže	53	E4

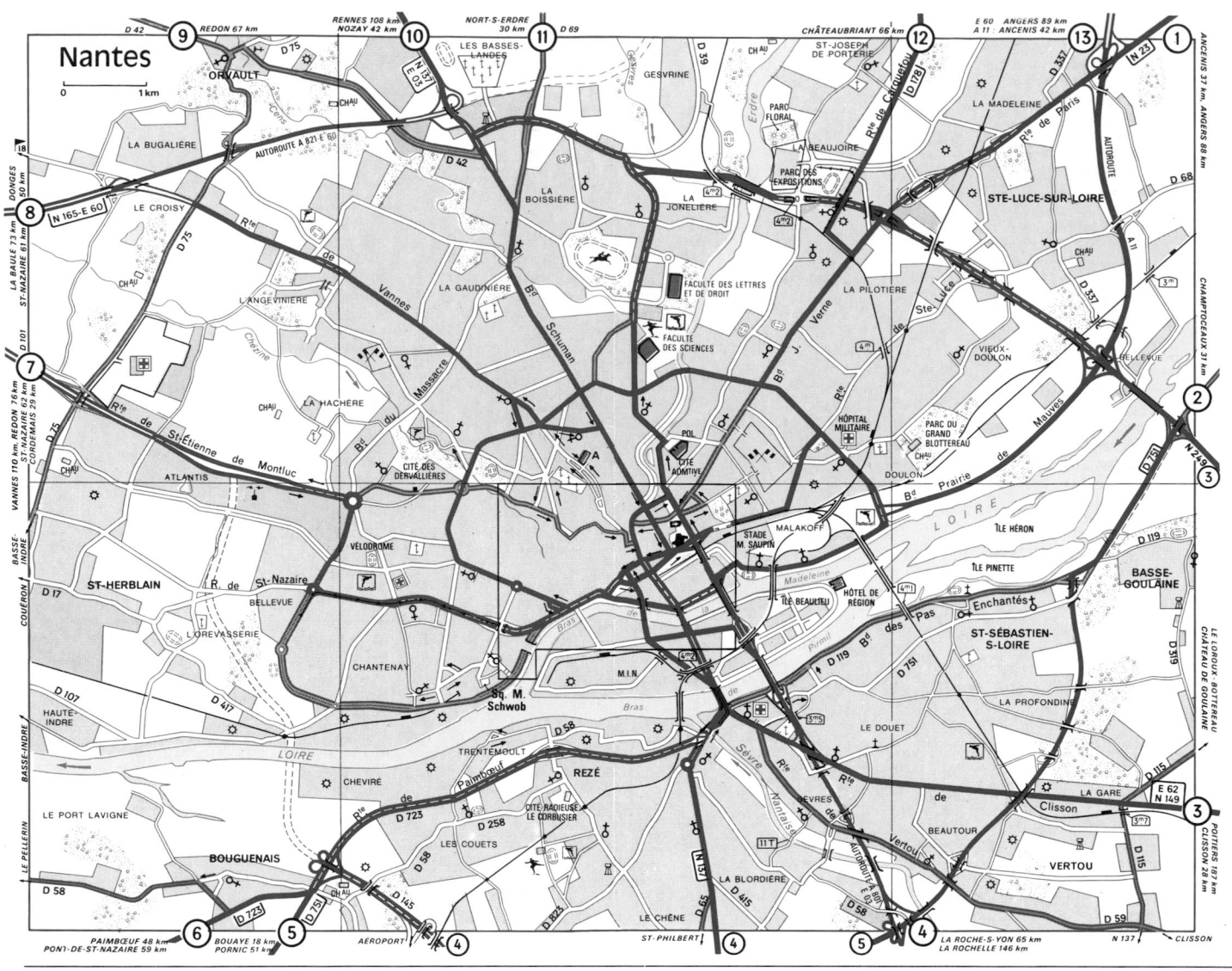

Nantes

N

Naab	55 F1	Nakskov	108 B4	Narcea, R	35 D1	Naustdal	100 A3	Navasfrías	39 D2	Néa Mihaniona	79 F3	Nedelišče	70 C1
		Näljänkä	99 E3	Nardò	65 F4	Nauvo	107 D3	Navatalgordo	39 F2	Néa Moní	85 E4	Nedervetil	102 C1
Naamijoki	98 C2	Na Logu	70 A2	Narew	112 C1	Nava	35 E1	Nave	60 B1	Néa Moudaniá	80 A4	Nedstrand	104 A3
Naantali	107 D3	Nalón, R	35 E2	Narila	103 E3	Nava, Colle di	31 F3	Nävekvarn	106 A4	Néa Péla	79 F3	Neede	17 D2
Naarajärvi	103 E3	Naltijärvi	95 D3	Narkaus	99 D2	Navacelles, Cirque		Navelli	63 F2	Néa Péramos (Stereá-		Needles, The	9 E3
Naarva	103 F2	Namdalseid	97 D4	Narni	63 E4	de	29 F3	Naver, L	2 C1	Eláda)	87 E1	Neermoor	47 E3
Naas	13 D4	Nämdöfjärden	106 B4	Naro	68 C4	Navacepeda	39 E2	Naveros	43 D4	Néa Péramos		Nefyn	6 A3
Näätämöjoki	95 F2	Náměšt	57 E1	Naro-Fominsk	111 F2	Navacerrada	40 A2	Navia	34 C1	(Makedonía)	80 C2	Negoiu	113 D4
Nabburg	56 B1	Namsen	97 D4	Nærøy	97 D4	Navacerrada, Pto		Navia de Suarna	34 C2	Neápoli (Kríti)	91 E4	Negorci	77 F3
Načeradec	57 D1	Namsos	97 D4	Närpes	102 B3	de	40 A1	Navia, R	34 C1	Neápoli		Negotin	73 F3
Náchod	112 A2	Namsskogan	97 D4	Närpio	102 B3	Navachica	44 A3	Navl'a	111 F4	(Makedonía)	79 D3	Negotino	77 E3
Naddvik	104 B1	Namur	50 C4	Narta	71 D2	Navaconcejo	39 E2	Náxos	88 C3	Neápoli		Negra de Urbión,
Nadela	34 B2	Namur (Prov)	50 C4	Nartháki	83 E2	Nava de la		Náxos Dias	88 C3	(Pelopónissos)	87 E4	L	36 B3
Nädlac	114 C1	Nancy	21 D4	Nartháki, Óros	83 E2	Asunción	40 A1	Náxos, N	88 C3	Néa Róda	80 B3	Negrar	60 C1
Nadur	68 B4	Nangis	19 F4	Narva	111 D1	Nava del Rey	35 E4	Nay	37 E1	Néa Sánda		Negratin, Emb del	44 B2
Nadvornaja	113 D3	Nannestad	105 D2	Narvik	94 B3	Navafria, Pto de	40 A1	Nazaré	38 A3	(Makedonía)	79 F2	Negreira	34 A2
Näfels	58 A2	Nant	29 F3	Nås	105 E2	Navahermosa	39 F3	Naze, The	11 D2	Néa Sánda		Nègrepelisse	29 D3
Nafpaktías, Óri	83 D4	Nanterre	19 F4	Näsåker	101 F2	Navalcán	39 F2	Nazilli	115 F4	(Thráki)	81 E2	Negru Vodă	115 E2
Nafpaktos	83 D4	Nantes	24 B2	Năsăud	113 D4	Navalcarnero	40 A2	Ndrejaj	76 C2	Néa Silata	80 A3	Neheim-Hüsten	17 F3
Náfplio	87 D2	Nantes, Canal		Nasbinals	29 F2	Navaleno	36 B3	Ndroq	76 C4	Néa Skióni	80 B4	Neiden	95 F2
Naggen	101 F3	de	22 C3	Naßfeld-Paß	59 F2	Navalmanzano	40 A1	Nea	101 D2	Néa Stira	84 B4	Neige, Crêt de la	27 D3
Nagold	54 C3	Nanteuil-le-		Našice	71 E2	Navalmoral de la		Néa Agathoúpoli	79 F3	Néa Tríglia	80 A4	Neila	36 B3
Nagu	107 D3	Haudouin	19 F3	Näsijärvi	102 C3	Mata	39 E3	Néa		Neath	8 C2	Neiße	53 F1
Nagyatád	114 A1	Nantiat	25 E4	Naso	69 D2	Navalperal de		Alikarnassés	91 D3	Néa Víssa	81 F1	Nejdek	53 E3
Nagykálló	112 C3	Nantua	26 C4	Nassau	51 F4	Pinares	40 A2	Néa Anhíalos	83 E2	Néa Zoí	79 E2	Nekromandío
Nagykanizsa	114 A1	Nantwich	6 C3	Nassereith	58 C2	Navaluenga	39 F2	Néa Artáki	84 B4	Néa Zíhni	80 B2	Efíras	82 B2
Nagykörös	112 B4	Nao, C de la	45 F1	Nässjö	109 D1	Navalvillar de Pela	39 E4	Néa Éfessos	79 F4	Nebel	47 F1	Neksø	109 D4
Nahe	48 A2	Náoussa (Kikládes)	88 C3	Nastola	107 F2	Navamorcuende	39 F2	Néa Epídavros	87 E2	Nebelhorn	55 E4	Nela, R	36 A1
Nahe R	54 B1	Náoussa		Næstved	108 C4	Navan	13 D3	Néa Fókeada	80 A4	Nebljusi	70 C4	Nelas	38 C1
Naila	53 D4	(Makedonía)	79 E3	Natalinci	73 D3	Navarra	36 C2	Neagh, L	13 E2	Nebra	52 C2	Nelidovo	111 E2
Napapiiri	99 D2	Nattaset	95 F3	Navarredonda de la		Néa Hili	81 E2	Nechranická		Nellim	95 F3
Nailloux	32 A1	Napoli	64 B4	Nattavaara	98 B2	Sierra	39 F2	Néa Iraklítsa	80 C2	přehr nádrž	53 E3	Nelson	6 C2
Nailsworth	9 D2	Napoli, G di	64 A4	Nättraby	109 E3	Navarrenx	28 B4	Néa Kalikrátia	79 F4	Neckar	55 D1	Neman	110 B3
Nairn	3 D3	Napoule, la	31 E4	Naucelle	29 E3	Navarrés	41 E4	Néa Kariá	81 D2	Neckarelz	55 D1	Neméa	87 D1
Najac	29 D3	Narberth	8 B2	Nauders	58 C2	Navarrete	36 B2	Néa Karváli	80 C2	Neckargemünd	54 C1	Nemirov	113 E3
Nájera	36 B2	Nærbø	104 A4	Nauen	49 D4	Navascués	37 D2	Néa Kerassoús	82 C2	Neckarsteinach	54 C1	Nemours	25 F1
Najerilla, R	36 B2	Narbolia	66 B3	Naul	13 D3	Navas del		Néa Kíos	87 D2	Neckarsulm	55 D2	Nemunas	110 C3
Nakkila	107 D1	Narbonne	32 B1	Naumburg	52 C2	Madroño	39 D3	Néa Koróni	86 C3	Nečujam	75 D2	Nenagh	12 C4
Nakło	112 A1	Narbonne-Plage	30 A4	Naunhof	53 D2	Navas de Oro	40 A1	Néa Mákri	88 A1	Neda	34 B1	Nene	10 C1
Nakovo	72 C1	Narcao	66 B4	Naussac, Bge de	29 F2	Navas de San Juan	44 B2	Néa Messángala	83 F1	Nédas	86 C2	Nénita	85 F4

Nenzing	58 B2		Nesle	19 F2
Neohoráki	84 A4		Nesoddtangen	105 D3
Neohóri (Etolía-			Nesseby	95 F1
Akarnanía)	82 C4		Nesselwang	55 E4
Neohóri (Évia)	84 B4		Ness, L	2 C3
Neohóri			Nestáni	87 D2
(Fthiótida)	83 E3		Nesterov	112 C2
Neohóri (Ípiros)	82 C2		Nestório	78 C3
Neohóri			Néstos	81 D2
(Kardítsa)	83 D2		Nesvik	104 A3
Neohóri			Nesviž	111 D4
(Magnissía)	84 A2		Neto	67 F3
Neohóri			Netolice	56 C1
(Pelopónissos)	86 C2		Netretić	70 C3
Neohóri (Thráki)	81 F1		Nettetal	17 D4
Neohóri			Nettuno	63 E3
(Trikala)	83 D1		Neuastenberg	17 F4
Néo Monastíri	83 E2		Neubeckum	17 F3
Néon Petrítsi	80 A2		Neubourg, le	19 D3
Néos Marmarás	80 B4		Neubrandenburg	49 D2
Néos Skopós	80 B2		Neubukow	48 C2
Néouvielle, Pic de	37 E2		Neuburg	55 F2
Nephin	12 B2		Neuchâtel	27 E2
Nephin Beg			Neu Darchau	48 B3
Range	12 B2		Neuenburg	47 E3
Nepomuk	56 C1		Neuenbürg	54 C2
Nera	63 E1		Neuendorf	49 D1
Nérac	28 C3		Neuenhaus	17 E2
Neráïda			Neuenkirchen	48 A3
(Amárandóos)	83 D2		Neuenstadt	55 D2
Neráïda (Neohóri)	83 D2		Neuerburg	54 A1
Neratovice	53 F3		Neufahrn	56 B2

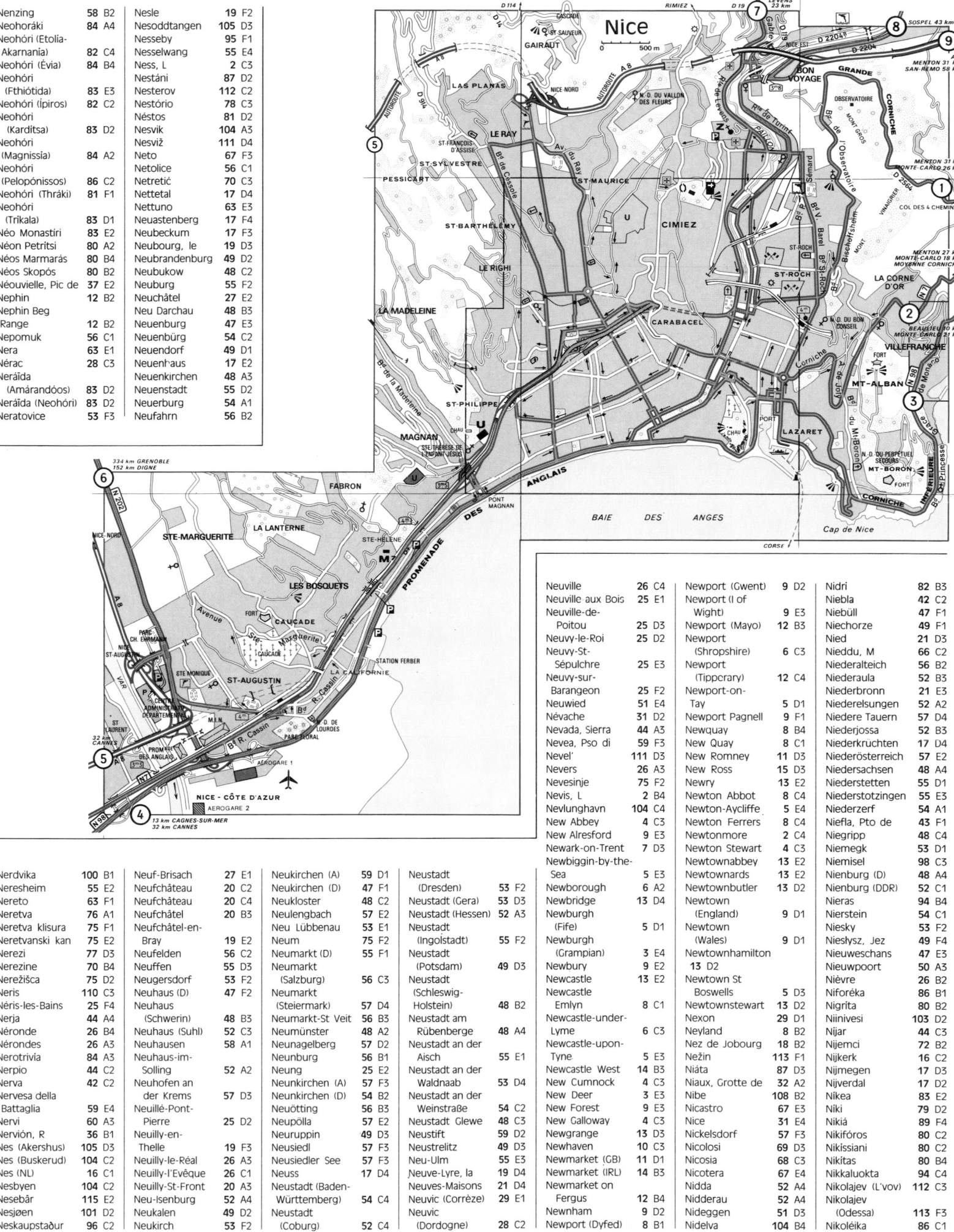

Nerdvika	100 B1	Neuf-Brisach	27 E1	Neukirchen (A)	59 D1	Neustadt		Neuville	26 C4	Newport (Gwent)	9 D2	Nidri	82 B3

Neustadt (Dresden) 53 F2

Nerdvika	100 B1	Neuf-Brisach	27 E1	Neukirchen (A)	59 D1	Neustadt (Dresden)	53 F2	Neuville	26 C4	Newport (Gwent)	9 D2	Nidri	82 B3
Neresheim	55 E2	Neufchâteau	20 C2	Neukirchen (D)	47 F1	Neustadt (Gera)	53 D3	Neuville aux Bois	25 E1	Newport (I of Wight)	9 E3	Niebla	42 C2
Nereto	63 F1	Neufchâteau	20 C4	Neukloster	48 C2	Neustadt (Hessen)	52 A3	Neuville-de-Poitou	25 D3	Newport (Mayo)	12 B3	Niebüll	47 F1
Neretva	76 A1	Neufchâtel	20 B3	Neulengbach	57 E2	Neustadt (Ingolstadt)	55 F2	Neuvy-le-Roi	25 D2	Newport (Shropshire)	6 C3	Niechorze	49 F1
Neretva klisura	75 F1	Neufchâtel-en-Bray	19 E2	Neu Lübbenau	53 E1	Neustadt (Potsdam)	49 D3	Neuvy-St-Sépulchre	25 E3	Newport (Tipperary)	12 C4	Nied	21 D3
Neretvanski kan	75 E2	Neufelden	56 C2	Neum	75 F2	Neustadt (Schleswig-Holstein)	48 B2	Neuvy-sur-Barangeon	25 F2	Newport-on-Tay	5 D1	Nieddu, M	66 C2
Nerezi	77 D3	Neuffen	55 D3	Neumarkt (D)	55 F1	Neustadt am Rübenberge	48 A4	Neuwied	51 E4	Newport Pagnell	9 F1	Niederalteich	56 B2
Nerezine	70 B4	Neugersdorf	53 F2	Neumarkt (Salzburg)	56 C3	Neustadt an der Aisch	55 E1	Névache	31 D2	Newquay	8 B4	Niederaula	52 B3
Nerežišca	75 D2	Neuhaus (D)	47 F2	Neumarkt (Steiermark)	57 D4	Neustadt an der Waldnaab	53 D4	Nevada, Sierra	44 A3	New Quay	8 C1	Niederbronn	21 E3
Neris	110 C3	Neuhaus (Schwerin)	48 B3	Neumarkt-St Veit	56 B3	Neustadt an der Weinstraße	54 C2	Nevea, Pso di	59 F3	New Romney	11 D3	Niederelsungen	52 A2
Néris-les-Bains	25 F4	Neuhaus (Suhl)	52 C3	Neumünster	48 A2	Neustadt Glewe	48 C3	Nevel'	111 D3	New Ross	15 D3	Niedere Tauern	57 D4
Nerja	44 A4	Neuhausen	58 A1	Neunagelberg	57 D2	Neustift	59 D2	Nevers	26 A3	Newry	13 E2	Niederjossa	52 B3
Néronde	26 B4	Neuhaus-im-Solling	52 A2	Neunburg	56 B1	Neustrelitz	49 D2	Nevesinje	75 F2	Newton Abbot	8 C4	Niederkrüchten	17 D4
Nérondes	26 A3	Neuhofen an der Krems	57 D3	Neung	25 E2	Neu-Ulm	55 E3	Nevis, L	2 B4	Newton-Aycliffe	5 E4	Niederösterreich	57 E2
Nerotrivía	84 A3	Neuillé-Pont-Pierre	25 D2	Neunkirchen (A)	57 F3	Neuve-Lyre, la	19 D4	Nevlunghavn	104 C4	Newton Ferrers	8 C4	Niedersachsen	48 A4
Nerpio	44 C2	Neuilly-en-Thelle	19 F3	Neunkirchen (D)	54 B2	Neuves-Maisons	21 D4	New Abbey	4 C3	Newtonmore	2 C4	Niederstetten	55 D1
Nerva	42 C2	Neuilly-le-Réal	26 A3	Neuötting	56 B3	Neuvic (Corrèze)	29 E1	New Alresford	9 E3	Newton Stewart	4 C3	Niederstotzingen	55 E3
Nervesa della Battaglia	59 E4	Neuilly-l'Evêque	26 C1	Neupölla	57 D2	Neuvic (Dordogne)	28 C2	Newark-on-Trent	7 D3	Newtownabbey	13 E2	Niederzerf	54 A1
Nervi	60 A3	Neuilly-St-Front	20 A3	Neuruppin	49 D3			Newbiggin-by-the-Sea	5 E3	Newtownards	13 E2	Niefla, Pto de	43 F1
Nervión, R	36 B1	Neu-Isenburg	52 A4	Neusiedl	57 F3			Newborough	6 A2	Newtownbutler	13 D2	Niegripp	48 C4
Nes (Akershus)	105 D3	Neukalen	49 D2	Neusiedler See	57 F3			Newbridge	13 D4	Newtown (England)	9 D1	Niemegk	53 D1
Nes (Buskerud)	104 C2	Neukirch	53 F2	Neuss	17 D4			Newburgh (Fife)	5 D1	Newtown (Wales)	9 D1	Niemisel	98 C3
Nes (NL)	16 C1			Neustadt (Baden-Württemberg)	54 C4			Newburgh (Grampian)	3 E4	Newtownhamilton	13 D2	Nienburg (D)	48 A4
Nesbyen	104 C2			Neustadt (Coburg)	52 C4			Newbury	9 E2	Newtown St Boswells	5 D3	Nienburg (DDR)	52 B3
Nesebár	115 E2							Newcastle	13 E2	Newtownstewart	13 D2	Nieras	94 B4
Nesjøen	101 D2							Newcastle Emlyn	8 C1	Nexon	29 D1	Nierstein	54 C1
Neskaupstaður	96 C2							Newcastle-under-Lyme	6 C3	Neyland	8 B2	Niesky	53 F2
								Newcastle-upon-Tyne	5 E3	Nez de Jobourg	18 B2	Niesłysz, Jez	49 F4
								Newcastle West	14 B3	Nežin	113 F1	Nieuweschans	47 E3
								New Cumnock	4 B3	Niáta	87 D3	Nieuwpoort	50 A3
								New Deer	3 E3	Niaux, Grotte de	32 A2	Nièvre	26 B2
								New Forest	9 E3	Nibe	108 B2	Niforéka	86 B1
								New Galloway	4 C3	Nicastro	67 E3	Nigrita	80 B2
								Newgrange	13 D3	Nice	31 E1	Niinivesi	103 D2
								Newhaven	10 C3	Nickelsdorf	57 F3	Nijar	44 C3
								Newmarket (GB)	11 D1	Nicolosi	69 D3	Nijemci	72 B2
								Newmarket (IRL)	14 B3	Nicosia	68 C3	Nijkerk	16 C2
								Newmarket on Fergus	12 B4	Nicotera	67 E4	Nijmegen	17 D3
								Newnham	9 D2	Nidda	52 A4	Nijverdal	17 D2
								Newport (Dyfed)	8 B1	Nidderau	52 A4	Níkea	83 E2
										Nideggen	51 D3	Niki	79 D2
										Nidelva	104 B4	Nikiá	89 F4

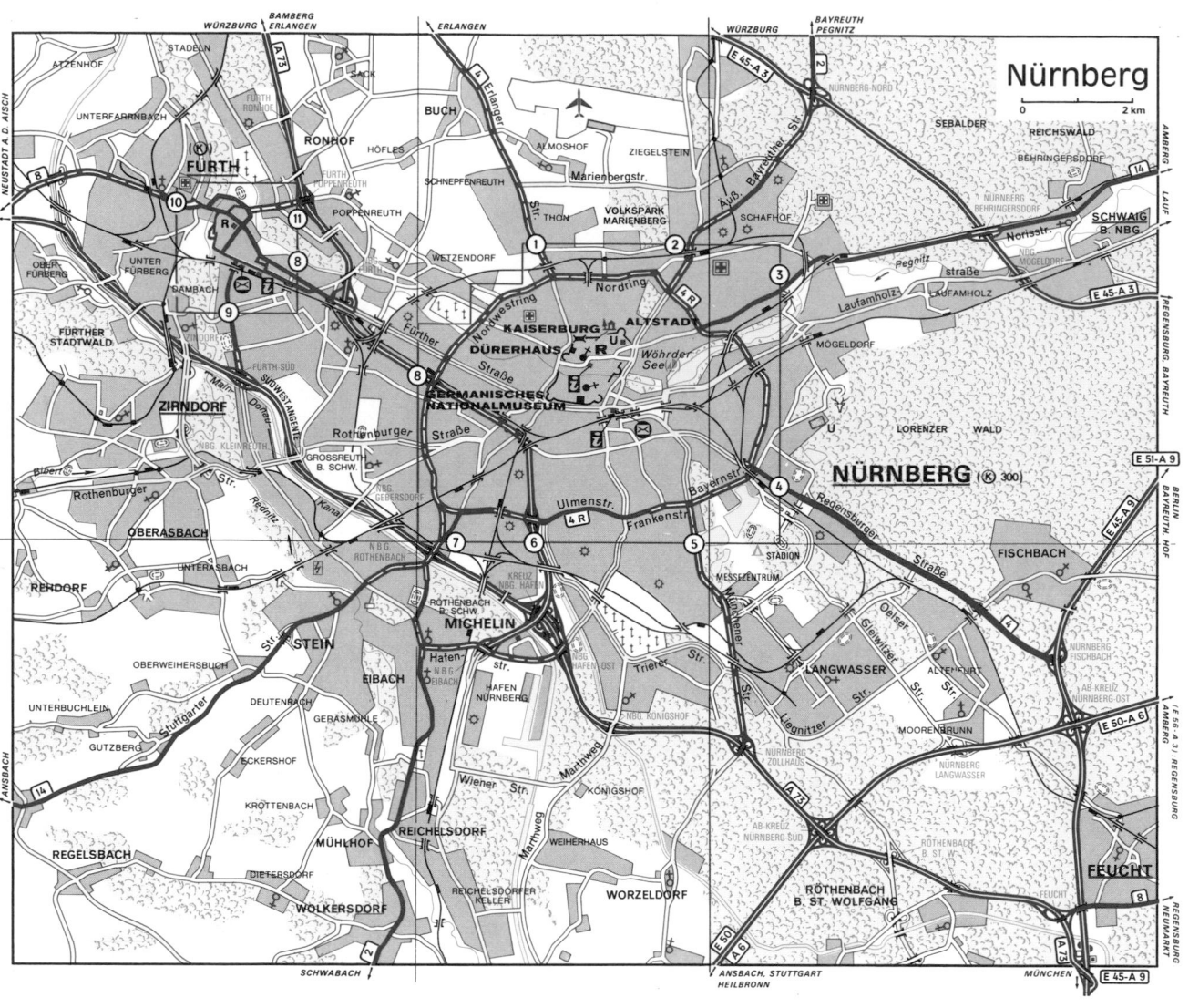

Nürnberg

0   2 km

Novales	37	D3
Nova Levante	59	D3
Novalja	70	B4
Nova Pazova	72	C2
Novara	60	A1
Novara di Sicilia	69	D2
Nova Siri	65	D4
Nova Topola	71	E3
Nova Vas	70	B2
Nova Vavos	76	B1
Nova Zagora	115	E2
Novelda	45	D1
Novellara	60	C2
Nove Mesto nad		
Váhom	112	A3
Noventa		
Vicentino	61	D1
Noves	30	C3
Nové Zámky	112	B4
Novgorod	111	D1
Novgorod-		
Severskij	111	F4
Novi Bečej	72	C2
Novi di Modena	60	C2
Novi Dojran	77	F3
Novigrad (Poreč)	70	A3
Novigrad (Zadar)	74	C1
Novi Grad	71	F3
Novigrad		
Podravski	71	D2
Novigradsko		
more	74	C1
Novi Karlovci	72	C2
Novi Kneževac	72	C1
Novi Ligure	60	A2
Novi Marof	70	C1
Novion-Porcien	20	B2
Novi Pazar	76	C1
Novi Pazar	115	E2
Novi Sad	72	C2
Novi Šeher	71	F4
Novi Senkovac	71	E2
Novi Slankamen	72	C2
Novi Travnik	71	E4
Novi Vinodolski	70	B3
Novo Brdo	77	D2
Novograd-		
Volynskij	113	D2
Novogrudok	111	D4
Novo Hopovo	72	C2
Novo Mesto	70	B2
Novo Mi loševo	72	C1
Novomirgorod	113	F2
Novoržev	111	D2
Novoselica	113	D3
Novo Selo (Bosna i		
Hercegovina)	71	E3
Novo Selo		
(Makedonija)	77	F3
Novoukrainka	113	F2
Novovolynsk	112	C2
Novo Zvečevo	71	E2
Novozybkov	111	E4
Novska	71	D3
Nový Bor	53	F3
Novyj Bug	113	F3
Nový Jičín	112	B3
Nowa Sól	112	A2
Nowe Warpno	49	E2
Nowogard	49	F2
Nowy Sącz	112	B3
Nowy Targ	112	B3
Noyant	23	F4
Noyers	26	B1
Noyers-sur-		
Jabron	30	C3
Noyon	19	F3
Nozay	23	D4
Nuasjärvi	99	E4
Nueva	35	E1
Nueva Carteya	43	F2
Nuévalos Monasterio		
de Piedra	36	C4
Nuevo Baztán	40	B2
Nufenenpass	58	A3
Nuhppir	95	E2
Nuijamaa	103	F4
Nuits-St-Georges	26	C2
Nules	41	E3
Nulvi	66	B2
Numana	61	F4
Numancia	36	B3
Numedal	104	C2
Nummela	107	E2

Nikopol	115	D2	Niwica	53	F1	Nomeny	21	D3	Nordhorn	17	E2	Norrby	98	A4	North York Moors		
Nikópoli	82	B3	Nizke Beskydy	112	C3	Nomexy	21	D4	Nordingrå	102	A2	Nørre Åby	108	B3	Nat Pk	7	D1
Nikopólis, Órmos	82	B2	Nizza Monferrato	31	F2	Nómia	87	E4	Nordkapp	95	E1	Nørre Alslev	108	C4	North Yorkshire	6	C1
Nikšić	76	B2	Njegoš	76	A2	Nonancourt	19	E4	Nordkinnhalvøya	95	E1	Nørre Nebel	108	A3	Norton	7	D1
Nilakka	103	D2	Njivice	70	B3	Nonant-le-Pin	19	D4	Nordkjosbotn	94	C3	Nørre Snede	108	A3	Nortort	48	A2
Nilivaara	98	B2	Njunis	94	C3	Nonaspe	37	E4	Nordkvaløy	94	B2	Nørre Vorupør	108	A2	Norwich	11	D1
Nilsiä	103	D3	Njupeskär	101	D3	None	31	E2	Nordland	97	E4	Nord-Lenangen	94	C2	Nosovka	113	E1
Nîmes	30	B3	Noailles	19	F3	Nonio	58	A4	Nord-Lenangen	94	C2	Norrfjärden	101	F3	Nossebro	108	C1
Nimféa	81	E2	Noáin	36	C2	Nontron	28	C1	Nordli	97	E4	Norrköping	106	A4	Nossen	53	E2
Nimféo	79	D3	Noarvaš	95	D3	Nónza	33	F2	Nördlingen	55	E2	Norrnäs	102	B3	Noss Head	3	D2
Nímos, N	93	E1	Noblejas	40	B3	Noord-Brabant	16	C3	Nordmaling	102	A2	Norrsunda	106	B2	Noteć	112	A1
Nin	74	C1	Nocera	64	B4	Noord-			Nordmark	105	E3	Norrsundet	106	B2	Nótia	79	E2
Ninove	50	B3	Nocera Tirinese	67	E3	Holland	16	C2	Nord-Ostsee-			Norrtälje	106	B3	Nótia Píndos	82	C1
Niort	24	C4	Nocera Umbra	61	E4	Noord-Oost-			Kanal	47	F2	Norrviken	108	C3	Nótios Evoikós		
Nipfjället	101	D3	Noceto	60	C2	Polder	16	C2	Nordøyane	100	A2	Norsjö	98	B4	Kólpos	84	B4
Nípsa	81	F2	Noci	65	E3	Noordwijk aan Zee	16	B2	Nordøyar	96	A3	Norsjø	104	C3	Nótio Stenó		
Niš	77	E1	Nodeland	104	B4	Noordzee	46	B3	Nordrana	97	E2	Norskehavet	96	B4	Kerkíras	82	B2
Nisa	38	C3	Nogara	60	C1	Noormarkku	102	B3	Nordreisa	94	C2	Nort	23	D4	Noto	69	D4
Nisa, Rib de	38	C3	Nogaro	28	B4	Nora	105	F3	Nordrhein-			Nörten-			Notodden	104	C3
Nišava	73	F4	Nogent	26	C1	Norberg	105	F3	Westfalen	17	E3	Hardenberg	52	B2	Notre-Dame-de-		
Niscemi	68	C4	Nogent-le-Roi	19	E4	Norcia	63	F1	Nordsee	47	B2	Northallerton	7	D1	Bellecombe	27	E4
Niška Banja	77	E1	Nogent-le-Rotrou	23	F3	Nord	20	A1	Nordseter	105	D2	Northam	8	C3	Nottingham	7	D3
Nissáki	82	A1	Nogent-sur-Seine	20	A4	Nord Beveland	16	B3	Nordstrand	47	F1	Northampton	9	F1	Nottinghamshire	7	D3
Nissan	109	D2	Nogueira de			Nordborg	108	A4	Nord Trøndelag	101	D1	Northamptonshire	9	F1	Nouan-le-Fuzelier	25	E2
Nisser	104	B3	Ramuin	34	B2	Nordby (Fanø)	108	A3	Norðurfjörður	96	A1	North Berwick	5	D2	Nousiainen	107	D2
Nissilä	103	D1	Nogueira, Sa de	34	C4	Nordby (Samsø)	108	B3	Nore (IRL)	12	C4	North Chan	13	E1	Nouvion	19	E2
Nissiros, N	89	F4	Noguera	41	D2	Norddeich	47	E3	Nore (N)	104	C2	North Downs	10	C3	Nouvion-en-		
Nissum Bredning	108	A2	Noguera Pallaresa,			Nordeide	100	A3	Norefjell	104	C2	Northeim	52	B2	Thiérache, le	20	B2
Nissum Fjord	108	A2	R	37	F2	Norden	47	E3	Nore, R	15	D3	Northern Ireland	13	D2	Nœux	19	F1
Nith	4	C3	Noguera			Nordenau	17	F4	Noresund	104	C2	North Esk	3	D4	Nouzonville	20	C2
Niton	9	E4	Ribagorçana, R	37	F3	Nordenham	47	F3	Norfolk	7	F3	North Foreland	11	D2	Nova Breznica	77	D3
Nitra	112	B3	Nohfelden	54	B1	Norderney	47	E3	Norg	17	D1	Northleach	9	E2	Nová Bystřice	57	D1
Nitry	26	B2	Noia	34	A2	Norderstedt	48	A2	Norheimsund	104	A2	North Ronaldsay	3	E1	Novaci		
Nittedal	105	D3	Noirétable	26	B4	Nordfjord	100	A3	Norra Bergnäs	98	A3	North Sound, The	3	E1	(Makedonija)	77	E4
Nittenau	56	B1	Noirmoutier	24	A3	Nordfjordeid	100	A3	Norra Gloppet	102	B2	North Tyne	5	F3	Novaci (Srbija)	72	C3
Nittendorf	55	F2	Noirmoutier, I de	24	A3	Nordfold	97	E1	Norråker	101	F1	North Uist	2	A3	Nova Crnja	72	C1
Nivala	102	C1	Noja	36	A1	Nordfolda	97	E1	Norra Kvarken	102	B2	Northumberland	5	E3	Novafeltria	61	E3
Nive	28	A4	Nokia	107	E1	Nordfriesische			Norra Kvill	109	E1	Northumberland			Nova Gorica (I)	59	F3
Nivelles	50	B3	Nola	64	B4	Inseln	47	E1	Norra Råda	105	E3	Nat Pk	5	E3	Nova Gorica (YU)	70	A2
Nivernais	26	B3	Nolay	26	B3	Nordhalben	52	C3	Norra Storfjället	97	E3	North Walsham	7	F3	Nova Gradiška	71	E3
Nivolet, Colle del	31	E1	Noli	60	A3	Nordhausen	52	C2	Norrbottens Län	98	B1	Northwich	6	C2	Nova Kasaba	72	B4

Nummi 107 E2
Nuneaton 9 E1
Nunnanen 95 D3
Nuñomoral 39 D2
Nunspeet 17 D2
Nuorajärvi 103 F2
Nuorgam 95 E2
Nuoro 66 B2
Nurallao 66 B3
Nürburg 51 E4
Núria 32 B3
Nurmes 103 E1
Nurmijärvi (Pohjois-Karjalan Lääni) 103 F1
Nurmijärvi (Uudenmaan Lääni) 107 E2
Nurmo 102 C2
Nürnberg 55 F1
Nürtingen 55 D3
Nus 27 E4
Nusse 48 B2
Nuštar 71 F2
Nuthe 49 D4
Nuttlar 17 F3
Nuttupera 103 D1
Nuutajärvi 107 E2
Nuvvos-Ailigas 95 E2
Nyåker 102 A1
Nybergsund 105 E2
Nyborg 108 B4
Nybro 109 E2
Nyírbátor 112 C3
Nyíregyháza 112 C3
Nykarleby 102 B2
Nykøbing F (Storstrøm) 108 C4
Nykøbing M (Viborg) 108 A2
Nykøbing S (Vestsjælland) 108 C3
Nyköping 106 B4
Nykvarn 106 B4
Nynäshamn 106 B4
Nyon 27 D3
Nyons 30 C3
Nýřany 53 E4
Nýrdalur 96 B2
Nýrsko 56 B1
Nyrud 95 F2
Nysa 112 A2
Nysa Łużycka 53 F1
Nysäter 105 E3
Nyseter 100 B3
Nysted 108 C4
Nyvoll 95 D2

O

Oadby 9 F1
Oakham 9 F1
Oanes 104 A3
Óassi 87 D1
Oban 4 B1
O Barco 34 C3
Obbola 102 B1
Obdach 57 D4
Obdacher Sattel 57 D4
Obedska bara 72 C3
Obejo 43 F2
Oberalppass 58 A3
Oberammergau 55 F4
Oberau 56 A4
Oberaudorf 56 B4
Oberdrauburg 59 E2
Oberessfeld 52 C4
Obergeis 52 B3
Obergrafendorf 57 E2
Obergrünzburg 55 E4
Obergurgl 58 C2
Oberhaslach 21 E4
Oberhausen 17 E3
Oberhof 52 C3
OberjochPaß 58 C1
Oberkirch 54 C3
Oberkirchen 17 F4
Oberkochen 55 E2
Obermarchtal 55 D3
Obernai 21 E4
Obernberg 56 C3
Obernburg 55 D1
Oberndorf (A) 56 C3
Oberndorf (D) 54 C3
Obernzell 56 C2
Oberölsbach 55 F1
Oberösterreich 56 C2
Oberprechtal 54 C3
Oberpullendorf 57 F3
Oberseebach 21 F3
Obersontheim 55 E2
Oberstaufen 55 E4
Oberstdorf 55 E4
Oberstein 54 B1
Obertauern 59 F1
Obertraun 59 F1
Oberursel 51 F4
Obervellach 59 E2
Oberviechtach 56 B1
Oberwart 57 F4
Oberwesel 51 E4
Oberwiesenthal 53 E3
Oberwölz 57 D4
Oberzeiring 57 D4
Óbidos 38 A3
Obilić 77 D2
Obing 56 B3
Obiou, l' 30 C2
Objat 29 D1
Obninsk 111 F3
O Bolo 34 C3
Obón 41 E1
Oborniki 112 A1
Obornjača 72 C1
Oborovo 70 C2
Obrenovac 72 C3
Obrež 72 C3
Obrov 70 A3
Obrovac (Split) 75 D1
Obrovac (Zadar) 74 C1
Obršani 77 E4
Obsteig 58 C2
Obudovac 71 F3
Obzor 115 E2
Obzova 70 B3
Očakov 113 F3
Oca, Mtes de 36 A2
Ocaña 40 B3
Oca, R 36 A2
Očauš 71 E4
Occhiobello 61 D2
Occhito, L di 64 B3
Očevlje 71 F4
Ochagavia 37 D2
Ochil Hills 5 D1
Ochsenfurt 55 E1
Ochsenhausen 55 E3
Ochtrup 17 E2
Ockelbo 106 A2
Öckerö 108 C1
Ocreza, R 38 C3
Ocrkavlje 76 A1
Ödåkra 108 C3
Odda 104 B2
Odden Færgehavn 108 B3
Odder 108 B3
Oddesund 108 A2
Odeceixe 42 A2
Odeleite 42 B2
Odelzhausen 55 F3
Odemira 42 A2
Ödemiş 115 F4
Odense 108 B3
Odenthal 17 E4
Oder 49 E3
Oderberg 49 E3
Oderbruch 49 E3
Oderbucht 49 E1
Oderhaff 49 E2
Oderzo 59 E4
Ödeshög 109 D1
Odessa 113 F4
Odet 22 B3
Odiel, R 42 C2
Odivelas 42 B1
Odivelas, Bgem de 42 B1
Odolo 60 B1
Odorheiu Secuiesc 113 D4
Odra 112 A2
Odžaci 72 B2
Odžak (Bosna i Hercegovina) 71 F3
Odžak (Crna Gora) 76 B1
Oebisfelde 48 B4
Oebro 105 F4
Oederan 53 E3
Oeiras 38 A4
Oelde 17 F3
Oelsnitz (Plauen) 53 D3
Oelsnitz (Zwickau) 53 D3
Oettingen 55 E2
Oetz 58 C2
Ofanto 64 C3
Ofenpass 58 C3
Offaly 12 C4
Offenbach 52 A4
Offenburg 54 C3
Offida 63 F1
Offranville 19 E2
Ofir 34 A4
Ofotfjorden 94 B3
Oggiono 60 A1
Ogliastro Cilento 67 D1
Oglio 58 C4
Ognon 27 D2
Ogošte 77 E2
Ogražden 77 F3
Ogre 110 C2
Ogulin 70 C3
Ohanes 44 B3
Óhi, Óros 88 A1
Ohiró 80 B1
Ohlstadt 56 A4
Ohorn 53 F2
Ohrdruf 52 C3
Ohre 48 B4
Ohře 53 E3
Ohrid 77 D4
Ohridsko Ez 77 D4
Ohringen 55 D2
Ohrit, Liq i 77 D4
Óhthia 82 C3
Ohthoniá 84 B4
Oijärvi 99 D3
Oijärvi L 99 D3
Oikarainen 99 D2
Oirschot 16 C3
Oise 20 B2
Oise (Dépt) 19 F3
Oisemont 19 E2
Oisterwijk 16 C3
Oitti 107 E2
Oituz 113 D4
Ojakylä 99 D4
Öje 101 E4
Öjebyn 98 B3
Ojén 43 E4
Ojos Negros 41 D2
Ojuelos Altos 43 E1
Öjung 101 E4
Okehampton 8 C3
Oker 48 B4
Oklaj 75 D1
Oknö 109 E2
Okol 76 C2
Oksbøl 108 A3
Oksby 108 A3
Øksfjord 95 D2
Øksfjorden 94 A3
Øksfjordjøkelen 94 C2
Øksnes 94 A3
Okstindan 97 E3
Okučani 71 E3
Okulovka 111 E1
Olafsfjörður 96 B1
Ólafsvík 96 A2
Öland 109 E2
Olan, Pic d' 31 D2
Olargues 32 B1
Olazagutía 36 B2
Olbernhau 53 E3
Olbia 66 B1
Oldcastle 13 D3
Oldebroek 17 D2
Oldeide 100 A3
Olden 100 A3
Oldenburg (Niedersachsen) 47 F3
Oldenburg (Schleswig Holstein) 48 B1
Oldenzaal 17 E2
Olderdalen 94 C2
Oldervik 94 C2
Oldfjällen 101 E1
Oldham 6 C2
Old Head of Kinsale 14 B4
Oldmeldrum 3 E4
Oldsum 47 F1
Oleggio 60 A1
Oleiros 34 B1
Oleiros 38 C2
Ølen 104 A3
Oléron, Ile d' 24 B4
Olesa 32 A4
Oleśnica 112 A2
Oletta 33 F2
Olette 32 B2
Olevsk 113 D2
Ølgod 108 A3
Olhão 42 B3
Olhava 99 D3
Oliana 32 A3
Oliana, Emb d' 32 A3
Olib 70 B4
Olib I 70 B4
Oliena 66 B2
Oliete 37 D4
Olimbía 86 C2
Olimbiáda (Makedonía) 80 B3
Olimbiáda (Thessalía) 79 E4
Ólimbos 93 D2
Ólimbos, Óros (Évia) 84 B4
Ólimbos, Óros (Pieriá) 79 E4
Ólinthos 80 A4
Olite 36 C2
Oliva 45 E1
Oliva de la Frontera 42 C1
Oliva de Mérida 39 D4
Olivares 40 C3
Oliveira de Azeméis 38 B1
Oliveira de Frades 38 B1
Oliveira do Bairro 38 B1
Oliveira do Douro 34 B4
Oliveira do Hospital 38 C2
Olivenza 38 C4
Olivenza, R de 38 C4
Olivet 25 E1
Olivone 58 A3
Ollería, Pto de l' 41 E4
Ollerton 7 D3
Ollières, les 30 B2
Olliergues 29 F1
Ollioules 31 D4
Ollöla 103 F2
Olmedillo de Roa 35 F4
Olmedo (E) 35 E4
Olmedo (I) 66 A2
Olmeto 33 F4
Olocau del Rey 41 E2
Olofström 109 D3
Olombrada 35 F4
Olomouc 112 A3
Olonzac 32 B1
Oloron Ste Marie 37 D1
Olost 32 A3
Olot 32 B3
Olovo 71 F4
Olpe 17 F4
Olsberg 17 F3
Olshammar 105 F4
Olst 17 D2
Ølstykke 108 C3
Olsztyn 110 B4
Olszyna 53 F1
Olt 115 D2
Oltedal 104 A3
Olten 27 F2
Oltenia 115 D1
Oltenita 115 E1
Olula del Río 44 C3
Olvega 36 C3
Olvera 43 E3
Omagh 13 D2
Omalí 79 D4
Omalós 90 B3
Omarska 71 D3
Ombrone 63 D1
Omegna 58 A4
Omiš 75 E2
Omišalj 70 B3
Omme Å 108 A3
Ommen 17 D2
Omodeo, L 66 B3
Omoljica 73 D3
Omorfohóri 83 E1
Ömossa 102 B3
Oña 36 A2
Oñati 36 B1
Oncala, Pto de 36 B3
Onda 41 E3
Ondara 45 E1
Ondárroa 36 B1
Oneglia 31 F3
OnesseetLaharie 28 A3
Onich 2 C4
Onkamo (Lapin Lääni) 99 E2
Onkamo (Pohjois Karjalan Lääni) 103 F2
Onkivesi 103 E2
Ons, I de 34 A2
Ontaneda 35 F2
Ontiñena 37 E3
Ontinyent 45 E1
Ontojärvi 99 F4
Ontur 45 D1
Onzain 25 E2
Oostburg 16 B4
OostelijkFlevoland 16 C2
Oostende 50 A3
Oosterbeek 17 D3
Oosterend 16 C1
Oosterhout 16 C3
Oostkamp 50 A3
Oostmalle 50 C3
OostVlaanderen 50 B3
OostVlieland 16 C1
Ootmarsum 17 E2
Opatija 70 B3
Opatovac 72 B2
Opava 112 A3
Opladen 17 E4
Oplenac 73 D3
Opočka 111 D2
Opole 112 A2
Opovo 72 C2
Oppach 53 F2
Oppdal 100 C2
Oppenau 54 C3
Oppenheim 54 C1
Opphaug 100 C1
Oppido Lucano 64 C4
Oppido Mamertina 67 E4
Oppland 104 C1
Oputten 16 C2
Opuzen 75 F2
Ora 59 D3
Oradea 112 C4
Oradour-sur-Glane 25 D4
Oradour-sur-Vayres 28 C1
Orahova 71 D3
Orahovac 77 D2
Orahovica 71 E2
Oraison 31 D3
Orajärvi 98 C2
Orange 30 B3
Orani 66 B2
Oranienbaum 53 D1
Oranienburg 49 D3
Oranmore 12 B3
Orašac (Hrvatska) 75 F2
Orašac (Srbija) 73 D3
Orasi 76 B3
Orašje 71 F3
Orăştie 114 C1
Oravainen 102 B2
Oravais 102 B2
Oravikoski 103 E2
Oravița 114 C1
Orb 30 A4
Orba 45 E1
Ørbæk 108 B4
Orbassano 31 E2
Orbe 27 D3
Orbec 19 D3
Orbetello 63 D2
Orbey 27 E1
Orbigo, R 35 D2
Orce 44 B2
Orce, R 44 B2
Orcera 44 B1
Orchies 20 A1
Orcières 31 D2
Orcival 29 E1
Orco 31 E1
Ordes 34 A1
Ordesa, Parque Nac. de 37 E2
Ordino 32 A2
Ordizia 36 C1
Orduña 36 B1
Orduña, Pto de 36 B1
Ore 101 E4
Orea 41 D2
Oreälven 102 A1
Orebić 75 E2
Örebro Län 105 F3
Öregrund 106 B3
Öregrundsgrepen 106 B2
Orei 83 F3
Orellana de la Sierra 39 E4
Orellana, Emb de 39 E4
Orellana la Vieja 39 E4
Orense 34 B3
Oréo 81 D2
Oreókastro 79 F3
Orestiáda 81 F1
Oresund 108 C3
Orfós, Akr 89 F4
Orgáni 81 E2
Organyà 32 A3
Orgañyà 37 F3
Orgaz 40 A3
Orgejev 113 E3
Orgelet 26 C3
Orgères-en-Beauce 25 E1
Orgon 30 C3
Orgosolo 66 B2
Orhi, Pic d' 37 D1
Orhomenós 83 F4
Oria 44 C3
Oria 65 E4
Oria, R 36 C1
Origny-Sainte-Benoîte 20 A2
Orihuela 45 D2
Orihuela del Tremedal 41 D2
Orimattila 107 F2
Oriní 80 B2
Oriolo 65 D4
Oripää 187 D2
Orissaare 110 B2
Oristano 66 B3
Oristano, G di 66 A3
Orivesi 102 C3
Orivesi L 103 F2
Orjahovo 115 D2
Ørjavik 100 B2
Ørje 105 D3
Orjen 76 A2
Orjiva 44 A3
Orkanger 100 C2
Örkelljunga 109 D3
Orkla 100 C2
Orkney Is 3 E1
Ørlandet 100 C1
Orlando, C d' 69 D2
Orlane 77 D1
Orlate 77 D2
Orléans 25 E1
Orlická přehr nádrž 56 C1
Orlovat 72 C2
Orly 19 F4
Orménio 81 F1
Ormília 80 B4
Órmos 79 F3
Órmos Korthíou 88 B1
Órmos Panagías 80 B4
Órmos Prinou 80 C3
Ormož 70 C1
Ormsjö 97 F4
Ormsjön 101 F1
Ormskirk 6 B2
Ormtjernkampen 104 C1
Ornain 20 C4
Ornans 27 D2
Orne (Calvados) 18 C4
Orne (Dépt) 20 B3
Orne (Meuse) 21 D3
Ørnes 97 E2
Ornós 88 C2
Örnsköldsvik 102 A2
Or'ol 111 F4
Orolik 72 B2
Orom 72 B1
Oron-la-Ville 27 E3
Oropesa (Castilla la Mancha) 39 F3
Oropesa (Valencia) 41 F3
Orosei 66 C2
Orosei, G di 66 C2
Orosháza 112 B4
Orpierre 30 C3
Orpington 10 C2
Orra 100 C3
Orsa 101 E4
Orša 111 E3
Orsajön 101 E4
Orsay 19 F4
Orsières 27 E4
Orsogna 64 A2
Orşova 114 C1
Ørsta 100 A2
Örsundsbro 106 B3
Orta Nova 64 C3
Orta San Giulio 58 A4
Orte 63 E2
Ortegal, C 34 B1
Orth 57 F2
Orthez 28 B4
Ortigueira 34 B1
Ortisei 59 D3
Ortles 58 C3
Ortnevik 104 B1
Orton 5 D4
Ortona 64 A2
Ortrand 53 E2
Örträsk 102 A1
Orubica 71 E3
Orune 66 B2
Orusco 40 B2
Orvalho 38 C2
Orvieto 63 E1
Órvilos, Óros 80 B1
Orvinio 63 F2
Orzinuovi 60 B1
Os 100 D3

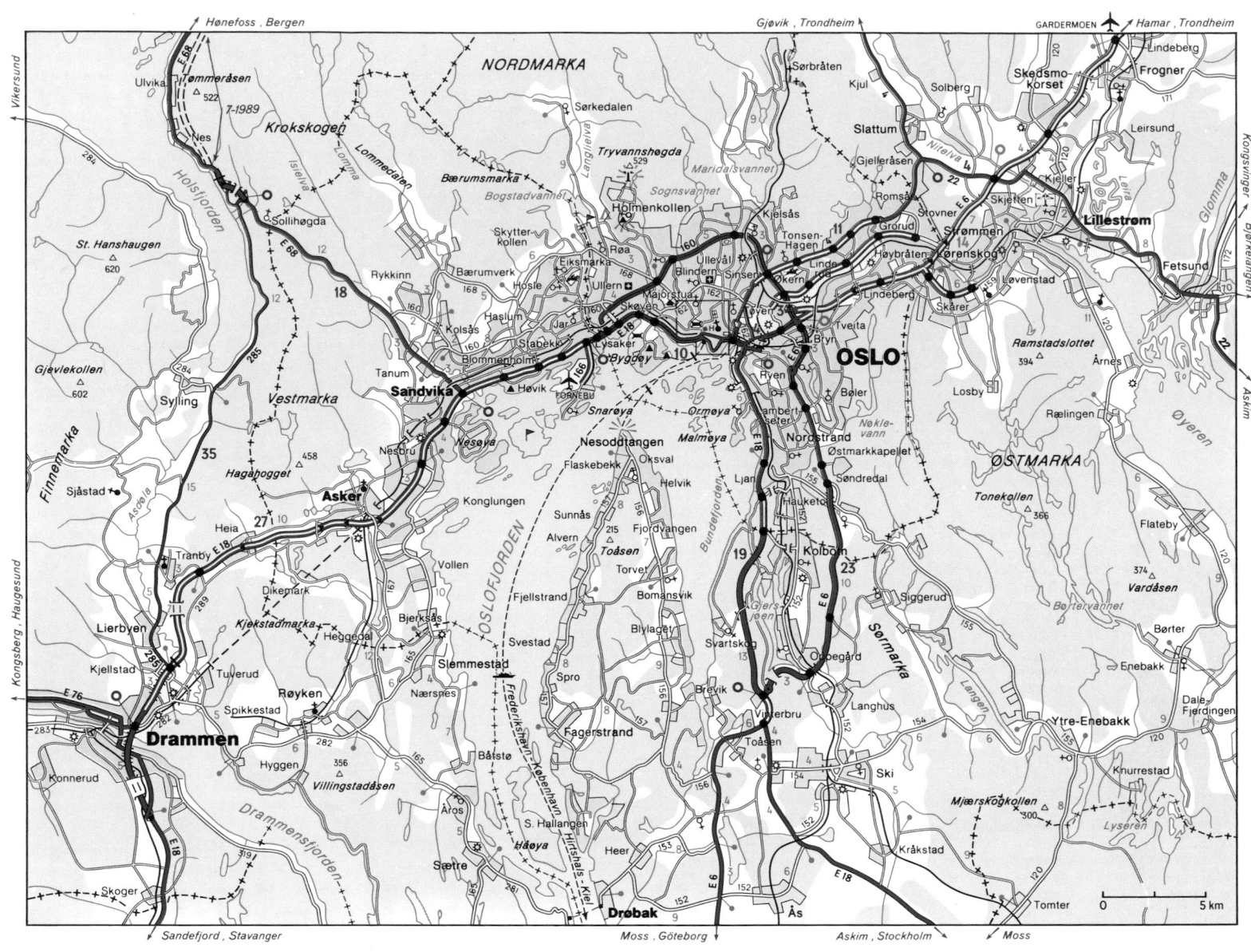

Osa de la Vega	40 B3	Óssa	80 A2	Ostfriesische		Oświęcim	112 B2	Ottobrunn	56 A3	Ourique	42 B2	Övre Fryken	105 E3
Osâm	115 D2	Ossa de Montiel	40 B4	Inseln	47 D3	Otanmäki	103 D1	Ottsjö	101 D2	Ourol	34 B1	Övre Pasvik	95 F2
Osby	109 D3	Óssa, Óros	83 F1	Östhammar	106 B3	Otava (CS)	56 C1	Ottweiler	54 B2	Ourthe	20 C1	Övre Soppero	95 D4
Oschatz	53 E2	Ossa, Sa de	38 C4	Ostheim	52 B4	Otava (SF)	103 E3	Otwock	112 B1	Ourville	19 D2	Ovruč	113 E1
Oschersleben	52 C1	Ossiach	59 F2	Ostia Antica	63 E3	Oteren	94 C3	Oxtaler	88 A2	Ouse, R.	7 D2	Owel, L	13 D3
Oschiri	66 B2	Ossiacher See	59 F2	Ostiglia	60 C2	Otešěvo	77 D4	Ötztal	58 C2	Oust	37 F2	Oxelösund	106 B4
Osečina	72 C3	Óssios Loukás	83 F4	Östmark	105 E3	Othem	109 F4	Ötztaleralpen	58 C2	Outes, Sa de	34 A2	Oxford	9 E2
Oseja de Sajambre	35 E2	Ossun	37 E1	Ost'or	113 E1	Othery	9 D3	Ouchy	27 D3	Outokumpu	103 E2	Oxfordshire	9 E2
Osen	96 C4	Ostaškov	111 E2	Ostra	61 E3	Óthris, Óros	83 E3	Oucques	25 E1	Outomuro	34 B3	Oxiá, N	82 C4
Osera de Ebro	37 D4	Østbirk	108 B3	Ostrach	55 D4	Otívar	44 A3	Oud Beijerland	16 B3	Outwell	10 C1	Oxiá (Stereá Eláda)	83 D3
Osijek	71 F2	Østby	105 E2	Östra Gloppet	102 B2	Otley	6 C2	Ouddorp	16 B3	Ouvèze	30 C3	Oxiá (Thessalía)	83 D2
Osilo	66 B2	Oste	47 F3	Östra Silen	105 D4	Otnes	100 C3	Oude Maas	16 B3	Ouzouer	25 F2	Oxie	108 C3
Osimo	61 F4	Osted	108 C3	Ostrava	112 B3	Otočac	70 C4	Oudenaarde	50 B3	Ouzouer-le-Marché	25 E1	Ox Mts, The	12 C3
Osinja	71 E3	Osterburg	48 C4	Oštrelj	71 D4	Otočec	70 B2	Oudenbosch	16 C3	Ovada	60 A2	Oyarzun	36 C1
Osipaonica	73 D3	Osterburken	55 D1	Ostritz	53 F2	Otok	72 B2	OudePekela	47 E3	Ovanåker	101 F4	Oybin	53 F2
Osipoviči	111 D4	Osterbybruk	106 B3	Ostróda	110 B4	Otoka	71 D3	Ouessant, Ile d'	22 A2	Ovar	38 B1	Øye	104 C1
Osječenica	71 D4	Østerby Havn	108 B2	Ostrog	113 D2	Otra	104 B4	Oughterard	12 B3	Ovčar Banja	73 D4	Øyer	104 C1
Oskarshamn	109 E2	Österbymo	109 E1	Ostrołęka	112 B1	Otranto	65 F4	Ouistreham	18 C3	Ovedskloster	109 D3	Øyeren	105 D3
Oskarström	108 C2	Österdalälven	101 D3	Ostrov (CS)	53 E3	Otsamo	95 E3	Oul	51 D4	Overath	17 E4	OyMittelberg	55 E3
Oslava	57 E1	Østerdalen	100 C3	Ostrov (RO)	115 E1	Otta	100 C3	Oulainen	99 D4	Øverbygd	94 C3	Oyntdartfjørdur	96 A3
Oslo	105 D3	Österfärnebo	106 A3	Ostrov (SU)	111 D2	Ottana	66 B2	Oulanka	99 E2	Overflakkee	16 B3	Oyón	36 B2
Oslo (Fylke)	105 D3	Osterfeld	53 D2	Ostrowiec		Ottaviano	64 B4	Oulankajoki	99 E2	Overhalla	97 D4	Oyonnax	27 D4
Oslofjorden	104 C3	Östergötlands		Świętokrzyski	112 B2	Ottenschlag	57 E2	Oulchy-le-Château	20 A3	Øverhörnäs	102 A2	Øystese	104 B2
Ösmo	106 B4	Län	109 E1	Ostrów		Ottensheim	57 D2	Oulu	99 D3	Overijssel	17 D2	Oyten	47 F3
Osnabrück	17 F2	Osterhofen	56 B2	Mazowiecki	112 B1	Otterburn	5 E3	Oulujärvi	99 E4	Overkalix	98 C2	Ozalj	70 C2
Ośno Lubuskie	49 F4	Osterholz		Ostrów		Otter Ferry	4 B2	Oulujoki	99 D4	Övermark	102 B2	Ožbalt	70 B1
Osogovija	77 F2	Scharmbeck	47 F3	Wielkopolski	112 A2	Otterlo	17 D3	Oulun Lääni	99 E4	Oversjuktan	97 F3	Ózd	112 B3
Osogovske		Osteria del Gatto	61 E4	Ostrožac (Bosna i		Otterndorf	47 F2	Oulunsalo	99 D4	Övertorneå	98 C2	Ozeblin	70 C4
planine	77 E2	Osterode	52 B2	Hercegovina)	70 C3	Otterøy	97 D4	Oulx	31 D2	Överum	109 E1	Ozieri	66 B2
Osoppo	59 E3	Osterøya	104 A2	Ostrožac (Bosna i		Ottersberg	47 F3	Ounasjoki	99 D2	Överuman	97 E3	Ozren	71 F3
Osor	70 B4	Östersund	101 E2	Hercegovina)	75 F1	Otterup	108 B3	Oundle	9 F1	Oviedo	35 D1	Ozren Devica	73 E4
Osorno	35 F3	Östersundom	107 F2	Ostsee	48 C1	Ottery St Mary	9 D3	Our	54 A1	Ovindoli	63 F2	
Osøyri	104 A2	Östervåla	106 B3	Osttirol	59 E2	Ottmarsheim	27 E1	Ouranópoli	80 B4	Øvre Anarjokka	95 D3	
Ospedaletti	31 E3	Øster Vrå	108 B2	Ostuni	65 E3	Ottnang	56 C3	Ource	26 C1	Øvre Årdal	100 B3	
Ospitaletto	60 B1	Osterwieck	52 B1	Osuna	43 E3	Ottobeuren	55 E3	Ourcq	20 A3	Øvre Dividalen	94 C3	
Oss	16 C3	Østfold	105 D3	Oswestry	6 B3			Ourense	34 B3			

P

Paakkila 103 E2
Paalasmaa 103 E1
Páamo de Masa, Pto de 35 F3
Paar 55 F3
Paasselkä 103 F3
Paavola 99 D4
Pabianice 112 B2
Pacaudière, la 26 B4
Paceco 68 A3
Pachino 69 D4
Packsattel 57 E4
Paço de Sousa 34 A4
Paços de Ferreira 34 A4
Pacov 57 D1
Pacy 19 E4
Padasjoki 107 E1
Padej 72 C2
Padđene 75 D1
Paderborn 17 F3
Paderne 42 B2
Padiham 6 C2
Padina 72 C2
Padinska Skela 72 C2
Padirac, Gouffre de 29 D2
Padjelanta 97 F1
Padornelo 34 C3
Padova 61 D1
Padrela, Sa da 34 B4
Padrón 34 A2
Padru 66 B2
Padstow 8 B3
Padul 44 A3
Paesana 31 E2
Paestum 64 B4
Pag 70 C4
Pag I 70 B4
Paganico 63 D1
Pagassés, N 83 F2
Pagassitikós Kólpos 83 F2
Paglia 63 D1
Pagny 21 D3
Pagóndas (Évia) 84 A3
Pagóndas (Sámos) 89 F2
Pagoúria 81 D2
Paguera 45 E3
Páhi 87 E1
Pahiá Ámos 91 F4
Pahís, Akr 80 C3
Paide 110 C1
Paignton 8 C4
Paijänne 103 D3
Páíko, Óros 79 E2
Paimbœuf 23 D4
Paimio 107 D2
Paimpol 22 C2
Painswick 9 E2
Paisley 4 C2
Paistunturit 95 E2
País Vasco 36 B1
Paittasjärvi 94 C4
Paiva, R 38 B1
Pajala 98 C1
Pájara 42 C4
Pajares, Pto de 35 D2
Paklenica Nac Park 70 C4
Pakoštane 74 C1
Pakrac 71 E2
Pakračka Poljana 71 D2
Paks 112 B4
Palacios de la Sierra 36 A3
Palacios del Sil 34 C2
Palacios de Sanabria 34 C3
Palade, Pso del 58 C3
Paládio 81 D2
Paladru 30 C1
Palafrugell 32 C3
Palagía 81 D2
Palagiano 65 E4
Palagonia 69 D3
Palagruža 75 D3
Palaia 60 C4
Palaiseau 19 F4
Palais, le 22 C4
Palamás 83 E2
Palamós 32 C3
Palancia, R 41 E3

Palanga 110 B3
Pala, Pto del 34 C1
Palas de Rei 34 B2
Palata 64 B2
Palatitsía 79 E3
Palatna 77 D1
Palau 66 B1
Palavas 30 B4
Palazzo del Pero 61 D4
Palazzolo Acreide 69 D4
Palazzolo sull' Oglio 60 B1
Palazzo San Gervasio 64 C3
Palazzuolo sul Senio 61 D3
Paldiski 110 C1
Pale 76 A1
Paléa Epídavros 87 E2
Palékastro 91 F4
Palena 64 A2
Palencia 35 E3
Paleohóra (Égina) 87 F2
Paleohóra (Kríti) 90 B4
Paleohóri (Grevená) 79 D4
Paleohóri (Halkidikí) 80 B3
Paleohóri (Ípiros) 82 B2
Paleohóri (Lésvos) 85 F3
Paleohóri (Pelopónissos) 87 D3
Paleohóri (Thessalía) 83 D1
Paleokastrítsa 82 A1
Paleókastro (Halkidikí) 80 A3
Paleókastro (Kozáni) 79 D4
Paleókastro (Sámos) 89 F2
Paleókastro (Séres) 80 B2
Paleókastro (Stereá Eláda) 83 D3
Paleokómi 80 B2
Paleópirgos (Stereá Eláda) 83 D4
Paleópirgos (Thessalía) 83 F1
Paleópoli (Ándros) 88 B1
Paleópoli (Samothráki) 81 E3
Paleós Kavála 80 C2
Paleós Xánthis 81 D2
Palermo 68 B3
Páleros 82 C3
Palérou, Órm 82 B3
Palestrina 63 F2
Palež 72 B4
Páli 89 F4
Paliano 63 F3
Palić 72 B1
Palídoro 63 E2
Palinges 26 B3
Palinuro 67 D2
Palioúri 80 B4
Paliouriá 79 D4
Paliseul 20 C2
Pälkäne 107 E1
Pälkem 98 B2
Pallas Ounastunturi 95 D3
Pallastunturi 95 D4
Pallice, la 24 B4
Palluau 24 B3
Palma 45 E3
Palmaces, Emb de 36 B4
Palma del Río 43 E2
Palma di Montechiaro 68 C4
Palmadula 66 A2
Palmanova 59 F3
Palmela 38 A4
Palmi 67 E4
Palo del Colle 65 D3
Palojoensuu 95 D3
Palojoki 95 D3
Palokki 103 E2
Palomäki 103 E1
Palomares del Campo 40 C3

Palomas 39 D4
Palomas, Pto de las 44 B2
Palombara Sabina 63 E2
Palombera, Pto de 35 F2
Palomera 41 D2
Pálos, Akr 88 B2
Palos, C de 45 D3
Palos de la Frontera 42 C3
Pals 32 C3
Pålsboda 105 F4
Paltamo 99 E4
Paltaselkä 99 E4
Paluzza 59 E2
Pámfila 85 F2
Pamhagen 57 F3
Pamiers 32 A2
Pampilhosa 38 B2
Pampilhosa da Serra 38 C2
Pampliega 35 F3
Pamplona 36 C2
Pamporovo 115 D3
Pamukkale 115 F4
Panagía (Ípiros) 82 C2
Panagía (Límnos) 85 D1
Panagía (Makedonía) 79 D4
Panagía (Thássos) 81 D3
Panagía (Thessalía) 82 C1
Panagjurište 115 D2
Panahaïkó, Óros 83 D4
Panarea, I 69 D2
Panaro 60 C3
Pancalieri 31 E2
Pančevo 73 D2
Pančićev vrh 77 D1
Pancorbo 36 A2
Pandánassa 87 E4
Pandeleimónas 79 F4
Pandino 60 B1
Pandokrátor 82 A1
Pandrup 108 B2
Panes 35 F2
Panetolikó, Óros 83 D3
Panetólio 82 C4
Panevėžys 110 C3
Pangbourne 9 E2
Pangéo, Óros 80 B2
Paniza, Pto de 36 C4
Pankajärvi 103 F1
Pankakoski 103 F1
Pankow 49 E4
Panórama (Dráma) 80 B2
Panórama (Thessaloníki) 80 A3
Panormítis 93 E1
Pánormos (Kikládes) 88 B2
Pánormos (Kríti) 91 D3
Päntäne 102 B3
Pantelleria 68 A4
Pantelleria, I di 68 A4
Paola 67 E2
Pápa 112 A4
Papádes 84 A3
Papádos 85 F3
Páparis 86 C2
Pápas, Akr 89 D2
Papasídero 67 E2
Papa Stour 3 F1
Papenburg 47 E3
Papikio 81 D2
Pápingo 78 C4
Pappenheim 55 F2
Papuk Mt 71 E2
Papuk (Reg) 71 E2
Parabita 65 F4
Paracin 73 E4
Paracuellos de Jiloca 36 C4
Parada de Cunhos 34 B4
Paradas 43 E3
Paradela 34 B3
Paradíssia 86 C2
Parádissos 81 D2
Parainen 107 D3
Parajes 34 C1
Parakálamos 78 C4
Parákila 85 F2
Paralía (Ahaḯa) 86 C1
Paralía (Lakonía) 87 E3

Paralía (Makedonía) 79 F4
Paralía (Stereá Eláda) 83 F4
Paralía Akrátas 87 D1
Parália Ástros 87 D2
Paralía Kímis 84 B3
Paralía Kotsikiás 84 A3
Paralía Skotínas 79 F4
Paralía Tiroú 87 E3
Paralímni 84 A4
Paralovo 77 D2
Paramé 18 B4
Paramera, Pto de 39 F2
Paramithiá 82 B2
Páramo del Sil 34 C2
Paranésti 80 C2
Parapanda 43 F3
Parapótamos 82 B1
Paraspóri, Akr 93 D2
Paray-le-Monial 26 B3
Parchim 48 C3
Pardubice 112 A3
Paredes 34 A4
Paredes de Coura 34 A3
Paredes de Nava 35 E3
Pareja 40 C2
Pareloup, Lac de 29 E3
Parentis-en-Born 28 A3
Párga 82 B2
Pargas 107 D3
Parikkala 103 F3
Parîngului, M 114 C1
Paris 19 F4
Parkalompolo 95 D3
Parkano 102 C3
Parla 40 A2
Parlavà 32 B3
Parma 60 B2
Parnassós, Óros 83 E4
Parndorf 57 F2
Párnitha, Óros 87 F1
Párnonas, Óros 87 D3
Pärnu 110 C2
Parola 107 E2
Páros 88 C3
Páros, N 88 B3
Parrett 9 D3
Parsberg 55 F2
Parsdorf 56 A3
Parseierspitze 58 C2
Parseta 49 F1
Parsteiner See 49 E3
Partakko 95 F2
Partanna 68 B3
Partenen 58 B2
Partenkirchen 55 F4
Parthenay 24 C3
Parthéni 89 E3
Partille 108 C1
Partinico 68 B3
Partizani 73 D3
Partizanske Vode 72 C4
Partney 7 E3
Partry Mountains 12 B3
Pasaia-Pasajes 36 C1
Pas de Calais 11 E3
Pas-de-Calais (Dépt) 19 E1
Pas de la Case 32 A2
Pas-en-Artois 19 F2
Pasewalk 49 E3
Pashalitsa 83 E2
Pasikovci 71 E2
Pašman 81 D2
Pašman I 74 C1
Passais 18 C4
Passà-Limáni 85 E4
Passás, N 85 F4
Passau 56 C2
Passavás 87 D4
Passero, C 69 D4
Passignano sul Trasimeno 61 D4
Passwang 27 E2
Pastrana 40 B2
Paštrik 76 C3
Pásztó 112 B4
Patay 25 E1
Pateley Bridge 6 C1
Patéras, Óros 87 E1
Paterna del Campo 43 D2
Paterna de Rivera 43 D4

Paternion 59 F2
Paternò 69 D3
Paternopoli 64 B3
Patersdorf 56 B2
P'atichatki 113 F2
Patiópoulo 82 C2
Patitíri 84 B2
Pátmos 89 E2
Pátmos, N 89 E2
Pátra 83 D4
Patraïkós Kólpos 82 C4
Patreksfjördur 96 A1
Patrington 7 E2
Pattada 66 B2
Patterdale 5 D4
Patti 69 D2
Pattijoki 99 D4
Patvinsuo 103 F2
Paúl 38 C2
Paularo 59 F2
Paulhaguet 29 F2
Paullo 60 A1
Pavia (I) 60 A2
Pavia (P) 38 B4
Pavilly 19 D3
Pavino Polje 76 B1
Pávliani 83 E3
Pávlos 83 F4
Pavullo nel Frignano 60 C3
Paxi 82 A2
Paxí, N 82 A2
Payerne 27 E3
Paymogo 42 C2
Payrac 29 D2
Pazardžik 115 D3
Pazin 70 A3
Pčinja 77 E2
Péage-de-Roussillon, le 30 B1
Peak District Nat Pk 6 C2
Peal de Becerro 44 B2
Peanía 87 F1
Peares, Emb de los 34 B2
Peç, N 76 C2
Peca 70 B1
Peccioli 60 C4
Pečenjevce 77 E1
Pech-Merle, Grotte du 29 D3
Pečigrad 70 C3
Pečinci 72 C3
Pecka 72 C4
Peckelsheim 52 A2
Pécs 114 B1
Pécsa Banja 76 C2
Pečurice 76 B3
Pedaso 61 E4
Pedersker 109 D4
Pedersöre 102 C2
Pédi 93 E1
Pedrafita do Cebreiro 34 C2
Pedrafita do Cebreiro, Pto de 34 C2
Pedrajas de San Esteban 35 E4
Pedralba (Castilla-León) 34 C3
Pedralba (Valencia) 41 E3
Pedras Salgadas 34 B4
Pedraza de la Sierra 40 A1
Pedrera 43 E3
Pedrizas, Pto de las 43 F3
Pedro Abad 43 F2
Pedro Bernardo 39 F2
Pedrógão (Alentejo) 42 B1
Pedrógão (Estremadura) 38 A2
Pedrógão Grande 38 B2
Pedrola 36 C3
Pedro Muñoz 40 B4

Pefkári 80 C3
Pefki 83 F3
Péfkos 78 C3
Pega 38 C2
Pegalajar 44 A2
Pegau 53 D2
Pegli 60 A3
Pegnitz 55 F1
Pego 45 E1
Pego do Altar, Bgem de 38 B4
Pegognaga 60 C2
Pegolotte 61 D1
Pehčevo 77 F3
Peine 52 B1
Peiting 56 A4
Peitz 53 F1
Pek 73 D3
Péla 79 E2
Péla (Nomos) 79 F3
Pelado 41 D3
Pelagie, Is 68 A4
Pelasgía 83 F3
Pelat, Mt 31 D3
Pelekános 79 D3
Pélekas 82 A1
Peletá 87 E3
Pelhřimov 57 D1
Pelinéo 85 E4
Pelister 77 E4
Peljašac 75 E2
Pelkosenniemi 99 E1
Pellegrino, M 68 B2
Pellegrue 28 C2
Pellerin, le 24 B2
Pellesmäki 103 E2
Pello 98 C2
Pellworm 47 F1
Pelopónissos 86 C2
Peloritani, M 69 D2
Peltosalmi 103 E1
Peltovuoma 95 D3
Pélussin 30 B1
Pelvoux, Mt 31 D2
Pembroke 8 B2
Pembroke Dock 8 B2
Pembrokeshire Coast Nat Pk 8 B1
Penacova 38 B2
Peña de Francia 39 D2
Peña, de Francia, Sade 39 D2
Peña de Oroel 37 D2
Peña Gorbea 36 B1
Peñalara 40 A1
Penalva do Castelo 38 C1
Penamacor 38 C2
Peña Mira 34 C3
Peña Nofre 34 B3
Peña Prieta 35 E2
Peñaranda de Bracamonte 39 F1
Peñaranda de Duero 36 A3
Peñarroya 41 E2
Peñarroya, Emb de 40 B4
Peñarroya-Pueblonuevo 43 E1
Penarth 9 D2
Peña, Sa de la 37 D2
Peña Sagra 35 F2
Peñas, C de 35 D1
Peñascosa 44 C1
Peñas de Cervera 36 A3
Peñas de San Pedro 44 C1
Peña Trevinca 34 C3
Peña Ubiña 35 D2
Peñausende 35 D4

Pendéli 87 F1
Pendéli Mt 87 F1
Pendeória 83 E4
Pénde Vrísses 80 A2
Pendine 8 B2
Peneda-Gerês, Pque Nac da 34 A3
Peneda, Sa da 34 A3
Penedono 38 C1
Penela 38 B2
Pénestin 22 C4
Penha 34 A4
Penhas da Saude 38 C2
Penhas Juntas 34 C4
Penhir, Pte de 22 A3
Penice, Pso del 60 A2
Peniche 38 A3
Penicuik 5 D2
Penig 53 D3
Peñíscola 41 F2
Penkun 49 E3
Penmaenmawr 6 A2
Penmarch, Pte de 22 A3
Pennabilli 61 E3
Penne 63 F1
Penne-d'Agenais 28 C3
Pennes, Pso di 59 D2
Pennines, The 6 C1
Peñón de Ifach 45 E1
Penrhyndeudraeth 6 A3
Penrith 5 D4
Penryn 8 B4
Penserjoch 59 D2
Pentland Firth 3 D2
Pentland Hills 5 D2
Pentrefoelas 6 B3
Pen-y-bont 8 C2
Penzance 8 A4
Penzberg 56 A4
Penzlin 49 D2
Peqin 76 C4
Perahóra 87 E1
Peraleda de Zaucejo 43 E1
Peralejos de las Truchas 40 C2
Perales del Alfambra 41 D2
Perales del Puerto 39 D2
Perales de Tajuña 40 B2
Perales, Pto de 39 D2
Peralta 36 C2
Peralta de Alcofea 37 E3
Peraíva 42 B2
Pérama (Ípiros) 82 C1
Pérama (Kérkira) 82 A1
Pérama (Kríti) 91 D3
Pérama (Lésvos) 85 F3
Pérama (Stereá Eláda) 87 F1
Peraméri 98 C3
Perá-Posio 99 E2
Peräseinäjoki 102 C2
Perast 76 B3
Peratáta 86 A1
Percy 18 B4
Perdido, M 37 E2
Pérdika (Égina) 87 F2
Pérdika (Ioánina) 82 C2
Pérdika (Thesprotía) 82 B2
Perdikáki 82 C3
Perdikas 79 D3
Peréa (Péla) 79 E3
Peréa (Thessaloníki) 79 F3
Perejaslav-Chmel'nickij 113 F2
Pereruela 35 D4
Pereval Jablonickij 113 F2
Pereval Srednij Vereck
Pereval Užok

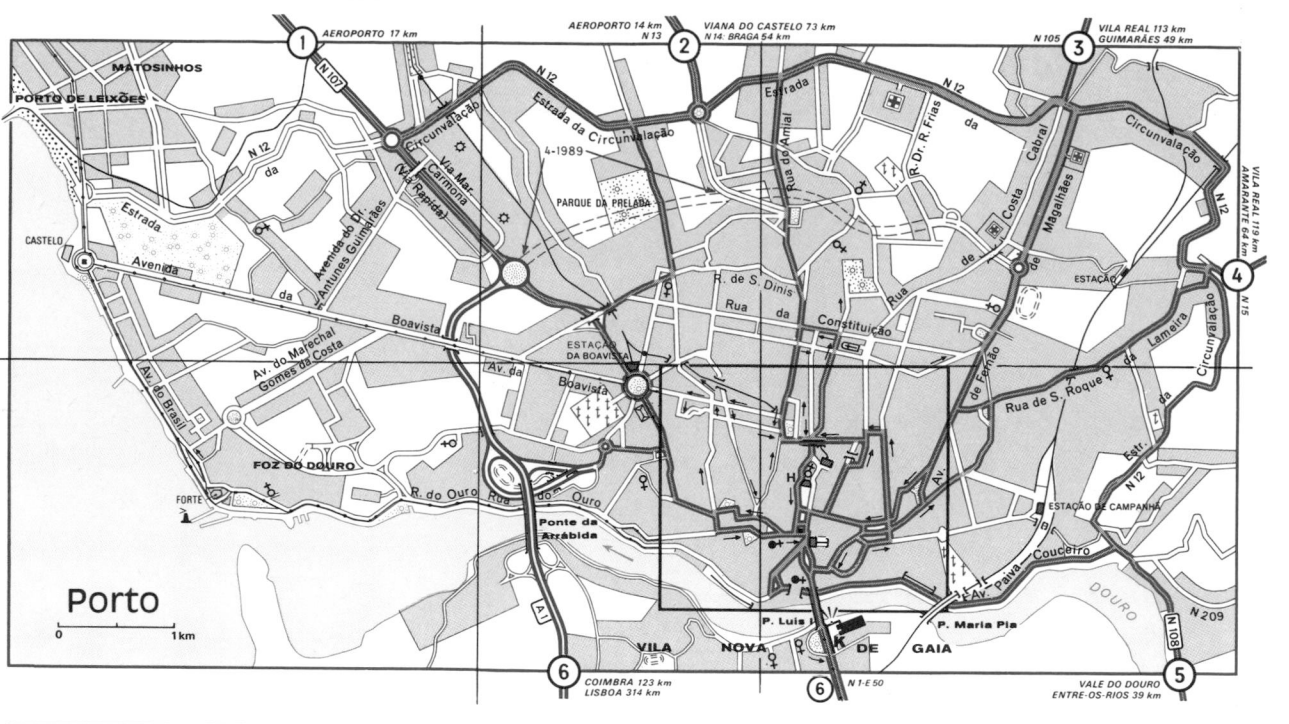

Porto

Pírgos (Makedonía)	79	F3
Pírgos (Pelopónnissos)	86	B2
Pírgos (Sámos)	89	E2
Pírgos (Stereá Eláda)	83	F4
Pírgos Diroú	87	D4
Pírgos Gerakíou	87	D3
Piriac	22	C4
Pirin	115	D3
Pirkkala	107	E1
Pirmasens	54	B2
Pirna	53	F2
Pirok	77	D3
Pirot	77	E1
Pirovac	74	C1
Pirsógiani	78	C4
Pirttikoski	99	E2
Pisa	60	C4
Pisciotta	67	D1
Pisek	56	C1
Piškorevci	71	E2
Pisogne	58	C4
Písses	88	A2
Pissodéri	79	D3
Pissónas	84	B4
Pissos	28	B3
Pisticci	65	D4
Pistoia	60	C3
Pisuerga, R	35	E4
Piteå	98	B3
Piteälven	98	B3
Pitești	115	D1
Pithagório	89	E2
Píthio (Thessalía)	79	E4
Píthio (Thráki)	81	F1
Pithiviers	25	F1
Pitigliano	63	D2
Pitlochry	3	D4
Pitomača	71	D2
Pittenweem	5	D2
Piva	76	B2
Pivka	70	A3
Pivnica	71	E2
Pivnice	72	B2
Pizarra	43	F3
Piz Buin	58	B2
Pizzighettone	60	B2
Pizzo	67	E3
Pizzoli	63	F2
Pjórsá	96	B2
Plabennec	22	A2
Plaćenska pl	77	D4
Plačkovica	77	F3
Plagiá (Makedonía)	79	F2
Plagiá (Thráki)	81	E2
Plagne, la	31	D1
Plaisance	28	B4
Pláka (Límnos)	85	D1
Pláka (Pelopónnissos)	87	E3
Pláka (Thráki)	81	E2
Pláka, Akr	85	D1
Pláka Litohórou	79	F4
Plakiás	90	C4
Planá	53	E4
Plana	76	A2
Planches-en-Montagne, les	27	D3
Plancoët	22	C3
Plandište	73	D2
Planica Mangrt	70	A1
Plánice	56	C1
Planina (Celje)	70	C2
Planina (Jesenice)	70	A1
Planina (Postojna)	70	A2
Planinica	73	E4
Planitz	53	D3
Plános	86	A1
Plansee	58	C1
Plasencia	39	D2
Plaški	70	C3
Plasy	53	E4
Platamona Lido	66	A2
Platamónas (Kavála)	80	C2
Platamónas (Piería)	79	F4
Platanákia	79	F2
Platanés	90	C3
Platani	68	B3

Períklia	79	E2	Pescolanciano	64	A2	Pétrola	45	D1	Pianello	61	E4	Pierre-de-Bresse	26	C3	Pílio	89	F3			
Perino	60	B2	Pescopagano	64	C4	Petróná	82	C3	Pianoro	61	D3	Pierrefitte	20	C3	Pílio, Óros	83	F2			
Períssa	91	E1	Pescorocchiano	63	F2	Petroșani	114	C1	Pianosa, I (Mare Adriatico)	64	C1	Pierrefitte-Nestaias	37	E2	Pillon, Col du	27	E3			
Perísta	83	D3	Peshkopi	77	D3	Petrotá	81	F1	Pianosa, I (Mare Tirreno)	62	B2	Pierrefonds	19	F3	Pilorí	79	D4			
Peristerá	80	A3	Pesiökylä	99	E3	Petrothálassa	87	E2	Piansano	63	D2	Pierrefontaine-les-Varans	27	D2	Pílos	86	C3			
Peristéra, N	84	B2	Pesmes	26	C2	Petroússa	80	B2	Piapaxaro, P	34	C2	Pierrefort	29	E2	Pilštanj	70	C2			
Perithório	80	B1	Pesočani	77	D4	Petrovac (Bosna i Hercegovina)	70	C3	Pias	42	B1	Pierrelatte	30	B3	Pina	37	D4			
Perívlepto	83	F2	Pêso da Régua	34	B4	Petrovac (Crna Gora)	76	B3	Piatra-Neamt	113	D4	Pieskehaure	97	F2	Piña de Campos	35	E3			
Perivóli	78	C4	Pesoz	34	C1	Petrovac (Srbija)	73	E3	Piave	59	E4	Piešt'any	112	A3	Pinar	43	E3			
Perivóli, N.	83	E2	Pessáni	81	F2	Petrovaradin	72	C2	Piazza al Serchio	60	B3	Pietersaaren mlk	102	C2	Pineda de la Sierra	36	A2			
Perivólio	83	D3	Peštani	77	D4	Petrovčić	72	C3	Piazza Armerina	68	C3	Pietersaari	102	C1	Pineda de Mar	32	B4			
Perjasica	70	C3	Pešter	76	C2	Petrovec	77	E3	Piazza Brembana	58	B4	Pietra Ligure	31	F3	Pinerolo	31	E2			
Perković	75	D1	Pestovo	111	F1	Petrovice	53	F4	Piazzola sul Brenta	59	D4	Pietralunga	61	E4	Pineto	64	A1			
Perleberg	48	C3	Pešurići	72	B4	Petrovići	72	B4	Piber	57	E4	Pietraperzia	68	C3	Piney	20	B4			
Perlez	72	C2	Petačinci	77	E1	Pettenbach	56	C3	Pibeste, P de	37	E1	Pietrasanta	60	B3	Pinhal de Leiria	38	A2			
Përmet	114	C4	Petäjäskoski	99	D2	Pettigoe	12	C2	Pićan	70	A3	Pietra Spada, Pso di	67	F4	Pinhal Novo	38	A4			
Pernå	107	F2	Petäjäves	103	D3	Petworth	9	F3	Picassent	41	E4	Pietrosu	113	D3	Pinhão	34	B4			
Pernaja	107	F2	Petalax	102	B2	Peuerbach	56	C2	Piccolo San Bernardo, Colle del	27	E4	Pieux, les	18	B3	Pinheiro	34	A4			
Pernarec	53	E4	Petalída, Akr	88	B3	Peura	99	D2	Picerno	64	C4	Pieve de' Burgondi del Cairo	60	A2	Pinhel	39	D1			
Pernes	30	C3	Petalídi	86	C3	Pewsey	9	E2	Pickering	7	D1	Pieve di Bono	58	C4	Piniós (Pelopónnissos)	86	C1			
Pernik	114	C2	Petalii, Nissí	88	A1	Peyrat-le-Château	29	D1	Pico	64	A3	Pieve di Cadore	59	E3	Piniós (Thessalía)	83	E1			
Perniö	107	E3	Petalión, Kólpos	88	A1	Peyrehorade	28	A4	Pico, Pto del	39	F2	Pieve di Soligo	59	E3	Pinkafeld	57	F3			
Pernitz	57	E3	Petaloúdes	93	F1	Peyresourde, C de	37	E2	Pico Ruivo	42	A3	Pieve di Teco	31	F3	Pinneberg	48	A3			
Pernštejn	57	E1	Pétange	21	D3	Peyriac-Minervois	32	B1	Picos de Europa	35	E2	Pievepelago	60	C3	Pino	33	F2			
Péronne	19	F2	Pétas	82	C2	Peyrolles	30	C4	Picote, Bgem de	34	C4	Pieve Santo Stefano	61	D4	Pinofranqueado	39	D2			
Perosa Argentina	31	E2	Petehovac	70	B3	Peyrol, Pas de	29	E2	Picquigny	19	F2	Pigádi	83	F3	Pinols	29	F2			
Pérouges	26	C4	Peterborough	9	F1	Peyruis	31	D3	Pídna	79	F3	Pigés	82	C2	Pinoso	45	D1			
Perpignan	32	B2	Peterhead	3	E3	Pézenas	30	A4	Piedicavallo	27	F4	Pigí	83	D4	Pinos Puente	44	A3			
Perrero	31	E2	Peterlee	5	E4	Pezinok	112	A3	Piedicroce	33	F3	Pigna	31	E3	Pinsk	113	D1			
Perreux	26	B4	Petersfield	9	F3	Pezoúla	81	D2	Piediluco	63	E2	Pigón, L	82	C1	Pintado, Emb de	43	D2			
Perros-Guirec	22	B2	Petershagen	17	F2	Pfaffenhofen	55	F2	Piedimonte d'A.	64	B3	Pihlajaveden as	102	C3	Pintamo	99	E3			
Persenbeug	57	D2	Pethelinós	80	B2	Pfäffikon	58	A2	Piedrabuena	40	A4	Pihlajavesi	102	C3	Pinto	40	A2			
Pershore	9	E1	Petilia Policastro	67	F3	Pfalzgrafenweiler	54	C3	Piedrafita	35	D2	Pihlajavesi L	103	F3	Pinzano al Tagliamento	59	E3			
Perstorp	109	D3	Petina	64	C4	Pfarrkirchen	56	B2	Piedrahita	39	E2	Pihlava	102	B3	Pinzolo	58	C3			
Perth	5	D1	Petkula	95	E4	Pfeffenhausen	56	B2	Piedralaves	39	F2	Pihtipudas	103	D2	Piobbico	61	E4			
Perthus, le	32	B3	Petlovača	72	C3	Pforzheim	54	C2	Piedras Albas	39	D3	Piikkiö	107	D2	Piombino	62	C1			
Pertisau	59	D1	Petoússio	82	B2	Pfreimd	56	B1	Piedra San Martín, Collado de la	37	D2	Piippola	103	D1	Pione	60	B2			
Pertoča	70	C1	Petra (E)	45	F3	Pfronten	55	E4	Piedras, Emb de	42	C2	Piispajärvi	99	F3	Pionsat	26	A4			
Pertoúli	83	D1	Pétra (Lésvos)	85	F2	Pfullendorf	55	D4	Piedrasluengas, Pto de	35	F2	Pikal'ovo	111	E1	Piotrków Trybunalski	112	B2			
Pertteli	107	E2	Pétra (Makedonía)	79	E4	Pfullingen	55	D3	Piedratajada	37	D3	Pikérmi	87	F1	Piove di Sacco	61	D1			
Pertuis	30	C3	Petralia	68	C3	Pfunds	58	C2	Pieksämäki	103	E3	Piła	112	A1	Piovene Rocchette	59	D4			
Pertunmaa	103	D3	Petrálona	80	A3	Pfungstadt	54	C1	Pielavesi	103	D2	Pilat-Plage	28	A2	Pipéri, N	84	C2			
Pertusa	37	E3	Petraná	79	E4	Phalsbourg	21	E4	Pielavesi L	103	D2	Pilas	43	D3	Pipriac	23	D3			
Perućac Vrelo	72	C4	Petrčane	74	C1	Philippeville	50	C4	Pielinen	103	F1	Pila, Sa de la	45	D2	Piqueras, Pto de	36	B3			
Peručko jez	75	D1	Petrel	45	D1	Philippsreut	56	C2	Pieljekaise	97	E2	Pilat, Mt	30	B1	Piran	70	A3			
Perugia	61	E4	Petrella, Mte	64	A3	Piacenza	60	B2	Piemonte	31	E2	Pilatus	27	F2	Pir'atin	113	F2			
Perušić	70	C4	Pétres	79	D3	Piadena	60	B2	Piennes	20	C3	Piléa	81	F2	Pireás	87	F1			
Péruwelz	50	B4	Petreto-Bicchisano	33	F4	Piana	33	E3	Pienza	61	D4	Piles	41	E4	Pirgadíkia	80	B3			
Pervenchères	23	F3	Petrič	115	D3	Piana d. Albanesi	68	B3	Pieriá	79	E3	Pilés	93	D3	Pirgetós	83	E1			
Pervomajsk	113	F3	Petrijevci	71	F2	Piancastagnaio	63	D1	Piéria, Óri	79	E4	Píli (Makedonía)	78	C2	Pírgi (Dráma)	80	B2			
Pesaro	61	E3	Petrína	86	C3	Piancavallo	59	E3	Pierowall	3	E1	Píli (Stereá Eláda)	87	F1	Pirgí (Híos)	85	E4			
Pescara	64	A1	Petrinja	71	D3	Piandelagotti	60	C3	Pierre-Buffière	29	D1	Píli (Thessalía)	83	D2	Pirgí (Kérkira)	82	A1			
Pescasseroli	64	A2	Petrodvorec	111	D1	Pian delle Fugazze, Pso	59	D4				Pilica	112	B2	Pirgí (Kozáni)	79	E3			
Peschici	64	C2	Petrohóri	83	D4	Pian del Voglio	60	C3				Pílio	84	A3	Pírgos (Íos)	88	C4			
Peschiera del Garda	60	C1				Pianella	64	A1							Pírgos (Kríti)	91	D4			
Pescia	60	C3																		
Pescina	63	F2																		
Pescocostanzo	64	A2																		

Plataniá (Makedonía) 80 C2
Platánia (Pelopónissos) 86 C2
Plataniá (Thessalía) 84 A2
Platanistós 88 A1
Platanítis 83 D4
Plátanos (Kríti) 90 B3
Plátanos (Pelopónissos) 87 D3
Plátanos (Thessalía) 83 F2
Platariá 82 B2
Plateau-d'Assy 27 E4
Plateés 87 E1
Pláti 81 F1
Platiána 86 C2
Platičevo 72 C3
Platikambos 83 E1
Platís Gialós (Kefaloniá) 86 A1
Platís Gialós (Míkonos) 88 C2
Platís Gialós (Sífnos) 88 B3
Platístomo 83 E3
Plattling 56 B2
Plau 48 C3
Plaue 49 D4
Plauen 53 D3
Plauer See (Potsdam) 49 D4
Plauer See (Schwerin) 48 C3
Plav 76 C2
Plavča 70 C3
Plavna 73 E3
Plavnica 76 B3
Plavnik *I* 70 B4
Plavnik *Mt* 70 B3
Playa de Gandía 41 E4
Playa de San Juan 45 E1
Pleaux 29 E2
Pleine-Fougères 18 B4
Pleinfeld 55 F2
Pleiße 53 D2
Plélan-le-Grand 23 D3
Plélan-le-Petit 22 C3
Pléneuf 22 C2
Plentzia 36 B1
Plépi 87 E2
Plešin 76 C1
Plestin 22 B2
Pleternica 71 E2
Plettenberg 17 F4
Pletvar 77 E3
Pleumartin 25 D3
Pleumeur-Bodou 22 B2
Pleven 115 D2
Pleyben 22 B3
Pliego 44 C2
Plítra 87 D4
Plitvice 70 C3
Plitvička jezera 70 C3
Plitvički Ljeskovac 70 C4
Plješevica 70 C4
Pljevlja 76 B1
Ploaghe 66 B2
Ploče 75 E2
Plochingen 55 D2
Płock 112 B1
Plöckenpaß 59 E2
Plöckenstein 56 C2
Pločno 75 E1
Ploërmel 22 C3
Ploiești 115 D1
Plomári 85 F3
Plomb du Cantal 29 E2
Plombières 27 D1
Plomin 70 B3
Plön 48 B2
Plonéour-Lanvern 22 A3
Płoń, Jez 49 F3
Płońsk 112 B1
Płoty 49 F2
Plouagat 22 C2
Plouaret 22 B2
Plouay 22 B3
Ploubalay 18 A4
Plœuc 22 C3
Ploudalmézeau 22 A2
Plouescat 22 B2
Plougasnou 22 B2
Plougastel-Daoulas 22 A3
Plougonven 22 B2
Plouguenast 22 C3
Plouha 22 C2
Plouigneau 22 B2
Ploumanach 22 B2
Plouzévédé 22 B2
Plovdiv 115 D3
Plumbridge 13 D2
Plungė 110 B3
Pl'ussa 111 D1
Pluvigner 22 C3
Plužine 76 A1
Plympton 8 C4
Plymstock 8 C4
Plzeň 53 E4
Po 60 C2
Poarta de Fier 114 C1
Pobierowo 49 F1
Poblet 37 F4
Pobrđe 76 C1
Počep 111 F4
Pöchlarn 57 E2
Počinok 111 E3
Počitelj 75 F2
Pocking 56 C2
Poćuta 72 C4
Pódareš 77 F3
Podbořany 53 E3
Podčetrtek 70 C2
Podensac 28 B2
Podersdorf 57 F3
Podgajci Posavski 72 B3
Podgarič 71 D2
Podgora 75 E2
Podgorač (Hrvatska) 71 F2
Podgorac (Srbija) 73 E3
Podgrad 70 A3
Podhum 75 E1
Podjuchy 49 E2
Podkoren 70 A1
Podlugovi 71 F4
Podnovlje 71 F3
Podogorá 82 C3
Podohóri 80 B2
Podol'sk 111 F2
Podol'skaja Vozvyšennost' 113 D3
Podpec 70 B2
Podrašnica 71 E4
Podravska Slatina 71 E2
Podromanija 72 B4
Podsreda 70 C2
Podsused 70 C2
Podturen 71 D1
Podujevo 77 D1
Podunavci 73 D4
Poel 48 C2
Poganovo 77 E1
Poggibonsi 60 C4
Poggio Imperiale 64 C2
Poggio Mirteto 63 E2
Poggio Renatico 61 D2
Poggio Rusco 60 C2
Pöggstall 57 E2
Pogoniani 78 B4
Pogradec 77 D4
Pohja 107 E3
Pohja-Lankila 103 F3
Pohjaslahti (Keski-Suomen Lääni) 102 C3
Pohjaslahti (Lapin Lääni) 99 D2
Pohjois-Karjalan Lääni 103 F2
Pohořelice 57 F1
Pohorje 70 B1
Poiana Brașov 113 D4
Poio 34 A2
Poiré, le 24 B3
Poirino 31 F2
Poissons 20 C4
Poitiers 25 D3
Põltsamaa 110 C2
Poix 19 E2
Poix-Terron 20 B2
Pojate 73 E4
Pojo 107 E3
Pokka 95 E3
Poklečani 75 E1
Pokljuka 70 A2
Pokupsko 70 C3
Polače 75 E2
Polacra, Pta de la 44 C4
Pola de Allande 34 C1
Pola de Gordón, la 35 D2
Pola de Laviana 35 E2
Pola de Lena 35 D2
Pola de Siero 35 D1
Polán 40 A3
Polcenigo 59 E3
Połczyn-Zdrój 110 A4
Polegate 10 C3
Poles 113 D1
Polesella 61 D2
Polessk 110 B4
Polhov Gradec 70 A2
Policastro 67 D1
Policastro, Golfo di 67 D2
Police 49 E2
Poličnik 74 C1
Policoro 65 D4
Polidéndri 84 B4
Polidrossos 83 E3
Poliegos, N 88 B4
Poliégou Folegándrou, Stenó 88 B4
Polígiros 80 A3
Polignano a Mare 65 E3
Poligny 27 D3
Polihnitos 85 F3
Polikárpi 79 E2
Polikástano 78 C3
Políkastro 79 F2
Polímilos 79 E3
Polinéri (Makedonía) 79 D4
Polinéri (Thessalía) 82 C2
Polipótamo 79 D3
Polipótamos 84 C4
Políraho 79 E4
Polirinía 90 B3
Polis, M 77 D4
Polissito 81 D2
Polistena 67 E4
Polithéa 82 C1
Politiká 84 A4
Poljana (Slovenija) 70 B1
Poljana (Srbija) 73 D3
Poljčane 70 C1
Polje 71 E3
Poljica 75 E2
Poljice 71 F4
Polla 64 C4
Pölläkkä 103 E2
Pöllau 57 E4
Polle 52 A1
Pollença 45 F2
Pollfoss 100 B3
Pollino, Mte 67 E2
Pollos 35 E4
Polmak 95 E2
Polock 111 D3
Polonnoje 113 D2
Polperro 8 B4
Poltava 113 F2
Polvijärvi 103 F2
Polzela 70 B2
Pomar 37 E3
Pomarance 60 C4
Pomarkku 102 B3
Pombal 38 B2
Pómbia 91 D4
Pomellen 49 E2
Pomezi 53 D4
Pomezia 63 E3
Pomigliano d'Arco 64 B4
Pommersfelden 55 E1
Pomokaira 95 E4
Pomorie 115 E2
Pomorze 110 A4
Pomovaara 95 E4
Pompei 64 B4
Pomposa 61 D2
Poncin 26 C4
Pondoiráklia 79 F2
Pondokómi 79 D3
Ponferrada 34 C2
Ponikovica 72 C4
Pons 28 B1
Ponsacco 60 C4
Pontacq 37 E1
Pontailler 26 C2
Pont-á-Marcq 19 F1
Pont-à-Mousson 21 D3
Pontão 38 B2
Pontardawe 8 C2
Pontarddulais 8 C2
Pontarion 25 E4
Pontarlier 27 D3
Pontassieve 61 D3
Pontaubault 18 B4
Pont-Audemer 19 D3
Pontaumur 26 A4
Pont-Aven 22 B3
Pont Canavese 31 E1
Pontcharra 31 D1
Pontchartrain 19 E4
Pontchâteau 23 D4
Pont-Croix 22 A3
Pont-d'Ain 26 C4
Pont-de-Beauvoisin, le 30 C1
Pont-de-Chéruy 26 C4
Pont-de-Claix, le 30 C2
Pont-de-Dore 26 A4
Pont-de-l'Arche 19 E3
Pont-de-Montvert, le 29 F3
Pont-de-Roide 27 E2
Pont-de-Salars 29 E3
Pont-d'Espagne 37 E2
Pont de Suert 37 F2
Pont-de-Vaux 26 C3
Pont-de-Veyle 26 C4
Pont-d'Oléron 28 A1
Pont-d'Ouilly 18 C4
Pont-du-Château 26 A4
Pont-du-Gard 30 B3
Ponte Arche 58 C3
Ponteareas 34 A3
Pontebba 59 F2
Pontecagnano 64 B4
Ponte Caldelas 34 A2
Ponteceno 60 B2
Ponte Ceso 34 A1
Pontecorvo 64 A3
Ponte da Barca 34 A3
Pontedecimo 60 A3
Ponte de Lima 34 A3
Pontedera 60 C4
Ponte de Sor 38 B3
Pontedeume 34 B1
Ponte di Legno 58 C3
Ponte di Piave 59 E4
Pontefract 7 D2
Pontelandolfo 64 B3
Ponte-Leccia 33 F3
Pontenelle Alpi 59 E3
Pont-en-Royans 30 C1
Ponte San Pietro 60 B1
Pontet, le 30 C3
Ponte Tresa 58 A4
Pontevico 60 B1
Pontfaverger-Moronvilliers 20 B3
Pontgibaud 29 E1
Pontigny 26 B1
Pontinia 63 F3
Pontinvrea 31 F2
Pontivy 22 C3
Pont-l'Abbé 22 A3
Pont-l'Evêque 19 D3
Pontlevoy 25 E2
Pontoise 19 E3
Pontones 44 B2
Pontón, Pto del 35 E2
Pontoon 12 B2
Pontorson 18 B4
Pontremoli 60 B3
Pontresina 58 B3
Pontrieux 22 C2
Pontrilas 9 D2
Ponts 37 F3
Pont-Ste-Maxence 19 F3
Pont-St-Esprit 30 B3
Pont St-Martin 31 E1
Pont-St-Vincent 21 D4
Pont-Scorff 22 B3
Ponts-de-Cé, les 23 E4
Pontsenni 8 C1
Pont-sur-Yonne 26 A1
Pontvallain 23 F4
Pontypool 9 D2
Pontypridd 8 C2
Ponza, I 63 F4
Ponziane, I 63 F4
Poole 9 E3
Poperinge 50 A3
Popinci 72 C3
Popoli 64 A2
Popovac 73 E4
Popovača 71 D2
Popova Šapka 77 D3
Popov Most 76 A1
Popovo 115 E2
Poppenhausen 52 B4
Poppi 61 D3
Poprad 112 B3
Porcari 60 C3
Porchov 111 D2
Porcuna 43 F2
Pordenone 59 E3
Poreč 70 A3
Pori 107 D1
Porjus 98 B2
Porkkalanselkä 107 E3
Porma, Emb del 35 E2
Porma, R 35 E2
Pornainen 107 F2
Pörnbach 55 F2
Pornic 24 A2
Pornichet 24 A2
Póros (Kefaloniá) 86 A1
Póros (Lefkáda) 82 B3
Póros (Póros) 87 F2
Póros, N 87 F2
Porozina 70 B3
Pórpi 81 D2
Porquerolles 31 D4
Porrentruy 27 E2
Porretta Terme 60 C3
Porriño 34 A3
Porsangen 95 E1
Porsangerhalvøya 95 D1
Porsgrunn 104 C3
Pórshöfn 96 C1
Portadown 13 D2
Portaferry 13 E2
Portaje, Emb de 39 D3
Porta, la 33 F3
Portalegre 38 C3
Portalé, Pto del 37 D2
Portalrubio 41 D2
Portariá 83 F2
Portarlington 13 D4
Port Askaig 4 B2
Portavogie 13 E2
Port-Bacarès 32 B2
Portbail 18 B3
Portbou 32 C3
Port Charlotte 4 A2
Port, Col de 37 F2
Port-Cros 31 D4
Port-de-Bouc 30 C4
Porte, Col de 30 C1
Port-Einon 8 C2
Portella Femmina Morta 69 D3
Port Ellen 4 A2
Portelo 34 C3
Port-en-Bessin 18 C3
Port Erin 6 A1
Pórtes 87 F2
Portet-d'Aspet, Col de 37 F2
Portezuelo 39 D3
Port Glasgow 4 C2
Portglenone 13 E1
Porthcawl 8 C2
Porthmadog 6 A3
Porthmós Elafonissou 90 A1
Portici 64 B4
Portile de Fier 114 C1
Portilla de la Reina 35 E2
Portillo 35 E4
Portillo de la Canda 34 C3
Portillo de Padornelo 34 C3
Portillo, Pto del 39 E2
Portimão 42 A2
Portimo 99 D2
Portinatx, Cala de 45 D3
Portishead 9 D2
Port-Joinville 24 A3
Port Láirge 15 D4
Portland, Bill of 9 D4
Port-la-Nouvelle 32 B2
Portlaoise 13 D4
Port-Leucate 32 B2
Port-Louis 22 B4
Portman 45 D3
Port-Manech 22 B3
Portmarnock 13 E4
Portnacroish 4 B1
Portnaguran 2 B2
Portnahaven 4 A2
Port-Navalo 22 C4
Porto (F) 33 E3
Porto (P) 34 A4
Porto Azzurro 62 C1
Pórto Carrás 80 B4
Porto Ceresio 58 A4
Porto Cervo 66 B1
Porto Cesareo 65 F4
Porto Cristo 45 F3
Porto de Envalira 32 A2
Porto de Lagos 42 A2
Porto de Mós 38 A3
Portodemouros, Emb de 34 B2
Porto do Barqueiro 34 B1
Porto do Son 34 A2
Porto Empedocle 68 B4
Portoferraio 62 C1
Portofino 60 A3
Port of Ness 2 B2
Porto Garibaldi 61 D2
Porto, G de 33 E3
Pórto Germeno 87 E1
Portogruaro 59 E4
Portohéli 87 E2
Pórto Kágio 87 D4
Pörtom 102 B2
Portomaggiore 61 D2
Portomarín 34 B2
Porto-Maurizio 31 F3
Porto Moniz 42 A3
Portomouro 34 A2
Portonovo 34 A2
Porto Petro 45 F3
Porto Pino 66 B4
Pórto Ráfti 88 A1
Porto Recanati 61 F4
Porto Rotondo 66 C1
Portorož 70 A3
Porto San Giorgio 61 F4
Porto Sant' Elpidio 61 F4
Porto Santo 42 A3
Porto Santo, I de 42 A3
Porto Santo Stefano 63 D2
Portoscuso 66 A4
Porto Tolle 61 D2
Porto Torres 66 A2
Porto-Vecchio 33 F4
Portovenere 60 B3
Portpatrick 4 B3
Portree 2 B3
Portrush 13 D1
Port-Ste-Marie 28 C3
Port-St-Louis 30 B4
Port St Mary 6 A1
Portsalon 13 D1
Pörtschach 70 A1
Portsmouth 9 F3
Portstewart 13 D1
Port-sur-Saône 27 D1
Port Talbot 8 C2
Porttipahdan tekojärvi 95 E4
Portugalete 36 B1
Portumna 12 C4
Port-Vendres 32 B2
Port William 4 C4
Porvoo 107 F2
Porvoonjoki 107 F2
Porzuna 40 A4
Posada 66 C2
Posadas 43 E2
Pöschenhöhe 56 C3
Pošechonje-Volodarsk 111 F1
Posedarje 74 C1
Posets, Pico 37 F2
Posio 99 E2
Positano 64 B4
Poßneck 52 C3
Possidi 80 A4
Possidonía 88 B2
Posta 63 F1
Postavy 111 D3
Postira 75 D2
Postojna 70 B2
Postojnska jama 70 A2
Poštorná 57 F1
Posušje 75 E1
Potami 80 C1
Potamiá 87 D3
Potamiés 91 E4
Potamós (Andikíthira) 90 A2
Potamós (Kíthira) 90 A1
Potamoúla 82 C3
Potenza 64 C4
Potenza *R* 61 E4
Potenza Picenza 61 F4
Potes 35 E2
Potídea, N. 80 A4
Potigny 18 C3
Potoci 75 F1
Potok 71 D2
Potós 80 C3
Potpećko jez 76 B1
Potsdam 49 D4
Pottenstein 57 E3
Potters Bar 9 F2
Pöttmes 55 F2
Potton 9 F1
Pouancé 23 D4
Pougues-les-Eaux 26 A2
Pouilly (Nièvre) 26 A2
Pouilly (Rhône) 26 B4
Pouilly-en-Auxois 26 C2
Poulaphouca Reservoir 13 D4
Poúlari, Akr 92 C1
Pouldu, le 22 B3
Pouliguen, le 24 A2
Poúlithra 87 E3
Poúnda 88 C3
Poúnda, Akr 84 B4
Pournári 83 E2
Pournári, Teh L 82 C2
Pourniás, Kólpos 85 D1
Pourri, Mt 31 D1
Poussu 99 F3
Pouyastruc 37 E1
Pouzauges 24 C3
Pouzin, le 30 B2
Považská Bystrica 112 B3
Poveda 40 C2
Povlja 75 E2
Povljana 70 C4
Povljen 72 C4
Povoa de Lanhoso 34 A4
Póvoa de Varzim 34 A4
Powerscourt 13 D4
Powys 9 D1
Poysdorf 57 F2
Pöytyä 107 D2
Poza de la Sal 36 A2
Požarevac 73 D3
Požega 72 C4
Požeranje 77 D2
Poznań 112 A1
Pozo Alcón 44 B2
Pozoblanco 43 F1
Pozo Cañada 44 C1
Pozo de Guadalajara 40 B2
Pozo Higuera 44 C3
Pozohondo 44 C1
Pozondón 41 D2
Pozozal, Pto 35 F2
Pozuelo (Castilla-la-Mancha) 44 C1
Pozuelo (Extremadura) 39 D2
Pozuelo de Calatrava 40 A4
Pozzallo 69 D4
Pozzomaggiore 66 B2
Pozzuoli 64 A4
Pozzuolo 59 F3
Präbichl 57 D3
Praća 76 A1
Prachatice 56 C1
Prada, Emb de 34 C3
Pradairo 34 C2
Pradarena, Pso di 60 B3
Pradelles 29 F2
Prádena 36 A4

Prades (E) 37 F4
Prades (F) 32 B2
Prado del Rey 43 D3
Pradoluengo 36 A2
Prägraten 59 E2
Praha 53 F4
Prahecq 24 C4
Prahova 115 D1
Prahovo 73 F3
Praia a Mare 67 E2
Praia da Barra 38 B1
Praia da Rocha 42 A2
Praia da Vieira 38 A2
Praia de Mira 38 B1
Praia de Santa Cruz 38 A3
Praia de Tocha 38 B2
Prali 31 E2
Pralognan 31 D1
Pra-Loup 31 D2
Prámanda 82 C2
Pramollo, Pso di 59 F2
Prangio 81 F1
Pranjani 72 C4
Prapatnica 75 D1
Prassiá 83 D2
Prassiés 90 C3
Præstø 108 C4
Prat de Compte 41 F1
Pratella 64 A3
Prati di Tivo 63 F1
Prato (Toscana) 60 C3
Prato (Umbria) 63 E1
Pratola Peligna 64 A2
Pratomagno 61 D4
Prato-Sornico 58 A3
Prats-de-Mollo 32 B3
Pravdinsk 110 B4
Pravia 35 D1
Praz 27 E4
Prebold 70 B2
Précy-sous-Thil 26 B2
Predappio 61 D3
Predazzo 59 D3
Preddvor 70 B2
Predeal 113 D4
Predejane 77 E1
Predel 70 A2
Predela 115 D3
Predil, Pso di 59 F2
Predjama 70 A2
Predoi 59 D2
Predošćica 70 B3
Pré-en-Pail 23 E3
Preetz 48 B2
Pregarten 57 D2
Preiner Gscheid 57 E3
Prekaja 71 D4
Prekestolen 104 A3

Preko 74 C1
Preljina 73 D4
Prelog 71 D1
Preločšica 71 D2
Premantura 70 A4
Prémery 26 A2
Premià de Mar 32 B4
Premilcuore 61 D3
Premnitz 49 D4
Premuda 74 B1
Premuda I 74 B1
Prenj 75 F1
Prenjas 77 D4
Prenzlau 49 E3
Prepolac 77 D1
Přerov 112 A3
Prerow 48 C1
Pré-St-Didier 27 E4
Preševo 77 E2
Presjeka 76 B2
Preslav 115 E2
Presolana, Pso della 58 B4
Prešov 112 B3
Prespansko Ez 77 D4
Pressath 53 D4
Pressbaum 57 E2
Prestatyn 6 B2
Presteigne 9 D1
Preste, la 32 B3
Prestfoss 104 C3
Přeštice 56 C1
Preston 6 B2
Prestonpans 5 D2
Prestwick 4 C2
Pretoro 64 A2
Prettau 59 D2
Prettin 53 D1
Pretzsch 53 D1
Preuilly 25 D3
Préveli 90 C4
Préveza 82 B3
Préveza (Nomos) 82 B2
Prevršac 71 D3
Prezid 70 B3
Pribini 71 E4
Priboj (Bosna i Hercegovina) 72 B3
Priboj (Srbija) 76 B1
Příbram 53 F4
Priego 40 C2
Priego de Córdoba 43 F3
Prien 56 B3
Prienai 110 C4
Prievidza 112 B3
Prigradica 75 E2
Prijeboj 70 C3
Prijedor 71 D3

Prijepolje 76 B1
Prilep 77 E3
Prilike 73 D4
Priluka 75 E1
Priluki 113 F1
Primaube, la 29 E3
Primel-Trégastel 22 B2
Primišlje 70 C3
Primolano 59 D3
Primorsk 111 D1
Primošten 75 D2
Primstal 54 B1
Princetown 8 C3
Prinés 90 C3
Prínos 80 C3
Prior, C 34 B1
Prip' at' 112 C1
Prisad 77 E3
Prislop 113 D3
Prisoje 75 E1
Priština 77 D2
Pritzerbe 49 D4
Pritzier 48 B3
Pritzwalk 48 C3
Privas 30 B2
Priverno 63 F3
Privlaka (Vincovci) 71 F2
Privlaka (Zadar) 70 C4
Prizren 77 D2
Prizzi 68 B3
Prnjavor (Bosna i Hercegovina) 71 E3
Prnjavor (Srbija) 72 B3
Proaza 35 D1
Probištip 77 E2
Probstzella 52 C3
Procida 64 A4
Pródromos 83 F4
Proenca-a-Nova 38 B3
Proevska Banja 77 E2
Profitis Ilías 93 E1
Profondeville 50 C4
Próhoma 79 F3
Prokletije 76 C2
Prokópi 84 A3
Prokuplje 77 D1
Prolom 77 D1
Prómahi 79 E2
Promahónas 80 A1
Promina, V. 75 D1
Promiri 84 A2
Pronsfeld 51 D4
Propriano 33 F4
Proskinás 83 F4
Prosna 112 A2
Prossedi 63 F3
Prossílio 81 D2
Prossotsáni 80 B2
Prostějov 112 A3

Próti 80 B2
Próti, N 86 B3
Protoklíssio 81 F1
Prötzel 49 E4
Proussós 83 D3
Provatónas 81 F2
Provence, Canal de 30 C4
Provenchères 21 E4
Provins 20 A4
Prozor 75 E1
Prudhoe 5 E3
Prukljansko jezero 75 D1
Prüm 51 D4
Pruna 43 E3
Prunetta 60 C3
Prut 113 D3
Prut 113 E4
Pružany 112 C1
Prvić 70 B4
Przasnysz 112 B1
Przełęcz Dukielska 112 C3
Przemyśl 112 C2
Przybiernów 49 F2
Psača 77 E2
Psahná 84 B4
Psáka 82 B2
Psális, Akr 88 A4
Psará 85 E4
Psarádes 78 C2
Psári, N 85 E4
Psári (Arkadía) 86 C2
Psári (Korinthía) 87 D1
Psári (Mt) 80 C3
Psáthi 88 B4
Psathópirgos 83 D4
Psathotópi 82 C2
Psérimos, N 89 F3
Psihró 91 E4
Psínthos 93 F1
Pskov 111 D2
Pskovskoje Ozero 111 D2
Ps'ol 113 F2
Pšov 53 E3
Psunj 71 E2
Pteléa 80 C2
Ptéri 83 D2
Ptolemaḯda 79 D3
Ptóo 84 A4
Ptuj 70 C1
Puchberg 57 E3
Pučišča 75 E2
Puckeridge 9 F2
Puçol 41 E3
Pudasjärvi 99 E3
Puebla de Alcocer 39 E4

Puebla de Almenara 40 B3
Puebla de Beleña 40 B1
Puebla de Benifasar 41 F2
Puebla de Don Fadrique 44 B2
Puebla de D. Rodrigo 39 F4
Puebla de Guzmán 42 C2
Puebla de la Calzada 39 D4
Puebla de la Reina 39 D4
Puebla del Caramiñal 34 A2
Puebla de Lillo 35 E2
Puebla de Obando 39 D3
Puebla de Sanabria 34 C3
Puebla de Trives 34 C3
Puebla Tornesa 41 F3
Pueblica de V. 35 D3
Puente de Domingo Flórez 34 C3
Puente de Génave 44 B1
Puente de los Fierros 35 D2
Puente Genil 43 F3
Puente la Reina 36 C2
Puente la Reina de Jaca 37 D2
Puentenansa 35 F2
Puente Nuevo, Emb de 43 E1
Puentes, Emb de 44 C2
Puentes Viejas, Emb de 40 B1
Puente Viesgo 35 F2
Puerto Castilla 39 E2
Puerto de Alcudia 45 F2
Puerto de Andratx 45 E3
Puerto de la Cruz 42 B4
Puerto de la Encina 43 E3
Puerto del Rosario 42 C4
Puerto de Mazarrón 45 D3
Puerto de Pollença 45 F2
Puerto de San Vicente 39 F3
Puerto de Sóller 45 E2
Puerto Lápice 40 B4
Puertollano 44 A1
Puerto Lumbreras 44 C3
Puerto Real 43 D4
Puerto Serrano 43 E3
Pugets-Théniers 31 E3

Puglia 65 D3
Puhos (Oulun Lääni) 99 E3
Puhos (Pohjois-Karjalan Lääni) 103 F3
Puhosjärvi 99 E3
Puhovac 71 F4
Puigcerda 32 A3
Puig Major 45 E2
Puignal 32 A2
Puig-reig 32 A3
Puigsacalm 32 B3
Puiseaux 25 F1
Puisserguier 30 A4
Pujols 28 B2
Pukë 76 C3
Pukiš 72 B3
Pukkila 107 F2
Pula (I) 66 B4
Pula (YU) 70 A4
Pulaj 76 B3
Puławy 112 C2
Pulborough 10 C3
Pulkau 57 E2
Pulkkila 99 D4
Pulpi 44 C3
Pulsnitz 53 E2
Pultusk 112 B1
Punat 70 B3
Punkaharju 103 F3
Punkalaidun 107 E2
Puokio 99 E4
Puolanka 99 E4
Purbach 57 F3
Purchena 44 B3
Purgstall 57 E2
Purkersdorf 57 E2
Purmerend 16 C2
Purnu 103 D3
Purullena 44 B3
Puruvesi 103 F3
Puškin 111 D1
Püspökladány 112 C4
Pustoška 111 D2
Pusula 107 E2
Puszcza 112 C1
Putanges 18 C4
Putbus 49 D1
Putgarten 49 D1
Putignano 65 E3
Putinci 72 C2
Putivl' 113 F1
Putlitz 48 C3
Puttelange 21 E3

Puttgarden 48 B1
Puula 103 D3
Puumala 103 E3
Puy de Dôme 29 E1
Puy-de-Dôme (Dépt) 29 E1
Puy de Sancy 29 E1
Puy-en-Velay, le 30 A2
Puy-Guillaume 26 A4
Puylaurens 29 D4
Puy-l'Evêque 29 D3
Puymirol 28 C3
Puymorens, Col de 32 A2
Pwllheli 6 A3
Pyhä-Häkki 103 D2
Pyhäjärvi (Hameen Lääni) 107 E1
Pyäjärvi (Oulun Lääni) 103 D1
Pyhäjärvi (Pohjois-Karjalan Lääni) 103 F3
Pyhäjärvi (Turun ja Porin Lääni) 107 D2
Pyhäjärvi L 103 D1
Pyhäjoki (Oulun Lääni) 99 D4
Pyhäjoki (Turun ja Porin Lääni) 107 D2
Pyhäjoki R 99 D4
Pyhältö 103 F4
Pyhäntä (Piipola) 103 D1
Pyhäntä (Ristijärvi) 99 E4
Pyhäranta 107 D2
Pyhäsalmi 103 D1
Pyhäselkä 103 F2
Pyhäselkä L 103 F2
Pyhätunturi 99 D2
Pyhatunturi 99 E2
Pyhävuori 102 C2
Pyhitysvaara 99 E3
Pyhrnpaß 57 D3
Pyhtää 107 F2
Pyla 28 A2
Pylkönmäki 103 D2
Pyrénées 37 E2
Pyrénées-Atlantiques 28 A4
Pyrénées-Orientales 32 B2
Pyrénées, Parc Nat des 37 E2
Pyrzyce 49 F3
Pyttis 107 F2

Q
Qaf'e Shllahut 76 C3
Qaf'e Shtamës 76 C4
Quakenbrück 17 E2
Quarré-les-Tombes 26 B2
Quarteira 42 B3
Quarto d'Altino 61 D1
Quartu San Elena 66 B4

Quatre Chemins 24 B3
Quatretonda 41 E4
Quedlinburg 52 C2
Queenborough 11 D2
Queen Elizabeth Forest Park 4 C2
Queensferry 6 B2
Quejigares, Pto de 40 A4
Queluz 38 A4
Queralbs 32 B3

Querfurt 52 C2
Quérigut 32 A2
Quero 40 B3
Quesada 44 B2
Quesnoy, le 20 A2
Questembert 22 C4
Quettehou 18 B3
Quiberon 22 C4
Quickborn 48 A2
Quiévrain 50 B4

Quigley's Point 13 D1
Quillan 32 B2
Quillane, Col de la 32 A2
Quillebeuf 19 D3
Quimper 22 B3
Quimperlé 22 B3
Quincinetto 31 E1
Quincoces de Yuso 36 A1
Quingey 27 D2

Quintana (Andalucía) 43 E2
Quintana (Extremadura) 39 E4
Quintana del Puente 35 F3
Quintana Martín Galíndez 36 A2
Quintanar de la Orden 40 B3

Quintanar de la Sierra 36 B3
Quintanar del Rey 40 C4
Quintana Redonda 36 B3
Quintanilha 34 C4
Quintanilla de Onésimo 35 F4
Quintin 22 C3
Quinto 37 D4

Quinzano d'Oglio 60 B1
Quipar, R 44 C2
Quiroga 34 C2
Quissac 30 B3
Qukës 77 D4
Quoich, L 2 C4

R

Raab 56 C2
Raab R 57 E4
Raabs 57 E1
Raahe 99 D4
Raajärvi 99 D2
Rääkkylä 103 F2
Raalte 17 D2
Raanujärvi 99 D3
Raasay 2 B3
Raasay, Sd of 2 B3
Raattama 95 D4
Rab 70 B4
Rab 70 B4
Rába 112 A4
Rabac 70 B3
Rábade 34 B1
Rabastens 29 D4
Rabastens-de-
Bigorre 37 E4
Rabat 68 B4
Rabe 72 C1
Rabka 112 B3
Rabrovo
(Makedonija) 77 F3
Rabrovo (Srbija) 73 E3
Rača (Kragujevac) 73 D3
Rača (Radan) 77 D1
Racconigi 31 E2
Rače 70 C1
Rachov 112 C3
Racibórz 112 A2
Račinovci 72 B3
Račišće 75 E2
Radalj 72 B3
Radan 77 D1
Rădăuţi 113 D3
Radbuza 56 B1
Rade 48 A3
Råde 105 D2
Radeberg 53 E2
Radebeul 53 E2
Radeburg 53 E2
Radeče 70 B2
Radechov 112 C2
Radenci 70 C1
Radenthein 59 F2
Radevowald 17 E4
Radici, Pso delle 60 C3
Radicondoli 60 C4
Radika 77 D3
Radimlje 75 E2
Radiovce 77 D3
Radlje 70 B1
Radljevo 72 C3
Radnice 53 E4
Radohinës, Maj'e 76 C2
Radojevo 73 D1
Radom 112 B2
Radomsko 112 B2
Radomyšl' 113 E2
Radotin 53 F4
Radovče 76 B2
Radovići 76 B3
Radoviš 77 F3
Radovljica 70 A2
Radovnica 77 E2
Radøy 104 A2
Radstadt 59 F1
Radstädter
Tauernpaß 59 F1
Radstock 9 D2
Raduša 75 E1
Radusa 77 D3
Radviliškis 110 C3
Radzyn' Podlaski 112 C2
Raesfeld 17 E3
Raffadali 68 B4
Rafina 88 A1
Ragama 39 F1
Raglan 9 D2
Rago 97 F1
Ragua, Pto de la 44 B3
Raguhn 53 D1
Ragunda 101 F2
Ragusa 69 D4
Rahden 17 F2
Ráhes 83 F3
Rahlstedt 48 B3
Raia, Rib de 38 B4
Rain 55 F2
Räisälä 99 E2
Raisduoddarhal'di 94 C2

Raisio 107 D2
Raittijärvi 94 C3
Rajac 73 F3
Raja-Jooseppi 95 F3
Rajamäki 107 E2
Rajince 77 E2
Raka 70 C2
Rakalj 70 A4
Rakitna 70 B2
Rakitnica 71 D2
Rakkestad 105 D3
Rakova Bara 73 E3
Rakovac 71 E3
Rakovica 70 C3
Rakovnik 53 E4
Rakvere 110 C1
Ralja 73 D3
Ram 73 D2
Ramacca 69 D3
Ramales de la
Victoria 36 A1
Ramallosa 34 A2
Ramberg 97 E1
Rambervillers 21 D4
Rambouillet 19 E4
Rambucourt 20 C4
Ramno 77 D2
Ramnoús 84 B4
Ramor, L 13 D3
Ramsau 56 B4
Ramsau 59 F1
Ramsele 101 F2
Ramsey
(Cambridge) 9 F1
Ramsey (I of Man) 6 A1
Ramsgate 11 D3
Ramsjö 101 E3
Ramstein 54 B1
Ramsund 94 B3
Ramundberget 101 D2
Ramvik 101 F2
Rana 97 D3
Ranalt 59 D2
Rance 22 C3
Ravenna 61 D2
Randaberg 104 A3
Randak 104 B3
Randalstown 13 E2
Randan 26 A4
Randanne 29 E1
Randazzo 69 D3
Randers 108 B2
Randijaure 98 A2
Randow 49 E2
Randsfjorden 105 D2
Råneå 98 C3
Råneälven 98 B2
Rangsdorf 49 E4
Rankweil 58 B2
Rannoch, L 4 C1
Ranovac 73 E3
Rantasalmi 103 E3
Rantsila 99 D4
Ranua 99 D3
Raon-l'Etape 21 E4
Rapallo 60 A3
Rapolano Terme 61 D4
Rapolla 64 C3
Rapperswil 58 A2
Rapsáni 83 E1
Raptópoulo 86 C3
Raša 70 A3
Räsälä 103 E2
Raša R 70 A3
Rasbo 106 B3
Rascafría 40 A1
Rasdorf 52 B2
Raseiniai 110 C3
Rasimbegov Most 77 E4
Rasina 73 E4
Raška 76 C1
Rasno 75 E2
Raso, C 38 A4
Rasquera 41 F1
Rastatt 54 C2
Rastede 47 F3
Rastegai'sa 95 E2
Rastenberg 52 C2
Rastenfeld 57 E2
Rasueros 39 F1
Rätan 101 E3
Rateče 70 A1
Ratekau 48 B2
Rates 34 A4
Rathdowney 12 C4

Rathdrum 13 D4
Rathenow 49 D4
Rathfriland 13 E2
Rathkeale 14 B3
Rathlin I 13 E1
Rath Luirc 14 B3
Rathmelton 13 D1
Rathmore 14 B4
Rathmullan 13 D1
Raticosa, Pso della 61 D3
Ratingen 17 E4
Ratkovac 76 C2
Ratkovo 72 B2
Ratten 57 E3
Rattenberg 59 D1
Rattersdorf 57 F3
Rattray 5 D1
Rattray Head 3 E1
Rättvik 101 E4
Ratzeburg 48 B2
Raubling 56 B3
Raucourt-et-Flaba 20 C2
Raudanjoki 99 D2
Raudaskylä 102 C1
Raufarhöfn 96 C1
Raufoss 105 D2
Rauha 103 E4
Rauhamäki 103 D3
Rauland 104 B3
Rauma (N) 100 B3
Rauma (SF) 107 D2
Rauris 59 E1
Rautalampi 103 D2
Rautas 94 C4
Rautavaara 103 E1
Rautio 102 C1
Rautjärvi 103 F3
Ravan 71 F4
Ravanica 73 E4
Ravanjska 70 C4
Ravanusa 68 C4
Ravello 64 B4
Raven 71 D2
Ravenna 61 D2
Ravensbrück 49 D3
Ravensburg 55 D4
Ravna Dubrava 77 E1
Ravna Gora 70 B3
Ravna Reka 73 E3
Ravne na
Koroškem 70 B1
Ravnište 77 D1
Ravnje 72 B3
Ravno 75 F2
Ravno Bučje 73 F4
Ravno, G. 75 E1
Rawicz 112 A2
Rawtenstall 6 C2
Rayleigh 11 D2
Rayol 31 D4
Räyrinki 102 C2
Ražana 72 C4
Ražanac 70 C4
Razboj 71 E3
Razbojna 77 D1
Raždaginja 76 C1
Razelm 113 E4
Razgrad 115 E2
Razlog 115 D3
Razlovci 77 F2
Raz, Pte du 22 A3
Reading 9 F2
Reales 43 E4
Réalmont 32 B1
Rebais 20 A4
Rebbenesøy 94 B2
Rebordelo 34 C4
Reç 76 C3
Recanati 61 F4
Recco 60 A3
Recey 26 C1
Rechnitz 57 F4
Rečica (SU) 111 E4
Rečica (YU) 70 C3
Recke 17 E2
Recklinghausen 17 E3
Recknitz 48 C2
Recoaro Terme 59 D4
Recuerda 36 A4
Recz 49 F2
Redange 21 D2
Red B 13 E1
Redcar 5 F4
Redditch 9 E1

Redhill 10 C3
Redon 23 D4
Redondela 34 A3
Redondo 38 C4
Redruth 8 B4
Ree, L 12 C3
Rees 17 D3
Reeth 6 C1
Refsnes 94 A3
Reftele 109 D2
Rega 49 F2
Regalbuto 69 D3
Regen 56 B2
Regensburg 56 B2
Regenstauf 56 B2
Reggello 61 D4
Reggio di Calabria 67 E4
Reggiolo 60 C2
Reggio nell' Emilia 60 C2
Reghin 113 D4
Regnitz 55 E1
Reguengos de
Monsaraz 42 B1
Rehau 53 D4
Rehburg-
Loccum 48 A4
Rehden 17 F2
Rehna 48 B2
Reichenau (A) 57 E3
Reichenau (CH) 58 B2
Reichenbach
(Dresden) 53 F2
Reichenbach
(Karl-Marx-Stadt) 53 D3
Reichertshofen 55 F2
Reichshoffen 21 E3
Reigate 10 C3
Reignier 27 D4
Ré, Ile de 24 B4
Reillanne 30 C3
Reims 20 B3
Reinach 27 F2
Reinbek 48 B3
Reinberg 49 D1
Reine 97 E1
Reinfeld 48 B2
Reinheim 54 C1
Reinli 104 C2
Reinosa 35 F2
Reinøy 94 C2
Reisaelva 94 C2
Reischenhart 56 B3
Reisjärvi 103 D1
Reiss 3 D2
Reit im Winkl 56 B4
Reitzenhain 53 E3
Reka 70 A3
Rekovac 73 E4
Remagen 51 E4
Rémalard 23 F3
Remeskylä 103 D1
Remich 21 D2
Remiremont 27 D1
Remolinos 36 C3
Remouchamps 51 D4
Remoulins 30 B3
Rempstone 7 D3
Remscheid 17 E4
Rémuzat 30 C2
Rena 105 D2
Renaix 50 B3
Renazé 23 E4
Renchen 54 C3
Rende 67 E2
Rendína
(Makedonía) 80 B3
Rendína
(Thessalía) 83 D1
Rendsburg 48 A2
Rengínio 83 F3
Rengsdorf 51 E4
Reni 113 E4
Renish Pt 2 A3
Renko 107 E2
Renkum 17 D3
Rennebu 100 C2
Rennerod 51 F3
Rennes 23 D3
Rennes-les-Bains 32 B2
Rennesøy 104 A3
Rennweg 59 F2
Reno 61 D2
Rensjön 94 C4
Rensvik 100 B2
Renwez 20 B2

Réole, la 28 B2
Replot 102 B2
Replotfjärden 102 B2
Repojoki 95 E3
Reposaari 102 B3
République, Col de
la 30 B1
Repvag 95 E1
Requena 41 D4
Réquista 29 E3
Rerik 48 C2
Resanovci 71 D4
Resavica 73 E3
Reschenpaß 58 C2
Resen
(Makedonija) 77 D4
Resen (Srbija) 77 E2
Resende 34 B4
Resia, Pso di 58 C2
Resita 114 C1
Resko 49 F2
Resmo 109 E3
Resna 76 B3
Resnik 73 D3
Ressons 19 F3
Restafjorden 94 C2
Restelica 77 D3
Resuttano 68 C3
Retezatului, M 114 C1
Rethel 20 B3
Rethem 48 A4
Rethen 52 B1
Réthimno 90 C3
Réthimno
(Nomos) 90 C3
Retiers 23 D3
Retortillo, Emb de 43 E2
Retuerta 41 D1
Retuerta del
Bullaque 39 F3
Retuerta, Emb de 36 A3
Retz 57 E2
Reuilly 25 E3
Reus 37 F4
Reusel 16 C4
Reuss 27 F2
Reuterstadt-
Stavenhagen 49 D2
Reutlingen 55 D3
Reutte 58 C1
Revard, Mt 27 D4
Revel 29 D4
Revesbotn 95 D1
Revigny 20 C4
Revin 20 B2
Řevničov 53 F3
Revolcadores 44 C3
Revonlahti 99 D4
Revsnes 104 B1
Reyðarfjörður 96 C2
Reykjavik 96 A2
Rēzekne 111 D2
Rezzato 60 B1
Rezzoaglio 60 A3
Rgotina 73 F3
Rhaeadr 8 C1
Rhayader 8 C1
Rheda-
Wiedenbrück 17 F3
Rhede 17 D3
Rhein 17 D3
Rheinbach 51 E4
Rheinberg 17 D3
Rheinböllen 54 B1
Rheine 17 E2
Rheinfelden (CH) 27 F2
Rheinfelden (D) 54 C4
Rheinhausen 17 D3
Rheinland-Pfalz 51 E4
Rheinsberg 49 D3
Rheinwaldhorn 58 B3
Rhêmes N.D. 31 E1
Rhenen 16 C3
Rheydt 17 D4
Rhinau 21 E4
Rhinow 49 D4
Rho 60 A1
Rhondda 8 C2
Rhône 26 C4
Rhône (Dépt) 26 B4
Rhône à Sète,
Canal du 30 B3
Rhosneigr 6 A2

Rhossili 8 C2
Rhüden 52 B1
Rhum 2 B4
Rhum, Sd of 2 B4
Rhune, la 28 A4
Rhuthun 6 B3
Rhyl 6 B2
Rhynern 17 E3
Rhynie 3 E4
Riaillé 23 D4
Riákia 79 E3
Rial 34 A2
Riaño 35 E2
Riaño, Emb de 35 E2
Rians 30 C4
Riansares R 40 B3
Rianxo 34 A2
Riaza 36 A4
Ribadavia 34 B3
Ribadelago 34 C3
Ribadeo 34 C1
Riba de Saelices 40 C1
Riba de Santiuste 36 B4
Ribadesella 35 E1
Ribarci 77 E2
Ribariće 76 C1
Riba-roja, Emb de 37 E4
Ribarska Banja 73 E4
Ribas de Campos 35 E3
Ribas de Sil 34 B2
Ribatejo 38 B3
Ribble 6 C2
Ribe 108 A3
Ribeauvillé 27 E1
Ribécourt 19 F3
Ribeira de Pena 34 B4
Ribeira, Emb de la 34 B1
Ribemont 20 A2
Ribera 68 B3
Ribérac 28 C1
Ribera de Cardós 32 A2
Ribera del Fresno 43 D1
Ribes de Freser 32 B3
Ribiers 30 C3
Ribnica (Bosna i
Hercegovina) 71 F4
Ribnica (Kočevje) 70 B2
Ribnica (Postojna) 70 A3
Ribnica na
Pohorju 70 B1
Ribnik 70 C2
Ribnitz-
Damgarten 48 C1
Ribolla 62 C1
Říčany 53 F4
Riccia 64 B3
Riccione 61 E3
Riceys, les 26 B1
Richelieu 25 D3
Richmond
(London) 9 F2
Richmond (Yorks) 6 C1
Richtenberg 49 D1
Rickling 48 A2
Ricla 36 C4
Ricobayo, Emb de 35 D4
Riddica 72 B1
Riec 22 B3
Ried
(Oberösterreich) 56 C3
Ried (Tirol) 58 C2
Riedenburg 55 F2
Riedlingen 55 D3
Riegel 54 C3
Riegersburg 57 F4
Riego de la Vega 35 D3
Riesa 53 E2
Riesi 68 C4
Riestedt 52 C2
Rietberg 17 F3
Rieti 63 E2
Rieumes 29 D4
Rieupeyroux 29 E3
Rieux 37 F1
Riez 31 D3
Riezlern 58 B2
Rīga 110 C2
Rigáni 83 D4
Rigeo 83 E2
Rigi 58 A2
Rignac 29 E3
Rignano Flaminio 63 E2
Rihéa 87 E3
Riihimäki 107 E2

Riisitunturi 99 E2
Riistavesi 103 E2
Riječa 72 B4
Rijeka 70 B3
Rijeka Crnojevića 76 B3
Rijssen 17 D2
Riksgränsen 94 B3
Rila 115 D3
Rila Mts 115 D3
Rillo 41 D2
Rillo de Gallo 40 C2
Rimavská-
Sobota 112 B3
Rimbo 106 B3
Rimini 61 E3
Rîmnicu Sărat 113 E4
Rîmnicu Vîlcea 115 D1
Rîmnio 79 E4
Rimske Toplice 70 B2
Rincón de la
Victoria 43 F4
Rincón de Soto 36 C3
Rindal 100 C2
Ringaskiddy 14 C4
Ringe 108 B4
Ringebu 100 C3
Ringford 4 C3
Ringkøbing 108 A3
Ringkøbing
Fjord 108 A3
Ring of Kerry 14 A4
Ringsaker 105 D2
Ringstad 104 A1
Ringsted 108 C3
Ringvassøy 94 B2
Ringwood 9 E3
Rínia 88 C2
Rinkaby 109 D3
Rinns Pt 4 A2
Rinteln 52 A1
Rinvyle Pt 12 A3
Río 83 D4
Riocavado de la
Sierra 36 A3
Riogordo 43 F3
Riola Sardo 66 A3
Riolo Terme 61 D3
Riom 26 A4
Riomaggiore 60 B3
Rio Maior 38 A3
Rio Marina 62 C1
Riom-ès-
Montagnes 29 E1
Rionero in Vulture 64 C3
Río, Punta del 44 B4
Rioseco de Tapia 35 D2
Rioz 27 D2
Ripač 70 C4
Ripanj 73 D3
Riparbella 60 C4
Ripatransone 61 F4
Ripley 7 D3
Ripoli 32 A3
Ripollet 32 A4
Ripon 6 C1
Riquewihr 27 E1
Risan 76 B2
Risbäck 97 E4
Risca 9 D2
Riscle 28 B4
Risle 19 D4
Risnes 104 B4
Risnjak 70 B3
Risør 104 C4
Risøyhamn 94 A3
Risøysundet 94 A3
Rissa 100 C1
Ristiina 103 E3
Ristijärvi 99 E4
Ristilampi 99 D2
Ristovac 77 E2
Risum-Lindholm 47 F1
Ritíni 79 E4
Ritoniemi 103 E2
Ritsóna 84 A4
Rittmannshausen 52 B3
Riudoms 37 F4
Riva 58 C4
Rivarolo Canavese 31 E1
Rive-de-Gier 30 B1
Rives 30 C1
Rivesaltes 32 B2
Rivière-Thibouville,
la 19 D3

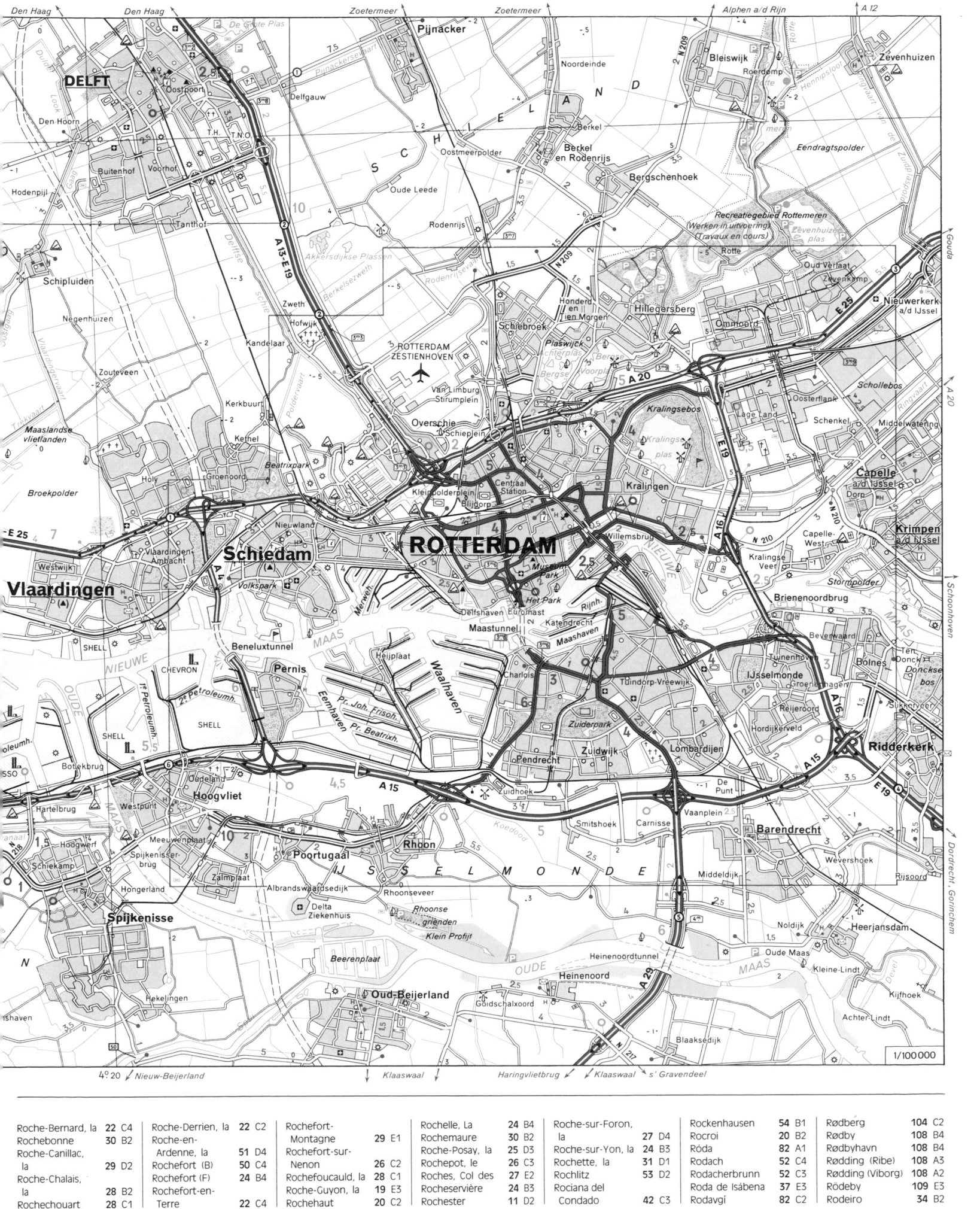

Roche-Bernard, la	22 C4	Roche-Derrien, la	22 C2	Rochefort-Montagne	29 E1	Rochelle, La	24 B4	Roche-sur-Foron, la	27 D4	Rockenhausen	54 B1	Rødberg	104 C2
Rochebonne	30 B2	Roche-en-Ardenne, la	51 D4	Rochefort-sur-		Rochemaure	30 B2	Roche-sur-Yon, la	24 B3	Rocroi	20 B2	Rødby	108 B4
Roche-Canillac, la	29 D2	Rochefort (B)	50 C4	Nenon	26 C2	Roche-Posay, la	25 D3	Rochette, la	31 D1	Róda	82 A1	Rødbyhavn	108 B4
Roche-Chalais, la	28 B2	Rochefort (F)	24 B4	Rochefoucauld, la	28 C1	Rochepot, le	26 C3	Rochlitz	53 D2	Rodach	52 C4	Rødding (Ribe)	108 A3
Rochechouart	28 C1	Rochefort-en-Terre	22 C4	Roche-Guyon, la	19 E3	Roches, Col des	27 E2	Rociana del Condado	42 C3	Rodacherbrunn	52 C3	Rødding (Viborg)	108 A2
				Rochehaut	20 C2	Rochesenvière	24 B3			Roda de Isábena	37 E3	Rødeby	109 E3
						Rochester	11 D2			Rodavgí	82 C2	Rodeiro	34 B2

Name	Pg	Grid
Rødekro	108	A4
Rodel	2	A3
Rodellar	37	E3
Roden	47	D3
Ródenas	41	D2
Rödermark	52	A4
Rodewisch	53	D3
Rodez	29	E3
Rodiezmo	35	D2
Rodi Garganico	64	C2
Roding	56	B1
Roditis	81	E2
Rodnei, M	113	D3
Rododáfni	83	D4
Rodohóri	79	E3
Rodolívos	80	B2
Rödön	101	E2
Rodonit, Gjiri i	76	C4
Rodópi (Nomos)	81	E2
Rodopi *Mts*	115	D3
Rodópoli	79	F2
Rodopós	90	B3
Ródos	93	F1
Ródos, N	93	F2
Rodováni	90	B3
Rodvattnet	102	A1
Rødven	100	B2
Rødvig	108	C4
Roermond	17	D4
Roeselare	50	A3
Rogač	75	D2
Rogača	73	D3
Rogačica (Kosovo)	77	E2
Rogačica (Srbija)	72	C4
Rogačov	111	E4
Rogaland	104	A3
Rogaška Slatina	70	C1
Rogatec	70	C2
Rogatica	76	A1
Rogatin	113	D3
Rogätz	48	C4
Rogen	101	D3
Rogen *L*	101	D3
Roggendorf	48	B2
Roggiano Gravina	67	E2
Roggosen	53	F1
Rogliano (F)	33	F2
Rogliano (I)	67	E3
Rognan	97	E2
Rogozna	76	C1
Rogoznica	75	D2
Rohan	22	C3
Rohr	52	B3
Rohrbach (A)	56	C2
Rohrbach (D)	21	E3
Rohrbrunn	52	A4
Rohrer Sattel	57	E3
Roignais	27	E4
Roine Mallasvesi	107	E1
Roisel	19	F2
Roissy	19	F4
Rojales	45	D2
Rök	109	D1
Rokiškis	110	C3
Røkland	97	F2
Rokovci	71	F2
Rokua	99	E4
Rokycany	53	E3
Røldal	104	B3
Rolfstorp	108	C2
Rolla	94	B3
Rollag	104	C3
Rolle	27	D3
Rolle, Pso di	59	D3
Rolvsøya	95	D1
Roma	63	E2
Romagnano Sesia	31	F1
Roman	113	D4
Romana	66	B2
Romanche	31	D1
România	73	D1
Romanija	71	F4
Romans	30	C2
Romanshorn	58	B1
Romantische straße	55	E3
Rombas	21	D3
Rombo, Pso del	58	C2
Römhild	52	B4
Romilly	20	B4
Romny	113	F1
Rømø	108	A3
Romont	27	E1
Romorantin	25	E2
Romsdalen	100	B2
Romsdalsfjorden	100	B2
Romsey	9	E3
Rona	2	B3
Ronaldsway	6	A1
Roncade	59	E4
Roncal	37	D2
Ronce	28	A1
Roncegno	59	D3
Roncesvalles	36	C1
Ronchamp	27	D1
Ronchi	59	F3
Ronciglione	63	E2
Roncobilaccio	60	C3
Ronda	43	E3
Rondane	100	C3
Ronda, Serr de	43	E4
Rønde	108	B3
Rondeslottet	100	C3
Rondissone	31	F1
Rondvassbu	100	C3
Rönnäng	108	C1
Rønne	109	D4
Ronneburg	53	D3
Ronneby	109	E3
Ronnebyån	109	E3
Rønnede	108	C4
Rönnöfors	101	E1
Ronse	50	B3
Roosendaal	16	B3
Roperuelos del Páramo	35	D3
Ropi	94	C3
Ropinsalmi	94	C3
Ropotovo	77	E3
Roquebillière	31	E3
Roquebrun	30	A4
Roquebrune-Cap-Martin	31	E3
Roquebrussanne, la	31	D4
Roquecourbe	32	B1
Roquefort	28	B3
Roquefort-sur-Soulzon	29	F3
Roque-Gageac, la	29	D2
Roquemaure	30	B3
Roquesteron	31	E3
Roquetas de Mar	44	B4
Roquevaire	30	C4
Rora Head	3	D1
Rore	71	D4
Røros	101	D2
Rørøy	97	D3
Rorschach	58	B1
Rørvig	108	C3
Rørvik (Nord Trøndelag)	97	D4
Rørvik (Sør Trøndelag)	100	C1
Ros'	113	E2
Rosà	59	D4
Rosal de la Frontera	42	C1
Rosarito, Emb de	39	E2
Rosarno	67	E4
Roscoff	22	B2
Ros Comáin	12	C3
Roscommon	12	C3
Roscommon (Co)	12	C3
Roscrea	12	C4
Rose (I)	67	E2
Rose (YU)	76	A3
Rosegg	70	A1
Roselend, Cormet de	27	E4
Rosell	41	F2
Rosendal	104	A2
Rosenheim	56	B3
Rosenhof	56	B2
Rosenthal	53	F3
Roses	32	C3
Roses, Golfo de	32	C3
Roseto degli Abruzzi	64	A1
Roßhaupten	55	E4
Rosheim	21	E4
Rosice	57	F1
Rosières	19	F2
Rosiers, les	24	C2
Rosignano Marittimo	60	C4
Roșiori de Vede	115	D2
Roskilde	108	C3
Roški slap	75	D1
Roßlau	53	D1
Roslavl'	111	E3
Rosmaninhal	38	C3
Røsnæs	108	B3
Rosolina Mare	61	D1
Rosolini	69	D4
Rosoman	77	E3
Rosova dolina	115	D2
Rosporden	22	B3
Rossano	67	F2
Rossan Pt	12	C1
Rosscarbery	14	B4
Roßdorf	54	C1
Rosses Point	12	C2
Rossija	111	E2
Rossio	38	B3
Rosskreppfjorden	104	B3
Rosslare	15	D4
Rosslare Harbour	15	D4
Rosslea	13	D2
Rossön	101	F1
Ross-on-Wye	9	D2
Røssvatnet	97	E3
Røssvik	94	A4
Rossvik	98	C3
Roßwein	53	E2
Rota	43	D3
Rotenburg (Hessen)	52	B3
Rotenburg (Niedersachsen)	48	A3
Roth	55	F1
Rötha	53	D2
Rothbury	5	E3
Röthenbach	55	F1
Rothenburg	55	F2
Rothenburg ob der Tauber	55	E1
Rothéneuf	18	B4
Rotherham	7	D2
Rothes	3	D3
Rothesay	4	B2
Rothwell	9	F1
Rotja, Pta	45	D4
Rotonda	67	E2
Rotondella	65	D4
Rotondo, M	33	F3
Rott (Bayern)	56	A3
Rott (Bayern)	56	B3
Rott *R*	56	B2
Rottach-Egern	56	A4
Rotten	27	F3
Rottenbach	52	C4
Rottenburg (Baden-Württemberg)	55	D3
Rottenburg (Bayern)	56	B2
Rottenmann	57	D4
Rottenmanner Tauern	57	D4
Rotterdam	16	B3
Rottne	109	D2
Rottneros	105	E3
Rottweil	54	C3
Rötz	56	B1
Roubaix	20	A1
Roudnice	53	F3
Rouen	19	E3
Rouffach	27	E1
Rougé	23	D4
Rougemont	27	D2
Rougemont-le-Château	27	E1
Rouillac	28	B1
Roujan	30	A4
Roulans	27	D2
Roulers	50	A3
Roundstone	12	A3
Rousay	3	D1
Roússa	81	E1
Rousses, les	27	D3
Rousset, Col de	30	C2
Rovaniemi	99	D2
Rovato	60	B1
Rovereto	59	D4
Roverud	105	D3
Roviés	83	F3
Rovigo	61	D2
Rovinj	70	A3
Roviśce	71	D2
Rovno	113	D2
Roxen	106	A4
Roxo, Bgem do	42	B1
Royal Canal	12	C3
Royal Leamington Spa	9	E1
Royal Tunbridge Wells	10	C3
Royan	28	A1
Royat	29	E1
Roybon	30	C1
Roye	19	F3
Royère-de-Vassivière	25	E4
Røyrvik	97	E4
Royston	9	F2
Röyttä	98	C3
Rožaje	76	C2
Rožanstvo	72	C4
Rozay-en-Brie	19	F4
Rozier, le	29	F3
Rožmberk	57	D1
Rožmitál	53	F4
Rožňava	112	B3
Rozoy	20	B2
Roztocze	112	C2
Roztoky	53	F3
Rozvadov	56	B1
Rrasë	76	C3
Rrëshen	76	C3
Rrogozhinë	76	C4
Rtanj	73	E4
Rtanj (Reg)	73	E4
Ruabon	6	B3
Rubbestadneset	104	A2
Rubena	35	F3
Rubeži	76	B2
Rubha a'Mhail	4	B2
Rubha Còigeach	2	C2
Rubha Réidh	2	B3
Rubi	32	A4
Rubiães	34	A3
Rubi de Bracamonte	39	F1
Rubielos de Mora	41	E3
Rubiera	60	C2
Rubio	35	F4
Rudare	77	D1
Rüdersdorf	49	E4
Rüdesheim	51	F4
Rudkøbing	108	B4
Rudn'a	111	E3
Rudna Glava	73	E3
Rudnica (Crna Gora)	76	B1
Rudnica (Srbija)	76	C1
Rudnik (Kosovo)	76	C2
Rudnik (Reg)	73	D4
Rudnik (Srbija)	73	D4
Rudo	76	B1
Rudolstadt	52	C3
Rue	19	E2
Ruecas, R	39	E4
Rueda	35	E4
Rueda de Jalón	36	C3
Ruelle	28	C1
Ruffec	25	D4
Ruffieux	27	D4
Rugby	9	E1
Rugeley	6	C3
Rügen	49	D1
Rugles	19	D4
Rugovska klisura	76	C2
Ruhla	52	B3
Ruhland	53	E2
Ruhner Berge	48	C3
Ruhpolding	56	B3
Ruhr	17	E3
Ruidera	40	B4
Rüjiena	110	C2
Ruka	99	E2
Rukatunturi	99	E2
Ruma	72	C2
Rumblar, Emb del	44	A2
Rumboci	75	E1
Rumburk	53	F2
Rumengol	22	B3
Rumenka	72	C2
Rumigny	20	B2
Rumilly	27	D4
Runcorn	6	B2
Runde	100	A2
Rundvik	102	A2
Runn	105	F2
Runni	103	D1
Runtuna	106	B4
Ruohtir	95	E2
Ruokojärvi	103	F3
Ruokolahti	103	F3
Ruokovesi	103	E2
Ruokto	98	B1
Ruoms	30	B2
Ruotsinpyhtää	107	F2
Ruovesi	102	C3
Rupa	70	B3
Rupea	113	D4
Ruppiner See	49	D3
Rupt	27	D1
Rur	17	D4
Ruše	70	C1
Ruse	115	D2
Ruševo	71	E2
Rush	13	E3
Rushden	9	F1
Ruski Krstur	72	B2
Rusko	107	D2
Rusko Selo	72	C1
Ruskele	98	A4
Rüsselsheim	51	F4
Russenes	95	D1
Russey, le	27	E2
Russi	61	D3
Rust	57	F3
Rustefjelbma	95	E1
Ruswil	27	F2
Rute	43	F3
Rüthen	17	F3
Ruthin	6	B3
Rüti	58	A2
Rutigliano	65	E3
Rutledal	104	A1
Ruuhitunturi	99	E2
Ruukki	99	D4
Ruuponsaari	103	D2
Ruurlo	17	D3
Ruvo di Puglia	65	D3
Ruwer	54	A1
Ruynes-en-Margeride	29	F2
Ružomberok	112	B3
Ry	108	B3
Rybinsk	111	F1
Rybinskoje Vodochranilišče	111	F1
Rybnica	113	E3
Rybnik	112	B3
Rychnov nad Kněžnou	112	A3
Ryd	109	D3
Ryde	9	E3
Rye	11	D3
Ryfylke	104	A3
Rygge	105	D3
Rykene	104	B4
Ryl'sk	113	F1
Ryman	49	F1
Rymättylä	107	D2
Rypefjord	95	D1
Rysjedalsvika	104	A1
Ryttylä	107	E2
Rzepin	49	F4
Rzeszów	112	C2
Ržev	111	F2

S

Name	Pg	Grid
Sääksjärvi	102	C2
Saal	55	F2
Saalach	59	E1
Saalbach	59	E1
Saale	52	C1
Saaler Bodden	48	C1
Saales	21	E4
Saalfeld	52	C3
Saalfelden	59	E1
Saane	27	E3
Saanen	27	E3
Saar	54	A1
Saarbrücken	54	B2
Saarburg	54	A1
Saaremaa	110	B2
Saarenkylä	99	D2
Saari	103	F3
Saariharju	99	E3
Saarijärvi	103	D2
Saarikoski	94	C3
Saariselkä	95	F3
Saariselkä (Reg)	95	F3
Saaristomeri	107	D3
Saarland	54	A2
Saarlouis	54	B2
Saas-Fee	27	F4
Šabac	72	C3
Sabadell	32	A4
Sabaudia	63	F3
Sabbioneta	60	C2
Sabero	35	E2
Sabiñánigo	37	D2
Sabini, Mti	63	E2
Sabiote	44	B2
Sablé	23	E4
Sables-d'Olonne, les	24	B3
Sables-d'Or	22	C2
Sæbo	100	A2
Sabóia	42	A2
Sabôr, R	34	C4
Sabres	28	B3
Sabrosa	34	B4
Sabugal	39	D2
Sæby	108	B2
Sa Calobra	45	E2
Sacavém	38	A4
Sacedon	40	C2
Saceruela	39	F4
Sacile	59	E3
Sacra di San Michele	31	E1
Sacramenia	35	F4
Sacratif, C	44	A4
Sada	34	B1
Sádaba	36	C2
Sado, R	38	A4
Sadurniño	34	B1
Saelices	40	B3
Safara	42	C1
Säffle	105	E4
Saffron Walden	10	C2
Safonovo	111	E3
Sagard	49	D1
S'Agaró	32	B4
Sagéika	86	B1
Sagfjorden	94	A4
Sagiáda	82	B1
Sagra, Sa de la	44	B2
Sagres	42	A3
Sagres, Pta de	42	A3
Sagunto	41	E3
Sagvåg	104	A3
Sahagún	35	E3
Sahalahti	107	E1
Šahinovići	71	E3
Sahl	108	A2
Sahloinen	103	D3
Saidus	110	B3
Saignelégier	27	E2
Saija	95	F4
Saillagouse	32	A3
Saillans	30	C2
Saimaa	103	E3
Saimaanranta	103	E4
Sains-du-Nord	20	B2
Sains-Richaumont	20	B2
St Abb's Head	5	E2
St Aegyd	57	E3
St-Affrique	29	E3
St-Agnant	24	B4
St-Agrève	30	B2
St-Aignan	25	E2
St-Aignan-sur-Roë	23	E3
St Alban	29	F2
St Albans	9	F2
St Alban's Head	9	E4
St-Amand-en-Puisaye	26	A2
St-Amand-les-Eaux	20	A1

St-A – Sal 187

St-Amand-Longpré 25 D2
St-Amand-Montrond 25 F3
St-Amans-des-Cots 29 E2
St-Amans 29 F2
St-Amans-Soult 32 B1
St-Amant 29 F1
St-Amant-Roche-Savine 29 F1
St-Amarin 27 E1
St-Ambroix 30 B3
St-Amé 27 D1
St-Amour 26 C3
St Andrä 70 B1
St Andreasberg 52 B2
St-André-de-Cubzac 28 B2
St-André-de-l'Eure 19 E4
St-André-de-Vézines 29 F3
St-André-les-Alpes 31 D3
St Andrews 5 D1
St-Anthème 30 B1
St-Antonin-Noble-Val 29 D3
St Anton 58 C2
St-Arnoult 19 E4
St Asaph 6 B2
St-Astier 28 C2
St-Auban 31 D3
St-Aubin-d'Aubigné 23 D3
St-Aubin-du-Cormier 23 D3
St-Aubin 18 C3
St-Aulaye 28 C2
St Austell 8 B4
St-Avold 21 D3
St-Aygulf 31 D4
St-Beauzély 29 E3
St Bees Head 4 C4
St-Benoît-du-Sault 25 E3
St-Benoît 25 F2
St-Bertrand-de-Comminges 37 E1
St-Béat 37 F2
St-Bénin-d'Azy 26 A3
St Blasien 54 C4
St-Blin 26 C1
St-Bonnet 31 D2
St-Bonnet-de-Joux 26 B3
St-Bonnet-le-Château 30 B1
St-Brévin 24 A2
St-Briac 18 A4
St-Brice-en-Coglès 18 B4
St Brides B 8 B2
St-Brieuc 22 C2
St-Calais 23 F3
St-Cast 18 A4
St Catherine's Pt 9 E4
St-Cergue 27 D3
St-Cernin 29 E2
St-Céré 29 D2
St-Chamas 30 C4
St-Chamond 30 B1
St-Chély-d'Apcher 29 F2
St-Chély-d'Aubrac 29 E2
St-Chinian 32 B1
St Christophen 57 E2
St-Ciers 28 B1
St-Cirq-Lapopie 29 D3
St-Clair-sur-l'Elle 18 C3
St-Clar 28 C3
St-Claud 25 D4
St-Claude 27 D3
St Clears 8 C2
St-Cyprien 29 D2
St-Cyprien-Plage 32 B2
St David's 8 B1
St David's Head 8 B1
St-Denis (Charente-Maritime) 24 B4
St-Denis-d'Orques 23 E3
St-Denis (Seine-St-Denis) 19 F4
St-Didier-en-Velay 30 B1
St-Dié 21 E4
St-Dier-d'Auvergne 29 F1
St-Dizier 20 C4
St-Donat-sur-l'Herbasse 30 C1
St-Eloy-les-Mines 26 A4
St-Emilion 28 B2
St-Etienne (Alpes-de-Haute-Provence) 30 C3
St-Etienne-Cantalès, Bge de 29 E2
St-Etienne-de-Baïgorry 28 A4
St-Etienne-de-Lugdarès 29 F2
St-Etienne-de-Montluc 24 B2
St-Etienne-de-St-Geoirs 30 C1
St-Etienne-de-Tinée 31 E3
St-Etienne-en-Dévoluy 31 D2
St-Etienne (Loire) 30 B1
St-Fargeau 26 A2
St-Félicien 30 B2
St Finan's B 14 A4
St-Firmin 31 D2
St-Florent (Cher) 25 F3
St-Florent (Corse) 33 F2
St-Florentin 26 B1
St-Flour 29 F2
St-François-Longchamp 31 D1
St-Fulgent 24 B3
St Gallen (A) 57 D3
St Gallen (CH) 58 B2
St Gallenkirch 58 B2
St-Galmier 30 B1
St-Gaudens 37 F1
St-Gaultier 25 E3
St-Genest-Malifaux 30 B1
St-Gengoux-le-National 26 C3
St-Geniez-d'Olt 29 E3
St-Genis-de-Stonge 28 B1
St-Genis-Laval 30 B1
St-Genix 30 C1
St-Geoire 30 C1
St Georgen (A) 56 C3
St Georgen am Langsee 70 B1
St Georgen (D) 54 C3
St-Georges 23 E4
St Georges Channel 8 A1
St-Georges-de-Didonne 28 A1
St-Georges-en-Couzan 29 F1
St-Germain-de-Calberte 29 F3
St-Germain-des-Fossés 26 A4
St-Germain-du-Bois 26 C3
St-Germain-du-Plain 26 C3
St-Germain-du-Teil 29 F3
St-Germain 19 F4
St-Germain-Laval 26 B4
St-Germain-Lembron 29 F1
St-Germain-les-Belles 29 D1
St-Germain-l'Herm 29 F1
St-Gertraud 58 C3
St-Gervais-d'Auvergne 26 A4
St-Gervais 27 E4
St-Gervais-sur-Mare 30 A4
St-Géry 29 D3
St-Gildas-de-Rhuys 22 C4
St-Gildas-des-Bois 23 D4
St-Gildas, Pte de 24 A2
St Gilgen 56 C3
St-Gilles-Croix-de-Vie 24 A3
St-Gilles 30 B4
St-Gingolph 27 E3
St-Girons 37 F2
St-Girons-Plage 28 A3
St Goar 51 E4
St Goarshausen 51 E4
St-Gobain 20 A3
St Govan's Head 8 B2
St-Guénolé 22 A3
St-Guilhem-le-Désert 29 F4
St-Haon-le-Châtel 26 B4
St Helens 6 B2
St-Hélier 18 B3
St-Hilaire-des-Loges 24 C3
St-Hilaire-de-Villefranche 28 B1
St-Hilaire-du-Harcouet 18 B4
St-Hilaire 32 B2
St-Hippolyte-du-Fort 29 F3
St-Hippolyte 27 E2
St-Honoré 26 B3
St-Hubert 20 C2
St-Imier 27 E2
St Ingbert 54 B2
St Ives (Cambs) 9 F1
St Ives (Cornwall) 8 A4
St-Jacques 23 D3
St-Jacut 18 A4
St Jakob 59 D2
St Jakob im Rosental 70 A1
St James 18 B4
St-Jean-Brévelay 22 C3
St-Jean-Cap-Ferrat 31 E3
St-Jean-d'Angély 24 C4
St-Jean-de-Bournay 30 C1
St-Jean-de-Daye 18 B3
St-Jean-de-Losne 26 C2
St-Jean-de-Luz 28 A4
St-Jean-de-Maurienne 31 D1
St-Jean-de-Monts 24 A3
St-Jean-du-Bruel 29 F3
St-Jean-du-Gard 30 A3
St-Jean-en-Royans 30 C2
St-Jean-Pied-de-Port 28 A4
St-Jeoire 27 D4
St Johann im Pongau 59 E1
St Johann in Tirol 59 E1
St John's Pt 13 E2
St-Jouin-de-Marnes 24 C3
St-Juéry 29 E3
St-Julien-Chapteuil 30 B2
St-Julien-de-Vouvantes 23 D4
St-Julien-du-Sault 26 A1
St-Julien-en-Genevois 27 D4
St-Julien 26 C3
St-Julien-l'Ars 25 D3
St-Junien 25 D4
St Just 8 A4
St-Just-en-Chaussée 19 F3
St-Just-en-Chevalet 26 B4
St-Justin 28 B3
St Keverne 8 B4
St Lambrecht 57 D4
St-Lary-Soulan 37 E2
St-Laurent (Calvados) 18 C3
St-Laurent-de-la-Salanque 32 B2
St-Laurent-du-Pont 30 C1
St-Laurent-en-Grandvaux 27 D3
St-Laurent-les-Bains 29 F2
St-Laurent-Médoc 28 B2
St-Laurent (Vendée) 24 C3
St-Laurent (Vienne) 28 C1
St-Léger 26 B3
St Leonhard (I) 59 D2
St Leonhard (Niederösterreich) 57 E3
St Leonhard (Tirol) 58 C2
St-Léonard-de-Noblat 25 E4
St Lorenzen 59 E2
St-Lô 18 C3
St-Louis 27 E2
St-Loup-Lamairé 24 C3
St-Loup-sur-Semouse 27 D1
St-Luc 27 F3
St-Lunaire 18 B4
St-Lys 29 D4
St-Macaire 28 B2
St Magnus B 3 F1
St-Maixent-l'Ecole 24 C3
St-Malo-de-la-Lande 18 B3
St-Malo 18 B4
St-Mamet-la-Salvetat 29 E2
St-Mandrier 31 D4
St-Marcellin 30 C1
St-Margarethen 48 A2
St Margaret's Hope 3 E1
St-Mars-la-Jaille 23 D4
St-Martin (Charente-Maritime) 24 B4
St-Martin-d'Auxigny 25 F2
St-Martin-de-Belleville 31 D1
St-Martin-de-Londres 29 F4
St-Martin-de-Seignan 28 A4
St-Martin-de-Valamas 30 B2
St-Martin-en-Bresse 26 C3
St-Martin (Pyrénées-Orientales) 32 B2
St Martin's 8 A4
St-Martin-Vésubie 31 E3
St-Martory 37 F1
St Mary's 8 A4
St Märgen 54 C4
St-Mathieu 28 C1
St-Mathieu, Pte de 22 A3
St-Maurice 27 E4
St Mawes 8 B4
St-Maximin-la-Ste Baume 31 D4
St-Médard-en-Jalles 28 B2
St-Méen 22 C3
St Michaelisdonn 48 A2
St Michael (Salzburg) 59 F2
St Michael's Mount 8 A4
St Michael (Steiermark) 57 E4
St-Michel-de-Maurienne 31 D1
St-Michel-en-Grève 22 B2
St-Michel-en-l'Herm 24 B4
St-Michel 20 B2
St-Michel-Mont-Mercure 24 C3
St-Mihiel 20 C3
St Monance 5 D2
St-Moritz 58 B3
St-Nazaire 24 A2
St-Nectaire 29 E1
St Neots 9 F1
St-Nicolas-d'Aliermont 19 E2
St-Nicolas-de-la-Grave 28 C3
St-Nicolas-de-Port 21 D4
St-Nicolas-du-Pélem 22 C3
St-Niklaas 50 B3
St Niklaus 27 F4
St-Oedenrode 16 C3
St-Omer 19 F1
St Oswald 59 F2
St-Pair 18 B4
St-Palais (Charente-Maritime) 28 A1
St-Palais (Pyrénées-Atlantiques) 28 A4
St-Pardoux-la-Rivière 28 C1
St Paul (A) 70 B1
St-Paul (Alpes-de-Haute-Provence) 31 D2
St-Paul (Alpes-Maritimes) 31 E3
St-Paul-Cap-de-Joux 29 D4
St-Paul-de-Fenouillet 32 B2
St-Paulien 29 F2
St-Paul-Trois-Châteaux 30 B3
St-Père-en-Retz 24 A2
St-Pé-de-Bigorre 37 E1
St-Pée 28 A4
St-Péray 30 B2
St Peter in der Au 57 D3
St-Peter-Ording 47 F2
St Peter Port 18 A3
St-Philbert 24 B3
St-Pierre (Charente-Maritime) 24 B4
St-Pierre-d'Albigny 31 D1
St-Pierre-de-Chartreuse 30 C1
St-Pierre-de-Chignac 28 C2
St-Pierre-Eglise 18 B2
St-Pierre-le-Moûtier 26 A3
St-Pierre (Morbihan) 22 C4
St-Pierre-sur-Dives 18 C3
St-Pois 18 C4
St-Pol-de-Léon 22 B2
St-Pol-sur-Ternoise 19 F2
St-Pons-de-Thomières 32 B1
St-Porchaire 28 B1
St Pölten 57 E2
St-Pourçain 26 A4
St-Privat 29 E2
St-Quay-Portrieux 22 C2
St-Quentin 20 A2
St-Rambert 30 B1
St-Rambert-d'Albon 30 B1
St-Rambert-en-Bugey 26 C4
St-Raphaël 31 E4
St-Renan 22 A2
St-Rémy-de-Provence 30 B3
St-Rémy-sur-Durolle 26 B4
St-Riquier 19 E2
St-Romain-de-Colbosc 19 D3
St-Rome-de-Tarn 29 E3
St-Saëns 19 E3
St-Satur 26 A2
St-Saulge 26 A2
St-Sauveur-en-Puisaye 26 A2
St-Sauveur-Lendelin 18 B3
St-Sauveur-le-Vicomte 18 B3
St-Sauveur-sur-Tinée 31 E3
St-Savin (Gironde) 28 B2
St-Savinien 24 C4
St-Savin (Vienne) 25 D3
St-Seine-l'Abbaye 26 C2
St-Sernin-sur-Rance 29 E3
St-Sever (Calvados) 18 C4
St-Sever (Landes) 28 B4
St-Sulpice-les-Feuilles 25 E4
St-Symphorien-de-Lay 26 B4
St-Symphorien-d'Ozon 30 B1
St-Symphorien 28 B3
St-Symphorien-sur-Coise 30 B1
St-Trivier-de-Courtes 26 C3
St-Trivier-sur-Moignans 26 C4
St-Trojan 28 A1
St-Tropez 31 D4
St-Truiden 50 C3
St Ulrich 59 D3
St-Vaast-la-Hougue 18 B3
St Valentin an der Haide 58 C2
St Valentin 57 D3
St-Valery 19 E2
St-Valery-en-Caux 19 D2
St-Valier 30 B1
St-Vallier-de-Thiey 31 D3
St-Varent 24 C3
St-Vaury 25 E4
St Veit 70 A1
St-Véran 31 E2
St-Vincent 27 F4
St-Vincent-de-Tyrosse 28 A4
St Vith 51 D4
St-Vivien-de-Médoc 28 A1
St-Wandrille 19 D3
St Wendel 54 B1
St Wolfgang 56 C3
St-Yorre 26 A4
St-Yrieix-la-Perche 29 D1
Ste-Adresse 19 D3
Ste-Anne-d'Auray 22 C4
Ste-Baume, la 31 D4
Ste-Croix-du-Mont 28 B2
Ste-Croix 27 D3
Ste-Croix, Lac de 31 D3
Ste-Croix-Volvestre 37 F1
Ste-Enimie 29 F3
Ste-Foy-la-Grande 28 C2
Ste-Foy-l'Argentière 30 B1
Ste-Geneviève-sur-Argence 29 E2
Ste-Hélène 28 B2
Ste-Hermine 24 B3
Ste-Livrade 28 C3
Ste-Lucie-de-Tallano 33 F4
Ste-Marie-aux-Mines 21 E4
Ste-Maure-de-Touraine 25 D2
Ste-Maxime 31 D4
Ste-Menehould 20 C3
Ste-Mère-Eglise 18 B3
Ste-Odile, Mt 21 E4
Ste-Sévère 25 F3
Ste-Suzanne 23 E3
Ste-Tulle 30 C3
Saintes 28 B1
Stes-Maries-de-la-Mer 30 B4
Saissac 32 B1
Šajkaš 72 C2
Sakarya 115 F3
Sakskøbing 108 B4
Sakule 72 C2
Säkylä 107 D2
Sala 106 A3
Salacgrīva 110 C2
Sala Consilina 64 C4
Salada 41 E3
Salakovac 73 D3
Salamajärvi 102 C2
Salamajärvi *L* 103 D2
Salamanca 39 E1
Salamina 87 F1
Salamina, N 87 E1
Saländi 87 E2
Salangen 94 B3
Salar 43 F3
Salardú 37 F2
Salas 35 D1
Salaš 73 F3
Salas de los Infantes 36 A3
Salazar, R 37 D2
Salbohed 105 F3
Salbris 25 E2
Salcombe 8 C4
Saldaña 35 E3
Sale 60 A2
Sålekinna 100 D3
Salem 55 D4
Salemi 68 A3
Sälen 101 D4
Salen (Highland) 2 B4
Salen (Mull) 4 B1
Salernes 31 D4
Salerno 64 B4
Salerno, Golfo di 64 B4
Salers 29 E2
Salève, Mt 27 D4
Salgótarján 112 B3
Salgueiro do Campo 38 C2
Sali 74 C1
Salice Terme 60 A2
Salies-de-Béarn 28 A4
Salies-du-Salat 37 F1
Salignac-Eyvigues 29 D2
Sallhll 115 F4
Salime, Emb de 34 C1
Salina, I 69 D2
Salinas (Andalucía) 43 F3
Salinas (Asturias) 35 D1
Salinas, C 45 F3
Salindres 30 B3
Sälinkää 107 F2
Salins 27 D3
Salisbury 9 E3
Salla 99 E2
Sallanches 27 E4
Sallent 32 A4
Sallent-de-Gállego 37 D2
Salles 32 A1
Salles-Curan 29 E3
Salling 108 A2
Salling Sund 108 A2
Salmerón 40 C2
Salmoral 39 F1
Salò 60 B1
Salo 107 E2
Salobreña 44 A4
Salona 75 D1
Salon-de-Provence 30 C4
Salonta 112 C4
Salorino 38 C3
Salor, R 39 D3
Salou 37 F4
Salou, C de 37 F4
Salpausselkä 107 F2
Salsbruket 97 D4
Salses-le-Château 32 B2
Salso 68 C3
Salsomaggiore Terme 60 B2
Salsta 106 B3
Saltash 8 C4
Saltburn-by-the-Sea 5 F4
Saltcoats 4 C2
Saltee Is 15 D4
Saltfjellet 97 E2
Saltfjorden 97 E2
Salto 34 B4
Saltoluokta 94 B4
Saltvik 106 C3
Saluggia 31 F1
Saluzzo 31 E2
Salvacañete 41 D3
Salvagnac 29 D3
Salvan 27 E4
Salvaterra de Magos 38 A3
Salvatierra-Agurain 36 B2
Salvatierra de los Barros 42 C1
Salvattera de Miño 34 A3
Salvetat-Peyralès, la 29 E3

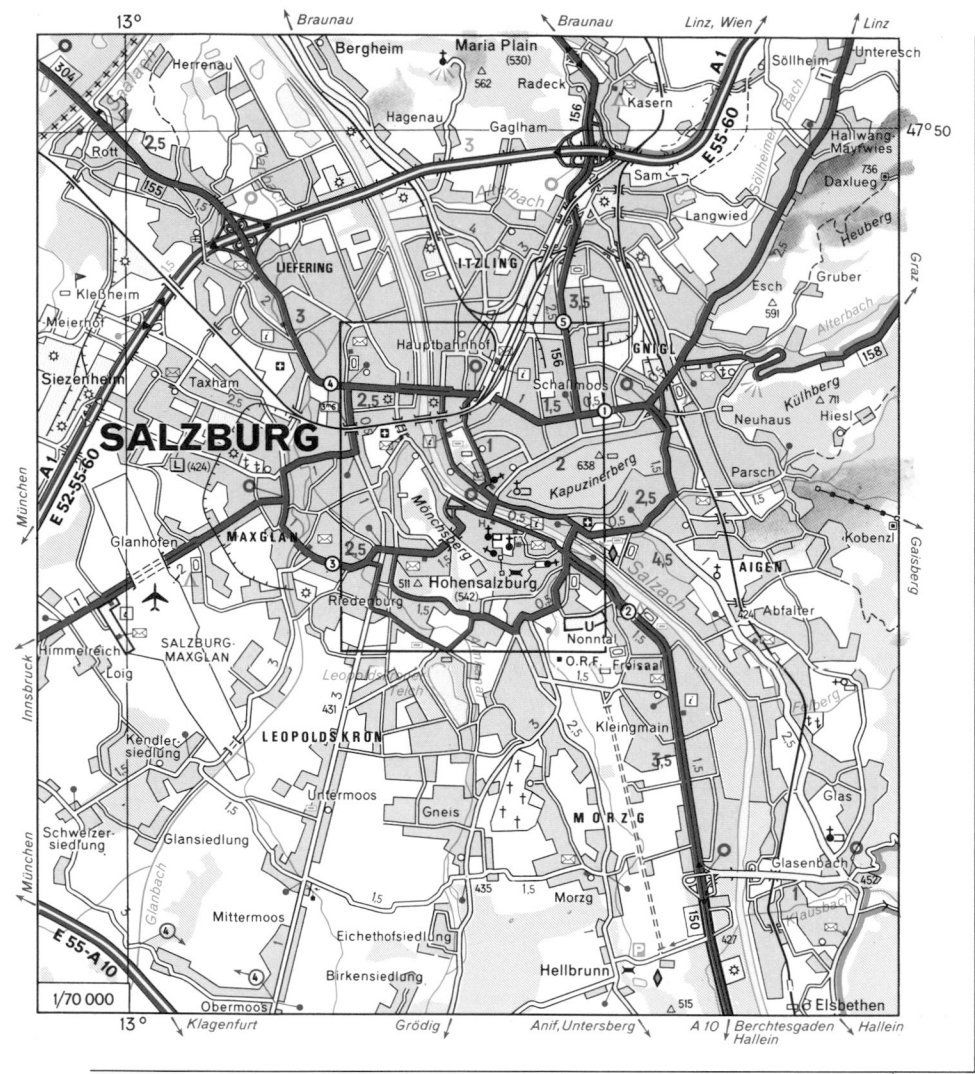

San Giovanni in Fiore	67 F2	San Millán	36 A2	San Vito sullo Ionio	67 F3		
San Giovanni in Persiceto	60 C2	San Millán de la Cogolla	36 B2	San Vittore del Lazio	64 A3		
San Giovanni Lupatoto	60 C1	San Millán de Lara	36 A3	Sana	71 D4		
San Giovanni Rotondo	64 C2	San Miniato	60 C4	Saná	80 A3		
San Giovanni Suergiù	66 B4	San Nicolás del Puerto	43 E2	Sanabria, L de	34 C3		
San Giovanni Valdarno	61 D4	San Nicolás de Tolentino	42 B4	Sanary	30 C4		
San Giuliano Terme	60 C4	San Nicolò		Sancergues	26 A2		
San Giustino	61 D4	San Nicolò Ferrarese	61 D2	Sancerre	26 A2		
San Glorio, Pto de	35 E2	San Nicolò Gerrei	66 B3	Sanchidrián	39 F1		
San Gottardo, Pso del	58 A3	San Ninfa	68 B3	Sancho, Emb de	42 C2		
San Ildefonso o la Granja	40 A1	San Pancrazio Salentino	65 F4	Sanclêr	8 C2		
San Isidro	44 C3	San Pedro	44 C1	Sancoins	26 A3		
San Isidro, Pto de	35 E2	San Pedro de Alcántara	43 E4	Sancti Petri	43 D4		
San Javier	45 D2	San Pedro del Arroyo	39 F1	Sancti Spiritus	39 D1		
San José (Andalucía)	44 C4	San Pedro de Latarce	35 E4	Sand (Hedmark)	105 D2		
San José (Ibiza)	45 D4	San Pedro del Pinatar	45 D2	Sand (Rogaland)	104 A3		
San Juan Bautista	45 D3	San Pedro de Mérida	39 D4	Sandane	100 A3		
San Juan de Alicante	45 E1	San Pedro Manrique	36 B3	Sandanski	115 D3		
San Juan de Aznalfarache	43 D2	San Pedro, Sa de	39 D3	Sandarne	101 F4		
San Juan de la Peña	37 D2	San Pellegrino, Pso	59 D3	Sandau	48 C4		
San Juan del Olmo	39 F2	San Pellegrino Terme	58 B4	Sanday	3 E1		
San Juan de los Terreros	44 C3	San Piero a Sieve	61 D3	Sandbach	6 C3		
San Juan del Puerto	42 C2	San Pietro, I di	66 A4	Sanddøla	97 D4		
San Juan, Emb de	40 A2	San Pietro in Casale	60 C2	Sande (D)	47 E3		
San Just Desvern	32 A4	San Pietro Vernotico	65 F4	Sande (Møre og Romsdal)	100 A2		
San Just, Sa de	41 E2	San Polo d'Enza	60 C2	Sande (P)	34 A4		
San Lazzaro di Savena	61 D2	San Quirico d'Orcia	63 D1	Sande (Vestfold)	104 C3		
San Leo	61 E3	San Rafael de Navallana, Emb de	43 F2	Sandefjord	104 C3		
San Leonardo de Yagüe	36 A3	San Rafael	40 A2	Sandeid	104 A3		
San Leonardo	59 D2	San Remo	31 F3	Sandfjellet	95 E1		
San Leonardo, Pso	64 A2	San Roque (Andalucía)	43 E4	Sandgerði	96 A2		
San Lorenzo (E)	36 B2	San Roque (Galicia)	34 A1	Sand in Taufers	59 D2		
San Lorenzo (I)	63 D1	San Rufo	64 C4	Sandnes	104 A3		
San Lorenzo de Calatrava	44 A1	San Salvador de Cantamuda	35 F2	Sandness	3 F1		
San Lorenzo de la Parrilla	40 C3	San Salvador	45 F3	Sandnessjøen	97 D3		
San Lucido	67 E3	San Salvo	64 B2	Sando	39 E1		
San Luis de Sabanillas	43 E4	San Sebastiano Curone	60 A2	Sandoméri	86 B1		
San Luis	45 F2	San Sebastián, Emb de	34 C3	Sandomierz	112 C2		
San Marcello	61 F4	San Sebastián	42 A4	Sandown	9 E3		
San Marcello Pistoiese	60 C4	San Severino Marche	61 F4	Sandoy	96 A4		
San Marco	67 E2	San Severo	64 C2	Sandøy	100 A2		
San Marco Argentano	67 E2	San Silvestre de Guzmán	42 C2	Sandrigo	59 D4		
San Marco dei Cavoti	64 B3	San Sperate	66 B4	Sandringham House	7 E3		
San Marco in Lamis	64 C2	San Stefano di Camastra	68 C3	Sandstad	100 C1		
San Marino	61 E3	San Stefano Quisquina	68 B3	Sandur	96 A4		
San Martino di Castrozza	59 D3	San Telmo	42 C2	Sandviken	106 B2		
San Martín de Castañeda	34 C3	San Valentino alla Muta	58 C2	Sandvikvåg	104 A2		
San Martín de la Vega	40 B2	San Vicente de Alcántara	38 C3	Sandwich	11 D3		
San Martín de Mondoñedo	34 C1	San Vicente de la Barquera	35 F1	Sandy	9 F1		
San Martín de Montalbán	39 F3	San Vicente de la Cabeza	35 D3	Sånfjället	101 E3		
San Martín de Valdeiglesias	40 A2	San Vicente del Raspeig	45 E1	Sangarcia	40 A1		
San Mateo	41 F2	San Vicenzo	62 C1	Sangerhausen	52 C2		
San Mateo de Gállego	37 D3	San Vigilio di Marebbe	59 D2	Sangis	98 C3		
San Mauro Forte	65 D4	San Vigilio, Pso di	60 C1	Sangonera, R	45 D2		
San Michele all' Adige	59 D3	San Vitero	34 C4	Sangro	64 A2		
San Miguel	45 D3	San Vito al Tagliamento	59 E3	Sangüesa	36 C2		
San Miguel de Escalada	35 E3	San Vito Chietino	64 A2	Sanguinaires, Iles	33 E4		
San Miguel del Arroyo	35 E4	San Vito dei Normanni	65 E3	Sanguinet	28 B4		
San Miguel de Salinas	45 D2	San Vito di C.	59 E3	Saní	80 A4		
		San Vito	66 C3	Sanitz	48 C2		
		San Vito lo Capo	68 A3	Sankt Olof	109 D3		

Salvetat-sur-Agout, la	32 B1	Sámos	89 F1	San Biagio Platani	68 B3
Salviac	29 D2	Sámos, N	89 E1	San Bonifacio	60 C1
Sælvig	108 B3	Samothráki	81 E3	San Candido	59 E2
Sálvora, I de	34 A2	Samothráki, N	81 E3	San Carlos de la Ràpita	41 F2
Salza	57 E3	Samper de Calanda	37 D4	San Carlos del Valle	40 B4
Salzach	56 B3	Sampeyre	31 E2	San Casciano in Val di Pesa	60 C4
Salzburg	56 C3	Samsø	108 B3	San Cataldo (Puglia)	65 F4
Salzburg (Prov)	59 E1	Samsø Bælt	108 B3	San Cataldo (Sicilia)	68 C3
Salzgitter-Bad	52 B1	Samtens	49 D1	San Cipirello	68 B3
Salzgitter-Lebenstedt	52 B1	Samugheo	66 B3	San Clemente, Emb de	44 B2
Salzhausen	48 B3	San	112 C2	San Clemente	40 C4
Salzkammergut	56 C3	San Adrián	36 C2	San Colombano al Lambro	60 B2
Salzkotten	17 F3	San Adrián, C de	34 A1	San Cosme	34 C1
Salzwedel	48 C4	San Agata de Goti	64 B3	San Cristóbal	42 C1
Šamac Slavonski	71 F3	San Agata di Militello	69 D2	San Cristóbal de Entreviñas	35 D3
Sama de Langreo	35 D1	San Agustín	40 B2	San Cristóbal de la Polantera	35 D3
Samarina	78 C4	San Amaro	34 B2	San Cristóbal de la Vega	39 F1
Samatan	28 C4	San Andrea Frius	66 B3	San Damiano d'Asti	31 F2
Sambatiki	87 E3	San Andrés del Rabanedo	35 D2	San Daniele del Friuli	59 E3
Sambiase	67 E3	San Antioco, I di	66 A4	San Daniele Po	60 C2
Samboal	40 A1	San Antioco	66 A4	San Demetrio Corone	67 E2
Sambor	112 C3	San Antonio	66 B1	San Donaci	65 E4
Sambre	50 B4	San Antonio Abad	45 D3	San Donà di Piave	59 E4
Sambuca di Sicilia	68 B3	San Antonio, C de	45 F1	San Emiliano	35 D2
Samedan	58 B3	San Bartolomé de las Abiertas	39 F3	San Esteban de Gormaz	36 A3
Sameiro, Mte	34 A4	San Bartolomé de la Torre	42 C2	San Esteban del Molar	35 D3
Samer	19 E1	San Bartolomeo in Galdo	64 B3		
Sámi	82 B4	San Benedetto del Tronto	61 F4		
Samikó	86 B2	San Benedetto in Alpe	61 D3		
Sammatti	107 E2	San Benedetto Po	60 C2		
Sammichele	65 E3	San Bernardino	58 B3		
Samnanger	104 A2	San Bernardino, Psodel	58 B3		
Samobor	70 C2				
Samodreža	77 D2				
Samoëns	27 E4				
Samokov (BG)	115 D3				
Samokov (YU)	77 D3				
Samora Correia	38 A4				
Samos	34 C2				
Samoš	73 D2				

San Esteban del Valle	39 F2
San Esteban de Pravia	35 D1
San Fele	64 C4
San Felice a Cancello	64 B3
San Felice Circeo	63 F3
San Felices de Los Gallegos	39 D1
San Felice sul Panaro	60 C2
San Felipe	40 C2
San Feliu de Guíxols	32 B4
San Ferdinando di Puglia	64 C3
San Ferdinando di Puglia	64 C3
San Fernando	43 D4
San Francisco Javier	45 D4
San Fratello	69 D2
San Gavino Monreale	66 B3
San Gemini	63 E1
San Giacomo	59 D2
San Gimignano	60 C4
San Ginesio	61 F4
San Giorgio del Sannio	64 B3
San Giorgio di Nogaro	59 F3
San Giorgio Ionico	65 E4
San Giorgio	31 E1
San Giorgio Piacentino	60 B2
San Giovanni a Piro	67 D2
San Giovanni di Sinis	66 A3

Sant Antoni de C. 32 B3
Sant Antoni, Emb de 37 F3
Sant'Apollinare in Classe 61 D3
Sant'Arcangelo di Romagna 61 E3
Sant Boi de Lluçanès 32 A3
Sant Celoni 32 B4
Sant Cugat 32 A4
Sant'Elia a Pianisi 64 B2
Sant'Elpidio a Mare 61 F4
Sant Esteve d'en Bas 32 B3
Sant'Eufemia, Golfo di 67 E3
Sant'Eufemia Lamezia 67 E3
Sant Gervàs 37 F3
Sant Hilari Sacalm 32 B3
Sant Hipòlit de Voltregà 32 A3
Sant Joan de les Abadesses 32 B3
Sant Julià de Lòria 32 A3
Sant Llorenc de Morunys 32 A3
Sant'Onofrio 67 E3
Sant Pau de Seguries 32 B3
Sant Pere de Roda 32 C3
Sant Pol de Mar 32 B4
Sant Ponç, Emb de 32 A3
Sant Quirze de Besora 32 B3
Sant Quirze Safaja 32 A4
Sant Ramon 37 F3
Sant Sadurní d'Anoia 32 A4
Santa Amalia 39 D4
Santa Ana 40 C4
Santa Anna, Emb de 37 E3
Santa Bàrbara (Catalunya) 41 F2
Santa Bárbara (Andalucía) 42 C2
Santa Bárbara Mt 44 B3
Santa Catarina 42 B3
Santa Caterina Pittinuri 66 A3
Santa Caterina Valfurva 58 C3
Santa Caterina Villarmosa 68 C3
Santa Cesarea Terme 65 F4
Santa Clara-a-Velha 42 A2
Santa Clara, Bgem de 42 A2
Santa Coloma de Farners 32 B3
Santa Coloma de Queralt 37 F4
Santa Colombo de Somoza 35 D3
Santa Comba Dão 38 B2
Santa Comba de Rossas 34 C4
Santa Comba 34 A1
Santa Cristina de Lena 35 D2
Santa Croce di Magliano 64 B2
Santa Cruz de Campezo 36 B2
Santa Cruz de la Palma 42 A4
Santa Cruz de la Sierra 39 E3
Santa Cruz de la Zarza 40 B3
Santa Cruz del Retamar 40 A2
Santa Cruz de Moya 41 D3
Santa Cruz de Mudela 44 A1
Santa Cruz de Tenerife 42 B4

Santa Cruz 36 C4
Santa Elena 44 A1
Santa Eufemia 43 E1
Santa Eugenia 34 A2
Santa Eulalia del Río 45 D3
Santa Eulalia de Oscos 34 C1
Santa Eulalia 41 D2
Santa Eulàlia 38 C4
Santa Fe 44 A3
Santa Fé 32 B4
Santa Fiora 63 D1
Santhià 31 F1
Santa Galdana, Cala 45 F2
Santa Gertrude 58 C3
Santa Giusta 66 B3
Santa Inés, Pto de 36 B3
Santa Liestra y San Quilez 37 E3
Santa Lucia d. Mela 69 D2
Santa Luz 34 C4
Santa Luzia 42 A2
Santa Magdalena de Pulpis 41 F2
Santa Margarida do Sádão 42 B1
Santa Margarida i Els Monjos 32 A4
Santa Margarita 45 F2
Santa Margherita 66 B4
Santa Margherita di Belice 68 B3
Santa Margherita Ligure 60 A3
Santa Maria Capua Vetere 64 B3
Santa Maria, C de 42 B3
Santa Maria da Feira 38 B1
Santa Maria d'Angeli 63 E1
Santa Maria del Campo Rus 40 C3
Santa Maria della Versa 60 A2
Santa Maria di Leuca,C 65 F4
Santa Maria la Real de Nieva 40 A1
Santa Maria la Real de Oseira 34 B2
Santa Maria Maggiore 58 A3
Santa Marina 35 E2
Santa Marina del Rey 35 D3
Santa Marinella 63 D2
Santa María de Huerta 36 B4
Santa María del Campo 35 F3
Santa María del Páramo 35 D3
Santa María de Nieva 44 C3
Santa María de Valverde 35 D3
Santa-Maria-Siché 33 F4
Santa Marta 39 D4
Santa Marta de Penaguião 34 B4
Santa Marta de Tormes 39 E1
Santa Olalla del Cala 43 D2
Santa Olalla 39 F3
Santa Pau 32 B3
Santa Pola 45 E2
Santa sa 45 E3
Santa Sofia 61 D3
Santa Sofia d'Epiro 67 E2
Santa Susanna 32 B4
Santa Tecla 34 A3
Santa Teresa di Riva 69 D2
Santa Teresa, Emb de 39 E2
Santa Teresa Gallura 66 B1
Santaella 43 E2

Santana (Estremadura) 38 A4
Santana (Madeira) 42 A3
Santana de Serra 42 A2
Santander 35 F1
Santanyí 45 F3
Santarém 38 B3
Santas Martas 35 E3
Santeramo in Colle 65 D3
Santes Creus 37 F4
Santesteban 36 C1
Santhià 31 F1
Santiago de Alcántara 38 C3
Santiago de Compostela 34 A2
Santiago de la Espada 44 B2
Santiago de la Ribera 45 D2
Santiago do Cacém 42 A1
Santiago do Escoural 38 B4
Santibáñez de Béjar 39 E2
Santibáñez de la Peña 35 E2
Santibáñez de la Sierra 39 E2
Santibáñez de Vidriales 35 D3
Santillana del Mar 35 F1
Santiponce 43 D2
Säntis 58 B2
Santisteban del Puerto 44 B1
Santo Domingo de la Calzada 36 B2
Santo Domingo de Silos 36 A3
Santo Domingo, Ptode 43 D1
Santo Estêvão (Beira Baixa) 38 C2
Santo Estêvão (Estremadura) 38 A4
Santo Estêvão, Rib de 38 A4
Santo Pedro da Torre 34 A3
Santo Severa 63 D2
Santo Stefano di Cadore 59 E2
Santo Stefano d'Aveto 60 B2
Santo Stino di Livenza 59 E4
Santo Tirso 34 A4
Santo Tomé 44 B2
Santok 49 F3
Santolea, Emb de 41 E2
Santomera, Emb de 45 D2
Santoña 36 A1
Santo-Pietro-di-Tenda 33 F2
Santorini, N 91 E1
Santuario de San Ignacio de Loyola 36 B1
Santuario d'Oropa 27 F4
Santu Lussurgiu 66 B3
Santurtzi 36 B1
Sanxenxo 34 A2
Sanza 67 D1
São Bartolomeu de Messines 42 A2
São Brás de Alportel 42 B3
São Cristóvão 38 B4
São Domingos 42 A1
São Gregório 34 B3
São Jacinto 38 B1
São João da Madeira 38 B1
São João de Tarouca 38 C1
São João dos Caldeireiros 42 B2
São José da Lamarosa 38 B3

São Leonardo 42 C1
São Mamede, Sa de 38 C3
São Manços 42 B1
São Marcos da Serra 42 A2
São Marcos do Campo 42 B1
São Martinho das Amoreiras 42 A2
São Martinho do Porto 38 A3
São Matias 42 B1
São Miguel de Machede 38 B4
São Pedro de Açor 38 C2
São Pedro de Moel 38 A2
São Pedro do Sul 38 C1
São Romão 38 C2
São Teotónio 42 A2
São Vicente, C de 42 A2
São Vicente da Beira 38 C2
Saône 26 C3
Saône-et-Loire 26 B3
Saorge 31 E3
Sapanca 115 F3
Sapataria 38 A3
Sápes 81 E2
Sapiéndza, N 86 C4
Sa Pobla 45 F2
Sapri 67 D1
Säräisniemi 99 E4
Sarajärvi 99 E3
Sarajevo 76 A1
Sarakiní 79 E2
Sarakiniko 84 B3
Saramon 28 C4
Sarandaporo 79 E4
Sarandáporos 78 C4
Sarandë 114 C4
Saraváli 86 C1
Saray 115 E3
Saraýköy 115 F4
Šarbanovac 73 E3
Sarbinowo (Gorzów Wlkp) 49 F3
Sarbinowo (Koszalin) 49 F1
Sárbogárd 112 B4
Sarca 58 C3
Sardara 66 B3
Sardegna 66 A2
Sardínia 82 C3
Sardoal 38 B3
Sardona, Piz 58 B2
Sarek 98 A1
Šarengrad 72 B2
Sarentino 59 D2
Särfjället 101 D2
Sargans 58 B2
Sariá, N 93 D2
Sari-d'Orcino 33 F3
Sarine 27 E1
Sariñena 37 E3
Sark 18 A3
Särkisalmi 103 F3
Särkisalo 107 D3
Sarlat-la-Canéda 29 D2
Sarmitunturi 95 F3
Särna 101 D3
Sarnano 61 F4
Sarnen 27 F2
Sarnico 60 B1
Sarno 64 B4
Sarnthein 59 D2
Sarny 113 D2
Sarö 108 C1
Sarón 35 F2
Sarone 59 E3
Saronída 87 F2
Saronikós Kólpos 87 F1
Saronno 60 A1
Sárospatak 112 C3
Sar Planina 77 D3
Sarpsborg 105 D3
Sarracín 35 F3
Sarral 37 F4
Sarralbe 21 E3
Sarrans, Bge de 29 E2

Sarre 21 E3
Sarrebourg 21 E4
Sarreguemines 21 E3
Sarre-Union 21 E3
Sarrià 34 B2
Sarrión 41 E3
Sarroch 66 B4
Sarsina 61 D3
Sars-Poteries 20 C2
Sarstedt 52 B1
Sarteano 63 D1
Sartène 33 F4
Sarthe 23 E4
Sarthe (Dépt) 23 F3
Sárti 80 B4
Sartilly 18 B4
Sarule 66 B2
Sárvár 112 A4
Sarvsjö 101 D2
Sarzana 60 B3
Sarzeau 22 C4
Sarzedas 38 C2
Sasa 77 F2
Saßnitz 49 D1
Sassari 66 A2
Sassello 60 A3
Sassenage 30 C1
Sassenberg 17 F3
Sassenheim 16 B2
Sassetta 62 C1
Sasso 63 E2
Sassoferrato 61 E4
Sassoleone 61 D3
Sasso Marconi 60 C3
Sassuolo 60 C3
Sástago 37 D4
Sasyk, Ozero 113 E4
Sátão 38 C1
Säter 105 F3
Satillieu 30 B1
Satolas 30 C1
Šator 75 D1
Satoraljaújhely 112 C3
Šatorina 70 B4
Satov 57 E1
Satow 48 C2
Sátres 81 D2
Satrup 48 A1
Satu Mare 112 C3
Saualpe 70 B1
Saucelle, Emb de 39 D1
Sauda 104 A3
Sauðárkrókur 96 B1
Sau, Emb de 32 B3
Sauerlach 56 A3
Sauerland 17 F4
Saugues 29 F2
Saujon 28 B1
Saukkovaara 99 E4
Sauland 104 C3
Sauldre 26 A2
Saulgau 55 D3
Saulieu 26 A2
Sault 30 C3
Saulxures 27 E1
Saumur 24 C2
Saundersfoot 8 B2
Sauris 59 D2
Saut du Doubs 27 E2
Sautet, Bge du 30 C2
Sautusjärvi 94 C4
Sauve 30 B3
Sauveterre-de-Béarn 28 A4
Sauveterre-de-Guyenne 28 B2
Sauveterre-de-Rouergue 29 E3
Sauxillanges 29 F1
Sauze d'Oulx 31 E2
Sauze, le 31 D2
Sauze-Vaussais 24 C4
Sauzon 22 B4
Sava (I) 65 E4
Sava (YU) 71 E3
Sávália 86 B1
Sävar 102 B1
Savelli 67 F2
Savenay 23 D4

Saverdun 32 A1
Saverne 21 E4
Savigliano 31 E2
Savignac-les-Eglises 28 C1
Savignano Irpino 64 C3
Savignano sul Rubicone 61 E3
Savigny-sur-Braye 23 F4
Saviñán 36 C4
Savine, Col de la 27 D3
Savines-le-Lac 31 D2
Savinja 70 B1
Savino Selo 72 B2
Savitaipale 103 E4
Sävja 106 B3
Savnik 76 B2
Savognin 58 B3
Savona 60 A3
Savonlinna 103 E3
Savonranta 103 F3
Sævråsvåg 104 A2
Sävsjö 109 D2
Savudrija 70 A3
Savukoski 95 F4
Sawbridgeworth 10 C2
Sáwel Mt 13 D1
Sax 45 D1
Saxmundham 11 E1
Saxnäs 97 F4
Sayatón 40 B2
Säynätsalo 103 D3
Säyneinen 103 E2
Sazadón, Pto de 35 D3
Sázava 112 A3
Scaër 22 B3
Scafa 64 A2
Scafati 64 B4
Scafell Pikes 5 D4
Scala di Santa Regina 33 F3
Scalasaig 4 B2
Scalby 7 D1
Scalea 67 E2
Scalloway 3 F2
Scalpay 2 B3
Scandiano 60 C2
Scanno 64 A2
Scansano 63 D1
Scanzano 65 D4
Scarba 4 B1
Scarborough 7 D1
Scardovari 61 E2
Scarinish 2 A4
Scarpe 20 A1
Scarriff 12 B4
Ščedro 75 E2
Ščepan Polje 76 A1
Scey-sur-Saône 27 D2
Schaalsee 48 B2
Schachendorf 57 F4
Schafberg 56 C3
Schaffhausen 58 A1
Schafstädt 52 C2
Schagen 16 C2
Schaprode 49 D1
Scharbeutz 48 B2
Schärding 56 C2
Scharhörn 47 F2
Scharmützelsee 49 E4
Scharnitz 59 D1
Schauinsland Feldberg 54 C4
Scheeßel 48 A3
Scheggia 61 E4
Scheibbs 57 E3
Scheifling 57 D4
Scheinfeld 55 E1
Schelde 50 B3
Schenefeld (Hamburg) 48 A3
Schenefeld (Itzehoe) 48 A2
Scherfede 52 A2
Schermbeck 17 E3
Scheßlitz 52 C4
Scheveningen 16 B3
Schia 60 B3
Schiedam 16 B3
Schieder-Schwalenberg 52 A1
Schiehallion 4 C1

Schierling 56 B2
Schiermonnikoog 47 D3
Schiermonnikoog I 47 D3
Schiers 58 B2
Schifferstadt 54 C2
Schildau 53 D2
Schilpario 58 C4
Schiltach 54 C3
Schio 59 D4
Schirmeck 21 E4
Schirnding 56 B2
Schkeuditz 53 D2
Schkölen 53 D3
Schladming 59 F1
Schlagsdorf 48 B2
Schlanders 58 C3
Schlangenbad 51 F4
Schleching 56 B3
Schlei 48 A1
Schleiden 51 D4
Schleiz 53 D3
Schleswig 48 A1
Schleswig-Holstein 48 A1
Schleusingen 52 C3
Schlieben 53 E1
Schliersee 56 B4
Schlitz 52 B3
Schlotheim 52 B2
Schluchsee 54 C4
Schlucht, Col de la 27 E1
Schlüchtern 52 B4
Schluderbach 59 E2
Schluderns 58 C3
Schlüsselfeld 55 E1
Schlutup 48 B2
Schmalkalden 52 B3
Schmallenberg 17 F4
Schmidmühlen 55 F1
Schmilka 53 F2
Schmölln (Leipzig) 53 D3
Schmölln (Neu-brandenburg) 49 E3
Schnackenburg 48 C3
Schnaittenbach 55 F1
Schneeberg (A) 57 E3
Schneeberg (D) 53 D4
Schneeberg (DDR) 53 D4
Schneverdingen 48 A3
Schoberpaß 57 D4
Schöckl 57 E4
Schönau 54 C4
Schönberg (A) 59 D2
Schönberg (Bayern) 56 C2
Schönberg (Karl-Marx-Stadt) 53 D4
Schönberg (Rostock) 48 B2
Schönberg (Schleswig-Holstein) 48 B1
Schönbrunn 57 F2
Schönebeck 52 C1
Schöneck 53 D3
Schönecken 51 D4
Schönefeld 49 E4
Schönewalde 53 E1
Schongau 55 F4
Schöningen 52 C1
Schönmünzach 54 C3
Schönsee 56 B1
Schönthal 56 B1
Schönwald 54 C3
Schönwalde 48 B2
Schoonhoven 16 C3
Schopfheim 54 C4
Schöppenstedt 52 B1
Schoppernau 58 B2
Schorndorf 55 D2
Schortens 47 E3
Schotten 52 A4
Schouwen Duiveland 16 B3
Schramberg 54 C3
Schrems 57 D2
Schrobenhausen 55 F2
Schröcken 58 B2
Schrozberg 55 E1
Schruns 58 B2
Schuls 58 C2
Schüttorf 17 E2
Schwaan 48 C2

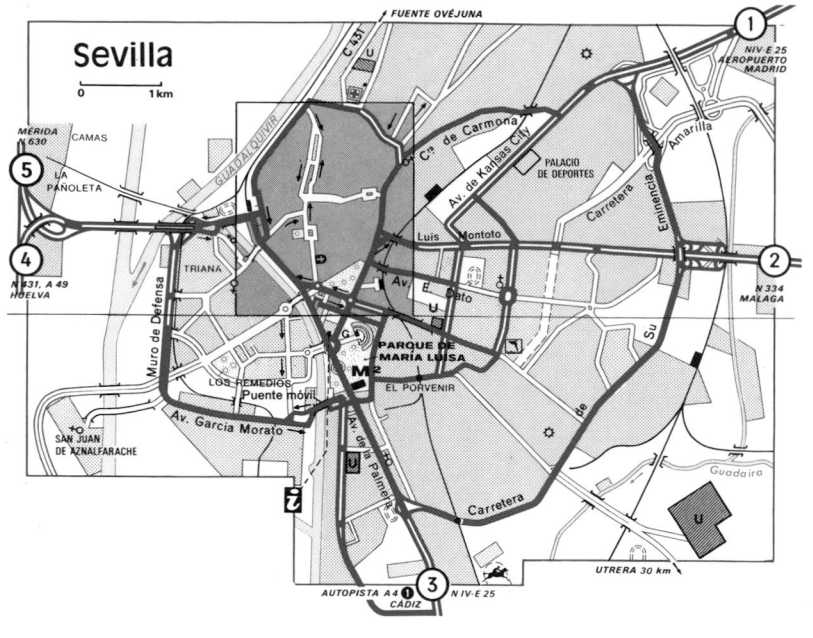

Sevilla

Sepino	64 B3	Severn, Mouth of the	9 D2	Sibinj	71 E3
Sepúlveda	36 A4	Severn,R	9 D2	Sibiu	113 D4
Sequeros	39 E2	Sever, R	38 C3	Sićevo	73 F4
Sequillo, R	35 E4	Seveso	60 A1	Sichar, Emb de	41 E3
Seraing	50 C4	Sevettijärvi	95 F2	Sicié, Cap	31 D4
Seravezza	60 B3	Sevilla	43 D2	Sicignano degli Alburni	64 C4
Seregno	60 A1	Sevilleja de la Jara	39 F3	Sicilia	68 B2
Serein	26 B2	Sevlievo	115 D2	Sicó	38 B2
Séres	80 B2	Sevnica	70 C2	Šid	72 B2
Séres (Nomos)	80 A2	Sevojno	72 C4	Sidári	82 A1
Serfaus	58 C2	Sèvre Nantaise	24 C3	Sideby	102 B3
Serfopoúla, N	88 B3	Sèvre Niortaise	24 C4	Sidensjö	102 A2
Seriate	60 B1	Sévrier	27 D4	Siderno	67 F4
Sérifos	88 A3	Sevsk	111 F4	Síderos, Akr	91 F3
Sérifos, N	88 A3	Sexten	59 E2	Sidiró	81 F2
Serifou, Stenó	88 A3	Seyches	28 C2	Sidirókastro	80 A2
Sermaize-les-Bains	20 C4	Seyda	53 D1	Sidirónero	80 C1
Sermide	60 C2	Seydisfjörður	96 C2	Sidlaw Hills	5 D1
Sermoneta	63 F3	Seyne	31 D3	Sidmouth	9 D3
Sernancelhe	38 C1	Seyne, la	31 D4	Siebenlehn	53 E2
Serón	44 B3	Seyssel	27 D4	Siedlce	112 C1
Serón de Nágima	36 B4	Sežana	70 A2	Sieg	51 E3
Serós	37 E4	Sézanne	20 B4	Siegburg	51 E3
Serpa	42 B1	Sezimovo-Ústí	57 D1	Siegen	17 F4
Serpeddi, P	66 B4	Sezze	63 F3	Siegsdorf	56 B3
Serpis, R	45 E1	Sfáka	91 F4	Siekierki	49 E3
Serra	41 E3	Sfakiá	90 C4	Siena	61 D4
Serracapriola	64 B2	Sfaktiría, N	86 C3	Sieppijärvi	98 C1
Serrada	35 E4	Sferracavallo	68 B2	Sieradz	112 B2
Serradifalco	68 C3	Sfikiá, L	79 E3	Sierck	21 D3
Serradilla	39 D3	Sfîntu Gheorghe	113 D4	Sierentz	27 E1
Serramanna	66 B4	Sforzacosta	61 F4	Sierninghofen	57 D3
Serrana, Pto de la	39 E3	's Gravendeel	16 C3	Sierpc	112 B1
Serra San Bruno	67 F3	's Gravenhage	16 B3	Sierra Boyera, Emb de	43 E1
Serravalle Scrivia	60 A2	Sgùrr Mór	2 C3	Sierra de Fuentes	39 D3
Serre Chevalier	31 D2	Sgùrr na Ciche	2 B4	Sierra de Yeguas	43 E3
Serre-Ponçon, Bge de	31 D2	Shaftesbury	9 D3	Sierre	27 E3
Serres	30 C2	Shanklin	9 E4	Sievi	102 C1
Serrières	30 B1	Shannon	12 B4	Sievin as	102 C1
Serrota	39 F2	Shannon, Mouth of the	12 A4	Sífnos, N	88 B3
Sersale	67 F3	Shannon, R	12 B4	Sífnou, Stenó	88 B3
Sertã	38 B2	Shap	5 D4	Sigean	32 B2
Servan	18 B4	Shapinsay	3 E1	Sigerfjord	94 A3
Sérvia	79 E4	Shebenik, Mal i	77 D4	Siggjarvåg	104 A3
Servian	30 A4	Sheelin, L	13 D3	Sighetu Marmaţiei	112 C3
Servigliano	61 F4	Sheep Haven	12 C1	Sighişoara	113 D4
Servol, R	41 F2	Sheep's Head	14 A4	Siglufjörður	96 B1
Sesa	37 D3	's Heerenberg	17 D3	Sigmaringen	55 D3
Sesena	40 A2	Sheerness	11 D2	Signy-l'Abbaye	20 B2
Sesia	27 F4	Sheffield	6 C2	Sigri	85 E2
Sesimbra	38 A4	Shefford	9 F2	Sigtuna	106 B3
Sesklo, N	93 E1	Shëmri (Shkodër)	76 C3	Sigüenza	36 B4
Sesma	36 C2	Shëmri (Tiranë)	76 C4	Sigulda	110 C2
Sessa Aurunca	64 A3	Shëngjin	76 C3	Siiddasjávri	94 B4
Sesta Godano	60 B3	Sheppey, I of	11 D2	Siikainen	102 B3
Šestanovac	75 E2	Shepshed	7 D3	Siikajoki	99 D4
Sestino	61 E3	Shepton Mallet	9 D3	Siikajoki R	99 D4
Sesto	59 E2	Sherborne	9 D3	Siilinjärvi	103 E2
Sesto Calende	60 A1	Shercock	13 D3	Sijarinska Banja	77 D1
Sesto Fiorentino	60 C3	Sheringham	7 F3	Sikaminiá	85 F2
Sesto San Giovanni	60 A1	's Hertogenbosch	16 C3	Sikås	101 E2
Sestola	60 C3	Shetland Is	3 E2	Siki	84 A2
Sestriere	31 E2	Shiel Bridge	2 C4	Sikiá (Makedonía)	80 B4
Sestri Levante	60 B3	Shieldaig	2 B3	Sikiá (Pelopónissos)	87 E4
Sestrunj	74 C1	Shiel, L	2 B4	Síkinos	88 C4
Sestrunj I	74 C1	Shijak	76 C4	Síkinos, N	88 C4
Sestu	66 B4	Shinás	79 E3	Sikióna	87 D1
Sesvete	70 C2	Shiniás	88 A1	Sikoráhi	81 E2
Séta	84 B4	Shin, L	2 C2	Sikoúrio	83 E1
Setcases	32 B3	Shínos	83 D3	Sikovuono	95 E3
Sète	30 A4	Shinoússa, N	88 C3	Sila, La	67 F3
Setenil	43 E3	Shipston-on-Stour	9 E1	Silandro	58 C3
Setermoen	94 B3	Shíza, N	86 C4	Silba	70 B3
Setesdalen	104 B3	Shkodër	76 B3	Silba I	70 B3
Setesdalsheiene	104 B3	Shkodrës, Liq i	76 B3	Silbaš	72 B2
Settebagni	63 E2	Shkumbin	76 C4	Sildegapet	100 A2
Settimo Torinese	31 E1	Sholári	80 A3	Şile	115 F3
Settle	6 C1	Shoreham	10 C3	Silis	44 B1
Settons, les	26 B2	Shpat, Mal i	77 D4	Siliqua	66 B4
Setúbal	38 A4	Shrewsbury	6 B3	Silistra	115 E1
Seudre	28 B1	Shrewton	9 E3	Silivri	115 E3
Seui	66 B3	Shropshire	9 D1	Siljan (N)	104 C3
Seulo	66 B3	Shupenzë	77 D4	Siljan (S)	101 E4
Seurre	26 C2	Sía, Pto de la	36 A1	Siljansnäs	101 E4
Sevastianá	79 E3	Siátista	79 D4	Silkeborg	108 A3
Sevenoaks	10 C3	Šiauliai	110 C3	Silla	41 E4
Sévérac-le-Château	29 F3	Sibari	67 E2	Silleda	34 B2
Sever do Vouga	38 B1	Sibbhult	109 D3	Silleiro, C	34 A3
Severn Bridge	9 D2	Sibbo	107 F2	Sillé-le-Guillaume	23 E3
		Sibbofjärden	107 F2	Sillian	59 E2
		Šibenik	75 D1		
		Šibenik Mt	75 E2		

Schwabach	55 E1	Scunthorpe	7 D2	Segura de los Baños	41 D1	Sella Nevea	59 F3
Schwäbisch Gmünd	55 D2	Scuol	58 C2	Segura, R	45 D2	Sella, Pso di	59 D3
Schwäbisch Hall	55 D2	Seaford	10 C3	Segura, Sa de	44 B2	Selles	25 E2
Schwabmünchen	55 E3	Seaham	5 E4	Sehnde	52 B1	Sellières	26 C3
Schwaigern	55 D2	Seaton	9 D3	Seia	38 C2	Sellin	49 D1
Schwalmstadt-Treysa	52 A3	Seaton Delaval	5 E3	Seiches	23 E4	Selm	17 E3
Schwalmstadt-Ziegenhain	52 A3	Sebečevo	76 C1	Seifhennersdorf	53 F2	Selmsdorf	48 B2
Schwandorf	56 B1	Sebeş	114 C1	Seignelay	26 B1	Selna	71 F3
Schwanebeck	52 C1	Sebež	111 D3	Seil	4 B1	Selommes	25 E2
Schwanenstadt	56 C3	Sebnitz	53 F2	Seiland	95 D1	Selongey	26 C2
Schwanewede	47 F3	Sečanj	73 D2	Seilandsjøkelen	95 D1	Seløy	97 D3
Schwarmstedt	48 A4	Secchia	60 C2	Seilhac	29 D1	Selsey	9 F3
Schwarza (A)	57 E3	Seckau	57 D4	Seille (Meurthe-et-Moselle)	21 D4	Selsey Bill	9 F3
Schwarza (DDR)	52 C3	Seclin	19 F1	Seille (Saône-et-Loire)	26 C3	Selters	52 A4
Schwarzach	59 E1	Secondigny	24 C3	Seinäjoki	102 C2	Seltz	21 F3
Schwarze Elster	53 E1	Sedan	20 C2	Seine	19 E3	Sélune	18 C4
Schwarzenbach	53 D4	Sedano	35 F2	Seine-et-Marne	19 F4	Selva	59 D3
Schwarzenbek	48 B3	Seda, Rib de	38 C3	Seine-Maritime	19 D3	Selvino	58 B4
Schwarzenberg	53 E3	Sedbergh	6 C1	Sein, I de	22 A3	Seman	114 B3
Schwarzenburg	27 E3	Séderon	30 C3	Seitenstetten	57 D3	Semeljci	71 F2
Schwarzenfeld	56 B1	Sedgefield	5 E4	Seitsemisen	102 C3	Semič	70 B2
Schwarzheide	53 E2	Sedičany	53 F4	Seixal	38 A4	Seminara	67 E4
Schwarzsee	27 E3	Sedico	59 E3	Seixo	34 B3	Semizovac	71 F4
Schwarzwald	54 C3	Sedilo	66 B2	Sejerø	108 B3	Semmering	57 E3
Schwaz	59 D1	Sedini	66 B2	Sejerø Bugt	108 B3	Semmering -Paß	57 E3
Schwechat	57 F2	Sedlare	77 D2	Sejm	113 F1	Semois	20 C2
Schwedt	49 E3	Sedlec-Prčice	53 F4	Sékoulas	86 C2	Semproniano	63 D1
Schweich	54 A1	Sée	18 C4	Šekovići	72 B4	Semur-en-Auxois	26 B2
Schweinfurt	52 B4	Seebenau	48 B4	Selargius	66 B4	Semur-en-Brionnais	26 B4
Schweinitz	53 E1	Seebergsattel	70 B1	Selassía	87 D3	Sena	37 E3
Schwelm	17 E4	Seeboden	59 F2	Selb	53 D4	Sénas	30 C3
Schwendi	55 E3	Seebruck	56 B3	Selbekken	100 C1	Sendim	34 C4
Schwenningen	54 C3	Seefeld	58 C1	Selbu	101 D2	Senez	31 D3
Schwerin	48 C2	Seehaus	56 C3	Selbusjøen	100 C2	Senftenberg	53 E2
Schweriner See	48 C2	Seehausen (Magdeburg)	52 C1	Selby	7 D2	Sengsengeb	57 D3
Schwerte	17 E3	Seehausen (Stendal)	48 C3	Selce	70 B3	Senigallia	61 F3
Schwetzingen	54 C1	Seeheim	54 C1	Selçuk	115 E4	Senise	65 D4
Schwielochsee	53 F1	Seelisberg	58 A2	Sele	64 C4	Senj	70 B3
Schwyz	58 A2	Seelow	49 E4	Selečka pl	77 E4	Senja Änderdalen	94 B3
Sciacca	68 B3	Sées	19 D4	Selenter See	48 B1	Senje	73 E4
Scicli	69 D4	Seesen	52 B1	Séléro	81 D2	Senlis	19 F3
Scilla	67 E4	Seevetal	48 A3	Sélestat	21 E4	Sennecey-le-Grand	26 C3
Scilly, Is of	8 A4	Seewalchen	56 C3	Selevac	73 D3	Sennen	8 A4
Scole	11 D1	Seewiesen	57 E3	Selfoss	96 A2	Sennestadt	17 F3
Sconser	2 B3	Sefkerin	72 C2	Séli	79 E3	Sennori	66 A2
Scopello	58 A4	Segesta	68 A3	Selia	90 C4	Senonches	19 E4
Scordia	69 D3	Segl	58 B3	Selianítika	83 D4	Senones	21 E4
Scorff	22 B3	Segni	63 F3	Seligenstadt	52 A4	Senorbi	66 B3
Ščors	113 E1	Segonzac	28 B1	Selinia	87 F1	Senožeče	70 A2
Scorzè	59 E4	Segorbe	41 E3	Selinunte	68 A3	Sens	26 A1
Scotch Corner	6 C1	Segovia	40 A1	Selishtë	76 C3	Senta	72 C1
Scotland	2 C4	Segré	23 E4	Selište	73 E3	Šentilj	70 C1
Scourie	2 C2	Segre	37 E3	Selje	100 A3	Šentjernej	70 C2
Scrabster	3 D2	Segre, R	32 A3	Seljord	104 C3	Šentjur	70 C2
Scridain, L	4 B1	Segura	38 C3	Selkämeri	102 B3	Šentvid na Šlemenu	70 B1
Scrivia	60 A2	Segura de la Sierra	44 B1	Selkirk	5 D3	Sépeaux	26 A1
Ščučin	110 C4	Segura de León	43 D1	Sellajoch	59 D3	Šepetovka	113 D2

Silloth	5 D4	Šišan	70 A4
Šilo	70 B3	Sisante	40 C4
Šilo	81 E2	Šišljavić	70 C3
Sil, R	34 C2	Sissa	60 B2
Sils	32 B4	Sissach	27 F2
Sils im Engadin	58 B3	Sissonne	20 B3
Siltakylä	107 F2	Sisteron	31 D3
Šilutė	110 B3	Sistiana	59 F3
Silvalen	97 D3	Sistranda	100 C1
Silvaplana	58 B3	Sitges	32 A4
Silvares	38 C2	Sithonía	80 B4
Silves	42 A2	Sitia	91 F4
Silvi Marina	64 A1	Sitnica	77 D2
Silvrettagruppe	58 B2	Sittard	17 D4
Silz	58 C2	Sittensen	48 A3
Simancas	35 E4	Sittingbourne	11 D3
Símandra	80 A3	Siuntio	107 E3
Šimanovci	72 C3	Siuro	107 E1
Simav	115 F4	Siurua	99 D3
Simaxis	66 B3	Siuruanjoki	99 D3
Simbach (Inn)	56 B3	Siusi	59 D3
Simbach (Isar)	56 B2	Sivac	72 B2
Simbruini, Mti	63 F2	Svaslı	115 F4
Simeto	69 D3	Síviri	80 A4
Sími	93 E1	Sívota	82 B2
Šimići	71 E3	Sívros	82 B3
Sími, N	93 E1	Siziano	60 A1
Simlångsdalen	108 C2	Sizun	22 B3
Simmerath	51 D4	Sjælland	108 C3
Simmern	54 B1	Sjællands Odde	108 B3
Simo	99 D3	Sjenica	76 C1
Simojärvi	99 E2	Sjeništa	76 A1
Simojoki	99 D3	Sjøåsen	97 D4
Simola	103 F4	Sjöbo	109 D3
Símonos Pétras	80 C4	Sjøholt	100 B2
Simonsbath	8 C1	Sjona	97 E2
Simonswald	54 C3	Sjötorp	105 E4
Simópoulo	86 B1	Sjoutnäset	97 E4
Simplonpass	27 F3	Sjøvegan	94 B3
Simrishamn	109 D3	Sjulsmark	102 B1
Sinaia	113 D4	Sjundea	107 E3
Sinalunga	61 D4	Sjusjøen	104 D2
Sinarádes	82 A1	Skåbu	100 C3
Sinarcas	41 D3	Skäckerfjällen	101 D1
Sindelfingen	55 D2	Skadarsko jez	76 B3
Sındırgı	115 F4	Skadovsk	113 F4
Síndos	79 F3	Skafidiá	86 B2
Sines	42 A1	Skaftá	96 B2
Sines, C de	42 A1	Skagafjörður	96 B1
Sinettä	99 D2	Skage	97 D4
Sineu	45 F2	Skagen	108 B1
Singen	55 D4	Skagern	105 E4
Singöfjärden	106 B3	Skagerrak	108 A1
Singra, Pto de	41 D2	Skaill	3 E1
Siniscola	66 C2	Skajálfandi	96 B1
Sinj	75 D1	Skála (Kefaloniá)	86 A1
Sinjajevina	76 B2	Skála (Lésvos)	85 F2
Sinni	65 D4	Skála (Pátmos)	89 E2
Sinnicolau Mare	114 C1	Skála	
Sinopoli	67 E4	(Pelopónissos)	87 D3
Sinsheim	55 D2	Skála (Stereá	
Sintra	38 C4	Eláda)	83 F3
Sinzig	51 E4	Skála Eressoú	85 E2
Siófok	112 B4	Skála Kaliráhis	80 C3
Sion	27 E3	Skaland	94 B2
Sioule	26 A4	Skála Oropoú	84 B4
Šipan	75 F2	Skála Potamiás	81 D3
Šipanska Luka	75 F2	Skála Rahoníou	80 C3
Šipka	115 D2	Skalavík	96 A4
Sipoo	107 F2	Skála Volissoú	85 E4
Sipoonselkä	107 F2	Skälderviken	108 C3
Šipovo	71 E4	Skålevik	104 B4
Sippola	107 F2	Skálfandafljót	96 B2
Šiprage	71 E4	Skalka	98 A2
Sira	104 A4	Skalohóri (Lésvos)	85 E2
Sira R	104 B4	Skalohóri	
Siracusa	69 D4	(Makedonía)	79 D3
Sirdalen	104 B4	Skaloti	80 C1
Sirdalsvatn	104 A4	Skælskør	108 B4
Siret	113 D3	Skamnéli	78 C4
Siret R	113 E3	Skandáli	85 D1
Sirevåg	104 A4	Skandári, Akr	89 F3
Sirig	72 C2	Skanderborg	108 B3
Sirino, Mte	65 D4	Skandzoúra, N	84 B3
Širitovci	75 D1	Skåne	109 D3
Sirkka	95 E4	Skånevik	104 A3
Sirma	95 E2	Skåningsbukt	94 C2
Sirmione	60 C1	Skånland	94 ·B3
Sirna, N	92 C1	Skänninge	106 A4
Široko Polje	71 F2	Skanör Falsterbo	108 C4
Sirolo	61 F4	Skara	109 D1
Síros, N	88 B2	Skaraborgs Län	109 D1
Siruela	39 F4	Skaramangás	87 F1
Sisak	71 D2	Skærbæk	108 A4
Skarberget	94 B4	Skotterud	105 D3
Škarda	74 B1	Skoulikariá	82 C2
Skåre	105 E3	Skoúra	87 D3
Skárfia	83 F3	Skoúrta	87 F1
Skärgårdshavet	107 D3	Skoútari	
Skärhamn	108 C1	(Makedonía)	80 B2
Skarnes	105 D3	Skoútari	
Skarplinge	106 B2	(Pelopónissos)	87 D4
Skarsvåg	95 E1	Skoutáros	85 E2
Skärvången	101 E1	Skövde	109 D1
Skarżysko-		Skrá	79 E2
Kamienna	112 B2	Skrad	70 B3
Skattungbyn	101 E4	Skradin	75 D1
Skatval	100 C2	Skradinski buk	75 D1
Skaulo	94 C4	Skreia	105 D2
Skaun	100 C2	Skrim	104 C3
Skee	105 D4	Skrolsvik	94 B3
Skegness	7 E3	Skrydstrup	108 A4
Skei (Møre og		Skudeneshavn	104 A3
Romsdal)	100 B2	Skuleskogen	102 A2
Skei (Sogn og		Skull	14 A4
Fjordane)	100 A3	Skultuna	106 A3
Skeiðarársandur	96 B2	Skuodas	110 B3
Skela	72 C3	Skuov'gilraš'ša	95 D2
Skellefteå	98 B4	Skurup	109 D3
Skellefteälven	98 B4	Skutskär	106 B2
Skelleftehamn	98 B4	Skutvik	94 A4
Skellig	14 A4	Skvira	113 E2
Skelmersdale	6 B2	Skye	2 B3
Skenderbeut, M i	76 C4	Slagelse	108 B3
Skender Vakuf	71 E4	Slagnäs	98 A3
Skepastó	80 B2	Slánčev Brjag	115 E2
Skerries	13 E3	Slancy	111 D1
Ski	105 D3	Slane	13 D3
Skíathos	84 A2	Slaney	15 D3
Skiáthos, N	84 A2	Slangerup	108 C3
Skibbereen	14 B4	Slano	75 F2
Skibby	108 C3	Slany	53 F3
Skibotn	94 C2	Šlapanice	57 F1
Skiddaw	5 D4	Slapská přehr	
Skidra	79 E3	nádrž	53 F4
Skien	104 C3	Slapská přehr	
Skierniewice	112 B2	Slatina (Bor)	73 E3
Skillingaryd	109 D2	Slatina (Bosna i	
Skiloundía	86 C2	Hercegovina)	71 E3
Skinári, Akr	86 A1	Slatina (Kraljevo)	73 D4
Skiniás	91 E4	Slatina	
Skinnarbu	104 B3	(Makedonija)	77 D3
Skinnskatteberg	105 F3	Slatina (RO)	115 D1
Skipagurra	95 F1	Slatine	75 D2
Skipton	6 C2	Slatinski Drenovac	71 E2
Skíros	84 C3	Slavgorod	111 E4
Skíros, N	84 C3	Slavinja	77 E1
Skíti	83 F1	Slavkovica	72 C4
Skive	108 A2	Slavkov u Brna	57 F1
Skivjane	76 C2	Slavnik	70 A3
Skjeberg	105 D3	Slavonice	57 D1
Skjern	108 A3	Slavonska Požega	71 E2
Skjersholmane	104 A3	Slavonski Brod	71 E3
Skjerstad	97 E2	Slavonski Kobaš	71 E3
Skjerstadfjorden	97 E2	Slavuta	113 D2
Skjervøy	94 C2	Sławno	110 A4
Skjønhaug	105 D3	Sławoborze	49 F2
Sklavopoúla	90 B3	Sleaford	7 D3
Sklíthro	83 F1	Slea Head	14 A3
Šklov	111 E3	Sleat, Sd of	2 B4
Skočivir	77 E4	Slettfjellet	94 C2
Škocjanske jame	70 A3	Sliedrecht	16 C3
Skodje	100 B2	Sliema	68 B4
Škofja Loka	70 A2	Slieve Bloom Mts	12 C4
Skofljica	70 B2	Slieve Donard	13 E3
Skog (Gävleborgs		Slieve Mish Mts	14 A3
Län)	101 F4	Slievenamon	14 C3
Skog (Västernorrlands		Slieve Snaght	13 D1
Län)	102 A2	Sligachan	2 B3
Skógafoss	96 B3	Sligeach	12 C2
Skogerøya	95 F2	Sligo	12 C2
Skoghall	105 E3	Sligo (Co)	12 B3
Skogstorp	105 F4	Sligo B	12 C2
Skogskloster	106 B3	Slišane	77 D1
Skólis	86 B1	Slite	109 F4
Skópelos (Lésvos)	85 F3	Sliven	115 E2
Skópelos		Sljeme	70 C2
(Skópelos)	84 B2	Šljivovica	72 C4
Skópelos, N	84 B3	Slobozia	115 E1
Skopí	91 F4	Slonim	112 C1
Skopiá	83 E1	Sloten	16 C1
Skopje	77 E3	Slough	9 F2
Skopós	79 D2	Slovac	72 C3
Skopun	96 A4	Slovenska Bistrica	70 C1
Skorenovac	73 D3	Slovenija	70 A2
Skorovatn	97 E4	Slovenj Gradec	70 B1
Skorped	101 F2	Slovenske Konjice	70 C1
Skotína	79 F4	Slovenské	
		Rudohorie	112 B3
		Slovinci	71 D3
		Slubice	49 F4
		Sluck	111 D4
		Sluderno	58 C3
		Sluis	16 A4
		Sluknov	53 F2
		Slunj	70 C3
		Słupsk	110 A4
		Slyne Head	12 A3
		Småland	109 D2
		Smålandsfarvandet	
			108 B4
		Smålands-stenar	109 D2
		Šmarje	70 C2
		Šmarješke Toplice	70 B2
		Šmartin	70 B2
		Smedby	109 E2
		Smederevo	73 D3
		Smederevska	
		Palanka	73 D3
		Smela	113 F2
		Smiqáda	81 E2
		Smilčić	74 C1
		Smilde	17 D1
		Smiltene	110 C2
		Smojmirovo	77 F3
		Smokovljan	75 F2
		Smøla	100 B1
		Smolensk	111 E3
		Smolevichi	111 D4
		Smólikas, Óros	78 C4
		Smoljan	115 D3
		Smorgon	111 D4
		Smyrahamn	104 A1
		Smygehamn	109 D4
		Snaefell	6 A1
		Snæfellsnes	96 A2
		Snaith	7 D2
		Snåsa	101 D1
		Snasahögarna	101 D2
		Snåsavatnet	101 D1
		Sneek	16 C1
		Sneem	14 A4
		Snežnik	70 B3
		Sniardwy, Jez	110 B4
		Snigir'ovka	113 F3
		Snillfjord	100 C2
		Snizort, L	2 B3
		Šnjegotina Velika	71 E3
		Snøfjord	95 D1
		Snøhefta	100 C3
		Snøtinden	97 E2
		Snowdon	6 A3
		Snowdonia Forest	
		and Nat Pk	6 A3
		Soave	60 C1
		Sobeslav	57 D1
		Sobra	75 F2
		Sobrado	34 B2
		Sobral da Adiça	42 C1
		Sobral de Monte	
		Agraço	38 A3
		Sobreira Formosa	38 C2
		Sobrón, Emb de	36 B2
		Søby	108 B4
		Soča	70 A2
		Soča R	70 A2
		Sočanica	77 D1
		Soccia	33 F3
		Sochaczew	112 B1
		Sochaux	27 E2
		Socol	73 D2
		Socovos	44 C1
		Socuéllamos	40 B4
		Sodankylä	95 E4
		Söderåkra	109 E3
		Söderbärke	105 F3
		Söderfors	106 B3
		Söderhamn	101 F4
		Söderköping	106 A4
		Södermanlands	
		Län	106 A4
		Söderskog	109 D3
		Södertälje	106 B4
		Sodražica	70 B2
		Sodupe	36 B1
		Soest (D)	17 F3
		Soest (NL)	16 C2
		Soestdijk	16 C2
		Sofádes	83 E2
Sofia	115 D2	Sommatino	68 C4
Sofiero	108 C3	Somme	19 E2
Sofikó	87 E1	Somme (Dépt)	19 F2
Sofó	83 E2	Sommen	109 E1
Sögel	17 E1	Sömmerda	52 C2
Sogliano al		Sommesous	20 B4
Rubicone	61 E3	Sommières	30 B3
Soglio	58 B3	Sømna	97 D3
Sogndal	100 B3	Somolinos	36 A4
Søgne	104 B4	Somosierra, Pto	
Sognefjell	100 B3	de	36 A4
Sognefjorden	104 A1	Sompio	95 F3
Sognesjøen	104 A1	Somport, Pto de	37 D2
Sogn og		Šomrda	73 E3
Fjordane	100 A3	Soncillo	35 F2
Soham	11 D1	Soncino	60 B1
Sohós	80 A2	Søndeled	104 C4
Soignies	50 B4	Sønderborg	108 B4
Soini	102 C2	Sønderby	108 B4
Soinlahti ·	103 D1	Sønder Felding	108 A3
Soissons	20 A3	Sondershausen	52 C2
Söke	115 E4	Søndersø	108 B3
Sokna	104 C2	Sondrio	58 B3
Soko Banja	73 E4	Songeons	19 E3
Sokolac	72 B4	Sonkajärvi	103 E1
Sokolov	53 D3	Sonnblick	59 E2
Sokołów Podlaski	112 C1	Sonneberg	52 C4
Sokosti	95 F3	Sonnewalde	53 E1
Sola (Rogaland)	104 A3	Sonogno	58 A3
Sola (Sogn og		Sonsbeck	17 D3
Fjordane)	104 A1	Sonseca	40 A3
Solana de los		Son Servera	45 F3
Barros	39 D4	Sonta	72 B2
Solana del Pino	43 F1	Sonthofen	55 E4
Solares	35 F2	Sontra	52 B3
Solberg	101 F1	Sopeira	37 F3
Solbergfjorden	94 B3	Sopilja	76 A1
Solčava	70 B1	Sopište	77 D3
Solda	58 C3	Sopoćani	76 C1
Sölden	58 C2	Sopot (PL)	110 A4
Soldeu	32 A2	Sopot (YU)	73 D3
Solent, The	9 E3	Sopotnica	77 D4
Solenzara	33 F4	Sopron	112 A4
Solesmes (Nord)	20 A2	Sora	64 A3
Solesmes (Sarthe)	23 E3	Soragna	60 B2
Solevåg	100 A2	Söråker	101 F3
Solf	102 B2	Sørarnøy	97 E2
Solferino	60 C1	Sorbas	44 C3
Solholmen	100 B2	Sorbe, R	40 B1
Solignac (Haute-		Sore	28 B3
Loire)	29 F2	Soresina	60 B1
Solignac (Haute-		Sørfjorden	104 B2
Vienne)	29 D1	Sør-Flatanger	96 C4
Soligorsk	111 D4	Sørfolda	94 A4
Solihull	9 E1	Sörfors	102 A1
Solin	75 D1	Sorga	52 B3
Soline	74 B1	Sorgono	66 B3
Solingen	17 E4	Sorgues	30 B3
Sölkerpaß	57 D4	Sørgutvik	97 D4
Söll	59 D1	Soria	36 B3
Sollana	41 E4	Soriano nel	
Sollefteå	101 F2	Cimino	63 E2
Sollenau	57 F3	Sørkjosen	94 C2
Sollentuna	106 B3	Sorø	108 B3
Sóller	45 E2	Soroki	113 E3
Sollerön	101 E4	Soroní	93 E1
Søllested	108 B4	Sørøya	95 D1
Solliès-Pont	31 D4	Sørøysundet	95 D1
Solnečnogorsk	111 F2	Sorraia, R	38 A4
Solofra	64 B4	Sørreisa	94 B3
Solosancho	39 F2	Sorrento	64 B4
Solothurn	27 E2	Sor, Rib de	38 B3
Solre-le-Château	20 B2	Sørrollnes	94 B3
Solrød	108 C3	Sorsakoski	103 E2
Solsona	32 A3	Sorsele	98 A3
Šolta	75 D2	Sorso	66 A2
Soltau	48 A3	Sort	37 F2
Solunska Glava	77 E3	Sortino	69 D4
Solunto	68 B3	Sortland	94 A3
Solvay	60 C4	Sortlandsundet	94 A3
Sölvesborg	109 D3	Sør Trøndelag	100 C2
Solvorn	100 B3	Sorunda	106 B4
Solway Firth	4 C4	Sørvågen	97 E1
Solynieve	44 A3	Sørvágur	96 A4
Soma	115 E4	Sørværøy	97 E1
Sombernon	26 C2	Sørvattnet	101 D3
Sombor	72 B2	Sos del Rey	
Someren	17 D4	Católico	37 D2
Somero	107 E2	Soses	37 E4
Somerset	9 D3	Sosnovyj Bor	111 D1
Someş	112 C4	Sosnowiec	112 B2
Sommarøy	94 B2	Sospel	31 E3

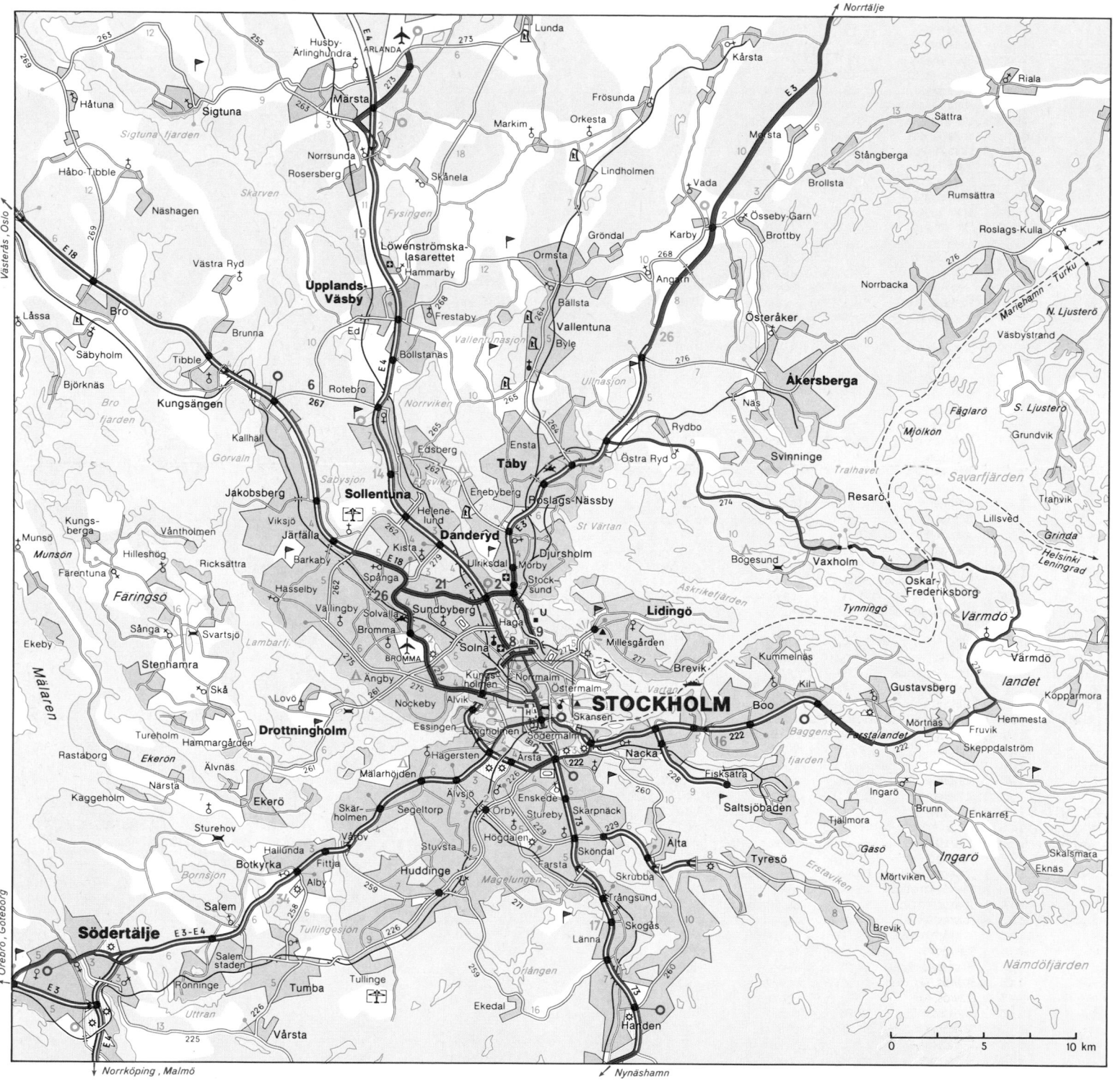

Šoštanj	70 B1	Souesmes	25 F2	Soure	38 B2	South		Spaichingen	55 D3	Spathí, Akr		Spiddle	12 B3
Sóstis	81 D2	Soufflenheim	21 F3	Sournia	32 B2	Queensferry	5 D2	Spakenburg	16 C2	(Pelopónissos)	87 F2	Spiekeroog	47 E2
Šostka	111 F4	Souflí	81 F2	Sourotí	80 A3	South Ronaldsay	3 E1	Spalding	7 E3	Spodnji Brnik	70 B2	Spielfeld	70 C1
Sotaseter	100 B3	Soúgia	90 B4	Soúrpi	83 F2	Southsea	9 F3	Spånda, Akr	90 B3	Spean Bridge	2 C4	Spiez	27 F3
Sotillo de la		Souillac	29 D2	Sousceyrac	29 D2	South Shields	5 E3	Spandau	49 D4	Speikkogel	57 E4	Spijkenisse	16 B3
Adrada	39 F2	Souilly	20 C3	Sousel	38 C4	South Tyne	5 D3	Spangenberg	52 B3	Spello	63 E1	Spilea Diroú	87 D4
Sotin	72 B2	Soulac	28 A1	Soustons	28 A4	South Uist	2 A3	Spanish Pt	12 B4	Spennymoor	5 E4	Spíli	90 C4
Sotira	79 E2	Soulaines-Dhuys	20 C4	Soutelo	34 B2	Southwell	7 D3	Sparlösa	108 C1	Sperhiáda	83 E3	Spiliá	83 E1
Sotkamo	99 E4	Soulinári	86 C3	Souterraine, la	25 E4	Southwold	11 E1	Spárta	87 E1	Sperhiós	83 E3	Spilimbergo	59 E3
Soto del Barco	35 D1	Soulíou, Óri	82 B2	Southam	9 E1	Souvála	87 F2	Spárti	87 D3	Sperillen	104 C2	Spilsby	7 E3
Soto de los		Soulópoulo	82 B1	Southampton	9 E3	Souvigny	26 A3	Spartivento, C		Sperlonga	63 F3	Spinalónga	91 E3
Infantes	35 D1	Soultz (Bas-Rhin)	21 E3	Southborough	10 C3	Sovata	113 D4	(Calabria)	67 E4	Sperrin Mts	13 D1	Spinazzola	65 D3
Soto de Luiña	35 D1	Soultz (Haut-Rhin)	27 E1	South Downs	9 F3	Sövdeborg	109 D3	Spartivento, C		Spétses	87 E3	Spincourt	20 C3
Soto de Sajambre	35 E2	Soúnio	88 A2	Southend	4 B3	Soverato	67 F3	(Sardegna)	66 B4	Spétses, N	87 E3	Špionica Donja	71 F3
Sotogrande	43 E4	Soúnio, Akr	88 A2	Southend-on-Sea	11 D2	Soveria Mannelli	67 F3	Spárto	82 C3	Spetsopoúla, N	87 E3	Špišić Bukovica	71 E2
Sotopalacios	35 F3	Souppes	25 F1	Southern Uplands	4 C3	Sovetsk	110 B3	Spas-Demensk	111 F3	Speyer	54 C2	Spišská-Nová Ves	112 B3
Sottomarina	61 D1	Source de la Loue	27 D2	South Esk	3 D4	Søvik	100 A2	Spáta	87 F1	Spey, R	3 D3	Spital	57 D3
Sottunga	106 C3	Source du		South Foreland	11 D3	Sož	111 E4	Spatharéi	89 E2	Spezzano		Spittal	59 F2
Sotuélamos	40 C4	Lison	27 D3	South Molten	8 C3	Sozopol	115 E2	Spathí, Akr		Albanese	67 E2	Spitz	57 E2
Soúda	90 C3	Sourdeval	18 C4	Southport	6 B2	Spa	51 D4	(Kíthira)	90 A1	Spezzano della Sila	67 E2	Spjelkavik	100 A2

Split	75 D2	Stansted	10 C2	Steine	104 A1
Spluga, Pso dello	58 B3	Stapar	72 B2	Steinestø	104 A2
Splügen	58 B3	Starachowice	112 B2	Steinfeld	17 F2
Splügenpass	58 B3	Stara Gradina	71 E2	Steinfeld	59 F2
Spodsbjerg	108 B4	Staraja Russa	111 E2	Steinfurt	17 E2
Špola	113 F2	Stara Moravica	72 B1	Steingaden	55 F4
Spoleto	63 E1	Stara Novalja	70 B4	Steinhaus	59 D2
Spornitz	48 C3	Stara Pazova	72 C2	Steinhausen	55 D3
Spotorno	60 A3	Stara Pl (BG)	115 D2	Steinheim (Baden-	
Spreča	71 F3	Stara Pl (YU)	73 F4	Württemberg)	55 E2
Spree	49 E4	Stará Role	53 E4	Steinheim	
Spreewald	53 E1	Staravina	77 E4	(Bayern)	55 E3
Spremberg	53 F1	Stara Vrata	70 C4	Steinheim (Nordrhein-	
Spresiano	59 E4	Stara Zagora	115 D2	Westfalen)	52 A2
Springe	52 A1	Stargard		Steinkjer	101 D1
Sprogø	108 B4	Szczeciński	49 F2	Steinnuder Meer	48 A4
Spurn Head	7 E2	Stårheim	100 A3	Steinpaß	59 E1
Spuž	76 B2	Stari	77 F3	Steinshamn	100 A2
Squillace, Golfo di	67 F3	Stari Bar	76 B3	Steinsland	104 A2
Squinzano	65 F4	Stari Begej	72 C2	Stekene	50 B3
Srb	71 D4	Starica	111 F2	Stelvio, Parco Naz	
Srbac	71 E3	Starigrad (Hvar)	75 D2	della	58 C3
Srbica	77 D2	Starigrad		Stelvio, Pso dello	58 C3
Srbija	73 D4	(Velebit)	70 B4	Stená Klissoúras	79 D3
Srbobran	72 C2	Stari Gradac	71 E2	Stenay	20 C3
Srđđevići	75 E1	Starigrad		Stendal	48 C4
Srebrenica	72 C4	Paklenica	70 C4	Stení	84 B3
Središče	70 C1	Stari Jankovci	72 B2	Stenlille	108 B3
Sredna Gora	115 D2	Stari Log	70 B2	Stenløse	108 C3
Srednje	71 F4	Stari Majdan	71 D3	Stenness	3 D1
Srednji kanal	74 C1	Stari Mikanovci	71 F2	Stenó	87 D2
Srednogorie	115 D2	Starnberg	56 A3	Stenó, Akr	88 B2
Sredska	77 D3	Starnberger See	56 A3	Stenó Ithákis	82 B4
Sremska		Starodub	111 F4	Sténoma	83 D3
Kamenica	72 C2	Starogard		Stenudden	98 A2
Sremska Mitrovica	72 C3	Gdański	110 A4	Stenungsund	108 C1
Sremska Rača	72 B3	Starokonstantinov		Stepanci	77 E3
Sremski Karlovci	72 C2		113 D2	Stepnica	49 E2
Srnetica	71 D4	Staro Nagoričane	77 E2	Stepojevac	72 C3
Srnice Donje	71 F3	Staro Petrovo Selo	71 E3	Stereá Eláda	83 D3
Środa		Staro Slano	76 A2	Sterkrade	17 E3
Wielkopolska	112 À1	Start Pt	8 C3	Stérna	
Srpska Crnja	72 C1	Starý Smokovec	112 B3	(Makedonía)	80 C2
Srpske Moravice	70 B3	Staßfurt	52 C1	Stérna	
Srpski Itebej	73 D1	Statland	97 D4	(Pelopónissos)	87 D2
Srpski Miletić	72 B2	Staußfurt	52 C2	Stérna (Thráki)	81 F1
Stabbursdalen	95 D2	Stavanger	104 A3	Sternberg	48 C2
Stade	48 A3	Staveley	7 D3	Stérnes	90 C3
Stádio	87 D2	Stavelot	51 D4	Sterup	48 A1
Stadskanaal	17 E1	Stavenisse	16 B3	Sterza, la	60 C4
Stadthagen	52 A1	Staveren	16 C1	Sterzing	59 D2
Stadtilm	52 C3	Stavern	104 C4	Stevenage	9 F2
Stadtkyll	51 D4	Stavrí, Akr	88 C4	Stevns	108 C4
Stadtlohn	17 E3	Stavrodrómi	86 C1	Stevns Klint	108 C4
Stadtoldendorf	52 A2	Stavrohóri	91 F4	Stewarton	4 C2
Stadtroda	52 C3	Stavrós (Évia)	84 B3	Steyr	57 D3
Stadtsteinach	52 C4	Stavrós (Imathía)	79 E3	Steyrermühl	56 C3
Stadt Wehlen	53 F2	Stavrós (Itháki)	82 B4	Stia	61 D3
Staffa	4 A1	Stavrós (Kríti)	90 C3	Stigliano	65 D4
Staffanstorp	108 C3	Stavrós (Thessalía)	83 E2	Stigtomta	106 A4
Staffelsee	56 A4	Stavrós		Stilfserjoch	58 C3
Staffelstein	52 C4	(Thessaloníki)	80 B3	Stilida	83 E3
Staffin	2 B3	Stavrós, Akr (Kríti)	91 D3	Stilo	67 F4
Stafford	6 C3	Stavrós, Akr		Stimánga	87 D1
Staffordshire	6 C3	(Thássos)	81 D3	Stípsi	85 F2
Stágira	80 B3	Stavroúpoli	80 C2	Stímfalía, L	87 D1
Stahle	52 A2	Steblevë	77 D4	Štimlje	77 D2
Stahovica	70 B2	Štěchovice	53 F4	Stintino	66 A1
Staines	9 F2	Steckborn	58 A1		
Stainz	57 E4	Steeg	58 C2		
Stajovce	77 E2	Steenbergen	16 B3		
Stalać	73 E4	Steenvoorde	19 F1		
Štalcerji	70 B3	Steenwijk	17 D2		
Stalida	91 E3	Stefáni (Ípiros)	82 B2		
Stall	59 E2	Stefáni (Stereá			
Stalle, Pso di	59 E2	Eláda)	87 F1		
Stallersattel	59 E2	Stefaniná	80 B3		
Stalowa Wola	112 C2	Stefanovíkio	83 F2		
Stamford	9 F1	Stege	108 C4		
Stamnes	104 A2	Stegersbach	57 F4		
Stams	58 C2	Steibis	55 E4		
Stamsund	94 A4	Steiermark	57 D4		
Stange	105 D2	Steigen	97 E1		
Stanišić	72 B1	Stein (A)	57 E2		
Stanišinci	73 D4	Stein (N)	105 D2		
Štanjel	70 A2	Steinach (A)	57 E2		
Stanke Dimitrov	115 D3	Steinach (DDR)	52 C3		
Staňkov	56 B1	Steinau	52 A4		
Stankovci	74 C1	Steinbach-			
Stanley	5 E4	Hallenberg	52 B3		
Stanós	80 B3	Stein (Baden-			
Stános	82 C3	Württemberg)	55 D4		
Stans	27 F2	Stein (Bayern)	55 E1		
Stansstad	27 F2				

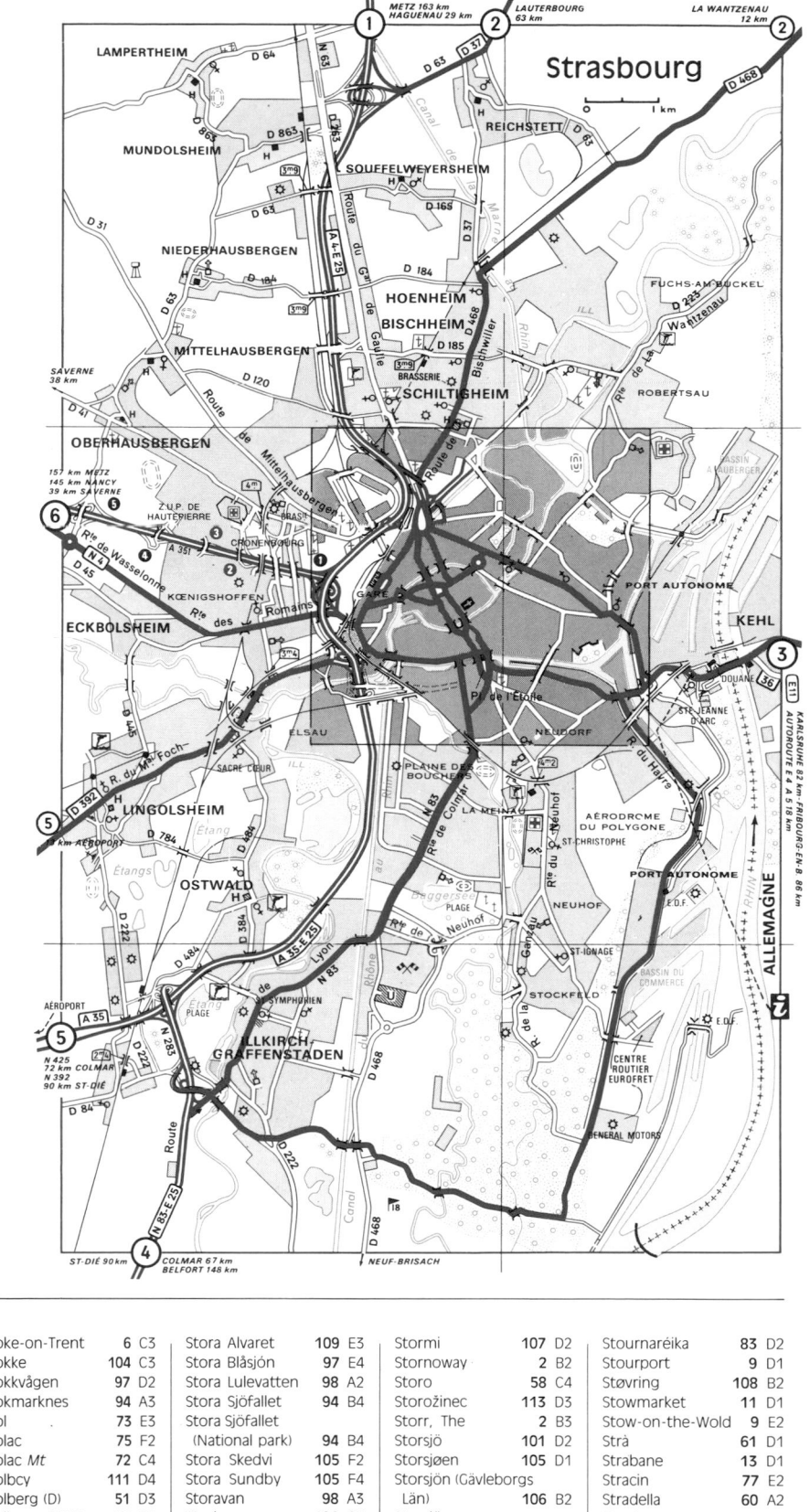

Strasbourg

Stoke-on-Trent	6 C3	Stora Alvaret	109 E3	Stormi	107 D2	Stournaréika	83 D2
Stokke	104 C3	Stora Blåsjön	97 E4	Stornoway	2 B2	Stourport	9 D1
Stokkvågen	97 D2	Stora Lulevatten	98 A2	Storo	58 C4	Støvring	108 B2
Stokmarknes	94 A3	Stora Sjöfallet	94 B4	Storožinec	113 D3	Stowmarket	11 D1
Stol	73 E4	Stora Sjöfallet		Storr, The	2 B3	Stow-on-the-Wold	9 E2
Stolac	75 F2	(National park)	94 B4	Storsjö	101 D2	Strá	61 D1
Stolac Mt	72 C4	Stora Skedvi	105 F2	Storsjøen	105 D1	Strabane	13 D1
Stolbcy	111 D4	Stora Sundby	105 F4	Storsjön (Gävleborgs		Stracin	77 E2
Stolberg (D)	51 D3	Storavan	98 A3	Län)	106 B2	Stradella	60 A2
Stolberg (DDR)	52 C2	Storby	106 C3	Storsjön		Stradsett	11 D1
Stolice	72 B3	Stord	104 A2	(Ljungdalen)	101 D2	Straelen	17 D3
Stolice Mt	73 E4	Stordal	100 B2	Storsjön		Stragari	73 D4
Stolin	113 D1	Store Bælt	108 B3	(Östersund)	101 E2	Strakonice	56 C1
Stollberg	53 E3	Storebø	104 A2	Storsjouten	97 E4	Stralsund	49 D1
Stöllet	105 E2	Storebro	109 E3	Storskarven	101 D2	Stranda	100 B2
Stolpen	53 F2	Store Heddinge	108 C4	Storslett	94 C2	Strandebarm	104 A2
Stølsheimen	104 B2	Store Molvik	95 F1	Storsteinnes	94 C3	Strandhill	12 C2
Stolzenau	48 A4	Store Mosse	109 D2	Storstrømmen	108 C4	Strangford	13 E2
Stómio	83 F1	Støren	100 C2	Storuman	97 F4	Strangford L	13 E2
Ston	75 F2	Storfjellet	97 F2	Storuman L	97 F3	Strängnäs	106 B3
Stone	6 C3	Storfjorden	100 B2	Storvik (N)	95 D2	Stranice	70 B1
Stonehaven	3 E4	Storfors	105 E3	Storvik (S)	106 A2	Stranorlar	12 C1
Stonehenge	9 E3	Storforsen	98 B3	Storvindeln	97 F3	Stranraer	4 B3
Stonglandet	94 B3	Storforshei	97 E3	Stotel	47 F3	Strasbourg	49 E2
Stopanja	73 E4	Storglomvatnet	97 E3	Stoúpa	86 C3	Straßburg	70 A1
Stör	48 A2	Storkow	49 E4	Stour	11 D2	Straßwalchen	56 C3
Storå	105 F3	Storlien	101 D2	Stourbridge	9 E1		

Stuttgart

0   2 km

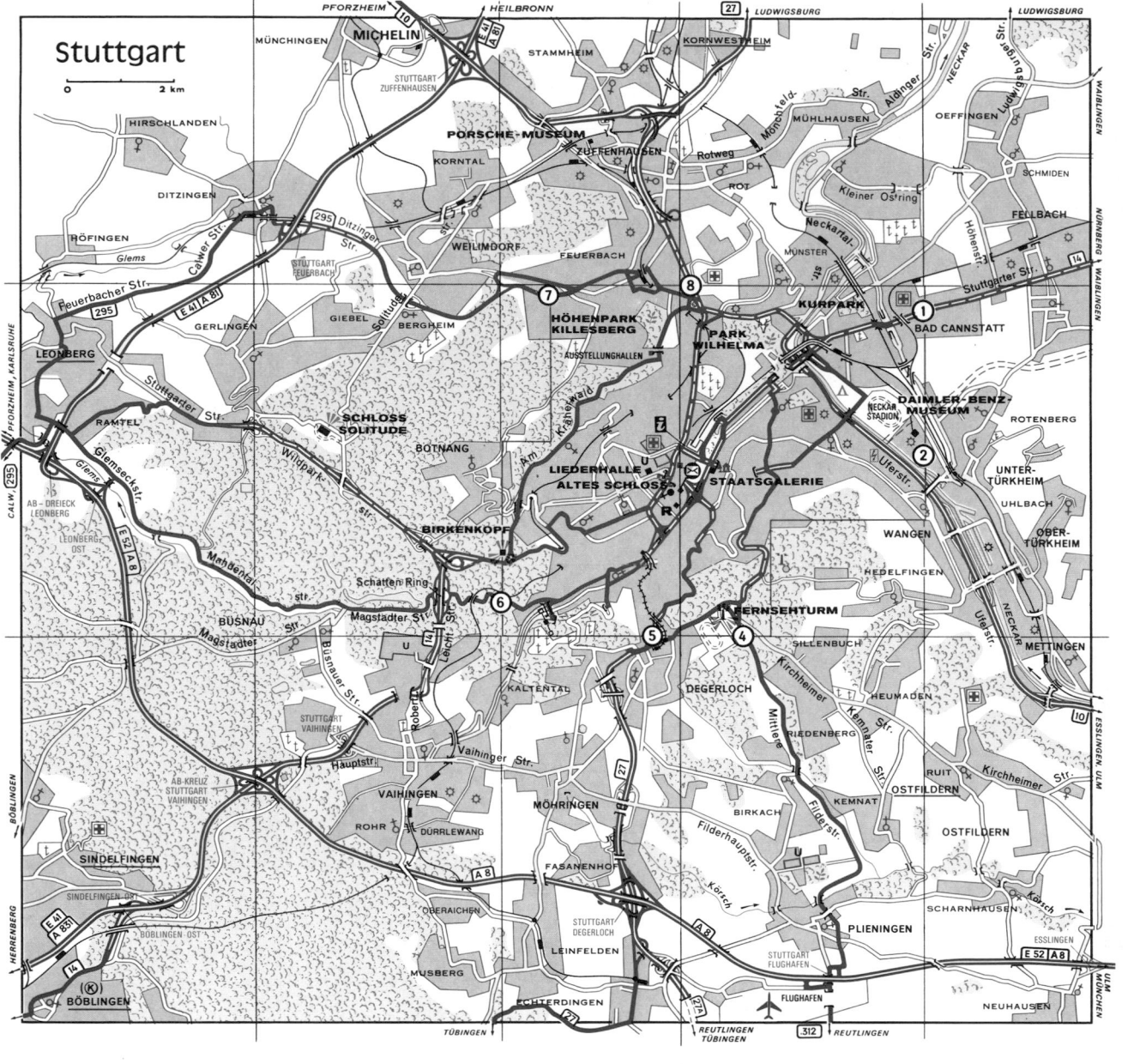

	Page	Grid
Suolijärvet	99	E2
Suolijoki	99	D2
Suomenlinna	107	E3
Suomenniemi	103	E3
Suomusjärvi	107	E3
Suomussalmi	99	F3
Suomutunturi	99	E2
Suonenjoki	103	E2
Suontee	103	D2
Suopelto (Kuopion Lääni)	103	D2
Suopelto (Mikkelin Lääni)	103	D3
Super-Besse	29	E1
Super-Molina	32	A3
Supetar	75	D2
Supetarska Draga	70	B4
Supino	63	F3
Šuplja-Stijena	76	B1
Surahammar	105	F3
Suraž	111	E4
Surbo	65	F4
Surčin	72	C3
Surduc	114	C1
Surdulica	77	E1
Surdup	76	B2
Sûre	21	D2
Surgères	24	C4
Súria	32	A3
Surnadalsøra	100	C2
Surrey	10	C3
Sursee	27	F2
Survilliers	19	F3
Susa	31	E1
Suså	108	C4
Sušac	75	E3
Susak	70	B4
Susak I	70	B4
Susch	58	B2
Susek	72	B2
Süßen	55	D2
Sušice	56	C1
Suspiro del Moro, Ptodel	44	A3
Susqueda, Emb de	32	B3
Sustenpass	58	A3
Susurluk	115	F3
Sutinjske Toplice	70	C2
Sutivan	75	D2
Sutjeska	73	D2
Sutjeska nac park	76	A1
Sutomore	76	B3
Sutri	63	E2
Sutterton	7	E3
Sutton	9	F2
Sutton Coldfield	9	E1
Sutton-in-Ashfield	7	D3
Sutton-on-Sea	7	E3
Suva gora	77	D3
Suva pl	77	E1
Suva Reka	77	D2
Suvasvesi	103	E2
Suvereto	62	C1
Suvobor	72	C4
Suvodol	77	E3
Suwałki	110	C4
Suze, la	23	F4
Suzzara	60	C2
Sval'ava	112	C3
Svalöv	108	C3
Svaneke	109	D4
Svanstein	98	C2
Svanvik	95	F2
Svappavaara	94	C4
Svärdsjö	105	F3
Svarstad	104	C3
Svarta	105	E4
Svartevatn	104	B3
Svartevatn L	104	B3
Svartisen	97	E2
Sværvolthalvøya	95	E1
Svattälven	105	F3
Svedala	108	C3
Sveg	101	E3
Svelgen	100	A3
Svelvik	104	C3
Svendborg	108	B4
Svenljunga	108	C2
Svensby	94	C2
Svenstavik	101	E2
Švermov	53	F3
Svetac	75	D2
Sveti Andrija	77	D3

	Page	Grid
Stratford-upon-Avon	9	E1
Strathaven	4	C2
Strathclyde	4	C2
Strathy Pt	3	D2
Stratóni	80	B3
Stratoníki	80	B3
Strátos	82	C3
Stratton	8	B3
Straubing	56	B2
Straumen (Bodø)	97	E2
Straumen (Fauske)	97	F1
Straumen (Møre og Romsdal)	100	B2
Straumen (Nord Trøndelag)	101	D1
Straumsjøen	94	A3
Straumsnes (Nordland)	97	E1
Straumsnes (Troms)	94	B2
Straupitz	53	E1
Strausberg	49	E4
Straža (Srbija)	73	E4
Straža (Vojvodina)	73	D2
Straža, G.	70	B2
Stražbenica	76	B1
Strážný	56	C2
Streatley	9	E2
Street	9	D3
Strehaia	114	C1
Strehla	53	E2

	Page	Grid
Streitberg	52	C4
Strengberg	57	D3
Stresa	58	A4
Streymoy	96	A3
Strezimirovci	77	E1
Strezovce	77	D2
Stříbro	53	E4
Strimónas	80	B2
Strimonikó	80	A2
Strimonikós Kólpos	80	B3
Strmac	71	E2
Strmica	75	D1
Strobl	56	C3
Strofádes, N	86	A3
Strofiliá	84	A3
Strojkovce	77	E1
Strokestown	12	C3
Stromberg	54	B1
Stromboli, I	69	D1
Stromeferry	2	B3
Strömfors	107	F2
Stromness	3	D1
Strömsbruk	101	F3
Strömsnäsbruk	109	D2
Stromstad	105	D4
Strömsund	101	F1
Ströms vattudal	101	E1
Strongoli	67	F2
Stronsay	3	E1
Stronsay Firth	3	E1
Strontian	2	B4
Stroud	9	D2

	Page	Grid
Strovlés	90	B3
Strub, Paß	59	E1
Struer	108	A2
Struga	77	D4
Struge	70	B2
Struma	115	D3
Strumble Head	8	B1
Strumica	77	F3
Strumica R	77	F3
Stryj	112	C3
Stryn	100	A3
Strzelce Krajeńskie	49	F3
Stubalpe	57	D4
Stubbekøbing	108	C4
Stubbenkammer	49	D1
Štubej	73	E3
Štubik	73	F3
Stubličke Toplice	70	C2
Stubline	72	C3
Stučka	110	C3
Stuckenborstel	48	A3
Studena	77	E1
Studenci	75	E1
Studenica	76	C1
Stugun	101	F2
Stühlingen	54	C4
Stuhr-Brinkum	17	F1
Stupnik	70	C2
Stura di Demonte	31	E3
Sturehov	106	B4
Sturminster Newton	9	D3

	Page	Grid
Sturup	108	C3
Stuttgart	55	D2
Stykkishólmur	96	A2
Styr'	113	D1
Suances	35	F1
Suardi	63	F2
Subbiano	61	D4
Subiaco	63	F2
Subijana	36	B2
Subotica	72	B1
Subotište	72	C3
Suc-au-May	29	D1
Suceava	113	D3
Sučevici	71	D4
Sučevita	113	D3
Suchań	49	F2
Suchiniči	111	F3
Süchteln	17	D4
Sucina	45	D2
Suck	12	C3
Sućuraj	75	E2
Sudbury (Derbys)	6	C3
Sudbury (Suffolk)	11	D2
Suddesjaur	98	A3
Sude	48	B3
Süderbrarup	48	A1
Suðuroy	96	A4
Suðuroyarfjørður	96	A4
Sueca	41	E4
Sueros	35	D2
Suffolk	11	D1
Suhl	52	C3
Suhopolje	71	E2
Suho Polje	72	B3

	Page	Grid
Šuica	75	E1
Suinula	102	C3
Suippes	20	B3
Suir, R	14	C3
Sukeva	103	E1
Sukobin	76	B3
Sukošan	74	C1
Sukovo	77	E1
Sukth	76	C4
Sula	113	F2
Suldal	104	B3
Suldalsvatn	104	B3
Sulden	58	C3
Sulęcin	49	F4
Sulina	113	F4
Sulingen	17	F2
Sulitjelma	97	F2
Sulitjelma Mt	97	F2
Sulkava	103	E3
Sully	25	F2
Sulmona	64	A2
Sultanhisar	115	F4
Sulz	54	C3
Sulzbach (Baden-Württemberg)	55	D2
Sulzbach (Saarland)	54	B2
Sulzbach-Rosenberg	55	F1
Sulzemoos	55	F3
Sumartin	75	E2
Sumba	96	A4
Sumburgh	3	F2

	Page	Grid
Sumburgh Head	3	F2
Sümeg	112	A4
Šumen	115	E2
Sumiainen	103	D2
Sumiswald	27	F2
Šumperk	112	A3
Sumy	113	F1
Sunart, L	2	B4
Sund	106	C3
Sunde (Hordaland)	104	A2
Sunde (Sør Trøndelag)	100	C1
Sunderland	5	E4
Sundern	17	F2
Sundini	96	A3
Sundom	102	B2
Sundsvall	101	F3
Sundsvallsbukten	101	F3
Suni	66	B2
Sunja	71	D3
Sunnansjö	105	F3
Sunndalen	100	C2
Sunndalsøra	100	B2
Sunne (Jämtlands Län)	101	F3
Sunne (Värmlands Län)	105	E3
Sunnemo	105	E3
Sunnylvsfjorden	100	B3
Suodenniemi	107	D1
Suolahti	103	D2

Sveti Ilija 75 E2
Sveti Janez 70 A2
Sveti Jovan
  Bigorski 77 D3
Sveti Naum 77 D4
Sveti Nikita 77 D2
Sveti Nikola 76 B3
Sveti Nikole 77 E3
Sveti Pantelejmon 77 D3
Sveti Rok 70 C4
Sveti Stefan 76 B3
Svetlogorsk
  (Belorussija) 111 E4

Svetlogorsk
  (Rossija) 110 B4
Svetlovodsk 113 F2
Svetozarevo 73 D4
Svetozar Miletić 72 B1
Svidník 112 C3
Švihov 56 B1
Svilaja 75 D1
Svilajnac 73 E3
Svilengrad 115 E3
Svingvoll 104 C1
Svinjar 71 E3
Svinoy 96 A3

Svištov 115 D2
Svitavy 112 A3
Svodđe 77 E1
Svolvær 94 A4
Svor 53 F3
Svorkmo 100 C2
Svoronáta 86 A1
Svorónos 79 F4
Svrljig 73 F4
Swadlincote 6 C3
Swaffham 11 D1
Swale 6 C1
Swalmen 17 D4

Swanage 9 E4
Swanley 10 C2
Swanlinbar 12 C2
Swansea 8 C2
Świdnica 112 A2
Świdwin 49 F2
Świebodzin 112 A2
Świecie 112 A1
Świecko 49 F4
Świerzno 49 F1
Swilly, L 13 D1
Swindon 9 E2
Swinford 12 B3

Świnoujscie 49 E2
Swords 13 D3
Sybil Head 14 A3
Syčôvka 111 F2
Sykäräinen 102 C1
Syke 17 F1
Sykkylven 100 A2
Sylene 101 D2
Sylling 104 C3
Sylt 47 F1
Sylt Ost 47 F1
Sylvenstein-
  Stausee 56 A4

Synod Inn 8 C1
Syötekylä 99 E3
Syre 3 D2
Sysmä 103 D3
Sysslebäck 101 D4
Syväjärvi 99 D1
Syväri 103 E2
Syvde 100 A3
Syvdsnes 100 A2
Syyspohja 103 E3
Szarvas 112 B4
Szczecin 49 E2
Szczecinek 110 A4

Szczeciński, Zalew 49 E2
Szczytno 110 B4
Szécsény 112 B3
Szeged 114 B1
Székesfehérvár 112 B4
Szekszárd 114 B1
Szentendre 112 B4
Szentes 112 B4
Szigetvár 114 B1
Szolnok 112 B4
Szombathely 112 A4

T

Tabanovce 77 E2
Tábara 35 D4
Tabarca, I de 45 E2
Taberg 109 D1
Tabernas 44 B3
Tabernes de
  Valldigna 41 E4
Taboada 34 B2
Tábor 57 D1
Tábua 38 B2
Tabuaço 34 B4
Tabuenca 36 C3
Täby 106 B3
Tachov 53 F4
Tadcaster 7 D2
Tafalla 36 C2
Tafjord 100 B3
Taganheira 42 A1
Taggia 31 F3
Tagliacozzo 63 F2
Tagliamento 59 E3
Taglio di Po 61 D2
Tahal 44 C3
Tahkvuori 103 E2
Taibilla, Sa de 44 C2
Taïgetos, Óros 87 D3
Tain 3 D3
Tain-l'Hermitage 30 B2
Taipadas 38 A4
Taipalsaari 103 E4
Taivalkoski 99 E3
Taivassalo 107 D2
Tajera, Emb de la 40 C1
Tajo, R 40 B2
Tajuña, R 40 B2
Takovo 73 D4
Taktikoúpoli 87 E2
Tálanda 87 E4
Talarrubias 39 E4
Talaván 39 D3
Talave, Emb de 44 C1
Talavera de la
  Reina 39 F3
Talavera la Real 39 D4
Talayuela 39 E2
Talayuelas 41 D3
Taldom 111 F2
Talgarth 9 D1
Talkkunapää 95 F3
Talla 61 D4
Tallante 45 D3
Tallard 31 D2
Tällberg 101 E4
Tallinn 110 C1
Talloires 27 D4
Tallow 14 C4
Talluskylä 103 D2
Talmont 24 B3
Tal'noje 113 E2
Talsi 110 B2
Talvik 95 D2

Tamames 39 E1
Tamar 8 B3
Támara 35 F3
Tamarite de Litera 37 E3
Tamási 112 B4
Tambre, R 34 A2
Tâmega, R 34 A4
Tàmelos, Akr 88 A2
Tamiš 72 C2
Tammela 107 E2
Tammisaari 107 E3
Tamnava 72 C3
Tampere 107 E1
Tamsweg 56 C4
Tamworth 9 E1
Tana 95 E1
Tana R 95 E1
Tanafjorden 95 E1
Tanágra 84 A4
Tanagro 64 C4
Tanamea, Pso di 59 F3
Tanaro 31 F2
Tancarville, Pont
  de 19 D3
Tandådalen 101 D4
Tandragee 13 D2
Tandsbyn 101 E2
Tandsjôborg 101 E3
Tangerhütte 48 C4
Tangermünde 48 C4
Tanhua 95 F4
Taninges 27 E4
Tanlay 26 B1
Tann 52 B3
Tännäs 101 D3
Tanndalen 101 D3
Tannheim 58 C1
Tannila 99 D3
Tanumshede 105 D4
Taormina 69 D3
Tapa 110 C1
Tapia de
  Casariego 34 C1
Tar 70 A3
Tara 72 C4
Tara R 76 B1
Taracena 40 B2
Tara klisura 76 B2
Tarancón 40 B3
Taranto 65 E4
Taranto, Golfo di 65 E4
Tarare 26 B4
Taraš 72 C2
Tarašča 113 E2
Tarascon (Ariège) 32 A2
Tarascon
  (Vaucluse) 30 B3
Taravo 33 F3
Tarayuela 41 E2
Tarazona 36 C3
Tarazona de la
  Mancha 40 C4
Tarbat Ness 3 D3

Tarbert (IRL) 14 B3
Tarbert
  (Strathclyde) 4 B2
Tarbert (Western Is) 2 B2
Tarbes 37 E1
Tarcento 59 F3
Tarčin 75 F1
Tardets-Sorholus 37 D1
Tardienta 37 D3
Tärendo 98 C2
Tärendöälven 98 C1
Targon 28 B2
Tàrgovište 115 E2
Tarifa 43 D4
Tarm 108 A3
Tarmstedt 47 F3
Tarn 29 D3
Tarn (Dépt) 29 E3
Tärnaby 97 E3
Tarna, Pto de 35 E2
Tärnäsjön 97 E3
Tarn-et-Garonne 29 D3
Tarn, Gges du 29 F3
Tarnobrzeg 112 C2
Tarnos 28 A4
Tarnów 112 B2
Taro 60 B2
Tarouca 38 C1
Tarp 48 A1
Tarporley 6 B3
Tarquinia 63 D2
Tarragona 37 F4
Tarrasa 32 A4
Tàrrega 37 F4
Tarrekaise 98 A2
Tårs 108 B4
Tarsia 67 E2
Tartas 28 B3
Tartu 110 C2
Tarvasjoki 107 D2
Tarvisio 59 F2
Täsch 27 F4
Tåsinge 108 B4
Tåsjo 101 F1
Tåsjön 101 F1
Tassin 26 C4
Tåstrup 108 C3
Tata 112 B4
Tatabánya 112 B4
Tatarbunary 113 E4
Tatry 112 B3
Tau 104 A3
Tauber 55 D1
Tauberbischofsheim
  55 D1
Taucha 53 D2
Tauerntunnel 59 E2
Taufers i. M. 58 C3
Taufkirchen 56 B3
Taulé 22 B2
Taunton 9 D3

Taunus 51 F4
Taunusstein 51 F4
Tauplitz 57 D4
Tauragė 110 B3
Taurianova 67 E4
Taurion 25 E4
Tauste 36 C3
Tauves 29 E1
Tavankut 72 B1
Tavannes 27 E2
Tavarnelle Val di
  Pesa 60 C4
Tavastila 103 F4
Tavaux 26 C2
Taverna 67 F3
Tavernelle 63 E1
Tavernes 31 D4
Tavignano 33 F3
Tavira 42 B3
Tavistock 8 C3
Tavolara, I 66 C1
Tavropós 83 D2
Tavropoú, Teh L 83 D2
Tavşanli 115 F3
Taw 8 C3
Taxenbach 59 E1
Taxiárhis 80 B3
Tay 5 D1
Tayinloan 4 B2
Tay, L 4 C1
Taynuilt 4 B1
Tayport 5 D1
Tayside 3 D4
Tazones 35 E1
Tczew 110 A4
Teano 64 A3
Teba 43 E3
Tebay 5 D4
Tech 32 B3
Techendorf 59 F2
Tecklenburg 17 E2
Tecuci 113 E4
Tees 5 E4
Teesside 5 E4
Teféli 91 D4
Tegéa 87 D2
Tegel 49 E4
Tegelen 17 D4
Tegernsee 56 A4
Teggiano 64 C4
Teguise 42 C3
Teide 42 A4
Teide Mt 42 A4
Teide, Pque Nac
  del 42 B4
Teignmouth 8 C4
Teijo 107 D3
Teil, le 30 B2
Teilleul, le 18 C4
Teisendorf 56 B3
Teisko 102 C3
Teixeiro 34 B1
Teixoso 38 C2

Tejeda, Sa de 43 F3
Tejo, R 38 A3
Tekeriš 72 C3
Tekija 73 E2
Tekirdağ 115 E3
Telč 57 E1
Telemark 104 B3
Télendos, N 89 E3
Teleno 34 C3
Telese 64 B3
Telford 6 C3
Telfs 58 C2
Telgte 17 E3
Tellingstedt 48 A2
Telti 66 B1
Teltow 49 D4
Témbi 83 E1
Tembleque 40 B3
Temerin 72 C2
Temmes 99 D4
Tempelhof 49 E4
Tempio
  Pausania 66 B1
Templemore 12 C4
Templin 49 D3
Temse 50 B3
Temska 73 F4
Tenala 107 E3
Ténaro, Akr 87 D4
Tenbury Wells 9 D1
Tenby 8 B2
Tence 30 B2
Tende 31 E3
Tende, Col de 31 E3
Tende, Colle di 31 E3
Tendilla 40 B2
Tenerife 42 A4
Tenhola 107 E3
Tenja 71 F2
Tennes 94 B3
Tennes 95 F4
Teno 95 E2
Tensta 106 B3
Tenterden 11 D3
Tentudia 43 D1
Teolo 61 D1
Teovo 77 E3
Tepelenë 114 C4
Teplá 53 E3
Teplice 53 E3
Ter 95 E4
Teramo 63 F1
Tera, R 35 D3
Ter Apel 17 E1

Termas de
  Monfortinho 39 D2
Terme Luigiane 67 E2
Termini Imerese 68 B3
Terminillo 63 F2
Terminillo, Mte 63 F2
Termoli 64 B2
Terneuzen 16 B4
Ternopol' 113 D2
Térovo 82 C2
Térpilos 80 A2
Terpní 80 B2
Terpsithéa 83 D4
Ter, R 32 B3
Terracina 63 F3
Terra de Basto 34 B4
Terradets, Emb
  dels 37 F3
Terrak 97 D4
Terralba 66 B3
Terranova di
  Pollino 67 E2
Terranuova Braccio
  lini 61 D4
Terras de Bouro 34 A3
Terrassa 32 A4
Terrasson-la-
  Villedieu 29 D2
Terrenoire 30 B1
Terriente 41 D2
Terschelling 16 C1
Teruel 41 D2
Tervakoski 107 E2
Tervo 103 D2
Tervola 99 D2
Tervuren 50 C3
Terzaga 40 C2
Tešanj 71 F3
Teslić 71 E3
Tessin 48 C2
Tessy 18 C3
Teste, la 28 A2
Tetbury 9 E2
Teterev 113 E2
Teterow 49 D2
Tetica 44 B3
Tetijev 113 E2
Tetovo 77 D3
Tetrákomo 82 C2
Tettnang 55 D4
Teuchern 53 D2
Teufen 58 B2
Teulada 66 B4
Teupitz 53 E1
Teuva 102 B3
Tevere 63 E2
Teviot 5 D3
Tewkesbury 9 E2
Texel 16 C1
Thabor, Mt 31 D1
Thale 52 C2

Thalfang 54 B1
Thalgau 56 C3
Thalheim 53 E3
Thalmässing 55 F2
Thalwil 58 A2
Thame 9 F2
Thames, R 11 D2
Thanes, K e 76 C4
Thann 27 E1
Thannhausen 55 E3
Thaon 27 D1
Tharandt 53 E2
Tharsis 42 C2
Thássos 80 C3
Thássos, N 81 D3
Thatë, Mal i 77 D4
Thau, Bessin de 30 A4
Thaya 57 F1
Thégonnec 22 B2
Theil, le 23 F3
Themar 52 C3
Thenon 29 D2
Theológos (Stereá
  Eláda) 83 F3
Theológos
  (Thássos) 80 C3
Théoule 31 E4
Thérain 19 F3
Thérma (Ikaría) 89 D2
Thermá
  (Makedonía) 80 B2
Thérma
  (Samothráki) 81 E3
Thermaïkós
  Kólpos 80 A4
Thérma Lefkádas 89 D2
Thérmi 79 F3
Thermi 85 F2
Thermissía 87 E2
Thérmo 83 D4
Thermopiles 83 E3
Thérouanne 19 F1
Thespiés 83 F4
Thesprotía 82 B2
Thesprotikó 82 B2
Thessalía 83 E2
Thessaloníki 79 F3
Thessaloníki
  (Nomos) 80 A3
Thetford 11 D1
Theux 51 D4
The Wash 7 E3
Thèze 28 B4
Thézenay 24 C3
Thíamis 82 B1
Thiaucourt 21 D3
Thiberville 19 D3
Thiéblemont-
  Farémont 20 C4
Thiendorf 53 E2
Thiene 59 D4
Thiers 26 B4
Thiesi 66 B2

Torino

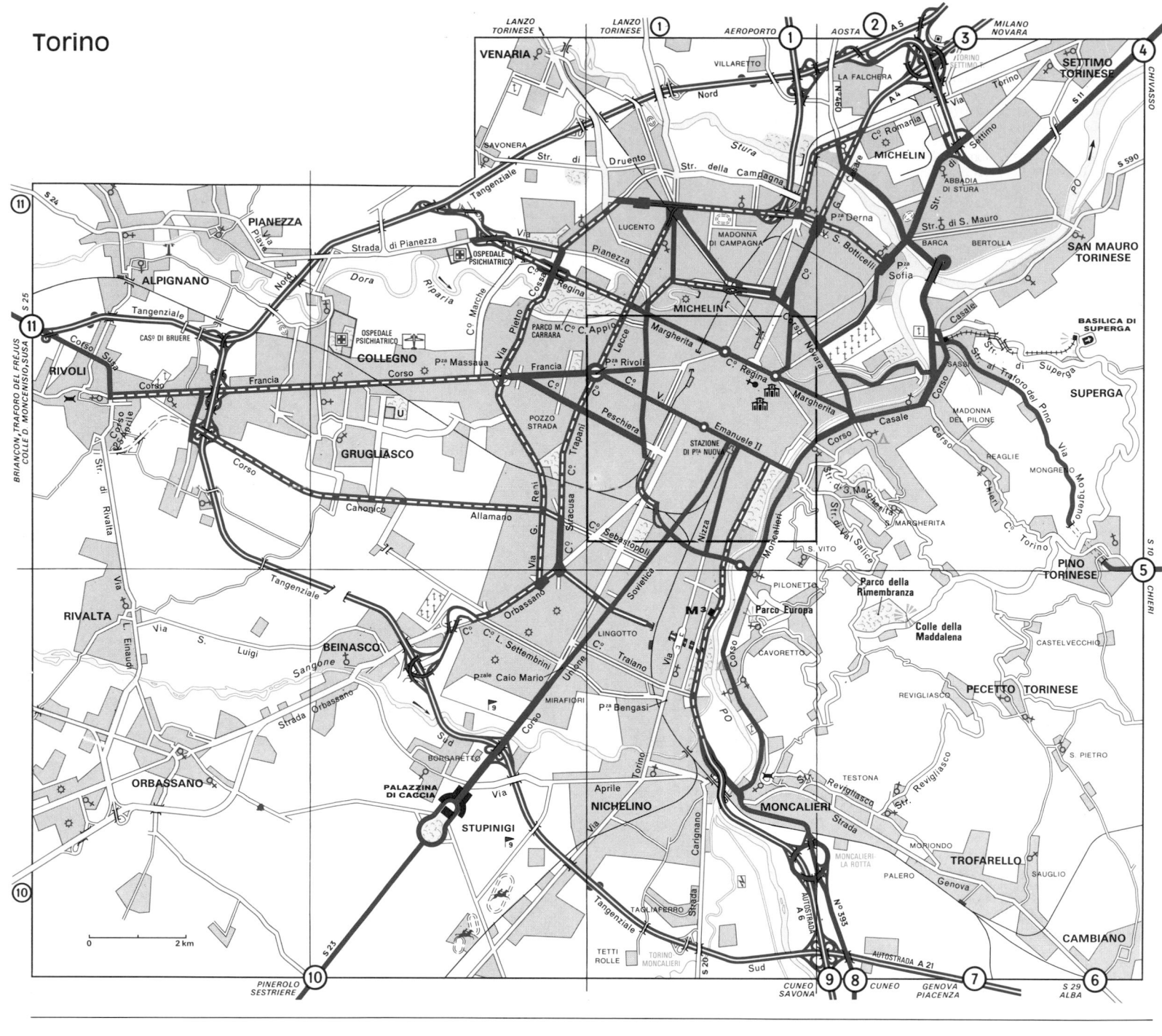

Thiessow	49 D1	Thornhill	4 C3	Tibro	109 D1	Tijola	44 B3	Tinchebray	18 C4	Tiree	2 A4	Titaríssios	83 E1
Thillot, le	27 E1	Thouarcé	24 C2	Tichvin	111 E1	Tikkakoski	103 D3	Tindari	69 D2	Tîrgo-Neamt	113 D4	Titel	72 C2
Thimariá	81 F2	Thouars	24 C2	Ticino	60 A1	Tikkala	103 F2	Tinée	31 E3	Tîrgoviște	115 D1	Titisee	54 C4
Thímena	89 E2	Thouet	24 C2	Ticino R	58 A3	Tikveš, Ez	77 E3	Tineo	35 D1	Tîrgu Frumos	113 E3	Titlis	58 A3
Thímena, N	89 E2	Thouría	86 C3	Tidaholm	109 D1	Tilburg	16 C3	Tingáki	89 F3	Tîrgu Jiu	114 C1	Tito	64 C4
Thiní, Akr	87 E2	Thoúrio	81 F1	Tidó	106 A3	Tilbury	10 C2	Tinglev	108 A4	Tîrgu Mureș	113 D4	Titograd	76 B3
Thionville	21 D3	Thráki	81 E2	Tiefenbronn	54 C2	Tílissos	91 D3	Tingsryd	109 E2	Tîrgu Secuiesc	113 D4	Titova Korenica	70 C4
Thíra	91 E1	Thrakikó		Tiefencastel	58 B3	Tillberga	106 A3	Tingvoll	100 B2	Tirig	41 F2	Titova Mitrovica	77 D1
Thíra, N	91 E1	Pélagos	81 D3	Tiefensee	49 E4	Tillières	19 E4	Tingvollfjorden	100 B2	Tírintha	87 D2	Titov Drvar	71 D4
Thirassía, N	91 E1	Thrapston	9 F1	Tiel	16 C3	Tilly-sur-Seulles	18 C3	Tinja	71 F3	Tiriolo	67 F3	Titovo Užice	72 C4
Thirsk	7 D1	Threshfield	6 C1	Tielt	50 A3	Tílos, N	89 F4	Tinn	104 C3	Tírnavos	83 E1	Titov Veles	77 E3
Thisted	108 A2	Thueyts	30 B2	Tienen	50 C3	Timanfaya, Parque		Tinnsjø	104 C3	Tirol	58 C2	Titov vrh	77 D3
Thíva	84 A4	Thuile, la	27 E4	Tiengen	54 C4	Nac. de	42 C3	Tínos	88 C2	Tirós	87 D3	Titran	100 B1
Thiviers	28 C1	Thuin	50 B4	Tierbmesvarri	94 C3	Timbáki	91 D4	Tiñosillos	39 F1	Tirrenia	60 C4	Tittmoning	56 B3
Thizy	26 C4	Thuir	32 C2	Tierga	36 C3	Tímbano	81 D4	Tínos, N	88 C2	Tirreno, Mare	68 B2	Tiumpan Head	2 B2
Thoissey	26 C4	Thum	53 E3	Tierp	106 A3	Tímfi, Óros	78 C4	Tiñoso, C	45 D3	Tirschenreuth	53 D4	Tivat	76 B3
Tholen	16 B3	Thun	27 E3	Tiétar, R	39 E2	Timfristós	83 D3	Tintagel	8 B3	Tirso	66 B2	Tiveden	105 E4
Tholey	54 B1	Thur	58 A1	Tigharry	2 A3	Timfristós Mt	83 D3	Tinténiac	23 D3	Tirstrup	108 B3	Tivenys	41 F2
Thollon	27 E3	Thüringen	58 B2	Tighnabruaich	4 B2	Timiş	114 C1	Tinto, R	42 C2	Tirteafuera, R	39 F4	Tiverton	8 C3
Tholó	86 C2	Thüringer Wald	52 B3	Tignes	31 D1	Timișoara	114 C1	Tiobraid Árann	14 C3	Tisa	72 C2	Tivissa	41 F1
Tholopotámi	85 E4	Thurles	14 C3	Tignes, Bge de	31 E1	Timmelsjoch	58 C2	Tione di Trento	58 C3	Tiscar, Pto de	44 B3	Tívoli	63 E2
Tholós	80 B2	Thurn, Paß	59 E1	Tiheró	81 F2	Timmendorfer		Tipasoja	103 E1	Tisnaren	105 F4	Tjaktjajaure	98 A2
Thomastown	15 D3	Thursby	5 D4	Tihío	79 D3	Strand	48 B2	Tipperary	14 C3	Tišnov	57 E1	Tjällmo	105 F4
Thônes	27 D4	Thurso	3 D2	Tihuta	113 D4	Timok	73 F3	Tipperary (Co)	12 C4	Tisvildeleje	108 C3	Tjeggelvas	98 A2
Thonon	27 D3	Thury-Harcourt	18 C3	Tiilikkajärvi	103 E1	Timoleague	14 B4	Tiranë	76 C4	Tisza	112 B4	Tjeldøya	94 B3
Thorens-Glières	27 D4	Thusis	58 B3	Tiistenjoki	102 C2	Timrå	101 F3	Tirano	58 C3	Tiszafüred	112 B4	Tjeldstø	104 A2
Thorikó	88 A2	Thy	108 A2	Tíjesno	74 C1	Timv. Peristéria	86 C3	Tiraspol'	113 E3	Tiszavasvári	112 C3	Tjentište	76 A1
Thorne	7 D2	Thyborøn	108 A2	Tijesno	74 C1	Tinahely	13 D4	Tire	115 F4	Titaguas	41 D3	Tjøme	104 C4

Tjong	97 E2	Topolovnik	73 E3	Torrejòn de la	
Tjørnuvik	96 A3	Topusko	70 C3	Calzada	40 A2
Tjøtta	97 D3	Torà de		Torrejón el Rubio	39 E3
Tkon	74 C1	Riubregòs	32 A3	Torrejón-Tajo, Emb	
Tobarra	44 C1	Torano Castello	67 E2	de	39 E3
Tobercurry	12 B2	Torbay	8 C4	Torre la Carcel	41 D2
Tobermore	13 D2	Torbole	58 C4	Torrelaguna	40 B1
Tobermory	2 B4	Torcello	61 D1	Torrelapaja	36 C3
Toberonochy	4 C1	Torchiarolo	65 F3	Torrelavega	35 F2
Toblach	59 E2	Tordera	32 B4	Torrellano	45 E2
Toce	58 A3	Tordesillas	35 E4	Torrelobatón	35 E4
Tocha	38 B2	Tordesilos	41 D2		
Tocina	43 D2	Tore	2 C3		
Todi	63 E1	Töre	98 C3		
Todmorden	6 C2	Töreboda	105 E4		
Todorići	71 E4	Torella d. Sannio	64 B3		
Todtmoos	54 C4	Toreno	34 C2		
Todtnau	54 C4	Torgau	53 E2		
Toe Head (GB)	2 A2	Torgelow	49 E2		
Toe Head (IRL)	14 B4	Torhout	50 A3		
Töfsingdalen	101 D3	Torigni	18 C3		
Toft	3 F1	Torija	40 B2		
Tofte	104 C3	Torino	31 E1		
Toftir	96 A4	Torio, R	35 D2		
Toftlund	108 A4	Torla	37 E2		
Tohmajärvi	103 F2	Törmänen	95 F3		
Toholampi	102 C1	Törmänmäki	99 E4		
Toijala	107 E2	Tormes, R	39 E1		
Toivakka	103 D3	Tormos	37 D3		
Toivala	103 E2	Tornavacas	39 E2		
Tojšici	72 B3	Tornavacas, Pto			
Tok	53 F4	de	39 E2		
Tokaj	112 C3	Torneälven	94 C4		
Tolbuhin	115 E2	Torneträsk	94 C3	Torrelodones	40 A2
Toledo	40 A3	Tornik	76 B1	Torremaggiore	64 B2
Toledo, Mts de	40 A3	Tornio	98 C3	Torremegia	39 D4
Tolentino	61 F4	Tornionjoki	98 C2	Torre Mileto	64 C2
Tolfa	63 D2	Tornjoš	72 C1	Torre Miró, Pto de	41 E2
Tolga	100 C3	Toro	35 D4	Torremocha	39 D3
Tollarp	109 D3	Törökszentmiklós		Torremolinos	43 F4
Tollense	49 D2		112 B4	Torrent	41 E4
Tølløse	108 C3	Toro, Monte	45 F1	Torrente de	
Tolmezzo	59 E3	Toróni	80 B4	Cinca	37 E4
Tolmin	70 A2	Toropec	111 E2	Torrenueva	44 B1
Toló	87 D2	Torpo	104 C2	Torre-Pacheco	45 D2
Tolosa (E)	36 C1	Torpoint	8 C4	Torre Pellice	31 E2
Tolosa (P)	38 C3	Torpshammar	101 F3	Torreperogil	44 B2
Tolox	43 E4	Torquay	8 C4	Torres del Río	36 B2
Tolva	99 E2	Torquemada	35 F3	Torres Novas	38 B3
Tolve	65 D4	Torralba de		Torres Vedras	38 A3
Tomar	38 B3	Calatrava	40 A4	Torrevieja	45 D2
Tomaševac	73 D2	Torrào	42 B1	Torrico de San	
Tomaševo	76 B2	Torre	38 C2	Pedro	38 C3
Tomašica	71 D3	Torre Annunziata	64 B4	Torri del Benaco	60 C1
Tomaszów		Torre Baja	41 D3	Torridon	2 B3
Lubelski	112 C2	Torre Beretti	60 A2	Torridon, L	2 B3
Tomaszów		Torreblanca	41 F3	Torriglia	60 A3
Mazowiecki	112 B2	Torrecaballeros	40 A1	Torrijas	41 D3
Tombebœuf	28 C3	Torrecampo	43 F1	Torrijo	36 C4
Tomelilla	109 D3	Torre Canne	65 E3	Torrijos	40 A3
Tomelloso	40 B4	Torrecilla	43 E4	Tørring	108 A3
Tomiňo	34 A3	Torrecilla en		Torrita di Siena	61 D4
Tomintoul	3 D4	Cameros	36 B2	Torroella de	
Tomma	97 D2	Torrecillas de la		Montgri	32 B3
Tømmervøg	100 B2	Tiesa	39 E3	Torröjen	101 D1
Tomra	100 B2	Torre de Abraham,		Torrox	43 F4
Tomtabacken	109 D2	Emb de	40 A3	Torsås	109 E3
Tona	32 B3	Torre de D. Chama	34 C4	Torsby	105 E3
Tonale, Pso del	58 C3	Torre de		Torshälla	106 A3
Tonara	66 B3	Embesora	41 E2	Tórshavn	96 A4
Tonbridge	10 C3	Torre de Juan		Torsken	94 B2
Tondela	38 B1	Abad	44 B1	Torsminde	108 A2
Tønder	108 A4	Torre del Aguila,		Tórtoles de	
Tongeren	50 C3	Emb de	43 D3	Esgueva	35 F4
Tongue	2 C2	Torre de la		Tortoli	66 C3
Tonnay-		Higuera	42 C3	Tortona	60 A2
Boutonne	24 C4	Torre del Bierzo	35 D2	Tortorici	69 D2
Tonnay-Charente	24 C4	Torre del Campo	44 A2	Tortosa	41 F2
Tonneins	28 C3	Torre del Greco	64 B4	Tortosendo	38 C2
Tonnerre	26 B1	Torre del Mar	43 F4	Toruń	112 B1
Tönning	47 F2	Torre de		Torup	108 C2
Tønsberg	104 C3	Moncorvo	34 C4	Tørvikbygd	104 B2
Tonstad	104 B4	Torre de Passeri	64 A2	Tory I	12 C1
Töpen	53 D3	Torre d. Impiso	68 A3	Toržok	111 F2
Topeno	107 E2	Torredonjimeno	43 F2	Torzym	49 F2
Topla	70 B1	Torre Faro	69 E2		
Toplica	77 D1	Torre Grande	66 A3		
Topli Do	73 E3	Torregrossa	37 F4		
Topliţa	113 D4	Torreira	38 B1		
Toploú	91 F4	Torrejoncillo	39 D2		
Topola	73 D3	Torrejoncillo del			
Topolčani	77 E4	Rey	40 C3		
Topol'čany	112 B3	Torrejón de Ardoz	40 B2		
Topólia	90 B3				

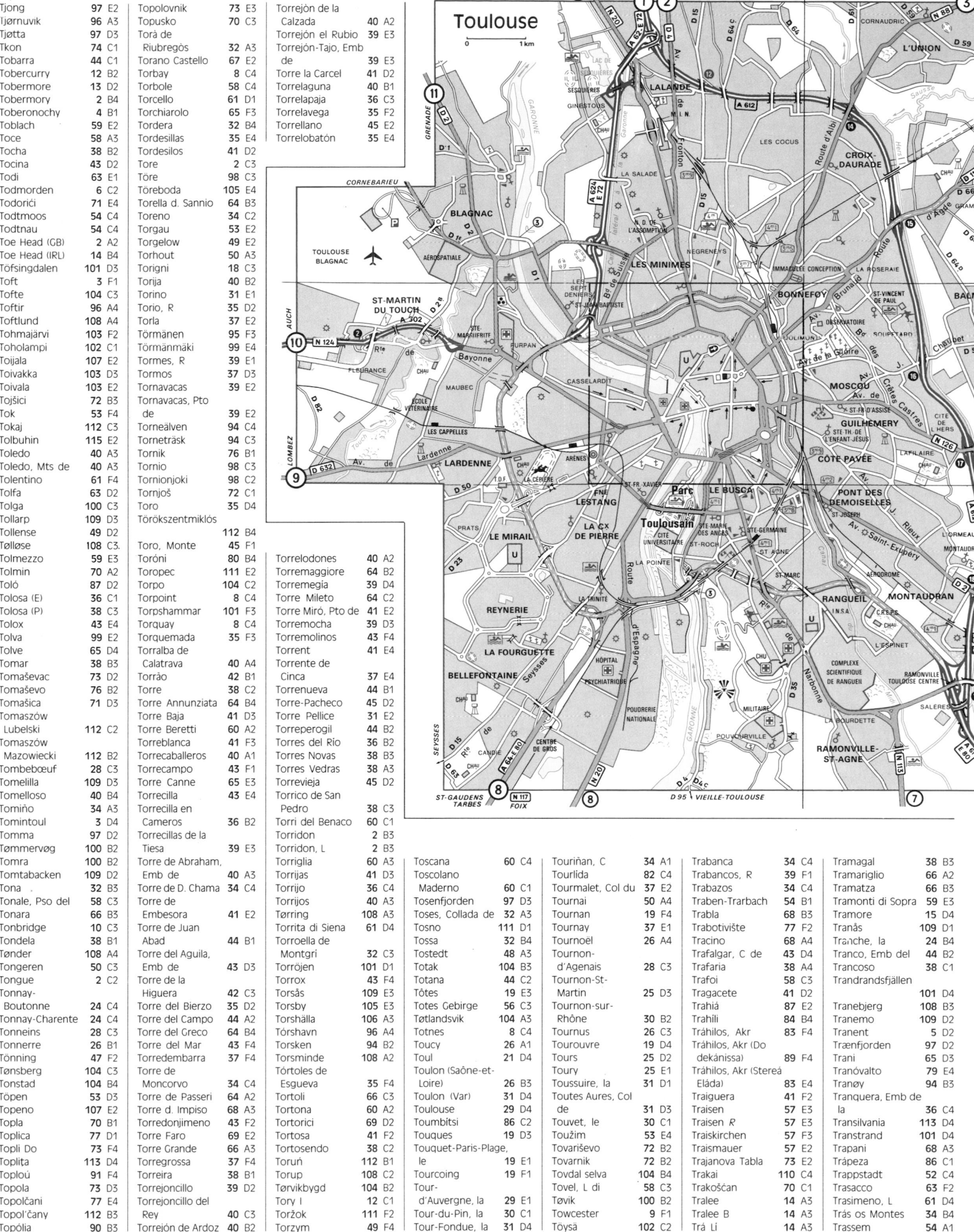

Toulouse

0   1 km

Toscana	60 C4	Touriñan, C	34 A1	Trabanca	34 C4	Tramagal	38 B3
Toscolano	60 C1	Tourlida	82 C4	Trabancos, R	39 F1	Tramariglio	66 A2
Tosenfjorden	97 D3	Tourmalet, Col du	37 E2	Trabazos	34 C4	Tramatza	66 B3
Toses, Collada de	32 A3	Tournai	50 A4	Traben-Trarbach	54 B1	Tramonti di Sopra	59 E3
Tosno	111 D1	Tournan	19 F4	Trabla	68 B3	Tramore	15 D4
Tossa	32 B4	Tournay	37 E1	Trabotivište	77 F2	Tranche, la	24 B4
Tostedt	48 A3	Tournoël	26 A4	Tracino	68 A4	Tranco, Emb del	44 B2
Totak	104 B3	Tournon-		Trafalgar, C de	43 D4	Trancoso	38 C1
Totana	44 C2	d'Agenais	28 C3	Trafaria	38 A4	Trandrandsfjällen	
Tôtes	19 E3	Tournon-St-		Trafoi	58 C3		101 D4
Totes Gebirge	56 C3	Martin	25 D3	Tragacete	41 D2	Tranebjerg	108 B3
Tøtlandsvik	104 A3	Tournon-sur-		Trahiá	87 E2	Tranemo	109 D2
Totnes	8 C4	Rhône	30 B2	Trahíli	84 B4	Tranent	5 D2
Toucy	26 A1	Tournus	26 C3	Tráhilos, Akr	83 F4	Trænfjorden	97 D2
Toul	21 D4	Tourouvre	19 D4	Tráhilos, Akr (Do		Trani	65 D3
Toulon (Saône-et-		Tours	25 D2	dekánissa)	89 F4	Tranóvalto	79 E4
Loire)	26 B3	Toury	25 E1	Tráhilos, Akr (Stereá		Tranøy	94 B3
Toulon (Var)	31 D4	Toussuire, la	31 D1	Eláda)	83 E4	Tranquera, Emb de	
Toulouse	29 D4	Toutes Aures, Col		Traiguera	41 F2	la	36 C4
Toumbítsi	86 C2	de	31 D3	Traisen	57 E3	Transilvania	113 D4
Touquet-Paris-Plage,		Touvet, le	30 C1	Traisen R	57 E3	Transtrand	101 D2
le	19 E1	Toúzim	53 E4	Traiskirchen	57 F3	Trapani	68 A3
Tourcoing	19 F1	Tovaríševo	72 B2	Traismauer	57 E2	Trápeza	86 C1
Tour-		Tovarnik	72 B2	Trajanova Tabla	73 E2	Trappstadt	52 C4
d'Auvergne, la	29 E1	Tovdal selva	104 B4	Trakai	110 C4	Trasacco	63 F2
Tour-du-Pin, la	30 C1	Tovel, L di	58 C3	Trakošćan	70 C1	Trás os Montes	34 B4
Tour-Fondue, la	31 D4	Tøvik	100 B2	Tralee	14 A3	Trassem	54 A1
		Towcester	9 F1	Tralee B	14 A3		
		Töysä	102 C2	Trà Li	14 A3		

Trasvase Tajo Segura, Canal de 40 C4
Traun 57 D3
Traun *R* 56 C3
Traunkirchen 56 C3
Traunreut 56 B3
Traunsee 56 C3
Traunstein 56 B3
Travemünde 48 B2
Travnik 71 E4
Trayas, le 31 E4
Trbovlje 70 B2
Trbuk 71 F3
Trbušani 73 D4
Trdinov Vrh 70 C2
Trebbia 60 B2
Trebbin 49 D4
Trébeurden 22 B2
Trebević nac park 76 A1
Třebíč 57 E1
Trebinje 76 A2
Trebisacce 67 F2
Trebišnjica 75 F2
Trebišov 112 C3
Trebnje 70 B2
Třeboň 57 D1
Tréboul 22 A3
Trebsen 53 D2
Trebujena 43 D3
Trecastagni 69 D3
Trecate 60 A1
Tre Croci, Pso 59 D2
Tredegar 9 D2
Tredozio 61 D3
Treene 48 A1
Treffort 26 C4
Treffurt 52 B3
Trefynwy 9 D2
Tregaron 8 C1
Trégastel 22 B2
Tregnago 60 C1
Tregony 8 B4
Tréguier 22 C2
Trehörningsjö 102 A1
Treia (D) 47 F1
Treia (I) 61 F4
Treignac 29 D1
Trelleborg (S) 108 C4
Trelleborg (SF) 108 B3
Trélon 20 B2
Tremblade, la 28 A1
Tremestieri 69 D2
Tremezzo 58 B4
Tremiti, I 64 C2
Tremp 37 F3
Trenčín 112 B3
Trendelburg 52 A2
Trentino-Alto Adige 58 C3
Trento 59 D3
Trent, R 7 D2
Trepča (Crna Gora) 76 C2
Trepča (Kosovo) 77 D1
Tréport, le 19 E2
Trepuzzi 65 F4
Tresco 8 A4
Trescore Balneario 60 B1
Tresenda 58 B3
Tresfjord 100 B2
Tresjuncos 40 B3
Treska 77 D3
Treskavica 75 F1
Tres Mares, Pico de 35 F2
Trešnjevica 73 E4
Trešnjevik 76 B2
Trespaderne 36 A2
Třešť 57 E1
Trets 30 C4
Tretten 104 C1
Treuchtlingen 55 E2
Treuen 53 D3
Treuenbrietzen 53 D1
Treungen 104 B4
Trevélez 44 A3
Trèves 29 F3
Trevi 63 E1
Trévières 18 C3
Treviglio 60 B1
Trevignario Romano 63 E2
Treviño 36 B2
Treviso 59 E4
Trévoux 26 C4
Trezzo sull' Adda 60 A1
Trgovište 77 E2
Trhové Sviny 57 D2
Triánda 93 F1
Tría Nissiá 92 C1
Triaucourt 20 C3
Tribanj Krušćica 70 C4
Triberg 54 C3
Tribsees 49 D2
Tricarico 65 D4
Tricase 65 F4
Tricesimo 59 F3
Trichiana 59 E3
Trie 37 E1
Trieben 57 D4
Trier 54 A1
Trieste 59 F4
Trieste, G di 59 F4
Trifels 54 C2
Trifili 81 F2
Triglav 70 A2
Trigóna 82 C1
Trigueros 42 C2
Trihonída, L 83 D4
Trijueque 40 B2
Tríkala (Makedonía) 79 F3
Tríkala (Nomos) 82 C1
Tríkala (Pelopónissos) 87 D1
Tríkala (Thessalía) 83 D1
Trikeri 83 F2
Trilj 75 E1
Trillevallen 101 D2
Trillo 40 C2
Trilofo 83 E3
Trim 13 D3
Trimouille, la 25 D3
Trindade 34 C4
Třinec 112 B3
Tring 9 F2
Tringia 82 C1
Trinità d'Agultu e V. 66 B1
Trinitapoli 64 C3
Trinité, la 22 C4
Trinité-Porhoët, la 22 C3
Trino 31 F1
Triora 31 F3
Trípi 87 D3
Tripiti, Akr 85 D2
Trípoli 87 D2
Triponzo 63 E1
Tripótama 86 C1
Triptis 53 D3
Trisanna 58 C2
Trischen 47 F2
Trittau 48 B3
Trittenheim 54 B1
Trivento 64 B2
Trizina 87 E2
Trlica 76 B1
Trnava 112 A3
Trnovo (Bosna i Hercegov ina) 75 F1
Trnovo (Slovenija) 70 A2
Trnova Poljana 75 D1
Troarn 18 C3
Trofa 34 A4
Trofaiach 57 E4
Trofors 97 E3
Trogir 75 D2
Troglav, V. 75 D1
Tróhalos 83 E1
Troia 64 C3
Tróia, Pen de 38 A4
Troina 68 C3
Trois Epis, les 27 E1
Trois-Moutiers, les 24 C3
Trois-Ponts 51 D4
Trojan 115 D2
Trojane 70 B2
Trollhättan 108 C1
Trollheimen 100 C2
Troms 94 C3
Tromsdalen 94 B2
Tromsø 94 B2
Trondheim 100 C2
Trondheimsfjorden 100 C1
Trondsheimsleia 100 B1
Tronö 101 F4
Tronto 63 F1
Troo 23 F4
Troon 4 C2
Tropea 67 E3
Trópea 86 C2
Tropojë 76 C2
Trosa 106 B4
Trossachs, The 4 C1
Trostan 13 E1
Trostberg 56 B3
Trouville 19 D3
Trowbridge 9 D2
Troyes 26 B1
Trpanj 75 E2
Trpezi 76 C2
Trpinja 71 F2
Trsa 76 B2
Tršić 72 B3
Trstenik (Kosovo) 77 D2
Trstenik (Pelješac) 75 E2
Trstenik (Srbija) 73 D4
Trsteno 75 F2
Trubčevsk 111 F4
Trubia 35 D1
Trubia, R 35 D1
Trubjela 76 B2
Truchas 34 C3
Truchtersheim 21 E4
Trujillo 39 E3
Trun 19 D4
Truro 8 B4
Trutnov 112 A2
Truyère, Gorges de la 29 E2
Tryde 109 D3
Trysiselva 100 D3
Tržac 70 C3
Trzcińsko-Zdrój 49 E3
Trzebiatów 49 F1
Trzebież 49 E2
Tržič Golnik 70 A2
Tsamandás 82 B1
Tsambika 93 F1
Tsangaráda 83 F2
Tsangário 82 B2
Tsaritsani 83 E1
Tsarkassiános 82 B4
Tsotili 79 D4
Tsoukaládes 82 B3
Tuaim 12 B3
Tuam 12 B3
Tua, R 34 B4
Tuath, L 4 B1
Tubilla del Agua 35 F2
Tübingen 55 D3
Tubre 58 C3
Tučepi 75 E2
Tuchan 32 B2
Tudela 36 C3
Tudela de Duero 35 E4
Tuella, R 34 C3
Tuerto, R 35 D2
Tuffé 23 F3
Tuheljske Toplice 70 C2
Tuhkakylä 103 E1
Tui 34 A3
Tuineje 42 C4
Tukums 110 B2
Tulach Mhór 12 C4
Tulare 77 D1
Tulcea 113 E4
Tul'čin 113 E3
Tulla 12 B4
Tullamore 12 C4
Tulle 29 D1
Tullgarn 106 B4
Tullins 30 C1
Tulln 57 E2
Tullow 13 D4
Tulppio 95 F4
Tulsk 12 C3
Tumba 106 B4
Tunbridge Wells, Royal 10 C3
Tundža 115 E3
Tunnhovdfjorden 104 C2
Tunnsjøen 97 E4
Tuohikotti 107 F2
Tuoro sul Trasimeno 61 D4
Tupalaki 95 E3
Turalići 72 B4
Turballe, la 22 C4
Turbe 71 E4
Turbie, la 31 E3
Turckheim 27 E1
Turda 112 C4
Turégano 40 A1
Turenki 107 E2
Turgutlu 115 F4
Turi 65 E3
Türi 110 C1
Túria, R 41 E3
Turija (Bosna i Hercegov ina) 71 F3
Turija (Srbija) 73 E3
Turija (Vojvodina) 72 C2
Turinge 106 B4
Turis 41 E4
Turjak 70 B2
Türkheim 55 E3
Turku 107 D2
Turmiel 40 C1
Turnberry 4 C3
Turnhout 50 C3
Türnitz 57 E3
Turnov 112 A2
Turnu Măgurele 115 D2
Turnu Roşu 113 D4
Turracherhöhe 59 F2
Turre 44 C3
Turriff 3 E3
Tursi 65 D4
Turtola 98 C2
Tuscania 63 D2
Tuse 108 C3
Tušilović 70 C3
Tustna 100 B2
Tutin 76 C1
Tutrakan 115 E2
Tuttlingen 55 D3
Turun ja Porin Lääni 107 D2
Tuturano 65 F3
Tutzing 56 A3
Tuulos 107 E2
Tuupovaara 103 F2
Tuusniemi 103 E2
Tuusula 107 E2
Tuxford 7 D3
Tuzi 76 B3
Tuzla 71 F3
Tvedestrand 104 C4
Tverrfjellet 100 B3
Tvøroyri 96 A4
Tweed, R 5 E2
Twelve Pins, The 12 A3
Twimberg 70 B1
Twist 17 E2
Twistringen 17 F1
Tydal 101 D2
Tyin 104 C1
Tyin *L* 100 B3
Týn 57 D1
Tyndrum 4 C1
Tynemouth 5 E3
Tynkä 102 C1
Tynset 100 C3
Tyräjärvi 99 E3
Tyresö 106 B4
Tyrifjorden 104 C3
Tyringe 109 D3
Tyristrand 104 C3
Tyrnävä 99 D4
Tyrone 13 D2
Tysfjorden 97 F1
Tysnesøy 104 A2
Tysse 104 A2
Tyssebotn 104 A2
Tyssedal 104 B2
Tysvær 104 A3
Tywi 8 C2
Tywyn 6 A3

U

Ub 72 C3
Ubaye 31 D2
Úbeda 44 A2
Überlingen 55 D4
Ubl'a 112 C3
Ubli (Crna Gora) 76 B2
Ubli (Lastovo) 75 E3
Ubrique 43 E4
Uchte 17 F2
Učka 70 B3
Uckange 21 D3
Uckfield 10 C3
Uclés 40 B3
Udbina 70 C4
Udbyhøj 108 B2
Uddevalla 108 C1
Uddheden 105 E3
Uddjaure 98 A3
Uden 16 C3
Udine 59 F3
Udovo 77 F3
Udvar 72 A1
Uebigau 53 E2
Uecker 49 E2
Ueckermünde 49 E2
Uelzen 48 B3
Uetersen 48 A2
Uetze 48 B4
Uffenheim 55 E1
Ugao 76 C1
Ugento 65 F4
Ugijar 44 B3
Ugine 27 D4
Uglič 111 F1
Ugljan 74 C1
Ugljan *I* 74 C1
Ugljane 75 E1
Ugljevik 72 B3
Ugra 111 F3
Ugrinovci 73 D3
Uherské Hradiště 112 A3
Uhingen 55 D2
Úhlava 56 C1
Uhrsleben 52 C1
Uig 2 B3
Uimaharju 103 F2
Uithoorn 16 C2
Uithuizen 47 D3
Ukkola 103 F2
Ukmergė 110 C3
Ukonselkä 95 E3
Ukraina 113 E2
Ukrina 71 E3
Ulcinj 76 B3
Uleåborg 99 D3
Ulefoss 104 C3
Uleila del Campo 44 C3
Ulëzë 76 C3
Ulfborg 108 A2
Uljanik 71 D2
Uljanovka 113 E3
Uljma 73 D2
Ullånger 102 A2
Ullapool 2 C3
Ulla, R 34 B2
Ullared 108 C2
Ullava 102 C1
Ulldecona 41 F2
Ullsfjorden 94 C2
Ullswater 5 D4
Ulm 55 E3
Ulmen 51 E4
Ulog 75 F1
Ulricehamn 109 D1
Ulrichsberg 56 C2
Ulsberg 100 C2
Ulsta 3 F1
Ulsteinvik 100 A2
Uludağ 115 F3
Ul'ugai'sa 95 E2
Ulva 4 B1
Ulverston 6 B1
Ulvik 104 B2
Ulvila 107 D1
Ulvsjö 101 E3
Ulzës, Liq i 76 C3
Umag 70 A3
Uman' 113 E3
Umbertide 61 E4
Umbrail, Pass 58 C3
Umbria 63 E1
Umbukta 97 E3
Umčari 73 D3
Umeå 102 B1
Umeälven 98 A4
Umhausen 58 C2
Umin Dol 77 E2
Umka 72 C3
Umljanović 75 D1
Una 71 D3
Unac 71 D4
Unari 99 D1
Unari *L* 99 D1
Uncastillo 37 D2
Unden 105 E4
Undersåker 101 D2
Undredal 104 B2
Uneča 111 F4
Unešić 75 D1
Úněšov 53 E4
Ungeny 113 E3
Ungilde 34 C3
Unhais da Serra 38 C2
Unhošt 53 F4
Unije 70 B4
Universales, Mts 41 D2
Unna 17 E3
Unnaryd 109 D2
Unnukka 103 E2
Unquera 35 F1
Unst 3 F1
Unstrut 52 C2
Unterach 56 C3
Unterhaching 56 A3
Unter-Schleissheim 55 F3
Unterwalden 27 F3
Unterwasser 58 B2
Unterweißenbach 57 D2
Upavon 9 E3
Upinniemi 107 E3
Upper L Erne 13 D2
Uppingham 9 F1
Upplands-Väsby 106 B3
Uppsala 106 B3
Uppsala Län 106 B3
Upton 9 E1
Uras 66 B3
Urbania 61 E3
Urbasa, Pto de 36 C2
Urbasa, Sa de 36 C2
Urbe 60 A3
Urbino 61 E3
Urbión, Sa de 36 B3
Urdos 37 D2
Ure 6 C1
Uredakke 97 E4
Urepel 36 C1
Urfahr 57 D2
Urfeld 56 A4
Urho Kekkonens kansallis puisto 95 F3
Uri (CH) 58 A3
Uri (I) 66 A2
Uriage 30 C1
Urjala 107 E2
Urk 16 C2
Urla 115 E4
Urlingford 14 C3
Urnäsch 58 B2
Urnes 100 B3
Uroševac 77 D2
Urovica 73 F3
Urquiola, Pto 36 B1
Urshult 109 D3
Ursprungpaß 59 D1

Urtivaara 95 D3	Usk 9 D2	Ustaritz 28 A4	Utajärvi 99 D4	Utrillas 41 E2	Uukuniemi 103 F3	Užgorod 112 C3
Ururi 64 B2	Usk R 9 D2	Uster 58 A2	Utåker 104 A3	Utsjoki 95 E2	Uurainen 103 D2	Uzin 113 E2
Ury 25 F1	Uskoplje 76 A2	Ustevatn 104 B2	Utbjoa 104 A3	Utsjoki R 95 E2	Uusikaarlepyy 102 B2	Uzunköprü 115 E3
Urziceni 115 E1	Üsküdar 115 F3	Ustibar 76 B1	Utebo 37 D3	Uttendorf	Uusikaupunki 107 D2	
Usagre 43 D1	Uslar 52 B2	Ustica, I di 68 B2	Utelle 31 E1	(Oberösterreich) 56 C3	Uvac 76 B1	
Uşak 115 F4	Ussat-les-Bains 32 A2	Ustikolina 76 A1	Utena 110 C3	Uttendorf	Uvac R 76 B1	
Ušće 73 D4	Ussé 25 D2	Ústi nad Labem 53 F3	Utiel 41 D3	(Salzburg) 59 E1	Uvdal 104 C2	
Usedom 49 E2	Usseglio 31 E1	Ustiprača 76 B1	Utne 104 B2	Uttoxeter 6 C3	Uzdin 72 C2	
Usedom I 49 E1	Ussel 29 E1	Ustka 110 A4	Utrecht 16 C3	Uudenmaan	Uzel 22 C3	
Useras 41 E3	Usselo 17 F4	Ustronie Morskie 49 F1	Utrecht (Prov) 16 C2	Lääni 107 F2	Uzerche 29 D1	
Usingen 51 F4	Ustaoset 104 B2	Ust'užna 111 F1	Utrera 43 D3		Uzès 30 B3	

V

	Vålberg 105 E3	Valdelinares 41 E2	Valdosa 36 A3	Valenciennes 20 A1	Valkenswaard 16 C4	Vallø 108 C3
	Valbo 106 B2	Valdemarsvik 109 E1	Valdres 104 C2	Valensole 31 D3	Valko 107 F2	Vallo della Lucania 67 D1
Vä 109 D3	Valbondione 58 B3	Valdemeca 41 D2	Valdres Flya 100 B3	Valentano 63 D2	Valladolid 35 E4	Valloire 31 D1
Vaajakoski 103 D3	Valbonë 76 C2	Valdemorillo 40 A2	Vale de Açor 42 B2	Valentigney 27 E2	Vallata 64 C3	Vallombrosa 61 D3
Vääkiö 99 E3	Valbonnais 31 D2	Valdemoro 40 A2	Vale de Cambra 38 B1	Valenza 60 A2	Vallbo 101 D2	Vallon-en-Sully 25 F3
Vaala 99 E4	Val Camonica 58 C4	Valdenoceda 36 A2	Vale de Estrela 38 C2	Våler (Hedmark) 105 D2	Valldal 100 B2	Vallon-Pont-d'arc 30 B3
Vaalajärvi 95 E4	Valcarlos 36 C1	Valdeobispo, Emb	Vale de Prazeres 38 c2	Våler (Østfold) 105 D3	Vall d'Alba 41 E3	Vallorbe 27 D3
Vaalimaa 103 F4	Valdagno 59 D4	de 39 D2	Vale, Emb de 37 F2	Valeria 40 C3	Valldemossa 45 E2	Vallorcine 27 E4
Vaals 51 D3	Valdahon 27 D2	Valdepeñas 44 A1	Valeggio sul	Valevåg 104 A3	Vall de Uxó 41 E3	Valls 37 F4
Vaaraslahti 103 E3	Valdaj 111 E1	Valdepeñas da	Mincio 60 C1	Valfabbrica 61 E4	Valle 104 B3	Vallsta 101 F4
Vaasa 102 B2	Val-d'Ajol, le 27 D1	Jaén 44 A2	Valença do Minho 34 A3	Valga 110 C2	Valleberga 109 D4	Valmiera 110 C2
Vaasan Lääni 102 C2	Valdajskaja	Valderaduey, R 35 D4	Valençay 25 E2	Val Gardena 59 D3	Valle Castellana 63 F1	Valmojado 40 A2
Vaassen 17 D2	Vozvyšennosť 111 E2	Valderas 35 E3	Valence-	Valgorge 30 B2	Valle d'Aosta 27 E4	Valmont 19 D2
Vabre 32 B1	Valdavia, R 35 E3	Val de Reuil 19 E3	d'Albigeois 29 E3	Valgrisenche 31 E1	Valle de Abdalajís 43 E3	Valmontone 63 F3
Vác 112 B4	Valdeazogues, R 43 F1	Valderiès 29 E3	Valence (Drôme) 30 C2	Valguarnera	Valle de la Serena 39 E4	Valogne 18 B3
Vaccarès, Etang	Valdecaballeros 39 E4	Valderrepisa, Pto	Valence (Gers) 28 C3	Caropepe 68 C3	Valle de los Caidos 40 A2	Valongo 34 A4
de 30 B4	Valdecabras 40 C3	de 43 F1	Valencia 41 E4	Valhelhas 38 C2	Valle de	Valoria la Buena 35 E4
Vacha 52 B3	Valdecañas, Emb	Valderrobres 41 F2	Valencia (Prov) 41 D4	Valíco della	Matamoros 42 C1	Valpaços 34 b4
Väddö 106 B3	de 39 E3	Valdestillas 35 E4	Valencia de	Forchetta 64 A2	Vallehermoso 42 A4	Valpalmas 37 D3
Vadehavet 108 A4	Valdecarros 39 E1	Valdeverdeja 39 E3	Alcántara 38 C3	Valimítika 83 E4	Vallejera, Pto de 39 E2	Val Passiria 59 D2
Vadheim 100 A3	Valdecebollas 35 F2	Valdevimbre 35 D3	Valencia de Don	Valíra 86 C3	Valle-Mosso 31 F1	Valpovo 71 E2
Vado Ligure 60 A3	Valdediós 35 E1	Valdezcaray 36 B2	Juan 35 D3	Valjevo 72 C3	Vallentuna 106 B3	Valprato Soana 31 E1
Vadsø 95 F1	Valdeganga 41 D4	Valdieri 31 E3	Valencia de las	Valjok 95 E2	Valleraugue 29 F3	Valras-Plage 30 A4
Vadstena 109 D1	Valdeinfierno, Emb	Valdihuela 39 F2	Torres 43 D1	Valjunquera 41 F1	Vallet 24 B2	Valréas 30 C3
Vaduz 58 B2	de 44 C2	Val-d'Isère 31 D1	Valencia del	Valkeakoski 107 E2	Valletta 68 B4	Valsamónero 91 D4
Vadvetjåkka 94 B3	Valdelacasa de	Valdobbiadene 59 D3	Ventoso 43 D1	Valkeala 107 F2	Vallgrund 102 B2	Valsavarenche 31 E1
Vaféika 81 D2	Tajo 39 E3		Valencia I 14 A4	Valkenburg 51 D3	Valli di Comacchio 61 D2	Valserine 27 D4
Vafiohóri 79 F2						
Vågaholmen 97 E2						
Vågåmo 100 B3						
Vågan 97 E1						
Vaganj 75 E1						
Vaganski vrh 70 C4						
Vágar 96 A3						
Våge 104 A2						
Væggerløse 108 C4						
Vaggeryd 109 D2						
Vágia 83 F4						
Vagioniá 91 D4						
Vagnhärad 106 B4						
Vagos 38 B1						
Vågsfjorden 94 B3						
Vågsøy 100 A3						
Vágur 96 A4						
Váh 112 B3						
Vähäkyrö 102 B2						
Vahto 107 D2						
Vái 91 F3						
Vaiano 60 C3						
Vaiges 23 E3						
Vaihingen 55 D2						
Vailly (Aisne) 20 A3						
Vailly (Cher) 26 A2						
Vainikkala 103 F4						
Vaisaluokta 94 B4						
Vaison-la-						
Romaine 30 C3						
Vaksdal 104 A2						
Vålådalen 101 D2						
Valadares 34 A4						
Valais 27 E4						
Valalta 70 A3						
Valamen 103 E2						
Valandovo 77 F3						
Val-André, le 22 C2						
Valareña 36 C3						
Valašské Meziříčí 112 B3						
Valax 107 F2						
Valberg 31 E3						

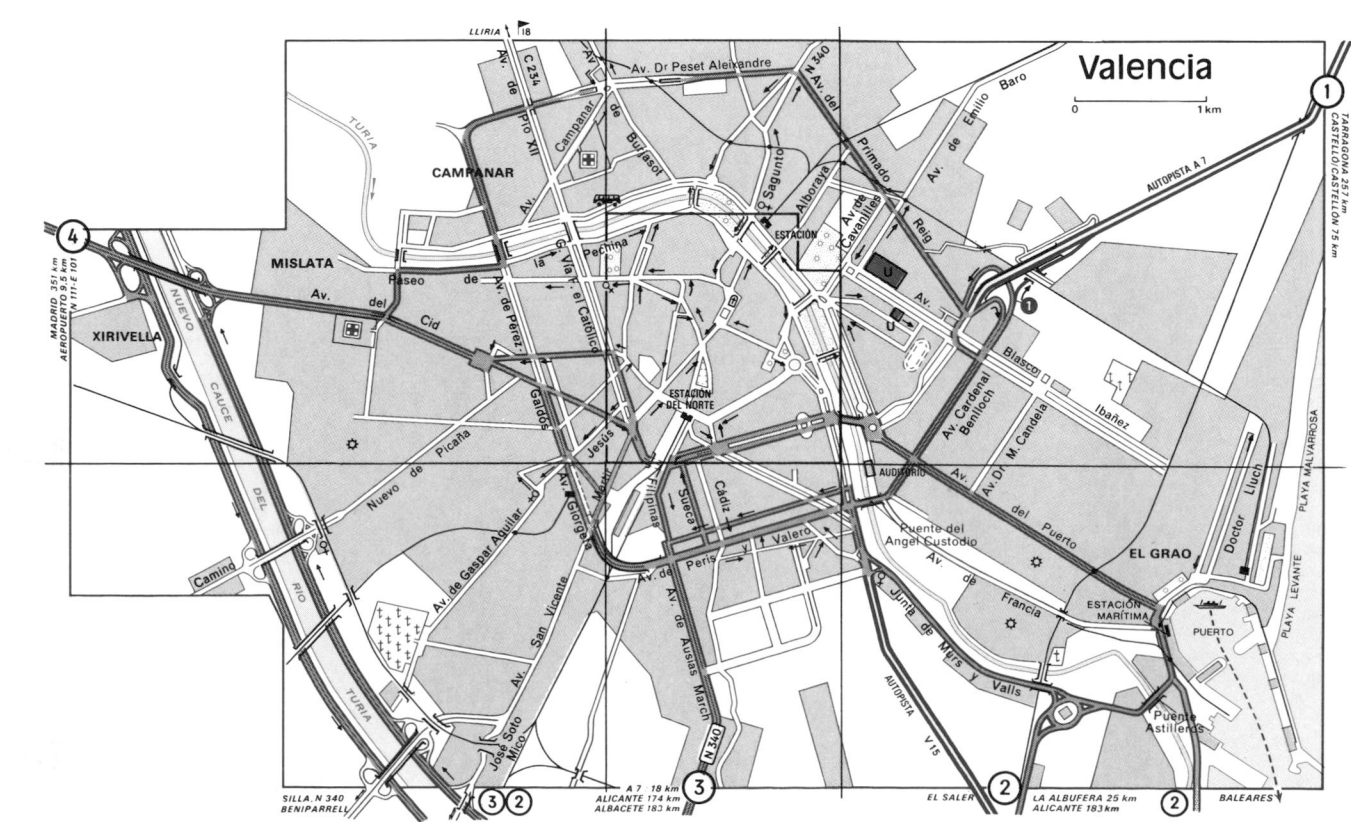

Valencia

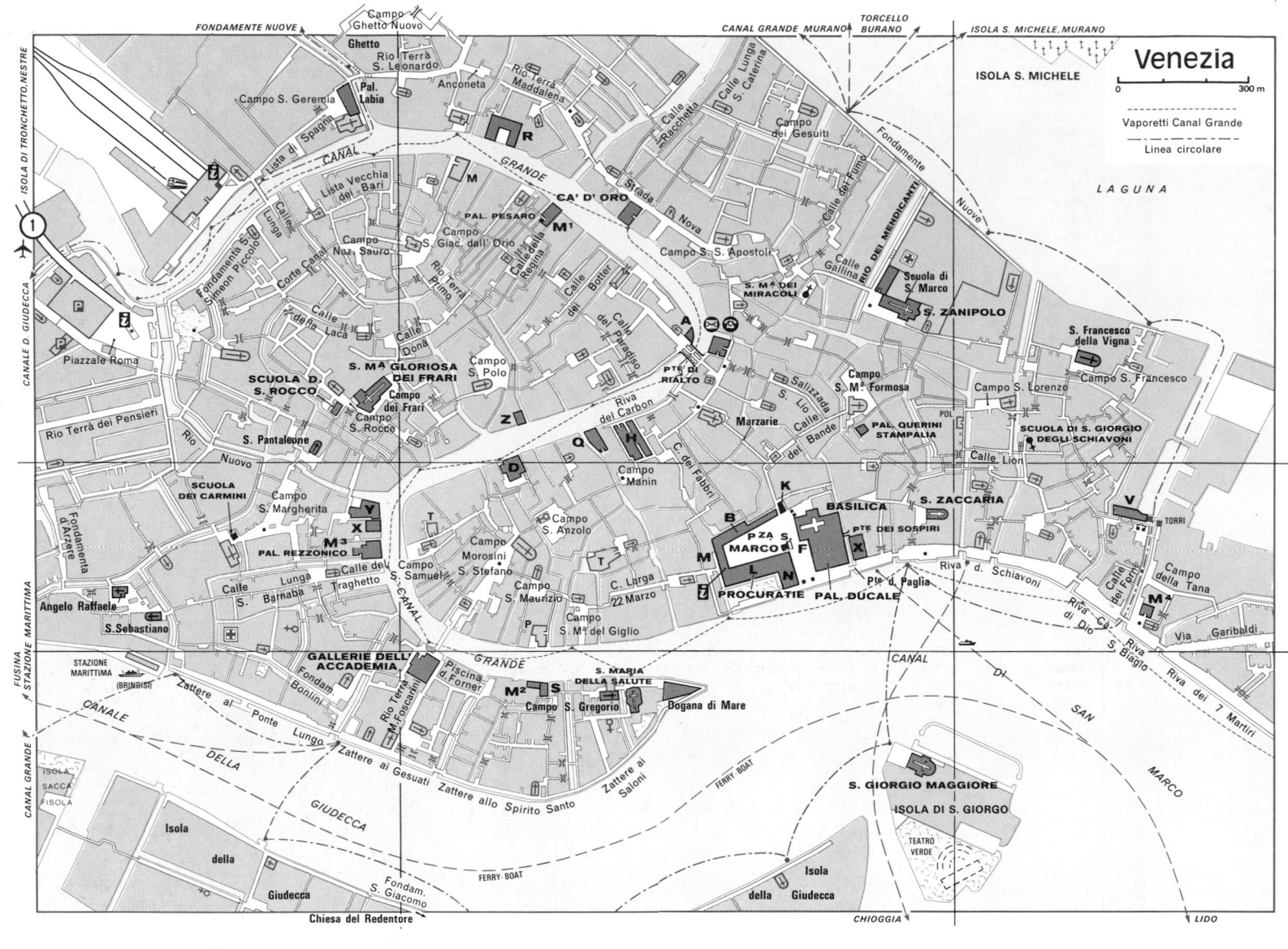

Venezia

Valset	100 C1	Vanån	101 D4	Varaždinske		Várkiza	87 F2	Vassiliká (Évia)	84 A3	Vathílakos		Veendam	47 D3
Valsjöbyn	101 E1	Vanda	107 E2	Toplice	71 D1	Värmlands Län	105 E3	Vassiliká (Lésvos)	85 F2	(Dráma)	80 C2	Veenendaal	16 C3
Vals-les-Bains	30 B2	Vandellòs	41 F1	Varazze	60 A3	Varmo	59 E3	Vassiliká		Vathílakos (Kozáni)	79 E4	Veere	16 B3
Valtellina	58 B3	Vänern	105 E4	Varberg	108 C2	Varna (BG)	115 E2	(Makedonía)	80 A3	Vathílakos		Vefsna	97 E3
Valtessiniko	86 C2	Vänersborg	108 C1	Vårbica	115 E3	Varna (YU)	72 C3	Vassiliká (Lefkáda)	82 B3	(Thessaloníki)	79 F3	Vefsnfjorden	97 D3
Val-Thorens	31 D1	Vangshylla	101 D1	Varda	72 C4	Värnamo	109 D2	Vassiliki (Thessalía)	83 D1	Vathípetro	91 D4	Vega	97 D3
Valtierra	36 C3	Vangsnes	104 B1	Várda	86 B1	Varnhem	109 D1	Vassilikó	84 B4	Vathís	89 F3	Vega de
Valtimo	103 E1	Vangsvik	94 B3	Vardar	77 E3	Varnsdorf	53 F2	Vassilikós	86 A2	Vatin	73 D2	Espinareda	34 C2
Váltos	81 F1	Vanha Vaasa	102 B2	Varde	108 A3	Värö	108 C2	Vassilis	83 E2	Vatnajökull	96 B2	Vegadeo	34 C1
Valtotópi	80 B2	Vanna	94 C2	Vardenik	77 E2	Varoš Selo	77 D2	Vassilítsa	78 C4	Vatne	100 B2	Vega de Valcarce	34 C2
Váltou, Óri	82 C2	Vännäs	102 A1	Vardø	95 F1	Várpalota	112 B4	Vassy	18 C4	Vatólakos	79 D4	Vegafjorden	97 D3
Valtournenche	27 F4	Vannavålen	94 C2	Vårdö	106 C3	Varpaisjärvi	103 E1	Västanbäck	101 F2	Vatopedíou	80 C4	Vegarienza	35 D2
Valun	70 B4	Vannes	22 C4	Vardoússia, Óri	83 D3	Värriötunturit	95 F4	Västanfyärd	107 D3	Vatra Dornei	113 D4	Vegårshei	104 C4
Valvasone	59 E3	Vannsjø	105 D3	Varel	47 F3	Vars	31 D2	Vastenjaure	97 F1	Vättern	109 D1	Vegas	35 E2
Valverde (Is		Vannsundet	94 C2	Vareleli	84 C4	Vars, Col de	31 D2	Västerås	106 A3	Vattholma	106 B3	Vegas del
Canarias)	42 A4	Vanoise, Massif de		Varengeville	19 D2	Vartdalsfjorden	100 A2	Västerbottens		Vaucluse	30 C3	Condado	35 E2
Valverde (La Rioja)	36 C3	la	31 D1	Varenna	58 B4	Vartholomió 20	86 B1	Län	98 A4	Vaucouleurs	20 c4	Vegesack	47 F3
Valverde del		Vanoise, Parc Nat de		Varennes-en-		Vartius	99 F4	Västerdalälven	101 D4	Vaud	27 D3	Veghel	16 C3
Camino	42 C2	la	31 D1	Argonne	20 C3	Värtsilä	103 F2	Väster Haninge	106 B4	Vau i Dejës	76 C3	Veghel	16 C3
Valverde de		Vansbro	105 E2	Varennes-sur-		Varvára	80 B3	Västernorrlands		Vaut të Dejës, Liq i	76 C3	Vegoritída, L	79 E3
Leganés	38 C4	Vans, les	30 B3	Allier	26 A4	Varvarin	73 E4	Län	101 F2	Vauvert	30 B4	Vehkalahti	103 F4
Valverde del		Vantaa	107 E2	Varennes-sur-		Varzi	60 A2	Västervik	109 E1	Vauvillers	27 D1	Vehmaa	101 D2
Fresno	39 D2	Vanttauskoski	99 D2	Amance	26 C1	Varzy	26 A2	Västmanlands		Vaux-le-Vicomte	19 F4	Vehmersalmi	103 E2
Valverde del Júcar	40 C3	Vaour	29 D3	Vareš	71 F4	Vasa	102 B2	Län	105 F3	Vávdos	80 A3	Veiðivötn	96 B2
Valøya	97 D4	Vaqueira	37 F2	Varese	58 A4	Vasarapera	99 E2	Vasto	64 B2	Växjö	109 D2	Veidnesklubben	95 E1
Våmb	109 D1	Var	31 D4	Varese Ligure	60 B3	Vásárosnamény	112 C3	Vatan	25 E3	Växtorp	108 C3	Veikkola	107 E2
Våmhus	101 E4	Vara	108 C1	Vårgårda	108 C1	Vascão, Rib do	42 B2	Väte	109 F4	Vayrac	29 D2	Veines	95 F1
Vamlingbo	109 F4	Varades	23 E4	Vargas	35 F2	Vasikkaselkä	95 F2	Vaterá	85 F3	V'az'ma	111 F3	Veinge	108 C2
Vammala	107 D1	Varallo	58 A4	Vargsund	95 D1	Vasil'kov	113 E2	Vateró	79 D4	Veberöd	109 D3	Veiros	38 C4
Vampula	107 D2	Varangerbotn	95 F1	Varhaug	104 A4	Vaskijärvi	107 D2	Váthia	87 D4	Vecht	17 D2	Vejen	108 A3
Vamvakás, Akr	85 F4	Varangerfjorden	95 F1	Vári (Kikládes)	88 B2	Vaskio	107 E2	Vathí		Vechta	17 F1	Vejer de la
Vamvakoú		Varangerhalvøya	95 F1	Vári (Stereá Eláda)	87 F1	Vaskivesi	102 C3	(Dodekánissa)	84 B4	Vechte	17 E2	Frontera	43 D4
(Pelopónissos)	87 D3	Varano de'		Varilhes	32 A2	Vaslui	113 E4	Váthi (Lefkáda)	79 F2	Vecinos	39 E1	Vejle	108 A3
Vamvakoú		Melegari	60 B2	Varimbómbi	87 F1	Vassarás	87 D3	Vathí (Makedonía)	92 C1	Vedelago	59 E4	Velada	39 F3
(Thessalía)	83 E2	Varano, L di	64 C2	Váris	79 D4	Vassés	86 C2	Vathí (Stereá		Vedrá, I	45 D4	Velagići	71 D4
Vanajavesi	107 E2	Varaždin	70 C1	Varkaus	103 E3	Vassieux	30 C2	Eláda)	82 B3	Vedungfjället	101 D3	Vela Luka	75 E2
												Velanídia	87 E4

Name	Page	Ref
Velate, Pto de	36	C1
Velayos	39	F1
Velbert	17	E4
Velburg	55	F1
Velde	101	D1
Velden (A)	70	A1
Velden (Nüberg)	55	F1
Velden (München)	56	B3
Veldhoven	16	C4
Velebit	70	C4
Velebitski kanal	70	B4
Velenje	70	B1
Velešta	77	D4
Velestíno	83	F2
Veleta, Pico	44	A3
Velež	75	F2
Vélez Blanco	44	C2
Vélez de Benaudalla	44	A3
Vélez-Málaga	43	F3
Vélez Rubio	44	C2
Velfjorden	97	D3
Veličani	75	F2
Veliés	87	E4
Velika	71	E2
Velika Drenova	73	E4
Velika Gorica	70	C2
Velika de Huelma	44	A3
Velika Jablanica	76	C2
Velika Jamnička	70	C2
Velika Kapela	70	B3
Velika Kladuša	70	C3
Velika Kopanica	71	F3
Velika Kruša	77	D2
Velika Morava	73	D3
Velika Mučna	71	D1
Velika Plana (Morava)	73	D3
Velika Plana (Prokuplje)	77	D1
Velika Tresta	73	E3
Veliki Alan	70	B4
Veliki Bastaji	71	E2
Veliki Gaj	73	D2
Veliki Grđevac	71	D2
Veliki Izvor	73	F3
Veliki Jastrebac	77	D1
Velikije Luki	111	E2
Veliki kanal	72	B2
Veliki Krš	73	E3
Veliki Popović	73	E3
Veliki Prolog	75	E2
Veliki Radinci	72	C2
Veliki Trnovac	77	E2
Veliki Vitao	76	A2
Veliki Zdenci	71	D2
Veliko Gradište	73	D2
Veliko Lašče	70	B2
Veliko Orašje	73	D3
Veliko Târnovo	115	D2
Velilla del R Carríon	35	E2
Veli Lošinj	70	B4
Velimlje	76	A2
Vélines	28	C2
Velingrad	115	D3
Velino	63	F2
Velino, Mte	63	F2
Veliž	111	E3
Veljun	70	C3
Velká Bíteš	57	E1
Velké Meziřiči	57	E1
Velkua	107	D2
Vellahn	48	B3
Velletri	63	E3
Vellinge	108	C3
Velopoúla	87	F3
Vélos	84	B4
Velpke	48	B4
Velten	49	D4
Velvendós	79	E4
Vemdalen	101	E3
Vemdalsskalet	101	E3
Vemhån	101	E3
Véna	81	E2
Venaco	33	F3
Venafro	64	A3
Venarey-les-Laumes	26	B2
Venaria	31	E1
Venčani	73	D3
Vence	31	E3
Venda Nova	34	B4
Vendas Novas	38	B4
Vendée	24	B3
Vendel	106	B3
Vendeuvre	26	B1
Vendôme	25	E2
Vendsyssel	108	B2
Veneheitto	99	D4
Veneta, Laguna	61	D1
Veneto	61	D1
Venezia	61	D1
Vengjaneset	104	A2
Venialbo	35	D4
Venjan	101	E4
Venjansjön	101	E4
Venlo	17	D4
Vennebeck	17	F2
Vennesla	104	B4
Vennesund	97	D3
Venosa	64	C3
Venosta	58	C3
Venray	17	D3
Venta	110	B3
Venta de Cruce	43	D3
Venta de Don Quijote	40	B3
Ventana, Pto de	35	D2
Venta Nueva	34	C2
Ventas de Huelma	44	A3
Ventimiglia	31	E3
Ventnor	9	E4
Ventotene, I	63	F4
Ventoux, Mt	30	C3
Ventspils	110	B2
Venturina	62	C1
Vera (E)	44	C3
Vera (N)	101	D1
Vera de Bidasoa	36	C1
Verbania-Pallanza	58	A4
Verberie	19	F3
Verbicaro	67	E2
Verbier	27	E4
Vercelli	31	F1
Vercel-Villedieu	27	D2
Verchnedvinsk	111	D3
Verdalsøra	101	D1
Verde, Col de	33	F3
Verden	48	A4
Verdikoússa	83	D1
Verdon	31	D3
Verdon, le	28	A1
Verdun (Meuse)	20	C3
Verdun (Saône-et-Loire)	26	C3
Verdun (Tarn-et-Garonne)	29	D3
Verfeil	29	D4
Vergato	60	C3
Vérgi	80	A2
Vergiate	60	A1
Vergína	79	E3
Vergio, Col de	33	F3
Vergt	28	C2
Véria	79	E3
Verin	34	B3
Verl	17	F3
Vermand	20	A2
Vermenton	26	B2
Vérmio, Óros	79	E3
Verna, Pzo di	69	D2
Vernet-les-Bains	32	B2
Verneuil	19	D4
Vernon	19	E3
Vérno, Óros	79	D3
Vernoux-en-Vivarais	30	B2
Verny	21	D3
Veroli	63	F3
Verona	60	C1
Verpillière	30	C1
Verran	101	D1
Verrès	27	F4
Versailles	19	F4
Versmold	17	F2
Verteillac	28	C1
Vertiskos, Óros	80	A2
Vertus	20	B4
Verucchio	61	E3
Veruela	36	C3
Verviers	51	D4
Vervins	20	B2
Verzuolo	31	E2
Verzy	20	B3
Vesanto	103	D2
Vescovato	33	F3
Veselí	57	D1
Vesijärvi	107	F2
Vesilahti	107	E1
Vesivehmaa	107	F2
Vesjegonsk	111	F1
Veskoniemi	95	F3
Vesle	20	B3
Vesoul	27	D2
Véssa	85	E4
Vest-Agder	104	B4
Vestby	105	D3
Vesterålen	94	A3
Vesterø Havn	108	B2
Vestertana	95	E1
Vestfjorden	97	E1
Vestfold	104	C3
Vestmanna	96	A3
Vestmannaeyjar	96	B3
Vestnes	100	B2
Vestone	58	C4
Vestre Jakobselv	95	F1
Vestvågøy	94	A4
Vésubie, Gorges de la	31	E3
Vesuvio	64	B4
Veszprém	112	B4
Veteli	102	C2
Veternica	77	E1
Vetlanda	109	E2
Vetralla	63	E2
Vetriolo Terme	59	D3
Vetschau	53	E1
Vettore, M	63	F1
Veules-les-Roses	19	D2
Veulettes	19	D2
Veurne	50	A3
Vevey	27	E3
Vévi	79	D3
Veynes	30	C2
Veyre	29	F1
Veyrier	27	D4
Vezdemarbán	35	D4
Vézelay	26	B2
Vézelise	21	D4
Vézénobres	30	B3
Vézère	29	D2
Vézins-de-Lévézou	29	E3
Vezzani	33	F3
Vezzano	58	C3
Via Appia	63	F3
Via Aurelia	60	C4
Via Casilina	63	E2
Via Cassia	63	D1
Viadana	60	C2
Via Emilia	61	D3
Via Flaminia	61	E3
Viana	36	B2
Viana do Bolo	34	C3
Viana do Castelo	34	A3
Vianden	21	D2
Viano do Alentejo	42	B1
Viar, R	43	D2
Vias	30	A4
Via Salaria	63	E2
Via Tiburtina		
Valeria	63	F2
Viaur	29	E3
Viborg	108	A2
Vibo Valentia	67	E3
Vibraye	23	F3
Vič	70	B1
Vic (E)	32	A3
Vic (F)	19	F3
Vicálvaro	40	B2
Vicdessos	37	D2
Vicenza	59	D4
Vic-en-Bigorre	28	B4
Vic-Fézensac	28	C4
Vich	32	A3
Vichy	26	A4
Vic-le-Comte	29	F1
Vico	33	E3
Vico del Gargano	64	C2
Vico Equense	64	B4
Vico, Lago di	63	E2
Vic-sur-Cère	29	E2
Victoria	68	B4
Vidå	108	A4
Vidago	34	B4
Vidauban	31	D4
Viddal	100	A3
Videbæk	108	A3
Vidiáki	86	C1
Vidigueira	42	B1
Vidin	114	C2
Vidio, C	35	D1
Viðoy	96	A3
Vidreres	32	B4
Vidrovan	76	B2
Vidsel	98	B3
Viduša	76	A2
Viechtach	56	B2
Viechtwang	56	C3
Vieira	38	A2
Vieira do Minho	34	B4
Viejo, Pto	39	D2
Viekinjärvi	103	F1
Vielha	37	F2
Vielle-Aure	37	E2
Vielmur	32	A1
Vielsalm	51	D4
Vienenburg	52	B1
Vienne	30	B1
Vienne (Dépt)	25	D3
Vienne R	25	D4
Vieremä	103	D1
Viernheim	54	C1
Vierraden	49	E3
Viersen	17	D4
Vierumäki	107	F2
Vierzehnheiligen	52	C4
Vierzon	25	F2
Vieste	64	C2
Vietas	94	B4
Vietri di Potenza	64	C4
Vietri sul Mare	64	B4
Vieux-Boucau	28	A3
Vieux Chaillol	31	D2
Vif	30	C2
Vig	108	C3
Vigan, le	29	F3
Vigeland	104	B4
Vigeois	29	D1
Vigevano	60	A1
Viggiano	65	D4
Vígla	82	C2
Vígla, Akr	91	D1
Vignale	31	F1
Vignanello	63	E2
Vignemale	37	E2
Vignes, les	29	F3
Vigneulles	20	C3
Vignola	60	C2
Vignole Borbera	60	A2
Vignory	26	C1
Vigo	34	A3
Vigo di Fassa	59	D3
Vigone	31	E2
Vigonza	61	D1
Vigrestad	104	A4
Vihanti	99	D4
Vihiers	24	C2
Vihtavuori	103	D3
Vihteljärvi	102	C3
Vihti	107	E2
Viiala	107	E2
Viinijärvi	103	F2
Viipustunturit	95	E3
Viitasaari	103	D2
Vik (Aust-Agder)	104	B4
Vik (IS)	96	B3
Vik (Nordland)	97	D3
Vik (Sogn og Fjordane)	104	B1
Vika	105	F2
Vikajärvi	99	D2
Vikanes	104	A2
Vikebukt	100	B2
Vikedal	104	A3
Vikersund	104	C3
Vikeså	104	A4
Vikevåg	104	A3
Vikingstad	106	A4
Vikna	97	D4
Vikoč	76	A1
Vikran	94	B2
Viksdalen	100	A3
Viksjö	101	F2
Viksjøfjell	95	F2
Viksta	106	B3
Vidå	108	A4
Vilada	32	A3
Viladamat	32	B3
Vila de Cruces	34	B2
Vila de Rei	38	B3
Vila do Bispo	42	A2
Vila do Conde	34	A4
Vila Fernando	38	C4
Vila Flor	34	C4
Vila Franca das Naves	38	C1
Vilafranca del Penedès	32	A4
Vila Franca de Xira	38	A4
Vila Fresca de Azeitão	38	A4
Vilagarcia de Arosa	34	A2
Vieira do Minho	34	B4
Vila Nova da Barquinha	38	B3
Vilanova de Arousa	34	A2
Vila Nova de Cerveira	34	A3
Vila Nova de Famalicão	34	A4
Vila Nova de Foz Côa	39	D1
Vila Nova de Gaia	34	A4
Vila Nova de Milfontes	42	A2
Vila Nova de Ourém	38	B3
Vila Nova de Paiva	38	C1
Vila Nova de Poiares	38	B2
Vilanova de Sau	32	B3
Vilanova i la Geltrú	32	A4
Vila Pouca de Aguiar	34	B4
Vila Praia de Âncora	34	A3
Vilar de Barrio	34	B3
Vila Real	34	B4
Vila-réal	41	E3
Vila Real de Santo António	42	B3
Vila-rodona	37	F4
Vila-seca	37	F4
Vila Velha de Ródão	38	C3
Vila Verde	34	A3
Vila Verde de Ficalho	42	C1
Vila Verde de Raia	34	B3
Vila Viçosa	38	C4
Vilches	44	A2
Vilejka	111	D4
Vilhelmina	97	F4
Vilia	87	E1
Viljakkala	102	C3
Viljandi	110	C2
Vilkaviškis	110	C4
Vilkovo	113	E4
Villa Adriana	63	E2
Villa Bartolomea	60	C1
Villablanca	42	C2
Villablino	35	D2
Villabona	36	C1
Villabrágima	35	E4
Villabuena del Puente	35	D4
Villacañas	40	B3
Villacarriedo	35	F2
Villacarrillo	44	B2
Villacastín	40	A1
Villach	59	F2
Villacidro	66	B4
Villada	35	E3
Villa del Prado	40	A2
Villa del Río	43	F2
Villadiego	35	F3
Villadossola	27	F4
Villaescusa de Haro	40	C3
Villafáfila	35	D4
Villafamés	41	E3
Villaflores	39	F1
Villafranca	36	C2
Villafranca del Bierzo	34	C2
Villafranca del Cid	41	E2
Villafranca de los Barros	43	D1
Villafranca de los Caballeros	40	B3
Villafranca di Verona	60	C1
Villafranca in Lunigiana	60	B3
Villafranca-Montes de Oca	36	A2
Villafranca Piemonte	31	E2
Villafranca Tirrena	69	D2
Villafranco del Guadalquivir	43	D3
Villafrati	68	B3
Villafrechos	35	E3
Villafruela	35	F4
Villafuerte	35	F4
Villagarcía del Llano	40	C4
Villager	35	D2
Villaggio Mancuso	67	F3
Villagonzalo	39	D4
Villaharta	43	E1
Villahermosa	44	B1
Villahoz	35	F3
Villaines-la-Juhel	23	E3
Villajoyosa	45	E1
Villa, la	59	D2
Villala	103	F3
Villalba	34	B1
Villalba de Guardo	35	E2
Villalba de la Sierra	40	C2
Villalba de los Barros	43	D1
Villalba del Rey	40	C2
Villalcampo, Emb de	35	D4
Villalcázar de Sirga	35	E3
Villalenga	36	C4
Villa Literno	64	A4
Villalón de Campos	35	E3
Villalonga	45	E1
Villalpando	35	E4
Villalpardo	41	D4
Villamañán	35	D3
Villamanrique	44	B1
Villamarchante	41	E3
Villamartín (Andalucia)	43	D3
Villamartín (Castilla-León)	35	E3
Villamassargia	66	B4
Villamayor	37	D3
Villamayor de Campos	35	E3
Villamayor de Santiago	40	B3
Villameca, Emb de	35	D2
Villa Minozzo	60	C3
Villandraut	28	B3
Villandry	25	D2
Villanova Monteleone	66	A2
Villanubla	35	E4
Villanueva de Alcardete	40	B3
Villanueva de Alcolea	41	F3
Villanueva de Alcorón	40	C2
Villanueva de Algaidas	43	F3
Villanueva de Argaño	35	F3
Villanueva de Arzobispo	44	B2
Villanueva de Bogas	40	A3
Villanueva de Cameros	36	B3
Villanueva de Córdoba	43	F1
Villanueva de Franco	40	B4
Villanueva de la Concepción	43	F3
Villanueva de la Fuente	44	B1
Villanueva de la Jara	40	C4
Villanueva de la Reina	44	A2
Villanueva de la Serena	39	E4
Villanueva de la Sierra	39	D2
Villanueva de las Torres	44	B2
Villanueva de la Vera	39	E2
Villanueva del Campo	35	D3
Villanueva del Duque	43	E1
Villanueva del Fresno	42	C1
Villanueva del Huerva	37	D4
Villanueva de los Castillejos	42	C2
Villanueva de los Infantes	44	B1
Villanueva del Rey	43	E1
Villanueva del Río y Minas	43	D2
Villanueva del Trabuco	43	F3
Villanueva de San Carlos	44	A1
Villa Opicina	59	F3
Villa Potenza	61	F4
Villaquejida	35	D3
Villaquilambre	35	D2
Villarcayo	36	A1
Villard-de-Lans	30	C2
Villar de Cañas	40	C3
Villardeciervos	35	D3
Villar de Domingo García	40	C2
Villardefrades	35	E4
Villar del Arzobispo	41	E3
Villar del Rey	39	D4
Villar de Peralonso	39	E1
Villarejo de Fuentes	40	C3
Villarejo de Orbigo	35	D3
Villarejo de Salvanés	40	B2
Villarente	35	E3
Villares de la Reina	39	E1
Villares del Saz	40	C3
Villargordo de Cabriel	41	D4
Villaricos	44	C3
Villarín de Campos	35	D4
Villarino	34	C4
Villarquemado	41	D2
Villarramiel	35	E3
Villarrobledo	40	C4
Villarroya	36	C3
Villarroya de la Sierra	36	C4
Villarroya de los Pinares	41	E2
Villarroya, Pto de	41	E2
Villarrubia de Santiago	40	B3
Villars	27	E3
Villars-les-Dombes	26	C4
Villarta de San Juan	40	B4
Villarubia de los Ojos	40	A4
Villasalto	66	C3
Villasana de Mena	36	A1
Villasandino	35	F3
Villa San Giovanni	67	E4
Villa Santa Maria	64	A2
Villasante	36	A1
Villa Santina	59	E3
Villasarracino	35	E3
Villasayas, Pto de	36	B4
Villaseco de los Reyes	39	E1
Villasequilla de Yepes	40	A3
Villasimius	66	C4
Villasor	66	B4
Villatobas	40	B3
Villatoro, Pto de	39	F2
Villatoya	41	D4
Villava	36	C2

Name	Page	Grid
Villavaara	95	F2
Villaverde del Río	43	D2
Villaviciosa	35	E1
Villaviciosa de Córdoba	43	E2
Villaviciosa de Odón	40	A2
Villavieja de Yeltes	39	D1
Villa Vomano	63	F1
Villé	21	E4
Villebois-Lavalette	28	C1
Villedieu, la	25	D3
Villedieu-les-Poêles	18	B4
Ville-en-Tardenois	20	B3
Villefagnan	24	C4
Villefort	29	F3
Villefranche-d'Albigeois	29	E3
Villefranche-de-Lauragais	29	D4
Villefranche-de-Lonchat	28	C2
Villefranche-de-Rouergue	29	E3
Villefranche-du-Périgord	29	D2
Villefranche-sur-Cher	25	E2
Villefranche-sur-Mer	31	E3
Villefranche-sur-Saône	26	C4
Villel	41	D2
Villemur	29	D3
Villena	45	D1
Villenauxe-la-Grande	20	A4
Villeneuve	30	B3
Villeneuve-de-Berg	30	B2
Villeneuve-de-Marsan	28	B3
Villeneuve-l'Archevêque	26	A1
Villeneuve-sur-Lot	28	C3
Villeneuve-sur-Yonne	26	A1
Villeréal	28	C2
Villers	19	D3
Villers-Bocage (Calvados)	18	C3
Villers-Bocage (Somme)	19	F2
Villers-Bretonneux	19	F2
Villers-Cotterêts	19	F3
Villers-devant-Orval	20	C2
Villersexel	27	D2
Villers-Farlay	27	D2
Villers la Ville	50	C4
Villers-le-Lac	27	E2
Villerupt	21	D3
Villerville	19	D3
Ville-sur-Tourbe	20	C3
Villeta Barrea	64	A2
Villiers-St-Georges	20	A4
Villingen-Schwenningen	54	C3
Villoldo	35	E3
Villoria	39	E1
Villotta	59	E3
Villuercas	39	E3
Vilnius	110	C3
Vilppula	102	C3
Vils (Bayern)	55	F1
Vils (Bayern)	56	B2
Vilsbiburg	56	B2
Vilseck	55	F1
Vilshofen	56	C2
Vilusi	76	A2
Vilvoorde	50	B3
Vimercate	60	A1
Vimianzo	34	A1
Vimieiro	38	B4
Vimioso	34	C4
Vimmerby	109	E1
Vimoutiers	19	D4
Vimpeli	102	C2
Vimperk	56	C1
Vinac	71	E4
Vinadio	31	E3
Vinaixa	37	F4
Vinalapó, R	45	D2
Vinaròs	41	F2
Vinay	30	C1
Vinça	32	B2
Vinča	73	D3
Vinchiaturo	64	B3
Vinci	60	C3
Vindafjorden	104	A3
Vindelälven	102	A1
Vindelfjällens N.R.	97	E3
Vindeln	102	A1
Vinderup	108	A2
Vindsvik	104	A3
Vingåker	105	F4
Vingelen	100	C3
Vingeveien	100	C3
Vinhais	34	C3
Vinica (Makedonija)	77	F3
Vinica (Slovenija)	70	C3
Vinjčani	77	E3
Vinje	104	B3
Vinkovci	71	F2
Vinnica	113	E2
Vinsternes	100	B2
Vinstra	100	C3
Vinstri	104	C1
Vintiländkaira	95	F4
Viñuelas	40	B2
Vinuesa	36	B3
Viotía	83	F4
Vipava	70	A2
Vipava R	70	A2
Vipiteno	59	D2
Vir (Bosna i Hercegovina)	75	E1
Vir (Hrvatska)	70	C4
Vir I	70	C4
Vira	75	D2
Vire	18	C4
Virgen	59	E2
Virgen de la Cabeza	43	F2
Virginia	13	D3
Virieu	30	C1
Virieu-le-Grand	27	D4
Virihaure	97	F1
Virkby	107	E3
Virkkala	107	E3
Virkkula	99	E2
Virksund	108	A2
Virmasvesi	103	D2
Virmutjoki	103	F3
Virolahti	103	F4
Virónia	80	A2
Virovitica	71	E2
Virpazar	76	B3
Virrat	102	C3
Virsbo	105	F3
Virserum	109	E2
Virsko more	70	C4
Virtasalmi	103	E3
Virton	20	C3
Virtsu	110	B2
Vis	75	D2
Vis I	75	D2
Visaurin	37	D2
Visby	109	F4
Visé	51	D3
Višegrad	72	C4
Višegradska Banja	72	C4
Viserba	61	E3
Viseu	38	C1
Viševica	70	B3
Viskan	108	C2
Viški kan	75	D2
Višnja Gora	70	B2
Višnjica	73	D3
Visočica	75	F1
Visočica R	73	F4
Viso del Marqués	44	A1
Visoki Dečani	76	C2
Visoko	71	F4
Visovac	75	D1
Visp	27	F3
Víssani	78	B4
Visselhövede	48	A3
Vissenbjerg	108	B3
Vissiniá	79	D3
Visso	63	F1
Vistabella del Maestrazgo	41	E2
Vistasväggi	94	B4
Vistheden	98	B3
Vistonída, L	81	D2
Visuvesi	102	C3
Vitaby	109	D3
Vitala	84	B4
Vitanovac	73	D4
Vitebsk	111	E3
Viterbo	63	E2
Vitez	71	E4
Vitigudino	39	D1
Vitina (Bosna i Hercegovina)	75	E2
Vitina (Kosovo)	77	D2
Vitlyčke	105	D4
Vito d'Asio	59	E3
Vítoli	83	D3
Vitolište	77	E4
Vitomirica	76	C2
Vitoria-Gasteiz	36	B2
Vitorog	71	E4
Vitoša	115	D2
Vitovlje	71	E4
Vitré	23	D3
Vitrey	27	D1
Vitry-en-Artois	19	F2
Vitry-le-François	20	B4
Vítsa	78	C4
Vitsand	105	E2
Vittangi	94	C4
Vittangiälven	94	C4
Vitteaux	26	B2
Vittel	27	D1
Vittoria	69	D4
Vittoriosa	68	B4
Vittorio Veneto	59	E3
Vittsjö	109	D3
Vitznau	58	A2
Viù	31	E1
Vivaro	59	E3
Vivel del R Martín	41	E2
Viver	41	E3
Viverio	34	B1
Viverols	29	F1
Viveros	44	B1
Vivier, le	18	B4
Viviers	30	B2
Vivonne	25	D4
Vizille	30	C2
Vižinada	70	A3
Vizitsa	83	F2
Vižnica	113	D3
Vizzavona	33	F3
Vizzavona, Col de	33	F3
Vizzini	69	D4
Vjosë	114	B4
Vlaardingen	16	B3
Vladičin Han	77	E1
Vladievci	77	F3
Vladimirci	72	C3
Vladimirovac	73	D2
Vladimirovo	77	F3
Vladimir-Volynskij	112	C2
Vlagtwedde	17	E1
Vlahává	83	D1
Vlahérna (Ípiros)	82	C2
Vlahérna (Pelopónnissos)	86	C2
Vlahiótis	87	D3
Vlahokerassiá	87	D2
Vlahomándra	83	D4
Vlahópoulo	86	C3
Vlanen	16	C3
Vlasenica	72	B4
Vlašić (Bosna i Hercegovina)	71	E4
Vlašić (Srbija)	72	C3
Vlasina Okruglica	77	E1
Vlasinsko jez	77	E1
Vlasotince	77	E1
Vlássio	83	D2
Vlásti	79	D3
Vlieland	16	C1
Vlihó	82	B3
Vlissingen	16	B4
Vlorë	114	B4
Vlotho	17	F2
Vltava	53	F3
Vobbia	60	A2
Vočin	71	E2
Vöcklabruck	56	C3
Vodice (Rijeka)	70	A3
Vodice (Šibenik)	74	C1
Vodna	73	E3
Vodňany	56	C1
Vodnjan	70	A4
Voe	3	F1
Vogatsikó	79	D3
Vogel	70	A2
Vogelsberg	52	A4
Vogelsdorf	49	E4
Voghera	60	A2
Vogošća	72	B4
Vohenstrauß	56	B1
Vöhringen	55	E3
Void	20	C4
Voikoski	107	F1
Voiron	30	C1
Voiteur	26	C3
Voitsberg	57	E4
Vojens	108	A3
Vojka	72	C3
Vojmsjön	97	F4
Vojnić	70	C3
Vojnik	70	B1
Vojska	73	D3
Vojtanov	53	D4
Vojvodina	72	C2
Vólakas	80	B1
Volary	56	C2
Volchov	111	E1
Volchov R	111	E1
Volda	100	A3
Voldafjorden	100	A2
Volders	59	D2
Volendam	16	C2
Volga	111	F1
Volímes	86	A1
Volissós	85	E4
Volkach	52	B4
Völkermarkt	70	B1
Völklingen	54	B2
Volkmarsen	52	A2
Volkovija	77	D3
Volkovysk	110	C4
Volmunster	21	E3
Voločisk	113	D2
Volokolamsk	111	F2
Volonne	31	D3
Vólos	83	F2
Vološin	111	D4
Volpiano	31	E1
Volta	60	C1
Volterra	60	C4
Voltri	60	A3
Volturara Appula	64	B3
Volturino, Mte	64	C4
Volturno	64	A3
Volvic	26	A4
Vólvi, L	80	B3
Volyn'	113	D2
Volyně	56	C1
Vónitsa	82	C3
Vonnas	26	C4
Voors	17	D2
Voorschoten	16	B3
Voorthuizen	16	C2
Vopnafjörður	96	C1
Vörå	102	B2
Vorarlberg	58	B2
Vóras, Óros	79	E2
Vorau	57	E3
Vorchdorf	56	C3
Vordernberg	57	E4
Vorderrhein	58	A3
Vorderriß	56	A4
Vordingborg	108	C4
Vorë	76	C4
Voreppe	30	C1
Vorey	30	A1
Vóri	91	D4
Vória Píndos	78	C4
Vóries Sporádes	84	C2
Vórios Evoïkós Kólpos	83	F3
Vório Stenó Kerkíras	82	A1
Vorma	105	D3
Vormsi	110	B1
Vorna	99	D4
Voroneţ	113	D3
Vorsfelde	48	B4
Vorskla	113	F2
Võrtsjärv	110	C2
Võru	110	C2
Vosges (Dépt)	27	D1
Voss	104	B2
Votice	53	F4
Votonóssi	82	C1
Voúdia	88	B4
Vouga, R	38	C1
Vouglans, Lac de	27	D3
Vouhorína	79	D4
Vouillé	25	D3
Voukoliés	90	B3
Voúla	87	F1
Voulgára	83	D2
Vouliagméni	87	F1
Voulkariá, L	82	B3
Voúlpi	83	D3
Voulte, la	30	B2
Vouraïkós	86	C1
Voúrinos, Óros	79	D4
Vourkári	88	A2
Vourliótes	89	E1
Voúrvoura	87	D2
Vourvouroú	80	B4
Voutás	83	F3
Vouvant	24	C3
Vouvray	25	D2
Voúxa, Akr	90	B3
Vouzela	38	B1
Vouziers	20	B3
Voves	25	E1
Vovoússa	78	C4
Voxnan	101	E4
Vöyri	102	B2
Voz	70	B3
Vozarci	77	E3
Voznesensk	113	F3
Vrå	108	B2
Vraca	115	D2
Vraca pl	77	D2
Vračev Gaj	73	D2
Vračevšnica	73	D4
Vrådal	104	B3
Vraháti	87	D1
Vrahiónas, Óros	86	A2
Vrahnéika	86	C1
Vrams-Gunnarstorp	108	C3
Vrana	70	B4
Vrancei, M	113	D4
Vranduk	71	E4
Vranica	71	E4
Vranja	70	A3
Vranjak	75	F2
Vranje	77	E2
Vranjska Banja	77	E2
Vranovská přehr nádrž	57	E1
Vran pl	75	E1
Vransko	70	B2
Vransko jezero	74	C1
Vrástama	80	B3
Vratarnica	73	F4
Vratnica	77	D2
Vratnik	70	B3
Vratno	70	C1
Vravróna	88	A1
Vražogrnac	73	F3
Vrbanja	72	B3
Vrbanja R	71	E3
Vrbas	72	B2
Vrbas R	71	E3
Vrbas klisura	71	E4
Vrbljani	71	D4
Vrbnica	77	D3
Vrbnik	70	B3
Vrboska	75	E2
Vrbovec	71	D2
Vrbovsko	70	B3
Vrčin	73	D3
Vrdnik	72	C2
Vreden	17	E3
Vrela	76	C2
Vrelo (Hrvatska)	70	C4
Vrelo (Srbija)	73	E4
Vreoci	72	C3
Vresse	20	C2
Vrésthena	87	D3
Vreta Kloster	106	A4
Vrginmost	70	C3
Vrgorac	75	E2
Vrh Kapele	70	C3
Vrhnika	70	A2
Vrhpolje	71	D4
Vría	79	E4
Vrínena	83	F3
Vríssa	85	F3
Vrisses	90	C3
Vrissiá	83	E2
Vrissoúla	82	B2
Vrlika	75	D1
Vrnjačka Banja	73	D4
Vrnograč	70	C3
Vrondádos	85	F4
Vrondamás	87	D3
Vronderó	78	C3
Vrondissí	91	D4
Vrondoú	79	E4
Vrondoús, Óri	80	B2
Vrossina	82	B1
Vrouhás	91	E3
Vrpolje (Osijek)	71	F2
Vrpolje (Šibenik)	75	D1
Vršac	73	D2
Vršani	72	B3
Vrsar	70	A3
Vrsi	70	C4
Vrška Čuka	73	F4
Vrtac	76	B2
Vrtoče	71	D4
Vrutok	77	D3
Vučitrn	77	D2
Vučjak	77	F3
Vučje	77	E1
Vučkovica	73	D4
Vue des Alpes	27	E2
Vuka	71	F2
Vukovar	72	B2
Vulcano, I	69	D2
Vulture, Mte	64	C3
Vuohijärvi	107	F2
Vuohijärvi L	107	F1
Vuokatti	99	E4
Vuokkijärvi	99	F3
Vuokojaure	94	C3
Vuoksenniska	103	F3
Vuolijoki	99	E4
Vuollerim	98	B2
Vuolvojaure	98	A2
Vuonislahti	103	F2
Vuonji	95	D2
Vuosjärvi	103	D2
Vuoskuvarri	95	D3
Vuostimo	99	E2
Vuotso	95	E3
Vyškov	57	F1
Vyšnij Voloček	111	E2

W

Waal	16	C3
Waalwijk	16	C3
Waasmunster	50	B3
Wabern	52	A3
Wachau	57	E2
Wachow	49	D4
Wächtersbach	52	A4
Waddeneilanden	16	C1
Wadebridge	8	B3

Wädenswil	58	A2
Wagenfeld	17	F2
Wageningen	17	D3
Waging	56	B3
Wagrain	59	E1
Wągrowiec	112	A1
Wahlstedt	48	A2
Waiblingen	55	D2
Waidhaus	56	B1
Waidhofen (Ybbs)	57	D3
Waidhofen (Thaya)	57	E2

Waidring	59	E1
Waischenfeld	52	C4
Waizenkirchen	56	C2
Wakefield	7	D2
Wałbrzych	112	A2
Walchensee	56	A4
Walcheren	16	B3
Walchsee	59	D1
Wałcz	112	A1
Wald	58	A2
Waldbröl	17	E4

Waldeck	52	A2
Waldenbuch	55	D3
Waldenburg	53	D3
Waldfischbach-Burgalben	54	B2
Waldheim	53	E2
Waldkappel	52	B3
Waldkirch	54	C3
Waldkirchen	56	C2
Waldkraiburg	56	B3
Wald-Michelbach	54	C1

Waldmünchen	56	B1
Waldsassen	53	D4
Waldshut	54	C4
Walensee	58	B2
Walenstadt	58	B2
Wales	8	C1
Wallasey	6	C2
Walldorf	54	C2
Walldürn	55	D1
Wallenfels	52	C4
Wallersdorf	56	B2

Wallerstein	55	E2
Wallingford	9	E2
Walls	3	F2
Walsall	9	E1
Walsrode	48	A4
Walsum	17	D3
Waltershausen	52	B3
Walton-on-the-Naze	11	D2
Waltrop	17	E3
Wanderup	48	A1

Wandlitz	49	E3
Wanfried	52	B2
Wangen	55	E4
Wangenbourg	21	E4
Wangerland-Hooksiel	47	E3
Wangerooge	47	E3
Wängi	58	A1
Wanna	47	F2
Wanne-Eickel	17	E3
Wantage	9	E2

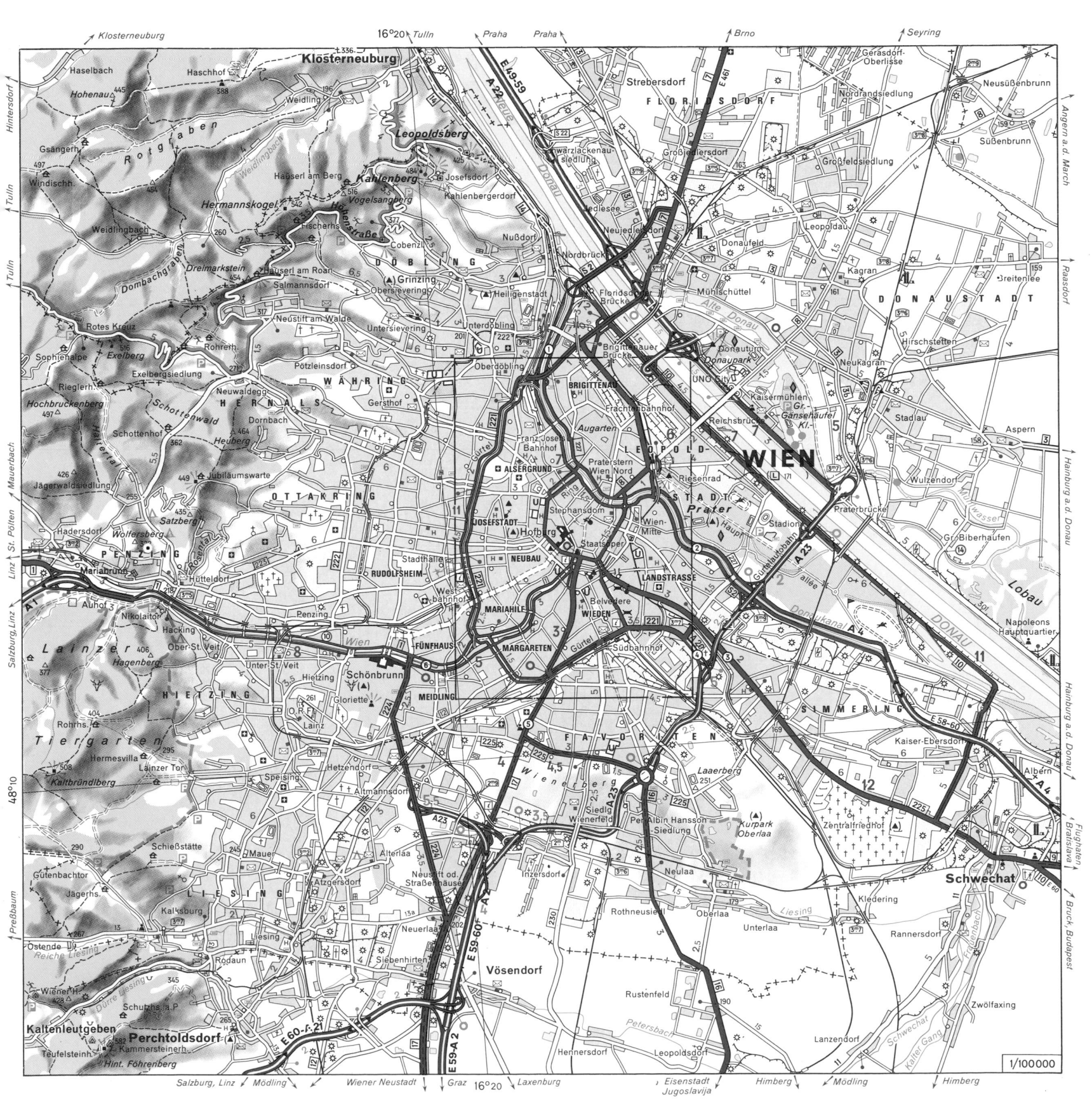

Name	Pg	Ref		Name	Pg	Ref		Name	Pg	Ref
Wantzenau, la	21	F4		Weener	47	E3		Wemding	55	E2
Wanzleben	52	C1		Weert	17	D4		Wemyss Bay	4	C2
Warburg	52	A2		Weferlingen	48	C4		Wendelstein	56	B4
Wardenburg	47	F3		Wegberg	17	D4		Wenden	52	D1
Ware	9	F2		Wegeleben	52	C1		Wengen	27	F3
Waregem	50	B3		Weggis	27	F2		Wenns	58	C2
Wareham	9	D3		Węgorzewo	110	B4		Werbellinsee	49	E3
Waremme	50	C3		Węgorzyno	49	F2		Werben	48	C3
Waren	49	D2		Wegscheid	56	C2		Werdau	53	D3
Warendorf	17	F3		Wehr	54	C4		Werder	49	D4
Warin	48	C2		Weibersbrunn	52	A4		Werdohl	17	E4
Warkworth	5	E3		Weichshofen	56	B2		Werfen	59	E1
Warmensteinach	53	D4		Weida	53	D3		Werl	17	F3
Warminster	9	E3		Weiden	56	A1		Werlte	17	E1
Warnemunde	48	C2		Weikersheim	55	D1		Wermelskirchen	17	E4
Warnow	48	C2		Weilburg	51	F4		Wermsdorf	53	E2
Warrenpoint	13	E3		Weil der Stadt	55	D2		Wernberg	56	B1
Warrington	6	B2		Weilheim (Baden-Württemberg)	55	D3		Werne	17	E3
Warstein	17	F3		Weilheim (Bayern)	56	A3		Werneck	52	B4
Warszawa	112	B1		Weimar	52	C3		Werneuchen	49	E4
Warszów	49	E2		Weinfelden	58	A1		Wernigerode	52	C1
Warta	49	F3		Weingarten	55	D4		Werra	52	B3
Warth	58	B2		Weinheim	54	C1		Wertach	55	E4
Wartha	52	B3		Weinsberg	55	D2		Wertach (R)	55	E3
Warwick	9	E1		Weismain	52	C4		Wertheim	55	D1
Warwickshire	9	E1		Weißbriach	59	F2		Werther	17	F2
Washington	5	E4		Weiße Elster	53	D3		Wertingen	55	E3
Wasselonne	21	E4		Weißenbach	58	C1		Wervik	50	A3
Wassen	58	A3		Weißenberg	53	F2		Wesel	17	D3
Wassenaar	16	B3		Weißenburg	55	F2		Wesenberg	49	D3
Wassenberg	17	D4		Weißenfels	53	D2		Wesendorf	48	B4
Wasseralfingen	55	E2		Weißenhorn	55	E3		Weser	47	F3
Wasserbillig	21	D2		Weißenkirchen	57	E2		Weser-Elbe-Kanal	48	C4
Wasserburg	56	B3		Weißensee	52	C2		Wesselburen	47	F2
Wasser-Kuppe	52	B3		Weißensee (L)	59	F2		Wessobrunn	56	A3
Wassertrüdingen	55	E2		Weissenstadt	53	D4		West Auckland	5	E4
Wassigny	20	A2		Weissenstein	27	E2		West Bridgford	7	D3
Wassy	20	C4		Weissfluhgipfel	58	B2		Westbury	9	D3
Wasungen	52	B3		Weißkirchen	57	D4		Westendorf	59	D1
Watchet	8	C3		Weißkugel	58	C2		Westenholz	48	A4
Waterfoot	13	E1		Weißwasser	53	F1		Westerburg	51	F4
Waterford	15	D4		Weitra	57	D2		Westerholt	47	E3
Waterford (Co)	14	C4		Weiz	57	E4		Westerland	47	F1
Waterford Harbour	15	D4		Wejherowo	110	A4		Westerlo	50	C3
Waterloo	50	B3		Weldon	9	F1		Westernbödefeld	17	F4
Waternish Pt	2	B3		Welgetschlag	57	D2		Western Isles	2	B2
Waterville	14	A4		Welland	9	F1		Wester Ross	2	C3
Watford	9	F2		Wellin	20	C1		Westerstede	47	E3
Wattens	59	D2		Wellingborough	9	F1		Westerwald	51	E3
Watton	11	D1		Wellington	9	D3		Westhofen	54	C1
Wattwil	58	A2		Wellington Bridge	15	D4		West Kilbride	4	C2
Watzmann	56	C4		Wells	9	D3		West Linton	5	D2
Waulsort	50	C4		Wells-next-the-Sea	7	E3		West Loch Tarbert	2	A2
Waveney	11	D1		Wels	56	C3		Westmeath	12	C3
Wavre	50	C3		Welsberg	59	D2		West Mersea	11	D2
Waxweiler	51	D4		Welschnofen	59	D3		Weston-Super-Mare	9	D2
Wear	5	E4		Welshpool	9	D1		Westport	12	B3
Wechsel	57	E3		Weltenburg	55	F2		Westray	3	E1
Wedel	48	A3		Welwyn Garden City	9	F2		Westray Firth	3	E1
Wedemark-Mellendorf	48	A4		Welzheim	55	D2		West Sussex	9	F3
				Wem	6	B3		West-Terschelling	16	C1

Name	Pg	Ref		Name	Pg	Ref		Name	Pg	Ref
West-Vlaanderen	50	A3		Wight, I of	9	E4		Wipper	52	C2
Wetherby	7	D2		Wigton	5	D4		Wipperfürth	17	E4
Wetter	17	E3		Wigtown	4	C3		Wisbech	10	C1
Wetteren	50	D3		Wigtown B	4	C4		Wischhafen	48	A2
Wettin	52	C2		Wijhe	17	D2		Wisełka	49	E2
Wettringen	17	E2		Wil	58	A2		Wishaw	4	C2
Wetwang	7	D1		Wildalpen	57	D3		Wisla	110	B4
Wetzikon	58	A2		Wildbad	54	C2		Wismar	48	C2
Wetzlar	51	F3		Wildeck	52	B3		Wissant	19	E1
Wexford	15	D3		Wildeshausen	17	F1		Wissembourg	21	F3
Wexford (Co)	15	D3		Wildon	57	E4		Wissen	51	E3
Weyer-Markt	57	D3		Wildspitze	58	C2		Witham	7	D3
Weyhausen	48	B4		Wildstrubel	27	E3		Witham	11	D2
Weyhill	9	E3		Wilfersdorf	57	F2		Withernsea	7	E2
Weymouth	9	D3		Wilhelmina kan	16	C3		Witney	9	E2
Weyregg	56	C3		Wilhelm Pieck-Stadt	53	F1		Witnica	49	F3
Whaley Bridge	6	C2		Wilhelmsburg (A)	57	E3		Wittdün	47	F1
Whalsay	3	F1		Wilhelmsburg (D)	48	A3		Witte	49	D1
Wharfe	6	C1		Wilhelmshaven	47	F3		Witten	17	E3
Whernside	6	C1		Wilhering	57	D2		Wittenberg	53	D1
Whitburn	5	D2		Wilkau-Haßlau	53	D3		Wittenberge	48	C3
Whitby	5	F4		Willebroek	50	B3		Wittenburg	48	B3
Whitchurch	6	B3		Willemstad	16	B3		Wittichenau	53	F2
White Bridge	2	C4		Willingen	17	F4		Wittingen	48	B4
Whitehaven	5	D4		Williton	8	C3		Wittlich	51	E4
Whitehead	13	E2		Wilmslow	6	C2		Wittmund	47	E3
Whiteness	3	F2		Wilnsdorf	17	F4		Wittow	49	D1
Whiten Head	2	C2		Wilsdruff	53	E2		Wittstock	49	D3
Whithorn	4	C4		Wilseder Berg	48	A3		Witzenhausen	52	B2
Whitland	8	B2		Wilster	48	A2		Władysławowo	110	A4
Whitley Bay	5	E3		Wilton	9	E3		Włocławek	112	B1
Whitstable	11	D3		Wiltshire	9	E3		Włodawa	112	C2
Whittlesey	9	F1		Wiltz	21	D2		Wöbbelin	48	C3
Wick	3	D2		Wimborne Minster	9	E3		Woburn	9	F2
Wickford	11	D2		Wimereux	19	E1		Woburn Abbey	9	F2
Wicklow	13	E4		Wincanton	9	D3		Woensdrecht	16	B4
Wicklow (Co)	13	D4		Winchcombe	9	E2		Woerden	16	C3
Wicklow Head	13	E4		Winchelsea	11	D3		Wohlen	27	F2
Wicklow Mts	13	D4		Winchester	9	E3		Woippy	21	D3
Widnes	6	B2		Windeck	51	E3		Woking	9	F3
Wiehe	52	C2		Windermere	5	D4		Wokingham	9	F2
Wiek	49	D1		Windischeschenbach	53	D4		Wołczenica	49	F2
Wieliczka	112	B3		Windischgarsten	57	D3		Woldegk	49	E2
Wieluń	112	B2		Windsbach	55	E1		Wolfach	54	C3
Wien	57	F2		Windsor	9	F2		Wolfegg	55	E4
Wiener-Neudorf	57	F2		Winkleigh	8	C3		Wolfen	53	D2
Wiener Neustadt	57	F3		Winklern	59	E2		Wolfenbüttel	52	B1
Wienerwald	57	E3		Winnenden	55	D2		Wolfhagen	52	A2
Wies (A)	70	B1		Winnigstedt	52	B1		Wolfratshausen	56	A3
Wies (D)	56	A4		Winnweiler	54	B1		Wolfsberg	70	B1
Wiesau	53	D4		Winschoten	47	E3		Wolfsburg	48	B4
Wiesbaden	51	F4		Winsen (Celle)	48	A4		Wolgast	49	E2
Wieselburg	57	E3		Winsen (Lüneburg)	48	B3		Wolin	49	E2
Wiesenburg	53	D1		Winsford	6	C3		Wolin (Reg)	49	E2
Wiesensteig	55	D3		Winsum	47	D3		Woliński Park Narodowy	49	E2
Wiesentheid	55	E1		Winterberg	17	F4		Wolkenstein	59	D3
Wiesenttal	52	C4		Winterswijk	17	D3		Wolkersdorf	57	F2
Wiesing	59	D1		Winterthur	58	A2		Wöllersdorf	57	F3
Wiesloch	54	C2		Wintzenheim	27	E1		Wollersheim	51	D3
Wiesmath	57	F3						Wollin	49	D4
Wiesmoor	47	E3						Wolmirstedt	48	C4
Wigan	6	C2								

Name	Pg	Ref
Wolsingham	5	E4
Wolsztyn	112	A2
Wolvega	17	D1
Wolverhampton	9	E1
Wolverton	9	E1
Wolznach	55	F2
Woodbridge	11	D1
Woodhall Spa	7	E3
Woodstock	9	E2
Wooler	5	E3
Worb	27	E2
Worbis	52	B2
Worcester	9	D1
Wörgl	59	D1
Workington	5	D4
Worksop	7	D2
Workum	16	C1
Wörlitz	53	D1
Wormerveer	16	C2
Wormhout	19	F1
Worms	54	C1
Worms Head	8	C2
Wörnitz	55	E2
Wörrstadt	54	C1
Wörth (Donau)	56	B2
Wörth (Main)	55	D1
Wörth (Rheinland-Pfalz)	54	C2
Wörther See	70	A1
Worthing	10	C3
Woświn, Jez	49	F2
Wragby	7	D3
Wrath, Cape	2	C2
Wrecsam	6	B3
Wrexham	6	B3
Wriezen	49	E3
Wrocław	112	A2
Wroughton	9	E2
Września	112	A1
Wulfen	17	E3
Wullowitz	57	D2
Wümme	48	A3
Wümme R	48	A3
Wünnenberg	17	F3
Wünsdorf	49	E4
Wunsiedel	53	D4
Wunstorf	48	A4
Wuppertal	17	E4
Würzburg	55	D1
Wurzen	53	D2
Wurzen-Paß	59	F2
Wusterhausen	49	D3
Wustrow (Rostock)	48	C1
Wustrow (Wismar)	48	C2
Wuustwezel	50	C2
Wye, R	9	D2
Wyk	47	F1
Wymondham	11	D1

X

Name	Pg	Ref		Name	Pg	Ref		Name	Pg	Ref		Name	Pg	Ref		Name	Pg	Ref		Name	Pg	Ref
				Xánthi (Nomos)	81	D2		Xerta	41	F2		Xilikí	83	E3		Xilóskalo	90	B3		Xirokámbi	87	D3		Xubia	34	B1
Xallas, R	34	A2		Xarrama, R	42	B1		Xertigny	27	D1		Xilís, Akr	87	D4		Xiniáda	83	E3		Xirókambos	89	E3		Xunqueira de Ambía	34	B3
Xanten	17	D3		Xàtiva	41	E4		Xesta, Pto de la	34	C1		Xilókastro	87	D1		Xinó Neró	79	D3		Xirolímni	79	D3				
Xánthi	81	D2		Xeresa	41	E4		Xifianí	79	E2		Xilopáriko	83	D2		Xinzo de Limia	34	B3		Xistral	34	B1				
				Xerovoúni	82	C2		Xilaganí	81	E2		Xilópoli	80	A2		Xiró	83	F3		Xódoto, Akr	89	D3				

Y

Name	Pg	Ref		Name	Pg	Ref		Name	Pg	Ref		Name	Pg	Ref		Name	Pg	Ref		Name	Pg	Ref
				Yecla	45	D1		Yesa	36	C2		Ylihärmä	102	C2		Ylläs	95	D4		Yoxford	11	E1		Yttermalung	105	E2
Yaiza	42	C4		Yeguas, Emb de	43	F2		Yesa, Emb de	37	D2		Yli-Kärppä	99	D3		Ylläsjärvi	95	D4		Ypäjä	107	E2		Yuncos	40	A2
Yalova	115	F3		Yeguas, R de las	43	F1		Yeşilova	115	F4		Ylikiiminki	99	D3		Ylöjärvi	102	C3		Yport	19	D2		Yunquera	43	E4
Yanguas	36	B3		Yell	3	F1		Yeste	44	C1		Yli-Kitka	99	E2		Yngaren	106	A4		Ypres	50	A3		Yunquera de Henares	40	B2
Yare	7	F4		Yell Sd	3	F1		Yeu, I d'	24	A3		Yli-Ii	99	D3		Yonne	20	A4		Yr Wyddgrug	6	B3		Yuste	39	E2
Yarmouth	9	E3		Yelmo	44	B2		Yèvre	26	A2		Yli-Muonio	95	D4		Yonne (Dépt)	26	A1		Yser	19	F1		Yverdon	27	E3
Yarmouth, Great	7	F4		Yeltes, R	39	D1		Y-Fenni	9	D2		Yli-Nampa	99	D2		York	7	D2		Yssingeaux	30	B1		Yvetot	19	D3
Ybbs	57	D2		Yenne	27	D4		Yıldız Dağları	115	E3		Yli-Olhava	99	D3		Yorkshire Dales Nat Pk	6	C1		Ystad	109	D4		Yvoir	50	C4
Ybbs R	57	D3		Yeovil	9	D3		Ylämaa	103	F4		Ylistaro	102	B2		Youghal	14	C4		Y Trallwng	9	D1		Yvoire	27	D3
Yebra	40	B2		Yepes	40	B3		Ylämylly	103	F2		Ylitornio	98	C2		Youghal B	14	C4		Ytterhogdal	101	E3				
				Yerville	19	D3		Yläne	107	D2		Ylivieska	102	C1												

Z

Zaandam	16	C2
Žabali	72	C2
Žabari	73	D3
Zablaće	75	D1
Žabljak (Durmitor)	76	B1
Žabljak (Titograd)	76	B3
Žabno	71	D2
Zabok	70	C2
Zabrddde	72	B3
Zadar	74	C1
Zadarski kanal	70	B4
Zadvarje	75	E2
Zafarraya	43	F3
Zafóra, Ni	92	C2
Zafra	43	D1
Žaga	70	A2
Žagań	112	A2
Zaglavak	72	C4
Zagorá	83	F2
Zagória	82	C1
Zagorje	70	B2
Zagreb	70	C2
Žagubica	73	E3
Zagvozd	75	E2
Zahara de los Atunes	43	D4
Zaháro	86	B2
Zahinos	42	C1
Zahna	53	D1
Záhony	112	C3
Zaidín	37	E4
Zajas	77	D3
Zaječar	73	F3
Zákinthos	86	A1
Zákinthos, N	86	A1
Zakopane	112	B3
Zákros	91	F4
Zala	112	A4
Zalaegerszeg	112	A4
Zalamea de la Serena	43	E1
Zalamea la Real	42	C2
Zalău	112	C4
Žalec	70	B2
Zaleščiki	113	D3
Zalew Wiślany	110	B4
Zalla	36	A1
Zálongo	82	B2
Zaltbommel	16	C3
Zalužnica	70	C4
Zambrana	36	B2
Zamora	35	D4
Zamość	112	C2
Záncara, R	40	B4
Zandvoort	16	B2
Zángano, Pto del	39	D4
Zanglivéri	80	A3
Zannone, I	63	F4
Zaorejas	40	C2
Zaostrog	75	E2
Zaovine Vežanja	72	C4
Zapadnaja Dvina	111	A4
Zapadnaja Dvina R	111	E2
Zapadna Morava	73	D4
Zapardiel, R	39	F1
Zapatón, R	39	D3
Zápio	83	E2
Zapponeta	64	C3
Zaprešić	70	C2
Zaragoza	37	D3
Zárakes	84	B4
Zaratán	35	E4
Zarautz	36	C1
Zarcilla de Ramos	44	C2

Zárkos	83	E1
Zarós	91	D4
Zaroúhla	87	D1
Zarrentin	48	B3
Žary	112	A2
Zarza la Mayor	39	D2
Zasieki	53	F1
Žaškov	113	E2
Žatec	53	E3
Zatoka Gdańska	110	B4
Zaton	75	F2
Zavala	75	F2
Zavattarello	60	A2
Zavidovići	71	F4
Zavlaka	72	C3
Zavratnica	70	B4
Zawiercie	112	B2
Žažina	71	C3
Zbaraž	113	D2
Zbraslav	53	F4
Žďár nad Sázavou	112	A3
Zdenac	70	C3
Zdice	53	F4
Ždrelac	74	C1
Ždrelo	73	E3
Zdunje	77	D3
Zduńska Wola	112	B2
Zebë, Maj'e	76	C3
Zebreira	38	C2
Žednik	72	B1
Zeebrugge	50	A3
Zeeland	16	B3
Zefiría	88	A4
Žegovac	77	D2
Žegra	77	D2
Žegulja	75	E2
Zehdenick	49	D3
Zeist	16	C3
Zeitz	53	D2
Zejtun	68	B4
Žekovec	70	B1
Zele	50	B3
Zelengora	76	A1
Zelengora (Reg)	76	A1
Zelenika	76	A3
Zelenogorsk	111	D1
Železná Ruda	56	C1
Železnik	72	C3
Železniki	70	A2
Železnogorsk	111	F4
Zelina	70	C2
Zélio	83	F3
Željezno Polje	71	F4
Zlatari	77	D1
Željin	73	D4
Zell (D)	54	B1
Zell (Oberösterreich)	56	C2
Zell (Tirol)	59	D2
Zella-Mehlis	52	C3
Zell am See	59	E1
Zellerrain	57	E3
Zeltweg	57	D4
Zelzate	50	B3
Zemun	72	C3
Zenica	71	F4
Zen'kov	113	F2
Žep	72	B4
Žepče	71	F4
Zerbst	53	D1
Zeri	60	B3
Zermatt	27	F4
Zernez	58	B3
Zerqan	77	D4
Zestoa	36	B1
Zeta	76	B2
Zetel	47	E3

Zeulenroda	53	D3
Zeven	48	A3
Zevenaar	17	D3
Zevgaráki	82	C4
Zevgolatió	86	C3
Zevio	60	C1
Zêzere, R	38	C2
Žiča	73	D4
Židlochovice	57	F1
Ziefsdorf	57	E2
Ziegenrück	52	C3
Zielona Góra	112	A2
Zierikzee	16	B3
Zierzow	48	C3
Ziesar	49	D4
Zi, Guri i	77	D4
Zijemlje	75	F1
Žilina	112	B3
Žilindar	76	C1
Ziller	59	D2
Zillertal	59	D2
Zimnicea	115	D2
Zinal	27	F4
Zirchow	49	E2
Žiri	70	A2
Žirje	74	C1
Zirl	58	C2
Zirndorf	55	D4
Zirndorf	55	E1
Žiros	91	F4
Zistersdorf	57	F2
Žitište	72	C2
Žitkovac	73	E4
Žitkoviči	113	D1
Žitomir	113	E2
Žitomisliči	75	F2
Žitoradđa	77	D1
Zittau	53	F2
Živinice	71	F3
Živogošće	75	E2
Žizdra	111	F3
Zjum	77	D2
Zlarin	75	D1
Zlarin I	75	D1
Zlata	77	D1
Zlatar	76	B1
Zlatar Bistrica	70	C2
Zlatarevo	77	F3
Zlatari	77	D1
Zlatarsko jez	76	B1
Zlatibor	72	C4
Zlatica	72	C4
Zlatni Pjasâci	115	E2
Zlatokop	77	E2
Zletovo	77	E2
Žljebovi	72	B4
Žlobin	111	E4
Zlot	73	E3
Žlutice	53	E4
Zmajevo	72	C2
Žman	74	C1
Žmerinka	113	E3
Žminj	70	A3
Znamenka	113	F2
Znojmo	57	E1
Zöblitz	53	E3
Zoetermeer	16	B3
Zogaj	76	C2
Zoločev	113	D2
Zolotonoša	113	F2
Žoltyje Vody	113	F2

Zonári, Akr	93	F1
Zóni	81	F1
Zonianá	91	D3
Zonza	33	F4
Zoodóhos Pigi (Makedonia)	79	E3
Zoodóhos Pigii (Pelopónissos)	87	F2
Zorita	39	E3
Zossen	49	E4
Zoúrvas, Akr	87	F2
Zoutkamp	47	D3
Zoutleeuw	50	C3
Zoúzouli	78	C4
Zrenjanin	72	C2
Zrin	71	D3
Zrinska gora	71	D3
Zrmanja, R	74	C1
Zrmanja	75	D1
Žrnovnica	75	D2
Zrze	77	D2
Zschopau	53	E3
Zschopau R	53	E3
Zubcov	111	F2
Zubin Potoku	76	C2

Žuč	77	D1
Zucaina	41	E3
Zuckerhütl	58	C2
Zudar	49	D1
Zuera	37	D3
Zufre	43	D2
Zufre, Emb de	43	D2
Zug	58	A2
Zugspitze	55	F4
Zuid Beveland	16	B4
Zuidelijk-Flevoland	16	C2
Zuid Holland	16	B4
Zuidlaren	17	D1
Zújar	44	B3
Zújar, Emb de	39	E4
Zújar, R	43	E1
Žukovka	111	F3
Zuljana	75	E2
Zumaia	36	B1
Zumárraga	36	B1
Zundert	16	C3
Zuoz	58	B3
Županja	71	F3
Žúpich	51	D3
Žur	77	D3

Zürich	58	A2
Zurrieq	68	B4
Zürs	58	B2
Zurzach	58	A1
Zusmarshausen	55	E3
Zusmarshausen	58	A1
Zvečan	77	D1
Zvenigorodka	113	E2
Zvijezda nac park	72	C4
Zvikovec	53	E4
Zvolen	112	B3
Zvonce	77	E1
Zvornik	72	B4
Zweibrücken	54	B2
Zweisimmen	27	E3
Zwenkau	53	D2
Zwettl (Niederösterreich)	57	D2
Zwettl (Oberösterreich)	57	D2
Zwickau	53	D3
Zwickauer Mulde	53	D3

Zwiefalten	55	D3
Zwiesel	56	C2
Zwijndrecht	16	C3
Zwolle	17	D2
Żyrardów	112	B1
Žut	74	C1
Žuta Lokva	70	C3
Zutphen	17	D2
Žužemberk	70	B2
Zvečan	77	D1
Žywiec	112	B3

Þ

Þingeyri	96	A1
Þingvallavatn	96	A2
Þistilfjörður	96	C1
Þjórsá	96	B2
Þórlákshöfn	96	A2
Þórshöfn	96	C1
Þórsmörk	96	B3

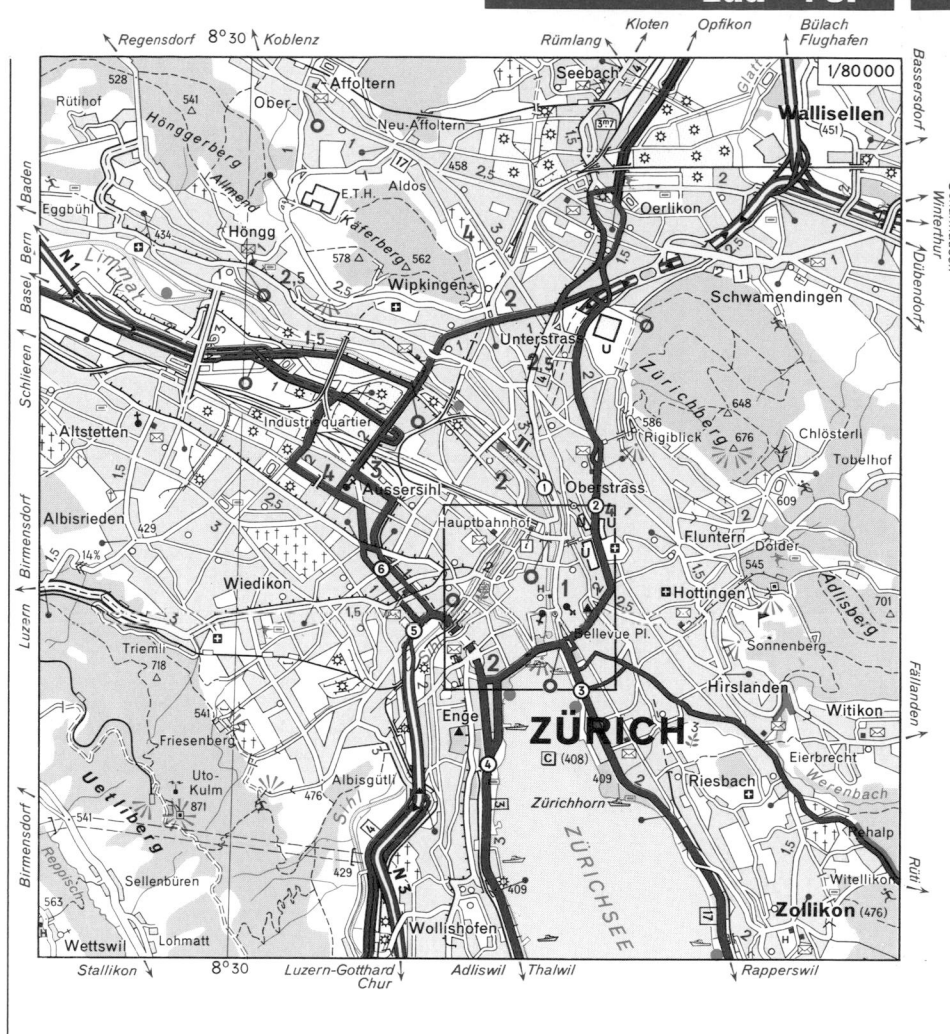

Notes